Anonymous

The Irish Crisis of 1879-80

Anonymous

The Irish Crisis of 1879-80

ISBN/EAN: 9783337384197

Printed in Europe, USA, Canada, Australia, Japan

Cover: Foto ©ninafisch / pixelio.de

More available books at **www.hansebooks.com**

THE IRISH CRISIS OF 1879-80.

PROCEEDINGS

OF THE

DUBLIN MANSION HOUSE

RELIEF COMMITTEE,

1880.

DUBLIN:
BROWNE & NOLAN, NASSAU-STREET.
1881.

CONTENTS.

	PAGE
LIST OF DUBLIN MANSION HOUSE COMMITTEE	v.
Sub-Committees	vi.
GENERAL REPORT	1
Foundation of the Committee	8
Sources of the Fund	16
Great Britain	17
Ireland	16
France	18
India	20
South Africa	22
United States	22
Canada and South America	23
Australasia	24
Manner of Distribution	27
The Executive Organisation	33
Progress of the Relief	34
The Western Isles	47
Dangers during the Summer	52
Conclusion	68
SPECIAL REPORTS :—	
FINANCIAL REPORT	81
Classification of Subscriptions	83
Balance Sheet	84 85
Seed Fund Balance Sheet	
REPORT OF INVESTIGATION HELD AT KILRONAN, ARANMORE, on 21st June, 1880, by JOHN ADYE CURRAN, Esq.	87
REPORTS ON THE CONDITION OF THE PEASANTRY OF THE CO. MAYO, by J. A. FOX, Esq.	105
REPORT OF THE MEDICAL COMMISSION, by Dr. SIGERSON and Dr. KENNY	123
Preliminary Report	129
District of Ballaghadereen	132
Charlestown District	135
Swineford and Foxford Districts	139
Districts of Ballina and Killala	143
Districts of Inniscrone (Sligo) and Louisburgh (Mayo)	147
Districts of Oughterard, Rosmuck, and Carraroe	150
Districts of Oranmore, Athenry, and Derrybrien	155
Final Report on Destitution Diseases in the West, by Dr. SIGERSON	161

[OVER.

CONTENTS.

APPENDICES.

I. First Meetings of Mansion House Committee	177
II. Deputation to LORD LIEUTENANT to obtain Seed Grant	181
III. Deputation to CHIEF SECRETARY in reference to Distress	189
IV. Insufficiency of Official Measures.—Mr. DILLON's Report	195
V. Closing Ordinary Meeting	199
VI. Final General Meeting	204
VII. Appeals, Forms, &c.	215
VIII. Correspondence	222
IX. Table of Distress	261
X. Constitution of Committees	295
XI. Letters of Irish Bishops	315
XII. Report of Donegal County Committee	325
XIII. Australian Correspondence	338
XIV. List of Subscriptions	345

DUBLIN MANSION HOUSE COMMITTEE.

The Right Hon. E. DWYER GRAY, M.P., Lord Mayor of Dublin,
Chairman.

RICHARD ALLEN, Esq.
CHARLES J. BRIDGETT, Esq.
MAURICE BROOKS, Esq., M.P.
GEORGE BROWNE, Esq., M.P.
Alderman CAMPBELL, J.P.
Alderman COCHRANE.
JAMES C. COLVILLE, Esq., J.P.
JOHN ADYE CURRAN, Esq.
Colonel DAYOREN.
MATHEW P. D'ARCY, Esq., D.L.
The Very Rev. The DEAN OF ST. PATRICK'S
GEORGE DELANY, Esq.
V. B. DILLON, Jun., Esq.
Very Rev. N. DONNELLY, R.C.A.
THOMAS DOWLING, Esq.
DAVID DRIMMIE, Esq.
DAVID DRUMMOND, Esq., J.P.
The Right Hon. The LORD EMLY.
The Hon. FREDERICK RICHARD FALKINER.
Very Rev. Canon FARRELL, P.P.
CHARLES J. FAY, Esq., M.P.
EDWARD FOX, Esq., J.P.
J. A. FOX, Esq.
WM. FINDLATER, Esq., M.P.
JAS. FROSTE, J.P., High Sheriff, Co. Clare
Captain GABBETT, M.P.
The Right Hon. E. GIBSON, M.P.
H. J. GILL, Esq., M.P., T.C.
Sir A. GUINNESS, M.P., D.L.
E. C. GUINNESS, Esq., D.L.
Colonel KING-HARMAN, M.P., D.L.
Alderman HARRIS.
Rev. MORGAN JELLETT, M.A., LL.D.
W. LANE JOYNT, Esq., D.L.
IGNATIUS J. KENNEDY, Esq., J.P., T.C.
JOSEPH E. KENNY, Esq., L.R.C.P. & S.
THOMAS KIERNAN, Esq.
E. H. KINAHAN, Esq., J.P.
Rev. WM. B. KIRKPATRICK, D.D.
W. DIGGES LA TOUCHE, Esq., D.L.
JAMES F. LOMBARD, Esq., J.P.
Dr. LONG, T.C.
Rev. T. LONG, A.M., Rector, St. Michan's

E. O. M'DEVITT, Esq.
RICHARD MARTIN, Esq., D.L.
G. W. MAUNSELL, Esq., D.L.
C. H. MELDON, Esq., M.P.
The Right Hon. The EARL OF MEATH.
Alderman M'DERMOTT.
Very Rev. Canon MONAHAN, D.D.
The Right Hon. VISCOUNT MONCK.
ANDREW T. MOORE, Esq., T.C.
The Most Rev. E. M'CABE, Catholic Archbishop of Dublin.
WILLIAM M'KENZIE, Esq.
WILLIAM M. MURPHY, Esq.
Very Rev. Dean NEVILLE, Rector, C.U.I.
PATRICK O'BRIEN, Esq., Melbourne.
JOHN O'CONNOR, Esq.
The O'CONOR DON.
The O'GORMAN MAHON, M.P.
The Right Hon. LORD O'HAGAN.
Dr. W. H. O'LEARY, M.P.
Very Rev. T. J. O'REILLY, R.C.A.
Lord FRANCIS F. G. OSBORNE.
ALEXANDER PARKER, Esq., J.P.
THOMAS PIM, Esq., Jun., J.P.
Hon. D. PLUNKET, M.P.
AMBROSE PLUNKETT, Esq.
Viscount POWERSCOURT.
J. TALBOT POWER, Esq., D.L.
Rev. W. GUARD PRICE.
Alderman PURDON.
HENRY ROE, Esq., D.L.
ABRAHAM SHACKLETON, Esq., J.P., T.C.
W. SHAW, Esq., M.P.
GEORGE SIGERSON, Esq., M.D., Ch.M.
P. J. SMYTH, Esq., M.P.
A. O. SPEEDY, Esq., L.R.C.S.I.
Colonel The Right Hon. T. E. TAYLOR, M.P.
The PROVOST OF TRINITY COLLEGE, Dublin.
Alderman HUGH TARPEY, J.P.
The Most Rev. R. C. TRENCH, Protestant Archbishop of Dublin.
JOHN WALLIS, Esq, J.P.
W. WILLIAMSON, Esq. (Todd, Burns & Co.)

THE PROTESTANT AND CATHOLIC ARCHBISHOPS AND BISHOPS OF IRELAND;
THE MODERATOR OF THE GENERAL ASSEMBLY OF THE PRESBYTERIAN CHURCH.

Examination Sub-Committee:

Alderman Tarpey
Rev. Canon Bagot
C. J. Bridgett
John Adye Curran
David Drummond
Colonel Davoren
V. B. Dillon, Jun.
George Delany
Rev. James Daniel

J. A. Fox
T. Maxwell Hutton
Alderman Harris
William Lane Joynt
Charles Kennedy
W. M. Murphy
Sir J. W. Mackey
Sir George B. Owens
With Hon. Secretaries and Treasurers

Publication Sub-Committee:

John Adye Curran
David Drimmie
Colonel Davoren
V. B. Dillon, Jun.

J. A. Fox
Thomas Pim
P. J. Smyth, M.P.
George Sigerson, M.D.
With Hon. Secretaries and Treasurers

Western Isles Sub-Committee:

William Lane Joynt
Rev. Canon Bagot
George Delany
Rev. James Daniel
V. B. Dillon, Jun.

P. M'Cabe Fay
T. Maxwell Hutton
Charles Kennedy
Sir George B. Owens
Lord F. Godolphin Osborne
With Hon. Secretaries and Treasurers

Finance Sub-Committee:

David Drimmie
Charles Kennedy
John Adye Curran

George Delany
T. Maxwell Hutton
With Hon. Secretaries and Treasurers

Clothing Sub-Committee:

J. F. Lombard
George Sigerson, M.D.
Maurice Brooks, M.P.

Jonathan Pim
John Wallis
William Lane Joynt
With Hon. Secretaries and Treasurers

Seed Sub-Committee:

Alderman Purdon
Sir James W. Mackey, D.L.
William Lane Joynt
J. F. Lombard

Richard Allen
Rev Canon Bagot
David Drummond
Charles Kennedy
With Hon. Secretaries and Treasurers

AUSTRALIAN SUB-COMMITTEE:

The LORD MAYOR
Alderman TARPEY
Canon BAGOT
CHARLES KENNEDY
V. B. DILLON, Jun.
Dr. SIGERSON

P. M'CABE FAY
Sir GEORGE OWENS, M.D.
Sir JOHN BARRINGTON
P. J. SMYTH, M.P.
The Right Hon. DAVID PLUNKET
With Hon Secretaries and Treasurers

TREASURERS:

E. DWYER GRAY, M.P., Lord Mayor.

His Grace The Most Rev. Dr. TRENCH
Sir JAMES W. MACKEY, D.L., High Sheriff
Alderman HUGH TARPEY

Sir JOHN BARRINGTON, D.L., Ex-Lord Mayor
JONATHAN PIM
WILLIAM LANE JOYNT, D.L.

HON. SECRETARIES:

R. W. BAGOT, Canon, LL.D.
JAMES DANIEL, P.P.
P. M'CABE FAY

T. MAXWELL HUTTON
CHARLES KENNEDY
Sir GEORGE B. OWENS

V. B. DILLON, Jun.

J. H. WRIGHT, *Assist.-Secretary.*

THE IRISH CRISIS OF 1879–80.

GENERAL REPORT.

The Mansion House Relief Committee was honoured by being entrusted with the largest share of the magnificent funds which the charity of friendly nations poured into Ireland during the last winter and spring, to stop the path of famine. Sums to the amount of £181,330 5s. 8d. were subscribed upon its appeals, and were distributed in more or less degree among 512,625 people, through the agency of 840 Sub-Committees. It was a great and onerous trust. It is due to those who, from the depths of remote continents, proffered their money unquestioningly at the first cry of want; it is due also to those who took the responsibility of standing as almoners between those distant benefactors and a population on the verge of famine—that, in rendering this final account of our stewardship, we should place on permanent record the circumstances which extorted our appeals to the charity of the world, the area and quality of the distress to which that charity was applied, the manner in which it was administered, the precautions by which it was guarded against partiality or imposition, and the blessed results which, under the favour of Divine Providence, have delivered Ireland from a ghastly period of suffering and death. Heretofore the reports of committees like this have been the melancholy records of efforts either undertaken too late, or, with all their noble generosity, undertaken upon too small a scale, to do more than palliate the horrors of almost unbridled pestilence and famine. We share with the other great charitable organizations of 1880 the satisfaction of believing that now, for the first time in a history painfully fruitful of famine precedents, a crisis which rendered 500,000 of the population foodless paupers has been grappled with and got under by the almost unaided arm of private benevolence. This has not been achieved without a terrible ordeal of suspense and suffering, during which thousands of lives hung upon the hazard of a weekly alms. The fearful imminence of the danger, while the recollection of it will always fill Irish hearts with gratitude to their deliverers, attaches a peculiar interest to the history of the extraordinary outburst of human sympathy, without limit of race, or creed, or distance, by which the force of the calamity was broken.

A Famine averted by Charity

CAUSES OF THE MOVEMENT.

<small>The losses during the Distress-Cycle, 1879-80</small>

The condition of Ireland, when the harvest of 1879 lay ruined, was of a character to dismay men of cool and moderate judgment. When the memory of facts has become less sharp, it will not be easy to realise by what an accumulation of old and new misfortunes a country of much natural fertility, inhabited by only 5,362,000 people over a cultivable area of at least 16,000,000 acres, was, towards the close of the nineteenth century, reduced by the mischances of three seasons to solicit the bread of charity for its people. It was, indeed, a crushing, and we may hope an altogether exceptional load of disaster, smiting every species of industry simultaneously. The tiller, the grazier, the commercial man, suffered alike under the blow. Bad seasons alone had destroyed £20,000,000 worth of crops within three years. In the <small>In Potatoes</small> single item of potatoes—still the staple food of the peasantry—the small cultivators had lost £11,570,000 upon the average value of the crop within the period, or £21,199,000 compared with a favourable year like 1876.* The REGISTRAR-GENERAL estimated the entire value of the crop of 1879 at £3,341,000, against an average value of £9,251,000. Agriculture of most other kinds had been steadily dwindling down; 519,307 acres out of a total tillage area of 5,500,000 acres had gone out of cultivation in ten years. The wheat culture was ruined. "In 1846, when this country had eight millions and a half of population, we were exporting £6,000,000 worth of cereals; in 1879 we had to import over £8,000,000 worth of the same produce to feed a population one-third less than it was then."† The breadth of land even under oats had <small>In Stock and Produce</small> declined by 320,000 acres, and the yield, from 21,125,552 cwts. in 1870, had sunk to 15,532,628 cwts. in 1879.‡ 50·2 per cent. of the entire surface of the country, and two-thirds of its wealth, were devoted to the raising of cattle; and the cheap transatlantic freights and the startling growth of the American live cattle trade had for the moment driven Irish cattle from the markets unsaleable. At the great fair of Ballinasloe in 1878 there were 52,597 sheep sold, and 6,378 unsold; in 1879, there were 29,777 sold at a depreciation of £1 10s. per head of ewes, and 15,186 unsaleable upon any terms. At the Banagher fair, in 1878, there were 17,000 sheep sold, and 1,550 unsold; in 1879, there were 2,900 sold at a loss, and 13,091 unsold. In the opinion of moderate and competent judges, £15,000,000 would not fully represent the depreciation in Irish stock during the year. Irish butter proved to be as ruinous a speculation as Irish stock and produce. The deep-seated depression in English trade had not merely reacted on the towns and paralysed commercial enterprise. It had dealt a fearful blow at the Irish butter trade by all but destroying the demand or turning it into foreign channels. By the double agency of lessened

---

* This is clearly demonstrated from official statistics in Dr. W. NEILSON HANCOCK's Papers on Ireland, 1880, p. 10. See also Dr. SIGERSON's Final Report, *infra*.

† Debate in Dublin Corporation, October 8, 1879.

‡ Agricultural Statistics of Ireland for 1879, p. 12.

production and falling prices, the Cork Butter Market alone sustained a dead loss of £308,000 on the season's operations, and the Tipperary Market a loss of £140,000 more.

Even before autumn revealed the ruin of the crops of 1879, a cry of suffering akin to panic ran through the agricultural classes, and was re-echoed in Parliament and in the Press by those who were most conversant with their condition. The first outlet of relief sought was an abatement of rents. Memorials, public meetings, and resolutions of Boards of Guardians appealed to the forbearance of landlords (and did not appeal in vain) upon the unvarying plea that the losses of two disastrous seasons, the depreciation of their stock and produce, and the stress of American competition had pressed the farmers to the earth. The Catholic clergy, assembled in their several deaneries, verified and reiterated the appeal. As early as June the 16th the clergy of the Catholic diocese of Galway put forth a declaration "from an intimate knowledge of the wants of our people," that "the present dire distress has not been equalled since the famine years." "Most humbly and respectfully do we implore of those in whose hands are placed the very lives of these poor people," said the clergy of the deanery of Cahirciveen about the same time "to come forward promptly and effectively to their relief." Eighty-seven traders of Cahirciveen published a declaration that "not since the dreadful famine years has the position of the farming class reached so low a level. Unable, as a rule, to meet liabilities already incurred, our forbearance saves numbers of them from total ruin." The clergy of Ossory, on the 3rd of July, called on the Government "to apply an efficacious and immediate remedy; otherwise the country will be exposed to a renewal of the horrors of the famine years." From Tralee, Killaloe, Dungarvan, Achonry, Cloyne, Tuam, and Ross, the cruel truth of the farmers' representations was no less unequivocally endorsed. It was not disputed: it was confessed, and even in many instances anticipated by the large, and often wholly spontaneous concessions of a considerable number of landlords, whose remissions of rent, ranging from 10 per cent. to a whole half-year's, began to fill a daily column in the newspapers from the commencement of June. The fear, however, that the crisis would outrun the power of private liberality, was already sinking into the public mind. On the 28th of June, in his place in the House of Commons, Mr. O'Donnell called the attention of the Government to "the resolutions of numerous Boards of Guardians and public bodies, and of the Catholic clergy, declaring the inability of the tenantry to pay existing rents in the present severe distress," and asked "whether the Government proposed to take any steps to alleviate the existing distress in Ireland?" The Chief Secretary for Ireland (Mr. Lowther) in his reply said: "It is a matter of satisfaction to the Irish Government that we have reason to believe the distress has not been so acutely felt in Ireland as in other parts of the United Kingdom," adding, "with regard to the last paragraph of the honourable gentleman's question, if he means by that, whether the Government have any intention of introducing a Bill in Parliament for the reduction of rents in Ireland, I may say we have no such intention"—a statement which was received with "laughter." The apprehension that the Executive had not quite realised the gravity of what was approaching, stimulated several Irish members before the breaking up of Parliament to utter impressive warnings that, in the words of Mr. GRAY, on the 8th of August, "The condition of affairs in Ireland was so grave as to call for the most earnest attention of the Government to the duty of devising some means of relief for the starving tenantry."

<small>Failure of the Harvest of 1879</small>

Things had come to this pass while the growing oat-crops were still reported to be luxuriant and before the blight had yet breathed upon the potatoes. It was felt that even a bountiful harvest would afford to the peasant farmers no barrier against a three years' accumulation of losses; and it turned out to be upon the whole the very worst harvest experienced in the present generation. The year was the wettest, and the temperature the lowest upon record.* The ripening months were simply a dreary procession of cold and broken showers. "The mean temperature of July was 3·9° below the average of the previous ten years, while that of August was 2·5° below the average." There were 17 wet days in August; 22 in September; 22 in October. During the six months ending September 30th, on whose character was to depend the fate of the harvest, cold rain fell upon 125 days out of 183—" that is to say," says the Registrar-General—" on two out of every three days." Notwithstanding the deplorable evidence of the weather, and the reports of blighted potato-fields, and inundated river-valleys, and rotting corn, which came fast and thick from every part of the country early in September, an impression in some manner gained ground among certain of the wealthier classes that either the alarm about the harvest was unreal, or that the extent of the damage to the crops was grossly exaggerated.

<small>Incredulity and its consequences</small>

Many benevolent persons at first suffered under the apprehension that the reports of a deficient harvest were simply forged to suit the purposes of political agitation, or to defraud the landlords of their rents, and that the fear of an absolute dearth of food was altogether chimerical. Incredulity of this description has been at all times in Ireland a clog upon the efforts of those who would open the eyes of the Government to the premonitory symptoms of distress, and has too often succeeded in creating a spirit of lethargy and suspicion which nothing short of the death-cries of a population in the pangs of famine could remove. A speaker was on his legs denying the existence of distress in Newry at the commencement of the Great Famine, when word was brought in that a man had just fallen dead of hunger on the streets;† and it was remarked, that, throughout that time of horrors, official persons chose every mincing term in the dictionary, except "famine," to describe the power which was slaying miserable victims around them by the thousand. We shall presently see how serious an impediment to charitable effort was this

---

* Dr. MOORE's "Meteorological Report," I. A. S., p. 19.
† Father O'ROBKE's "History of the Great Famine."

dead-weight of cynical unbelief, which, beginning by deriding the testimony of public speakers and newspaper writers, was no less stubborn when that testimony came to be solemnly endorsed by 1,404 Catholic Priests, 835 Protestant Clergymen, 722 Justices of the Peace, 508 Medical Officers, 977 Poor-Law Guardians, and the 6,171 other Members of the Local Relief Committees. Not the least evil of thus discrediting the moderate testimony of those who are versed in the affairs of the people is that the very exaggeration which is deprecated is directly encouraged; and men who, to a sympathetic hearer, would speak under the responsibility of weighing well their words, are sometimes driven into loose or heated statements in the hope of gaining an audience for truths which they have a burning interest in making known; the result commonly being to increase the suspicions and confuse the facts on both sides.

About the main facts of the condition of Ireland when the harvest was gathered, however, there was no longer room for confusion. The harvest was the worst since the famine years. Two-thirds of the potato-crop were rotted and gone, and the 250,000 people, to whom it was the staff of life, would, by the beginning of the new year, be without food or the means of buying it; 500,000 people more stood upon the verge of ruin. A gloomy foreboding settled down upon the people's hearts. Some vague sense of drifting towards an abyss took possession of them. The portents which preceded the Great Famine seemed to be slowly reproducing themselves; cries of warning, incredulity, reproaches, delays, unpreparedness, and all the while the spectre of a foodless winter drawing nearer. A famine like that of the winter of 1846 no sane man expected in the winter of 1879, no more than those who raised the alarm in 1845 anticipated so horrible an extent of calamity a year afterwards. But that men did not exaggerate when they proclaimed that a calamity, comparable to nothing since the famine years, had overtaken the country, and, that as far as human foresight went, there was as much to dismay a thoughtful Irishman, looking abroad over his country, in the autumn of 1879 as in the autumn of 1845, and more, we shall make abundantly clear by the official figures. The three substantial guarantees against any wholesale reproduction of the scenes of the Great Famine were, that the population was less, that Indian meal was to be bought in any quantity at moderate prices, and that a considerable part of the agricultural classes had raised themselves above the condition of absolute dependence on the potato. An advantage that, perhaps, counted for still more, was a Government which accepted the responsibility for the lives of the people, and, behind that Government, an active and organised public opinion, prompt to discern danger, eager in its criticisms, constant in its admonitions to officials, and commanding, by the medium of the telegraph, an instant influence over the sympathy and assistance of nations at opposite ends of the globe.

Upon the other hand, the Irish problem, in the autumn of 1879, was beset with perplexities which were altogether absent in 1845. The one all-embracing misfortune of the famine years was the failure of the potato-crop. The grain-crops of 1845 and 1846 were favourable, even abundant; and, until the abrogation of the duty on foreign corn had a monopoly of the markets. The winds and rains of 1879 not alone destroyed 2,500,000 tons of potatoes, they wrought a deficiency of 800,000 cwts. of wheat (four-ninths of the fair produce), 5,000,000 cwts. of oats, and 1,500,000 tons of turnips. That is to say, according to the Chancellor of the Exchequer's official computation in the House of Commons, the Irish farmers had suffered a dead loss under all heads by the years' tillage alone of £10,000,000 sterling*—being more than the total loss in 1846, and being "nearly equal to the whole valuation of the land of Ireland, exclusive of buildings." † Remember that this blow descended upon a class who had already lost £1,671,000 worth of potatoes alone the year before, and £3,989,000 worth the year before that; whose cattle had been depreciated in value by at least £15,000,000 in a single year; whose butter trade had sustained a loss of at least £700,000; who had drawn £8,699,000 of their savings out of banks to stop the gap ‡ within the same period; and whose losses in the matter of potatoes alone in the three years equalled in the aggregate the whole estimated losses when the famine of 1846 was at its height. Nor does this represent the depth of the calamity Two classes of losers have to be carefully distinguished from one another—the class who hardly suffered directly at all in 1845-47, and the class who, to the kind of losses incidental to those years, added new ones no less crushing. True, the large farmer class had grown larger and wealthier since 1845; 70 per cent. of the small holdings had been consolidated with that object in the meantime; but, whereas that class remained in almost undiminished affluence after the potato failure of 1845, and stood as bulwarks of employment and charity among their famine-stricken countrymen, it was they who now reeled under the heaviest pecuniary (although not the most immediately vital) losses; whose capital had been for three seasons running out by millions to pay rents which were not earned, and cover losses extending over every branch of their business; wh owere feeding cattle at a loss, raising dairy produce at a loss; and whose very existence was threatened if the gigantic competition of America should go on increasing. These men were themselves above the dread of hunger, if it should come to the worst, for a season or two more, but their resources were gone, their courage crushed; they had cut down their expenditure to the point of much personal privation; as an employing class they were for the moment effaced, and the 90,000 or 100,000 agricultural labourers who looked up to them for employment became suddenly aware that there was no employment to be had upon any terms wherever they turned their despairing eyes. Thus, even in favoured districts, removed from the traditional area of distress, there

Misfortunes of the Large Farmers

Who were effaced as an Employing Class

* The estimated value of the Irish crops had decreased from £32,758,000 in 1878 to £22,743,000 in 1879—and 1878 was itself a year of disaster.
† Dr. NEILSON HANCOCK's Papers on Ireland.
‡ Statistics on Savings in Ireland, 1880.

arose the double phenomenon of a farming class paralyzed by losses and the fear of further losses, and a landless labouring population huddled together in the towns, without the smallest prospect of subsistence.

And if this was the condition of those parts of the country emancipated from dependence upon the potato-crop, let us now try to realize to what a condition those vast tracts along the western seaboard had sunk, to which the potato-crop was still the vital condition of existence, when that crop lay miserably rotting in the fields and pits. To say that the farmers lost £8,000,000 by the potato-crop of 1879 as compared with a good year like 1876, or that they lost £20,000,000 on that head alone in three years, conveys no adequate measure of the disaster unless we remember that proportionately the overwhelming preponderance of that loss fell upon the shoulders not of the wealthier class of large farmers, with whom the potato was an altogether subsidiary article of produce, but upon the small holders, to whom it was the prop and mainstay of existence. To understand this, let us look a little more closely at the figures. The immense county of Donegal, which has an area of 585,000 nominally cultivable acres (mostly mountain grazing lands) against 564,000 acres of unproductive bogs and barren mountains, lakes, rivers, roads, and fences, had 47,734 acres under potatoes in 1879, with 31,485 occupiers and their families to be fed thereon. The county of Kildare, with 355,936 cultivable acres to less than 40,000 worthless ones, devoted only 8,764 acres to potatoes, and had only 8,948 occupiers, of whom 4,095 held above fifteen acres a-piece.* Again contrast the case of the unhappy county of Mayo, 1,318,129 acres in extent, valued in all at £314,302, with the rich county of Meath with little more than a third the area (578,247 acres) valued at nearly double that figure (£544,888); the one with 44 per cent. of its surface a barren wilderness, the other with 1·9 per cent. of bog and marsh, and ·0 per cent. of barren mountain land; the one having to sustain 37,027 families of occupiers out of its poverty, the other only 11,730 comparatively flourishing occupiers of the richest lands in the island. Mayo staked 58,067 acres of potatoes upon the chances of the harvest; Meath only 12,069. That is to say, three-fourths of the destruction of the potato-crop fell upon the counties of the western coast, which were both the poorest and the most vitally dependent upon it; upon a race of small farmers, moreover, whose store-cattle had lain upon their hands as so many useless food-consumers; who were, therefore, proportionately as severe losers in this respect also as the graziers; who, in two of the poorest counties of Connaught alone, had lost £250,000† of English wages, and within about fifty of the poorest parishes in those counties had lost £50,000 more by the collapse of the kelp trade. At the same time it became known, to the horror of the public, into what a condition of life this avalanche of misfortunes had already sunk some 50,000 of those cottier-tenants; driven, for the most part, by the events which followed the Great Famine from the more

---

*Agricultural Statistics, p. 34.
Dr. NEILSON HANCOCK's Paper on Irish Migratory Labourers.

fertile tracts into the waste boglands and the crevices of the rocky seaboard, and weighted with considerable rents even here; supporting life upon the food of animals in dwellings to which civilized communities would not consign their dogs; able to grow little except potatoes on their sterile patches; forced to put down year after year the same constantly deteriorating race of seed upon the same worn and exhausted soil; wrestling, season after season, with hunger; feeding half the year upon potatoes, and lying at the mercy of small dealers to tide them over the remaining six months with advances of Indian meal upon whatever terms of credit they chose to dictate; forced to borrow more, and able to repay less after each of these three last calamitous seasons, and now at last beaten to the very brink of the gulf, without food, money, or credit.

Credit at an end

The discovery of the universal extinction of credit it was which precipitated the crisis. Famine had been staved off from January to August, 1879, by almost desperate credit. Two food-dealers alone in the little town of Castlerea had £40,000 due to them by the peasants, although they had only been repaid 15 per cent. of the previous year's credits.* Advances to the amount of £14,000 were totted up in the traders' books in the poor village of Oughterard, the valuation of the entire Union in which it is situated being only £14,897. But the credit of peasantry and shopkeepers alike had now touched bottom. The remnant of the potato harvest once eaten out, nothing stood between the western peasants and an unspeakable fate—nothing, except the power of the State or the charity of the world. Still another terrible menace—one which Sir STAFFORD NORTHCOTE, in his speech at the Dublin Mansion House, on October 9th, anticipated would turn out to be the most serious of all—was the prospect of a fuel famine; the peat, which alone can be burned in the cabins of the western peasantry, having lain for months, even to the verge of winter, at the mouths of the cuttings in the bogs drenched through with moisture.

FOUNDATION OF THE COMMITTEE.

The situation in Autumn

The summary of the situation, then, in the autumn of 1879, was this:—that, if the landlords and the shopkeepers, themselves sorely pressed, chose to exercise their legal right of seizing upon the harvest in satisfaction of their debts, all the conditions of wholesale famine were at hand; that, considering the sacrifices to which the forbearance of both these classes had already submitted, and the solemn sense of brotherhood in misfortune which had come over nearly the entire community, this was happily an improbable contingency; but that even if the landlords should (as they afterwards did) forego several millions of rent, and the shopkeepers several millions of debt due to them, there

---

* This apparently incredible fact, which was first stated in the *Freeman's Journal*, was afterwards verified by the special correspondent of the *Daily News*, and by Professor BALDWIN, Assistant Commissioner to the Royal Agricultural Commission, who inspected the books.

would still remain, beside 100,000 of the pauper labouring class, immense tracts along the entire western coast from Donegal to Cork, where the population were drifting straight into the horrors of a famine. It followed that, although no moderate thinker could apprehend that the approaching winter would see the country desolated to anything like the extent of 1846 and 1847, the premonitory conditions were in almost every respect more depressing than those of 1845,* and that an equal disregard of those conditions now would produce in the following years a still more terrible calamity than that which followed the blundering apathy and vain warnings of 1845.

An appeal Charity deferred why?

Long before the Mansion House Committee was formed, most of the men who afterwards contributed to establish it foresaw that such a movement was inevitable. It was for three reasons deferred to the last moment to which it could be safely deferred. In the first place, the landlords having remitted (as is calculated) at least £3,000,000 of rents, and the traders having almost nowhere attempted to exact their accounts by force of law, the potato harvest, such as it was, might be trusted to keep the people alive until about the opening of the new year, while a few weeks providential dry warmth in October turned a considerable portion of the sodden peat into fuel, and so to a great extent dissolved anxiety on that score. In the second place, the persistence with which in some quarters the harvest was still asserted to be an average one, and the distress decried as partly or even wholly an imposture, as well as perhaps the exaggerations into which the sense that their danger was ignored or made light of threw the panic-stricken people, disposed many to wait until the course of events should reveal the precise character of the crisis in a way that would put all further controversy on the subject to silence. Above all, it was felt that not alone would such charitable funds as we had any right to count upon be in all probability inadequate to the emergency, but that private charity, even if it could be made a principal means of coping with a widespread national calamity, would both breed the vices of mendicancy among the people and absolve the State from what was generally conceived to be the duty of meeting a national catastrophe out of the national funds.

Feeling that a National Catastrophe should be met out of the National Funds

The Central Relief Committee, analogous to our own, which was founded in Dublin in the years of the Great Famine, was only able to collect £83,934 17s. 11d., of which £20,000 was granted from a British charitable organization; and it was conceded that if the descriptions of the impending distress were not wicked fictions, it would take a million of money even to appease the pangs of hunger with the coarsest and scantiest food. Nobody dared to anticipate the golden tide of charity which the first cry of destitution, received with coldness and suspicion nearer home, set flowing from two mighty young nations at the furthermost ends of the globe. Nobody had the right to anticipate it. The country had been already at least twice in this century paraded before the world as an object of charity. The world had most nobly

---

* Dr. HANCOCK's Papers on Ireland, p. 9.

poured balsam into its wounds. The kindly burst of sympathy from our kith beyond the seas, the ready pledge of brotherhood from generous strangers all the world over, had brought no bitterness and had left no memories but those of gratitude and love. Nevertheless, there was a certain pang of humiliation and shame in the thought of appealing for the alms of distant nations before any sufficient attempt was made to utilise the resources of our own. The country was suffering deeply in every part, dangerously in some parts. But it was not bankrupt. It had reserves of capital. The unappropriated surplus of the Church Temporalities Fund represented a sum of £5,000,000 of Irish money, specially dedicated to extraordinary Irish needs. The country formed part of the wealthiest empire in the world. The self-respect of the people themselves revolted against the idea of national mendicancy. "Work, not alms," was the burden of the cry which resounded through the country all the autumn and winter from public meetings, Boards of Guardians, and assemblages of the Catholic clergy. A meeting of the Irish Catholic Hierarchy, held on the 14th of October, deputed four prelates of their body—the Archbishops of ARMAGH and DUBLIN, and the Bishops of ELPHIN and CLONFERT—to wait upon the LORD LIEUTENANT, at Dublin Castle, in order to urge upon his Grace that a prompt system of employment upon useful public works was the main requirement of the time. The Corporation of Dublin, with only one dissentient, adopted a resolution on the 30th of October, on the motion of Mr. GRAY, pressing the Government to make timely provision for the approaching emergency, and declaring: "That in the opinion of this Council the best means of discharging this primary duty of Government without pauperising and demoralizing large numbers of the industrial population of the kingdom, is by the prompt institution, on an adequate scale, of reproductive works by which employment would be provided for the people." Seventy Irish members of Parliament signed a memorial to the EARL OF BEACONSFIELD, the Prime Minister, in which they most earnestly urged upon the Government, through him, the necessity of taking immediate steps to prevent or mitigate as far as possible the threatened calamity. "We believe," said the memorialists, "that this can be best done by affording assistance to works of a permanent and useful character. Promptness is absolutely necessary, as delay will only result as on former occasions in ill-considered and unproductive expenditure. If the law does not give the Government power to meet the emergency we would urge the desirability of summoning Parliament for a short winter session." The MARQUIS OF HAMILTON headed an influential deputation of noblemen and gentlemen of all political hues to the CHIEF SECRETARY to solicit a loan from the Treasury for the institution of a great and useful public work in southern Donegal. In fact, the general conviction in Ireland was that £1,000,000 advanced out of Irish funds and expended either in the autumn or in spring upon a comprehensive and well-considered scheme of public works or assisted industry in the more afflicted districts, would break the back of the more urgent distress; that that amount

Movement for Public Works

distributed in wages would practically replace the exhausted credit of the peasantry, at least in the article of their humble food; that, instead of sinking under the temptations of organized and recognised beggary, the people would spring eagerly at the chance of feeding themselves and paying their way by honest labour; that trade confidence would revive with the circulation of money in districts from which money had almost disappeared; and that not only would a dangerous emergency have been thus tided over without suffering or demoralization, but that a permanent addition to the producing power of the country would have been made, by the extent of land that would have been drained and reclaimed, by the railways, roads, and fishery piers that would have been constructed in the very districts where those advantages were most lamentably wanting, and where the ordinary course of enterprise could never have supplied them. A similar course of policy was urged in vain upon the Government of Sir ROBERT PEEL in 1845, when famine was preventible, and was embraced the next year when famine had become ungovernable.

In the meantime, evidence was piled upon evidence to show that widespread distress, and over extensive districts absolute destitution, was at hand; and the sense of gloom and uneasiness grew deeper. The Catholic Clergy of the diocese of Clogher, comprising the Priests of Monaghan and of large districts of Fermanagh, Tyrone, Donegal, and Louth, came to a remarkable resolution, "commending the melancholy state of the country to the consideration of our rulers, who are bound to look to us, and calling on the Irish Members of Parliament to force our condition on the attention of the Government before it is too late." The Bishop and Priests of the diocese of Kilmore, in a declaration published on the 16th of October, spoke of it as "a question which we know to be one of life or death to many persons," and —speaking of the labouring population of a district which was supposed to be one of the most comfortable in Ireland—"without money, without credit, and without work, they must, if not soon and generously aided, become the victims of famine, pestilence, and death." The Government, meanwhile, maintained an attitude of watchful reserve. They undertook the responsibility of dealing with the emergency as it arose. A popular impression ran abroad that they were not fully persuaded of the reality of the danger, and that their distrust, as well as perhaps the feelings engendered by an intense agrarian agitation in Ireland, had communicated an equal degree of incredulity in England. The *Times* announced on the 17th of September—"There is the best reason for believing that the losses of the Irish farmer have been trifling compared with those of the English farmer. Food has been and is everywhere cheap and plentiful." On the 27th of September, wrote the *Daily Telegraph*—"The harvest in Ireland has not turned out badly on the whole, for the rains that have deluged England, have more or less avoided the sister island, where the amount of moisture has not much exceeded the usual average."* The LORD

_{Prospects growing gloomier}

_{Discouraging attitude of the Government}

---

* Dr. MOORE's Official Returns show that there were 22 rainy days in that month in Ireland.

LIEUTENANT, in his speech, at the Newry Cattle Show Banquet, on the 17th of August, had described the occasion as one "marked by very great commercial, and, to a certain extent, agricultual depression;" adding, "I believe the agricultural distress which exists in England is far more oppressive and far more severe at the present time than it is in Ireland." The Chancellor of the Exchequer (Sir STAFFORD NORTHCOTE), speaking at a banquet in the Dublin Mansion House on the 9th of October, declared "that there had been a good deal of exaggeration of the loss or failure of the harvest in many parts of the country," and seemed to attach more importance to the prospect of a dearth of fuel. Mr. MITCHELL HENRY, M.P., a Member of the Royal Agricultural Commission, stated in public, that the two Assistant Commissioners (Professor BALDWIN and Major ROBERTSON), whom the Government had appointed to visit the western coast, had been "so horrified with the impending destitution," that they had made a special report to the Government. This was some days before the deputation of Bishops went to Dublin Castle to ask for public works. They received a discouraging reply. The PRIME MINISTER was unable to find leisure to receive seventy Irish Members of Parliament upon the subject. November passed. Employment had almost vanished. Crowds of hungry labourers in Skibbereen, Kilmallock, Dungarvan, Kilkenny, and other places, invaded the workhouses, clamouring for work or food. In the more stricken districts the small farmers were actually consuming their seed potatoes. The instinct of charity was already stirring. People in the Australian cities were straining eagerly for some definite hint of how much was needed, and when. Early in December, the COMTE DE PARIS sent £10 into Connemara. Still, earlier, the BISHOP OF DETROIT, U.S., remitted £824 15s. to the ARCHBISHOP OF CASHEL, as the contribution of his diocese, and a first instalment of £200 reached the BISHOP OF ROSS from the diocese of Cleveland, Ohio. On the 16th of December, the LORD MAYOR OF DUBLIN received a telegram from Adelaide, South Australia, inquiring whether assistance was needed, and who would receive it? It was the first act in the history of the Mansion House Committee—the first presage of that extraordinary outpouring of sympathy which was, in a few months, to fill the coffers of this Committee with more Australian money than the Central Relief Committee of the Great Famine time could collect from the whole world.

The Duchess of Marlborough's Fund

Two days afterwards the people of England were startled by a letter in the *Times* of the 16th December, from Her Grace the DUCHESS OF MARLBOROUGH, making an eloquent and urgent appeal to English benevolence for the relief of distress in Ireland. "There will be extreme misery and suffering," she wrote, "among the poor, owing to the want of employment, loss of turf, loss of cattle, and failure of the potatoes, unless a vigorous effort of private charity is got up to supplement the ordinary system of Poor Law relief." "After anxious consideration," Her Grace had decided to form a committee of ladies, over which she would herself preside, to take charge of whatever funds should be entrusted to her for distribution, and she entreated her countrymen of the sister isle "generously to contribute to the relief of the miserable sufferers by the inclemency of the season which, added to the rainy climate and ungenial soil of the West, have well nigh produced a famine of food and fuel." Two days subsequently Her Grace solicited the LORD MAYOR OF LONDON to aid her, impressively adding: "The distress will, I fear, be terrible this winter unless private benevolence will come to our assistance." Her Grace's action, inspired, as it was known to be, by the fullest official knowledge of the situation, created a deep impression of surprise, and awakened a great response in England; and the courage with which the DUCHESS OF MARLBOROUGH initiated her appeal, the zeal with which she prosecuted it, the unflagging energy with which she undertook a principal part in the vast operations necessitated by the large funds entrusted to her, and the spirit of anxious sympathy with the people which inspired and sustained her, will always remain among the most gracious recollections of these gloomy months.

It was now evident that no large scheme of public employment was to be looked for; and that not alone was charity left to be the only weapon against starvation, but that charity, to be effectual at all, must be sought at once. A great land-owner like the Hon. Col. KING-HARMAN, M.P., might still declare in the *Times*:* "I cannot hope, nor dare I write a word to express a belief, that the (DUCHESS OF MARLBOROUGH'S) demand, however well responded to, will meet the present crisis," and might exclaim: "Allow the worst against us and this remains—our people are starving and are willing to work." The BISHOP OF ACHONRY, aching with the sight of three hundred pallid faces gathered about his door on Christmas Eve, beseeching food, might cry out with a terrible force: "We, Irish priests and bishops, are custodians of morality and order. It is our duty to counsel peace and preach loyalty. But it is hard to instil loyalty or promote peace when there is question of empty stomachs and an unsympathetic Government." But "our people are starving" was the one imperative fact of the moment. Fifteen hundred applicants "to our horror" swarmed into Clifden on the 21st December to share the £12 10s. which was all that the local Relief Committee had to give them. Mr. MITCHELL HENRY, M.P., had "never seen men so changed" as the peasants of the Letter hills; "pale, thin, bloodless, and without a smile, their condition is absolutely without hope." It was no longer a time for national punctilio or sighs for what might have been. Upon Christmas Eve the citizens of Dublin were summoned hurriedly together in the Oak Room of the Mansion House by the then Lord Mayor (Sir JOHN BARRINGTON) to deliberate upon the situation. A short adjournment was found necessary owing to the inconvenience of the day and the informal manner in which the meeting had been summoned; in order also to arrive at settled opinions whether the charitable movement to be here inaugurated was to be an independent organization or should constitute itself ancillary to the Ladies' Committee formed by the DUCHESS OF MARLBOROUGH;

Hope of Public Works at an end

First Meeting at the Mansion House

* December 25th.

whether it should confine its operations to the dangerous distress which was gaining head in Dublin itself or extend them to the whole field of Irish misery. The adjournment was made still further desirable by the fact of its being the eve of the periodical change in the Mayoralty, when the new Lord Mayor, on whose responsibility the movement must be carried on, was about to accede to office. So strongly did the feeling run even still that private charity could only purchase off the danger for a time, and that State employment on reproductive works was the only thorough-going specific for the crisis, that Mr. V. B. DILLON, Jun., and several other gentlemen called on the meeting not to separate without addressing some representation to that purport to the Government. The meeting, however, preferred not to embarrass itself before it was well formed with a subject which might either have been thought to fall outside the strict bounds of a charitable movement or have occasioned controversy among men who had no controversy as to the existence of dire distress, and the necessity of grappling with it promptly. Upon this last point, which was the main point, the meeting thought as one man. "I have come up from the West within a few days," said Sir ARTHUR GUINNESS, M.P., "and I can say most truly that any subscriptions to any amount, however large, that can be obtained will be very inadequate to meet the necessities of the case. There are hundreds—for all I know, thousands—of families whose supply of potatoes has been nearly consumed. Their credit is at an end, and what is to happen to these people unless the hand of the charitable comes in to afford relief to the starving, I don't know."

The Adjourned Meeting

The adjourned meeting was held on Friday, the 2nd of January, 1880, in the Oak Room of the Mansion House, where only the previous day the incoming Lord Mayor of Dublin (the Right Hon. EDMUND DWYER GRAY, M.P.) had been receiving the congratulations of the citizens on assuming office. There was a complete fusion of creeds, ranks, and parties in the attendance. The Protestant Archbishop of Dublin (the Most Rev. Dr. TRENCH) was present to assist at the foundation of a movement in whose operations for many months his matured wisdom, hearty sympathy, and conciliatory spirit bore a constant and influential part. The Catholic Archbishop (the Most Rev. Dr. McCABE), who was unavoidably absent, commissioned the Rev. T. J. O'REILLY specially to represent him. The Conservative and Liberal members for the City and the University; numbers of leading Catholic and Protestant clergymen; the ex-Lord Mayor (Sir JOHN BARRINGTON, D.L.); the High Sheriff (Sir J. W. MACKEY); the RECORDER OF DUBLIN; members of Parliament, magistrates, and other influential persons of every political and religious denomination, mingled cordially in a union which has never once been broken, even by a division, during the trying vicissitudes of six anxious months. The ARCHBISHOP OF DUBLIN moved the LORD MAYOR into the chair. In doing so, he congratulated them all that the honour and the responsibility of guiding this movement had fallen to one who, they were all confident, would bring it to a successful issue. That the movement was essentially non-political and non-sectarian was the first point emphasized in the short speech of the LORD MAYOR. That there could by any possibility be a rivalry between it and kindred charitable organisations he disclaimed in the most distinct way. "I take it that every man who has come here," he said, "recognises in the most grateful spirit the gracious and generous manner in which Her Grace the DUCHESS OF MARLBOROUGH has acted on this occasion (hear, hear); and if it be the view of this meeting that another relief fund should be originated, I presume you will select men to form a committee of the fund who will take care that there shall be no clashing between the two organisations (hear, hear)." It was the unanimous view of the meeting that another fund should be originated—that, in the words of SIR ARTHUR GUINNESS there was "room—ample room"—for both of them, and ample need for every penny they could glean—that, in fine, while the DUCHESS OF MARLBOROUGH would appeal, it was hoped successfully, in quarters where an Irish committee might fail of influence, a committee representing all ranks and sections of Irish opinion would possibly command a readier access to unbounded fields of Australian and American assistance. So that point was settled. The question whether the movement was to be a civic or a national one was decided by the very composition of the meeting. The grand object was to create a committee who should command confidence; over what area or in what manner they would distribute relief might be safely confided to their discretion, and could be limited only by the limit of distress, wherever it showed itself. The resolution which called this committee into existence was in the following terms :—

<small>Origination of Mansion House Fund</small>

"That the poorer classes in many parts of Ireland must, during the coming season, suffer great distress, involving absolute destitution, if extraneous aid be not liberally and promptly supplied; and that, without interfering with the beneficent efforts for a similar purpose already instituted, a Fund be now opened for the Relief of Distress in Ireland, to be called 'The Dublin Mansion House Relief Fund.'"

It was proposed by Sir ARTHUR GUINNESS (now LORD ARDILAUN); and Mr. P. J. SMYTH, M.P., who seconded it, and who "felt, very profoundly, that dire necessity alone could justify the appeal for extraneous aid," confessed with sorrow that that dire necessity had arisen. Incidentally it was mentioned that the BISHOP OF RAPHOE declared that already in ten at least of the twenty-five parishes of Donegal, "the condition of the people could not be much worse, short of absolute famine;" and Mr. GEORGE BROWNE, M.P., stated that he knew, from personal experience, that, in the greater part of Mayo, the crop of potatoes was already exhausted, and in two months more the people would be without food, or the hope of buying it. But nobody any longer dreamed of debating the necessity for the new organization: its composition was the chief business of the meeting. A representative Committee was nominated, the Treasurers and Secretaries appointed, and a subscription list commenced upon the spot.

SOURCES OF THE FUND.

<small>Universality of the Response</small>

We have traced the circumstances which impelled the Mansion House Committee to throw itself upon the charity of mankind, for the lives of the peasantry. We propose now to detail how its appeals were prosecuted, and how they were answered in every region of the globe; how messages were flashed free around the world for charity sake, and tens of thousands of pounds were flashed back; how men in the young Australian cities, French noblemen, African diamond-diggers, Mahommedans and Hindoos, the Canadian Parliament, the great-hearted citizens of the United States, the exiles in remote South American cities, were stirred by the same impulse, assembled to utter the same sentiments, and rushed into the same noble rivalry of beneficence: and by what an unparalleled exertion of human sympathy many thousands of the helpless Irish peasants were snatched from the agonies of famine.

IRELAND.

<small>Smallness of Irish Subscriptions accounted for</small>

The meeting which called the Mansion House Committee into being subscribed £1,500 then and there. Within a few weeks the Irish subscriptions (which were chiefly Dublin subscriptions) exceeded £4,000. In the end they reached the sum of £8,324 18s. 4d. In considering the smallness of this sum, it will be borne in mind that it offers no criterion whatever of the sacrifices made in Ireland to cope with the distress. It represents mainly the contributions of the citizens of Dublin. It represents only a small part even of these. Many munificent contributions from Dublin had found their way to the DUCHESS OF MARLBOROUGH'S Fund before this Committee was formed. Many more were made in the shape of a separate diocesan collection at the churches. Not only this, but the distress in Dublin itself had grown to such a head, owing to the inflow of pauperised agricultural labourers, and the paralysis of all sources of employment, that it was found necessary, in order that foreign subscriptions might go intact to purchase food for the famishing peasantry, to institute a separate Dublin Charities Fund, whose whole revenues were subscribed in Dublin. The resources of the traders in the towns, of the landowners, and the large farmers, had been enormously encroached upon by the same causes which brought starvation to the doors of their poorer countrymen. The large farmers had lost millions of capital, and were standing aghast at the future. The landlords in general had been obliged to relinquish portion, and in the more afflicted districts the entire, of their rents; and were many of them themselves beset with grievous pecuniary embarrassments. The greater number of those who could still afford to be generous preferred to exercise their generosity by providing employment locally for the people; and princely examples, such as that of Sir ARTHUR GUINNESS, might be cited, where not only employment, but food and clothing were thus placed within reach of the peasantry without the fact being evidenced in any public subscription list. The merchants and shopkeepers of the towns, again, had borne a crushing share of the general disaster; millions of the depreciation in the value of crops and stock, were simply represented by so much swollen bad debts in the shopkeepers' books, and by their own shaken credit; nevertheless, apart from innumerable cases in which Indian meal was still doled out of the shops in pure charity, local subscriptions were organized even in darkly distressed neighbourhoods; and in towns like Nenagh, Skibbereen, Tipperary, Ballina, Dungarvan and Arklow, sums of £300 or £400 were raised and expended locally before recourse was had to outside organisations for a single shilling. Nay, the generosity of the distressed peasantry to each other—the readiness with which a cottier removed by only a few weeks' supply of potatoes from starvation would share his little store with some wretch whom gaunt starvation had already in its grasp—forms one of the sweetest and most touching, as it was one of the commonest, pictures of these terrible months; and the amount of their humble contributions to keep each other alive, at a time when the hope of human help was vague, and when looking into each other's eyes they beheld what seemed to them the light of death, will probably rank as the most precious of all in a Record more enduring than this. Add to all this, that some of the wealthier classes in the few districts unvisited by distress held somewhat selfishly aloof as soon as their sense of responsibility was removed by the unexpected munificence of the foreign contributions—that the country was paying £1,011,888 in taxes for the support of its paupers, even in 1879, against £523,000 twenty years before;* that it was paying £117,275 in out-door relief alone, against £8,239 in 1859; that the number of paupers actually in the workhouses reached 59,870 in February, 1880, the highest number during the Famine of 1846, having been 51,802; and that in the spring of 1880, there was the enormous number of 117,454 persons receiving relief at the expense of the taxpayers—many of them themselves little removed above the necessity of relief—and it will be readily seen that the £8,204 subscribed to the Mansion House Fund from Ireland is no measure of the enormous sacrifices which the crisis imposed upon the great bulk of the Irish people.

GREAT BRITAIN.

The Committee was no sooner formed than the LORD MAYOR, as its Chairman, despatched an identical telegram to the Mayors of the great English and Scotch municipalities soliciting their co-operation. Within a few days after that appeal the MAYOR of BOLTON remitted subscriptions to the amount of £130 in response; Birmingham followed with a first instalment of £100 on the 16th January; Manchester with £250 on the 19th of January; Cardiff with £200 on the 21st January; Birmingham with £100 more; Wigan with £150; Sheffield with £500 on the 26th January; Glasgow with

The Response from England

---

* Local Government Board Report for 1879. In 1880 of course the poor rate will have been much greater.

£750 on the 13th of February; and so on until the English and Welsh subscriptions reached a total of £16,941 17s. 5d.; and the Scotch subscriptions a total of £2,805 6s. 2d. Considerable as these sums are, it must not for the honour of the British name be supposed that they were the full measure of British sympathy in a crisis which imperilled the lives of thousands of their Irish fellow-subjects. In the first place a long period of agricultural and commercial depression had produced a considerable degree of poverty and privation throughout large districts in England; while the confusion in many English minds between the distress in Ireland and the formidable political movement to which it had given birth or sustenance, alienated beyond doubt a large mass of English sympathy. In the next place, the London Mansion House Fund, usually the main channel of British charity, was subsidiary to and an affluent of the DUCHESS OF MARLBOROUGH's Ladies' Committee; and by its means and through the agency of the English newspapers, the largest proportion of British subscriptions found their way to that organisation. Certain misunderstandings arose between the Duchess of MARLBOROUGH's Committee and this Committee, for which this Committee most certainly was in no way responsible. They were, no doubt, caused by a desire on the part of Her Grace's Committee to obtain as large contributions as possible in aid of their charitable objects. These matters were sufficiently dealt with at the time, and are only referred to here because they no doubt had an effect in checking subscriptions to this Committee from England, where statements circulated by the DUCHESS OF MARLBOROUGH's Committee had a wider circulation than that obtained by the subsequent corrections from this Committee, which their publication necessitated.

FRANCE.

Formation of the French Committee

The bond of affection which has always united the French and Irish peoples, especially in hours of misfortune for either, emboldened the Mansion House Committee from the beginning to look to France as one of the traditional friends of the starving Irish peasants. Accordingly Mr. J. P. LEONARD was requested to take measures for the formation of a Committee in the French Capital, and Mr. P. J. SMYTH, M.P., was deputed to represent this Committee, and convey the appeal of the Irish people. On the 21st of February, largely through the indefatigable energy of Mr. J. P. LEONARD, a "Comité de Secours aux Irlandais" was formally constituted, which included many of the most illustrious names in France. His Eminence the CARDINAL ARCHBISHOP OF PARIS was its President, and the roll of the Committee included four Dukes, nine Counts, the Vice-President of the Chamber of Deputies, seven Senators, ten Deputies, and representatives of the Bar, of the French Academy, and of the Bank of France. The Executive Committee, upon whose shoulders the burthen of the movement chiefly fell, was composed of General DE CHABAUD LATOUR, M. CONNELLY, Conseiller à la Cour de Cassation; Comte DE FLAVIGNY, whose interest in Ireland

had been warmly enkindled by his father's mission of thanks to Ireland after the war of 1871; M. C. GODELLE, Député de la Seine; M. le Duc ROCHEFOUCAULT DE BISACCIA, M. LABOULAYE, Senator; Mr. J. P. LEONARD, M. le Comte O'CONNELL, Vicomte O'NEILL DE TYRONE, Docteur RIANT, Secretary of the Society of Aid for the Wounded; and M. l'Abbé D'HULST, Vicar-General of Paris; with Comte DE FLAVIGNY as General Secretary; Comte O'CONNELL as Treasurer, and M. SIMONNET as Secretary of the Committee. Notwithstanding the cloud of depression which was passing over France itself, and the gigantic tax just imposed upon the charity of the French people for the relief of the sufferers by the inundations in Spain, the movement prospered beyond anticipation. Diocesan collections were instituted by order of the bishops in every diocese of France; 29,000 francs were subscribed from Arras, 25,000 from Rennes, 18,000 from Toulouse, 17,000 from Versailles, 13,000 from Tours, 11,000 from Bayeux, and Verdun, 8,000 from Metz; the CARDINAL ARCHBISHOP OF PARIS decreed a collection in every parish, of the capital in a pastoral letter overflowing with tenderness and goodwill for Ireland; the celebrated Père MONSABRÉ uttered a magnificent appeal from the pulpit of the Madeleine, which produced over 22,000 francs; Madame la Maréchale DE MACMAHON herself, and some of the greatest ladies of France, were among the collectors; the officers of various regiments of Chasseurs and of the Line, religious orders, associations of workmen, and members of the aristocracy, poured in their contributions; and, before June, there was realized a fund of 842,104 francs. In order to avoid doing any violence to the susceptibilities exhibited with reference to the destination of the English subscriptions, the Paris Committee decided to divide its receipts into three equal portions, one of which was entrusted to the Catholic Archbishop of DUBLIN, for division among the Irish bishops, the second to the Mansion House Committee, and the third to the British Ambassador at Paris, Lord LYONS, for transmission to the Duchess of MARLBOROUGH'S Committee; the motive of this partition being admirably expressed in the declaration:—
"Absolument étranger lui-même à toute préoccupation politique, le Comité Français déclare n'avoir d'autre mobile qu'un sentiment de reconnaissance et sympathie pour l'infortune, d'autre ambition que celle d'être un intermédiaire utile entre l'Irlande qui souffre et la France qui se souvient." Remembering that 200,000 francs in addition to the sums received by the Paris Committee, were transmitted direct to Ireland by the French bishops, that 103,000 francs more were subscribed on the separate appeal of the Paris journal, *l'Univers*, and that the total aid received from that generous nation amounted to at least 700,000 francs,* the Mansion House Committee have some reason to congratulate themselves upon having given the initiative to the work of opening up this noble fund of charity, and evoking so memorable a pledge of sympathy and affection from France to Ireland.

<small>Greatness of the Response</small>

---

* Rapport lû à l'Assemblée Générale du Comité de Secours, p. 18.

INDIA.

The advantages of Free Telegraphing.

The Mansion House Committee possessed one inestimable means of enkindling foreign sympathy, which this is the place most gratefully to record. They enjoyed the privilege of constant telegraphic communication, free of cost, with those regions of the Eastern and Western Continents where the most liberal aid might be expected; and were thus enabled not only to convey the first decisive announcement to those countries that the crisis had come, but to acknowledge the remittances and announce the different stages of the distress to Committees separated by many thousands of miles with as much facility and at as little cost as if they were within the circuit of the penny post. This tremendous advantage was the fruit of a mission to London, undertaken by Mr. V. B. DILLON, Jun., shortly after the formation of the Committee. By the kind and powerful introduction of Viscount MONCK, Chairman of the Anglo-American Telegraph Company, Mr. DILLON was fortunate enough to secure not only from that great Company, which gave the control of the American telegraph system, but from the Eastern Extension Company, which opened up free communication with India and Australia, the generous concession that all the charitable appeals and telegrams of the Committee should be forwarded free of cost throughout the continents traversed by these world-wide systems. The advantage was completed by the offer of the American Associated Press to transmit the appeals of the Committee, free of charge, throughout the American cities. Without these concessions, literally thousands of pounds must have been risked in sending the telegrams which were thus despatched without cost, or, the telegrams remaining unsent, our distant benefactors must have continued in perplexity and uncertainty as to the situation in Ireland, until the rich remittances which saved so many thousands of Irish lives would either never have come or have come too late.

Madras

In India, for example, the telegraphed appeal of the LORD MAYOR of DUBLIN was the first reliable assurance that any calamity in the remotest degree resembling Famine was fastening upon Ireland. No sooner was the uncertainty dispelled, than a powerful wave of sympathy rolled over that great empire. A preliminary meeting of a few gentlemen in the Madras Club, on the 24th of January, at which Brigadier-General O'CONNELL was moved to the chair, and the Hon. Mr. Justice KERNAN and Colonel BERESFORD were the chief speakers, subscribed 2,450 rupees before they parted, and gave the first impulse to the movement in the Southern Presidency. This was but the precursor of the immense meeting of natives and Europeans that assembled at Patcheaffah's Hall, on the 10th of February, under the presidency of the Chief Justice of Madras (SIR CHARLES TURNER) at which not only did the Bishop of MADRAS and most of the great European functionaries pledge their energies to the movement, but the sympathy of the most distinguished native Indian citizens of Madras was testified upon the grounds so pithily summarised by the Hon. G. N. GUJPATI RAO, when he said : "It is our bounden duty to assist suffering humanity in Ireland, not only because the united British people have assisted us largely during our late famine; not only because the Irish Members of Parliament have always advocated the cause of India; not only because our army is largely recruited from the Irish people, and to them we owe the preservation of our country; not only because our statesmen, judges, lawyers, and orators have largely come from Ireland and benefitted this country by their skill, erudition and political sagacity; not only because Ireland and India are identical in their several governments in many ways; but also because our sympathy demands that we should assist our fellow man when he has become houseless, foodless and clotheless through no fault of his own." Before the Madras collection closed, £6,898 8s. had been remitted by the Honorary Secretary, Mr. MICHAEL GOULD, to this Committee.

The movement in Bombay was inaugurated by a great public meeting on the 28th of January, at which the Governor of that Presidency took the chair, and at which the heads of the Parsee, Hindu and Mohammedan communities vied with the great European officials in the warmth of their language and in the munificence of their subscriptions. The prosecution of the work devolved upon a Committee numbering one hundred and sixty of the foremost citizens of Bombay. An attempt was made to divert the entire proceeds to the Duchess of MARLBOROUGH's Fund, on the ground of a political difference between the LORD LIEUTENANT of Ireland and the LORD MAYOR of Dublin; but the Hon. Mr. MOWATT pointed out the invidiousness of excluding the Mansion House Committee from any share of the subscriptions, seeing that the first intimation received in Bombay of the need of any subscriptions at all was the telegram of the LORD MAYOR, as Chairman of that Committee. The Hon. MORARJEE GOCULDASS even went the length of declaring that he would withdraw from the Committee if this course were taken, observing that "the native community would not subscribe to a fund which was to be administered governmentally, for that was what they would regard as the practical meaning of handing over the whole of the money to the wife of the Viceroy." The money was ultimately divided in equal shares between the two Irish Central Committees; and the amount which reached this Committee from Bombay, was £3,600. The movement spread to Bengal, where, on the 19th of February, a Committee composed of the LIEUTENANT-GOVERNOR, nearly all the great officers of Government, with three Maharajas and a number of other native dignitaries was formed, with the Hon. RIVERS THOMPSON at the head of the executive Sub-Committee; the Hon. J. O'KINEALY, the Hon. KRISTODAS PAL, and Mr. J. W. O'KEEFFE as Honorary Secretaries; and Mr. H. W. J. WOOD as Honorary Treasurer. The proportion of the Bengal Subscription remitted to the Mansion House Committee amounted to £4,490.

A still more remarkable impulse of spontaneous native sympathy moved the people of the great State of Hyderabad to make to the distant Irish sufferers the generous donation of £2,740, of which his Highness the NIZAM himself contributed 20,000 rupees; his Minister, Sir SALAR JUNG, 4,000 rupees;

the AMIR-I-KABIR, 4,000 rupees; and twelve of his Nawabs over 1,000 rupees a piece. Even amidst the snows and horrors of an Afghan campaign, the British troops had thoughts and helpful messages for those who were face to face in Ireland, with a more ignoble death than death in battle; and a collection of £239 11s. 1d., sent home from Candahar, almost at the same moment with the news which, perhaps, sealed the fate of many a kind-hearted donor, was one of the most affecting incidents of a charitable movement which, from every part of the world, thrilled Ireland with emotion and surprise.

The effort originated in Hong Kong by the Governor, the Right Hon. Sir J. POPE HENNESSY, produced £2,128 5s.

SOUTH AFRICA.

From the South African Diamond Fields came another extraordinary testimony of good-will. Griqua Land West, whose whole white population does not exceed 20,000, despatched to this Committee, on the first signal of distress, the sum of £1,196. If any names should be singled out of the whole generous mass of subscribers, it should be those of Mr. MOSES CORNWALL who appears to have been the guiding spirit of the movement, and that of Chevalier LYNCH, the active and accomplished President of the Committee. The Cape Colony is represented in the subscription lists of the Mansion House Committee by £140, and Natal by £71.

THE UNITED STATES.

The New York Committee

From the outset of the danger the eyes of Ireland turned trustfully to that great nation, which has given hospitable and prosperous homes to many millions of our race, and which, in former epochs of Irish suffering, was foremost and most splendid in the munificence of her succour. Public feeling in the United States had indeed long dwelt with anxiety and suspense upon the deepening clouds which were closing over Ireland. We have already enumerated gifts which arrived unasked from across the Atlantic early in December. On the 19th December a number of gentlemen who had been active in ministering to the Irish distress of 1862, met in the office of the Industrial Savings Bank in New York to talk over the increasing rumours of destitution in Ireland,—RICHARD O'GORMAN, HENRY L. HOGUET, EUGENE KELLY, WILLIAM WATSON, JAMES LYNCH, THOMAS BARBOUR, Judge JOHN R. BRADY, and Judge CHARLES P. DALY. They sought information from this Committee immediately on its formation, as to the dimensions of the crisis. They received for answer the appeal of the Mansion House Committee "to all Irishmen and all friends of Ireland to aid in our efforts to save the people from destruction. We would point to the constitution of our Committee," added the appeal, "which comprises representative men of the highest character and position in the country, and of all creeds and politics, as an assurance both that this appeal is justified, and that any funds entrusted to us shall be distributed in the manner best calculated to meet the emergency." The New

York Irish Relief Committee was there and then constituted. The first pledge of its activity was a cheque for £1,600 on the 21st January.

The amount received from the United States by this Committee did not reach as large a sum as might have been anticipated both from this beginning and from the fact of the Anglo-American Telegraph Company and the American Associated Press having generously enabled us to telegraph our appeals free of charge over the American Continent—a privilege that was largely availed of. This was due to the circumstance of strong attacks having been made in America upon the constitution and motives of this Committee—attacks which were abundantly refuted, on the highest authority, as reference to the Appendix will show—and which, probably, no person either in Ireland or America would now be disposed to repeat or to attempt to sustain. The Mansion House Committee do not desire, at this distance of time, to revive a regrettable incident, and it is alluded to only in order to explain how it came to pass that so comparatively small a proportion of the generous charity of the United States reached this Committee. Portion of it went to form the new Relief Fund of the Irish National Land League; another portion was absorbed in the separate American Fund founded by the *New York Herald;* still another separate Relief Fund was constituted in Philadelphia, and the greatest amount of all was transmitted directly to the Irish bishops, in order to cure all possible jealousies upon the subject. Of the munificent charity, thus divided into many channels—all, we are glad to think, uniting in the long run in the same healing influence upon Irish misery—this Committee received sums amounting to £11,244 12s. 3d. In addition to the achievements of private charity, an official mark of sympathy from the Government of the United States must not be overlooked, who, following the remarkable precedent of the "Jamestown" and the "Macedonian" in 1847, commissioned the United States frigate "Constellation" (Captain POTTER) to proceed to Ireland with a cargo of relief provisions. The LORD MAYOR of DUBLIN and Mr. W. LANE JOYNT, D.L., were deputed by this Committee to welcome the representatives of America upon their arrival at Cork Harbour; and it may be hoped that the cordial, and even enthusiastic attentions paid throughout Ireland to the officers of the "Constellation,"—(in whose honour the LORD MAYOR and LADY MAYORESS gave a great ball in the Mansion House, and whose commander, as representative of the United States, was invested with the freedom of the city of Dublin),—have been accepted, as they were intended, as some slight tokens of the profound gratitude with which all ranks and classes of the Irish people were inspired by the unexampled generosity of America.

Marginalia: Division of American Subscriptions

CANADA AND SOUTH AMERICA.

Across the Canadian frontier Ireland found friends no less staunch. The Parliament of the Dominion set apart the magnificent vote of 100,000 dollars as an Irish Relief Fund, confiding it to the Colonial Secretary

Marginalia: The Canadian Parliament

(Sir M. H. BEACH, Bart.) for allocation at his discretion. Upon his invitation the fund was administered by delegates chosen in an equal proportion from the Duchess of MARLBOROUGH'S Committee and from the Mansion House Committee. The LORD MAYOR, to whom this Committee entrusted the choice of its three delegates, nominated Mr. V. B. DILLON and Mr. THOMAS PIM, Jun., as his colleagues. Following the limitations prescribed by the COLONIAL SECRETARY, the money was mainly applied to the origination of reproductive public works upon the Western coast, the erection of fishing harbours, and the equipment of the pauper fishermen with boats and gear. Over and above the vote of the Dominion Parliament, this Committee was made the depositary of 20,000 dollars appropriated to the relief of Irish distress by the Government of the Province of Ontario; and the splendid examples thus set by the provincial governments were imitated by private contributions in every part of the Dominion, Newfoundland alone affording £1,800. Nor were the scattered Irish colonies of the South American coast deaf to the distant murmurs of distress. Upon the initiative of Mr. DENIS M. GALLAGHER, one of the most representative gatherings ever beheld in British Guiana assembled in Georgetown, Demerara, early in May, under the presidency of Mayor FORSHAW, at which a movement was inaugurated which yielded £486 5s. 6d. to the funds of this Committee. In the city of Buenos Ayres, largely owing to the exertions of Mr. EDWARD P. MULHALL, and of Messrs. EDWARD CARROLL and MICHAEL CASEY, Trustees to the Fund, another great movement sprang up, and contributed £3,802 9s. 8d. to the coffers of this Committee.

AUSTRALASIA.

Astonishing generosity of Australasia

But it is not too much to say that the money which saved the famishing Irish peasants at the most critical moment of the year—the aid which filled the gap where famine was rushing in—the subscriptions which astonished Ireland most by their magnificence, by their promptness and by their modesty, and the memory of which lingers most fondly in the popular heart—were the subscriptions literally showered upon this Committee from the Colonies of the Australasian Continent. Frequently though the members of this Committee have striven by votes and letters to express the gratitude and wonder with which these phenomena filled their hearts, we are conscious that the debt remains still imperfectly acknowledged, if it can ever be repaid. "At a time when the reality of the distress was doubted by many even here at home," in the words of Mr. SMYTH, M.P., "the heart of Australia was moved. No special appeal was made to her generosity; no deputations visited her shores; yet for four months a continuous stream of gold flowed to us from that country." It was not the mere magnitude of the sums sent that was most surprising (though places like Melbourne and Sydney sometimes transmitted more money in a single instalment than the opulent city of London afforded this Committee during the whole course of the distress); it was the electric sympathy with which the

Its spontaneity and promptness

appeal was no sooner heard than answered, or even anticipated; it was the suddenness with which this Committee was inundated with gifts from unknown givers. While persons nearer home were calculating and demurring, the people of Australia demanded no other authority than the circular telegram of the LORD MAYOR of DUBLIN to spring to action, and cover the Colonies with a network of Irish Relief organizations. Their plan of remittance was no less swift. The subscriptions, as soon as they were lodged in the local bank, were telegraphed to London, and were made immediately available; so that the moneys collected in remote cities of Australia or New Zealand one week were feeding the famished peasants of Connemara the next. They wasted no time in telegraphing explanations, or preambles or subscription lists. The effect of those huge anonymous remittances descending week after week struck the popular imagination with something of the wonder of a magic shower of gold. The fact stands, we think, unexampled in the history of human charity, that £62,735 had been thus remitted from Australia before this Committee could discover how it came or whom to thank; and it was only after several months that, the name of Sir JOHN O'SHANASSY having been found to be identified with the Melbourne remittances, the LORD MAYOR of DUBLIN was able, in a letter addressed to that distinguished man, to pour out the heartfelt gratitude of the Irish people to their unknown deliverers, asking him to transmit their thanks to the people of all the Colonies. Even still we are without knowledge of the history of that extraordinary movement, other than the broad facts relating to a few of the great towns; what is true of the splendid sacrifices of these would beyond doubt hold of hundreds of places whose bare names have reached us with their moneys.*

South Australia

We have already mentioned that Adelaide enjoys the distinction of having been the first in its own country or in any country to suggest the formation of the Mansion House Committee. On the 16th of December, for the information of a meeting summoned in the excitement of recent news from Ireland, the MAYOR of ADELAIDE telegraphed to the LORD MAYOR of DUBLIN: "Does the present distress in Ireland warrant action being taken here for its relief?" When the meeting came together on December the 19th, no answer had been returned from Dublin; the speakers found themselves surrounded with perplexity and uncertainty; the only information they possessed as to the character of the Irish Crisis was contained in extracts from Irish newspapers quoted by Mr. M. T. MONTGOMERY; all that was certain was that there was grievous distress in Ireland and that the Colonists had set their hearts upon relieving it. The resolution taken there and then, at the instance of Rev. Father BYRNE, the Catholic Vicar-General, as proposer, and of the Hon. J. C. BRAY, M.P., as seconder, pledged the people of Adelaide to raise an Irish Relief Fund forthwith, and to forward it to the LORD MAYOR OF DUBLIN "for equitable distribution." How well the pledge was kept may be estimated by the fact that South Australia alone yielded £7,836 10s. to the

* See Australian and New Zealand Correspondence in Appendix.

funds of this Committee. The first cheque actually made available in Dublin was a first instalment of £500 from Brisbane on the 13th of January. On the 15th arrived £2,000 from Sydney, and three days afterwards £1,500 more; on the 18th, a cheque through the Union Bank of Australia for £5,000 conveyed the magnificent first fruits of the movement in Melbourne; on the 20th, Adelaide followed with £1,000; and so proceeded the generous competition till Australia proper, Tasmania, and New Zealand had piled together the memorable gift of £94,916 16s. 8d. to suffering Ireland. The foundations of the Melbourne organisation were laid at an influential public meeting held in the Town Hall under the presidency of the Mayor (the Right Worshipful GEORGE MEARES). All ranks and nationalities were blended in the work. Deep sympathy and perfect impartiality with regard to internal political differences in Ireland were the key-notes of the meeting. Its representative character will be best judged from the composition of the Executive which had Sir JOHN O'SHANASSY, K.C.M.G., M.P., as chairman; the Right Worshipful the MAYOR, Treasurer; Mr. W. B. DALY, Vice-Chairman; Mr. E. G. FITZGIBBON, Convener of Meetings; and Messrs. L. DOYLE and L. KENYON, Hon Secs.; while the General Central Committee included—Sir W. H. F. MITCHELL, Sir C. GAVAN DUFFY, Sir BRYAN O'LOGHLEN, Sir CHARLES MACMAHON, Sir SAMUEL WILSON, the Hon. N. FITZGERALD, M.L.C.; the Hon. T. SUMMER, M.L.C.; the Hon. WM. CAMPBELL, M.L.C.; the Hon. A. FRASER, M.L.C.; the Hon. W. WILSON, M.L.C.; the Hon. JAS. MUNROE, M.L.A.; the Hon. Dr. HEARN, M.L.C.; Messrs. P. MORNANE, R. HARPER, M.L.A.; J. G. DUFFY, M.L.A.; J. WILSON (Crowlands), J. TUSHEY, D. WHITE, W. CROSS, P. FAGAN, E. L. ZOX, M.L.A.; P. KELLY, J. H. GRAVES, M.L.A.; A. K. SMITH, M.L.A.; SIMEON COHEN, JOHN M'GEE, J. B. PERRINS, ANDREW TOBIN, JAMES ORKNEY, Aldermen MOUBRAY, HAM, and O'GRADY. The Melbourne subscriptions amounted altogether to £31,314 19s. 11d. In Sydney, where the movement had received its nurture from Mayor FOWLER, Mr. P. A. JENNINGS, C.M.G.; Mr. J. HOURIGAN, J.P.; Mr. H. E. A. ALLEN, Mr. J. P. GARVAN, Mr. J. DAVIES, M.L.A., and many others whose very names have remained hidden, collections to the amount of £1,600 in all the Catholic churches of the archdiocese formed but one of the many shapes in which the generous infection spread rapidly through the colony, until the contribution of New South Wales amounted to £28,000. What has been thus briefly indicated in relation to the chief centres of population holds with equal if not more intensity of Geelong, of Brisbane, of Hobart Town (Tasmania), of Wellington (New Zealand), of Auckland, of Dunedin, of Christchurch, of Womat, and of many another generous settlement, whose succours were as prompt, as kindly, and as splendid as the £1,100 subscribed by the railway employees of Victoria. Altogether, Queensland subscribed £12,069 2s. 9d.; Western Australia, £1,214 17s. 5d.; Tasmania, £3,619 6s. 3d.; New Zealand, £10,427 2s. 6d.; Fiji, £315. It deepens the indebtedness of this Committee to the people of the Australian Colonies that although telegrams of a character which had caused misapprehension elsewhere were disseminated also in

Australia they never caused the slightest wavering in the direction which the charity of the Australian people had from the beginning taken, and which it persevered in to the end.

SUMMARY OF SUBSCRIPTIONS.

The summary of the resources possessed by the Mansion House Committee is briefly this:—From Europe, £32,153 8s.; from Asia, £20,576 8s. 9d.; from Africa, £1,407; from America, £26,875 14s. 2d.; and from Australasia, £94,916 16s. 8d., making, together with unclassified foreign subscriptions, and grants to the amount of £3,000 from the American funds remitted to the ARCHBISHOP OF TUAM; £854 5s. 10d. contributed for the purpose of giving grants for seed; and £178 7s., interest allowed by National Bank on current balances a total available income of £181,665 9s. 1d.

Summary of Subscriptions

MANNER OF DISTRIBUTION.

The initial consideration forced upon the Mansion House Committee was, by what local agency this great charitable trust fund could be most prudently and most effectively devoted to its object. Two areas of distribution presented themselves: the Poor-Law Union or the parish. The objections to a distribution by Unions were found to be numerous and decisive, and were only counterbalanced by the saving of laborious correspondence, which a Central Committee must derive from restricting its cares to some eighty Union Committees, instead of letting them range over some 840 parochial ones. In the first place, the Union boundary, being an artificial one for rating purposes, cut through in all directions the ancient divisions into parishes, which in Ireland are the natural and settled groupings of population: thus arbitrarily binding together districts with little common interest in or knowledge of each other. Again, outdoor relief being in all the distressed Unions discouraged, and in some altogether withheld, the Boards of Guardians could claim no special acquaintance with the necessities of the poor outside the workhouse walls; while, without entering into the justice of the feeling, it is certain that, in many of the most afflicted Unions, the composition of those Boards was viewed with suspicion and dislike by the mass of the indigent population. The circumstance that the Union system would exclude the Catholic clergy (in many of the most needy neighbourhoods, the only persons really cognisant of the depth of the distress), from all potential voice in the allocation, and would substantially place it in the discretion of one irresponsible person (the Chairman of the Union), would have alone been an almost insuperable objection. The system, when adopted by another Committee as the basis of distribution, had to be broken through at many points to be in any sense workable. Moreover, this Committee had to reflect that, in handing over vast charitable sums practically to the Boards of Guardians, they absolved landowners and the richer part of the ratepayers, in Unions that were still solvent, from bearing their part in the support of the poor who refused to bury themselves in the workhouses; and the notorious disinclination of Boards of Guardians, in the distressed districts,

Area of Distribution

to grant outdoor relief, made it at least possible that they would have at once relieved their rates, and maintained a character for generosity, by not merely an unequal, but a lavish partition of the charitable funds. But, even if the objections touching the composition of Union Committees could have been surmounted, these Committees must have proved quite unequal to the strain of transmitting varying weekly supplies of food to a few dozen remote centres, many of which, in the distressed districts (as Kilkerin from Clifden, or Achill from Newport), were some twenty miles of wild country asunder. They must have simply fallen back upon Sub-Committees, without any restraining sense of responsibility or honourable trust, and thus doubled the delay and complexity of the relief operations, without giving any more substantial guarantee against waste than the occasional observations of an inspector. The aim of the Mansion House Committee was to gather together the representative men of all religious and political hues in a neighbourhood; to make certain of their intimate personal acquaintance with the condition of the district; to enforce a system of accounts, under which every shilling of expenditure would be brought weekly under their own eyes and under the scrutiny of the Central Committee; and, having organized such a body, under such a system, to trust freely that the same sentiments of honourable responsibility and scrupulous economy, which actuated the General Committee, would be found equally potent in the local representative Committees: without imposing upon them the idle and vexatious system of inquisition, which was found to work so unhappily in the crisis of 1846-7. Within the parish area alone were found all the elements of such an organization: the Roman Catholic and Protestant clergy, the dispensary doctor, the magistrates, traders, and Poor-Law Guardians, daily face to face with the actual aspect of affairs; with interests, sufficiently divergent to create a wholesome check without lessening the common bond of a vital interest in the unhappy people; able to come together constantly without inconvenience, to act promptly, and to concentrate the relief within a moderate and compact area. Even the parish limits were found to be too great in a few of the scattered mountain parishes, where almost the whole population was depending upon charity for life: and in these isolated instances, subdivisions were made rather than imperil human lives for the sake of the symmetry of a system.

The Local Committee System

The first condition insisted upon, in the formation of a Local Committee, was that the clergy of all denominations, the dispensary medical officer, and a certain number of prominent laymen of all persuasions in the parish, should be invited to co-operate. In only three instances throughout Ireland, was there found the slightest difficulty in combining the Catholic and Protestant clergy in hearty brotherhood, on the Committees. The exceptions were parishes in Connemara where the Protestant clergymen happened to be also members of the Irish Church Mission Society. It was agreed on all hands that a union of the conflicting elements in these three localities was impossible, and that it was equally impossible to withdraw grants

Composition of Local Committees

from places literally threatened to be devoured by famine. The sage counsel of the Protestant ARCHBISHOP OF DUBLIN was, under the circumstances, cheerfully followed; and by a unanimous resolution of the 5th February, proposed by the Very Rev. DEAN NEVILLE, Rector of the Catholic University, and seconded by the Rev. CANON BAGOT, the Distribution Committee were authorised to put an end to the difficulty, by making grants to two Local Committees in the same neighbourhood in those special cases where it was sufficiently proved to be impossible to form a Committee in common. It was the only occasion on which, during six trying months, any shadow of religious division vexed the plain course of charity. It served simply to throw into stronger light the heartiness with which, upon more than eight hundred Local Committees in every corner of the country, Catholic, Protestant, and Presbyterian were found working side by side with the same unity, loyalty, and breadth of sympathy which were the foundation-stones of the Central Committee.

That the wisest and best-informed elements of the population were in fact collected into the Local Committees entrusted with the immediate dispensation of relief, will be recognised at a glance when we submit, as the result of a careful analysis of their composition, the fact that these Local Committees were composed of 1,404 Catholic Clergymen, 835 Protestant Clergymen, 508 Medical Officers, 977 Poor Law Guardians, and 6,171 other lay members. The rules under which they were embodied, and the queries which they were obliged to answer before becoming entitled to a grant, ensured that, in entering upon their work, they would take pains to form a clear and accurate judgment of the condition of their districts; that they would estimate the number of those entitled to relief, and check that number weekly, according to the variations of the distress; that they would set forth the circumstances of every applicant on the relief-roll, the number and ages of his family, the extent of his holding (if any), and the amount and duration of the relief afforded to him; with such other particulars touching population, valuation, amount of poor-rate paid, and other available resources of any kind, as should afford the Central Committee some basis of comparison between the necessities of different districts. The local organisations being thus powerfully constituted, being saddled with the responsibility of their returns, and working under a system which, while affording the Local Committees a large and honourable discretion, enabled the Central Committee to take a weekly survey of the needs and expenditure of every district, it was felt that any system of inspection, to be effectual, would involve the employment of an expensive staff, and could only ensure the accuracy of the local accounts, which our own system submitted to an ample weekly test; or, if the inspectors were empowered to override the judgment of the Local Committees with respect to particular recipients of relief, it would open the gate at once to the collisions which destroyed the local relief system in 1847. No general system of inspection was, therefore, established by this Committee; and the visits paid at various periods to different parts of the distressed districts by the LORD MAYOR, Mr. LANE JOYNT, Rev. Canon BAGOT, Lord FRANCIS G. OSBORNE, Mr. J. A. FOX, Mr. J. A. CURRAN, and Dr. SIGERSON, were made, not with a view to submitting Local Committees to a harassing inquisition, but in order to gain information for the guidance of the Central Committee in reference to particular phases of the distress. The principal remaining matter, in which the Mansion House Committee insisted upon a uniform and inflexible rule, was that relief should be given only in the shape of food, fuel, or clothing, and should, under no circumstances, be dispensed in money. The latter stipulation was an obvious barrier against imposition. The rule restricting the expenditure to food, fuel, or clothing, was dictated by the feeling that the charity invoked on behalf of a starving population was due, in the first instance at all events, to those who were stripped of the common necessaries of existence. The fuel-famine having been providentially averted by the dryness of the early winter, that item was practically struck out of the expenditure. Owing to the large sums devoted by other charitable Committees to the purchase of clothing, our expenditure on that head also was confined to a distribution of clothes, shoes, and blankets among the all but naked creatures of the remote western coasts and islands. Substantially speaking, therefore, the Mansion House Fund went in almost unbroken bulk to feed those who had no other food under heaven.

The Relief mainly in Food

Danger of the Land lying uncropped

One great temptation beset the Committee to violate its rule. It had hardly been formed when the terrible cry arose that the famishing people were devouring their store of seed-potatoes, and that, unless they were in some manner provided with new seeds, the land must remain untilled, and the partial famine of 1879-80 widen into a wholesale and ungovernable famine in 1880-81. It was pressed upon the Committee that, side by side with the relief of present want, the obvious destination of charity should be the prevention of incomparably greater want, at the very juncture when public charity must be exhausted; that the allocation of any large portion of our fund to the purchase of seeds would even act in relief of the food-supply, by encouraging the peasantry to eke out a subsistence for a few weeks longer upon the remainder of their wretched seed-potatoes; and, that the seed-potatoes which would so disappear, having lost almost all power of reproduction, and being, in fact, the certain seeds of potato failures in the future, the substitution of a new stock would not alone banish immediate famine, but be a source of permanent abundance. The strength of these considerations pressed painfully upon the Committee, but their duty as trustees of a fund subscribed to relieve actual and existing distress; the alarming rapidity with which that distress was every day extending and intensifying; the consciousness that their fund was at that moment the mainstay of many thousand lives, and that the amount or duration of the foreign assistance which fed it was of its nature precarious; the strong persuasion also that the State alone could or ought to deal with the clearly-defined danger of the land of the country being left in general barrenness; and that even the whole resources of this Committee invested in the purchase of seeds, would but cover a patch in the desert, while relaxing the responsibility of the State, and raising dangerous hopes among the peasantry—all united powerfully to confirm them in their resolution to direct all their energies, first and above all, to grapple with the hunger which was at the people's doors. The Sub-Committee, who were appointed to deliberate upon the subject reported, through their Chairman, Mr. P. J. SMYTH, M.P., their opinion, "that strenuous efforts should be at once made to bring within reach of the small farmers seed-potatoes and oats of the best quality, but that funds subscribed for the relief of immediate distress were not available for that purpose." Their view was unanimously endorsed by the General Committee, upon the 23rd of January; they did not, however, neglect the terrible warning that seed-time was approaching and would find the peasantry without seeds to sow. At the instance of the Rev. CANON BAGOT, who was one of the earliest to appreciate the danger, and one of the most energetic in removing it, a deputation consisting of the LORD MAYOR, the Most Rev. ARCHBISHOP TRENCH, the HIGH SHERIFF, the Rev. CANON BAGOT, Mr. GEORGE BROWNE, M.P., Mr. W. LANE JOYNT, Alderman PURDON, Alderman TARPEY, Mr. CHARLES KENNEDY, and Mr. P. J. SMYTH, M.P., was appointed to wait upon the LORD LIEUTENANT and the CHIEF SECRETARY FOR IRELAND, to press upon them the urgent necessity of immediately providing the small farmers with seeds. This Committee feel some pride in having thus contributed to this result; that the Government shortly afterwards adopted and carried into law a Bill of Major NOLAN, M.P., which empowered the Poor Law Guardians of Unions scheduled as distressed to borrow money without interest for the purchase of seed oats and potatoes, which they were authorised to issue at cost price, in moderate quantities, and upon reasonable terms of repayment to the humble class of farmers rated under £15. Considering that it took over £500,000* to compass the partial distribution of seeds effected under this Act through the agency of a cautious Government department, it will be seen how futile must have been any expenditure which we could have devoted to that object; the entire balance remaining in the hands of the Mansion House Committee on the 1st of March, when the Seeds Act received the Royal assent, being £42,186 16s. 6d.

Deputation to the Lord Lieutenant

The wisdom of the resolution to make the supplying of food to the destitute the first charge upon their funds, was in another respect strongly brought home to the Committee; for the only other great charitable organisation, which was then in full activity, having set aside a sum of £80,000 for seed-potatoes,† and having only a small balance remaining, the Mansion House

---

* Annual Report of the Local Government for Ireland, 1880, p. 14.

† This sum was expended by the DUCHESS OF MARLBOROUGH'S Committee in supplying seeds to those cottier landholders and others, whom the Seeds Act left out of account, and in this way was a source of much benefit. The amount of a separate Seeds Subscription, which was opened by the energy of the Rev. Canon BAGOT in connection with the Mansion House Fund, was similarly expended.

Committee suddenly found themselves charged with the principal support of over 400,000 persons, whom grants at the rate of £10,000 a week, together with the assistance furnished from the private remittances to the Irish Bishops, barely sufficed to keep in existence upon the slenderest and coarsest rations.*

Nature of the Food Supply

The expenditure of the Local Committees was, thus, not merely limited to the purchase of food, but practically of only one kind of food, and that the humblest and cheapest—Indian meal. From a close scrutiny of the local vouchers, it appears that £165,480 of the entire fund went into the item of food alone. Ground Indian corn had come to be the ordinary sustenance of the Irish peasantry for several months of the year; its cheapness enabled a small sum to spread relief over an astonishingly large area; while the unpalatable nature of the diet was little likely to tempt those who were not reduced to a dire pitch of destitution. The ordinary course of trade was not disturbed in the purchase of food. It was bought at current market price, as far as possible from local dealers, with the effect of reviving confidence by circulating money through the exhausted veins of trade, as well as of securing a food-supply more conveniently and as cheaply. The possibility of exacting labour as a test of distress was early and anxiously considered, and was decisively rejected as impracticable. There were innumerable works of public advantage calling for attention in the distressed districts; and there was a strong public feeling that their accomplishment would have offered the healthiest and most enduring form of State assistance. But Local Charitable Committees had not only no authority to undertake works which were under public jurisdiction;

Labour Test found impracticable

they had no machinery for setting them in motion upon any systematic plan; they had no staff to enforce a regular or efficient labour system; and while men would in many cases be tempted to keep up the pretence of desultory labour, to their own demoralization and to the neglect of their farms, the very persons who were in sorest need of relief, and who would be debarred by feebleness or age from public labour, would possibly perish neglected. Wherever peculiar local circumstances rendered useful employment possible, the Local Committees were not only authorised, but were strongly exhorted to enforce it. This plan was in several districts, as for instance in Skibbereen, Cahirciveen, and Ballina, found to be productive of solid good, especially where industry upon men's own farms was made the condition of relief. But for the reasons above enumerated, the general enforcement of a labour-test was not attempted and was not possible.

County Committees projected

The framework of the Local Committees having been laid, it occurred to the Mansion House Committee to complete the organization by forming representative County Committees, which would both act in relief of the tremendous strain of correspondence upon the central body, and, possibly, apportion the parish grants with a more intimate knowledge than a National

---

* The number of persons relieved by the Mansion House Committee for the week ending 28th February, was 512,625; for the week ending 27th March, 488,335. Grants to the amount of £11,945 were made between the 1st and the 9th of March.

Committee, and with less bias than a purely local one. One such Committee we were fortunate enough to be able to count upon—the Donegal County Committee, of which the Catholic and Protestant bishops, the leading landowners, clergymen, and representative men of all complexions were members; which, throughout the burden and heat of the crisis, in one of the gloomiest theatres of distress, undertook the charge of a pauper population, which, at one season of the year, numbered 80,000 souls; and of whose administration of the £14,495 entrusted to them by this Committee, no breath of complaint was ever uttered. But Donegal was in this respect exceptionally happily circumstanced. It was almost entirely situated within one diocese, and the diocesan organization worked smoothly around a recognised common centre. The other counties, where the distress was of sufficient magnitude to make County Committees desirable—for instance Galway and Mayo—were divided into separate dioceses, and were composed of vast and barren tracts, with little railway communication, or intercommunication of any kind between districts, in many cases sixty or even eighty miles apart; and it was at once seen that the few gentlemen from inland towns who alone could undergo the inconvenience of meeting together as County Committees, would be at far greater disadvantage than the Central Committee in dealing with the sequestered regions upon the seaboard, of whose circumstances they were ignorant, and whose necessities demanded instant and exceptional means of relief. Except in the case of Donegal, the project of intermediary County Committees was abandoned; the Central Committee assumed the whole burden of supervising the affairs of 840 Local Committees; and, for those desolate thousands, who were all but perishing on the islands and coasts of the Western Ocean—for whom Local Committees were helpless, and whose danger outran all common danger—the Western Isles' Sub-Committee was founded early in February, to make them its special and unstinted care.

THE EXECUTIVE ORGANISATION.

It will be understood that the guidance of an organisation thus widespread, involving the consideration of many hundred weekly applications, with the innumerable inquiries, correspondences, and comparisons arising thereout, imposed upon this Committee a labour of some magnitude. In the first months, especially before the exact extent of the distress was probed, or the relief system in full work, the task was one which those who had best reason to understand it, would not willingly face again for any less inspiring object than the saving of human life. The concentration in Dublin of the whole expense and trouble of superintending the local organisations, instead of having the labour and the cost divided among eighty local centres, involved necessarily a considerable addition both to the outlay and the labour thrown upon the Central Committee. A staff of clerks, to perform the enormous mass of scrivenery, accounts, and returns accruing daily, was the least of our requirements. The advantage of possessing the Mansion House, not only for the meetings of the Committee, but for the transaction of every detail of its business, was very great. For more than six months the whole ground floor of the Mansion House was continuously occupied by day, and during a considerable part of the nights, by Sub-Committees, secretaries, and clerks. With the advantage of this suite of offices; of the machinery of forms, books, returns, and checks, devised by Mr. DILLON; with the assiduous daily and nightly labours of numerous members of the Committee, and the loyal co-operation of their paid assistants, we are glad to think that the multifarious business daily thrust upon the Committee in all its branches, was despatched as smoothly and as promptly as the crisis demanded. The major portion of the labour, and the most critical portion, devolved upon the Examination Sub-Committee: it was they who sifted the tri-weekly mass of applications; who collated the returns from the different districts; who, from the answers to searching queries, from comparisons of population, valuation, Poor-law taxation, and amount of help received from other charitable organizations, proportioned the grants to the varying necessities of the districts, and who conducted the multitudinous correspondence therewith related. The other Sub-Committees were the Publication Committee, which directed the appeals to and correspondence with foreign nations; the Western Isles' Committee, charged with provisioning the islands of the Western Coast; the Finance Committee, which transacted the financial affairs of the Fund; the Seeds Committee, which administered the special fund contributed for the distribution of farm seeds; and the Clothing Committee, charged with the selection and transmission of the clothing ordered by the General Committee.

PROGRESS OF THE RELIEF.

State of Affairs at commencement of the year

Let us recall the state of affairs amidst which the relief operations of the Mansion House Committee began. We propose to show, from the testimony of independent eye-witnesses, that, in the beginning of January, before that relief had begun to tell, absolute Famine had raised its head in many places; and that, if the hand of public charity had not interposed, and that quickly (all hope of State employment having disappeared), the interval between horrible privations and a more horrible death must have been soon passed. The official estimate was, that about two-thirds of the whole potato-crop had perished. That meant, as Dr. NEILSON HANCOCK observes, that the loss in some districts must have been nearly total. The BISHOP OF ELPHIN estimated that "scarcely one-tenth of the potato-crop in Roscommon was fit for human food." "There are thousands of families," his Lordship wrote,

Evidence of various Eye Witnesses

concerning his own diocese, on the 12th of January, "already suffering from hunger, and if relief does not speedily reach them, famine, sickness, and death will soon visit their desolate cabins." "I am personally aware," wrote the Hon. Secretary of the Miltown (Co. Galway) Relief Committee, on its formation in January, "that many families are living upon yellow meal since the last week of November. Many are in such straits that they have depended for the last three months on the charity of neighbours only less wretched than themselves." The Priests of Aran Island walking through one of its villages, saw children "entirely, absolutely naked" shivering in the fireless chimney corner.* In the parish of Muinteravara upon Bantry Bay, there were families "actually starving on boiled turnips and salted sprats."† A Correspondent of the *Freeman's Journal*, who travelled through the distressed districts of the West at the critical period in January before the Relief had made itself felt, visited hundreds of families wasting away in actual starvation; existing upon a chance meal of stirabout begged from neighbours only less bare than themselves; digging the potato-fields over again for a few forgotten roots, or cowering in their cabins all day, in order not to excite the pangs of hunger; a family of nine in Dinas Island, existing on periwinkles; the greater portion of the population of Inishark living upon a sort of sea-weed, called *sloucaurn;* "broken-spirited, half-clad men, women, and children squatted in the darkness around the turf ashes, or ravening their horrid mess of sea-weed or periwinkles; their potatoes gone since Christmas; nothing to sow, nothing to fish with, nothing to pawn; children without a rag of underclothing; sick men and women without a drop of milk or tea to wet their lips with; hollow cheeks, lustreless eyes, and broken hearts." "With sorrow and a bleeding heart I have to confess to you," wrote the Rev. M. KILLEEN, P.P. Kilshanny (Co. Clare), "that the blackness of death seems hanging over us; the strong men are growing weak and faint." A Catholic Priest of Galway stated to the Special Correspondent of the London *Standard*, that he knew a family of eleven persons all told, who had not had a meal for four days.‡ Many of the people of Ferriter (Co. Kerry), "once comfortable," their parish priest vouched, were, in January, living on boiled Swedish turnips, which they begged from their more fortunate neighbours. ‖ In Pettigo (Co. Fermanagh), men who came to the Priest's house, looking for relief, "fainted with hunger and exhaustion."§ The Protestant Rector of Cahirciveen having opened some small relief works to employ the starving people, one of the first men who came to seek employment dropped dead at his gate, the doctor said from heart disease, the people said from want as well.

The *Standard* Correspondent, whose investigations did much to dispel the incredulity which was even then largely prevalent in England, observes in a letter from Galway, on the 13th of January: "The more I examine and investigate the condition of things here, the more thoroughly convinced am I that it is impossible to overestimate the gravity of the situation. There will be something far more serious to occupy the public mind soon, than the excitement attending the service of a few ejectment processes. A few of the landlords are anxious to assist the people, others stand apart and will do nothing, while many others are to be met with who deny the existence of any distress

* Letter of Rev. J. A. CONCANNON, P.P., and Rev. D. W. FAHEY, C.C., January 29.
† Letter of Rev. J. BOWEN, P.P.   ‡ *Standard*, January 14th.
‖ Letter to the BISHOP of KERRY.
§ Letter of Rev. J. M'KENNA, P.P., to Mansion House Committee.

at all. I have conversed with several, and have heard all the above opinions propounded, but I am bound to say, that I have met with no one who, on being pressed, did not acknowledge that things were bad, and certain to become worse during the summer, for all credit is at an end, and the people can hope for no food from their holdings till August, when the crops will come in." In another letter he remarks:—" I have met persons during my journey, who laugh at the idea of famine in the West, and who say sincerely enough : ' I can't see it;' but such persons do not understand the long-suffering, patient, unobtrusive character of these poor people. They dread the name of want, almost as much as they dread its presence, and so seek to conceal their sufferings even from each other. Hence they will approach the verge of starvation before they ask for relief." Nevertheless, the Correspondent, as he entered Caherciveen, found swarms of these much-enduring creatures in the streets, "squatting in rows along the kerbstones, crouching in dozens at the corners, sitting on doorsteps, waiting and watching for food the livelong day. . . . . All life and spirit seem crushed out of them, their energies are prostrate, they can think about nothing but hunger. If you meet them on the foot-paths they do not turn aside ; if you push them gently from your path, they move mechanically, as if unconscious of the presence of external objects. Humanity shrinks startled and appalled from the contemplation of such abject misery, and nothing but the feeling of deep responsibility could induce me to write it." * In Killarney, which enjoyed the rare and all but singular advantage of having 800 heads of families in the employment of the EARL OF KENMARE, the Correspondent, leaving the open streets, passed (in the company of the dispensary medical officer and of a priest deputed by the bishop to accompany him) "through crowded lanes and alleys, where the cabins of the poor were clustered thickly together ; and I shall never forget the scenes of poverty and wretchedness which were here revealed, although I should vainly attempt to describe them. In one wretched house we found a family of eight persons. The father had not had a day's work for two months, and the mother assured us that her little ones had not tasted food since the morning of the previous day. Huddled on a wisp of straw, which lay on the damp floor, and covered merely with an old quilt, the hungry children had cried themselves to sleep, but the noise of our visit disturbed them, and they renewed their clamours in piteous appeals to ' Mammy ' for something to eat. Not an article of furniture, save a broken bench, was in the house, all had been sold or pawned for food; the Sisters of Mercy had given them their last meal; the eldest child was to go to the convent that evening, and, should she fail to get food, the poor creatures would continue supperless. My companions gave this destitute family the price of a supper, and we went our way, and saw able-bodied men lying upon wretched straw couches, believing that by remaining quiet, they could better resist the pain of hunger which gnawed at

* *Standard*, January 26th.

their vitals. . . . . Farther on we came to the cabin of a family, who had once been better off; they were now reduced to the lowest extremity, and, horrible to relate, the mind of the mother had given way before the pangs of hunger, and she had become insane. 'I have been attending this woman,' said the medical man to me, 'and I believe that she has gone mad from starvation.' Need I write more? I prefer to spare your readers the recital of further tales of misery. I am sick and weary from the contemplation of such scenes, and I fervently pray it may never be my lot to witness them again."* Dr. KEARNEY, writing from Carna, Connemara, on the 22nd January, declared that there were over 500 families in the parish, in absolute want at that moment. "Several families here of six, seven, and eight members, have not had a morsel of food for the last fortnight, except by rooting at the soil from sunrise to sunset, in order to pick up the stray potato that escaped at the first digging." "If not relieved before the end of this week," wrote the Rev. P. GREALY, C.A., from the same place, on the 26th January, "I fear we will have many inquests."

The special correspondent of the *Daily Telegraph* gave still more horrible pictures, if possible, of his experiences. Of the first cabin he entered at Kildonay, he said:—"I never saw anything in the way of a home in a civilized country—and I have seen a good deal—more appalling than this." In a neighbouring cabin the family dinner of eight persons consisted of a single cabbage. "These Kildonay people," he wrote on the 6th January, "and their neighbours all along the Donegal coast, as well as up in the highlands, will soon be starving. There is the fact—the very hardest of facts—and the Government and the people of Great Britain, having to look it in the face, had better do so at once, lest a worse thing happen, and it be said that the unfortunates have actually perished for want of aid." "Oh! sir, we are all alike," said a poor fellow to him in Murrisk (Co. Mayo), "and if the Lord don't open a gap for us soon, we're all done." "In many places," he wrote from Connemara, on January 12th, "the question is one of famine impending, but here the grisly spectre has arrived, and stalks abroad though the country seeking its victims. Proofs of this are unhappily forthcoming in any number." Another observer † takes a dozen cases precisely in the order in which he visited the houses, good, bad, and indifferent, upon his route through Allbrack, (in the neighbourhood of Slyne Head), and there is reason to think the result represents faithfully the condition of the distressed populations at the initiation of the relief. "No 1.—A squatter, evicted from his farm, and living on a patch of conacre; potatoes gone since November, seeds and all; living since by pawning; nothing now left to pawn; not a potato in the house for supper, unless the *vannithee* could beg some; didn't know how much rent or debt he owed—more than he could pay till the day of his death. No. 2.—A tall haggard man; had not sown a potato last year; had no money to buy the

* *Standard*, January 20th.   † *Freeman's Journal*, January 28th.

seed. How had he lived since?—(with a ghastly smile)—The third part of the time starving; sometimes catching a fish, if a neighbour would lend him a boat; sometimes doing an odd day's work at the Castle at 1s. 6d. a day, 1s. a day of which was stopped for rent; had not got breakfast, and did not know where to get supper. Father FLANNERY held out some cheering hope that relief would be forthcoming in a week. The man turned fiercely—'In a week! If you get anybody that will bury me then, it will be enough for me.' No. 3.—Potatoes for a week besides seed; three children lying sick, unable to keep the half-rotten potatoes on their stomachs; mother crooning sullenly over the fire, and would hardly look up to answer. No. 4.—Nine in family; father without shoe or stocking, clad in a piece of ragged sail-cloth; ashamed, like most of his neighbours to appear at Mass; sowed 2½ bushels of seed potatoes last year; ate the last of them, seeds and all, before Christmas; nothing to feed nine mouths for the last fortnight except the relief meal; used to make two and three tons of kelp when it fetched £6 or £7 a ton; was glad enough last year to give it for 80s.; has no earthly means of raising a penny, or seeding his land. No. 5.—Father, mother, and six children, for the last three weeks, depending on charity for a meal a day and for turf; had to burn a box, and some of the timbers of the roof for firing; the relief meal being out, they had no supper for the night, 'Only there are good neighbours still, thanks be to his Holy Name.' (The turf famine has scourged this district more severely than any other I know, the fuel having not only to be brought five miles on people's backs, but to be paid for in cash). No. 6.—Five children; mother dying of consumption; lying in her everyday clothes on the ground close to the fire, with her little children mutely grouped around her; potatoes for another fortnight, but not a drop of milk to moisten the dying woman's lips. No. 7.—Father proudly exhibited a fortnight's potatoes, besides a bushel of seeds, with the air of a man of fortune; 'To tell the truth, though, we haven't a rag of clothes to go to Mass, nor a blanket itself, that is not in the pawn.' No. 8.—Will be able to live unaided until St. Patrick's Day, and, in this wilderness of misery worse than his, must expect no compassion. No. 9.—Seven children; for nine weeks without potatoes; father shoeless; no turf, and no money to buy it; would have died already only for the relief, 'and small loss' (he gloomily said); a quarter of a stone of flour 'with nine divides,' the only sustenance of the family for two days; not a scrap of breakfast that morning, and had yet to beg a supper; offered an old table to a neighbour the previous evening for a supper of potatoes, and could not get them; bed and clothes in pawn; 'enough debts to drown a ship;' 'not as much rags between us as would clothe a child.' No. 10.—Five in family; a poor woman, two days after her confinement, lying on a pallet in the chimney corner, with a quilt over her everyday clothes; her husband had to sell quarter of his seed potatoes to buy some turf during her lying-in, 'and indeed, unless dry potatoes, sorra the penny I had to reach her any comfort in life in her weakness.' (This was one of the most respectable farmers in the townland, and he accepted the Priest's furtive shilling with as warm gratitude as if it were a fortune). No. 12.—A *prauca* (lowest type of a Connaught hut) of the most frightful kind, built against rocks, and flat-roofed with green sods and wattles; entered three steps under ground by a door less than four feet high; inhabited by two old women, one of whom was lying on the floor in her clothes, almost speechless and insensible, dying, if I can believe the testimony of all her neighbours, of absolute starvation; her old fellow lodger and her daughter solemnly averred that she had not tasted anything of any sort except cold water for three whole days, and that when they managed to beg some potatoes, her stomach refused to retain any food; I cannot doubt that the unfortunate old creature was in one of the last stages of starvation. I was glad to fly from the horrors of the place, while my reverend companion was administering the last Sacraments to the dying woman."

We have thought it best to allow eye-witnesses to tell, in their own words, the condition of things which the Mansion House Committee and the sister charitable associations were face to face with, at the outset of their career. Over nearly the whole western half of the island hung a cloud of impending famine; along the sea-coast, famine was actually at its work, slowly wasting the strength of the people to the point of pestilence and death. Suddenly through the gloom, began to pierce the light of the world's sympathy and help. Charitable grants began to be distributed just at the moment when, in many districts, the charity of the wretched people towards each other had done its last office, and when the miserable beings, reduced to a meal a day of turnips, shell-fish, or sea-weed, had already sunk into the torpor which is the second stage of starvation. So urgent was the necessity, so heartrending were the panic-stricken letters which poured in from places reduced to extremities like this, that at their first meeting in January the Mansion House Committee, in several cases, unanimously suspended standing orders for the purpose of despatching aid to Committees not yet formally constituted, rather than prolong the pangs of the starving people by one unnecessary hour. It may be judged with what a wild rush the unhappy people clutched at the first earnest of relief. One of the most dismal spectacles of those times, was the ragged famished crowds that came like spectres out of the darkness of their cabins, swarming around the doors of the Relief Committees by day and night, in rain and frost, with gaunt piteous faces, in their thin rags, waiting patiently for the first wretched dole of Indian meal. The Swinford Committee, at their first distribution, on the 16th of January, sat far into the night, and distributed 1,000 tickets for two stones of Indian meal apiece; yet there were between 300 and 500 more fathers of families still left empty-handed, who travelled long distances, and waited all day and night in the streets in expectation of a similar wretched pittance.* "On yesterday, our day of meeting at Belleek" (County Fermanagh), "to afford relief," wrote

Margin notes: Condition of Actual Famine in the West; First influence of the Relief

---

* Letter of the Very Rev. DEAN DURCAN, P.P., V.F., 17th January.

the Chairman of the Local Relief Committee, "the crowd was so great, looking for anything at all we could give, that it occupied the Committee up to two hours after night to get through our list of applicants, and we had to give up the task nearly in hopeless despair of knowing what to do to get the shivering creatures away. It was sad to see hundreds crowded together, around the door of where the Committee met, waiting from twelve o'clock noon to eight at night, under drenching rain, for whatever little we could give." The rush at the first distribution in Collooney (County Sligo) "was so large that it took several policemen and others to keep the passage clear."*
"I had this evening (22nd January)," says the Rev. M. O'Donnell, P.P., Foxford, "to address five hundred starving creatures from my window, as I could not open the door. It was only after night closed, when these creatures were induced to leave with empty stomachs, that we were able to hold our meeting." "Those people who still entertain doubts as to the intensity of distress in Connemara," says the Correspondent of the *Standard*, writing from Loughrea, on the 15th January, "would, I feel sure, be readily induced to alter their opinions could they only have witnessed the spectacle exhibited a few days since in the little town of Clifden. Here a Local Relief Committee has been established, and, an instalment of money having been forwarded from Dublin, the Committee at once applied it to purchase food for the hungry people. This public tender of relief at once revealed the misery of the poor creatures who thronged to obtain it. Hungry and half naked, without clothes and without credit, they had cowered for weeks in their cabins, ashamed to appear before their neighbours in the open day, and venturing only to move about when the friendly shades of night came to veil their wretchedness. But now the news was abroad that bread for the hungry ones might be had for the asking, and, in the wild rush to obtain it, all other considerations were forgotten. Women and children, half naked, rushed through the streets and besieged the doors of the Committee-rooms, and provision-stores. The women were wrapped in pieces of old patch-work quilts. An old blanket, or a piece of sacking was substituted for a cloak, and, in some cases an old corn sack was used for the same purpose. It was manifest that every article of clothing, on which money could be raised, had been disposed of.
. . . . . The presence of so much misery was sickening, and afforded a sight which will not readily be forgotten." At Cahirciveen, the same cautious observer confesses himself fairly overpowered by "the shrieks of woe and piteous supplications which burst from the famishing crowd" around the Rev. Canon Brosnan's door, at the announcement that there was no more relief for the day. "I saw men, borne forward by their fellows, falling on their knees at the door-step, and, with big tears in their eyes, declare that they were starving. It was too much for the Priest's resolution, and with a hurried apology to me for his seeming inconsistency, he turned to the poor creatures

* Letter of Mr. George Helen, 19th January.

again: 'If I had to sell my house and its contents, they shall not starve,' said he, and I am certain that he meant it." More wonderful even than the sufferings of the people, was their self-control during that dangerous period, before the relief-system had yet fully developed itself, and while many were enduring the torments of seeing relief in sight without being able to taste it. Except that a bread-van was robbed in Sligo, and some bread-shops broken into by roughs in the city of Cork, and that a band of starving wretches boarded a schooner laden with meal off Errismore, thinking it was relief meal, and when told that it was private property went quietly away; there is not a single instance recorded in which the hungry and excited crowds, sick with waiting, and often waiting in vain, in the towns of the distressed districts, proceeded to any act of outrage or plunder. *Self-control of the People*

By the end of January the Relief Organisation had penetrated to every district where life was in danger, and for the moment the terrors of starvation were banished. A thrill of relief and gratitude ran through the rescued people. The thanks of Carna will sufficiently exemplify the rest:—"The people are grateful beyond expression or description, and pray for you and all their benefactors. Hundreds would have died here from hunger already if you had left us to our fate."* The Mansion House Committee had dispensed their fund, however, with a sparing hand, and only in districts menaced with immediate and deadly danger. It was felt, as it turned out, that the distress must increase every week, as the store of potatoes of the small farmers ran out; it was found to be spreading in an alarming form to counties far outside the original zone of distress; and the Committee had to face the prospect, that, the Government measures in the direction of public employment having collapsed, hundreds of thousands of starving people would be thrown for six months to come upon the uncertain resource of foreign charity. First, with regard to the unanticipated extent of the distress;—the taint which was darkest on the Western coasts was suddenly discovered to have eaten its way into the very heart of hitherto flourishing inland regions. In counties like Longford, Tipperary, Monaghan, Waterford, Antrim, Leitrim, Fermanagh, Roscommon, and Cavan, not only were bands of foodless labourers roaming through the towns, but the cruel blows of the last three years had crushed the small farmers in the dust, and reduced them in many districts almost to the condition of their brethren of the Western wilds. Major PERCY, the resident magistrate of what used to be reputed the wealthy town of Nenagh, visited the homes of the unemployed poor there, in February, "and he declared he was quite unprepared, even with all his experience of distress in India, to realise the extent of the poverty and misery that met his gaze." "Really, the poor people are on the point of dying; their appearance is appalling:" was the report of the Belleek (County Fermanagh) Committee. The Very Rev. Dr. CLEARY, P.P., Dungarvan (now Bishop of Kingston, in *Completion of the Relief System* *Unanticipated extent of the Distress* *In the North*

---

* Letter of the Rev. FATHER GREALY, Chairman of the Local Committee.

Canada), in acknowledging a grant of £100 on the 19th of February, reminds the Mansion House Committee that, "your generous charity will enable us to save our poor from starvation for not more than six days." The Rev. THOMAS CUMMINS, C.C., as early as the 20th of January, knew of thirty-three homes in Scotstown, County Monaghan, where there was neither food nor fire, and related a visit made by him to a patient in a hovel where he found the family, seven in all, striving to cheat hunger "by lying on cold beds, in a fireless room, with cold, empty stomachs;" adding the terrible words, "I fear my patient is now a cold corpse among them, and if I was constituted judge and jury over the cause of her death, my verdict would be 'want of food.'" From Moybologue, Co. Cavan, the Rev. J. E. H. MURPHY, B.A., Clk., wrote, on the 12th February:—"No case of death by actual starvation has as yet, thank God, occurred, to the knowledge of the Committee; but unless immediate relief be procured from some source, we know not what fearful results a delay of even so short a time might bring forth. Many of the small farmers are destitute of food, of fuel, and of clothing. They are at the present moment eating, or have already eaten, their seed potatoes and seed corn, to preserve life. Many of them are perishing for want of ordinary clothes, and, what is far more serious, have no bedclothes to protect them at night from the wintry cold." The Rev. W. THOMPSON, Rector of Cushendall, County Antrim, described the condition of the people of that neighbourhood as "impoverished to an extent unknown since '47." In Arklow (County Wicklow) the whole fishing population owed their lives to charity. "It is painful and humiliating to have to acknowledge that even in this, the premier county of Ulster, there exists distress deepfelt and widespread," said an appeal from Kilcoo, County Down, on the 12th of February, signed, among others, by the Hon. S. WARD, by Mr. J. P. KINGSCOTE, J.P.; by the Rev. CHARLES PARKHURST, M.A., Incumbent; and the Rev. H. CONNOR, P.P. "Nothing but sheer necessity can force our people to acknowledge want and ask relief." Again, from Plumbridge, County Tyrone:—"You may think it strange to have before you an appeal for relief from so prosperous a county as Tyrone. Even here, not long since, everyone would have thought so likewise. This parish, if not rich, had few poor. Now all is changed." In March there was no county in Ireland in which there were not at least two Local Relief Committees receiving grants from the Mansion House Fund. There were 37 such Committees in Cavan, 42 in Limerick, 18 in Longford, 22 in Tyrone, 13 in Westmeath, 19 in Monaghan, 37 in Tipperary, 11 in Kilkenny, and so on, according to the pressure of the distress, and the power to cope with it out of the local resources.* In the City of Dublin itself dangerous symptoms of distress had shown themselves; processions of unemployed labourers marched through the

---

* £7,010 was granted by this Committee for the relief of the distress in Cavan; £7,710 in Leitrim; £3,910 in Tipperary; £1,090 in Westmeath; £9,335 in Roscommon; £3,275 in Limerick; £2,315 in Monaghan; £11,065 in Sligo; £2,225 in Tyrone. The smallest amount granted to any county was £95 to Wexford.

streets; and various strong claims to a portion of the Mansion House Fund were pressed upon this Committee. The Sub-Committee, to which the applications were submitted, while acknowledging the exceptional intensity of the distress, declared that "a city like Dublin could not, with propriety, appeal for outside aid to relieve distress within its precincts." As, however, many of the Dublin subscribers had contributed on the understanding that the city should not be excluded, it was recommended that a portion, and that not a large portion, of the money subscribed in Dublin, should be used for the relief of distress in Dublin; with the distinct understanding and declaration, that no further city claim upon the Fund should be entertained. The grants, amounting to £625, which were upon the strength of that recommendation divided among the city charitable organisations (being, as it was reckoned, about one-tenth of the Dublin subscriptions), constituted the only assistance furnished by this Committee in Dublin. The grievous distress which unquestionably prevailed in the city was taken in charge by a separate City of Dublin Relief Committee, with a separate fund, which the Lord Mayor inaugurated with a subscription of £500. The establishment of an independent civic organisation saved the Irish capital the humiliation of begging bread for its poor, at the same time that it liberated the Mansion House Fund in its entirety for the relief of distress of a more desperate type elsewhere. *The Distress in Dublin left to be dealt with by a Special Civic Fund*

While the demands for help were thus starting up, here, there, and everywhere, in spite of the tight rein kept upon places with any capacity left to help themselves, the steps taken by the Government with the object of providing employment, had altogether failed to lessen the strain upon the charitable funds. In November the Government had offered loans on favourable terms to landowners, for the improvement of their estates, and to local sanitary authorities for useful works, with the object of creating employment for unskilled labour. This project having proved practically a dead letter, the landowners were in January invited to take loans, to be expended in labour upon their estates, upon the liberal terms of having to pay only 1 per cent. interest, no interest at all being charged for the first two years, and the period of repayment being spread over 35 years. Considerable sums were applied for under this generous power; but it was found that the districts where the distress was sorest, were precisely those in which the landowners were unwilling to incur loans upon any terms; and, in the result, no appreciable amount of employment from that source reached the labouring classes, until the back of the distress was broken.* At the same time the LORD LIEUTENANT was empowered by the Government to convoke Extraordinary Baronial Sessions, in districts where the alternative measure had no effect, and to make advances at 1 per cent. interest, repayable in fifteen years, for such public works as the Sessions might sanction, under the heads of fencing, repairing,

---

* The Local Government Board Annual Report states, that up to its date (17th April, 1880), of £1,245,583 applied for by landowners, £134,460 had been issued, and of £143,962 applied for by sanitary authorities, £7,937 had been issued. It is believed that the bulk of the advances were made to a few great landed proprietors.

or levelling existing roads, or making new ones. One hundred and six such Baronial Sessions were actually summoned by the LORD LIEUTENANT. But, in some of the needy districts (as at Clifden), the Justices refused point-blank to saddle bankrupt baronies with taxation, which, in the universal indigence of the cesspayers, must come out of the pockets of the landowners. In others, the cesspayers consented to bear the taxes, and passed large presentments for public works; but the works passed at the Baronial Sessions had to be first approved of by the Commissioners of Public Works, (who in most cases rejected them altogether); those which survived had to be submitted to the Government, who referred them to the Local Government Board, who referred them to their Local Inspectors for reports; which reports were in turn transmitted by the Local Government Board to the Government, with whom the final decision lay. During this process of circumlocution, the season had advanced to sowing-time, and the danger of drawing men away from tilling their lands was made the apology for deferring the baronial works until midsummer, or throwing them overboard altogether.

Deferred till Summer or thrown overboard

The special measures of the Government having thus failed to afford any substantial co-operation, the whole brunt of the relief fell upon the charitable organisations, and, to far the largest extent, upon this Committee. The DUCHESS OF MARLBOROUGH'S Committee had, from the beginning, restricted its scope to Connaught and the Atlantic seaboard, and its grants applied only to the class of occupiers of small holdings of land who could not legally (until the abrogation of the Gregory quarter-acre clause in March) receive Poor-law relief without surrendering their holdings. In relation to the entire labouring population, therefore, and throughout all the remaining area of distress, the Mansion House Committee was, with the exception of the National Land League, the only then existing source of dependence. The extent of the responsibility thus involved, even altogether outside the original focus of distress, may be estimated by the fact that, of the sixty-six Unions officially scheduled, under the Relief of Distress Act, as distressed districts, thirty-eight Unions are situated outside the range of the DUCHESS OF MARLBOROUGH'S Committee's operations: that is to say, Connaught, Donegal, Clare, Kerry, and Cork; and that the Extraordinary Baronial Sessions convoked by the LORD LIEUTENANT were spread over no less than sixteen counties.* Under these circumstances, every succeeding week in January and February brought forth new Local Committees, and increased demands upon the existing ones. The Mansion House Committee found themselves constrained to admit the claims of 102 new Local Committees in the period from the 17th to the 28th of February. On the last day of February there were 631 of these Committees in operation, and the total number of persons on the relief lists during the last week of that month was 512,625 (a large proportion of whom, however, were partially relieved by the munificent

The People dependent on Charity for Food

---

* Annual Report of the Local Government Board, pp. 9 and 12.

grants transmitted from America to the Irish Bishops, and from other sources). It had required an expenditure of £45,049, concurrently with at least as much more from all other eleemosynary sources, to feed the destitute until then with scanty doles of Indian meal. That that duty was, however, fulfilled, with as little privation to the sufferers, and as careful precaution against fraud as is, perhaps, possible in the case of a wide-spread voluntary charitable organisation, we do not care to show so much by the votes of thanks of the Local Committees which were during the period constantly and fervently poured forth, as by the united voice of the Irish Bishops, whose means of information were unrivalled, and who were themselves above all suspicion of local bias, as well as by the verdicts of public bodies still less likely to be charged with partiality towards this Committee. For example, the Grand Jury of the County of Cork, assembled at the Spring Assizes (J. M'CARTHY O'LEARY, Esq., D.L., Foreman), passed an unanimous resolution, proposed and seconded by two of the most prominent Conservative landowners in that county, "offering their grateful acknowledgments to the Executive Committee and the subscribers to the Mansion House Fund, for the large sums of money forwarded by them for the relief of distress in this county." The Grand Jury of the County of Kerry at the same time (HENRY A. HERBERT, Esq., M.P., Foreman), passed a resolution, proposed by Mr. E. DE MOLEYNS, and seconded by Mr. J. E. BULLER, "That we express our appreciation of the efforts made and carried out by the Mansion House Committee for the relief of the distressed districts in this county."

Up to March there was no visible barrier whatever between the people and starvation, except the charitable funds, and the MARLBOROUGH Committee grants for food having about this time practically ceased, the Mansion House Committee had no alternative but to encounter the daily increasing ravages of distress, with ever-increasing inroads upon their Fund. The Relief of Distress Act, passed on the 15th of March, altered the situation. It enabled Boards of Guardians, in Unions scheduled as distressed, to grant out-door relief in food or fuel to the small farmers, without the surrender of their holdings, and to such other able-bodied persons as they deemed fit objects of relief. Upon the 19th of March, the LORD MAYOR impressed gravely upon the Mansion House Committee the advisability of utilising the new Act so as to relieve the tremendous strain upon the charitable funds, and husband their resources for the still more trying months to come. They were now spending at the rate of £13,000 a week; their balance was under £40,000; they had no reason to anticipate that the magnificent Australian funds, which were their main reliance, could continue to flow in with the same volume as heretofore. If they went on maintaining their present grants, their resources would be exhausted in six weeks; at the very time when, the spring work being over, the distress promised to be more acute and desperate than ever. The Relief Act (he argued) placed the Guardians of the scheduled Unions in the position of giving food and fuel to the poor, and that was practically what

Increasing Demands upon this Fund

The Relief of Distress Act

Proposed reduction of the charitable Grants

this Committee had hitherto been doing. If they reduced their grants, the Guardians could not reasonably shirk the duty of making good the deficiency to the poor. There were other circumstances which seemed to render a curtailment of the grants, not merely feasible, but desirable. Owing to the operation of the Seeds Act, an unusual breadth of tillage was being laid down; and, although the small farmers were too poor to pay for labour, there still sprang up sufficient employment in many districts to enable the agricultural labourers to be removed from the relief lists. It was stated also, that in a few isolated instances, labourers who could find work preferred to be supported in idleness by charity. All these considerations moved the Mansion House Committee to adopt a resolution :—

"That, in view of the enormous and increasing demands upon the Mansion House Fund, and the fact that the distress is likely to be more severe in some weeks hence, when the spring work is over, and seeing that Boards of Guardians are empowered to grant out-door relief, in food and fuel, to Unions scheduled under the 3rd section of the Relief of Distress (Ireland) Act, 1880, it is desirable that in such Unions the Local Committee should see that the provisions of the said Act, and the order of the Local Government Board thereunder are put in force, but not in such manner as to interfere with the cultivation of their own land by small landholders now in receipt of relief; be it therefore resolved that a circular be issued to the Local Committees, directing their attention to the provisions of the Act, and requiring them, so soon as the Guardians of the Union are prepared to afford adequate out-door relief under the 3rd section thereof, to confine, save in special and exceptional cases, the relief given by means of the Mansion House Fund, to small farmers cultivating their own lands, and with instructions to supply to the Guardians of their Union, and to require from them lists of those relieved by both respectively, so as to guard against relief being given to one person from more than one source, and similarly in the case of other relief organisations, if such exist within the districts; and that the Local Committees be required to notify to this Committee all cases where the Guardians fail to carry out the provisions of the Act, or to fix a sufficient scale of relief. That the Publication Committee be appointed to carry out the foregoing resolution, with instructions to place themselves in communication with the other Committees, in order to secure, so far as possible, uniformity of action, with power to adopt a joint form of circular with the other two Committees."

The Act proved inoperative.

The result showed that the new Relief Act was substantially as ineffectual as those which had preceded it. From various causes, the Boards of Guardians could not be spurred into any general system of out-door relief, such as would replace the charitable grants, should they be diminished or withdrawn. In the Unions where the distress was most aggravated, any attempt to feed the people at the expense of the ratepayers, must simply have swamped the entire ratepaying body in common ruin. In many Unions it took several thousand pounds a week, in various forms of alms, to keep the population alive. Such a burden imposed upon a body of ratepayers who, in the language of the Belmullet Local Committee, "are not themselves half so independent, nor so sure of their daily food, as the paupers to whose support they must contribute if they have it," would have reduced them to ruin before a month. In many other Unions the Guardians had availed themselves liberally of the Seeds Act, and had purchased from £4,000 to £8,000 worth of seed corn and potatoes; which they considered to be as heavy a responsibility as their ratepayers should bear. But there were others where these excuses failed; where the poor-rate was still low, where the distress was within reasonable bounds, and where the well-to-do portion of the community had not hitherto, in taxation or subscriptions, borne their full share of the sacrifices of the time. This was so strongly felt, that for several months the Mansion House Committee did not relax their efforts with the Local Government Board, to stimulate the recalcitrant Guardians into a more generous policy. But the Act was not mandatory, and the Guardians shunned the sacrifice. In these circumstances a wail of terror went up at the prospect of a withdrawal or reduction of the Mansion House grants. "For God's sake," Dean M'Manus telegraphed to the LORD MAYOR from Clifden, "do not abandon us. If help is withheld for a week, hundreds will die." In almost identical words, the Protestant Rector of Moylough, Rev. Canon TAIT, LL.D., uttered the warning: "If for a single week the supplies are cut off, we shall have hundreds starving on every side." One good result came of the action of the Mansion House Committee: any person who could possibly find subsistence by his labour was carefully eliminated from the relief-lists. But as fast as the labourers found employment, fresh batches of the small farmers were coming to the end of their food supply, and there was reason to fear they would be driven to devour the seed-potatoes just supplied to them, if their wants were not otherwise supplied while they were tilling their farms. Despite all the efforts of vigilance and economy, therefore, the last week of March found the relief-lists still exhibiting the enormous total of 488,335 persons. Providentially, if the demands upon the charitable funds had not greatly diminished, neither had the flow of the world's charity.

Consternation at the Reduction of the Grants

THE WESTERN ISLES.

It is necessary shortly to explain now the special machinery applied to the relief of the islands of the Atlantic coast and the necessity for it. These islands number about thirty in all, and contain 22,510 souls. They are scattered at wide intervals along the whole western coast from Donegal to Cork. Although in many cases separated from the mainland by a channel only a few miles wide, they lie open to the full rage of a tempestuous ocean which, from November to May, beats around them with such fury that even the hardy fishermen of the islands are frequently for whole fortnights together afraid to tempt the waves. Owing to the want of sheltered landing-places, the passage to the islands is still more perilous for large craft, and even the

Special circumstances of the Western Isles

mountainous shores they adjoin are for the most part almost as inaccessible and forlorn as the islands. Upon these desolate prisons amidst the Atlantic, it suddenly became known that men were sinking by slow starvation unknown to the world. The worst that could be said of isolated cases upon the mainland was, save in a few exceptional cases, true of the entire island population. If ever there was poverty genuine, poignant, terrific, and unmerited, it was theirs. Their little food crops had withered so utterly away that it was often difficult to find an altogether sound potato in a basketful or a basketful in a whole ridge. Every smallest remnant of their simple wealth had disappeared under the last three years' avalanche of losses; their stock, their furniture, the very clothes on their backs and the blankets off their wretched beds. Valuable fishing grounds lay at their doors; but such boats as they possessed were too crazy, and their fishing-gear too rotten and primitive to yield them any sufficient return for the dangers of these wild seas. If they burned kelp, as upon the islands in Kilkerrin Bay, or if they migrated yearly to Scotland for the harvest, as from Achill, they had suffered their share of the year's loss of £50,000 in the one industry, and of £250,000 in the other. Helpless alike on sea and shore, shivering in rags around their empty fireplaces, friendless and alone in their solitude of angry waters, they had shortened their rations as in a besieged city until in January they were existing for the most part upon a meal a day of rotten potatoes, turnips, coarse dried fish, or boiled *sloucawn*. Before them, famine; around them a misery which (in the words of Mr. LANE JOYNT after he had beheld it) " language could not describe "— which (said Lord FRANCIS GODOLPHIN OSBORNE) " almost drives me to despair of relieving it "—a misery so abject that when a gunboat was despatched a short time before to one of the Blasket Islands to enforce payment of county cess, the crew of the gunboat no sooner saw the unhappy creatures they had come to overawe, than they clubbed together and paid the amount of the demand out of their own wages. The Mansion House Committee recognised that the starving islanders could be rescued by none of the ordinary methods, since upon most of the islands there was nobody above the fear of starvation to organise a Local Committee, and even if such a body could be supplied with funds the people must inevitably have perished before the money could be turned into food and the food transported to the islands. A Western Isles Committee, composed of Mr. WILLIAM LANE JOYNT (Chairman), Lord FRANCIS GODOLPHIN OSBORNE, Rev. CANON BAGOT, and Mr. GEORGE DELANY, with the Honorary Secretaries, was formed early in January to organise a special food-supply for the service of the islands. In this matter the most cordial co-operation was established between this Committee and the DUCHESS OF MARLBOROUGH'S Committee, as well as subsequently the Committee of the *New York Herald* Fund. One hundred tons of Indian meal were promptly collected in equal shares by the two Committees at convenient depots upon the coast, and the danger, delay, and destruction of food by sea-water which the ordinary carriage by schooner would have involved were avoided by the valuable co-operation of

Co-operation of the various Committees

the Admiralty authorities, who placed a fleet of four of Her Majesty's gunboats at the disposal of the Committee for convenience of transport. Mr. H. A. ROBINSON, Local Government Inspector, who superintended the first distribution of fifty tons among the islanders of the Mayo and Galway coasts in the latter end of February, described in his report the eagerness with which the Kilkerrin islanders swarmed out in their boats when the reliefship came in sight, until "before the vessel was ten minutes anchored the sea was black with boats running into one another, coming stern on alongside, getting their ropes entangled with the screw and with each other; every island sending its contingent to add to the excitement and confusion." The sale of sea-weed at £1 18s. a boatload, Mr. ROBINSON found to be all that was left to the peasantry as a means of livelihood. "To this add a few pigs for which there is a fair demand, and a few cattle for which at the present time there is none, and this ends *the best* of the Kilkerrin Bay islanders' resources." "If the physical appearance of the people may be taken as a criterion," Mr. ROBINSON says, speaking of Inishark, "I never saw a more pale and wretched-looking community. They nearly all appeared to have come to an end of their supplies, and the hundredweight of meal recently distributed to them *was the only adjunct to their seaweed and boiled limpets* . . . . . Clothing, too, among the children is sadly needed. Many of them had nothing on whatever except a patch of flannel which scarcely went round their shoulders." A special correspondent of the *Standard*, who accompanied Mr. ROBINSON on his cruise, gave still more affecting accounts of the condition of the islanders. "There cannot be the slightest doubt in the world," he wrote from Dinish Island, "that but for the relief benevolently given then, these people would now be dying of actual hunger and want." "If aid had not been sent to the inhabitants of Turbot Island, I cannot see how they could have escaped a terrible death by starvation." "During a fortnight's tour in these desolate islands, I have not seen a single article of clothing that could be called finery." "Destitution in its most awful forms has overwhelmed the unhappy inhabitants of Innishark. Their condition when we landed on the islands and inspected their cabins, was little short of death by slow starvation." "The most extreme poverty and want are everywhere visible. Naked and without food, many of the people are slowly starving to death." "Powerfully built frames are worn and emaciated, and many a day must elapse before they regain even the small amount of strength necessary to cultivate their wretched holdings." These are but a few of the expressions of horror to which a moderate and conscientious observer found himself driven by his experiences of the Western Isles. The Indian meal so sparingly divided among the islands was welcomed as manna; and £500 was promptly placed at the discretion of the Western Isles Committee to supply in some measure the frightful want of clothing among the unhappy people which was revealed by Mr. ROBINSON's report. Henceforward the transport of food to the islands was performed by a regular and carefully organized service of gunboats at the joint expense of the two Committees. The labour of personally apportioning and distributing these food-cargoes over hundreds of miles of a stormy and dangerous coast was undertaken on the part of this Committee by Lord FRANCIS GODOLPHIN OSBORNE. The DUCHESS OF MARLBOROUGH'S Committee, on their part, cordially accepted him as their representative, too. His task extended over more than three months, during which he visited every remotest island in those boisterous seas, from the desolate islets of Donegal to those which cluster in Roaring-water Bay inside Cape Clear. His reports from the various islands were harrowing in the extreme. "I have visited many houses both in Boffin and Shark," he reported on the 11th of March, "and I have no hesitation in stating, that the poverty and distress exceed all that I had been prepared for, and that on these islands, and on all the islands on the West Coast, had it not been for the relief distributed by the various Committees, there must have been innumerable cases of actual starvation and death." "My heart grows sick at the sights I see," he writes of Lettermullen. "The people's patience and endurance is marvellous, and I think any man who sees what I have seen, and murmurs at our ordinary troubles, must be indeed hard to learn any lesson." Many of the islands upon the Cork and Kerry Coast he found to be not only entirely dependent upon charity for food, but "quite destitute of fuel," although, speaking of his experiences of the South generally, he did not consider the actual want nearly so great in the South as in the West, and was proportionately circumspect in his distributions there. Innisboffin, off the Donegal Coast, he declared to be the most abjectly miserable place he had yet seen, and in the neighbouring Tory Island, although the pasturage was so barren as to appear almost incapable of supporting animal life, the people were "skinning the land," in order to burn the dried sods for fuel. The entire population of 1,800 persons on Arranmore (County Donegal), were, "with scarcely an exception, wholly dependent upon the small amount of relief which they received from the Relief Committees. "The amount," he adds, on the 12th May, "which the present state of the funds allows to be distributed to the different families is barely sufficient of itself in any case to maintain life, and in many cases where the families are exceptionally large, it is really quite inadequate." Neither turf nor water was to be got on the adjoining Island of Inishkeragh, inhabited by 13 families, both were obliged to be brought from the main land. "What motive have I to exaggerate?" he wrote from Sligo on the 25th of May, when he had all but completed his circuit of the coast. "I long and pine day and night to see things less utterly miserable than I am still forced to see them." The islands provisioned during Lord FRANCIS OSBORNE'S cruise were saved at least from the extremities of famine. Henceforward, their frightful misery was alleviated by every means that the liberality of the united Committees, and the most tender and anxious care of humane men, could devise. Towards the end of March H.R.H. the DUKE OF EDINBURGH arrived to take command of the relief squadron on the Western Coast, and invited representatives of the

Lord Francis Osborne's Reports

different Committees to confer with him at Galway upon the most efficient system of distribution. Mr. LANE JOYNT was deputed thither with full powers to represent the Mansion House Committee; and a system of joint relief was there concerted between HIS ROYAL HIGHNESS and the representatives of the DUCHESS OF MARLBOROUGH'S, the *New York Herald*, and the Mansion House Committees, which, if it could not quite dissipate the misery of the islands, beyond all question secured to the population throughout the summer as near an approach to abundance of food and comfort of clothing as has, perhaps, ever brightened their joyless lives. The DUKE OF EDINBURGH superintended the distribution of the relief, and when he returned to England bore strong testimony to the impression of sickness and horror made upon him by the sufferings and endurance of the Western peasants. Mr. LANE JOYNT, who accompanied HIS ROYAL HIGHNESS in his explorations of the islands off the Galway Coast, conveyed to the Mansion House Committee in impressive terms, the two convictions to which he had been driven by his experiences in the West—(1), that he had beheld, with his own eyes, "an amount of poverty and misery, that it would be impossible to exaggerate and most difficult to pourtray," and (2), that the charitable funds alone had prevented privation from going the length of death. The cargo of the American relief ship "Constellation" formed at this time an important factor in the supplies to the Western Islands. Its distribution was confided to the *New York Herald* Committee, through its active representative, the Rev. Dr. HEPWORTH; the DUKE OF EDINBURGH made a special trip to Cork Harbour, with his flotilla of gunboats, to proffer his assistance in carrying out the beneficent purpose of the American people; and the cargo was in the space of a week or two in process of consumption in the most necessitous nooks upon the Atlantic Coast. HIS ROYAL HIGHNESS was shortly afterwards summoned away from Ireland by the death of his mother-in-law, the EMPRESS OF RUSSIA. The relief service, devolved thenceforward upon Captain DIGBY MORANT, R.N., who, like the officers and men of his fleet, threw himself heart and soul into the work, and whose official report of his operations, though framed with the blunt terseness of a gallant seaman, conveys with awful force the extent of wretchedness that had to be coped with along that grand but desolate coast. The sum of £4,445 4s. 11d. was expended from the Mansion House Fund upon the recommendations of the Western Isles' Committee, and it is generally felt that no part of the Fund was applied to the alleviation of more appalling distress, or was attended with more unmixed blessings to the Irish poor.

<small>The Duke of Edinburgh's experiences</small>

DANGERS DURING THE SUMMER.

Promise of a good harvest

The half-a-million's worth of new seeds distributed through the country under the Seeds Act had brought a greater breadth of land under tillage than had been seen for years in the distressed districts, and a mild and sunny spring was opening a vision of hope to the farmers. But at least four months lay between them and the gathering of the harvest—four months of absolute dependence upon charity for existence—months, too, which the experiences of previous Irish famines had marked out as the time of the year when suffering sounded its deepest depths. To save the people from perishing while a bountiful crop was ripening under their dying eyes—to cover four lingering months of destitution, while the distress was growing ever wider, and their funds beginning to fail—was now the all-absorbing anxiety which began to press upon the Mansion House Committee at almost every meeting. The demands for food were not abating, nor likely to abate. The labourers, when the spurt of spring employment was over, fell back into pauperism. The small farmers who would have starved to death during March only for the charitable grants, would starve only for them now all the same. Except that the opening of the fishing season might prove to be an adjunct of relief on parts of the Western Coast, no new resource had cropped up. Public works there were none. The Poor Law Guardians had set their faces against out-door relief. The DUCHESS OF MARLBOROUGH's Committee had all but discontinued their grants of food. Hundreds of thousands of hungry people had come to look up to the Mansion House Committee for the weekly pittance of Indian meal which kept body and soul together. On the other hand the Mansion House Fund was running out faster than it was coming in. The Australian subscriptions—*grande decus columenque rerum !*—were beginning to be closed. Pare and scrutinise the grants as they might, the Committee could barely retain six weeks' supply in hands, while ten or twelve hungry weeks more loomed before them, after charity should have divided its last crust. To increase their anxieties, certain incautious expressions published on the high authority of the Trustees to whom the DUCHESS OF MARLBOROUGH, when leaving Ireland, had entrusted the remnant of Her Grace's Fund, were construed in England and abroad as an intimation that the worst of the distress was over; with the effect that the apathy and incredulity which weighed upon all charitable efforts in the beginning took fresh courage and had to be combated over again. The expressions were afterwards explained or recanted by those who had used them; but the harm had been done. The weekly contributions rapidly thinned. Either the Mansion House Committee must forthwith reduce or withdraw their grants, and take chance for the Poor Law proving equal to the emergency; or keep the people alive as long as they could and warn the Government with all their might in the meantime, that upon their head must in a few weeks lie the **responsibility**.

Danger of the people dying while it was ripening

The Mansion House Fund running out

Fresh Subscriptions checked

This alternative was strongly brought to the notice of the Committee, on the 17th of April, by a report presented to them by Mr. JAMES H. TUKE as the result of nearly two months' experiences in Donegal and parts of Connaught. Mr. TUKE's well-known experience as a representative of the Society of Friends during the great famine, as well as the careful and moderate character of his investigations, gave great weight to his conclusions. The first of these conclusions was, that as regards the Unions bordering on the sea-coast, throughout the whole of the district he had visited, the question of absolute distress and need for help was only one of degree, attaining its maximum in the Gletnies Union in Donegal, and in portions of the Unions of Clifden and Oughterard in Galway. Of the penury and destitution of these districts, he said, the fact that in several electoral divisions seventy or eighty per cent., or more, of the population needed to have their daily food supplied, told its own tale; that there were also Unions or portions of Unions in Mayo and other parts of Connaught, nearly equally needing help was beyond doubt. His second conclusion was that the whole of these districts would continue to need assistance until the crops then being planted were ready for use; that in fact, "for four or five months to come food will need to be found for many thousands of the little farmers and cottiers of the West." As the public measures of relief were not promising, and as the influx of charitable subscriptions was not likely to continue, Mr. TUKE saw but two courses open to the Mansion House Committee under these circumstances:—the one, a general reduction of the present scale of grants over the whole area now assisted; the other, a contraction of this area to the poorest districts in the West, with a distribution therein at nearly the present rate: and he unhesitatingly declared that the latter course was the one which suggested itself to his judgment. But Mr. TUKE judged of the area of distress only from his visits to three counties; and, if he found so terrible a pitch of destitution in these, a visit to counties like Cavan, or Leitrim, or Monaghan would have given him perhaps a truer idea of the difficulty of contracting the area of assistance. The LORD MAYOR, who, being in Cork to welcome the Officers of the "Constellation" about this time, took advantage of his stay in order to visit some of the Western regions of that county, declared himself appalled by the picture of misery he saw on Long Island and around Schull. The condition of affairs which he saw on the Western Coast of Cork make him shudder to think what was likely to occur unless the relief supplies could be kept up. The LORD MAYOR's misgivings as to Cork were confirmed by all sorts of evidence as to districts still further removed from the regions generally reckoned to be the strongholds of distress, Mr. ANCKETELL, D.L., who came up to Dublin in search of relief for his unhappy neighbours, described the mountainous districts of Monaghan to be in a state of actual starvation. The Kilcoo (Co. Down) Committee claimed (April 29) that no district in Ireland exceeded their own in misery; reported the spread of dysentery and diarrhœa from improper food; and were apprehensive that, "notwithstanding all our efforts to save them, many will perish." The

Rector of Kiltubrid, Carrick-on-Shannon (the Rev. SAMUEL E. HOOP) reported that many of the small farmers were compelled from weakness, consequent on want of food, to give up labour on their own farms, "as they can't stand work without food;" and declared he could bear it no longer, if he was forced to witness the sight of hundreds of famishing people each moment crowding around his door entreating for relief, while he was compelled to tell them, in their starvation and despair, that not having received any grant for the previous ten days he could give them no issue of meal. And this not merely reveals the condition of places with some repute for prosperity, but points to the fact that from the beginning the Mansion House Committee had discriminated carefully between the wholesale misery of the extreme West, and the more limited, though often equally acute, description of distress in the less stricken parts of the country. In this latter class of cases, the grants had been all along upon a small scale, and had been repeated only upon the most urgent evidence of hunger. "You say that the grant ought to be sufficient until the 24th instant," expostulated the Rev. E. MAYNE WADSWORTH, Rector of Dunseverick, Bushmills (County Antrim), on the 14th of April. "If our Committee had been informed of a certain date for your grant to be spent in, we must have left families without one meal in the day. What are we to do? I believe there is not greater want in any part of Ireland, than in this place. On Monday and yesterday, persons were at the glebe-house in a starving condition, and I had to relieve them out of my own pocket, and from very small means. I ask again, what are we to do?" It was evident that the margin of curtailment was small.

Distinction observed all along between different shades of Distress

Nevertheless, the consideration of Mr. TUKE's report, and the grave considerations submitted to them by the LORD MAYOR upon his return from the South, determined the Committee to try an almost desperate experiment in this direction. The harvest in the South promised to be an early one, its prospects looked bright, and probably in about two months more the new potatoes there would be well in; but the LORD MAYOR did not hesitate to say that far from the distress lessening, he was every day more and more convinced that they were only just entering upon the most dangerous part of the year. He asked them to consider whether they could meet the problem of undiminished want and failing resources, (1) by devising some means of raising new funds, (2) by concerting some plan of common action with the other charitable organisations, or (3) by ascertaining whether there were any of the distressed districts which were not at starvation point, and cutting them off. Upon the 29th of April, the Examination Sub-Committee had to make the grave announcement that out of 142 applications submitted for their consideration the previous day (the largest number since the commencement of the distress) they had been obliged, in view of the steady decrease in the Mansion House Fund, and the increasing intensity of the destitution in many districts, to refuse or defer no less than 63, and to intimate in 28 other instances, that the grants must be considered final. The

The Committee driven to further curtailments

principle upon which the Examination Committee proceeded was to encourage, as far as possible, the action of those Boards of Guardians that had made fair use of their power to grant out-door relief, and to refuse grants altogether to those Unions where, the rates being still low, the Guardians had selfishly thrown the entire burden of relief upon the charitable funds. It was hoped in this way to stimulate the Guardians to assume some part at least of the functions which were growing too much for unassisted charity. The expectation proved to be a delusive one. With few exceptions, the Guardians murmured about the burdens they had already incurred, and could not be induced to move. The Local Government Board could not be induced to compel them. They need not regard a man as technically "destitute," it appeared, as long as he was receiving charitable relief; and if men were struck off the charitable relief lists, they would, in all likelihood, die before the Poor Law machinery could be put in motion. Those Local Committees, whose supplies were curtailed or cut off, appealed to the Guardians, and appealed in vain; then a cry of panic and suffering broke forth far and wide. The Kilmore Committee (Co. Leitrim) were obliged to reduce their grants of three quarters of a stone of meal per head, per week, to the same quantity per fortnight. "The consequence is," wrote the Rev. Mr. BAMBRICK, "I have seen men tottering along more like skeletons than like living men." "We will be driven into the workhouse ourselves like sheep," was the reply of the Castlebar Guardians to an appeal for more outdoor relief. The BISHOP OF CLONFERT himself besought the Loughrea Guardians without avail. "Unless we receive for the next three months," was the report from Addergoole, "constant and generous grants to relieve the alarming distress of our people, we shall have renewed in this parish, in their worst aspects, the famine scenes of '46." It was the unanimous opinion of the Manorhamilton Committee that the distress had at no time been more acute than it was now. The Rev. B. MULHOLLAND entreated the Mansion House Committee not to let the retrenchment commence with Donaghedy (Co. Tyrone). "A larger number than ever of my people are destitute, and three-fourths of the people on the mountains have nothing to live on." The Rev. Mr. Nangle, of Dromahair (Co. Leitrim), mentioned an instance where a man and his wife and eight children were living for eight days upon one stone of Indian meal and some turnips; "a few weeks after the man became insane." In Forkhill, (Co. Armagh), the charitable supplies being cut off, the parish priest and the rector had to borrow £15, rather than send a thousand hungry applicants away empty handed. "For God's sake" they cried, "send us some good tidings before Sunday, or we must send our people home with the sad news that they must die of starvation, unless the fever which has began its work gives them a quicker release." "If your Committee refuse to grant relief to the starving people," wrote the Rev. Mr. M'CAUSLAND, [Rector of Castlerea, (Co. Roscommon), "while funds are in their hands, upon them must rest the responsibility." "The results of the diminished supplies," said the BISHOP

The consequences

of KILLALA, "are complaints, destitution, and sickness." Epidemics of low fever were breaking out in various directions.

Retrenchment at its lowest point

Retrenchment had now gone as far as anybody dared to push it. The weekly grants, which used to average £8,000 and £9,000, were clipped down to little more than £5,000. The piteous importunities which every day's post brought forth, were resisted as long as it was possible to resist them without endangering human life. Nevertheless, while the cry was swelling that the worst of the distress was yet to come, the Committee's balance was sinking steadily to £30,000, and every device for calling new sources of charity into play was discouragingly received. Upon the 8th of May, the sum of £10 only was received, while the disbursements, attenuated though they were below any other period of the distress, reached £1,070. Upon that same day an important step was taken to impress upon the new Government, which had just come into office, that the charitable organisations could not bear the strain much longer, and that the duty of the State towards hundreds of thousands of its starving subjects could not be any further deferred. A body

Deputation to the Chief Secretary

of the most influential members of the Mansion House Committee waited upon the new Chief Secretary for Ireland (Mr. FORSTER), at Dublin Castle, as a deputation, to enforce this view. The LORD MAYOR explained in the most forcible way the position of the Committee. They had spent £37,000 in March, £33,000 in April, in feeding the people. They had evidence which they deemed convincing, that the distress was not likely to be in any degree mitigated before the end of July, and the coming in of the harvest. Their present resources would only furnish a month's relief, and they had no sanguine hope that charity could do much more for them. They saw no organisation at present in existence which could take up their work. What they feared was, the shock that might ensue in the period of transition between any sudden cessation of charitable relief, and the organisation of any other system of relief to replace it—a transition attended with such deadly consequences in 1847—and they took this method of giving timely warning of the danger, so that the Government might make full preparation, while the charitable funds still lasted, for some other organisation to keep the people from starvation until the coming in of the harvest. The Protestant ARCHBISHOP OF DUBLIN declared it to be the settled conviction of all who were acquainted with the history of the distress, that the suffering of the people was as intense now as it had been at any time, and that there was no ground for expecting that it would be abated for the next two months or more. Mr. JONATHAN PIM (an honoured veteran in the relief of Irish distress), thoroughly agreed with the LORD MAYOR, both as to the probable duration of the distress, and as to the danger that would arise whenever the charitable funds should be worn out. Mr. BROOKS, M.P., and Mr. P. J. SMYTH, M.P., added their solemn words of warning; and the Rev. Canon BAGOT pointed out how ineffectual the present system of Poor Law relief must be in the case of the small farmers, who now principally swelled the relief lists, since, apart from their abhorrence of craving assistance at the workhouse gates, they were mostly ratepayers, taxed for the relief of the poor at a moment when they were themselves in a state of actual pauperism. The reply of the CHIEF SECRETARY was a grave and earnest one. He wanted no argument, he said, to convince him of the existence of distress—not, he trusted, what it was in 1847, but beyond doubt very severe. He was not at all surprised that the deputation were very much alarmed about the condition of the people for the next two or three months, for he fully expected that the months of June and July, and perhaps part of August, would be in some respects the worst they would have to deal with. But having himself thrown upon the late Government the responsibility of preventing starvation in Ireland, he declared in the most distinct terms that he would not shirk that responsibility now. He announced what was being done with the machinery bequeathed to him by the late Government. Of the loans to landowners for employment, £189,000 had been issued, and £26,000 actually spent. The baronial presentments which were passed months before, had hitherto lain in the Government offices. Mr. FORSTER announced that the expenditure of £76,000 had now been sanctioned on this head, and would commence at once. He hoped that these two sources of employment would do a good deal towards getting the people over the interval between this and the harvest. But should they prove inadequate, and should it be found quite impossible to extract relief from the the ratepayers, he admitted frankly it would be the duty of the Government to step in and resort to other measures. In the meantime, he appealed to the charitable Committees not to be discouraged from continuing their labours, and, if possible, to strike out some common plan of action for the relief of that class of misery which neither the Government nor the Poor Law could deal with. *His encouraging Reply*

Incontestably, the sincere and thoughtful tone of Mr. FORSTER's reply, followed up as it was by a spirit of earnest and active endeavour in every branch of the administration, did much to tranquillise public anxiety. It made manifest that at all events the gravity of the danger was appreciated, and that its developments were being watched with sympathetic vigilance by the responsible authorities. Two days afterwards, the CHIEF SECRETARY sent a subscription of £50 to the Mansion House Fund, with a note to the LORD MAYOR, in which he said :—" What you told me last Saturday, about the distress in the West, confirmed as it is by what I hear from other quarters, makes me feel that there is still pressing need for charitable aid between now and next harvest." This was followed on May 20th, by the munificent subscription of £500, from the new Lord Lieutenant of Ireland, Earl COWPER, K.G., who accompanied it with a kindly letter, in which he said in the first place :—" I am convinced from all I hear and from all I read, that there is still much need of private charity in Ireland;" and in the second place, "I am satisfied that the money entrusted both to the DUCHESS OF MARLBOROUGH's Committee and to the Mansion House Committee, has been well administered, and that fewer mistakes have *Fresh impulse to Subscriptions* been made than could reasonably be expected in so vast and complicated a task." These, with some temporary fillip in the subscriptions, and the ever-growing clamour of hunger, stimulated the Mansion House Committee to make one more effort to replenish their exhausted means. A powerful statement was drawn up by Professor SIGERSON and sent abroad, showing that while destitution, now complicated with fevers, still prevailed, and must continue to prevail with unabated rigour for several months, the resources of charity were drawing rapidly to an end, and that within a few weeks, if further generosity did not renew their store, the Mansion House Committee would be forced "formally to resign into the hands of those whom the State appoints to watch over its safety, the full charge of the suffering lives which have hitherto been the subject of their care, and must still be the object of their painful solicitude." Indeed the necessity of either continuing their efforts upon an adequate scale, or of discontinuing them altogether, was now constantly borne in upon the Committee. The good intentions of the Government were slow in bearing fruit. The truth was, that the lines they were obliged to travel in were so unworkable that no amount of pressure or energy could make the paltry and scattered sources of public employment act in substitution for an organisation like ours. A series of searching queries submitted to the Local Committees* revealed the fact, that within an area in the County Cavan, in which the Mansion House Committee were relieving 39,354 persons, the expenditure upon Baronial Public Works (most of which had not even been commenced on the 1st of June), would yield about $1s.\ 2\frac{1}{2}d.$ to each distressed individual; that in Mayo, in 35, or more than half of the districts relieved by the Mansion House Committee, no public works whatever were contemplated; in 26 districts more, where the money had been voted to set them on foot, no part of the money had been expended up to the 1st of June, and even were the whole sum voted for the County in process of expenditure, it would amount to an allowance of $1s.\ 4d.$ per head of the distressed population; and that in Galway the results were almost equally absurd as a pretence of relief. There was even a suspicion, to which the BISHOP OF KILLALA did not hesitate to give voice, that influential persons, interested in keeping down county-cess, were upon one pretext or another keeping the works postponed until the harvest should come in, when they would be allowed to collapse as unnecessary. The loans to landowners had proved in the same way to be fitful and insignificant as measures of relief. In the poorest districts the landowners had borrowed nothing; and most of those who did borrow, were good resident landlords who would have given pretty nearly the same amount of employment in any case to those around them. The remarkable energy developed in official quarters was beginning to induce Boards of Guardians, here and there, to make considerable additions to their outdoor relief lists; but this was the only respect in which the pressure upon the charitable funds was sensibly lessened.

<small>But the Government Relief Machinery could not be got to work</small>

* These were prepared by Mr. DILLON, whose subsequent Report was ordered by the Committee to be submitted to the attention of the Government.

Upon the other hand the evidence of undiminished want and suffering was never more overwhelming. If those who contributed nothing to the distress had not so persistently attempted to shelter their own meanness, or prejudice, by discouraging the charity of others, it would be absurd to quote testimony to a fact which every official from the LORD LIEUTENANT down, and every person of credit acquainted with the relief operations throughout the country, confessed. The Catholic clergy of the Diaconate of Castlebar, published in the latter end of May, " a solemn declaration that a terrible crisis presses most heavily upon our people, and that unless the Government comes to their assistance, no efforts of the charitable Committees can save the people from death by hunger." From another province, the clergy of the Deanery of Caherciveen, speaking for the whole barony of Iveragh, solemnly declared that the LORD MAYOR'S representation of the state of the country, was, " unhappily but too true, and that the instant and thorough action of the Government is absolutely necessary to save the people's lives." They acknowledged with gratitude that these districts had shared liberally of the charitable funds: "but with troubled and anxious hearts, we, who behold the people's saddening condition, declare before Heaven, that the cries of our people are fiercer, and their efforts greater now than ever to get food." " During spring operations," wrote the BISHOP OF CLONFERT, on the 17th May, " we forbore to importune you, as the poor struggled on to subsist; but now the present and coming months are the truly crucial ones." " Limited as the supplies of the Central Committees have been of late," said the BISHOP OF KILLALA, "if stopped before harvest will come to the relief of the people, famine and starvation will be the result." And the BISHOP OF RAPHOE, as the mouthpiece of the Donegal County Committee, declared, on the 18th of May, that at no previous period of the distress were they in such danger of a sudden collapse, as when the last generous grant from the Mansion House reached them. Indeed the Mansion House Committee had ample material from the personal investigations of its own members in the distressed districts to estimate the pressure of distress. The LORD MAYOR had been in the South. Mr. LANE JOYNT had made various visits ranging over Kerry, Limerick, Clare, Galway, Antrim, and Donegal. Lord FRANCIS OSBORNE had been nearly over every inch of the distressed seaboard. Rev. Canon BAGOT had been through West Cork and Kerry, towards the end of May, and through the inland regions of Mayo early in June. The conclusion at which they all arrived, and which the reports of Mr. Fox, and of the Medical Commissioners, Dr. SIGERSON and Dr. KENNY, in the succeeding month, effectually established, was that the people had been preserved from starvation mainly by the instrumentality of the Mansion House grants; that the great majority of them were still depending on charity for their daily food; and that the result of curtailing the charitable supplies had been in many instances to throw the Local Committees into debt, to submit the people to incredible hardships, and to a large extent to sow the seeds of the fever epidemics which shortly began to appear.

Critical position of this Committee

A grievous anxiety then began to weigh heavily upon the Mansion House Committee, their balance having by the 17th June shrunk to £11,000, and their appeal for fresh funds having fallen perfectly unheeded in England, whether they should any longer attempt to cope with this tremendous mass of misery; whether, in fact, their continued existence might not, in the words of the Catholic ARCHBISHOP OF DUBLIN, "be quoted as a justification for the non-intervention of Government." So strongly did these apprehensions take possession of the Committee that, at one period, some of the most thoughtful and influential of its members had all but resolved on suspending the labours of the Committee altogether, should their appeals remain unanswered, and, having divided the balance among the most necessitous of the Local Committees, to leave the rest to the Government. The Examination Committee actually reported in favour of this course, as in their opinion "the only one open to your Committee to save the people in the distressed part of Ireland from actual starvation, during the time that would necessarily elapse between any sudden stoppage of relief, without notice, on the part of your Committee, and the taking up of the position by those upon whom, but for your intervention, the duty of providing for the lives of our suffering and destitute poor would have devolved." They were dissuaded, however, by the strong and earnest advice of the LORD MAYOR, and others; that to dissolve this Committee, would be to embark the unhappy people upon an unknown sea; that there was still a balance of £60,000 in the hands of the different charitable Committees; that their own last appeal for funds had not had time to fructify; that the summer was advancing rapidly and brightly; that the new potatoes promised to be fit for eating in the South early in July; and, that a full third of their burden being thus removed, one more vigorous effort of charity would possibly land the people safely in the midst of a bountiful harvest. They struggled on. Their perseverance was rewarded with

They struggled on

a fairly steady reflux of subscriptions; although in England the spirit of suspiciousness destroyed all chance of any general impulse of charity. No device for husbanding the funds or calling forth new ones was neglected. The Boards of Guardians were, at Mr. DILLON'S suggestion, appealed to earnestly to make a generous use of their powers, recalling how largely the operations of this Committee had hitherto lessened the incidence of the poor rate upon the owners and occupiers of property. The possibility even of an amalgamation or of concerted action between the various charitable Committees was frequently and cordially examined. One of the first acts of the Mansion House Committee on coming into existence, had been to appoint a deputation to proffer co-operation, and to devise if possible some working arrangement with the DUCHESS OF MARLBOROUGH'S Committee; as, unhappily, one of the first letters upon their minutes was one which repulsed these overtures. Throughout their career the Mansion House Committee constantly held out a friendly hand to every sister organisation; most cheerfully shared in the Marlborough Committee's operations upon the Western coasts; proffered their aid to the Philadelphia Fund Committee; threw open their whole sources of information to the Committee of the *New York Herald* Fund, and placed their entire machinery of Local Committees, organised with so much labour and cost, at their service. The Lord Mayor himself, whom political circumstances had brought into collision with distinguished personages identified with the Marlborough Fund, offered upon several occasions to withdraw from all part in the operations of this Committee, if his withdrawal could tend, in the slightest degree, to a complete and cordial understanding between all the charitable organisations. It would serve no useful pupose to rake up the circumstances under which these overtures were frustrated; it is enough to say that any common administration of the different funds was found to be less desirable, and still more impracticable at the eleventh hour, than it had proved to be at the beginning. At the same time this did not prevent the interchange of information between the several organisations, and the allocation of grants, as far as possible, by the light of each other's returns.

Towards the beginning of July the demands upon this fund began to abate in the extreme South. The unprecedented warmth of the summer had hastened the harvest by several weeks; and, as the ripening crept further northwards, Local Committee after Committee closed its books and bade farewell to the Mansion House Commitee with warm-hearted words of gratitude. But a long and horrible ordeal had still to be passed through before the peasantry of the West and North had anything to hope for from their later harvest—an ordeal which was, in many respects, the most disastrous to human life that they had as yet endured. Disease was now fastening in a terrific way upon the West. The effects of a uniform Indian-meal diet, often unmoistened by milk, and often only parboiled for want of fuel, had been heightened in many cases during the last month, owing to the straitened charitable funds and the consequent diminution of rations; and had produced the inevitable crop of famine-sickness, springing up at a dozen scattered places simultaneously, and making an easy prey of its attenuated victims. Already, in May there had been sixty homesteads on the Island of Garumna affected by fever, and a hundred and five in the district of Kilmaine. It was now made known for the first time to the public (and there is reason to fear to the Government also), through the medium of correspondence addressed to the Mansion House Committee,* that a disease which, whatever its technical description, was in every substantial respect famine-fever, had arisen simultaneously in various distressed districts of Mayo and Galway. Mr. J. A. Fox had at this time undertaken, at the request of the Mansion House Committee, a personal investigation into the present stage of distress in Mayo, and the prospects of its continuance. We will have occasion presently to notice the flood of light which Mr. Fox's carefully-drawn reports threw upon the effect and administration of the Mansion House relief in the West; but the very first of them made it sufficiently

---

* A Special Correspondent of the *Freeman's Journal* at the same time exposed the extent of the epidemic and the inefficiency of the measures for its treatment.

manifest, not merely that many thousands in North Mayo had been for months, and were still, indebted to charity alone for their existence, but that to the rest of their privations were now added fever epidemics of alarming extent and intensity. The fact that most of the cases reported bore the character of malignant typhus was immediately seized upon to show, that the epidemics were not traceable to destitution, since (it was asserted) typhus fever was "quite a distinct disease" from famine-fever.* This allegation appeared to the Mansion House Committee to involve so important a question, touching the present health and future sustenance of the distressed populations, that upon the 28th of June they requested Dr. SIGERSON to form a Medical Commission to investigate upon the spot the character and origin of the prevalent form of disease.

<small>Medical Commission as to the Character of the epidemics</small>

That task was performed by Dr. SIGERSON (who associated with himself Dr. JOSEPH E. KENNY, a physician of extensive experience in Dublin), in a manner which gained the applause of high medical authorities, and which to a great extent, shaped the course of the Government into a resolute subjugation of the epidemics, and in every respect confirmed the Committee's estimate of Dr. SIGERSON's high scientific and professional reputation. Dr. SIGERSON set out by showing that typhus fever, instead of being the somewhat benign and commonplace disease that the minimists would seem to hint, was in reality the deadliest of those which followed in the train of the great Famine, and was quite as closely identified with periods of destitution and distress, and as distinctly traceable to deficient alimentation, as the comparatively mild relapsing (or so-called "famine") fever. The specific form of fever, prevailing in the West, was therefore of secondary importance, compared with the consideration of the conditions in which the disease had arisen. These conditions the Medical Commission examined for themselves in different foci of disease, in Mayo and Galway; and the evidence was found to be everywhere overwhelming that the different forms of disease, existing in different districts, or side by side—maculated typhus, typhoid, and relapsing fever—were all the direct offspring of frightful destitution. It was found that all the families, in which the disease had first shown itself, had been compelled to subsist on the relief meal allocated by the Local Committees, and that, as a rule, none others had been attacked. The only exceptions to this rule were the cases of certain Medical Officers, and a very few others, to whom the fever had extended by contagion, from the distressed. The attempt to account for the epidemics upon the ground of the unsanitary condition of the peoples' dwellings, was disposed of by showing among other proofs that one of the most miserable villages in the Charlestown district, where every principle of sanitary science was set at defiance, had been remarkably free from fever for a number of years, until the present frightful period of destitution enfeebled the bodies of the villagers, and opened the door to maculated typhus; while on the other hand, habitations in the neighbouring town of Swinford, whose

<small>Found to be directly traceable to Destitution</small>

---

* Dr. GRIMSHAW, Registrar-General, one of the Hon. Secs. of the MARLBOROUGH Committee, went to much pains to elaborate this untenable distinction.

unsanitary conditions rivalled, if they did not exceed, those of the rural village, were perfectly free from the inroads of typhus, because the poor of the town were safe from at least the extreme privations of their country brethren. The Commissioners' own recorded experiences among the sufferers established in fact beyond all controversy, that deficient nutrition was invariably the principal, and in many cases unquestionably the only cause in the production of the prevalent disease. A few of the scenes which came under their notice are conclusive upon this point, as well as pitiful beyond the power of words to express :—

"Entering one house, fairly circumstanced, we were received by the mother, pale, worn, feeble, scarcely able to move about, after a severe attack of fever. Two or three children, convalescents, were sitting in the kitchen, and in an inner room lay, far advanced in maculated typhus, her father-in-law, husband, and two grown-up daughters. Until a few days ago she had to attend to all. Even now, though an old woman had been got as nurse, the sick son had been obliged to take the sicker father into his bed, in order to restrain him whilst delirious. This house is worse than a fever-ward—it is a fever-furnace. The family, throughout this terrible time of illness, have been dependent for very life upon the support of the Local Relief Committee. Other cases have their own peculiarly painful features. In one, at Carne, the young husband is a victim; in another the wife lies sick, with scarce a rag of bed-clothes. At Ballintadder, in a musty dark room, two children were tossing in fever upon some straw on the floor, and another ailing upon the poor bed. In an adjoining cabin, five children had been ailing together; two were up when we entered, and three lying in fever, 'heads and points' on an old bedstead, covered with a couple of potato sacks. In the midst of their affliction the father gives a refuge to an infirm and aged sister. It may be mentioned, as adding to the sombre character of the scene, that these people are under notice of ejectment. . . . . At Upper Lurga, we came within sight of a lonely cabin on a bleak moor, of which a few acres had been reclaimed. All was darkness within the house, whence came moans of pain and invocations. Hearing the voice of the owner saluting us, we requested the window to be opened. There was no window—nothing but a shutter. When this was thrown back, we found the earthen floor covered with victims of the destitution fever. At the entrance, their feet near the door-way, lay side by side two grown young women, aged respectively 21 and 19; beyond, with her head almost touching theirs, was a younger girl, aged 14, recovering, but unable to move. On the left side, on the floor, lay the mother of the family in her day clothes. There was scarcely straw enough to keep them off the ground, not enough to hide its hardness, doubly hard to the aching backs of fever patients. What scanty covering they had could not be called bed-clothes. The only person to nurse or attend on all, was the worn and wretched parent, aged 50, trembling with weakness from want and watching as he stood, and expecting every hour to be stricken down, when all would be left to die 'within the walls.' It was impossible to find that they had been exposed to any source of infection. There was no one ill of all they knew; 'and why the strange disease should have come to us, on this wild moor,' exclaimed the mother, 'we cannot know—God alone knows.' They had been passed over in the first six or seven distributions, and had to sell a little calf to buy Indian meal; their cow had run dry, but they had got, for a little time, some quantity of milk from one lent by a brother. For months they had had nothing but Indian meal to eat, and brownish bog-water to drink. These are cases of famine-typhus if ever famine-fever existed."*

The reports of the Medical Commission not merely established the connection between the distress and the fevers. That was afterwards amply acknowledged by the Medical Commissioners sent down by the Local Government Board. But these reports furthermore bristled with suggestions towards grappling with the epidemic and remedying the barbarous inefficiency of the Poor-law system of relief—suggestions to which the Chief Secretary for Ireland acknowledged himself in Parliament to be in a large degree indebted for the vigorous measures by which the epidemic was ultimately got under. They even formulated some remedial measures, beyond the immediate purview of the hour—for example, the provision of cottage-hospitals in remote districts; light spring conveyances to replace the present lumbering and jolting vans, which answer as ambulances for the conveyance of the sick to hospital; an improved medical service; the admission of clergymen to the Boards of Guardians, and, above all, some such legislation as would raise the social condition of the peasantry, and liberate them from the inroads of destitution-diseases for the future. The strength of public opinion thus evoked, and, there is reason to believe, the example of anxious and unstinted activity shown by Mr. FORSTER to the subordinate authorities, produced perhaps as great an effort as the Irish Poor law system was capable of, towards the eradication of the fever-epidemic. The Board of Guardians in the worst of the fever-centres had been already dissolved, and the Vice-Guardians appointed in their stead had orders now to spare no expense in preserving human life. The anxieties of the Charitable Relief Committees, however, continued to be very grave. Mr. Fox's reports disclosed the continuance of distress in its most dreadful forms. He found whole masses of the population depending for life upon the scanty doles of Indian meal served out by the Local Committees, living in miserable hovels, "which are a shocking reproach to the civilization of the nineteenth century;" the children often nearly naked; the bedding long since pawned; the sick and the healthy flung together upon truckles of old straw, covered by the dirty sacks which conveyed the seed potatoes in the spring; men, women, and children often lying upon earthen floors saturated with damp; some families dragging on existence upon half rations of Indian meal moistened with milk given for charity, others without a morsel of food except cooked cabbage, "in numerous cases, neither milk, meal, nor cabbage about the premises." Except that some of the Boards of Guardians had been driven to increase their out-door relief lists, he found at the same time that no amount of energy or good-will could redeem the original feebleness of the

The activity of the Poor-Law Officials stimulated

Continuance of shocking destitution in the West

---

* The Commissioners subsequently add the sad note, that this poor mother and her two elder daughters died, but at least not without the comforts that prompt generosity could procure for them.

Government measures of relief, or construct, out of the disjointed machinery of scattered baronial and private employment and workhouse relief, any adequate substitute for the swift and all-embracing system of the charitable organizations. The people were, to use a phrase that was not exaggerated, "wild for work;" in many of the less stricken districts work was beginning to be obtainable; but in the poorest neighbourhoods, either the landowners were spending nothing, or were, in some instances, deducting their rents out of the men's wages, and either there were no baronial works at all on foot, or the contractors were obliged to defer the payment of wages until the works were "certified." The LORD MAYOR first mooted a suggestion which was at that time working in many minds, that a Government which could break through the trammels of red tape might have effectually and at one-fifth the cost quelled the distress, by dividing among the Charitable Committees a grant sufficient to enable them to furnish adequate relief supplies until the gathering of the harvest; and Mr. PARNELL, M.P. actually proposed in Parliament the allocation of £200,000 out of the Church Surplus Fund for that purpose. The proposal was parried on the plea of the nearness of the harvest and of the easy terms upon which Boards of Guardians were under the new Relief Act proffered money for outdoor relief.* The Mansion House Committee had only to concentrate their strength more and more upon the strongholds of distress; to enlarge their grants in these places, as the demands in other directions began to slacken; and, by every method that suggested itself to recruit their funds for the final period of distress. Mr. HENGLER kindly offered the proceeds of an equestrian entertainment amounting to £100. The most notable of the methods adopted was a diocesan collection suggested by Mr. DRIMMIE. It is worthy of record that, with the exception of the noble contribution of £780 remitted from the Diocese of Waterford, by the Most Rev. Dr. POWER, and of £89 from five parishes of the Diocese of Kildare and Leighlin, the readiest response to the appeal of the Mansion House Committee came from the most sorely-tried western and northern dioceses. The collections remitted by the BISHOPS OF KILLALA and RAPHOE, while the smallness of the amount was a painful proof of the intensity of the calamity which had swept these dioceses bare, were a most touching assurance of the generosity, already so often and so sorely taxed, of the few in the community who had anything left to give. "I am sorry," said the BISHOP OF RAPHOE, "that the amount is so small, but knowing, as I do, the condition of the people, I am surprised that it is even so much. Such as it is, they have given it with all their hearts. I have been delighted to learn that even those who have suffered severely have endeavoured to give some little token of their gratitude for the munificent aid which has come to them

New Outdoor Relief Act

The final period of Distress

---

* The new Relief Bill, introduced by Mr. FORSTER, enacted by its second clause, that the Local Government Board might grant to the Boards of Guardians in any scheduled Union "such moneys as they may find necessary, having regard to the financial condition of such Union, and the presence of distress within its limits, to aid in giving outdoor relief, provided that the entire sum so granted shall not exceed £200,000." But this liberal provision only became law at the commencement of August—when the need for it was practically over.

F

from the Mansion House. In some instances, even the Protestant poor, not awaiting the collections in their own churches, have sent their little offerings to the parish priests." The venerable ARCHBISHOP OF TUAM, finding that any fresh burden on his afflicted people would be a cruelty, remitted instead the magnificent sum of £3,000 to the Mansion House Committee, out of the large American and Australian funds entrusted to His Grace for distribution, expressly describing the gift as "additional evidence of my warm appreciation of the successful labours of that Committee."

<small>The harvest</small>

Aids like these bridged over the dangerous month of July—"pre-eminently the hardest period of the distress," reported the Moygowna Committee, on July 12th; a time when "never was relief more needed" in Enniscrone; when, in another part of Mayo, the hungry people had almost torn the unripe potatoes out of the ground. At length the sunny summer bore its fruit. Over the greater part of the country, in the beginning of August, the people, with thankful hearts, were tasting the firstlings of a fairly abundant harvest. In the unhappy West, partly owing to the unkindly nature of the soil, partly to the inferior seeds in some instances foisted upon the people under workhouse contracts, the evil-omened blight once more wrought havoc in the potato fields, and, it is to be feared, in some districts, prepared the way for another grievous winter. But for the present the people were surrounded with humble abundance, the spectre of hunger was gone; and, with thanksgivings to Divine Providence—with a thrill of gratitude to those far away brothers and benefactors, who, under that Providence, had been their deliverers from the Shadow of Death—the people rose up with renewed courage to face the menaces of the future. The closing meetings of the Mansion House Committee were brightened with the news of Relief Committees dissolving on all sides, and making their last act an act of fervent gratitude to the Central Committee, and to those who filled its hands. The last General Meeting of this Committee for the Distribution of Relief, was held on the 14th of August, 1880. Mr. DRIMMIE brought up the balance sheet struck by the Finance Committee, and accompanied it with a clear and terse analysis of the expenditure. The rest of the proceedings were words of mutual congratulation, such as, if they are ever pardonable, were pardonable among colleagues, whom seven months of voluntary labours had bound together in a memorable and successful struggle to preserve the lives of many thousands of their countrymen. In reply to votes of thanks passed to himself as Chairman, and to the LADY MAYORESS for giving the use of the Mansion House to the Committee, the LORD MAYOR expressed in warm terms his obligations to his colleagues, upon whom, he said, more than upon himself the burden of the work had fallen.

<small>Dissolution of the Local Committees</small>

"We have outlived attack," said the LORD MAYOR, "and I think our work will prove that Irishmen of all creeds, when a great crisis comes, can combine for a great national object, and accomplish it successfully. It is the pride of this Committee, representing all parties and all creeds, that, during our many meetings, we never had one single division. I believe that this Committee, and other charitable organisations have saved the country from a terrible calamity. Only the other day I was looking at the returns of what the Government had done, and I can say with confidence that if we had to depend upon the Government—and I do not use the word in a party sense, but I mean the executive Government—the people would have starved. It is now they are beginning to distribute money—now when the harvest is coming in. The Government were warned twelve months ago, that nothing could avert this calamity. But from some cause or another—I will not say whose fault it was—their action was not sufficiently prompt to avert or assist in grappling with the famine. The Relief Committees—the DUCHESS OF MARLBOROUGH's Committee, this Committee, the Land League Committee, and the *New York Herald* Committee—stepped into the breach, and did the work; and I have not the slightest false shame in saying, that this Committee has deserved well of the country, and has done a national work, of which every member should feel proud. When the report of our proceedings reaches the public, I do feel that it will be admitted on all hands that we did our best to deserve success, and that not one of us spared any exertion or effort to secure the proper distribution of the large sums entrusted to our care."

Where every member of the Committee co-operated so loyally to secure the great object for which it was formed, it is hard to select names for special mention. We are restrained by this difficulty, and by the delicacy attending any reference by a Committee to its own members, from saying here much that anybody acquainted with the working of the Committee must deeply feel. But we cannot in common justice conclude this report without expressing the special obligations of the Committee to Alderman TARPEY, for his assiduous labour on the Examination Sub-Committee; to Mr. V. B. DILLON, Jun., who planned the ground-work of the relief system, and carried it to a successful end; to Mr. JOHN ADYE CURRAN, who conducted the correspondence with the Local Committees; to Mr. CHARLES KENNEDY, for his constant attendance to and supervision of the working of the organisation; to Mr. W. LANE JOYNT, for his labours in connection with the supply of food and clothing to the Western Islands; to LORD F. G. OSBORNE, who superintended the distribution of supplies to the Islands; to Mr. DAVID DRIMMIE, who transacted the principal part of the financial business of the Committee; to Professor SIGERSON, M.D., for his services on the Publication Sub-Committee, and on the Medical Commission in conjunction with Dr. J. E. KENNY; to the Rev. Canon BAGOT, the founder of the Seeds Fund; to Mr. J. A. FOX, for his reports concerning the condition of Mayo; to Mr. DAVID DRUMMOND, Rev. J. DANIEL, P.P., Mr. T. MAXWELL HUTTON, and Colonel DAVOREN, for their close attention to the work of the different Sub-Committees; and especially to the Most Rev. Dr. TRENCH, for his assistance in every vicissitude of a trying time. None but their colleagues can know the labour, often extending into the night and early morning, which these and other gentlemen devoted to a work which at one time threatened to overwhelm them, and any words of thanks from their colleagues would be a trifling recompense compared with the satisfaction of knowing that their sacrifices for the alleviation of the sufferings of their fellow-countrymen have not been made in vain.

CONCLUSION.

Little remains to be written, the Committee would fain believe, to satisfy the subscribers to the Mansion House Fund, that their money has been administered, under an anxious sense of responsibility, with as much economy and as little abuse, as the best labour and skill of the Members of this Committee could ensure, and in the result effectually to the saving of human life. The total expenses incurred in receiving and dispensing the Fund—including cost of telegrams, postage, stationery, printing, salaries, advertising, travelling expenses, inspection of Local Committees, and incidentals—amount (as appears from the Report of the Finance Sub-Committee) to £3,425 17s. 3d. The principal item therein is that of £1,084 9s. for the salaries of Assistant Secretary, Clerks, and Accountants. It will be remembered that to the minutest local detail the relief system was organized and directed from Dublin, and that the expenses which would have otherwise been distributed over a number of local centres were concentrated entirely upon the Dublin Executive. Whoever calls to mind the prodigious labour of setting 840 Local Committees in motion, maintaining a constant and minute correspondence with the bulk of them for eight months, sifting complaints, checking returns, and, at the same time, keeping up a voluminous postal and telegraphic correspondence of appeals and acknowledgments with Committees in all parts of the globe, will appreciate the meaning of these figures, and will understand that it was only by the physical, as well as mental labour, extending frequently far into the nights, undergone by Members of the Committee; and only by the circumstance that the free use of the Mansion House swept the item of rents off the balance-sheet, that the Dublin newspapers inserted advertisements at largely reduced rates, and the American and Eastern Telegraph Companies transmitted thousands of pounds' worth of telegrams, free of cost—it was only in consequence of many happy contingencies of this sort, that so vast a task was compassed at so moderate an expense. The £1,527 spent in circulating 27,000 copies of the Committee's appeal throughout the world, and Final Report, was the only other sum out of £180,000 that did not go directly to feed or clothe the objects of the subscribers' bounty. There being no lack of local food-dealers, too, and the money being spent upon the spot, the cost of transit of food, and of local storehouses and clerks, which formed so great a portion of charitable expenditure in the times of the Great Famine, was altogether obliterated. Save in one or two exceptional instances, the Local

Committees employed no paid assistance of any kind, but simply issued tickets which were honoured in the contractors' shops.

So much for expenses of administration; the efficiency of the system of Local Committees—both as to the grants made to them, and as to the grants made by them—is a question to be approached with more diffidence. No charitable organisation ever invented probably could, at a few weeks' notice, have assumed the charge of half a million destitute persons, and more or less supported them for months, without making mistakes. The Mansion House Committee are sensible that, in dividing so considerable a sum, among so vast a population, and under so many varying circumstances, they cannot claim freedom from those irregularities in grants to which errors of judgment, or defective information, must occasionally give rise. Many things, no doubt, were done, and many things left undone, which an absolutely perfect system would have corrected. They are content to accept the fact, that there has not been a single jarring note in the too generous public praises which their efforts have met with among persons of all degrees in Ireland, as a recognition that they have at least done their best, and that their errors produced no serious harm. If the same test can be taken as a criterion of the action of the Local Committees, it may be anticipated that these bodies will be found to have been still more worthy of the confidence of the subscribers to this Fund, and of the gratitude of the unhappy people to whom they were the immediate ministers. The rivalries of local traders, or the querulousness of unsatisfied applicants for relief, now and again gave rise to complaints; which invariably, however, were either too transparent to call for investigation at all, or, when investigated, turned out to be wholly groundless. Persons, too, who were not subscribers to the Fund, and who systematically discouraged others from subscribing, were occasionally found whispering vague insinuations of imposition, either by or upon the Local Committees; but all efforts to fasten them to facts or particulars were fruitless. One tangible charge— and one alone—was levelled against a Local Committee. It was made by the land agent and the Protestant Rector of the Aran Islands against the Aran Sub-Committee. The complaint was no sooner formulated than the Mansion House Committee deemed it sufficiently important to be at once and searchingly investigated. Mr. JOHN ADYE CURRAN, B.L., was selected by the Mansion House Committee to proceed to the Aran Islands, and bring the persons interested on both sides face to face, at a formal investigation on the spot.

Mr. CURRAN's cool and well-reasoned judgment, which will be found in a Special Report, exhibits the result. It was charged that the Protestant Rector had been excluded from the Sub-Committee, and the explanation was found to be that this was one of these exceptional cases in which, at the suggestion of the Protestant ARCHBISHOP OF DUBLIN, the Mansion House Committee had agreed to make grants to two separate Committees, if necessary, in the same district. The Rector had not formed a separate Committee, because the only

Protestant on the islands requiring relief had received it plentifully. It was charged that the agent had been studiously kept off the Committee; and there was written proof that he had been requested, and given several opportunities to join. Finally it was alleged that relief was refused to persons who worked for the Rector, or frequented a Protestant shopkeeper's shop; and, upon the evidence he has so lucidly set forth, Mr. CURRAN reported that not only was there no evidence given that destitute people had been refused relief by the Committee for either of these reasons, but that he was affirmatively satisfied to the contrary, by the proofs put before him. The matters thus satisfactorily cleared up formed the only tangible charge of partiality or mismanagement against a Sub-Committee which came to the ears of the Mansion House Committee. That persons sometimes received small quantities of Indian meal, who were not wholly destitute, is very likely true. That here and there the judgment of the Local Committees may have been imposed upon by even grosser abuses is, according to all human experience, probable, though it has never appeared in evidence. The only certain circumstance which gave a colour to the inuendos sometimes put forth in idleness, and sometimes in malice, but always without name, or date, or detail, was, that in cases where small farmers were stripped of everything else beside, the possession of one cow (or in some cases even more), was not held to be a bar against their receiving relief. These half-starved animals (which the poor people often pinched themselves to a meal a day to keep alive), were at the time perfectly unsaleable; they afforded the only chance of moistening the unvarying mess of Indian meal stirabout with milk for children and sick persons; a single cow was sometimes, as in Achill, owned "in shares" by three or four families; and the policy, as well as the humanity, of not driving the people to part with their last hope of ever again stocking their little farms, is so obvious, that it is unnecessary to defend a discretion which was, according to all the evidence, wisely and sparingly used. The members of this Committee who at various times, and in different parts of the country had opportunities of observing the working of the local bodies—The LORD MAYOR, Mr. LANE JOYNT, Mr. J. A. FOX, Rev. Canon BAGOT, Lord FRANCIS OSBORNE, Dr. SIGERSON, and others—returned but the one report of their experiences: that the Local Committees were discharging their painful and thankless task upon the whole with complete efficiency, and with wonderful devotion; that the Protestant and Catholic clergy had no rivalry but in sympathy and self-sacrifice for the sake of the suffering people; that the accounts were scrupulously kept, and the work of relief performed, upon the whole, swiftly, thoroughly, and judiciously. In 1846-47, the want of Local Committees, such as these, was one of the most effectual allies of the Famine. "At any time," it has been well written, "the want of an educated, intelligent body of men to carry out the various local measures must be severely felt; but its pressure was almost overwhelming, when the whole population of many districts were fed by the hands of strangers."* When we read upon the same excellent authority that "this want of the necessary machinery for administering relief in the districts which most required it, had more effect than any other circumstance in impeding the exertions requisite to relieve the sufferings of the destitute in that time of calamity"—we cannot dwell with too much gratitude upon the good fortune which, in this latest ordeal, raised up even in the most desolate regions of the country, bodies of men who, surrounded daily by the most repulsive forms of misery, never shrank from their posts, until, by their patience, wisdom, courage, and labour, the time of trial passed into the time of returning plenty. Nor should it go unrecorded of the people who were fed by the world's charity, that they concealed their sufferings until starvation was entering their doors; that their self-respect rebelled to the last against the beggar's trade; that "work, not alms," was the cry of their hearts, until it was stifled by the pangs of hunger; that throughout the uncertainties and privations of seven months' dependence upon public charity, their endurance, peacefulness, and thankfulness to all who had a kindly word, or did a kindly deed for them, gave a certain dignity to their honest poverty; and that no sooner did the harvest offer them its first promises of subsistence than they quitted the life of mendicants as eagerly as they had embraced it reluctantly. Upon the whole, perhaps, no other people could have passed through a prolonged period of enforced mendicancy with less taint of demoralisation; and no people ought, perhaps, to have been exposed to the test.

In the result, a Famine which must have swept away many thousands of the population was stayed by the hand of private charity—and of private charity almost alone—until the bounty of the Almighty came in to banish it altogether. That we do not over-rate the saving of human life is now confessed by everybody possessed of official or local knowledge of the facts. Mr. Fox's reports teem with the evidence of Catholic Bishops, Landowners, Chairmen of Boards of Guardians, Doctors, and Clergymen of all persuasions, that charity alone stood between vast masses of the population and a terrible death. Within the last six weeks of the distress, beyond doubt, the vigorous co-operation of the Government relieved private charity of a considerable portion of its care. 92,619 persons were on the 24th July, receiving more or less substantial doles of outdoor relief; 22,680 men were at the same time employed upon baronial works;† and it may, perhaps, be assumed that as many more found employment under the loans to the landowners. But, roundly speaking, during the entire perilous interval between January and July, the money of Australia and America and their generous sister nations

---

* Transactions of the Central Relief Committee of the Society of Friends, during the Famine in Ireland, in 1846 and 1847, Chap. I., p. 13.

† Official return of the Board of Works, 30th June. Many of the men here taken credit for, however, were only employed for short intervals of a week or two.

was the sheet-anchor of the Irish peasantry; it provided their daily food for many thousands who, without it, must have lain down to die, or gone to choke the distant workhouses of bankrupt unions, never to raise their heads again among men. Whether this was not too great a tax to lay upon private charity, and too great a risk to run upon the chance of private charity proving equal to it, are questions which unhappily may not impossibly be again matter of grave concern in the government of Ireland. We deem it a duty to record it as our opinion that the tax upon the humanity of distant communities, the uncertainty of the results, the shame of craving alms throughout the world, and the danger of demoralisation in distributing them, were all too great to have been left for so long a time to be the only resource of an immense area of a country, possessed of unappropriated national funds of its own, and bound closely to the richest nation in the world.

The tax upon Private Charity and the risk too great.

Nor should it be forgotten, in felicitations upon the happy issue of the crisis, that it was only by an extraordinary chain of providential coincidences that the distress was prevented from receiving developments which would have broken all bounds of private effort. We have seen that, up to the beginning of October, Her Majesty's Ministers considered the danger of a fuel famine the worst omen of the time. The peat which, as fuel, was even more to the Western peasants than the potato, as food, was, up to that period, lying on the bogs dripping with moisture; a few more rainy weeks, and a winter as inclement as the preceding one might have fastened down upon the unhappy people and killed them off like flies in their fireless cabins; for even if coal could have been distributed in sufficient quantity through the almost inaccessible mountain villages of the West, the peasantry had no grates to burn it in. This fearful danger was averted by an autumn and a winter of exceptional mildness; which both saved the fuel generally,* and protected the half-clad and half-fed people from the ravages of cold and wet. Again, there was the contingency of the landlords and creditors swooping upon the remnants of the harvest for their rents and debts, and leaving the small farmers naked on the brink of winter; it had occurred before in 1845, and to a large extent even in 1846, and might occur again. The unheard of forbearance of both classes of creditors, and in some degree the desperation of the peasantry, left the harvest, such as it was, almost in its integrity for food, and thereby cut off four months' dependence upon charity. The State may justly claim the credit of having, by its adoption of the principle of Major Nolan's Seeds Bill, removed still another danger, which was, perhaps, the most imminent of all—the danger of one-third of the cultivated land of the country lying waste for want of seeds. This Committee can perhaps claim the credit of having first brought the danger and the remedy to the notice of the Government. Whoever reflects how great a sum of money it required to keep the people

The chain of coincidences that mitigated the crisis

The Fuel-Famine averted

Landlords' and creditors' forbearance cut off four months' dependence on charity

The advances of seeds

---

* There were exceptions to this rule, many localities (as will be seen from the Medical Reports) suffered considerably from insufficiency of fuel.

supplied with the bare necessaries of life—even after they had been providentially saved from a fuel famine—after they had been remitted millions of debt—after their land had been seeded for them—while many of them were paying no rents—while the weather, whose mildness which had sheltered them from disease, through the winter and spring, was brightening their harvest-fields with early promise—cannot think without a shudder to how large an extent we owe it to the accidents of seasons and other coincidences that the calamities of 1879-80 did not end in a catastrophe. For it must be recollected that the Mansion House Fund was only one of many agencies employed to mitigate the crisis. Beside the £180,000 subscribed to this Fund, sums amounting to about £300,000 more were distributed between the DUCHESS OF MARLBOROUGH'S Committee, the *New York Herald* Fund Committee, the National Land League, the Canadian Fund Committee, and the Philadelphia Fund Committee.

The earliness of the harvest

The largest share of the American subscriptions—according to one calculation, £200,000—was forwarded to the Irish Bishops for separate distribution; £26,530 was thus remitted to the ARCHBISHOP OF TUAM alone. The individual remittances from America and Australia to friends in Ireland, will be, perhaps, moderately estimated at £150,000 more. If to this magnificent tribute of £830,000 of private charity, we add the £189,720 claimed to have been issued to landowners for relief employment, the £55,987 returned as the expenditure upon baronial relief works, and the extra charges for outdoor relief, which are probably underestimated at £200,000, we shall have, in round numbers, £1,270,000 applied to the alleviation of seven months' distress without being able to do much more than satisfy the immediate cravings of want; and this, without taking into account that some £4,000,000 of rents and debts were, if not wiped out, at least suspended during that time, that £500,000 more were loaned for seeds, that therefore, four months' food was available at the beginning of the crisis, and that an unusually early harvest shortened its continuance for fully three weeks longer, at a juncture when every form of charity was exhausted. Nor can we truly say that, with all that timely warnings, glorious generosity, zeal, organisation, and immense expenditures like those we have enumerated could do, there has not remained much suffering, and, it is to be feared, some contributory elements of the increased mortality of the year. Dr. SIGERSON, while he shows that in the quarter in which the charitable relief organisations started, the death-rate fell from 1·6 per 1,000 in excess, to 1 per 1,000 in excess of the rate for the corresponding quarters of the past five years, notes, that the death-rate nevertheless remained exceptionally high; and is driven to the conclusion that many must have quietly succumbed to their sufferings, and silently died out. There is, unfortunately, too much reason to suppose that, before the Relief organisations were in existence, and afterwards, when the funds were running low, a long course of privations, or of uniform and meagre diet, predisposed the enfeebled bodies of many of the sufferers to disease. But the more we dwell upon the dimensions, the perils, and difficulties of the

With these advantages it took £1,270,000 to keep the people alive

Irish Crisis of 1879-80, the more humbly should we bow in thankfulness to the Almighty for the issue.

Advantages over the time of the Great Famine

To compare the circumstances of the Great Famine with those of that through which we have just passed, the premonitory omens in each case being almost equally dark—the scarcity and dearness of food, the immense freights, the difficulties of transporting provisions, the absence of local organisation or of local traders, the confusion, the blundering, the waste of millions of money and hundreds of thousands of lives, *then ;* and the plentifulness of cheap food in the markets, on the very spot, in the remotest places, *now*—the vigorous local organisations, the ease with which our appeals were in a moment made to travel round the world and bring back noble help almost as quickly;—to think of how blight and inclemency and sickening disappointment dogged the unhappy people season after season in that horrible time, while the benignity of the seasons cheered and a bounteous harvest ended in one season our own period of agony—and then to contrast the depopulated, emaciated, horror-stricken and helpless Ireland that emerged from the Great Famine, with our own milder sufferings and happier deliverance—is not to lessen the gravity of the dangers we have escaped from, but to produce two lasting impressions upon the Irish heart. One of thanksgiving to the Almighty that He has vouchsafed to order all things so well towards the mitigation of the calamity and to multiply the means of meeting it. The other, of abiding gratitude and affection for the far-away kinsmen and brothers all the world over, by whose magnificent gifts many thousands tottering on the brink of a miserable death have been spared to breathe their prayers on Irish soil to-day for their preservers.

Shall this crisis close the history of Irish Famines?

Shall the crisis of 1879-80 close the history of Irish famines? Whether periods of distress are to recur or no, the lessons of the last twelve months have pointed out some particulars in which the Irish poor-laws must be materially changed, if they are to be effectual. The Boards of Guardians must be brought to harmonise with the interests of the great bulk of the population, that they may respond sensitively to the pressure of real want, without overburdening the body of ratepayers. A ready means of bringing

Defects of the Poor-laws.

this about would seem to be the admission to Boards of Guardians, as in England, of clergymen, who alone know the secrets of the Irish poor, and whose energy, firmness and administrative capacity were manifested in the late ordeal no less conspicuously than their noble loyalty to the suffering people. Poor-law Boards thus leavened might, perhaps, safely be trusted to make poor-law relief a reality in those districts where it at present conveys no meaning except the idea of a distant workhouse—half hospital, half prison—for the sick and worthless;—to enforce some system of sanitation in the dwellings of the poor;—to make provision for the treatment of epidemic disease locally in those remote regions of the Western unions, where conveyance to the workhouse hospital would involve dangerous risk and torment to the patients;—

and, above all, to frankly recognise the invincible abhorrence of the workhouse entertained by the Irish peasantry, by a liberal dispensation of outdoor relief in cases where, in the normal state of the existing law, the alternative of semi-starvation in their cabins is the surrender of their little farms and homes. In order to equalise the financial burden upon every portion of the population, it seems to be inevitable that the whole Union should be taxed at a uniform rate. The present system of charging each electoral division separately with the support of its own poor is unjust to the towns in times of agricultural prosperity, and ruinous to the country in periods of agricultural distress; and, while in the richer agricultural districts it holds out a direct incentive to landlords and large farmers to drive the labourers into the towns, in the poorest districts, whose wealth, such as it is, is concentrated in the towns, the property owners and shopkeepers thereof are exempted from the responsibility of assisting in the support of the starving cottiers by whom in better times they live and grow rich. An amelioration of the law in these respects is, in our opinion, essential to bring about the relief of honest poverty, if the Poor-law system is to mean anything beyond a set of expensive establishments for the accommodation of vagabonds and almshouses for the aged.

At the same time it must not be concealed that, in the Unions where distress is apt to be most poignant, such is the poverty of almost the whole population, that no possible re-casting of the Poor-law system can render it adequate as a relief organisation in times of pressure—much less succeed in averting them. That, should the present economic conditions remain unchanged, such periods of pressure must arise again, and may not find the world in such a mood of benevolence, or relief organisations in such a state of preparedness to resist them, is the lesson which gives most concern to everyone having an interest in, or a responsibility for, the future of Ireland. Into a discussion of these conditions, the constitution of the Mansion House Committee forbids us to enter. It would perhaps involve political controversy, in which many members of this Committee, united loyally for the relief of actual suffering, might be found ranged upon opposite sides. There are, however, some grounds of opinion common to all, and there is imperative necessity for giving it expression. It is agreed that the condition of things, under which a fertile and in many places thinly-populated island is reduced twice in each generation to crave alms at the doors of the nations, that a large section of its people may not starve to death, is a shameful and intolerable scandal. It is admitted that, unless thousands of persons are to be left oscillating between poverty and starvation, at the mercy of the seasons, some redistribution of the population along the unreclaimed Western sea coasts, which are the perpetual lurking places of distress, is inevitable. Whether that redistribution should take the ignominious form of expatriation for the people, or of transference to these extensive tracts in the interior of the country, which are at present only half utilized, or not utilized at all, is a question which we cannot here

Under present economic conditions Famine must recur

These conditions a scandal

discuss. It is only too evident, at the same time, that Irish agriculture in general is not merely threatened by an intensifying foreign competition, but suffers from a deep internal malady, which unnerves industry, discourages improvement, causes division between those who own and those who till the soil, habituates the peasantry to ambitionless lives of squalor, and leaves the wealth of the soil neglected or mocked with half a tillage.

The deep internal malady of Ireland

Thirty years ago the Society of Friends, in concluding their benevolent labours during the Famine of 1846–47, proposed the question :* "What circumstances can account for the inactivity and want of improvement which characterise the Irish tenantry? The civic population are more industrious and energetic; and the same men who are indolent on their farms in this country, exhibit a different character when they emigrate to America. It is a strange phenomenon to see landlords almost ruined by the taxation required for supporting pauper labourers in the workhouses; while millions of acres are wholly waste or imperfectly cultivated, and millions of money are lying at a low rate of interest in the funds. There are no doubt various causes for the depressed condition of Ireland; but it is an important question for public consideration, how far that depressed condition has resulted from injudicious legislation. If there be any legal impediments to the prosperity of the country, they should be first removed, and a free scope left for human exertion, before it can be right to condemn the people for improvidence or want of industry. The state of the law respecting land is universally admitted to be complicated and uncertain. A thorough reform appears essential to the improvement of the social condition of the country." What direction that reform is to take is, now as then, a source of heart-burnings and perplexity. Some moderate principles developed in the Report of the Society of Friends have, however, ripened into pretty general acceptance "The possession of land (p. 115) should be so far considered as a trust for the benefit of society at large, that no private arrangements should be permitted to interfere with the public good, by impeding those improvements which may be necessary to render the soil as productive as possible. In the absence of all restrictions, the interests of the individual owner perfectly coincide with those of society, and will secure for the public the best management and the largest production." The restrictions which then existed exist in great measure still—the system of entails which tie the hands of so many owners for life ; the cumbrous and expensive machinery for the transfer of land, which practically forbids the buying or selling of land in small parcels ; the landlord's right of summary seizure of the tenants' goods under the law of distress with the effect of lowering the tenant's credit and of enabling landowners to hire their lands to the highest bidder without regard to the value of the land or the character of the tenant; and finally, all the resulting demoralisation among

The necessity of Land Reform enforced after the Great Famine

---

* Transactions of the Central Relief Committee of the Society of Friends, during the Famine in Ireland, in 1846 and 1847, p. 110

the tenantry, whom "the heavy expenses of a transfer of land in moderate lots deprives of the opportunity of investing their savings in land and thus becoming the farmers of their own estates, and upon whom the want of a secure tenure of their farms under the existing system has the inevitable effect of impeding improvement."* Few will now dispute that a necessary part, if not the whole, of land reform in Ireland must consist in "the removal of all restrictions, whether of law or practice, which interfere with the free use of the land for the purposes of human industry"—"that the laws ought to be such as would enable every member of the community to sell or to purchase any quantity of land, with the smallest practicable delay, expense, and risk." Whether the remedy should stop here, or in what other form the unrest and insecurity which paralyse the peasant's arm may be removed, is a question not so germane to our present purpose, as that responsible statesmen should attack the problem resolutely and at once. It is as true now as when the Society of Friends reported, that improvement is at a stand still for want of a secure tenure—that "in many parts of Ireland leases are rare, and the occupants hold merely from year to year"—that "if the tenant have no lease he knows that any additional value he may give to his farm, whether by his capital or his industry, renders him liable to a demand of an increased rent." It is, unhappily, no less true now than then, that, following in the wake of a period of distress, "the agrarian outrages which have so deeply stained the character of Ireland, have lately appeared in an aggravated form where they were least expected to arise." Far be it from us, as from that benevolent society, "to extenuate the enormity, or to palliate the guilt of these dreadful outrages; yet they have exciting causes, which should, if possible, be removed." In reading these calm and solemn lessons taught by a Famine which swept away two millions of the Irish population, we cannot reflect without melancholy, that the thirty years which have rolled by since those pages were written should find us emerging from another famine, surrounded by the same phenomena of a fruitful soil and a starving population, a war of classes, a stain of crime, and the self-same prostration of national energy attributed to the self-same causes. "There is no time to lose in effecting these reforms. The present state of the country, while it exhibits some indications of improvement, is such as to cause deep anxiety even in the most hopeful." This was written in 1852. Another famine; and Mr. JAMES H. TUKE, who assisted nobly in the work of the Society of Friends during the former famine, revisited the country.* "And still the question remains"—he wrote in the spring of 1880—"How can this almost universally disaffected tone be changed into one of content and loyalty? The

Thirty years ago and to-day

---

* Transactions of the Central Relief Committee of the Society of Friends, during the Famine in Ireland, in 1846 and 1847, p. 110.
* A Visit to Donegal and Connaught in the Spring of 1880, by JAMES H. TUKE, Author of "A Visit to Connaught in the Autumn of 1847," page 89.

Conclusion

position seems to me one of the greatest gravity, and I cannot believe that any Government can long exist without having it forced upon them."

Shall another kind stranger, in another generation, utter the same dreary warning and tell the same woful tale of a people who thrive everywhere unless at home, stagnating and perishing of hunger in their own beautiful land? Or shall the crisis now so happily tided over by the wondrous hand of human charity, be the last that shall make Irishmen blush to behold their country exhibited as an almshouse, supported by the compassion of the world?

Signed on behalf of the Mansion House Relief Committee.

E. DWYER GRAY, M.P., LORD MAYOR,
Chairman.

R. W. BAGOT, CANON, LL.D.,
JAMES DANIEL, P.P.,
P. M'CABE FAY,
T. MAXWELL HUTTON,
CHARLES KENNEDY,
GEORGE B. OWENS, KNT.,
V. B. DILLON, JUN.,
} *Hon. Secretaries.*

DUBLIN, *7th December,* 1880.

SPECIAL REPORTS.

I.—FINANCIAL REPORT.

II.—REPORT OF INVESTIGATION held at Aranmore, by J. ADYE CURRAN, Esq., Barrister-at-Law.

III.—REPORT on the Condition of the Peasantry of the County of Mayo, by J. A. FOX, Esq.

IV.—REPORT of the MEDICAL COMMISSION on the causes and extent of the Fever Epidemic in the West, by GEORGE SIGERSON, M.D., Ch.M., and J. E. KENNY, L.R.C.S.

FINANCIAL REPORT.

The Finance Committee of the Mansion House Fund for the Relief of the Distress in Ireland, in submitting their report on the Balance Sheet presented herewith, desire to draw attention to a few items in the statement which appear to them deserving of special notice. The total receipts amount to £181,665 9s. 1d., of which £180,097 5s. 6d. have been contributed for the general purposes of the Committee, £535 10s. 9d. for specified distribution, £854 5s. 10d. for the purpose of giving special grants for seed, and £178 7s. 0d. interest allowed by the National Bank on current balances. It is interesting to notice that from Australia and New Zealand an amount has been received exceeding half the entire contributions. Individual subscriptions have been received from all parts of the world, as will be seen by classification list on page 83.

The largest individual subscription received was from the Maharajah of VIZIANAGRAM, £1,000; his Grace the Archbishop of TUAM, out of funds entrusted to him for the relief of distress, forwarded £3,000 to this Committee; the smallest was 1s., "a widow's mite." An alphabetical list of every subscription has been prepared, and is issued with the Committee's report. With reference to the disbursement of the fund it may be mentioned that 844 Local Committees were established throughout the districts in which the greatest distress prevailed, but these by amalgamation were reduced to 769. Through these agencies £166,899 have been dispensed in providing food, fuel, and clothing for the destitute.

The account shows that £4,445 4s. 11d. has been expended by the Western Isles Committee in the purchase of meal and clothing for the Islanders on the Western coast, and the Seed Committee expended the special contributions received for the purpose, together with £47 1s. 9d. for carriage, making in all the sum of £933 7s. 1d. in the purchase and distribution of seeds. In addition, special grants, amounting to £289 11s. 4d., have been made for the purchase of clothing, flour, milk, extract of meat, &c., for fever-stricken patients, and for distribution on the Western coasts. Contributions amounting to £535 10s. 9d., forwarded with special instructions for distribution in specified places, have been disposed of in accordance with the wishes of the donors. A list of grants made, arranged in counties, has been prepared, and is issued with the Committee's report. During the progress of the work of the Committee it was resolved to publish a pamphlet detailing the circumstances which led to the formation of the Committee, giving an account of its proceedings, and appealing for help, 50,000 copies were distributed at home and abroad at a cost of £1,077 14s. 11d. for printing and postage.

It will also be observed that by a resolution unanimously adopted by the Committee, a sum £450 was specially allocated as grants of £150 each to the families of Drs. DONOVAN and ROBINSON, of Skibbereen, and Dr. GREALY, of Oranmore, who died of fever caught in discharge of their duty as Dispensary Officers attending the poor during the late distress, for the relief of which this Committee was organised.

Under the heading of "Expenses" it will interest the Committee to have information regarding some of the larger items:—£189 3s. 3d. was expended on telegrams transmitted abroad, notwithstanding the fact that the Great Eastern and Anglo-American Telegraph Companies transmitted our messages free. This expenditure was most judicious, and, as the Committee are aware, was the means of bringing in contributions amounting to many thousands of pounds. The stationery, printing, and scrivenery, amounting to £677 13s. 10d., include stationery and all printed matter supplied to our 840 Local Committees. The salaries paid amount to £1,009 9s., an item of expenditure which was kept at this moderate figure through the personal exertion of members of Committee, who devoted time unsparingly in carrying on the work. Advertising amounts to £794 19s., and comprises appeals in newspapers throughout the United Kingdom, and the insertion of lists of subscriptions thrice weekly in the Dublin daily papers. This item would have been considerably larger but for the great liberality of the proprietors of the different papers, who made large reductions from their usual charges. In the incidental expenses there is included an item, £7 10s., rent of temporary office, which is the only outlay for rent, as through the great kindness of the LORD MAYOR and LADY MAYORESS, and at a great sacrifice of personal comfort, ample office accommodation in the Mansion House was placed at the disposal of the Committee. The total expenses incurred in receiving and dispensing the fund—including cost of telegrams, postage, stationery, and printing, salaries, advertising, and travelling expenses, inspection of Local Committees, and incidentals—amount to £3,425 17s. 3d.

The Committee desire to place on record their appreciation of the valuable assistance rendered by Mr. J. H. WRIGHT, the Assistant Secretary, and by Mr. A. J. PHILIPPS, the Accountant.

The Finance Committee beg to report in conclusion, that the balance in Bank to the credit of the fund is £2,586 7s. 10d., which amount, with any further contributions which may be received, will be reserved for special distribution under the direction of the Trustees appointed by the Committee for this purpose.

Signed on behalf of the Finance Committee,

DAVID DRIMMIE.

CLASSIFICATION OF SUBSCRIPTIONS
RECEIVED BY THE
MANSION HOUSE RELIEF COMMITTEE.

			£ s. d.	£ s. d.	£ s. d.
EUROPE:					
ENGLAND AND WALES	Collections		13,268 15 11		
	Individual Subscriptions		3,673 1 6	16,941 17 5	
SCOTLAND	Collections		2,643 18 3		
	Individual Subscriptions		161 7 11	2,805 6 2	
IRELAND	Collections		2,123 10 7		
	Individual Subscriptions		6,201 7 9	8,324 18 4	
FRANCE	Collections			4,081 6 1	32,153 8 0
ASIA:—					
INDIA	Collections			18,360 3 9	
CHINA	Do.			2,128 5 0	
ARABIA	Do.			82 0 0	20,570 8 9
AFRICA:—					
GRIQUA LAND WEST	Collections			1,196 0 0	
CAPE COLONY	Do.			140 0 0	
NATAL	Do.			71 0 0	1,407 0 0
AMERICA:—					
UNITED STATES	Collections		11,111 3 1		
	Individual Subscriptions		133 9 2	11,244 12 3	
CANADA	Collections		9,468 3 3		
	Individual Subscriptions		45 3 1	9,513 6 4	
NEWFOUNDLAND	Collections			1,800 0 0	
LA PLATA	Do.			3,802 9 8	
BRITISH GUIANA	Do.			486 5 6	
MAURITIUS	Do.			29 0 5	26,875 14 2
AUSTRALASIA:—					
VICTORIA	Collections			31,314 19 11	
NEW SOUTH WALES	Do.			28,000 0 0	
QUEENSLAND	Do.			12,000 2 9	
SOUTH AUSTRALIA	Do.			7,836 10 0	
WESTERN AUSTRALIA	Do.			1,214 17 5	
TASMANIA	Do.			3,010 6 3	
NEW ZEALAND	Do.			10,427 2 6	
FIJI	Do.			315 0 0	
AUSTRALIA	Individual Subscriptions			119 17 10	94,916 16 8
MISCELLANEOUS FOREIGN INDIVIDUAL SUBSCRIPTIONS				1,703 8 8	
ARCHBISHOP OF TUAM, SPECIAL CONTRIBUTION				3,000 0 0	4,703 8 8
TOTAL					£ 180,632 16 3

Dr.   BALANCE SHEET OF TH[E]
                                                      December

1880, December 2nd.	£	s.	d.	£	s.	
TO AMOUNT OF SUBSCRIPTIONS RECEIVED TO DATE	180,007	5	6			
DITTO CONTRIBUTED FOR SPECIFIED DISTRIBUTION	535	10	9			
	180,632	16	3			
Less Amount allocated to Seed Fund	31	19	6			
				180,600	16	
„ FUND CONTRIBUTED SPECIALLY FOR GRANTS FOR SEED	854	5	10			
Add Amount allocated from General Fund	31	19	6			
				886	5	
„ INTEREST ALLOWED BY NATIONAL BANK ON CURRENT ACCOUNT				178	7	
				£181,665	8	

We have carefully examined all Details comprised in above Account as set ou[t]
with entries, and we certify the Account to be correct.
The form of Accounts devised by the Committee, and the very careful and
Committee to present a highly satisfactory statement of the distribution of the Fun[d]

35, DAME-STREET, DUBLIN,
    5th *January*, 1881.

MANSION HOUSE RELIEF FUND.
2nd, 1880.

Cr.

1880, December 2nd.		£	s.	d.
By Grants made as follows :—				
TO LOCAL COMMITTEES FOR FOOD, FUEL, AND CLOTHING		160,899	0	0
TO WESTERN ISLANDS:				
Meal £2,236 10 11				
Clothing 1,978 10 7				
Cost of distribution .. 229 14 5		4,445	4	11
FOR SEED, AS PER SPECIAL CONTRIBUTIONS FOR				
THIS PURPOSE £886 5 4				
Carriage on do. 47 1 9		933	7	1
AMOUNT SPECIALLY DISTRIBUTED PER CONTRA ..		595	10	9
SPECIAL GRANTS:				
Purchase of Shoes £433 0 8				
In Clothing, Flour, Milk, Extract of Meat, &c. 289 11 4				
Families of deceased Doctors 450 0 0				
Carriage on Flour, &c. 9 8 4		1,182	0	4
DISTRIBUTED BY MEMBERS OF COMMITTEE TO SPECIAL				
CASES		130	0	0
COST OF PUBLICATION OF PAMPHLET AND REPORT OF				
COMMITTEE'S PROCEEDINGS, FOR CIRCULATION AT				
HOME AND ABROAD:				
Printing £1,178 6 0				
Postage 349 8 11		1,527	14	11
By Expenses (including Costs of Appeal and of Organisation and Distribution of Funds)				
SALARIES:—Assistant Secretary and Clerks ..£1,009 9 0				
Auditors' Fee 25 0 0		1,034	0	0
STATIONERY, PRINTING, AND SCRIVENERY		677	13	10
ADVERTISING IN UNITED KINGDOM		704	19	0
TRAVELLING EXPENSES, including Cost of Inspection of Local				
Committees		311	5	6
TELEGRAMS:—Foreign £189 3 3				
Home 63 10 5		252	13	8
POSTAGE		103	15	9
WAGES, Porter and Messenger		68	10	0
BANK CHARGES, STAMPS, &c.		35	7	5
INCIDENTALS, including Car Hire, Rent of Temporary Offices, &c.		147	3	1
BALANCE transferred to Trustees		2,586	7	10
		£181,005	0	1

...ooks kept by the Committee; we had all vouchers produced to us, compared vouchers
manner in which they were kept, very much facilitated the Audit, and enabled the
at its disposal.

KEVANS & KEAN,
Chartered Accountants.

MANSION HOUSE RELIEF COMMITTEE.

SEED FUND BALANCE SHEET.

	£ s. d.	£ s. d.		£ s. d.	£ s. d.
To Amount contributed by Sheffield and Lincolnshire Railway Company	610 0 0		By Amount granted for Seed		807 3 8
" Do. by Irish Peasantry Relief Fund London	105 0 0		" Freights £11 2 0		
" Do. Citizens of Oxford allocated from Total Collection at request of Contributors	100 0 0		" Do. paid out of General Fund 47 1 9		58 3 9
" Do. Collection, Rouen, France	39 5 10		" Sundry disbursements, including Hire of Sacks, Watchman, Bank Charges, &c.		67 19 8
	£854 5 10				
" Amount voted from General Fund	31 19 6				
		886 5 4			
" Do. for Carriage	...	47 1 9			
		£933 7 1			£933 7 1

We have examined Details and Vouchers for above Account, and found all correct.

35, DAME-STREET, DUBLIN,
5th January, 1881.

KEVANS & KEAN,
Chartered Accountants.

REPORT OF INVESTIGATION

HELD AT

KILRONAN, ARANMORE,

ON

MONDAY, the 21st day of JUNE, 1880,

BY

JOHN ADYE CURRAN,

MEMBER OF THE COMMITTEE.

MY LORD MAYOR, MY LORDS AND GENTLEMEN,

I beg to lay before you, as members of the Dublin Mansion House Committee, the following report of an investigation held by me at Kilronan, Aranmore, on Monday, the 21st June, 1880, on the subject of certain charges preferred verbally, by letter, and in the public press, against your Aran Sub-Committee, by the Rev. WILLIAM KILBRIDE, Protestant Rector of the Islands, and THOMAS H. THOMPSON, Esq., Agent to the Digby Estates.

Before coming to the proper subject matter of this report, a few words on the Islands themselves, and what I saw there, may not be out of place.

The Aran Islands are three in number, and lie some 30 miles to the W.S.W. of Galway. Aranmore or Inishmore, the largest of the three, is about 11 miles long by 1¾ mile wide at its broadest part. Inishmain or the Middle Island is some 8 miles in circumference, and Inishere the eastern, or, as it is sometimes called, the southern Island, is about half the size of Inishmain. There is a pier at Kilronan in Inishmore, which is of great use during the fine season, but, as I was informed, is utterly incapable of affording sufficient protection to boats during the fierce gales that prevail in Winter. The total area of the Islands comprises 11,288 acres, and the population is something over 3,000. The surface of the Islands is very barren, consisting mainly of limestone rock, seamed here and there with patches of rich soil, in which the potato, the principal, if not the only crop on the Islands, seems to grow most luxuriantly, as if it were out of the bare rocks themselves. At the present time, potatoes meet the eye at every point. They form the chief support of the inhabitants, and I am glad to be able to add, the growing crop promises to be a most plentiful and healthy one. Nothing else appears to grow or thrive on the Islands, save in one small favoured and sheltered spot—an oasis in the desert—the residence of the Rev. WM. KILDRIDE, which forms a very pleasing contrast to the wild appearance of the rest of the Island of Aranmore. Whatever soil there is on the Island is very shallow, and more affected by a dry season than one could imagine without seeing it.

Fishing and the manufacture of kelp are also a means of support to a considerable number of the inhabitants. There is no fuel on the Islands, and the turf has to be carried over in hookers from the opposite shores of Connemara.

The distress caused by the failure of the potato crop, has been this year intensified by a very bad fishing season. The drought in the early Summer dried up, to a considerable extent, any pasturage on the Islands, and the result has been, that starvation has been only kept off by the grants from the Relief Committees. The Aran Committee will require further aid to tide them over their difficulties for some weeks to come.

Communication with the main land is carried on by hookers, which ply to and from Galway, and other points on the coast. A good sized yacht carries the post bag, passengers and merchandise three times a week to and from Galway during the Summer months; and twice a week during the remainder of the year, weather permitting; an important qualification at Aran, where communication during the Winter months is frequently interrupted by storms for weeks together, and very much interfered with during the Summer by calms which prevent the sailing of the hookers. I was placed in the position of being made personally to feel the latter inconvenience, as I was detained on the Island for a considerable time after I had concluded the business I had to do, by a calm which gave the ocean the appearance of a sheet of oil for some days.

There are also a number of canoes, or corachs, used by the natives for fishing and other purposes, which are, however, only suited for fine weather, being constructed of ribs of wood covered with canvas. I was informed in Galway that during the Summer months, commencing with July, the steamer plying between that city and Ballyvaughan, calls once a week at Kilronan.

Having regard to the secluded position of these Islanders, one is not surprised to find that their customs, manners and dress are very primitive. They seem to be a fine looking, sturdy race of men, physically superior in every respect to the peasantry of the neighbouring main land. The ordinary shoe worn by both men and women is a piece of raw hide, stitched over the toes and at the heels, and fastened to the foot by means of a piece of fishing cord running across the instep. The Islands abound in ruins and ancient monuments, and the cliff scenery is magnificent. The Protestant Church stands in the centre of the village of Kilronan. The Catholic Church is some two miles away from the village. The Curate officiates every Sunday (weather permitting) on the two smaller Islands, leaving Kilronan on Saturday evening or sometimes on Sunday morning, and finishing his very arduous duties with late Mass on the South Island.

There is one small inn at Kilronan dignified by the very grand title of the "Atlantic Hotel." It is not at all so bad as it looks, and the hostess, Mrs. COSTELLOE, certainly endeavours to make up for her lack of accommodation by her earnest endeavour to please, and to make one as comfortable as possible, and to judge by her bill, handed me when leaving, the modern civilisation of high charges has not as yet reached the proprietor of the "Atlantic Hotel."

The flannel supplied by the Dublin Committees proved at the time a great boon, but I heard many complaints, some of which I was enabled to verify, as to its inferiority. The flannel I saw on the children certainly presents a marked contrast with the splendid stuff the people themselves make; and I am of opinion that wool purchased for them to make flannel of, would have been of more lasting benefit. The corduroy sent down proved of little value, as the salt water and air caused it to split up in every direction after a few days' use.

I left Dublin on Friday, the 18th June, and, thanks to the kind services of a friend in Galway, was enabled to leave that place about 12 o'clock on the next day, Saturday, for Aran. An Islander named COSTELLOE and his son happened to be returning at that hour with some cargo from Galway to Kilronan, where they live; they own a fine substantial hooker, and I went across with them, and afterwards returned in the same boat. So pleased was I with father and son, both remarkably intelligent men, that to any person fond of a sail in a thoroughly safe boat, I commend the trip and the skipper.

In presenting my report I shall avoid, as far as possible, discussing any matter not directly bearing upon the action of the Aran Sub-Committee, and I may add I pursued the same course on the Island.

However, in order that you may be the better enabled to form an opinion as to the wisdom of the conclusion at which I have arrived, it is necessary that you should be aware that there has existed on the Islands, for many years, a very bitter feeling between the present Protestant Rector and the Catholic Priests. I refused at the investigation entering into any matters resulting from that feeling, or into the causes of it, save in so far as it might be shown that the destitute suffered in any manner therefrom; and whatever be my opinion as to the merits or demerits of either side, I refrain from expressing it, and sincerely regret that where all should be peace and unity, so much strife exists.

The Catholic clergy on the one hand complain that the Rev. WM. KILBRIDE unduly interferes in religious matters with those of the Islanders who work for or are brought into contact with him, or those acting in concert with him. On the other hand, he and Mr. THOMPSON complain that the priests have been endeavouring to prevent the Catholics on the Island from working for Mr. KILBRIDE, or for a Protestant shopkeeper named CHARD; and that they have also been endeavouring to crush the latter by preventing the people from buying at his shop. This ill-feeling existed long prior to the creation of the Aran Sub-Committee, and I only refer to it, that you may the better understand the statements made before me at this investigation.

The following correspondence took place between the Rev. WM. KILBRIDE and Mr. THOMPSON and myself, and resulted in the inquiry being fixed to take place on the following Monday morning at 10 o'clock:—

ATLANTIC HOTEL, *Saturday.*

DEAR REV. SIR,

The Mansion House Committee have thought it proper to have an investigation on the spot into certain charges made by Mr. Thomas H. Thompson against the Aran Committee. Should these charges be well founded, we shall at once take steps to provide you with funds to relieve those of your persuasion who are destitute, and have been neglected. Will you, therefore, with Mr. Thompson, be kind enough to fix some hour to-morrow, if possible, at which I may be able to call a meeting of the Aran Sub-Committee, to which I invite your presence, and when you shall be afforded every opportunity and facility for substantiating any complaint you may have. In suggesting to-morrow, Sunday, I merely have regard to my personal convenience, as I do not wish to remain on the Island longer than what is absolutely necessary.

Faithfully yours,
JOHN ADYE CURRAN,

REV. W. KILBRIDE. *Member of Mansion House Committee.*

ATLANTIC HOTEL, *Saturday, June* 19*th.*

DEAR SIR,

The Mansion House Committee have thought it proper to have an investigation on the spot into certain charges made by you against the Aran Sub-Committee; I have written to Rev. W. Kilbride on the subject. Will you, therefore, with him, kindly fix some hour to-morrow, if possible (but in this suit your own and his convenience), at which I may be able to call a meeting of the Aran Sub-Committee, to which I invite your presence, and when you shall be afforded every opportunity and facility for substantiating any complaint you may have. In suggesting to-morrow, Sunday, I merely have regard to my personal convenience, as I do not wish to remain on the Island longer than what is absolutely necessary.

Faithfully yours,

THOMAS H. THOMPSON, Esq. JOHN ADYE CURRAN.

KILRONAN, ARAN ISLAND, *June* 19*th.*

DEAR SIR,

Your letter took me altogether by surprise after such a long delay; Sunday duties will absolutely prevent me from attending such an investigation as you propose, but, even if no such duties intervened, I should be very unwilling to engage in such a thoroughly secular business on such a day. I never made any charge in either public or private about any neglect having been shown to any *Protestants* in this place. At the Mansion House I stated that I had only two requiring relief, and that I could supply myself their wants.

The charges I made were of a general kind against the Committee, to show that it was utterly unfit, from its composition, mode of management, and general conduct, to carry on such a work. I mentioned exclusive dealing carried on against a shop through and by this Committee. Now, in my opinion, unless you have full power both to summon and swear all the witnesses who may be called or required, such an inquiry cannot by any possibility be held, as would satisfy either party or elicit the facts of the case, so as to bring out the truth. If you have this power, then I would be glad to assist in this investigation, although it will be attended with some loss to myself, as I had intended going to Galway on Monday about some law business. If you would kindly let me know whether you have power to summon witnesses, and also intend holding a thorough investigation on the whole *subject*, *embracing* all details, then I will let you know whether I will postpone my Galway business. If possible I will do so, but would feel very much obliged if you will kindly let me know by bearer whether you can act in the manner aforesaid.

I am, dear Sir, yours faithfully,

J. ADYE CURRAN, Esq.,   WILLIAM KILBRIDE.
Atlantic Hotel, Aran.

19th June, 1880.

DEAR SIR,

In reply to your note just received, I beg to say that I do not think Sunday would be a suitable day for the investigation into the charges made against the Aran Relief Committee.

I think the investigation will occupy more time than you may think. Permit me to ask whether you have power to examine on oath, for otherwise any investigation might prove abortive. It appears to me that some notice should have been given that the Dublin Committee intended to hold this inquiry, for it so happens that I had made arrangements to leave the Island on Monday. If, however, you have authority to hold the investigation in the way above stated, I shall of course remain.

Yours truly,

THOMAS H. THOMPSON.

ATLANTIC HOTEL, *June 20th*.

DEAR REV. SIR,

I have not the power either to summon or swear witnesses. I came down to investigate all complaints against the Sub-Committee in reference to the mode and objects of its relief. I suggested Sunday as a matter of personal convenience, but at the same time can quite respect your objection to that day. If you choose to attend, select your own day, but I should be obliged for an answer by bearer.

Yours faithfully,

REV. W. KILBRIDE.   JOHN ADYE CURRAN.

ATLANTIC HOTEL, *June 20th*.

DEAR SIR,

I only suggested Sunday, as very much of my time is not my own; but if you wish to be present and go on with your charge, select your own day; at the same time I may say that I have power neither to summon nor swear witnesses. I made enquiries at 1, Clare-street, before finally determining to come down, and found you were here, and not expected there for some time. Kindly state your final intention per bearer, and also let me know to what place shall I send you an answer to your letter of the 15th instant, which I received the day before I left Dublin.

Faithfully yours,

THOS. H. THOMPSON, Esq.   JOHN ADYE CURRAN.

KILRONAN, *Sunday.*

DEAR SIR,

I am rather pressed for time at present, or I would answer your note more fully; however, towards the middle of the day I will write to you more at large on the subject you inquire about.

I am, dear Sir, yours faithfully,

J. ADYE CURRAN, Esq.,
Atlantic Hotel.

WM. KILBRIDE.

KILRONAN, 20*th June*, 1880.

DEAR SIR,

I will let you know in the course of the day what I shall do.

Yours truly,

THOS. H. THOMPSON.

It will be better to address me in Dublin in answer to mine of 15th.

KILRONAN, *Sunday.*

DEAR SIR,

Since the *Freeman's Journal* of the 9th of June reached the Island, the intimidation has been so great that I feel certain that most, if not all those whom I might count upon as witnesses, would be afraid to come forward now in any such way. In proof of this, I need only refer you to the sergeant of police here, and he can inform you of the public meetings and speeches made at them during the week before last. He can also inform you of the formidable procession on last Sunday, both before and after Mass, and also that it was enough to strike terror into most.

The magistrate, too, I am sure, would give such information as would tend to show that the people would be afraid to come forward.

Under these altered circumstances, I am greatly afraid that I could get no voluntary witnesses to testify to past acts of the Sub-Committee. Under the compulsion of a summons they would come forward. This would serve them as an excuse for acting in opposition to those around them. Please see the police sergeant, as I have no doubt that he will corroborate these statements. Taking all these things into account, I have no doubt but that an investigation carried on without a power of summoning witnesses, and examing them on oath, would be barren of results, unfair to myself, and worthless. However, I shall be willing to attend at the time and at the place you may appoint for the intended inquiry.

I am, dear Sir, yours faithfully,

J. ADYE CURRAN, Esq.,
Atlantic Hotel.

WILLIAM KILBRIDE.

20*th June*, 1880.

DEAR SIR,

I have read the Rev. Mr. Kilbride's note to you, and I agree with him as to the unlikelihood of getting voluntary witnesses in the matter upon which you have come down, and for the reasons which he gives. I shall postpone leaving the Island, however, as I intended to-morrow, and will attend any investigation you may hold at any hour you name.

Yours very truly,

JOHN ADYE CURRAN, Esq.

THOMAS H. THOMPSON.

ATLANTIC HOTEL, *June* 20*th*.

REV. DEAR SIR,

I must decline holding an investigation into charges made by you and Mr. Thompson, at which the parties making the charge say they will only attend as spectators, and which you yourself say would be "barren of results, unfair to you, and worthless."

Neither do I think it part of my duties to go about making the inquiries suggested by you from the police sergeant and others. I cannot but come to the conclusion that neither of you wish for the investigation.

I return to Galway this evening if possible.

Faithfully yours,

REV. W. KILBRIDE.   J. A. CURRAN.

ATLANTIC HOTEL, 20*th June*, 1880.

DEAR SIR,

I came down here to investigate charges made by you and Rev. W. Kilbride against the Aran Sub-Committee. When you say that you agree with Rev. W. Kilbride's letter, I can only say that I must decline making any inquiry into charges when the parties making the charge say they cannot produce evidence for reasons, the validity of which I certainly must take the liberty of questioning.

Faithfully yours,

THOS. H. THOMPSON, Esq.   JOHN ADYE CURRAN.

P.S.—You cannot blame me if I believe that you have shirked an investigation into the charges made by you against the Sub-Committee.

KILRONAN, *Sunday*.

DEAR SIR,

Your note just received. I must protest most loudly against your interpretation of my last note in answer to yours. I never said that I would be a mere spectator; all I wanted to show was that there would be almost insuperable difficulties in the the way of procuring evidence on account of recent proceedings here. In referring you to the sergeant, I merely did so for fear that you might have doubted my word. I consider, too, that your being unable to examine witnesses on oath is also a great impediment in the way of arriving at any satisfactory conclusion. I shall (D.V.) be ready to attend your meeting, as I told you plainly in my last letter, at whatever time or place you may appoint, although it may be even at the greatest disadvantage to me.

I am, dear Sir, yours truly,

J. ADYE CURRAN, Esq.   WM. KILBRIDE.
Atlantic Hotel.

KILRONAN, *June* 20*th*, 1880.

DEAR SIR,

You came down here as you say to investigate charges made by me against the Aran Sub-Committee. Allow me, however, to say that your appearance was rather sudden, without notice, and without the qualifications necessary to make an inquiry useful. Now I beg to say that I am in no way shirking an investigation, and, as I told you, am ready to attend at any time to-morrow, not as a mere spectator, but to give all the help circumstances permit.

Yours truly,

THOMAS H. THOMPSON.

I had no intention of holding an inquiry at which the parties making the charge, the subject-matter of investigation, would attend only as it were under protest and as spectators, but the last two letters changed in my opinion the aspect, and I immediately wrote a short note to the two gentlemen, stating that I should hold the inquiry, subject to their convenience, at 10 o'clock next morning (Monday).

Having regard to the fact that the magistrate, Mr. JAMES O'FLAHERTY, was referred to by Mr. KILBRIDE, I wrote to that gentleman enclosing him copy extract from Mr. KILBRIDE's letter, and inviting his presence at the inquiry; and I may pass from this matter in saying, that Mr. O'FLAHERTY, who is a Protestant magistrate resident on the Island, very kindly came down next morning, was present at the greater part of the investigation, and in answer to me stated publicly that he was not aware of any intimidation existing on the Island, but that he had heard rumours to which he attached no weight, and in which he did not believe.

On Monday morning all the parties assembled in a large room recently built in the Inn. Mr. THOMPSON and Rev. W. KILBRIDE were present, as was also Mr. CHARD. The Members of the Sub-Committee also attended: Rev. JOHN CONCANNON, P.P.; Dr. BODKIN, and Rev. D. W. FAHEY, C.C. Their Secretary, Mr. E. N. FITZGERALD, a teacher in the National School, had left the Island sometime before. Mr. O'FLAHERTY, J.P., was, as I have stated, also present.

Before the proceedings commenced, Mr. THOMPSON stated, that both he and Mr. KILBRIDE laboured under considerable difficulties in consequence of my not having the power to summon or swear witnesses. I endeavoured to explain to him that in asking for the inquiry he had said nothing about requiring a sworn one, and that a gentleman of his experience should have known that at any investigation held by a body composed as the Mansion House Committee is, there was no power either to summon or swear witnesses, and I told him that as I was there at his own request to investigate charges made by him, I consider the objections as coming from him rather late.

I then proceeded to deal with the several charges in their order.

I first took up the charge made in writing by Mr. KILBRIDE, in the following language:—

"The charges I made were of a general kind against the Committee, to show that it was utterly unfit, from its composition, mode of management and general conduct, to carry on such a work. I mentioned exclusive dealings carried on against a shop through and by this Committee."

The charge of Mr. THOMPSON on the same subject was contained in his letter of the 4th May to this Committee, in which he stated that "he, Mr. THOMPSON, *had been studiously kept off the Committee.*"

Mr. THOMPSON stated, that according to our rules clergymen of all denominations should be on the Relief Committees, and that in consequence the Rev. W. KILBRIDE was so entitled. I explained to him that such had been our fixed rule, but that at a Meeting of the Mansion House Committee, held on the 5th February, the Most Rev. Dr. TRENCH, Archbishop of Dublin, being in the chair, a resolution was passed allowing, in some places, the formation of what I might call exclusive Committees, and that the Aran was one of the few Committees we found it necessary to allow to be formed without the presence on it of the Protestant Rector.

I further told him that we should have allowed Mr. KILBRIDE at any time to have formed a Committee to relieve those of his own persuasion in distress, but for the fact that he had informed your Committee there were but two Protestants on the Island needing relief, and those he was able to provide for himself.

In answer to me Mr. KILBRIDE stated, he had now only one of his persuasion requiring help, and that he had no complaint against the Committee on that subject, as that party had received plentiful relief.

Neither gentleman appeared to be aware of the resolution of the 5th February, at the time they made the charge, nor until I informed them of its having been passed. And having regard to what I have stated, and to the fact that the formation of the Aran Committee, without the presence on it of the Rev. W. KILBRIDE'S name as a Member, was permitted under that resolution by you, I could not come to the conclusion that the absence of the Reverend Gentleman's name from the Committee rendered it utterly or at all unfit, from its composition, to carry on the work of relief.

The next matter I had to consider was, the alleged exclusion of Mr. THOMPSON from the Committee. To use his own words, in his letter, "he had been studiously kept off." I have come to the conclusion that this charge has no foundation, and that upon admitted facts and letters. Early in February, the Committee wrote the following letter to Mr. THOMPSON :—

ARAN ISLANDS, GALWAY BAY.

To THOMAS H. THOMPSON, Esq.,

SIR—We beg leave to inform you that a Relief Committee has been formed in Aran. We are in receipt of a very considerable sum of money from the Mansion House Fund. In compliance with the Rules of this Fund, we beg to request your kind co-operation on our Committee in dispensing the relief for the destitute.

We beg to remain, Sir, your obedient servants,

JOHN A. CONCANNON, for the Committee.

To that letter Mr. THOMPSON on the 18th February, replied as follows :—

1, CLARE-STREET, 18*th February*, 1880.

GENTLEMEN,

I am in receipt of your invitation to co-operate in the relief supplied by the Mansion House Committee. Not being at present on the Island, I am unable to comply with the request.

Yours obediently,

THOMAS H. THOMPSON.

On his next visit to the Island, Mr. THOMPSON saw the Parish Priest, the Rev. JOHN A. CONCANNON ; he was asked again to join, but refused, unless he was first shown the lists and accounts kept by the Committee.

The Parish Priest told him that every matter would be open to his inspection as a Member of the Committee, but refused to allow him to see any of their books, unless he first signified his intention of becoming a Member. This Mr. THOMPSON refused to do. The matter ended there, and I fail to see in what manner he has been studiously, or at all, *kept* off the Committee. It is not every member of the public who has a right to see your books; to give such a right, I think it necessary the party should have subscribed to your funds, or be a member of one of your Committees, and, as a matter of fact, Mr. THOMPSON has not as yet sent any subscription to your funds.

Again Mr. O'FLAHERTY, the Magistrate, was asked by Dr. BODKIN, one of the Committee, to join them, and he refused, giving as his reason that he could not give the time, and was not in a position to know as much about the wants of the poor as the Parish Priest and the Doctor.

The Rev. W. KILBRIDE then made a charge against the Committee, that they had a paid Secretary. Though denying Mr. KILBRIDE's right to interfere in this matter, one dealing with the internal management of our Committee, still I explained to him that having a paid officer was, to a considerable extent, a matter of discretion with our Sub-Committees. In some cases it would be almost impossible to have accurate accounts kept, unless a person whom the Committee could command and expect to do the duty were employed, as we required weekly accounts, as a rule, to be sent in, and that we had permitted payment of a Secretary in many cases. Mr. KILBRIDE also complained that numbers of the people frequently were left unrelieved; but he gave no evidence to satisfy me on that point.

He stated that on several occasions, women in the street complained to him on the subject, both in the night and during the day; but early in the investigation I was able to satisfy my own mind that Mr. KILBRIDE allowed himself to be made the dupe of some few of the people on the Islands, who, having received relief from the Committee, or when refused such on proper grounds, found that they had only to go to the Reverend Gentleman, and make some complaint against the Sub-Committee, to ensure their being listened to by willing ears, and, in some instances, their receiving that relief a second time; and I also endeavoured to explain to him that you, or any Committee acting under you, could not possibly be expected thoroughly to relieve the destitute, and that all that could be expected from you, or that you could expect from your Sub-Committees, would be to give fairly according to your or their means, and I saw no reason to come to the conclusion that the Sub-Committee at Aran had not properly and fairly distributed their funds.

Mr. KILBRIDE then complained that the Committee had not given any of their meal orders to a shopkeeper on the Island named CHARD. I refused to investigate that matter, or to interfere with the discretion of the Sub-Committee, as to the parties from whom they bought the meal and other provisions, and I told him, which was the fact, that you had so refused in every one of the very many cases where such complaints had been made to you, on the part of, or by dissatisfied shopkeepers in the districts of the various Sub-Committees; but that if he showed me that the poor had in any manner suffered by such a course of action, I should, of course, at once interfere. But Mr. KILBRIDE was unable to, or at all events did not, give me any evidence on this point, nor did he even suggest, except by his inference, that the poor had in way suffered by the subject matter of the complaint, or that they were at all ever refused relief, because of their frequenting Mr. CHARD's shop.

I was satisfied upon the evidence, that in some instances certain parties had been requested not to frequent Mr. CHARD's shop. The Catholic Clergy may have had their own reasons for such a course: into the validity of those reasons I declined to enter as outside the scope of my inquiry, save in so far as it could be shown to me that destitute people had been refused relief by the Committee on that account; not only was no such evidence given, but I was affirmatively satisfied by the evidence supplied by the Committee that, whatever the wishes of the Clergy were on the subject, in no case was any destitute person refused relief because of his or her frequenting the shop.

The next charge was one made by Mr. THOMPSON in a letter dated 2nd June, and addressed to me.

"I was informed by letter that last Saturday week ten heads of families were put on one list. This was called the 'Soupers' List.' All these were refused relief. The reason assigned was that some worked for Mr. KILBRIDE, others for Mr. CHARD, and others again went to his shop.

Now, at the very onset, Mr. THOMPSON told me that he went too far in stating that "any reason was assigned," that that was only the inference of Mr. KILBRIDE from whom he had derived the information. I told him that the reason assigned seemed to me to be the "gravamen" of the charge, but that I should receive any evidence as to the first portion of it he had to produce; Mr. KILBRIDE then produced a number of written statements and one declaration, which, he said, had been made by parties who were now too much intimidated to come forward.

I refused at the time to receive them, and informed Mr. KILBRIDE that, apart altogether from my view of such evidence as a lawyer, it would be most unfair to the Aran Sub-Committee if, at an investigation on the spot called for by him and Mr. THOMPSON, I accepted from him written statements which you might have had before you in Dublin, without the necessity of a local inquiry, and the veracity of which the Sub-Committee had no opportunity of testing.

I was further convinced of the propriety of insisting upon strict proof being given as to what was contained in these written statements, by the fact that, as shown to me by Mr. KILBRIDE, they all appeared appended to an intended letter to a leading Dublin journal, in which all the charges made against the Sub-Committee were reiterated.

While discussing the matter, Mr. KILBRIDE on the one hand asserting, and the Committee on the other denying, the existence of any intimidation, Dr. BODKIN requested Mr. KILBRIDE to give him the names of those parties he said were so intimidated, and whose attendance he was unable to procure. This was done, and, in less than five minutes, the Doctor having picked them out of a large crowd waiting outside the hotel, paraded all the parties named before us in the room, apparently, to my mind, much to the Reverend Gentleman's surprise, if not disgust.

MARY FLAHERTY was then called, and in answer to the Rev. WILLIAM KILBRIDE, she stated that she was the wife of a man named PATRICK FLAHERTY, a blaster by trade; her husband was in the habit of working for Mr. KILBRIDE, and sometimes for Mr. CHARD. She attended to get relief on the 22nd May, heard her husband's name called out by Rev. Mr. FAHEY; that gentleman did not say he would not give her husband any relief, nor did he say anything about a "Soupers' List"; she got relief every time it was going, always got her rights.

Mr. KILBRIDE then proceeded to cross-examine this woman out of a written document, to which he said she had put her mark in the presence of Mr. THOMPSON and himself, and in which he alleged she made a statement at variance with that now made. She got very much excited, but stoutly maintained she was telling me the truth; it further appeared that she was in constant employment at the Police Barracks, earning, according to the number of constables, a sum not exceeding twenty-two shillings per month, with her board and certain perquisites; her mother and mother-in-law were on the relief list, and her family have received, from time to time, relief to the value of £4 15s. 7d.

Mr. THOMPSON and the Rev. WILLIAM KILBRIDE said it was quite evident the woman had been intimidated from telling me the truth, as she had told it to them when putting her mark to the statement.

I could not help believing that there had been a species of intimidation practised in this case, but not by the parties suggested.

One can well imagine a scene enacted during a period of deep distress, in a room in the house of the Rev. WILLIAM KILBRIDE, in which this nervous, excitable, poor, ignorant, uneducated woman, in the presence of her husband's employer, standing face to face with the agent to whom her husband had to pay his rent, might easily be induced, if not coerced, by that husband, himself unscrupulous, to make or sign with her mark a statement which, he considered, might be palatable to those two gentlemen, and which they no doubt believed at the time to be true.

The observations I shall presently make upon PATRICK FLAHERTY's own evidence will throw more light upon this matter.

Mrs. JAMES GILL was the next witness examined by Mr. KILBRIDE; she denied she had ever been refused relief; she was never put on the "Soupers' List;" on one occasion Father FAHEY read a list of names down, her's was on it. He said he should ask Father JOHN (the Parish Priest) before giving them anything; she afterwards got relief in the evening. She worked for Rev. WILLIAM KILBRIDE.

It further appeared that this woman's husband was in almost constant employment, under Rev. WILLIAM KILBRIDE, on board the yacht which carries the post to and from Galway.

CELIA GILL, a daughter of Mrs. JAMES GILL, was next examined; she remembered on one occasion that her mother got meal, afterwards on the same day she, CELIA, met Father FAHEY, who said that he had seen her leaving CHARD's shop five times that day. Her mother got the meal about 12 o'clock, and this observation was made some time later in the day.

The Rev. WILLIAM KILBRIDE did not pretend these two witnesses were not telling the truth, and, from their evidence, I was asked to draw two conclusions:—first, that relief had been improperly withheld until after the Rev. JOHN CONCANNON had been consulted, and, secondly, that the conversation with the daughter was an intimation that no more relief would be granted until the family ceased visiting Mr. CHARD's shop.

Upon investigation I find that this family received from your Aran Sub-Committee relief to the amount of £6 18s 4d., and, I think that if Father CONCANNON acted at all wrongly, he did so in advising that any relief should have been given on the occasion to this family, having regard to the fact that two members of it were working. I have already stated that the Catholic Clergy were anxious their flock should not visit Mr. CHARD's shop; I told them I did not approve of this, but, at the same time, I had no right to interfere with their action, which, upon investigation, I might have found justified; but I came to the conclusion, that no anxiety on the part of the Priests to keep the people out of the shop interfered with the giving of relief by the Committee to the GILLS, or to any other family on the Islands; and, as the best evidence of this, I may refer to the fact, that shortly before the conversation of Father FAHEY with CELIA GILL, he had without remonstrance given relief to the mother for the family, though not only was her daughter visiting Mr. CHARD's shop, but she herself, and her husband, were working for Rev. WILLIAM KILBRIDE at the time.

The next witness examined by Rev. WILLIAM KILBRIDE was a Mrs. MOGAN, wife of MICHAEL MOGAN, who also worked for Mr. KILBRIDE.

She denied ever having heard a list of Soupers called out; she was given plenty of relief whenever she required it, and had no complaint to make against the Committee. I ascertained from the books of the Committee that her family had received relief to the value of £6 3s.

The Rev. WILLIAM KILBRIDE informed me that this woman had also put her mark to a statement at variance with what she now said. The observations I have already made upon the evidence and statement of Mrs. FLAHERTY apply equally in this case.

Mrs. O'DONNELL, wife of PATRICK O'DONNELL, was then examined by Mr. KILBRIDE.

She stated that for two months she had received no relief except 4s. 6d. and 3s. 6d. worth the last two occasions.

She, on one occasion, with three or four others, was called a Souper by Father FAHEY; she was refused relief, that is, she did not come in for it for two months, because she was not sent for.

In answer to Rev. D. W. FAHEY, she said her husband and son were working all this time, and at the time of the refusal they were getting 17s. per week between them. There were three or four names called out. Father FAHEY said nothing but called her a Souper. An order for 2s. was sent lately, but she sent it back; she could not give any reason for so doing. Father FAHEY said to her, not to let anything he said make her go to CHARD'S, or stop out of it, but to earn an honest shilling wherever she could.

Mr. CHARD then stated young O'DONNELL was working on and off with him about three days every week. He understood from Mrs. O'DONNELL that her husband was working for Mr. KILBRIDE; he did not want the people to come to his shop.

From the books of the Committee I ascertained that the O'DONNELLS had received relief to the value of £6 9s. 5d.

PATRICK FLAHERTY, husband of the first witness, was then examined by the Rev. WILLIAM KILBRIDE, and said: I was present at the distribution of relief on 18th May last, heard Father FAHEY say to B. FLAHERTY, "go down to Mr. CHARD, he knows what side to put the spoon before you."

I got no relief that day, no reason was given for the refusal. Heard Father FAHEY say, "come on now, let us read out the Soupers' List;" he read out 10 names including mine. I got no relief.

I was working for a fortnight at the time, but not for Mr. KILBRIDE or Mr. CHARD. My wife earns 22s. at the outside every month, in addition to her food and perquisites, at the Police Barrack; she is always there. She got relief lately from Dr. BODKIN to the extent of 5s. My wife's mother also gets relief. My mother was plentifully supplied; Father FAHEY gave me 20s. for potatoes, and Mr. KILBRIDE gave me also a similar amount.

Just as the witness had given the last answer, there was a commotion at the door of the room in which we were sitting. Those on the outside of the crowd were suddenly thrust aside, and Mrs. FLAHERTY, the wife, sprang in, caught hold of her husband in a manner less polite than determined, and calling out that she would allow him to tell no more lies, disappeared with him in her grasp, from the room and down the narrow stairs. The entire incident occupied less time than it has taken me to narrate the circumstance.

After the disturbance, caused by Mrs. FLAHERTY'S sudden appearance and rapid exit with her husband in custody, had subsided, Mr. KILBRIDE informed me, that after such an exhibition of intimidation, he could not possibly proceed further with that branch of the inquiry.

I saw no evidence of intimidation in the act of Mrs. FLAHERTY, but I did see evident signs of deep anger on her part against her husband for telling, what she believed to be, a false story, and against those who, she thought, were backing up her husband in his acts, and I reminded the Reverend

Gentleman that, as a matter of fact, he had examined the witnesses whose names he had given Doctor BODKIN, and that none of them had suggested they had been ever refused relief because they worked for him or Mr. CHARD, or visited the shop of the latter; but as he, Mr. KILBRIDE, complained that several of the witnesses produced by him had given evidence, which, he alleged, was at variance with their written statements to him and Mr. THOMPSON, I told him that if he produced a written statement made to him by any person, showing as a fact that relief had been refused in consequence of the party having gone into Mr. CHARD's shop, or worked for him, Mr. KILBRIDE, or Mr. CHARD, I should take that statement and report it to you. Mr. KILBRIDE replied that he had no statement actually containing such an averment, which was only an inference of his own, and that he had withdrawn that part of the charge; he also stated that one woman, then sick in bed and too ill to attend, had made such a complaint to him; but I did not consider I could act on such testimony.

I also informed the Reverend Gentleman that, if he sent me copies of the statements of the various witnesses examined, I should lay them before you. This he has not done.

I then asked for a list of the ten names he alleged were put on the "Soupers' List." Mr. KILBRIDE gave me the following names, and I annex the amount of relief given to those parties by your Committee at Aran:— Patrick O'Donnell, £6 9s. 5d.; Anthony O'Donnell, £5 18s. 6d.; James Car, £3 6s.; Patrick Dignam, £4 8s.; Patrick Folan, £3 19s. 5d.; James Gill, £6 18s. 4d.; Widow Kearns, £3 17s. 6d.; Michael Mogan, £6 3s.; Patrick Flaherty, £5 3s.; James Coleman, £6 2s. 6d.; Widow Harvey, £2 0s. 6d.; Patrick Flaherty, £4 15s. 7d.; Mrs. Dillane, £3 17s. 6d.; Sullivan and Fallon, £2 5s. 4d.

The Widow HARVEY is the only Protestant on that list. Mr. KILBRIDE said he was able to supply her wants himself, notwithstanding which the Committee seems to have given her moderate relief, the amount of which however satisfied the Reverend Gentleman, as he himself informed me. The other names are those of Catholics, therefore the word "Souper," in its ordinary acceptation, did not apply to them.

The Rev. D. W. FAHEY, C.C., then stated the case for the Committee; he denied the charges made against them, and contrasting the evidence of FLAHERTY with that of his wife, asked me not to rely on it as trustworthy, and related a circumstance that had occurred lately:—FLAHERTY received one pound's worth of seed potatoes from the Rev. WILLIAM KILBRIDE, and a like amount from himself. One evening, shortly afterwards, he met FLAHERTY near his garden, the latter, pointing up towards his land, told him, Father FAHEY, that there was a portion of it ready to receive potatoes, but yet unplanted, as he had not sufficient seed; doubting his veracity, he, Father FAHEY, went to his land, and digging with his hand, found, not only the place indicated, but the entire of his holding, fully planted.

The Rev. WILLIAM KILBRIDE objected to this statement being made in the absence of FLAHERTY, who, he understood, was prepared positively to contradict it.

Father FAHEY replied that he had intended asking him the question, but was deprived of the opportunity of cross-examining him by his sudden disappearance with his wife, but that it appeared strange that the Rev. WILLIAM KILBRIDE seemed to know all about the interview, so as to be able to assert FLAHERTY would contradict his, Father FAHEY's, statement before it had been mentioned by him.

In reply to me, the Rev. D. W. FAHEY said that the Committee, according to their means, had given relief fairly to all those in distress on the Islands, and had never refused relief to any person for any of the reasons suggested by the Rev. WILLIAM KILBRIDE, that a list of parties in employment was made out in whose cases relief was either discontinued or lessened so long as the employment lasted.

It certainly seemed strange to me that when Father FAHEY was under examination the Rev. WILLIAM KILBRIDE abstained from asking him any question as to the truth or falsehood of the charges made against the Committee.

The Rev. D. W. FAHEY could not be said to be an intimidated or untruthful witness. Charges were brought against him and the other Members of the Committee, by the Rev. WILLIAM KILBRIDE, through his mouth-piece Mr. THOMPSON. Those charges failed in proof, for reasons, the validity of which I shall for a moment admit, yet when brought forward face to face with the Rev. D. W. FAHEY under examination, neither has the courage to ask him whether those charges were well founded, though each must have been aware that the admission by Father FAHEY of the truth of even a portion of them would have been strong corroboration of their case.

Finding neither Mr. KILBRIDE nor Mr. THOMPSON put the questions, I put them myself with the above result.

The next charge was contained in the words :—" From what funds were the people from the South Island, in February last, and also at the Great Land League Meeting, held in the School-house, Kilronan, fed and recreated with bread and porter?"

Mr. THOMPSON withdrew this charge, on being informed by the Rev. J. A. CONCANNON that no part of the sum so spent, amounting to something under £2, had been taken out of the Mansion House Fund.

The next charge was contained in the words :—" From whence came the £30 given, as reported, to the tenants of Kilronan, nominally to buy seed after all their ground was planted : this money, rumour states, was given on the 9th April to buy seed potatoes, although the majority of those planting it had their land planted at the time ; rumour further reports that most of this money was returned to be kept as a defence fund for legal expenses ?"

The Rev. J. CONCANNON stated that the sum referred to formed a part of a sum of £40 given to him by the Archbishop of TUAM, and that any of it that remained over he divided among some of those poorest on the Island. Mr. THOMPSON said he was satisfied with this explanation, and withdrew the charge so far as it affected your Committee.

This closed the evidence on both sides, and, having given the matter most careful consideration, I am of opinion that the Rev. WILLIAM KILBRIDE has failed in the charge he made against the constitution of the Aran Sub-Committee, and I agree with Mr. O'FLAHERTY, when that gentleman says, that it is composed of those who, above all others, are best suited to know the wants of the poor.

Mr. THOMPSON's own letter of the 18th February is the best answer to his charge of having been studiously kept off the Committee.

There was no evidence adduced before me, which would warrant me in suspecting, much less coming to the conclusion, that the relief had been unfairly or improperly distributed.

The only remaining charge pressed against the Committee is deprived of much, if not of all, of its sting, in consequence of the latter portion of it—that in which it is alleged the Committee assigned the reasons mentioned for the refusal of relief—having been withdrawn by Mr. THOMPSON and the Rev. W. KILBRIDE: the latter gentleman stating that he could not press that part of the charge further than as his own inference from the facts stated.

I believe that a list of names was made out from week to week by the Committee, not of "Soupers," for, with one exception already alluded to, they were all Catholics, but of men and women, who were at the time, or had been during the week, earning money: these parties were refused, and properly refused relief. The Rev. W. KILBRIDE and Mr. CHARD were two of the principal, if not the principal, employers on the Island, and it followed as a necessary result that many persons must have been refused relief from time to time in consequence of their working for either of those gentlemen.

The term "Souper," in its ordinary and well-known signification, has no representant on the Aran Isles; there are on them, I believe, but some two or three who have changed their religion; but recollecting the ill-feeling between the clergy of both denominations, to which I have alluded, which was well-known to the people, and the evident anxiety of the Catholic Clergy to prevent as much as possible members of their flock being brought into contact with either the Rev. W. KILBRIDE or Mr. CHARD, I have no doubt but that the list made out from time to time of those who were working for those two gentlemen, became to be known commonly among the Islanders as the "Soupers' List."

In such a sense only had the expression any meaning. I was thoroughly satisfied that none of the parties complaining had ever been refused relief when working for either the Rev. W. KILBRIDE or Mr. CHARD, because of their employers, but were properly refused on account of their being in employment, and earning money.

I was also satisfied that some few parties on the Islands considered the relief as a matter of right, to which they were entitled, whether working or idle. Take for instance the case of Mrs. O'DONNELL, whose complaint against, and ill-feeling towards, the Committee, arose simply in consequence of their properly refusing to give her relief, at a time when both her husband and son were earning substantial weekly wages; again, another class was represented by PAT FLAHERTY, who having received as much as he could from the Committee, found that a complaint well put together ensured his finding a willing sympathizer in the Rev. W. KILBRIDE.

I did not believe the greater part of FLAHERTY's statement, and it is a strange fact that the only two on the Island, FLAHERTY and Mrs. O'DONNELL, who before me accused the Rev. D. W. FAHEY of having used the word "Souper," were parties, members of whose families were in constant employment, and who never should have got a shilling's worth from our Relief Fund. It is also a coincidence that all those who were examined before me, or who had made statements to Mr. KILBRIDE or Mr. THOMPSON, were themselves, or some members of their families were, in the employment of the former gentleman.

Some of these parties imposed upon the Rev. W. KILBRIDE, relying upon the ill-feeling to which I have alluded. The following is a case typical of many:—The Committee properly refuse a man relief because he is working; he happens at the time to be working for the Reverend Gentleman, or Mr. CHARD. The party refused at once goes with his tale to the Rev. W. KILBRIDE, giving as a reason for the refusal, not that he was working, but that he was working for him or Mr. CHARD. The statement is reduced to writing, disappointment and anger both tend to exaggeration, and Mr. KILBRIDE should not be surprised, if in his calmer moments the man reverts to the truth, which is harmless, and refuses to adhere to the exaggeration, in which lies the point of the charge.

In every case in which any person was refused relief, it was either proved or admitted that he or she, or some member of the family, was working. The Committee positively assured me, and I believe them, that no person had ever been refused relief for the reasons suggested by Mr. KILBRIDE, or Mr. THOMPSON, that they, of course, struck parties off while working, only to put them on the list again when thrown out of employment; I had no evidence before me, nor did I see any reason for believing or suspecting, that any persons had been at any time refused relief because of their frequenting Mr. CHARD's shop. Into the discussion of any other matters, as I have said, I refused to enter, and upon the whole and for the above reasons I think the Aran Committee have thoroughly cleared themselves of all charges brought against them by either the Rev. WILLIAM KILBRIDE or Mr. THOMAS H. THOMPSON, all which I submit as my report.

JOHN ADYE CURRAN.

20, GARDINER'S PLACE,
29th June, 1880.

REPORTS
ON THE
CONDITION OF THE PEASANTRY
OF THE
COUNTY OF MAYO,
DURING THE FAMINE CRISIS OF 1880,
BY
J. A. FOX,
Member of the Committee.

FIRST REPORT,

On the Results of his Recent Inspection of Certain Districts in Mayo, submitted at the usual Meeting of the Committee held on the 3rd July, 1880.

I HAVE the honour to report that, having arrived in Mayo on the 25th inst., in obedience to a resolution of the Mansion House Committee, I have since made such inquiry in and inspection of the northern district as has satisfied me that the funds entrusted to the various Sub-Committees, in that part of the county, have been well and properly distributed. Everywhere, throughout an area extending over some three hundred square miles, I have found the books produced for my inspection voluntarily, and kept with remarkable fidelity, recollecting the amount of unpaid labour which is involved in their keeping. Abuses in the distribution of relief there may have been at an earlier period in the year, but such abuses, if they occurred, were inevitable. And, on the whole, I have been astonished at witnessing the pains which have been taken to prevent them.

Such singular freedom from misapplication of the funds may be due, in some measure, perhaps, to the fact that the books containing lists of the destitute poor, and the accounts generally, are virtually under the control, if not always in the custody of the local clergy, who, as the destitution deepens in intensity, naturally become more and more alive to the necessity for a strict economy in the distribution of relief amongst the most deserving objects of charity only.

At Ballaghaderreen I found, to my regret, that the Catholic Bishop, who is Chairman of our Committee there, was absent, but his Administrator, the Rev. Mr. STENSON, gave me most valuable assistance in his place. Typhus fever had broken out, and had extended to some ten or twelve families altogether already. Here, as elsewhere, the people were stricken with terror at the proximity of a disease, accompanied by delirium in some of its stages, which might have the effect of depriving them of the consolations of religion at the hour of death; and had it not been for some Sisters of Charity in the neighbourhood, the dead might have been left without burial for an inconvenient period. Two of those ladies had undressed, washed, and coffined a destitute woman the day of my arrival, carrying her remains into the street after extraordinary labour. Theoretically, the Poor Law System is supposed to provide for such an emergency, but practically the poor fever patients who cannot be removed to the workhouse are barbarously allowed to die in their wretched hovels without either nursing or attendance.

In the same manner the Poor Law system provides in theory that no man shall die of starvation, while it will be my painful duty now to report, on unimpeachable authority, that many thousands of human beings would have died of starvation during the past few months except for the relief doled out by the various charitable committees throughout North Mayo during that period; and what the fate of this destitute population must be, should our funds fail before the gathering of the harvest, will be abundantly shown by my subsequent observations. Many thousands of persons—men, women and children—are wholly supported by the charity of these committees throughout the wide area, extending from Ballaghaderreen, in one direction, to Curry, on the borders of the adjoining County of Sligo, on the other; and by another route, as far as Attymas, Ballyhaunis, Foxford and Kiltymagh, &c. The clearest and most convincing evidence has been laid before me that it is to this source alone so many persons are indebted for their existence to this date, and that if the supply be now suddenly cut off, they must inevitably perish during the next six weeks.

Acting in the spirit of the resolution of the Mansion House Committee, composed of gentlemen of various politics and parties, I have been careful not to confine my inquiries amongst any particular creed or class; while, at the same time, I have taken the precaution of seeing with my own eyes many of the recipients of relief in their miserable hovels, which, so far as I have yet observed, are a shocking reproach to the civilization of the nineteenth century. I have sometimes wished I were accompanied by the LORD MAYOR, or Archbishop TRENCH in my travels, though I do not believe that tongue, or pen, however eloquent, could truly depict the awful destitution of some of those hovels. The children are often nearly naked. Bedding there is none, everything of that kind having long since gone to the pawn-office, as proved to me by numerous tickets placed in my hands for inspection in well-nigh every hovel. A layer of old straw, covered by the dirty sacks which conveyed the seed potatoes and artificial manure in the spring, is the sole provision of thousands —with this exception, that little babies in wooden boxes are occasionally indulged with a bit of thin, old flannel stitched on to the sacking. Sometimes even charity itself had failed, and the mother of the tender young family was found absent, begging for the loan of some Indian meal from other recipients of charitable relief—the father being in almost every instance away in England labouring to make out some provision for the coming winter.

Men, women, and children sleep under a roof and within walls dripping with wet, while the floor is saturated with damp, not uncommonly oozing out of it in little pools. The construction and dimensions of their hovels are, as abodes of human beings, probably unique. On the uplands they are mostly built of common stone walls without plaster, and are often totally devoid of the ordinary means of exit for the smoke, as it may also be almost said they are devoid of anything in the shape of furniture. On the low-lying lands, on the other hand, they may be briefly described as bog holes, though by a merciful dispensation of the architect these are undoubtedly rendered somewhat warmer by their very construction out of the solidified peat and mud. Their dimensions are even more extraordinary still, varying from 12 feet by 15 feet down to one half that limited space. Yet all of them are inhabited by large families of children, numbers of whom sleep on a little straw spread on the bare ground, with nothing to cover them save the rags and tatters worn during the day. I invariably found them on the occasion of my visits crouching around the semblance of a fire, lighted on the open hearth. And this at midsummer, shewing how terribly low must be the vitality amongst them.

I refrain from describing more minutely the particular cases of want and destitution which came under my notice. I could not describe them, and any attempt of mine for the purpose would fall far short of the reality. It was only when I was accompanied by a Catholic priest I could get an insight into their appalling character. Alone, some of the most destitute tried to screen from me the poverty of their truckle beds, upon which the straw was often so thin that I could touch the bare boards with my hand. These received me with a dull, passive surprise, wondering what might be the object of my curiosity in so wretched a country. And even the priest himself had occasionally to use no little persuasion to overcome this modest feeling, by assuring them that I was present in the capacity of a friend, only desirous of ascertaining the extent of their poverty. Everywhere the condition of the children was dreadful, having nothing but the Indian meal, badly cooked, to live upon, and the parents only too glad if the charitable funds provided the family with half enough even of that. Sometimes there was a miserable cow about the premises—for, in every case, I am referring to the class of small farmers, mostly residing on three to five acres of land, which in North Mayo is generally found to be reclaimed bog or mountain slope: and this cow was supplying milk, principally *gratis*, to a small number of children other than the owner's, to mix with the Indian meal. Occasionally people appealed privately to my companion on no account to cut off the charitable supplies from the possessor of the cow, seldom worth more than a few pounds, and just then unsaleable in any market, as the animal was the hope of so many little ones. At other times cooked cabbage, without a morsel of condiment save salt, was found where there was no meal, and in some instances one was found mixed with the other. But, in numerous cases, there was neither milk, meal, nor cabbage about the premises, and in those I gave some temporary relief, to fill up the interval till the next general distribution of the Local Committee; yet in the most destitute cases hardly a word of complaint was uttered on the subject, it being a habit with, if not the nature of, the Mayo peasant submissively to ascribe his lot in times of scarcity as well as plenty to the "will of Providence."

Everywhere the Mansion House Committee is spoken of with unvarying gratitude, which is all the more genuine now that people know its funds are nearly exhausted. But, without being invidious, it is only just to mention that the efforts of the *New York Herald* Committee in behalf of the destitute children are also warmly appreciated. Mr. JOHN BARRETT, the District Inspector of National Schools, to whom I am indebted for much useful information, told me, amongst other things, that the bit of dry bread given from that fund brought so many children to school that often in the course of his inspection he could only obtain a way through the crowd with difficulty.

Of course the correspondence addressed to the Mansion House daily for many months past reveals the opinions of the Catholic clergy throughout North Mayo, as to the number of persons in their respective parishes who are in danger of death from starvation, should charitable sources of relief fail. All I can add is, with an intimate knowledge of the general tenor of that correspondence, that it is in nowise exaggerated, and not seldom falls short of the reality. But I made it my duty to call on the Protestant clergy in every district where I could find them. The Rev. Canon LITTLE, who is rector of three parishes, has authorised me to say that, in his opinion, two thousand people in the neighbourhood of his rectory, which is on the borders of Kilmovee, are on the verge of starvation, and that any stoppage of charitable relief before the harvest, must immediately produce what he described as a "catastrophe." The Rev. Mr. CONSTABLE, Rector of Swinford, has pledged himself to me in like manner as regards the still larger population in that district; while the Rev. Mr. COSTELLO, Rector of Kilmactighe, assured me after much deliberation, that at least one hundred families, numbering perhaps six or seven hundred souls, are slowly starving in his parish, as revealed by their physical appearance from day to day, and that any stoppage of charitable relief at this juncture would result in their almost immediate death.

Invariably the Catholic priests speak with cordiality and gratitude of the humane and disinterested co-operation of the Protestant clergy, who are themselves suffering from grievances of their own, in this time of trial; and I cannot refrain from saying that when all the present misery and wretchedness have passed away, they will at least have left behind them many lasting friendships arising out of such co-operation.

The testimony of a number of medical men I have seen is substantially the same, amongst them Dr. DILLON, Ballaghaderreen; Dr. PHILIPS, Carrycastle; Dr. BURKE, Kiltymagh; and Dr. CONRY, Swinford, a young medical officer of the Union, who has entirely too much to do, pending the recovery from fever of another medical gentleman in the district, considering the alarming spread of the disease in and about Swinford. The Catholic clergy, to whom I am indebted for so much valuable information, as well as for their indispensable company in visiting the hovels of the destitute, are the Rev. Mr. STENSON, Ballaghaderreen; the Rev. Mr. DURCAN, Carrycastle; the Rev. Mr. LOFTUS, Charlestown; the Rev. Mr. CONLAN, Swinford; and the Very Rev. Canon O'DONOHOE, of Curry, on the borders of Sligo county, a highly accomplished ecclesiastic, whose testimony is very remarkable. Having observed that he constantly spoke of the destitution as being extreme in the Mayo parishes, and scarcely alluded to his own, in which I thought I saw as much misery as elsewhere, I put him the usual formula at parting, as to what might happen in certain eventualities. He took off his hat for a moment, and, speaking with great solemnity, declared " in the presence of Almighty God," that three hundred and fifty families in his parish would die of starvation.

Yet, notwithstanding this desperate condition of things, the police informed me that there was no crime, small or great, in the district referred to, and a retired sub-inspector of the Force pointed out a large house in Bellaghy, filled from floor to ceiling with the pawned goods of the poor, which, he added, was not even protected by the presence of anyone on the premises at night—such is the unimpaired honesty of this starving people. Everywhere they are clamouring for work, the women and children as well as the men, and force themselves on the baronial contractors in spite of them. In several instances I saw boys and girls of tender years engaged in breaking stones on the roadside—surely the least likely work at which one would expect to find such persons—and without even the wire gauze protection for the eyes, so commonly worn by adults employed on similar labour in England. But the baronial works are absurdly limited in their scope, and cannot furnish any substantial means of relief; while in many cases the contractors being unable or unwilling to pay the labourers at the end of the week, or even a fortnight, the condition of the latter is more pitiable still, inasmuch as their share of the charitable relief may have been, as it sometimes has been, cut off in the meanwhile, on the very natural supposition that they could be no longer in need.

I made it my business to see two or three contractors in person, to ascertain the truth or falsehood of such an incredible state of things. To secure perfect impartiality I selected a Protestant contractor and two Catholic contractors. The first, a Mr. HENRY STEWART, near Ballaghaderreen, told me that public report is only too true; but he had that day (Saturday), out of regard for the destitute condition of the people, gone to the bank, and paid the wages of his workmen out of his own pocket, though when he might be paid himself he did not know. The second contractor was a Mr. DONOHOE, near Curry, also a highly respectable man, who said that when the men first came upon some sanitary works, in which he was engaged, seeing that they were not able to work through want of nourishment, he arranged to pay them in some cases daily in advance, and found that they revived in a wonderful manner with the food which they were able thus to obtain. The last was a contractor near Swinford, who could not get his works "certified," and so could only pay some three out of twenty-two men employed upon them. He endeavoured to obtain a survey from me, but I had by this time convinced myself that as an attempt to provide a substantial means of temporarily relieving a destitute and starving people, the entire system of baronial works, like the system of outdoor relief, is an organised burlesque.*

It is but right to say, however, that as far as Mr. FORSTER, the Chief Secretary, himself is concerned, he is vindicating his well-known character for personal and political sincerity. At Carrick-on-Shannon, before entering Mayo, and everywhere in Mayo itself, I found proofs abundant of his efforts to set the boards and public bodies in rapid motion. But he is dealing with a number of machines running on parallel lines, completely disjointed, which it is physically impossible to make use of for any practical purpose in an emergency like the present. Important officials and leading county personages, whom I am not permitted to name as I have named others, are distinctly of opinion that he should place a sufficient sum in the hands of our well-organised and respectable committees, to provide the destitute with immediate employment under the circumstances.

That some of the smaller landholders are meanwhile themselves very badly off, I had given me many touching proofs; while few of the larger landholders have availed themselves of the government offer of a loan, even where they made a formal application for such, as published in the newspapers some months ago. The same thing happened in 1847, as anyone who is familiar with the history of the period must know; but it is no part of the duty of my report to dwell upon or investigate the reasons, and so I confine myself to stating the fact. Some of the landowners are behaving nobly, as, for instance, Captain ARMSTRONG, who, in his capacity of Chairman of the Tubbercurry Board of Guardians, is also Chairman of the Duchess of MARLBOROUGH's Committee. This gentleman will not allow any tenant on his extensive estate to accept charitable relief, having provided them all with abundant employment, without even troubling the Board of Works for the money. Others, perhaps, are not behaving so nobly, as, for instance, an absentee Irish peer, drawing thirty thousand a year out of the country, whose tenants are everywhere living upon the Indian meal which we have had so much labour in collecting from the four quarters of the globe. And it may not be without interest to remark here, that five of the largest Mayo landed proprietors are absentee gentlemen of rank, whose estates alone extend over an area of 369,000 acres. The Parliamentary returns prepared by the Local Government Board set forth the valuation of this vast acreage, for taxation purposes, as £71,000, which pro-

* For a fuller report as to the insufficiency (and practical inutility) of the baronial works in a crisis like the present, see page 121.

bably represents a rental of £100,000 a year; in other words, a sum largely in excess of the total amount distributed throughout the county by the various charitable organisations during the present crisis. It is no more than stating a fact, provocative of no controversy, to add, that the resident gentry of Mayo have now, as was the case in 1847-8, not only no sympathy with the absentee landlords, but that they would on the contrary, and for obvious reasons, gladly see the system of absenteeism discouraged by the heaviest penalties practicable.

Many of the shopkeepers, as well as the landowners, are behaving with generosity in the present crisis, and it would be very unjust to stigmatise either, as a class, with the want of practical sympathy displayed by some.

The whole country is sown with potatoes and corn to an extent never before remembered, and this is in some measure due to the splendid gifts of seed and manure bestowed on the people by the Catholic Bishop of Achonry, Dr. M'CORMACK, from the charitable funds placed in his hands. The potato crop looks most promising, though the corn has been a little shaken by the prevailing winds and rains. But it is apprehended by all classes of people that the claims upon the harvest are so numerous and heavy, the fruits of it will not be available to the farmers beyond a period of a few months, when the present condition of things must recur, as it would require several prosperous harvests to make up for the losses of the past three years. At Swinford Quarter Sessions, the other day, there were some two thousand processes entered, and it is said the number might have been increased tenfold, if the shopkeepers and landowners were as rapacious as they are often represented to be. But the Judge adjourned the Sessions till October on account of the fever, and has thus mercifully secured the fruits of the harvest, in that district at least, to many. Having taken occasion to inquire of some of the shopkeepers how came it that they had entrusted persons of such small means with so much credit, the answer was invariably the same; it was because they had and have still implicit confidence in the probity of their customers. The probity of the Mayo farmers is invariably acknowledged. It is stated, however, by the clergy, and generally believed, that too many of them have to pay heavily for the favour, which can scarcely be considered an advantageous accommodation under the circumstances.

As to the question of fever, in addition to the cases at Ballaghaderreen, there are some cases at Carrycastle, but it is more widespread at Charlestown and Swinford. It is undoubtedly typhus; yet, where the patients are able to survive removal in an ordinary open cart, without springs, to the workhouse, many miles off, they frequently recover under the humane and skilful treatment which, it is but just to say, they receive in the hospital attached. But still, those who cannot be removed are barbarously left to die in their hovels without nursing or attendance, whether the Poor-law system be responsible or not. Again, at Charlestown, where accompanied by Mr. J. Mulligan, a kindly member of the local Committee, I entered many of the houses for the purpose of personally inspecting them, I found that they had not been generally whitewashed either inside or out, though typhus prevails there to an extent sufficiently alarming. The medical officer at Swinford meanwhile informs me that he is watching two cases near Ballyhaunis which have all the symptoms of what is technically called relapsing fever—that is, real famine fever*—those symptoms being vomiting, diarrhœa, extreme prostration, with that pinched, anxious look said to be so characteristic of the disease, and a "thready" pulse, but without any spots as in typhus. The number of cases of typhus itself in the workhouse hospital is forty-six.

The Board of Guardians has been dissolved, with much advantage to the poor, and even the baronial works are being placed under inspectors, the contractors having been abolished also in the neighbourhood of Swinford. Still, the amount of money to be expended is wholly inadequate as a means of substantial relief, and if gratuitous relief be now substituted, the number and status, as well as the pay, of the relieving officers should be at once increased and improved.

The Mayo farmers had to part with their pigs long ago, and they have lately sustained a severe loss only second to that of the potatoes, which I have nowhere seen noticed. They were accustomed to keep large numbers of hens, whose eggs, taken in exchange for other food by the shopkeepers, helped materially to support their families. During the past ten months, but particularly since January last, the hens have been seized with an epidemic like cholera, and fully 90 per cent. of them have succumbed to the disease, which is fatal in a single night.

It is greatly feared that the people will, in their craving for a change, as well as a sufficiency of food, dig up the new potatoes before they have become fit for eating, and that the result will bring a terrible scourge upon themselves as well, which in their present exhausted state they would be quite unable to resist. I drove twenty-two miles to a large meeting of the Catholic clergy at Bohola, on Wednesday last, upon whom, in the course of conversation, I took the liberty of impressing this fact, with a view to warn their people against such a risk; but the general opinion appeared to be that the risk will be run in spite of all warning, and it was even suggested that the most destitute will ravenously feed upon the potatoes a month before the usual time.

I have only to observe, in conclusion, for the information of the Committee, that I returned to Dublin last night, after exactly a week's travelling through a part of Mayo, which is typical of a great portion of the county, as I believed my report to be of much too urgent and important a nature to be otherwise delivered; but I propose to return to the country after a day or two, for the purpose of inspecting and reporting upon other districts in obedience to the resolution of the Mansion House Committee.

* See Reports of Medical Commission *infra*.

SECOND REPORT,

On the Results of his Recent Inspection of Certain Districts in Mayo, submitted at the usual Meeting of the Committee held on the 22nd of July, 1880.

I have the honour to report that, in obedience to a further resolution of the Mansion House Committee, at their meeting of the 3rd inst., I lately proceeded to Mayo a second time, selecting a different part of the county, for the purpose of inquiry and inspection, from that which occupied my attention on the occasion of my former visit. At Ballyhaunis I had the advantage of meeting the Catholic Bishop of Achonry, Dr. M'CORMACK, to whose splendid gifts of seed I referred in my previous report, and also Mr. HENRY BRETT, formerly and for many years County Surveyor of Mayo, and still holding the same important office in Wicklow County. The Bishop, like every person of position whom I have yet met, expressed it as his firm conviction that, were it not for the merciful operations of the Relief Committees, many thousands of persons must have died of starvation in North Mayo alone during the past six months; and also that, perhaps, even now, we may not be beyond the contingency of a great calamity, arising out of various causes, such as the still possible failure of the potato crop, the general indebtedness of the small farmers to the landlords and the shopkeepers, even if the crop should prove to be a bountiful one, and the absence of useful or remunerative employment for the people during the winter months, to enable them to tide over their difficulties next year.

Mr. BRETT is of opinion now, as in 1847, that public employment should take the form of the reclamation of waste lands, together with the encouragement of a better system of husbandry amongst the small farmers; and I understood it to be his intention to report to this effect to the Government, by whom he is employed on special service in Mayo at the present time. His facts and figures are of paramount importance just now, since even a Land Bill, fashioned upon the lines of the most pronounced reformers, could not bring any immediate accession of prosperity to a population wanting "elbow room," so to speak, and suffering from chronic starvation in consequence of such want. Speaking of the waste lands, he observed, that there are at least four baronies in the West which might afford scope for an early experiment in reclamation, not only without pecuniary loss, but with infinite economic gain to the State, viz.:—

		Average value per Acre.	
		s.	d.
Erris (Mayo) ...	232,888 acres	1	1
Boylagh (Donegal) ...	158,517 ,, ...	1	3
Ballynahinch (Galway) ...	194,584 ,, ...	1	4
Ross (Galway) ...	98,000 ,, ...	1	5

Mr. BRETT, whose long connection with Public Works in Ireland lends the weight of practical experience to his opinions, is clearly convinced that the whole of this enormous acreage, which includes neither deep bog nor mountain top, is capable of complete reclamation. And, moreover, he can point out, he says, "numerous instances in the counties of Mayo and Sligo, as well as in Wicklow and Waterford, of reclamation effected at considerable expense where the produce of the lands in two years defrayed the entire cost of outlay."

As an elaborate proposal of the same character was submitted to Parliament by Lord John Russell when Premier in 1847,—(*vide* Hansard, 25th January in that year)—and was only defeated through the selfishness of Sir Robert Peel, a similar scheme, having for its primary object the introduction of the "idle hands" upon the "idle lands," can scarcely be deemed a thing beyond the domain of practical politics in 1880, more especially since it involves neither "confiscation" nor "spoliation."

There has been destitution and privation in the neighbourhood of Ballyhaunis, Knock, and Claremorris, as elsewhere, but the squalor and misery are not so widespread as in the Swinford district. At Claremorris I visited the Workhouse, accompanied by the Medical Officer, who showed me over the entire place, including the Fever Hospital, in which I was glad to find no more than two patients, one of whom was convalescent, and both technically described as of "simple continued fever." The Workhouse is well kept, and as the Guardians have supplied lime for white-washing purposes *gratis* throughout the Union, where required, it may be that this freedom from fever is due to such sanitary precautions. The Union is supplied with an ambulance, old fashioned, but not uncomfortable, and the employment of nurses to attend the destitute fever patients in their own houses, where they are incapable of the fatigue of removal to the hospital, has been formally authorised when necessary.

The Clerk of the Union favored me with some statistics which will be of interest to the Committee. The number in the house is only 169, but the number on out-door relief has increased from 192, as it stood last year, to 588, as it stood on the 5th June last. The amount of relief given is, however, extremely small, varying from one and sixpence to three and sixpence weekly for each family. Again, in the single electoral division of Murneen, where our Local Committee is relieving 300 families, the Guardians are only relieving four. Amongst the remaining statistics furnished me by the Clerk of the Union, I find what I anticipated in my previous report, that there is the greatest disparity between the amounts applied for by way of public loan, and the amounts finally issued, whether as regards the landowners' private purposes, or as regards the baronial works. In Claremorris Union, for instance, of the £10,970 applied for by the landowners, only £2,780 was actually issued up to the 5th of June, an amount not likely to be increased, since the low rate of interest offered by Government is no longer available. And of the £2,409 applied for, for expenditure on baronial works, only £920 had been actually issued to the same date.

From Claremorris I drove to the residence of Mr. ARTHUR CREAN, J.P.,

Chairman of the Board, and a landowner, who received me with the same courtesy, and even cordiality, which I have experienced at the hands of all classes in Mayo in the course of my inquiries. Mr. CREAN was not in the least reticent in furnishing me with fresh proof as to the terrible nature of the crisis through which we are passing. This gentleman frankly acknowledged that, though his Board had been steadily increasing the quantity of out-door relief since February last, thousands of persons must have died of starvation throughout the Union but for the help afforded by the Relief Committees, the Poor Law machinery being, in his opinion, incapable of dealing with any such widespread and exceptional destitution. The full weight of this testimony can only be estimated relatively, as regards the county generally, by recollecting my previous observation as to the fact that the squalor and misery around Claremorris were not so apparent to me as in other districts. Like the BISHOP OF ACHONRY, and for the same reasons, Mr. CREAN cannot altogether free himself from gloomy forebodings as regards the immediate future, should nothing in the shape of public employment be found for the destitute population during the coming winter.

At Claremorris, as at Ballaghaderreen and Swinford, something like vitality is maintained amongst the convent school children, by the indefatigable exertions of the Nuns in supplying them with food and clothing, in contrast with the sad appearance of those in the ordinary roadside schools, often greatly and unhealthily overcrowded, whose wan and pinched countenances betoken their half-starved condition.

At Attymas I made a house-to-house inspection through a very wretched mountainous district, where the destitution was in several cases so urgent, I had to relieve them then and there with my own hands. The Parish Priest, the Rev. Mr. O'GRADY, showered blessings on the heads of Miss HORT, of the Duchess of MARLBOROUGH'S Committee, and Mr. EDMUND PERY, a local landowner, and High Sheriff of the county, whose benevolence has passed into a proverb. This gentleman being a member of our local Committee, I felt it my duty to call upon him. His testimony was substantially that of others, with this gratifying addition, that having oftentimes investigated alleged abuses in the distribution of the Mansion House Fund, he could never find a single one verified. The condition of the people of Mayo, owing to a variety of causes, was always precarious, he said, and the first touch of misfortune placed them on the very verge of starvation. Last year, he went on to observe, they were visited by a series of misfortunes, namely, a continued failure of their crops including that of flax, and depreciation in the price of stock, together with a falling off in the supplies usually furnished by employment in England; and lastly, an entire stoppage of credit on the part of the banks and shopkeepers.

Of the misfortunes mentioned by Mr. PERY, it is instructive to point out that the depreciation in money value of crops in Ireland in 1879 alone, as compared with 1878, is shown by the Registrar General to amount to £10,014,788; of which the loss on potatoes is reckoned at £4,238,484, the latter crop being estimated at 22,273,520 cwts., as against a ten years' average of 60,000,000 cwts. However widely diffused, such a loss must have fallen with exceptional severity on Mayo.

At Backs the destitution partakes of much the same extreme character, whole families trying to eke out an existence on a single acre of wretched land, lying in patches amongst boulders of various sizes, which often conceal the village hovels even at a short distance. Here, too, I found, on some of the smallest of small farms even for Mayo, unhappy cases requiring immediate relief, while the kind of sleeping accommodation available for young and innocent children, was too shocking to examine minutely. Everywhere around there is the loveliest scenery, and everywhere, also, alas! misery and wretchedness indescribable, and wholly out of sympathy with the beauties of a district singularly favoured by nature.

At Castlebar I called on the Very Rev. Canon M'GHEE, P.P., and the Rev. Mr. DE BURGHE SIDLEY, the Protestant clergyman, both of whom testified as to the fearful consequences which must have ensued but for the operations of the Relief Committees around that district. Mr. SIDLEY, like Mr. BRETT, entertains strong convictions as to the advisability of reclaiming the waste lands, while Canon M'GHEE instanced the clamours of the people about him for employment, by relating how numbers of women even came with hammers to force themselves upon the baronial works. This gentleman, in conjunction with his fellow-members, had taken the precaution, as far back as February last, to call in the services of the Relieving Officers of the Union, for the purpose of preparing a tabular statement shewing the number of cattle, sheep, pigs, &c., held by each individual within the area covered by the operations of our local Committee, with a view to enable the latter to exercise the utmost possible discrimination in distributing relief. The authentic information thus obtained entirely surpassed their very worst anticipations. The small farmers around, it was shown, had been gradually compelled by their extreme poverty to part with everything in the shape of saleable stock with few exceptions.

Here, too, I was introduced to Sir CHARLES KNOX-GORE, Foreman of the Grand Jury, and a large landowner, who spoke to me in the frankest manner as to the perilous time over which we have passed. He, like Mr. EDMUND PERY, volunteered the statement that every alleged abuse in the distribution of the Relief Funds vanished into thin air on investigation. Sir CHARLES thinks a supreme effort should me made to keep the Funds going until the 15th of August, before which date the potatoes will be quite unfit for human food. At Castlebar, also, I called on Mr. JAMES DALY, the proprietor of the *Telegraph*, an active member of our local Committee in that town, and much regretted not to have found him at home, as he is said to be in a position to supply valuable information as regards the condition of the people. Both Sir CHARLES GORE and Mr. STANDISH M'DERMOTT, ex-Chairman of the Swinford Board of Guardians, invited me to call upon them for further conversation, should I be remaining longer in the country, but the time at my disposal was limited, and caused me to lose this opportunity of acquiring additional information from gentlemen of their station.

From Castlebar I proceeded to Crossmolina, where I again made a house-to-house inspection throughout a twenty-two miles' drive. Everywhere I saw evidence of great destitution, though not so extreme as I had witnessed in some other districts. And this makes the evidence of the Parish Priest, the Rev. Dr. COSTELLO, and that of Mr. Joseph PRATT, of Enniscoe, the heir to considerable estates in this and a neighbouring county, the more remarkable. I missed seeing the Protestant clergyman, upon whom I called, and who is working cordially with the Catholic priest, but, as Mr. PRATT is a Protestant gentleman, the evidence of two such independent witnesses may be considered sufficiently impartial and conclusive. It is to the effect that the scenes of 1847, well remembered by Dr. COSTELLO, and often described to Mr. PRATT by his father, might have been repeated as early as February in the present year, but for the Relief Committees, and primarily here, as elsewhere, but for the Mansion House Committee.

Sir CHARLES GORE, who, in his capacity of Chairman of the Board of Guardians, is also Chairman of the Duchess of MARLBOROUGH'S Committee in Ballina, advised me, at parting, to trust implicitly to Mr. PRATT, who is himself a Grand Juror of the county, a Poor Law Guardian, and an active member of the same Committee. The Catholic Bishop of Killala, Dr. CONWAY (Chairman of our local Committe,) upon whom I called to pay my respects, also, like Sir CHARLES GORE, spoke in the most flattering terms of Mr. PRATT, on account of the representations made to him from time to time by his priests. The testimony of such a man is, then, as important as any country gentleman's testimony can well be, and the entire purport and substance of Mr. PRATT'S lengthened conversations with me was as strong, if not stronger, than that of any Catholic priest or Protestant clergyman with whom I came in contact throughout my travels in Mayo. He is most fully in accord with the Rev. Dr. COSTELLO as to the awful crisis through which the country has been passing, and he, with much feeling, expressed it as his firm conviction that deaths from starvation may have occurred, and probably did occur at Crossmolina, shortly after Christmas, in spite of all their precautions. Of one such death at least he was "quite sure"—another proof that the operations of the Mansion House Committee did not commence a day too soon. Mr. PRATT is further of opinion that, however abundant the harvest may be, it will be necessary to provide the people with public employment during the winter months, to avoid a recurrence of the crisis next year; and he also suggested that we should not break up our Committee even when our funds fail, but that we should maintain our organisation in Dublin for the purpose of influencing the Government while any cause for anxiety continues, as at present, to exist.

The last district of which I have to speak is Foxford, where I received every possible assistance in my inquiries from the Protestant vicar, the

Rev. Mr. EAMES, as well as from Major RUTTLEDGE FAIR, a local landowner, both of whom are acting in cordial co-operation with the Parish Priest, the Rev. Mr. O'DONNELL, who was unfortunately absent during the period of my visit. In his absence, I was accompanied in my house-to-house inspection by another member of our Committee, Mr. SHIEL, the Local Registrar, for whose services I feel myself extremely indebted. We visited more than thirty hovels of the poor, principally in the townlands of Culmore and Cashel, in which I beheld scenes of wretchedness and misery wholly indescribable. In some of those hovels evicted families had lately taken refuge, so that the overcrowding added to the other horrors of the situation. In one hovel, in the townland of Cashel, we found a little child, three years old, one of a family of six, apparently very ill, with no person more competent to watch it than an idiot sister of eighteen : while the mother was absent begging committee relief, the father being in England. In another an aged mother, also very ill, lying alone, with nothing to eat save long-cooked Indian meal, which she was unable to swallow. In another, in the townland of Culmore, there were four young children, one of whom was in a desperate condition for want of its natural food—milk—without which it was no longer capable of eating the Indian meal stirabout, or even retaining anything whatever on its stomach. I took off my glove to feel its emaciated little face, calm and livid as in death, which I found to be stone cold. My companion gently stirred its limbs, and after a while it opened its eyes, though only for a moment, again relapsing into a state of coma, apparently. It lay on a wallet of dirty straw, with shreds and tatters of sacking and other things covering it. The mother was in Foxford begging for relief, the father being in England in this case also. In no Christian country in the world probably would so barbarous a spectacle be tolerated, except in Ireland.

It is but right to add, that the mother of one of the evicted families, whose husband was in England, acknowledged with much gratitude some assistance which she had received from the funds of the Land League. And, speaking of evictions generally, they are everywhere frankly acknowledged to be the work, not of the old hereditary landowners, but more commonly of those newcomers who, having purchased land in the Encumbered Estates Court as an investment, are devoid of any sentiment save that of a desire for a profitable return for their money ; though of course there are exceptions, and even notable ones, amongst both classes.

Meeting Captain SPAIGHT, Poor Law Inspector, at Foxford, on my return, he begged it as a personal favour that I would report to him what I might see wrong in my travels through the country. I at once gave him the contents of my note book; but with the distinct intimation that I should here publicly charge the Poor Law System with culpable negligence, and a clear evasion of the Act of Parliament, in not making proper provision for the prolonged absence of the Dispensary Doctor at Foxford. I say "proper provision," because the calling in of another medical man, from a remote Dispensary district, ten miles off, alone probably too large and too populous to receive sufficient attention at his hands, does not constitute any such provision. Captain SPAIGHT, who appears to be very earnest in the attempt to discharge his duties, offered to send milk to the village next morning; but as I had already secured those cases temporary relief at my own hands, I intimated further to him that medical attention, rather than milk, was now urgently required, though not to be had. The Registrar of Foxford informed me that the number of persons actually in, or recovering from fever in the neighbourhood, is at present thirty-five, yet not the slightest effort has been made, up to the present, to whitewash or otherwise disinfect the tainted houses.

Emigration is proceeding rapidly in Mayo, especially amongst the class of single young women. From the parish of Charlestown alone more than eighty had gone, up to the middle of June, while from Backs more than a hundred have left to the present date. Persons in America, who had not been heard of for many years, are now moved by reports of the famine to send money for their friends to enable them to emigrate. And here the question arises, is there no benevolent organisation in existence for the protection of this defenceless class of young people at Liverpool and elsewhere, on their journey to their new and distant home? Surely the good work done by Mrs. CAROLINE CHISHOLM in a past generation should now inspire some amongst her own sex, if not others, to emulate her fame as the "Emigrant's Friend."

Fortunately, the crops have not yet been seriously affected by the heavy rains, though the blight is apparent in many places sown by the old seed-potatoes. I had some dug for inspection at Crossmolina, and cutting through the root with my penknife, found the disease distinctly marked. But there is much confidence that the Champions will escape, for even the stalks resist those strong winds to which those of the other seeds succumb. Elsewhere, as at Crossmolina, the affected potatoes were described as "Pink Eyes," but it is greatly feared that White Rocks, so called, have been imposed upon the peasantry as Champions in many cases.

Passing on to the subject of relief works, I have everywhere found them fitful, wholly insufficient, and otherwise unsatisfactory, as explained in my previous Report. Having a few hours to spare at Athlone on Sunday, I visited the Vice-Chairman of one of our Local Committees, St. Peter's and Drum, who told me that in his district the contractors could not get their works "certified," and so the unfortunate labourers employed upon them were without their wages, while the works were themselves stopped. Yet it is only just to the Government to say, that they are sending many additional officers through the country, to try and facilitate matters, but there is apparently no fixed plan in their operations; while the local bodies are everywhere confused and undecided, or unwilling, in voting additional funds for expenditure. Meanwhile there is unlimited scope for road-making in Mayo, for nowhere else, perhaps, are the public highways so dangerous to life and limb. Yet, at best, even this can scarcely be described as work of a reproductive character, or of permanent utility. Indeed, many of the baronial works which I saw in operation, in the shape of bog road fences, would scarcely withstand a sharp rain-storm, which would speedily reduce them to their original elements of peat and mud. On the other hand, what might be done in the way of reclaiming waste lands is often visible to the eye as well as to the imagination. In many districts through which I travelled I saw patches of meadow and smiling cornfields, where only a few years ago there was nothing but savage bog and moorland.

The great evil of the times in Mayo is not the question of rent, but rather the circumstance that the holdings of the small farmers are deficient in quantity as well as quality. This it is that necessitates the annual flight to England, an evil in itself, to enable them to eke out even a miserable existence on their return. If it could be remedied without injustice to "vested interests," you might have a prosperous and contented peasantry, instead of one whose present condition is a scandal to the Empire. To render that condition less degraded meanwhile, some modification of the existing Poor Law System is obviously necessary.

The smallness of the amount of Poor Law relief distributed in Ireland as compared with England is not generally known. In 1878, 85,000 persons only were relieved in Ireland, at a cost of £990,000, while in England, 748,000 persons were relieved, during the same period, at a cost of £7,688,000. Taking the population of Ireland at one-fourth of that of England, it will be seen that the Poor Law relief distributed in Ireland, the poorer country, is not one-half what it is in England, the richer country.

In conclusion, I have to report that I have everywhere found the books of the Local Committees kept with scrupulous exactness, and the utmost possible discrimination used in the distribution of relief. I was only once called on to investigate a complaint, which was made to me by a shopkeeper at Swinford, to the effect that the Catholic and Protestant clergy had thought fit to employ a paid secretary, at wages of 15s. a week. Believing the complainant's intention to be one of pure benevolence, conceived in the interests of the poor, I proposed to call a meeting of the Committee at once, dismiss the paid official, and appoint the shopkeeper himself honorary secretary on the spot. The proposition alarmed him: he excused himself, and I was suffered to go in peace. I may say that the destitute population of Swinford is enormous; that the Catholic priests and the Protestant rector are rivals in one respect only, as to who shall excel the other in kindness to the poor; and that even the appointment of paid secretary, which was indispensable, was conferred upon the present holder of the laborious office as a matter of business in which charity had some part.

I am much indebted to the Rev. Mr. CONMEY, P.P., of Backs, the Rev. Mr. O'DONOHUE, C.C., of Ballyhaunis, and, in an especial manner, to the Very Rev. Canon BOURKE, P.P., of Claremorris, for assistance and useful information. On this occasion I have not found it necessary to trouble the police with my inquiries; but I have ascertained from the clergy and magistrates that the peace of North Mayo continues unbroken, while the honesty of the starving peasantry is the theme of every tongue. I now invite the members of the Committee to question me upon any point of interest in my Report, so as to afford me an opportunity of verifying my statements by referring to the authority upon which they are made.

APPENDIX TO REPORT,

On the subject of the Baronial Relief Works, submitted at the usual Meeting of the Committee, held on the 12th of June, 1880.

I am desirous of bringing under the notice of the Committee some facts of an important character derived from information lately supplied by our Local Committees in Mayo and Galway as regards the public works either projected or in actual operation in those counties.* On a recent occasion I took the opportunity to cite the County of Cavan as a typical illustration of what might be expected from those works in the way of relief throughout the kingdom. Instead, however, of confining myself to this, an isolated case, I have now gone through the returns from two of the largest, and at the same time the most impoverished counties in the West. Those returns exhibit the question as it stood on the first of the present month, just twelve days ago, and the result will show that no appreciable alteration has taken place since.

We have sixty-four Committees altogether in Mayo, of which all but a few have supplied us with the required information. The total amount of money voted for expenditure within the wide area covered by those Committees is £11,583, while the destitute population more or less dependent on the Mansion House Fund for subsistence within the same area is represented to be 171,493. Assuming that this money was really expended, it would be equal to an allowance of about one and fourpence to each individual on the relief lists throughout the county. But as a matter of fact, in thirty-five —that is, rather more than one-half—of the districts relieved by our Committees, no such public works have been heard of at all; while in twenty-six districts where the money was voted to set them on foot, they had not, for one reason or another, even been commenced on the 1st of June, on which date they were really in operation in three districts in the county only, so far as the information supplied to the Mansion House enables us to judge. The sums being spent in a few favoured districts are comparatively insignificant, as for instance at Kilmaclasser, near Westport, where £64 is to be distributed amongst a destitute population of 1,445 souls. So much for Mayo.

Turning now to Galway, we have returns from seventy-five out of our ninety Committees spread over that county. The facts and figures are in a like

---

* The information in question was contained in returns made by the Local Committees in response to inquiry forms drawn up by Mr. V. B. Dillon, jun., and issued by the Publication Committee.

K

manner equally disappointing. The total amount of money voted for expenditure within the area covered by those Committees is £13,360 9s., while the destitute population more or less dependent on the Mansion House Fund for subsistence within the same area is 132,732. If the money was really expended amongst this population, the share falling to each individual would be about two shillings, or some eight-pence more than the portion of the destitute individual in the adjoining county. But unhappily the story is just the same in Galway as in Mayo. In forty-one—that is, rather more than one-half—of the districts relieved by our Committees no public works have been projected at all; while in twenty-seven districts, where the money was actually voted for expenditure, the works in question had not been even commenced on the 1st of June. The sums to be expended in the few fortunate districts are often equally insignificant in Galway as in Mayo, as for instance, at Annaghdown, where £101 15s. is the portion of a destitute population of 2,000 souls.

But even those figures admit of a further qualification, inasmuch as the works in question, which mostly consist in making or repairing roads, are in many cases apparently entrusted to contractors, who are often represented to us as undertaking them at a price considerably below the sum voted. Again, with regard to the projected works in both counties which had not commenced on the 1st of June, the reply of the Local Committees is often eloquent in its hopelessness. In answer to the query, "When are the works to be commenced?" it is sometimes merely observed, "Cannot say; perhaps never." This was the case at Ballindine, in Mayo, where £200 had been voted for expenditure amongst a destitute population of 3,000. At Cumner, in Galway, the patience of the Committee being exhausted, the reply is, "The works won't commence till a number of people have died of starvation;" while at Belclare, in the same county, exasperated in a like manner by the delay, the Committee having informed us that the long-expected employment had not commenced, add, "And when it will be commenced is only known in Heaven and to the Board of Works."

It has often been cynically observed that a man may prove anything from statistics. I can only say, having gone carefully through them, that the individual who could envolve any degree of hope from these, would be, not a man, but a magician. Even if the public works were in full operation throughout the two Counties of Mayo and Galway—and the information supplied by our Local Committees, show that such is the case within the limited area of some nine parishes only—any hopes that may have been raised as to the probability of their proving a source of substantial relief in the present crisis, are wholly illusory and without foundation. The returns from which I have been quoting are not without their use, however, inasmuch as they exhibit, in a very striking light, the wisdom of the Lord Mayor in refusing to adopt any course which might lead to a premature dissolution of the Mansion House Committee.

REPORT
OF THE
MEDICAL COMMISSION,
BY

GEORGE SIGERSON, M.D., Ch. M.,

Dean of the Faculty of Science, C.U.; Licentiate of the King and Queen's College of Physicians; Member of the Royal Irish Academy; Fellow of the Linnean Society, London; Member of Council of Statistical Society, Dublin; and Ex-Member of Council of British Association; Corresponding Member of the Scientific Society, Brussels; and of the Anthropological and Clinical Societies, Paris, &c.;

AND

JOSEPH E. KENNY, L.R.C.S. (Edin.),

Visiting Physician to the North Dublin Union, and Ex-Medical Officer to the Coleraine Street Dispensary.

PREFACE.

THE prolonged existence of severe distress, of which painful descriptions reached the Mansion House Committee from clergymen of all creeds, medical officers, magistrates, and various competent witnesses, gave early cause for apprehension lest wide-spread disease should supervene.

Soon isolated outbreaks began to be recorded. From Castletown Berehaven, in the County Cork, Canon CARMODY wrote, on the 21st of January, that several farmers were starving, and others trying to eke out life on garbage. "To add to our misfortune," he continued, "we have a great number of poor people here sick of measles, and some also sick of fever. I have every reason to know that several of these poor sick creatures are suffering the greatest privations." The fever epidemic increased as the distress continued, and made victims amongst the medical profession.

At the Committee Meeting of April 14th, a letter was read from the Dean of Ross, announcing the death of Dr. ROBINSON, at Skibbereen, of fever caught in the discharge of his duty whilst attending the sick on Clear and Hare Islands. Mr. LANE JOYNT mentioned that this was the second medical man who had been sacrificed to the relief of the people on the islands named,—Dr. O'DONOVAN, jun., having previously lost his life.

Although the first tidings of the existence of an epidemic of destitution-disease reached the Committee from the South, the sickness seems to have there remained localised, in the most distressed district. The case was different as regards the generally poorer and more neglected population of the Western province. One district after another, not adjoining, but wide apart, reported that fevers had begun to make their appearance amongst the destitute peasants. It seemed as though, when a certain point of suffering from continued privation had been reached, the disease should manifest itself—the earliness of its invasion being, in individuals and in districts, in direct proportion to the degree of distress endured.

The existence of disease was only reported incidentally, and in some localities it had continued for a considerable time before notice came to the Mansion House Committee. The first recorded observation sent from the West, came from Kilmaine parish, in the County Mayo, and was contained in the following terse communication from the local organisation: "The gentlemen of your Committee will best understand the frightful state of this district by simply putting before them the following facts: The fever patients number 103, and such is the fear entertained by the people that we have failed to get a nurse at any payment, so that in order to assist those suffering from that disease, our Committee had to run into debt before they received your last instalment. Our relief list contains 441 families (2,207 individuals), whose destitution it is impossible to exaggerate, and heart-rending to witness."

On May 12th, a communication was made in reference to a grave outbreak of fever along the coast of Galway; over fifty or sixty houses in the large island of Garumna, it was stated, were afflicted with fever. Dr. SIGERSON remarked that, at a very early stage of the Committee's existence, he had mentioned his apprehension that fever would supervene upon starvation. Famine did not necessarily show itself by immediate death. It first showed itself by a general lowering of the system, and by the accessibility of the constitution to various diseases, which would not have attacked people in strong health. The fact that fever had occurred in several places already, and that, according to their reports, it appeared to be extending its area, and to be appearing in new places, ought to make them apprehend that, in a short time, they would hear that fever had become more general in the distressed parts of the country than it was at present; therefore it was their absolute duty, by giving food and by putting pressure on the guardians, wherever possible, to take precautions against the occurrence of those diseases which supervened upon insufficient nutrition. Mr. J. A. FOX, in confirmation of these remarks, mentioned that they had, that day, received four or five reports of fever having broken out in various parts of the country, and in each letter it was stated to be distinctly attributable to diminution or uniformity of food. Further reports having come in, the subject was again referred to, May 28th, and extracts from the Registrar-General's Quarterly Returns of Births, Marriages and Deaths were quoted by Dr. SIGERSON in corroboration. The Mansion House

Committee, in consequence, embodied in its Address this reference to the existence of disease:—" It is a lamentable truth that the fever which follows famine has already made its appearance in several places; and when we recall the ravages caused by it in 1847, this manifestation of the disease naturally gives rise to the most grave apprehensions."

Attention was drawn, on June 18th, to the intelligence published in the medical papers, that Dr. O'DEA had been stricken down with fever at Oranmore, and that Dr. GREALY, temporarily appointed in his place, had contracted the disease, and, after a short illness, had succumbed. In connection with this, Dr. SIGERSON proposed the following resolution, which was seconded by Sir GEORGE OWENS and unanimously adopted:—" That the LORD MAYOR, as Chairman of this Committee, be requested to represent to the Government the services of those members of the medical profession who have fallen victims to epidemic fever, the result of exceptional distress and famine, in order that due recognition of their services be taken, and an allowance be made to their families." This resolution was supported, amongst others, by Mr. CHARLES KENNEDY, and by Professor HAUGHTON, who said that these lamentable deaths, and others which they all remembered in '46 and '47, would lead to a consideration of the general question that must sooner or later be taken up—that is, whether gentlemen occupying positions such as those they now referred to should not be placed in a position similar to that occupied by others in the Army and Navy Department. In accordance with the resolution, a letter was addressed by the LORD MAYOR to the Right Hon. W. E. FORSTER, Chief Secretary, stating the prevalence of disease, and its consequences. "In many cases, the sickness appears to be the direct result of the insufficient and unvaried diet of the poor, dependent for their existence on doles of Indian meal,—in all cases, unquestionably, the extension of disease has been facilitated owing to the great diminution of vital resistance in constitutions enfeebled by privations." From fevers, engendered under these exceptional circumstances of general distress, three medical officers had died, and it was suggested that the State might be fairly asked to recognise their exceptional services by making a grant to the families of those who fell victims. Receipt of this letter was duly acknowledged.*

Whilst this discussion was taking place, the following description of the condition of fever-stricken Charlestown was on its way to the Mansion House, from the Local Relief Committee, the signature of whose Honorary Secretary it bears:—

"I am very sorry to have to say that the state of this poor parish is daily becoming more alarming. The famine fever (and a most dangerous type) is now

* Subsequently a grant was made to the families of Drs. O'Donovan and Robinson, from the Royal Bounty Fund. At its final meeting, the Mansion House Committee unanimously allocated £150 to the representatives of the three medical officers who had fallen victims, to serve both as a recognition of their services and as an encouragement to others who should have similar dangers to encounter.

very prevalent, and making such progress that I fear there will not be ere long a village in all the parish free of it. Of course, the destitute were the first to be visited by this awful disease, but, like death itself, it respects not persons, and very shortly makes its unwelcome visits to the well-to-do and independent. I have seen three pass by me this week to the workhouse, from the little village in which I reside. Only the week before I saw the widow borne to the grave from her orphans, and only the wall separates me from where the wife of a respected member of our Committee lies dangerously ill. Only a fortnight since, on the same day, and forth from the same house went the corpses of the grandmother and grandchild, and the son now lies dangerously ill in the workhouse."

The extension of the disease was commented on and described in the public Press, more especially in the *Freeman's Journal*, which sent a special correspondent to the distressed districts. Subsequently, the *Irish Times* acted in a similar manner. Some persons, in official circles, took objection to the disease being regarded as famine-fever, and propounded certain views. One opinion seemed to exclude the operation of famine, unless mesenteric fever were present; another, unless land-scurvy were noticed; another, if typhus fever were observed. In consequence of this, the subject was again considered at a meeting of the Mansion House Committee, June 28th, when the LORD MAYOR suggested that a Medical Commission should be issued. The following is an extract from the proceedings of that date :—

The LORD MAYOR said, with reference to the fever, he noted that, at a meeting of the DUCHESS OF MARLBOROUGH's Committee yesterday, Dr. GRIMSHAW said it was stated to him that it was not true famine-fever but typhus. *

Mr. DILLON—He said it was reported to him, that means an official report to him as Registrar-General.

* At the subsequent meeting of the Duchess of Marlborough's Committee, the following proceedings are recorded :—

"THE EARL OF MEATH.—Is not typhus fever quite a distinct disease from famine-fever?
"Dr. GRIMSHAW.—Yes, decidedly.
"THE EARL OF MEATH.—Then the fever now prevailing in Swineford is not of the same type as that which broke out after the famine of '47?
"Dr. GRIMSHAW.—Certainly not.
"THE EARL OF MEATH.—I should like it to go forth that such a thing as famine-fever does not exist."

Even as regards "famine" (*i.e.* mild relapsing) fever there was official evidence of its existence. In the Official Return of Births, Marriages, and Deaths, for the first quarter of the year, the following statement appears from the local Medical Officer, Laurencetown Dispensary District, Ballinasloe : " A case of famine or relapsing fever came under my notice last week." Dr. Ryan, Dispensary Officer, New Pallas, reported to the Tipperary Board of Guardians, on the 3rd February, that "whole families were in actual starvation. Famine fever had crept into the district, and he was attending three patients. Two days previously in Old Pallas, a young man aged 21, died of starvation. . . . The poor fellow was on a bed in a dark cabin, with a cup of water beside him. He had no clothes on him. Never did he witness such a sight." On the 6th February, Dr. Laffan reported two cases of starvation to the Cashel Board of Guardians. Others of the Medical Officers have testified to the existence of relapsing fever, as will be found in the accompanying Reports. In the same Quarterly Return, the Medical Officer of Inisbofin, Clifden, relates, "that a woman died, and her death was due to the want of the necessaries of life, at least accelerated by such want." Other cases of deaths, resulting from starvation, were reported in the public press, in the first months of the year, with particulars of Coroners' inquests, and evidence of the Medical Officers,—*e.g.* at Corofin, Kenmare, and Fermoy.

The LORD MAYOR said he really did not know whether typhus consequent on starvation and want was not something very much of the same class, but they had a gentleman on the Committee, who would be pre-eminently qualified to give them information as regards the character of this fever, if he would favour the Committee by going down to Mayo. If Dr. SIGERSON had time to go down and give them information on the subject, it would be exceedingly valuable.

Dr. SIGERSON said the observations of the Lord Mayor did him very high honour, and he would, of course, place his services immediately at the disposal of the Committee, but just for two or three days his engagements would prevent him leaving town; after that time, however, he would be free. There appeared to be a misconception abroad with regard to this matter of disease. It first was mentioned in the *Daily Chronicle*, a London paper, which stated that famine fever was reported from Ireland. The writer said it was to be hoped that this was a mistake—that it was only typhus fever. It would appear from that and other observations that typhus fever was a somewhat benign disease, and, being a common-place disease, could have no connection with distress. That was a most grievous mistake. Following upon famine they might have typhus, typhoid, and relapsing fever. They were different in type, and that was a subject which was, no doubt, highly interesting to the nosologist, but that difference was not a matter of very great importance to the patient suffering under the disease or the country afflicted by such a scourge. They were all catching diseases, and might spread largely throughout the country. Therefore, the difference mentioned did not affect in any degree the principal points at issue. Any of these diseases might occur sporadically and not necessarily as a consequence of famine; they might have "famine fever," relapsing fever, occurring in London, where it had occurred, and elsewhere. It was originally noticed in Scotland, and having shown itself very prevalent in Ireland after the famine, it received the name of famine fever. One question was, whether it had now occurred in Ireland. They had in the Registrar-General's Reports a statement made by one of the local Registrars that he had himself seen a case of famine fever. Typhus fever showed itself during the famine of 1846 and 1847 in great abundance, and that was undoubtedly, a result of privation, starvation, and depression of the powers of mind and body. If that type were somewhat more familiar to us in Ireland than relapsing fever, it was due to the fact that in Ireland the populations in the West, and where it occurred, had been badly nourished. Typhus had not been found in other countries to the extent to which it had prevailed in Ireland. It was practically unknown in France until the time of the Crimean War, and it was rather an exception in countries where the population were well fed. So far from being in any respect a benign disease, from some statistics that had been made in the London Hospital, it was found the percentage of deaths was greater in typhus than in relapsing fever. The treatment in all these cases must proceed on the same principle—the patients required such nutritious diet as they could get, and such things as were opposed to the depression which was produced by these disastrous diseases. It was abolutely necessary to notice now emphatically and clearly that any statement which would seem to suggest that typhus fever was not a consequence of privation was a statement contrary to all their scientific knowledge (hear, hear). And any statement which would go to point out that they could have no fever of any particular consequence in a country unless it were "famine-fever," was also utterly opposed to all their medical knowledge, and he thought they ought in all their statements oppose the granting of the name of famine fever to that particular type of fever known as relapsing fever; the three fevers he had mentioned might all of them be, and unquestionably were, in certain cases, famine-fevers. In relapsing fever the patient retained his consciousness, appeared to recover, and then was liable to a relapse. The other fevers depended, just like it, upon a privation of nourishment, insufficient clothing, and the huddling of the people together, causing the disease to spread. Whether it was relapsing fever in Charlestown or not was a secondary question; the main question was, was it a disease consequent upon insufficient diet and hardships.

A resolution was passed that Dr. SIGERSON should visit the West of Ireland to report on the fever, and authorising him to take another medical man with him as an Assistant Commissioner.

Mr. DRIMMIE suggested that Dr. SIGERSON should visit Oranmore, where it was reported that two doctors had died.

In compliance with the request of the LORD MAYOR and Committee, Dr. SIGERSON, accompanied by Dr. KENNY, preceeded to the West, and the following Reports were transmitted to the Committee.

The Commissioners visited each locality, without giving previous intimation of their intention. In not one instance did they find an abuse of the charitable funds; in point of fact, it was too manifest that the distribution of food was very insufficient both as regards quantity and quality. A few complaints were made, but they came from those who, having some small means, had not been granted relief; and it is highly to the credit of their clergy that, notwithstanding threats of refusing to pay dues, such complaints were possible. They prove that the funds were rigorously reserved for the most distressed. The general resignation, good order, and absence of a mendicant spirit in the districts visited were highly remarkable.

To all with whom the Commissioners had occasion to confer, whose names are recorded in these pages, and in particular to their Lordships the Bishops of CLONFERT, ACHONRY, and KILLALA, the thanks of the Medical Commissioners are sincerely tendered.

These Reports have been printed, in accordance with a unanimous resolution of the Mansion House Committee, at its closing ordinary meeting, August 14th, when Dr. SIGERSON's final Report was read, and the following proceedings took place:—

Mr. DILLON said he had great pleasure in moving that the Report be adopted and printed. It was very desirable that the entire series of Reports that had been presented by Dr. SIGERSON and Dr. KENNY should be printed in a book form and distributed amongst the members of the House of Commons. They threw a great deal of light on the condition of the West of Ireland. He had observed that in the discussion that took place on the previous night in the House of Commons, Mr. FORSTER recognised the value of these reports, and stated that in many instances their recommendations had been adopted.

Sir GEORGE OWENS seconded the motion.

The LORD MAYOR (Mr. E. D. Gray, M.P.,) in his concluding remarks, said:—

To Dr. SIGERSON, Dr. KENNY, and Mr. J. A. FOX, our thanks are also due for their most valuable Reports; and to these gentlemen gratitude is, indeed, due, not only from the Committee, but from the country, for having, without reward, except the reward of their own consciences, given the services they did—who went and personally inspected the localities, and gave us those Reports, the value of which was recognised in the House of Commons and by the Government, who have acted on suggestions of these gentlemen. These Reports will be a lasting record of the work done by this Committee.

PRELIMINARY REPORT

BY

GEORGE SIGERSON, Esq., M.D.,

Member of the Mansion House Committee, appointed to visit the West of Ireland, on the outbreak of Fever in that Province.

My Lord Mayor, my Lords and Gentlemen,

Having, at your request, undertaken to inquire as to the causes of certain fever outbreaks, and their relations to the continued distress, I deem it requisite to place this preliminary statement before you. The question has been raised as to whether or not the fever mentioned is "famine fever;" and from some observations made elsewhere, it would seem that certain speakers consider that but one kind of fever follows famine, and that this must be relapsing fever. Particular emphasis has been given to the denial that the fever admittedly prevailing in some localities in the West is similar to that observed "after the famine of 1847," and the country has been congratulated thereupon, and informed that typhus fever is quite a distinct disease from famine fever. It is important, in presence of such assertions, to place the facts immediately in their true light.

Periods of distress, involving physical privations and mental depression, have been shown, on unquestionable authority, to be accompanied by various diseases. Of these "continued fevers" may be said to be the chief, so far as Ireland is concerned: they have been classified as Typhus, Typhoid, and Relapsing. Typhoid fever, sometimes termed enteric, pythogenic, and mesenteric fever, may be eliminated from present consideration. It is not now in question. MURCHISON, indeed, states that destitution does not predispose to this fever, and that the wealthier classes are more liable to it than the poor; but GRISOLLE has found that, as regards France, misery aggravates the disease, and augments the mortality. It existed during the famine years, though it is nowhere described as the "famine fever."

With respect to typhus, and relapsing fevers, it is admitted that distress acts as a predisposing cause in relation to both. Even MURCHISON, who would connect the latter disease more directly with famine, has declared that "destitution and deficient alimentation are the most powerful predisposing causes of typhus." Of the two, he confesses the latter to be far the more dangerous to human life. "Relapsing, or famine fever," he remarks, "is far from being a fatal disease. As compared with typhus, or pythogenic (typhoid) fever, its rate of mortality is extremely small." Hence we should rather desire that the mild relapsing (or so-called "famine" fever) had made its appearance than regard typhus fever as the preferable visitant.

The following extracts from the report of the Census Commissioners for the year 1851 will show that typhus fever did unmistakably prevail during the years of the great famine. At first, it seems to have held almost exclusive possession of the country; later on, concurrently with it, there came an epidemic of mild relapsing (so-called "famine") fever in 1847: but typhus fever appears to have regained its empire in 1848.

"1845. Prevalent diseases: inflammatory fever, small-pox, and scarlatina. Typhus fever greatly on the increase in some districts, and becoming rife in others."

"1846. Typhus fever raging to an alarming extent in Mayo. In Cavan, great prevalence of 'fever' of 'a fatal kind,' [therefore not to be called 'famine fever.']"

"1847. Typhus fever specifically mentioned at Oranmore. 'Malignant fever' (typhus) widely prevalent. 'The fever embraces various types,— the simple, the petechial' (spotted typhus), 'the typhoid, and the purpuric.' Relapsing fever noticed from Roscommon, Wexford, Cork, and Dublin, as an epidemic. But at the Kilmainham Temporary Hospital, Dr. CURRAN describes the roadside as strewn with victims of 'the terrible typhus.' BASCOMBE writes that 'virulent small-pox committed great havoc, and then typhus prevailed in Ireland.' In the Liverpool petition to Parliament is found the complaint that the Irish immigration to that town produced most disastrous consequences. 'Dysentery, diarrhœa, small-pox, and typhus abound.'"

"1848. The occurrence of relapsing fever is noticed. 'True maculated typhus fever also prevailed to a great extent, and, towards the spring of 1848, altogether supplanted the less dangerous form of epidemic (relapsing) fever.'"

The foregoing extracts will be considered, I presume, abundantly to demonstrate that typhus fever, which, as we have seen, may be a consequence of destitution, prevailed in a predominant manner throughout the great famine period. This, in fact, has already been declared by medical authorities intimately conversant with the diseases which then afflicted the country. Whilst the Census Commissioners, in their above mentioned Report, group, under the head of "famine fever," typhoid, typhus, and short relapsing fever, they also make special mention of the ravages of Irish typhus. Other authorities are still more specific. Dr. LYONS, in his classic work on fever, has remarked that "the spotted typhus, it is well known, is historically associated in Ireland and elsewhere with great famine periods, and a depressed and impoverished state of the population." And in a passage which, though written twenty years ago, might seem to have been composed yesterday, and in reference to recent allegations, he justly observes: "Whilst I admit the frequent occurrence of relapsing fever in Ireland, I must be allowed to record here my protest against the statements recently circulated, on very insufficient data, that relapsing fever constituted the large majority of the famine fevers in Ireland. The contrary of this I believe to be the case; and, having had large and extended experience in the last great famine fever visitations of Ireland in 1846, 1847, and 1848, I can certify that the maculated typhus was the disease which chiefly prevailed, whilst the relapsing fever presented itself only at the close of the great typhus visitation. To cite no other proof: we may note that the deaths from fever in Ireland in the ten-year period, 1841—1851, amounted to over 200,000, a mortality which it is impossible to account for on the supposition that the prevailing epidemic was one of relapsing fever, which is certainly by no means a very formidable or fatal disease."

Finally, side by side with statements made by the Earl of MEATH and Dr. GRIMSHAW to the effect that " typhus fever is quite (decidedly) a distinct disease from famine fever," I would set the following emphatic declaration made by a most experienced and eminent authority, the late Dr. STOKES. Demurring to the limited application of the term "famine fever," he remarks:—" In the epidemic of 1847-8, which followed the disastrous famine of Ireland, the contagious nature of the disease was too well established, as shown by the terrible mortality of the members of the medical profession, and of many of the country gentlemen. Now, if ever the characters of typhus were shown it was then. Every form of continued fever occurred —in thousands of cases—relapsing fever, typhoid or enteric fever, and the worst form of typhus that could be seen."

Having thus made briefly manifest the relations of distress to different types of fever, and to typhus fever in particular, it is obvious that an inquiry into the specific form of fever prevailing in the Western districts must be of secondary importance to the consideration of the conditions in which the disease has arisen, especially if that disease be one so closely identified with periods of destitution and distress as typhus fever. In this investigation, I am happy to say that, using the privilege given me by the Committee, I have been fortunate in obtaining the co-operation of Dr. J. E. KENNY, whose experience as physician to the North City Dispensary district, where much poverty exists, renders his assistance of peculiar value.

I have the honour to remain,
My Lords and Gentlemen,
Your obedient Servant,
GEORGE SIGERSON, M.D., Ch.M., &c.,
Dean of the Faculty of Science, C.U.

3, *Clare-street, July 2nd,* 1880.

DISTRICT OF BALLAGHADEREEN (CO MAYO).

REPORT OF DR. SIGERSON AND DR. KENNY.

July 6th, 1880.

LORD MAYOR AND GENTLEMEN,

In compliance with the desire of the Mansion House Committee to procure an exact professional account of the conditions and causes of the fever which has broken out in the Western distress districts, we have the honour to submit the following as our report in connection with the district of Ballaghadereen. With the cordial permission of Dr. M'DERMOTT, the Medical Officer, we have visited all the cases of fever in the neighbourhood, and we have made a careful inquiry into the circumstances under which they occurred.

The first fact which forcibly struck us was, that all the families in which the disease had shown itself had been compelled to subsist on the relief meal allocated by the Local Committee. The next fact was, that none others of the inhabitants but these distressed families have as yet been attacked. The disease in question is maculated typhus—a disease which, as demonstrated in Dr. SIGERSON's preliminary report, depends most particularly on deficient nutrition, and has been peculiarly associated with great distress periods in Ireland.

The fever showed itself here, as far as can be determined, simultaneously in two places about three-quarters of a mile distant. One is in the town of Ballaghadereen, the other on the elevated land adjoining. In one case, communication with Charlestown is traceable; in the other, no conveyance of infection is discoverable. As this case is of greater interest, we shall briefly note it first:

The K—— family inhabits a cabin about three-quarters of an English mile from the town, in an elevated district. The sanitary conditions of the household are not worse than those which characterise other humble cabins in which no disease exists. This family numbers eleven members, and has stood in need of relief from the beginning of the Committee's existence. Owing to the great pressure of claimants and to limited means, three distribution days passed before it received any relief. Since then the rate of relief has been three stones of Indian meal a-week on three occasions, but usually only two stones per week. No other relief was obtained. Some small quantity of milk was occasionally got from a cow aged from 15 to 16 years. Here a daughter, aged about nine, and the mother of the family, were stricken down by typhus in the order in which they are named, and finally a second daughter. The mother died; the two children are convalescent.

In the case of this family deficient alimentation must be distinctly arraigned as the great predisposing agent in the causation of the fever. The amount of nourishment which each person could derive from the scanty daily dole of Indian meal was plainly insufficient for the support of health, and in the struggle for existence the weakest first gave way to disease.

In the case of the family M——, all the members had been also on the relief list since the beginning, with the exception of one daughter, formerly at service in Charlestown. In this place she seems to have caught the typhus infection, and returning, she, and subsequently her mother and sister, fell sick. Here again, the mother perished; the daughter's recovering slowly. The remaining cases present no facts for special remark beyond the circumstance that, being all in abject poverty, the debility of their constitutions made them fit subjects for the invasion of the disease.

In all, eight persons have been attacked (so far as is known), of whom one-fourth (two mothers) have fallen victims. As the average mortality in the London Fever Hospital is 20·89 per cent., it is obvious that the mortality here (25 per cent.) is in excess of the standard. Judging from the evidence of distress and suffering which came before us in the course of our investigation of the condition of other poor families, we consider there is grave reason to apprehend an increase in the number of fever cases in this locality. The symptoms of physical privation and mental depression were but two frequent.* Most of those persons whom we saw, have had to depend solely on the allocations of Indian meal, without milk or other adjunct; it was a rare luxury when "white water" (composed of a little oatmeal and much water) could be obtained.†

* One example, out of many, may be here given of distress. The F—— family consisted of five persons, of whom the father had recently gone to England to seek work. The remaining four were receiving relief from the local Committee, at the rate of one quarter pound of Indian meal and one quarter pound of oatmeal each daily. They had no milk. The bed-clothes had been pawned to eke out a subsistence. No out-door relief was granted them. Curious to learn how the father had procured money to proceed to England, we made the inquiry. Then only the mother confessed that she had pawned her jacket and petticoat to obtain his passage-money. The poor woman was pregnant.

The rate of distribution of the Indian meal, according to the testimony of the recipients, and of the Rev. Mr. O'Hara, appears to have been about half a pound per head daily; it was sometimes less. Yet, neither in this locality, nor in any other, did the distressed ask us for alms—not in one instance. All seemed sad in spirit: a child was not heard to laugh or seen to play, in wide districts.

† The official report of the Registrar of Frenchpark (Co. Roscommon), another dispensary district of the same Union, gives the following picture of the condition of the people in the first quarter of the present year:—

"The sanitary state of the district is satisfactory; the principal prevailing disease is bronchitis, which is principally caused by want of clothing and food. The privation of the poor is something awful. I have known men to stand working knee-deep in water a whole day, and their only food was Indian meal, and not enough of that same, without milk, or sugar and water even. I have visited patients who were actually lying on peat, without any covering but their clothes." [The Registrar here gives the particulars of one case: a young man in fever, whose mother and three sisters had no bed to lie on, as a specimen of the hardships endured for want of proper bedding accommodation.] "I think the people ought to have oatmeal substituted for Indian, and in cases of sickness money ought to be given to enable the people to buy nourishment, not Indian meal, as it proves injurious to the aged and sick."

We beg to submit the following recommendations:—

1st. In order to prevent as far as possible an increase of fever, it is most desirable that the great predisposing cause here—deficient alimentation—be made an end of. Poor families, in which there are many children, those at all events in most distress, should be at once enabled to obtain an improved and less monotonous diet—that is to say, oatmeal, potatoes, milk, should be supplied them for a few weeks, until the danger be over.

2nd. A light ambulance should be provided for the conveyance of the sick. Nothing of the kind is to be found. Some four or five years ago an old breadvan (in which the sick person was deposited and shut in) was used. It was driven by a ragged lunatic. On one occasion formerly a sick woman was placed in the "well" of a car, her legs dangling out, and so driven to hospital. The only conveyance at present is a common cart. The results plainly must be that the sufferers or their friends will object to removal, and that the physician cannot risk the life of patients by ordering removal, when they are suffering from grave depressing diseases, even though these are infectious.

3rd. It is of urgent importance to establish a small hospital in Ballaghadereen. The dispensary district contains a population of 16,000 persons, mostly poor, and covers an area of 18 by 11 English miles. Some parts of the parish are distant twenty English miles from the Castlerea Union Hospital, and the conveyance of sick persons for such a distance must be often perilous, and in inclement weather almost necessarily fatal. At hand we find a spacious military barracks, which, until recently, was in charge of one or two policemen as caretakers, and in which at present there are but six or eight married policemen. One wing of this might be at once employed, with the best effect, for the purposes of an hospital, and placed under the willing care of the Sisters of Charity. If this were done, there would be no want of nurses, such as now exists; no reluctance to reveal the presence of fever, little trouble in removing patients, and, consequently, far less danger of the spread of infectious disease.

4th. Finally, as on the State devolves the duty of providing for the due disposal of the remains of the unfriended dead, we are of opinion that, where a person dies of the prevailing disease, without willing kindred to provide for his interment, the Medical Officer should be granted power to requisition the aid of one or more policemen, as sanitary assistants, for the purpose. It should be impossible for salaried agents of order to stand aloof, whilst two frail women are obliged, out of charity, to coffin and carry down from an upper story the remains of the deserted dead.

We have the honour to remain,
Your obedient Servants,

GEORGE SIGERSON, M.D., CH.M.
J. E. KENNY, L.R.C.S., &c.

Ballaghadereen.

CHARLESTOWN DISTRICT (CO. MAYO).

SECOND REPORT OF DR. SIGERSON AND DR. KENNY.

12th July, 1880.

LORD MAYOR AND GENTLEMEN,

It seemed to us necessary to remain three nights in Charlestown fever centre in order not only to investigate thoroughly the health-condition of the district, but also to give what medical assistance we could, where it was much required. There cannot be a question as to the distress being here also, the principal, and, in many cases, probably the only cause in the production of maculated typhus—the prevalent disease. All the families whom we visited, and we visited almost all where fever exists, or did exist, were families whose necessities had compelled them to appeal to the Relief Committee at an early period.* There was but one exception, and, in this instance, it was reluctantly confessed that, previous to the outbreak of the fever, this family had been forced to live on only two meals a day. This family and all the others have been wholly dependent on the action of the Relief Committee, whose labours have been incessant, under the direction of a pastor, the Rev. THOMAS LOFTUS, who seems to have been placed here by a special Providence. But for this, Charlestown might have been a charnel-house.

Typhus fever appears to have first made its appearance in the town in the house of the M—— family, all of whose members have been on the relief list since January. Though we made searching inquiries, we could not discover that the disease had been communicated by infection, and consequently we are disposed to regard it as arising here spontaneously

---

* The official report of the Registrar of this dispensary district (Lowpark), supplies the following authentic account of the condition of this locality in the first months of the year:

"I cannot adequately describe the amount of want and destitution I have witnessed in this district during the past two months, and which is fast increasing. The small land-holders are in great straits, their credit gone, and having been obliged to sell the few miserable head of cattle they possessed to keep themselves and families from starvation, and every article of clothing worth anything sent to the pawn-offices. Not one resident landlord, or even one qualified to be a Poor Law Guardian, in the electoral division I reside in. The Guardian lives in another county and union. This being my native place, and knowing the state of this part of the country and the people intimately, I must say their state can scarcely be worse."

In corroboration of part of this description, it may be added that we were much struck by the absence of cattle—the emptiness of the pastures, so to speak, in this and other areas. Grass was going to waste for want of stock. With respect to the portion of this statement descriptive of the exceptional distress, that has received a most painful confirmation in the great outbreak of typhus.

First a child fell sick, then mother, father, and second child, in the order named. A considerable number of other poor families next became its victims.

The character of the disease was markedly shown by its course, which we traced; for whilst it mowed down those whose constitutions had been debilitated by privations, it has hitherto generally spared families in fair circumstances. Sporadically, throughout the rural districts, the maculated typhus has shown itself, in isolated places, remote from the town, where the inmates had remained apart without communication with any fever-stricken person. Here the one thing common to all was severe distress; and here, as elsewhere, it is impossible to avoid coming to the conclusion that deficient alimentation was the prime factor in the causation of the disease. Sanitary imperfections, undoubtedly, are to be found in town and country; but time after time we have had occasion to observe dwellings surrounded by extremely bad sanitary conditions quite free from the invasion of the fever, whilst others at a little distance were assailed, though better circumstanced. The house of M'D——, for instance, at Kilgariff, dark as a cavern and foul as a byre, with a manure pit half full of stagnant water at the door, was devoid of all fever, though it was the worst habitation we saw in this district. Hence we must give to sanitary imperfections a position of secondary importance.

The scenes which came under our notice were often most heart-rending. Take one case:—

Entering one house, fairly circumstanced, we were received by the mother, pale, worn, feeble, scarcely able to move about after a severe attack of fever. Two or three children, convalescents, were sitting in the kitchen, and in an inner room lay, far advanced in maculated typhus, her father-in-law, husband, and two grown-up daughters. Until a few days ago she had to attend to all. Even now, though an old woman had been got as nurse, the sick son had been obliged to take the sicker father into his bed in order to restrain him whilst delirious. This house is worse than a fever ward—it is a fever furnace. The family, throughout this terrible time of illness, have been dependent for very life upon the support of the Local Relief Committee.

Other cases have their own peculiarly painful features. In one, that of O'H——, at Carne, the young husband is a victim; in another, that of J——, the wife lies sick, with scarce a rag of bed-clothes. At Ballintadder, in a musty, dark room, two children were tossing in fever on some straw on the floor, and another ailing on the poor bed. In an adjoining cabin five children had been ailing together; two were up when we entered, and three lying in fever, "heads and points," on an old bedstead, covered with a couple of potato sacks. In the midst of their affliction the father gives a refuge to an infirm and aged sister. It may be mentioned, as adding to the sombre character of the scene, that these people are under notice of ejectment.* We had to leave the car on the high road, and follow a rugged way, made through the bog by the tenants, for the distance of about three-quarters of an English mile, in order to reach their habitations. These two are the only fever-smitten families who have as yet received out-door relief, so far as we could ascertain.

One other case to conclude with. After a drive of three miles from Charlestown to Upper Lurga, over a most uneven road, we came within sight of a lonely cabin on a bleak moor, of which a few acres had been reclaimed. Descending at some distance, we made our way to the place on foot. All was darkness within the house, whence came moans of pain and invocations. Hearing the voice of the owner, D——, saluting us, we requested the window to be opened. There was no window—nothing but a shutter. When this was thrown back we found the earthen floor covered with victims of the destitution fever. At the entrance, their feet near the doorway, lay side by side two grown young women, aged respectively 21 and 19; beyond, with her head almost touching theirs, was a younger girl, aged 14, recovering, but unable to move. On the left hand side, on the floor, lay the mother of the family in her day-clothes. There was scarcely straw enough to keep them off the ground, not enough to hide its hardness, doubly hard to the aching backs of fever patients. What scanty covering they had could not be called bed-clothes. The only person to nurse or attend on all was the worn and wretched parent, aged 50, trembling with weakness from want and watching as he stood, and expecting every hour to be stricken down, when all would be left to die "within the walls." It was impossible to find that they had been exposed to any source of infection. There was no one ill of all they knew; "and why the strange disease should have come to us on this wild moor," exclaimed the mother, "we cannot know; God alone knows." They had been passed over in the first six or seven distributions, and had to sell a little calf to buy Indian meal; their cow had run dry, but they had got, for a little time, some small quantity of milk from one lent by a brother. For months they had had nothing but Indian meal to eat, and brownish bog-water to drink. These are cases of famine typhus if ever famine fever existed.

We repeat that no out-door relief had reached these cases. Throughout the district there was no trace of disinfection, nor could we find any disinfectant in Charlestown, except a minute quantity obtained by a private individual. An infected house still remained, as it had been closed by the chairman of our Committee, not yet disinfected. Our suggestions in reference to this and other matters have, however, been cordially received by Captain Spaight, the Local Government Board Inspector.

Wherever we found exceptional cases of distress, we made a small donation to meet immediate wants, and took measures to secure better

---

* Action was deferred, owing to the postponement of the Swineford Assizes, on account of the prevalence of fever; but the evictions were subsequently carried out.

provisions for the stricken sufferers. The jars of Liebig's Extract sent here by the Mansion House Committee have been of great use. As many of the families in remote parts found it almost impossible to obtain milk (so valuable for fever patients) we telegraphed for cans of condensed milk, which arrived before we left Charlestown, and which will do excellent service.

In conclusion, we lay before your Committee the following suggestions, which we trust will be acted upon by the proper authorities:—

1st. The police should be directed to act as sanitary assistants, and to proceed forthwith to disinfect all places requiring disinfection. They should likewise be required to help in the removal of the sick, and not make it necessary that the pastor should himself have to carry out patients.

2nd. Charlestown should be recognised as a fever centre until the time of danger be past. A vice-guardian should reside here to keep all subordinates active. An assistant medical man ought to be appointed, and a small temporary hospital might be fitted up, with a proper staff of nurses, not now to be found.

3rd. The sick should be immediately supplied with milk, flour, and oatmeal, and some stimulants; the diet of the convalescent families should be other and better than Indian meal, if they are to recover; and the dietary of the distressed should be universally and at once improved, if the extension of this terrible disease is to be arrested.

We have the honour to remain,
Your obedient Servants,
GEORGE SIGERSON, M.D.
J. E. KENNY, L.R.C.S.

Swineford.

SWINEFORD AND FOXFORD DISTRICTS.

THIRD REPORT OF DR. SIGERSON AND DR. KENNY.

July 16th, 1880.

LORD MAYOR AND GENTLEMEN,

If disrespect for sanitary precepts sufficed of itself to cause the production of maculated typhus, that disease should be endemic in Faheens. This hamlet, which is within a few miles of the town of Swineford, is unique of its kind. No road nor lane leads to it, nor are any streets to be found within it. On leaving the highway we had to get over two or three fences, follow the course of a stream, traverse a field path, and finally (under a heavy shower) we crossed the wall of a mire-pit, trod along its margin, and were at once in the centre of an irregular group of cabins. Each cabin has its midden-stead or manure-pit, the narrow borders of which serve as paths. There are about forty habitations, some huddled together, others straggling apart.

Now, contrary to all pre-conceived theories, this hamlet has been remarkably free from fever for a number of years. Testimony to this effect is borne by the energetic clergyman, the Rev. Mr. CONLAN, who, during the four years of his mission here, knew of but one case, and that in the vicinity of Faheens. MAURICE C——, himself a convalescent, recalling this case, marks it out as an exception in his long experience as a resident in the village. The professional knowledge of Dr. O'GRADY (fortunately recovering from an attack of typhus caught in the zealous discharge of his duty) confirms this evidence, during a decade of years. Though to some it may appear strange that such a thing should be, it will not surprise those who have read the account given of a very similar hamlet* in the pages of STOKES, and who recall the pointed admonition to sanitarians by that illustrious authority, warning them against permitting theories to take precedence of facts. †

---

* Similar, but much worse, for "where the tenement had not the casement of a dung-pit or yard, or right to part of the common way, the manure was stored *in* the dwelling-house. But nevertheless, this town has always been a remarkably healthy place." It is suggested that there were two great advantages in favour of health:—an ample supply of the very best water, and smoky houses—peat smoke having antiseptic properties.—Stokes' *Continued Fevers*. Appendix A. London: Longmans. 1874. (Edited by J. W. Moore, M.D.)

† Discussing the causes of fever (cap. V., *loc. cit.*) Dr. Stokes expressed his belief that "too much stress had been laid upon miasmata resulting from imperfect drainage, or the want of ventilation, and of public cleanliness in general." They may, he admits, deteriorate the physical and moral condition of the people, and so help to increase the mortality of an existing epidemic. There is, he points out, a tendency in many minds to attribute great phenomena to too limited a cause or causes. Thus, some form of essential disease arises and spreads, imperfect sewerage is discovered and the evil abated; then "the sanitarians triumphantly appeal to the circumstance as proving that the outbreak was the direct result

What, then, has been the cause of the outbreak of maculated typhus in Faheens, since sanitary disrespect did not produce it? Not infection, we find; for the person in whom the disease first appeared, Mary C——, and who died of it, was noted for her home-staying disposition; whilst the village, on account of its secluded position and poverty, has little intercourse with other parts. The adult males (here as elsewhere in Mayo), being generally away, labouring in England, do not, of course, go forth and return daily. Owing to their absence, the women and the children (when these are not at school) are engaged either about their houses or in field and bog work in the vicinity of their homes. There is but one element discoverable making this season to differ from preceding seasons, and that element is the pressure of exceptional distress.

The victims to the disease here, as in other places, were those whom want compelled to appeal to the local relief committee. On the dole granted them, and on that alone, had the family subsisted in which the fever first manifested itself. The Committee, owing to the great demands of a large parish, was unable to give this family of five persons more than two stones weekly of Indian meal, and they themselves could not procure milk. Of the five, four fell sick, and two of these four died. It is superfluous to add that such results must be attributed to the very deficient alimentation.

Once a focus of fever has been created, it is, of course, likely to spread by infection and thus the disease extended through several families in Faheens, whose names were amongst the first on the relief lists. At Cullaun, likewise, where the fever appeared early, the family had been forced by misfortune on the relief list at the very beginning of the year.

Now, as a counter test, we may refer to certain habitations in the town of Swineford. There are some cabins here whose unsanitary conditions rival, if they do not exceed, those of the houses at Faheens. Some are sunken under the level of the street, green and grimy externally; dark, dirty, and smoky within; whilst a few feet from their doors stretches a decomposing dung heap. There has been no fever in these. Neither has there been fever in others, small, overcrowded, and foul to look at, which are to be observed in another direction. The inmates, though poor, of these town cabins, have not had to suffer the extreme privations of their rural compeers, and have thus escaped the inroads of the fever, although the unsanitary conditions of the cabins were equal in all.

of the alleged nuisances, and perhaps of them alone. By this line of argument many sanitarians, who have not received a scientific education, and who know but little of the history of disease, hold that such removable influences may originate diseases, which are themselves dissimilar. But the question before us is: Are those influences in this country the sole or the chief cause of fever? It is difficult to believe that they are, "because, in poor dwellings in Ireland, where such influences are but too constant and too general, the production of fever, whether sporadically or epidemically, is inconstant and irregular in the highest degree. Why should these causes produce fever at one time, and not at another? Why should districts remain for years free from fever, whilst the supposed exciting cause remains in full force? Or, again, why, if the cause be constant, should the epidemic character of the fever vary?"

Having procured lists of the admissions, ages, and deaths of fever patients admitted to Swineford for the past month, we have carefully tabulated them, taken per-centages, and compared the results with those recorded by MURCHISON. Children taken with typhus generally escape death—a circumstance familiar to Irish physicians—but we regret to be forced to the conclusion that for patients of more advanced years, these tables show a greater mortality than the standard named. This is manifestly the case if we compare the results which concern ages above twenty, and very markedly evident if, eliminating ages above sixty, we compare facts relating to ages from twenty to sixty. As we cannot doubt that due care was bestowed on the patients in hospital, we must infer that their constitutions, even in the prime of life, were so enfeebled by lack of sufficient food as to diminish their chances of recovery.

Swineford, a passably prosperous town, is well-nigh free from typhus. The cases which we have seen in its environs are convalescent. In the Foxford district we have seen several convalescent cases, and some still suffering. Before leaving the latter locality the discovery of certain other cases of typhus fever was reported to us. It should be added that disorders other than typhus fever may result from insufficient nutrition. Gastric troubles of various kinds may first show themselves; these we found numerous in the Charlestown district. Then, at a more intense degree, come dysentery, diarrhœa, and typhoid, of which we found numerous examples in the Swineford and Foxford districts. The history of the cases uniformly showed that the sufferers, children in most instances, had been compelled to subsist for a long time on Indian meal porridge, without milk. It gives us pleasure to bear our testimony to the courtesy, goodwill, and humanity of the vice-guardians, and the medical and lay inspectors of the Local Government Board. The reforms now made fulfil, to a certain extent, the desires already expressed in our reports, and some suggestions which we took the liberty to offer have been promptly acted on. Disinfectants have been sent over in quantity to Charlestown, and an improved diet has been ordered for the sick and convalescent. On our arrival at Swineford, we found that the dietary of the distressed had been judiciously varied by the allocation of one third oatmeal to two-thirds Indian meal. At Faheens, however, the inhabitants informed us that they had, up to the day of our arrival, received nothing but Indian meal, insufficient in quantity, from the relief officer. The vice-guardians have ordered that this be rectified.

We are, indeed, happy to state that, whatever theories may be afloat, the authorities here act upon the principle that a variation of the dietary, and more and better food, are the best remedies against the increase and extension of the destitution-diseases. This is the principle we have advocated; at the same time we desire to see a more common use of disinfectants, to prevent spread of fever by infection, and we trust that the houses at Faheens and elsewhere will be promptly disinfected. For that purpose, we would again recommend that the services of the police should be availed of.

From whatever cause, whether from over-work, want of system, or want of good will, the relieving officers do not (in certain instances) appear to carry out efficaciously the task laid upon them. In some cases we have found families fairly relieved and duly grateful, in other instances families have been apparently overlooked. Nor is it becoming that crowds of women from rural places should remain all day, and late into the night, beseeching aid in the town. All who merit assistance should be promptly relieved in the forenoon, and all others dismissed at once.

We have the honour to remain,
Your obedient Servants,
GEORGE SIGERSON, M.D., Ch.M.
J. E. KENNY, L.R.C.S.

Ballina.

P.S.—We regret to state that the death has been reported to us of the poor mother whose exclamation in reference to the strange disease coming to them on the wild moor we noted in our last. Before dying, at all events, she had something better than bog-water to moisten her parched lips.*

---

* Unhappily, we are informed, her two elder daughters have since fallen victims. Thus, out of that family of five persons, only the aged father and his youngest child survive.

DISTRICTS OF BALLINA AND KILLALA.

FOURTH REPORT OF DR. SIGERSON AND DR. KENNY.

19*th July*, 1880.

LORD MAYOR AND GENTLEMEN,

Wherever we pass, we find, as a rule, that many more cases of destitution-diseases exist than have come under the cognizance of the officials. Their reports, consequently, do not always give an adequate idea of the amount of sickness prevailing in a given area. Families, stricken with fever, are very reluctant to make the fact known, because all intercourse with their neighbours would be immediately stopped. They would be regarded as plague-stricken, and their houses avoided by all. Hence they do not, in very many instances, inform even the Dispensary Medical Officer, and thus numerous cases may exist over a large district, whilst only a very few have been brought under his notice.

Thus, in one of the districts which we examined (Charlestown), we found it stated that there was but one case of fever present; within this same area we ourselves witnessed nineteen victims of fever (distinctly maculated typhus in every case, save two). These were confined to bed. In addition to these, within the same district, we investigated the circumstances of seven families, who, having suffered from typhus fever, had members convalescent indeed, but still presenting in their enfeebled frames the after-consequences of the disease. It is quite plain that, to judge from the facts concerning this district, official statistics relating to disease lack a solid foundation. Let it be understood, however, that we do not give this as a type of what occurs elsewhere: we mention it here to emphasise our statement regarding what we have observed in other localities, namely, that many cases of destitution-disease do exist which are not on the official register. This fact will, we believe, be frankly acknowledged by the Medical Officers themselves.

The health of the inhabitants of Ballina was considered to be so good that, on Saturday, July 17, the Guardians contemplated dismissing the assistant relieving officer. On the previous day, however, the Rev. Mr McNULTY having mentioned to us the names of ten families in the vicinity of the town, of whom thirty-eight individuals were fever victims, some lying, some convalescent, we proceeded to inspect several of these families. Within a mile of the town we entered the cottage of W. B———, by the road-side. On the left, lay the emaciated father, still unable to rise, and a daughter aged nine, in maculated typhus; on the right, lay the mother, struck down a day or two before by the same disease. A sick infant occupied the cradle, and another child, recently suffering from fever, was able to go about. The man had, like others, concealed his distress in the beginning, and only got relief-meal from the Committee in February. They had had no milk, and were able to obtain only an insufficient amount of Indian meal; sweetened water, or weak, cheap coffee replaced the milk for the children. It was then remarked by those who brought the aid that the semi-starved baby was covered with long, downy hair on the face, arms, and hands. We note this because (though unknown to those who narrated it) such a growth was occasionally observed in victims of disease during the great Famine.

In this family there are eight persons in all, utterly helpless. The amount of out-door relief they have received during their illness has been at the rate of two shillings and sixpence a-week. This, of course, is quite insufficient to provide an adequate supply of proper nutriment for such an afflicted family. Without going into further details, we may say that the other cases visited were found to be more or less similarly situated.

All have been recipients of aid in Indian meal from the beginning; and to the fact that the dole here has been somewhat larger than in certain other districts we attribute the comparatively slight mortality. Indian meal, however, even when sufficient in quantity, has not approved itself capable of sustaining healthy life by itself, or with the scanty adjuncts obtainable by the distressed. This we find to be likewise the opinion of Dr. SCOTT, the Dispensary Medical Officer of Ballina, who has observed the occurrence of fever, in previous years, at seasons when the poorer families were reduced to Indian meal as a continuing diet. In connection with this subject, it should be borne in mind (when previous fevers are mentioned) that for the last two years the peasantry suffered severely, and that the registry of last year presented an unexampled rate of mortality. The beneficent intervention of Relief Committees has prevented that excess of deaths from being this year exceeded.

We are happy to say that the Ballina Guardians, on being apprised of the true state of things, receded from the intention of dismissing the assistant relieving officer, and have given directions in favour of liberal relief, which, it is to be hoped, will be duly carried into execution. The economic advantage of prompt assistance in cases where infectious disease afflicts the poor ought to be thoroughly understood. Want of such aid may cause the spread of the disease in ways that we have already mentioned, and in the following manner:—When, early in spring, K—— died (of fever), the family took the blanket from his bed and pawned it, in order to procure money to bury him. Another instance of the same kind is reported to us as having happened last autumn, when the bed itself was pawned. Of course, these articles had not been previously disinfected by the hapless poor. It is unnecessary to point out how such actions may be efficient in spreading disease.

To Kilcummin and Rathlacan, a distance of about fifteen English miles, we proceeded on Saturday, from Ballina, passing through Killala. The Board of Guardians here appeared to be under the impression that the health of the Union left little to be desired: a careful examination of the state of the localities, named above, has, however, led us to entertain a directly different opinion as regards these areas.

At Kilcummin we observed four or five cases of fever, and here the type seemed to vary from that we had hitherto studied, and relapses to show themselves, as noted by Dr. McNulty, the efficient Medical Officer of the district. These patients, though in distress, and on the Committee lists, were somewhat less badly off than those in whom maculated typhus, without relapse, had been observed. The relapses came on without being traceable to dietetic errors. It has been remarked by the gentleman named that here, and at Foghill, fever prevailed before the distribution of relief; that it diminished as aid was granted, and that it began again to show itself when the amount of relief given was decreased.

Rathlacan surpasses any village we have yet seen for the number and variety of the fever cases within it. This irregular group of cabins is situated on shelving rocks, sloping towards the entrance of Killala Bay, at its western side. Its position ought to enable it to rank amongst the healthiest of hamlets. The houses number about forty-five, nearly a hundred fewer than in former times. The evening had fallen when we visited it, and thus all the inmates were at home. Rocky ledges and loose stones form the streets. In the centre of the village is a well, not altogether free from the suspicion of soakage. Passing from cabin to cabin, we discovered, with interest and surprise, that the hamlet might be regarded as a museum of assorted fevers. Maculated typhus in one house was followed by typhoid in the next; a third showed an example of fever with relapses; and a fourth a specimen of dysenteric diarrhœa. There were, in all, eleven cases of fever, where the persons were confined to bed; two cases of convalescence from fever; and two or three cases of other ailments in this unduly portioned and strangely fortuned village. All the families have been receiving aid, in Indian meal, from the Committee, since its beginning; and are manifestly very poor, though the men combine fishing with cultivation of small plots of ground. Milk was rarely and but scantily to be had. Only one family in this village had been reported as sick to the active medical officer of the district, Dr. Madden, who promptly saw the patients and ordered relief.

On investigating the matter, we learned with amazement, that the guardians diminish considerably the relief ordered, after the first week,—so that the sufferers are deprived of due nourishment when they most require it. Rathlacan is some eight English miles from Killala; and we are informed by the Rev. Mr. CONWAY that the most remote parts of the district are nearly twenty-three English miles distant from hospital. But there is no vehicle save a common, springless country cart, for the conveyance of patients. The Rev. Mr. NOLAN, Chaplain of the Union Workhouse, informs us that there is no place for fever patients there, except a disused ward over the chapel, frequented daily by the inmates. It would certainly be a perilous experiment to attempt to place them there, but all such danger is avoided in a very effective, but singular manner. Dr. MADDEN, Dispensary Officer of Ballycastle, has stated to us that he was informed by Mr. JAMES MAY, Relieving Officer, that the latter had received directions not to admit any fever cases into the workhouse, as there is no fever hospital in the Union!

This is beyond comment. If prompt measures be not taken by a liberal increase of properly varied food to the yet healthy inhabitants, and of appropriate nourishment for the sick, Rathlacan will soon be a thorough plague-spot. Due sanitary action should be immediately taken, and carefully carried out. Utterly deficient alimentation and imperfect sanitation combine to create the diseases here. In connection with this subject, it may be added that the condition of the poor would have been much bettered had the work of pier-building on the neighbouring shores been commenced.

From Rathlacan we crossed Killala Bay to Inniscrone, in which several new cases of typhoid, or enteric fever, have appeared within the last few days. There is here a startling absence of sanitary care on the part of the authorities, whose neglect should be at once remedied, and a due amount of out-door relief given where at present it is denied. In relation to this district, we shall make further observations in our next report.

We have the honour to be,

Your obedient Servants,

GEORGE SIGERSON, M.D., CH.M.

J. E. KENNY, L.R.C.S., ETC.

Castlebar.

DISTRICTS OF INNISCRONE (SLIGO) AND LOUISBURGH (CO. MAYO).

FIFTH REPORT OF DR. SIGERSON AND DR. KENNY.

July 26th, 1880.

LORD MAYOR AND GENTLEMEN,

INNISCRONE, a favourite watering-place in the West, is well situated on the eastern shore of Killala Bay. Its position, like that of Rathlacan on the opposite side, should entitle it to a more than usually fair bill of health. The land slopes downward towards the sea, the cottages are somewhat cleaner than others we have seen, and the people in ordinary years must be rather better-circumstanced. Nevertheless, this hamlet and the adjoining area have suffered vastly from fever (chiefly typhoid) throughout the past season. Some cases occurred in the closing months of last year; but the disease began to show its greatest severity after the end of January. In the small hamlet of Inniscrone the fever visited twenty-four houses, where thirty-one females and forty-seven males have suffered from its presence. Of these (including one case close by) four persons have died. At least as many more have been fever-stricken in the adjoining district.

It is a noteworthy thing that all who have suffered from fever, with scarce an exception, had been suffering from distress. Their names are on the list of the Local Relief Committee. It is, therefore, imperative to conclude that insufficient alimentation here again has acted as the chief predisposing cause. The distribution of Indian meal was, owing to straitened means, necessarily irregular, and often very scanty. Milk was rarely to be had. Out-door relief was seldom given, and (it was stated) only to those who could work. Again, the wages of many who did labour were, in case of State-aided works, withheld from the labourers for rent arrears. Hence such work did not add to the resources of the distressed, who were compelled to subsist on what charitable doles of Indian meal they could obtain. As a consequence, there was great moral and physical depression in the district. In the village we observed the most marked neglect of due sanitary care on the part of the local authorities. An open sewer passes by the road-side, close to a well, along a number of cottages, the inmates of which have to step over it before reaching the highway. Typhoid fever had shown itself in these cottages, finding a ready prey in the enfeebled constitutions of the inhabitants, and extending in the usual way.

The M—— family dwell near, in a neat, clean cottage, fairly furnished, and not overcrowded. Two of the younger members, we were informed, had just recovered from the disease; four were lying when we entered: the father, in febricula, his son, aged fifteen, and his two daughters, aged respectively seventeen and twenty, suffering from typhoid fever. There had been no aid given by the Relieving Officer. There were no disinfectants used. Commenting on the existence of the sewage stream and pools, we were informed by the Rev. Mr. IRWIN that, at the March Extraordinary Presentment Sessions, he had called attention to this nuisance, but all action with regard to it was refused. We cannot doubt that such strange neglect must bear the blame of having contributed to the extension of this deplorable disease. Another instance of unwise parsimony must be mentioned in the refusal of the Guardians of Dromore West to appoint an assistant relieving officer to a district which, extending over four parishes, was so severely stricken with fever. It is self-evident that one individual could not attend to the wants of such an area, if its inhabitants had been properly relieved. They were not, and the disease had full sway.

The food of the distressed should have been promptly improved, and a suitable dietary supplied to the sick. Generally, we were informed that no relief was given to the fever-smitten. At Corballa, we found that in the case of the family of B——, a small sum was given; the family numbered nine members; when eight of these were sick, a dole of three shillings and fourpence was granted—being about one-fourth of what the Swineford Vice-Guardians considered necessary in a case where seven members of a family were ill. Near at hand we found another fever-case, that of the girl C——, which had not been reported to the Medical Officer. No outdoor relief had been received, and we were pitifully told that the yellow meal did not agree with her, it "turned on the stomach." The mother had been sick, and the father died after four days' acknowledged illness. There are, probably, many such cases which have not been reported.* With respect to the type of disease prevailing in the district, it has been principally typhoid fever; there have been some instances of typhus, however, and we have noted certain cases which presented the characteristic symptoms of relapsing, or so-called famine-fever. The patients had experienced pains, green vomitus, and perspired profusely; there was temporary convalescence, and, then, after an interval, a relapse supervened. In one instance, the symptoms during the relapse were more severe than on the first invasion of the disease.

---

* From the Rev. Mr. O'Hara, Adm., a list of thirty-eight fever-stricken patients has been received, being the number which came under his notice since his arrival in the parish of Castleconnor, May 8th. Other cases, however, had previously occurred. "There is no attempt whatever," he writes, "made in the direction of nursing these patients, and as to removing them to the Union hospital, seven miles off, it is never thought of. In fact, I am told it would take a pair of strong horses to draw the Workhouse ambulance, and I am not aware of its having been ever used."

Inniscrone is almost eight English miles distant from the Union Hospital (Dromore West); the most remote part of the district is about thirteen miles. As in the Killala Union, there is no conveyance but a common country cart.

LOUISBURGH.

On our way to this region, we were informed that some cases of fever had appeared at Clonkeen, near Castlebar. It was further stated that the Rev. Mr. WALTERS and Dr. LYDON have themselves been obliged to coffin and carry out the corpse of a person named D——, who had died of the much-dreaded disease. At Louisburgh, we were told that a magistrate's order having been issued for the removal of the fever-patient K——, the Relieving Officer asked help from the police, which was refused.

This district appears to have suffered to an almost similar extent with Inniscrone. One hundred and twelve persons are known to have been affected with fever, and of these six died. It is acknowledged in this, as in other localities, that many cases have, in all probability, been concealed. Dr. GRIFFIN tells us that he believes there were many cases to which his attention was not called. As to the cause of the disease, he has no hesitation in ascribing most of the cases to improper alimentation, whilst not overlooking the action of sanitary causes. At present there are but few confined to bed, but there are many convalescents throughout the district, who require a dietary that they cannot get. At Culaghan, we visited the O'M—— family, regarded as in better circumstances than many. First, a child took sick at school; the disease extended, till four members of the family were prostrated. The father died of the fever, and the widow is striving on with the aid of her children, the eldest, a girl, being eleven years of age. A boy, still unwell, is partly able to sit up. To reach this hamlet, we had to cross over fences, bogs, and rock-ledges, for there is neither road nor lane to Culaghan. In many cases, it appears, all or nearly all, the members of the families attacked were prostrated by disease. In four instances, five members were stricken; in two instances, six; in one family, eight suffered; and in another, that of F. D——, the father, mother, and the ten children were all smitten by the fever. The type of fever which principally prevailed was typhus. Some cases of relapsing fever were observed by Dr. GRIFFIN, at Coolacoon, and we noted its occurrence, in the case of B——, at Finnue.

As regards the question of relief, none of these sorely-stricken families, save four (of whom two were soon put off the list), obtained any out-door relief. They had all been on the lists of the Relief Committees for months before their sickness; and, with the few exceptions mentioned, they had only this charity to depend on throughout. The Relieving Officer (a bailiff on the estate of a great absentee proprietor) had, we found, earned the thanks of distressed families by suggesting their names to the Local Committee. The Rev. Mr. JOYCE informed us that the same official (personally humane) was directed to attend meetings of the Local Committee, and to remove from the list of out-door relief the names of such as received relief there. That list, however, must be in miniature. Public and sanitary works are much required, especially at Louisburgh, where the people are still drawing water from the river, below the out-fall of a small open sewer. One well appears to be judged sufficient to supply the wants of the township. Perhaps the most painful circumstance in connection with the question of destitution-disease, in this area, is the fact that some of the first cases of fever showed themselves amongst the children at school. It was stated that they brought home the fever with them. The schoolmaster, himself, a man extremely prudent, caught the infection from them, and died of it. Struck by a circumstance which differentiates this district from others already visited, we made inquiries, and found that this locality, unlike the rest, had received no grants to provide food for the school-children. The coincidence is too marked to be accidental. There is a lesson here, which, we trust, will be borne in careful remembrance.

The vast extent of this district, including as it does some islands, and the rugged character of large portions of it, render conveyance of patients to Westport (a long day's journey from Gowlan), a thing practically impossible. A cottage hospital at Louisburgh would be of undoubted service.

The potato blight has, unfortunately, made its appearance here to a very considerable extent. Even the Champions show spots on the leaves and decay at the roots, but not to an alarming degree as yet.

GALWAY COUNTY.

DISTRICTS OF OUGHTERARD, ROSMUCK AND CARRAROE.

Judging from what has come under our own observation, there has been much more effort made to provide, by public road works, for the employment of the distressed and the improvement of the county in Galway, than in Mayo, where it is much required. In the southern county, also, there has been a certain amount of out-door relief granted, which, however, has been inadequate to the necessities of the time. Here, as in Mayo, it is evident that numbers would have perished but for the prompt action of the Relief Committees. The distress, of course, must continue until August ushers in the harvest, and, it is feared by competent authorities, that disease will re-appear or increase if the peasantry are obliged to have recourse too soon to the unripe tubers, especially when unable to obtain meal. With these preliminary observations, we now proceed to refer to special localities:—

OUGHTERARD.

In this district the Medical Officer, Dr. BRERETON, informed us that he had not this year remarked any cases of purpura hæmorrhagica (land scurvy), which he noticed here previously. On the other hand, there has been a large number of cases of typhus, typhoid, "gastric" and scarlet fevers, and some diphtheria, which appears to have been very fatal. The number of visiting tickets had, in a given space, increased from thirty to eighty-four, or nearly threefold, and a medical assistant would, we were told, have been of advantage. From the Rev. Mr. CRADDOCK we received a list giving the names and residences of fifty-two persons who had been suffering from the various diseases. Everyone of these had been on the lists of the local Committees, otherwise, it was stated, they would have starved, so destitute were they. We visited the H—— family at Tullaghacot, of whom five had been sick; two were still lying in typhus. This family had been first on the Committee's relief list. Some out-door relief had been given, but the visit of a nurse (were it but for a few days to give proper instructions in dealing with the sick), and the employment of disinfecting agents, are much to be desired.

It should be added that deficient or improper food acts as a predisposing cause for all the diseases named.

ROSMUCK.

Remote, in one of the wildest parts of Connemara, lies the district of Rosmuck, composed of mountains, moors, granite rocks, long winding creeks, intricate straits, and many islands, occasionally inaccessible. Green patches of ripening crops, fenced by high walls of loose stones, and interspersed by erratic boulders and pyramids of great grey pebbles, gathered from the field, attest the incessant industry of the peasant, striving against innumerable obstacles. Large breadths of this district are utterly without roads, or even lanes. Sea-wrack for manure, turf for fuel, crops for market —all must be carried on the backs of men or horses, to or from the shore or distant highway when necessary. Then, with a thrust of the hand, the stones fall from the loosely-built walls, and a gap is made for the passage of the burthen.

To visit fever-stricken Camus,* a portion of this district, we had to

---

* Mr. Tuke visited Camus on the 2nd of April, and thus describes its aspect then: "Half-a-mile away, and, I would venture to say, no one would think it possible that any human being could live or even find foot-hold on this rock-strewn shore; but by degrees you see the little "smokes" arising, and here and there little dark stripes of land, which show that the ground is being prepared for the potatoes they *hope* to obtain, for they have none left to plant. Then you see, peering above the rocks, little dark heads of men, women and childen, who, attracted by the unwonted sight, come out of their cabins to reconnoitre. As you walk among them on landing, they watch you with curious eyes: they do not beg, and cannot answer your inquiries, for most do not understand, and few can talk, English. In one house which I entered, three children, under one covering, ill with fever, were lying on the ground; others also were ill. For these miserable places among the rocks they were each paying from £4 to £8 a-year. This would seem incredible at any time. No wonder that none had paid their rent last year. I heard that the agent had talked about evicting them, but I think had deferred his intention." The landlord of this place, and of a vast tract besides, is Mr. Berridge, an Englishman. "He is non-resident, and so far as I can hear," writes Mr. Tuke, "does nothing for his tenants."

The reference which Mr. Tuke makes to the prevalence of the Irish language here, may also be applied to other districts. Indeed, in almost all the localities we visited, a

take to a boat, and after a long row up a sinuous creek, to traverse a slippery shore of rocks covered with shaggy sea-wrack. Our way next lay over pathless bogs, fields, and through new-made gaps, to cabins whose reedy roofs rose but little above the grey walls that divide the fields. Some of the doors were only breast-high, and the interior was often correspondingly small. Smoke often filled the inside, for there was no lime with which to build a chimney, though in some cases an ingenious screen of interwoven reeds supplied its place. In one bare, cold, and almost empty cabin we found a poor mother, MARY J——, lying on the ground, in fever, with none to tend her but a son. Her anxiety was all about him, lest he should catch the disease. The son stated that the Relieving Officer had first refused relief, saying he was able to support her (yet they are very poor); then informed him nothing could be given until he should see the Medical Officer, who lives on an island in the centre of his immense district. After her illness had lasted three weeks, two-pence worth of bread and some half-pint of wine had been obtained.

In another case, that of J. H—— (five in family), a child aged eight was lying ill of typhus fever, and the mother was within a few days of her confinement. She was apprehensive lest she should be unable to obtain a nurse when her time came, owing to the sickness in her house. The father stated that, having made application, the Relieving Officer told him nothing could be done until he took the ticket to Oughterard for the sanction of the Guardians. This involved a distance of from fifty to sixty English miles, going and returning. In other cases we found that some small amount of out-door relief had been given, and we consider the system (not the well-intentioned official) is to blame. In one case we found that a nurse had been obtained, and the Relieving Officer stated that he was prepared to pay for a nurse in the confinement case, *if* the poor man could procure one! Twenty-nine fever cases had been reported to him, of whom three had died. Here, more even than in other parts, the people have withheld knowledge of their condition when fever-stricken, particularly where one of the males was spared to labour at the charitable works, lest he should be struck off. Even their priest, the Rev. Mr. KEANE, has not been informed in many cases until danger of death approached. Where that did not threaten, the disease was concealed:

CARRAROE.

What we have said with regard to ill-fated Camus holds good also, in a more intense degree, as regards Carraroe, especially Carraroe North, where much sickness has prevailed amongst the half-fed, half-clad peasantry.

knowledge of the Gaelic language must be requisite for the full performance of their duties, by all who, like clergymen, physicians and others, have to deal closely with the people. Medical terms are not, for instance, well understood, even by those peasants who speak English, and mistaken answers have been given (*i.e.*, tending to confound typhoid with typhus), as was ascertained by questioning the speakers in their native tongue. Then they express themselves with correctness, and often with remarkable grace.

whose appearance was more forlorn than that of any others we have yet beheld.

Neither Camus nor Carraroe are islands: they are portions of the mainland. Yet, such is the absence of roads here, they are only accessible by sea from Rosmuck. The distance by water to Carraroe South cannot be less than six or seven miles, through difficult channels. Midway, we had to leave the boat and travel over an isthmus, at low tide, of stones, slippery with fuci, across which it was necessary for the men to drag the boat. There being no pier, our course on landing lay again over a broad shore of shaggy rocks. If we refer particularly to such points as these, it is in order that you may realize the difficulties presented to the conveyance of the sick to an hospital some thirty miles away! Consider also that these are obstacles to the visits of Medical Officer and clergymen. In rains and storms, their course must be painful and dangerous; whilst, in winter, if overtaken by darkness, or tossed by tempests, there is imminent risk of life. Hence, we would urge that, in all such districts, the channels should be improved where necessary, and small boat-piers built where so much required.

Carraroe South is almost a repetition of Camus, with its grey granite walls; but the cabins here are a shade better, and some employment has been furnished by the making of a small road, which cannot be completed, we are told, for want of funds. Carraroe North, however, is worse than even Camus. In some parts, the laborious peasants have succeeded in forming fields and raising scanty crops; but, over a wide range, the eye beholds nothing save a dreary expanse of brown bog, broken at intervals by white reefs of granite rock. There have been nineteen cases of fever reported to the Relieving Officer in the Carraroes, Clynagh, and Kuranbeg since the 1st of April; but more have, confessedly, existed. It is our duty to add that (as in the instance of the Ballintadder fever-families) notices of eviction had been obtained against the peasants of the Carraroes.*

* The social condition of Carraroe was thus described by the Duke of Argyll, in a debate on the "Compensation for Disturbance Bill," in the House of Lords, in August, 1880. Having referred to "inconsiderate evictions," as the acts of new proprietors, he illustrated the "injudicious exercise of the rights of property" by the case of Carraroe, in the county Galway:—

"On the whole townland," he said, "there were 89 tenants, with families numbering in the whole 515 souls; their rent was £137 7s., or 30s. each. They were of the smallest class of occupiers. There were 1,934 acres in the townland, of which 110 were arable, under crops. The whole stock of the farms consisted of only 4 horses, 110 cattle, 62 sheep, and 14 pigs. The total valuation of the stock and crops—everything—was £1,423, or about £2 15s. for every soul in the townland. One-third of the acreage was arable. I think that was a case clearly in which the tenantry were so reduced, as you may see from the valuation of their stock and crops, that it was impossible they could pay their rent after the three years of the worst harvests we have had for a long period. In this case notices of eviction were served. I rather think in the time of the late Government they were enforced or attempted to be enforced, by, I believe, only 20 men. There was a general resistance to the service of those ejectments; and when we came into office the Irish Government had to reinforce the police to the extent of 200 men. You had in that case at the mercy of the landowner a whole population of upwards

M

Obviously, there could be no more efficacious way of disseminating infectious disease over the country than by compelling persons sick in fever, or just convalescent, to quit their isolated dwellings and wander about, seeking shelter from others, probably at a distance and not yet smitten. Whilst the disease is thus being spread, the mortality must be increased among the homeless wanderers.

Hence, it ought to be the first policy of the State, in such cases, to suspend the power of eviction until the risk of infection shall have disappeared. The conditions of such a suspension it is not for us to suggest, but, as regards the vital importance of such a measure, no doubt can be possible.

The occurrence of scarlet fever (a most catching and dangerous disease) in the district should give emphasis to our recommendation. In Kilbrickan alone, it appears, there have been about twenty cases of scarlet fever since the 1st of June. There are also two cases of typhus in children, as reported to us, in this place. Five children died of scarlatina, giving thus the highest percentage of mortality. Some are stated to have turned black after death. It is unquestionable that bad food operates as a predisposing cause as regards this disease also; and, on investigation, we learned that the schools in the Rosmuck district had received no grants for food. Thus, both in Louisburgh and in Rosmuck, where no food-grants were made to the schools, the children have suffered in a most special degree from disease.

In conclusion, we have to add that in both districts, but particularly in this, the children suffer from want of clothes. In Carraroe North, above all, the spectacle was the saddest we have seen. The men were almost all barefooted, even where using spades or "loys." All—men, women and children (bright-eyed and intelligent) were wearing—we cannot say clothed with—dilapidated pieces of flannel, hanging about them in shreds, too threadbare for patching. As they stood in groups on the rocky shore of that bare land, blessing our departing boat, their presence added not animation but desolation to a scene not to be paralleled in Christendom.

We remain, Gentlemen,
Your obedient Servants,
GEORGE SIGERSON, M.D., CH.M.
J. E. KENNY, L.R.C.S.

Galway.

of 500 souls, who, under the existing law, without one shilling of compensation" [though they had reclaimed the land from barrenness!] "without one shilling to carry them to America, because they were evicted for non-payment of rent." They would have had to go forth, also, suffering from diseases engendered by hardships and famine.

DISTRICTS OF ORANMORE, ATHENRY, AND DERRYBRIEN.

SIXTH REPORT OF DR. SIGERSON.

August 3rd, 1880.

My Lord, Mayor and Gentlemen,

A zone of health interposes between disease at Oughterard and disease at Oranmore. The favoured region is that of the City of Galway and its precincts. Under ordinary circumstances, towns suffer at least as severely as the rural districts from infectious diseases, which find special facilities for appearing and spreading in their overcrowded lodgings, squalid tenement houses, and unwholesome lanes. This season, however, the towns of Ballina, Swineford and Galway, which enjoy a certain amount of comfort, have practically escaped the diseases that, in their immediate neighbourhood, have afflicted the rural population and villages on which the pressure of distress bore most severely.

Where, as in this instance, the boundaries of distress map out the topography of disease, cause and effect are too manifestly connected to escape recognition by all impartial minds.

One case of typhus fever, at Culnainue, near Oughterard, could be traced to Oranmore, and there seemed to be a disposition, in one quarter, to refer most cases to this centre. But against this is the fact that the infection was not conveyed from Oranmore to Galway City, whither many of the fever patients were removed to hospital. Only six miles separate these two places (and Galway has rarely been so free from fever), whilst Oughterard lies some eighteen miles beyond the latter city. Tracing the course of infection is useful, when carried out under rigidly scientific rules, but it must not be ignored that the causes which generate certain diseases in one locality will operate in another also.

Oranmore has no claim to be considered as a special manufactory of fevers. Situate on rising ground, at the eastern extremity of Galway Bay, in a fairly wooded country, it has many natural advantages over other fever-stricken places. Its cottages are rather above the average as regards cleanliness. According to the statement of an inhabitant, the Registrar of the district, there was not a more healthy place in the West of Ireland than Oranmore. Dr. O'Dea states that, since he became Medical Officer in 1877, he has not had a single case of an epidemic nature, in the town or immediate neighbourhood, until recently. This year, however, the locality was smitten with great severity by fevers, and this year the people had suffered greatly from the cumulative effects of distress. The District Registrar attributes the prevalence of disease entirely to the distress. The fever first showed itself in the case of a poor family named M—— (about a mile from the village), whose cottage is in fair sanitary condition. It was impossible to refer back to any source of infection. The family is composed of the two parents, and nine children. All had been compelled to subsist on Indian meal since before Christmas. They had not had a sufficiency of milk. First, one child sickened; then, in a few days, eight were lying together; and, finally, the eldest was stricken down. They were convalescent when I visited the house. In all, during their sickness, they appear to have received about fifteen shillings' worth (in money and nutriment) as out-door relief—an amount manifestly insufficient during the long continuing disease of so many sufferers. Other cases very soon after showed themselves, not only in Oranmore, but in the villages and country around. Though reaching by infection some persons in good circumstances, the disease chiefly confined itself to the distressed, whose names were on the lists of the local relief committee. The Rev. Mr. QUIN informs me that the committee was only able to give one cwt. of Indian meal a fortnight to the worst cases, and largest families. As in all other localities, this meal could not have been sufficiently boiled, for the simple reason that fuel was very scarce: two or three smouldering sods hardly dispelled the darkness and cold from the hearth of any cabin we entered. In this district, it appears, the poor people were extremely badly off as regards fuel (which they have to import from other places), especially during the wet weather. When the fine season came, they used the sun-dried droppings of cattle.

Only forty-four cases of fever are on the register for the past two quarters, but it is now needless to repeat that such records give an inadequate idea of the amount of disease in a district. After careful investigation, with the assistance of the Medical Officer and the clergyman, a list of one hundred and thirty-two cases was obtained. Seven are quite recent cases, mostly still lying, but the patients are persons in fair circumstances, to whom the disease extended by infection. Fourteen deaths occurred. Some of these happened in peculiarly painful circumstances. In Glenascoil a family of seven were stricken down with fever; the father and mother succumbed, and five children were left orphans. In Renvile a family of nine were fever-smitten; here, again, the parents were taken, and seven children orphaned. Dr. O'DEA having caught the infection of typhus from one of his poor patients, a temporary substitute was procured in the person of Dr. GREALY. This young physician was not himself long at work until he also was seized, and, unhappily, succumbed, a victim to the disease. Dr. O'DEA having become convalescent, was ordered off duty for a month by his medical attendants; but, incredible as it may sound, he was called back to work at the expiry of a fortnight, and only obtained a respite by paying half the salary of a substitute. Such an occurrence as this must tend to discourage Medical Officers from the zealous discharge of their functions, in cases of extra danger, and, consequently, it calls for such a reform in their position as should secure them extra encouragement in cases of extra risk and labour, which epidemics bring.

The types of fever which were observed here were typhoid, and a form was noticed in many termed "gastric," owing to the prominence of symptoms referable to that region. Similar observations have been made elsewhere. Vomiting at the commencement was not infrequent. There were no relapses remarked in this locality. It is worth noticing that gastric symptoms were common in the year of the great famine, and that the type of fever at Oranmore, in 1847, was typhus, not relapsing fever.

The necessity for prompt and liberal action, whenever distress occurs, could not be better exemplified than by the consequences of the recent fever-outbreak in this district. Confessedly the result of privations, had the distress been foreseen and prevented, these destitution-diseases would not have afflicted the suffering poor, spread from them to their more comfortable neighbours, nor, extending still more widely, have made other distant localities pay tribute to disease and death. To the west, Oughterard, to the east, Athenry and Craughwell, have cause of complaint on this account. It should be added that, although the out-door relief granted was not sufficient, the strain upon local resources was greater than in many other places. The last cess struck for the support of the poor, made the rate four shillings and ninepence in the pound; and it is apprehended that the next may increase it to over seven shillings. In such cases, the State should come to the aid of a district suffering pressure from exceptional causes.

ATHENRY.

Proceeding at night to Athenry, long stretches of the road were found converted into miniature lakes, through which the horse splashed more than fetlock-deep. There is no need to seek far for the proper subject of a work of public utility, where highways become, after rains, impassible to all, but barefoot, pedestrians. In the town and immediate neighbourhood of Athenry there have occurred about thirty-four cases of fever within the last four months: a very unusual number, as I was informed by the Relieving Officer. Some were still suffering. Four died. Having examined a case, in one cottage, and traced the infection to another, I visited the latter. Here the mother became first affected, but could refer the disease to no extern cause. She had been ailing in health for some time before, unable even to go to Mass, and was not therefore likely to contract the disease from others. The family was supposed to have some means; but, on investigation, it was found that their twelve sheep had died in spring, their potatoes had failed, and they had been subsisting on Indian meal since the latter end of January. Their one cow gave milk, which was shared with a sick neighbour. Soon after the mother, four of the children were likewise fever-smitten; when she became convalescent, another of the children and the husband were stricken. One child was still suffering, and the husband I found to present the characteristic maculæ of typhus. The family numbers eight members, for the support of whom, during this grievous illness, the meagre sum of five shillings a-week was granted. No nurse appears to have been provided, even when mother and children were lying. In this case, no extern source of infection was discovered; but the Rev. Mr. M'Philpin informed me that some early cases appeared in the direction of Oranmore.

At Craughwell, the Rev. Mr. Geoghegan mentioned that two families had been attacked, and that, in both instances, the infection of the fever had been distinctly traced to Oranmore. There is no need to insist on the great desirability of preventing the formation of a fever-focus, and of hindering the extension of the disease, when once a centre has been constituted. Its power of radiation is greatly reduced when the pressure of distress is diminished. Centres may be formed, having little or no radiation, where the general condition of the people is somewhat above the lowest. This was the case at Craughwell.

The same rule holds good as regards two incipient foci, at places south of Loughrea. At Annaghbride, one case recently occurred, and the patient died (July 26th). The family had suffered privations; their sheep had died; they had but one cow, and were living on Indian meal. The distress has been much felt, the Rev. Mr. Griffin informs me, and the children lack sufficient clothing; but there does not exist such abject poverty here as we have elsewhere observed. Several miles distant, in a different direction, at Sunnagh, another centre formed. Here two families have been attacked. In one, a young boy died; in the other, the disease, after running through the family (a child first showing the symptoms), carried off the mother. The disease was stated to be a virulent form of maculated typhus. I was informed by the Rev. Mr. Raftery that both families were very poor, and subsisting on the grants of the Committee. These did not amount to more than two shillings' worth of food per week for a family of nine persons.

DERRYBRIEN.

By far the poorest and most desolate portion of this region is the mountain district in the direction of Woodford and Derrybrien. The latter place, about eighteen English miles south of Loughrea, is reached by a hilly road, passing for about twelve miles through upland moors, bogs, and long stretches of barren mountain, made all the more dismal, at the time of my journey, by lowering clouds and falling rain. Along this weary way patients must be brought, summer and winter, some from a distance of over twenty English miles to Loughrea; and such a journey, even in a spring conveyance, must cause much suffering, especially to those who experience the aching pains of typhus. At Derrybrien the industry of the peasantry has partly clothed the mountain sides with crops. In this mountainous region a fever centre was formed, and the disease spread considerably and very fatally. As to the origin of the disease, there are contradictory reports. Some think the mother of the family brought the infection from a southern district near Scariff. Hence, I thought it necessary to inquire as to the hygienic state of that locality, and Dr. SAMPSON, of Scariff, gives this reply to a telegram:—" Twelve cases of typhus fever occurred in Mountshannon district. Eight of those were treated in hospital. Two deaths in the twelve." The statement of the victims, and of the survivors in the family, was, however, to the following effect:—Although not amongst the distressed, the mother worked in the field, and there caught cold. She was ailing, and had not left home for months. Subsequent exposure during a long journey to Loughrea Market and back, at night, developed the disease. The invalid husband succumbed a few days after her death. I may add that, as a rule, the fever, so far as we have seen, first attacked either a child, or a parent enfeebled in health. The weakest were most subject to the invasion of the fever. Here, both parents died, in the course of a few days, and, as no physician had been called in, the infectious nature of the disease was not suspected, and there was a wake. When its nature was revealed, the people, as usual, held aloof; and, in one case, I was informed by the Rev. Mr. CALLAGY, the convalescents had to carry out the victim of the fever. Judging from personal observation of a case now lying, the type here prevalent is maculated typhus. This is confirmed by the opinion of the Medical Officer, Dr. BLACKTON, who states that two cases of typhus have also shown themselves in miserably poor families, at Cloonco, near Woodford. In Derrybrien, the disease has run through a number of distressed families, whose names are on the relief list, whilst reaching to a few others besides.

The disease has been exceedingly virulent in this mountain district. Of thirty-one fever-stricken patients, seven died of the disease, thus giving a very high percentage. One other death occurred, the circumstances connected with which illustrate very sadly the want of a ready mode of obtaining nursing attendance in remote country districts. In this case, all the members of the family were stricken down by disease, some simultaneously, some successively. One is still lying in maculated typhus. The father and mother died of it; there was no nurse, and one son, in the delirium of disease, got out of bed, and, wandering abroad over the fields in the night, never returned; he was finally discovered drowned in a pool of water. So melancholy an event as this should induce the creation of cottage-hospitals in every remote locality like Woodford, where, as Dr. BLACKTON justly remarks, it would be of the greatest utility.

A sufficient amount of out-door relief appears to have been given in this district to the fever-stricken families; but, generally, the grants of out-door relief are few in number and small in quantity.

With much regret, I have to mention that the potato-blight appears to have shown itself rather widespread and well-marked, from the neighbourhood of Galway City to the mountains of Derrybrien. The oats, which have hitherto presented so fair a promise have, in many parts, been beaten down and "lodged," owing to the recent heavy rains.

I remain, Gentlemen,
Your obedient Servant,
GEORGE SIGERSON, M.D., Ch.M.

P.S.—As during this portion of the medical investigation into the state of the distressed districts I was deprived of the co-operation of Dr. J. E. KENNY, I desire to take this opportunity of bearing my testimony to his assiduous labour, and of tendering him my personal thanks for his valuable assistance.

Loughrea.

DR. SIGERSON'S FINAL REPORT
ON DESTITUTION-DISEASES IN THE WEST.

August 14th, 1880.

My Lord Mayor, my Lords and Gentlemen,

When you requested me to conduct a medical investigation into the nature and causes of the fevers reported to your Committee from various distressed districts, west of the Shannon, there existed some conflict of opinion in reference to the connection, as cause and effect, between the privations of the sufferers and the form of fever observed. It was, for instance, stated that the disease was distinctly different from famine-fever; that it was merely an outbreak of typhus, and an effort was made to show that it had no relationship to the prevailing distress. On the other hand, it was alleged that famine-fever did afflict the country. In the observations which I had the honour of addressing to you, on the occasion of your request, I pointed out that it was a serious error to suppose that relapsing (or so-called famine) fever alone was a consequence of distress. Typhus, typhoid, and relapsing fevers might, all of them, supervene in a period of privation, and therefore the aim of any medical inquiry should be to ascertain not so much the presence of a particular fever-form as the circumstances under which it arose. Of the diseases named, typhus was shown to be a far more formidable visitant than relapsing (technically termed "famine") fever. These statements, formally set out in my preliminary Report, were there supported by extracts from authoritative documents, showing that the several fevers mentioned had all been recognised during the period of the great famine, and that, of the three, maculated typhus had been the most constant and by far the most fatal associate of the famine years.

It is gratifying to observe that no such conflict of opinion is now manifested. The connection between the distress and the fevers, in the stricken districts, has since been amply acknowledged. The reports of the Medical Commissioners sent down by the Local Government Board, are, in principle, accordant with the opinions placed before you in my preliminary Report, and, in fact, confirmatory (so far as they extend) of the results of the researches of my colleague and myself. Our investigation embraced a greater area.

With these prefatory remarks, I have the honour to submit the following general observations, in the tenor of which my colleague, Dr. Kenny, completely concurs:—

1st. According to the official calculations, the money-value of the crops in Ireland was over ten millions sterling less last year than in 1878. Nearly one-half of this loss was due to failure of the principal food-crop of the humbler classes. The standard of comparison, however, is a low one, as will be seen by what follows. The produce of the potato-crop during the last three years was greatly below what it had been in the preceding three-year period.

In 1874	... ...	3,551,601 tons.
1875	... ...	3,512,884 „
1876	... ...	4,154,785 „

In the last three-year period the produce stood as under:—

In 1877	... ...	1,757,275 tons.
1878	... ...	2,526,504 „
1879	... ...	1,113,676 „

To the immense cumulative loss represented by these figures must be added serious loss arising from deficient crops of wheat and oats. The depreciation in the money value of horned cattle may be judged from the fact that of the 9,916 animals offered for sale at the great October fair of Ballinasloe, 8,297 were taken away unsold. These losses fell with extreme severity on the smaller land-occupiers, and must have reduced many of them to great straights. The depression of trade in America and Britain, lessening the demand for labour, deprived them of much assistance from wage-earning kinsfolk, and the necessary stoppage of credit by shopkeepers, after the last bad harvest, combined with other enumerated causes, left many thousands without any resource.

That the physical and moral depression of the people told upon the health of the nation is manifest from the official Quarterly Returns. Throughout last year, the birth-rate was lower and the death-rate higher than in the corresponding quarters of the quinquennial period, 1874-78. From the Return relating to the last quarter of last year I take the following noteworthy extracts:—" The birth-rate of Ireland is again under the average of the corresponding quarters of the previous five years to the extent of 1 per 1,000 of the estimated population. The death-rate is above the average for the same period, and is the highest registered in the fourth quarter of any year since registration of deaths commenced in the year 1864." Having pointed out that the weather in the first two of these three months was " comparatively much more favourable than it had been during the preceding portion of the year," and mentioned that the month of December became unusually severe, and contributed much to increase the death-rate, the Registrar-General proceeded to state that " the suffering caused by the extremely bad harvest and depression of trade is no doubt, to a considerable extent, a cause of the excessive death-rate of Ireland during the past quarter." It should be added that many of the local Registrars referred the prevalence of chest diseases, and other ailments, as well as their fatality, largely to the want of a sufficiency of fuel and food. With special regard to fever, I find that the Registrar of Castleconnor mentions that he had " a few cases of fever of a low type, which," he says, " I believe were due principally to the bad diet the people have to live on, owing to the unwholesome quality of the potatoes, as well as the great diminution in quantity." This is the Inniscrone district, which was subsequently so much stricken by fever. At Kilkelly, Swineford, the Registrar reported an epidemic of typhus fever. From Oughterard, the Registrar of Cloonbur, No. 1 district, wrote that " typhus has appeared in isolated cases, and, I fear, will become more general, the result of bad and insufficient food.' The foreboding has been sadly justified. Some of the local Registrars expressed themselves as looking forward with great anxiety to the coming quarter.

By tabulating the death totals of the country, the relationship of the increase of deaths to the accumulating pressure of the distress will be rendered more plain.

In 1876	...	...	...	...	...	92,324
1877	...	...	...	...	...	93,543
1878	...	...	...	...	...	99,629
1879	...	...	...	...	...	105,432

It will be seen from these figures that 19,194 more persons died in the last two, than in the first two years. If the space of six years be considered, it will be found that the average death-rate of the first four years amounted to 93,985. Judged by this standard, there was, in 1878, an excess of 5,644 deaths; and, last year, a still greater excess of 11,447 deaths.

2nd. With the beginning of the present year the various relief Committees came into operation, and their beneficent influence may be inferred from the fact that the death-rate, which, in the previous quarter, had been 1·6 per 1,000 in excess, now fell to 1 per 1,000 in excess of the rate for the corresponding quarters of the past five years. It remained, as will be observed, still much above the average. As the food, which the funds of the Committee permitted them to distribute, was insufficient in quantity and quality to maintain health by itself, and as the inhabitants of the most distressed districts were, as a rule, unable to supplement it by any adjunct, save weak coffee, sugar and water, or simply water, destitution-diseases appeared in several districts, and manifested themselves largely amongst the most distressed class. The anæmic and emaciated countenances of very many first struck the attentive observer. Next, further symptoms of deficient alimentation were shown by gastric disorders, aggravated dyspepsia, dysentery, and dysenteric diarrhœa. The same cause, operating in a more intense degree, or on more enfeebled constitutions, resulted in the production of fevers of different types. The first, most active, and most fatal of these was, unquestionably, maculated typhus—the customary and formidable associate of distress. Many foci were discovered, spontaneously formed and directly due to the impoverished and reduced condition of the victims. In some districts, specified in our Reports, this fever prevailed almost or entirely alone. Typhoid fever, however, was occasionally present, and in one district (that of Inniscrone) it appears to have been the principal disease. In two localities, both fevers were present, in not very dissimilar proportions. The marked predominance of gastric symptoms, referable to alimentary causes, has made some observers note the presence of a form of this fever known as "gastric." There were some hybrid forms, and many instances of slow convalescence. Some cases of relapsing fever were observed by the Medical Officers in the Dispensary Districts of Lawrencetown, Swineford, Killala, and Louisburgh. At the two last-named places we had the advantage of seeing the patients; and, at Inniscrone and Corballa, the description of their symptoms, given by two convalescents, showed that they had also suffered from the same form of disease. In these two cases, and in a case at Finune (Louisburgh), the characters of the type appeared to be especially well-marked. This form of fever is technically named (in some handbooks) "famine-fever." It has been already shown in the preliminary Report that this is a misleading, because, apparently, an excluding appellation. Relapsing fever has no title to be termed famine-fever, *par excellence*. It was the last and least formidable of the fevers by which Ireland was stricken in the great famine-period. Here it did not show itself under the pressure of worse conditions than those which helped to generate the maculated typhus; in point of fact, the latter was the disease which manifested itself in those persons and places that had suffered most severely from the urgency of the distress. The results of our investigations, as regards the dependence of disease upon distress, bear out in every particular the statements made in the preliminary Report, which I had the honour of addressing to your Committee. The words of STOKES there quoted to describe the diseases of the great famine, apply with fidelity to those which supervened (though in a much less degree) on the recent distress, "Now, if ever the characters of typhus were shown, it was then. Every form of fever occurred—relapsing fever, typhoid or enteric fever, and the worst form of typhus that could be seen."

3rd. There can be no question as to the fact that the assistance granted by the relief committees has availed to save thousands of human lives. This was the deliberate conviction of medical officers, clergymen, and others well-qualified by their close acquaintance with the condition of the peasantry to form a correct judgment. Several of the local Registrars have borne explicit testimony to the same effect, in the Quarterly Returns. All that we have seen of the utter dependence of vast numbers of the peasantry on the periodical doles of Indian meal goes to confirm their opinion. Again and again, we were told, in every district, that the distressed people owed their very existence to the action of the Mansion House Committee, to which all were most grateful. The exceptional high death-rate, however, demonstrates that many must have quietly succumbed to their sufferings, and silently died out. It is everywhere declared that the distribution of Indian meal has been of vital service, but it is evident that this article of diet, although sufficient to withstand the immediate effect of starvation, is very inadequate, by itself, to maintain health. Many of those whom we found stricken with fever and other diseases had been compelled to subsist for four, five, or six months on Indian meal, generally insufficiently boiled (owing to want of fuel); as adjuncts, they had very rarely any milk; in one or two districts, weak coffee; in some, sweetened water; and in not a few cases, water only. Now, the absolute necessity of a mixed dietary has been shown by experiment. The continued use of a food element much superior to Indian meal has been found inadequate long to sustain life. Thus Dr. STARK, in 1769, lived on bread and water 44 days; bread, water and sugar, 29 days; bread, water and olive oil, 24 days—in all, 97 days: his health then failed, and he died in consequence. MAGENDIE, having fed dogs on pure wheaten bread and water, found that they did not last longer than fifty days. On the other hand, dogs survived when fed on gluten, which is rich in a variety of food principles. Now, according to ROBIN, Indian meal is remarkable for the absence of gluten. The result of the analyses of grain from different places vary. POLSON gives 8·8 as the percentages of albuminoids in American maize; they rise to over fourteen per cent. in Odessa and Alsacian wheat, and to above twenty per cent. in Egyptian and Polish grain (BOUSSINGAULT and PELIGOT). In oats, they vary from over ten to over fifteen per cent. (ANDERSON, KROCKER). According to the table given in Dr. MAPOTHER's useful Manual, the percentages of nitrogenized matter in Indian meal, wheat flour, and oatmeal stand at 9, 11 and 12. It will thus be seen that, as regards albuminoids, Indian meal takes the lowest rank, and is only half as rich in them as some oats and some wheat. Hence the experiments which go to prove that neither man nor certain animals can live more than two or three months on bread and water, must be taken as doubly conclusive against the idea that Indian meal and water, sweetened or not, could support the human frame in health for four or five months. Destitution-diseases are the logical consequences of the attempt.*

---

* To an important fact, in corroboration of this, my attention was called by Sir John Lentaigne. As Inspector of the Reformatory and Industrial Schools of Ireland, he found that the Superioress of the Industrial Schools at Oughterard had, during the distress-period, been compelled to withdraw the children under her charge from the National School, owing to the fact that various skin and other affections had shown themselves amongst its ordinary pupils. These ailments were recognised as the direct consequences of the mal-nutrition of these children, by Indian meal. When proper and sufficient food was given them, through means supplied by the Charitable Committees, the ailments were stayed and erased. Then, it was found possible to send the Industrial School children to the National Schools.

The following extract from the reply of Mrs. Martyn, the Superioress referred to, bears witness to the fact :—

"OUGHTERARD, *December 15th*, 1880.—I can fully corroborate the statement made last summer to Sir John Lentaigne in regard to the diseases prevalent among the children attending our National Schools. I hesitate not to say that sores and other more serious disorders were the consequence of Indian meal used as a sole means of support. The appearance of some children was frightful, and had it not been for the bread and milk so

It may be added that the connection between insufficient alimentation and disease, previously demonstrated by the eminent mind of Corrigan, was fully acknowledged by the Census Commissioners in 1851, when dealing with the famine-period. "It is scarcely possible," they remarked, " to lessen the physical strength of a people by withholding their customary amount of food, or to alter suddenly the chemical constituents of that people's usual source of sustenance, without rendering them liable to epidemic disease: whilst it is without the range of all probability that depression of mind, amounting to despair, consequent upon parents witnessing the lingering starvation of their offspring, or children observing the haggard looks and wasted forms of their parents and near relations, could occur without producing fatal results upon the human frame."

4th. The invasion of the disease was disavowed and resisted, usually, as long as possible. Men working in the field or bog insisted they had only caught a cold, and held out until forced to take to bed. A few, " put it over them standing." It was touching to see one boy persevering in work, though taken with nausea and retching; and another, a debilitated convalescent from fever, endeavouring to labour in the field, but compelled to sit down and rest from time to time. The words of the Census Commissioners may be again quoted, when they say that " more females were attacked with fever than males." They add—" Another peculiarity of the great famine-fever" (under which name they include typhus, typhoid, and relapsing) " of 1846-50, was the number of children and very young persons attacked by it—to an extent far greater than any previous records of fever have elicited." These have been marked characteristics of the fevers of this recent distress-period. In every district, large numbers of children and young people have been attacked—nearly all the members of a large family being often stricken down simultaneously. It happened frequently that a child was the first attacked, and, in two districts, where food had not been granted for school-children, these were prominently the earliest sufferers from disease. Insufficiency of proper food, and above all

bountifully bestowed by Charitable Committees, the greater number of the children of this locality must have fallen victims to disease. We were afraid to let the little ones of our Industrial School go to the National Schools during that season of starvation so happily averted by good friends. I only regret that we cannot continue to many, each morning, that substantial meal which restored health and colour to the worn frames and wan faces of our suffering charge, now dependent on dry potatoes of a bad description."

The children in some of the other and remoter districts had yet more privations to suffer than those of Oughterard, and the consequences must have been fully as deplorable. It is worth noting here that the pellagra disease, which affects the poorest inhabitants of certain portions of Milan, Piedmont, the Landes, the Pyrenees, and parts of Spain, has been attributed to the use of vitiated Indian meal. The disease first attacks the skin, next the digestive mucous membrane, and finally the central nervous system. According to Balardini, Costallat, and Robin the disease is due to the development, beneath the epidermis, of the spores of the *Ustilago carbo* (Tulasne), a minute fungus parasitic on the grain, which have been detected in the meal. One case of an adult near Killala presented some symptoms which resembled those of the first stage of pellagra. But the subject is one that requires continued observation.

deprivation of milk, tell heavily against the health of the children, in every such crisis.* Next to the children, their mothers appear to have been especially liable to the invasion of destitution-fever. In many places, the grown men having left to seek employment in Britain and America, the mothers had to work at agricultural labour, with debilitated constitutions. In all cases, it could be elicited that where a little milk was procurable, they deprived themselves of it, and gave that little to nourish the youngest children. Having advised (on giving some aid) that milk should be obtained for the feeble children, the mother's assent was prompt—" I would take it from my heart to give it to them." In this spirit they have acted. In some places, both parents have succumbed, but the mortality amongst the mothers of the West is one of the most marked and painful characteristics of the recent destitution-diseases.

5th. It has been alleged, occasionally, that the peasantry are reckless in the matter of fever, and spread the disease by holding wakes. Our experience gives this a complete contradiction.† In two cases only could

* Sir John Lentaigne, in his Report on the Industrial and Reformatory Schools, remarks on the persistent injury to the constitutions of children, from the privations in food, clothing, and care to which they had been subjected. He summarises the statistics given by the late Sir William Wilde, Census Commissioner in 1857, as to the frightful prevalence of famines in this country, where, "during the last century twenty-five out of the one hundred years were years of absolute want." The evil consequence to the health of the survivors was shown by the fact that an excessive proportion of them have suffered from certain affections (e.g. blindness). "The last Census returns taken in 1871" observes Sir J. Lentaigne, "fully corroborate those remarks, and they show that a greater proportion of deaf, dumb, and blind then existed in Ireland than in any other portion of the United Kingdom; the numbers being 1 in every 445 of the population in Ireland, while in England and Wales the proportion was 1 in every 686, and in Scotland 1 in every 658." From 1849 to 1859, inclusively, 118,895 cases of ophthalmia, principally among children under 15 years of age were treated in the Union Workhouses, besides vast numbers in the rural districts and cities. Sir J. Lentaigne truly remarks that "these figures afford incontrovertible evidence of the calamities that insufficient nurture periodically brings on the inhabitants of certain districts of this island. Then, again, a fatal fever, from the same cause, has for hundreds of years lurked here and there, and whenever the food of the people fails, through adverse atmospheric disturbance, this fever is ready to burst out with increased malignancy of type."
Special attention is called to "the necessity which exists for ameliorating the condition of the children in the famine districts of the West by the supply of sufficient clothing as well as food for their use," for "without sufficient food and clothing, their physical and mental organism and functions cannot be sufficiently developed." Coarse poor bulky diet is not readily assimilated by the digestive organs of children. Warmth is a condition of health for them, as well as good food. Death by starvation has been asserted to be death by cold, and application of external warmth is the first and most effective remedy in the cure of persons dying from starvation. "Where food is scanty, sufficient fire and clothing are absolutely necessary: yet the young children, in the poverty-stricken districts of the West were, during the last winter, to a large extent without proper clothing, until supplied by the Relief Committees. Besides, from continual rains the turf could not be dried. In one school in Galway, when the District Inspector of the National Board visited it for examination by results, the weather was so cold at the time that the ink in the bottles was frozen, and the turf so wet that it would not kindle; in another school at the time he inspected it, only 6 boys out of 45 had a second article of clothing to wear, their dress consisting solely of a flannel tunic tied round the waist."—*Eighteenth Report of the Inspector appointed to visit the Reformatory and Industrial Schools of Ireland*, 1880.

† Another ungrounded statement alleged a prevalence of drinking habits among the peasantry of the distressed districts. This was in distinct contradiction with the facts observed during a month's close and vigilant examination of the peasants' homes throughout

infection be traced to this cause; and in both instances it was believed that the victims had died of non-infectious diseases. This happened early. So soon as the infectious nature of the malady was known, the people left the stricken families in as perfect isolation as possible. When obliged to inform one young mother that her child, who was ailing, had been attacked by "the strange disease," she began to lament, and, to some words of consolation, she replied, "Ah, if it had been any other sickness!—but now no one will come near our threshold." The difficulties, in the way of having the sick removed, and the dead coffined and carried forth, to which we have adverted in the local Reports, are striking illustrations of the strong desire of the inhabitants of a fever-stricken district to hold aloof from infection. It has also been alleged, at times, that typhus is endemic in Ireland, as though that were an excuse for its existence. This statement does not apply to some of the localities visited, nor does it account for the exceptional prevalence of fever in all; but, on the other hand, it excuses nothing, for it is the strongest condemnation of the poor conditions under which the humbler classes in the stricken districts live. Continental writers refer to the continuance of typhus in Ireland and Silesia as symptomatic of the insufficient alimentation of their peasantry. PROUST, the distinguished author of the "Traité de l'Hygiène," remarks in that work on the deplorable position of those populations, in Ireland, Silesia and Algeria, where it suffices that one failure of their food-crop should happen to plunge them into distress and typhus. It concerns the honour of their respective Governments, he says, to endeavour, so far as may be possible, to guard against those great catastrophes "which place a large portion of mankind under the constant menace of starvation and typhus."

6th. The habitations of the peasantry stand generally in need of

---

Connaught, from its northern shore to its southern boundary. In no district was there any sign remarked of anything conflicting with perfect sobriety; even the fever-stricken patients had none of those stimulants which were required for their sustainment and recovery. The slander was circumstantial, and asserted a great increase in the consumption of spirits in the country. To this the following extract from an English journal gives a refutation:—

"The days when England freed itself of its financial difficulties by a liberal increase in the consumption of spirits seem to be coming upon us again. If the power for gratifying the taste for strong drinks can be accepted now, as it certainly was a few years ago, as a sure test of a nation's prosperity, this country must be fast returning to its halcyon days of happiness. During the first three quarters of 1878, there were retained for consumption in England alone a little over 11,900,000 gallons of spirits. In the corresponding period of 1879, the quantity had diminished to less than 11,600,000 gallons. This year has been marked by a considerable increase in the consumption, and the number of gallons drunk has more than recovered the ground lost two years ago. In the other countries of the United Kingdom the decrease has been progressive since 1878, but the falling-off is not so rapid as it was twelve months since. In Scotland there has been a respectable decrease in the last two years of nearly 300,000 gallons.

"In Ireland the decrease has been still greater. Last year the quantity consumed was nearly half a million of gallons less than in its predecessor, and in 1880 there is a further diminution of 230,000. When the apostle of temperance proclaimed last week that the recent distress in Ireland had been aggravated by an increase of drink, he was undoubtedly speaking without his book."—*Pall Mall Gazette*, December 14th, 1880.

improvement, and this could readily be secured by means of such encouragement as may be found in other countries, and some other parts of this island. The houses in the West are built of stone—not of hardened clay, as in our eastern districts, where the practice of making "mud" cabins appears to have been introduced from England, in which country "clob-walls" and "wattle-and-dab" houses were once common, and where (*e.g.*, in Lancashire) the mud cabin is still to be seen. The manure pit is usually before the door, an arrangement not peculiar to Connaught. Formerly frequent in England (Shakespeare's father was fined for keeping an obstructive dung-heap in front of his house, in the town of Stratford), it is still common in parts of Germany, Scotland and Ulster. Fevers are not endemic there, as they should be if this were an efficient cause. Turf-mould, with which the midden-steads in the West are copiously supplied, is a good deodoriser, so that they are in reality less offensive to health than to the eye, in many cases. Nor ought the green colour of the pools to be regarded as a sign of putrefaction, for it is, on the contrary, due to the growth of myriads of minute algæ—plants whose existence tends to purify the fluids in which they develop.

Often the same roof covers, and the same walls enclose, domestic animals and their owners. This system has many disadvantages, but cannot be regarded as altogether adverse to health, seeing that, in the districts where the system prevails, the death-rate is not greater but less than elsewhere, and large families of fine children abound. It is to be noticed that, during this season of distress and disease, the number of cattle to be housed was smaller than in better and healthier times.* One is reminded of the description given by Tacitus of the children of German chief and slave, who passed their days on the same ground, mixed with the same cattle, were reared up in dirt, ran about naked, and yet "grew up to that size and strength of limb which we behold with wonder." I may mention, in addition, that a distinguished Paris physician informed me that he cured the delicate constitutions of his own children and those of many of his patients, by making them sojourn for a time in the midst of a great cattle-stable in the vicinity of that city. As a rule, the Irish cabins in the

---

* The testimony of the Relieving Officer in the Ballaghadereen District, and of others, elsewhere, was to the effect that "tenants who had three or four cows two years ago had none now." Mr. Tuke cites the evidence of a police-constable, engaged in collecting returns of stock and crops, in Oughterard District, to show the great reduction in numbers and quantity. Usually, the peasantry made a strenuous effort to retain one or two cattle, suffering hunger rather than part with them, and with the hope of recovering their former position. But empty stalls almost universally showed that they had been forced to surrender some of their few cattle.

Perhaps, not the least striking sign of poverty was the almost complete absence of domestic pets, throughout large districts. Dogs were rare, except with herds, and cats scarcely to be seen in any cabin. In one cottage, a cat sat by the head of a fever-stricken child; in another, a half starved kitten crouched by a smouldering sod. Where there was not food enough for the poor children, there was none for "*les bouches inutiles.*"

West, even the poorest, have two doors, in order that one may be constantly open during the day, blow the wind as it will; at night, when closed, the air enters tolerably freely beneath and around them. Much discomfort is caused in not a few cabins by the prevalence of smoke, when fuel can be got. This is not owing to any peculiar predilection on the part of the Irish peasantry. WHITAKER remarked that the common people in the North of England and Cheshire "had their fire in the midst of the house, and no chimney above to discharge the smoke," so late as the seventeenth century. Here, the defect is caused by the inability of the peasant to build a proper chimney-tube, the place of which is sometimes supplied by a screen of reeds. Kindly counsel and judicious help would amply avail here, as elsewhere, to amend all that needs improvement in the condition of the habitations of the peasantry. But, whilst it is highly desirable that such improvements should be affected, it must be noted that many places, where they are most required, have been free from fever for long periods, and that many others have totally escaped. Inasmuch as the diseases showed themselves when and where distress most prevailed, not where sanitary defects seemed most prominent, it is imperative to conclude that, excepting exceptional cases, deficient alimentation was the prime predisposing cause in all such instances.

This conclusion is confirmatory of the opinions of the most eminent Irish physicians. GRAVES, remarking on the tendency to attribute the origin of typhus to the unwholesome emanations produced by decomposition, observes that, "In Ireland, facts do not bear out this hypothesis." STOKES describes a village, whose unsanitary condition was much worse than any we saw, and adds that it had escaped endemical disease. He also quotes the evidence of Dr. PRATT, resuming the experience of nearly a quarter of a century as Dispensary Officer in districts where manure-pits were as close and unseemly as any we beheld; "in such places," he adds, "a case of fever of any type rarely occurs, the average length of life is high, and illness, except common colds and infantile diseases, is almost unknown." When fever does make its appearance, after severe distress, in these localities, its efficient cause must be obvious.

7th. It was noted, in 1846, that a fatal epizootic attacked domestic fowl. The same fact must be recorded for a considerable portion of Mayo, as, in Ballaghadereen, Charlestown, Swineford and Foxford districts, it was the universal complaint that the poultry had been largely destroyed by disease. There was no marked premonitory sign; frequently, after laying, the hens would lie down and die. The loss has been felt very severely by their peasant owners. Elsewhere this disease did not prevail, but fatal sickness amongst sheep was mentioned as having existed in the districts of Rossmuck and Athenry.

II.

The experience gained from a close study of the recent crisis induced us to offer certain suggestions with the aim of obviating some observed deficiencies. Several of these were happily adopted. In addition, it seems desirable to enumerate here, in conclusion, such remedial measures as might serve to correct defects, and avert in the future the errors of the past. These measures may be divided into two classes: 1st, Medical; 2nd, General.

Medical Remedial Measures.

1st. At present, in many districts, the hospital centres are too far apart to subserve all the uses that should be expected from them. Hence it is extremely desirable that cottage-hospitals should be established in districts remote or difficult of access. These small hospital-homes would make the peasantry familiar with proper medical aid, and supply nurses when required. By this means the sick would be tended, and the peasantry, losing their dread of the distant workhouse hospital, would give early notice of infectious disease, and assist in its isolation and arrest. Large numbers, now, do not report to the Medical Officer, and many more cases of disease occur than are recorded.

2nd. Light spring conveyances, suitable for the carriage of the sick, should be at once provided, where none exist. There can be no excuse for employing common carts, the jolting of which would, in many cases, prove injurious, and, in some, fatal, to patients whose removal might otherwise be an advantage.* Some of the ambulances (relics of the Crimean War) are too cumbersome to be readily managed or easily used in

---

* The following description by the special correspondent of the *Freeman's Journal*, June 29th, 1880, will enable the reader to realise the conveyance of the sick in open, springless carts, which are still continued in some localities mentioned:—

"On Saturday I passed one of these carts on its way to Swineford. A woman lay moaning in fever in it, her burning head resting on her daughter's lap. The cart jumped and jolted over every stone and ruggedness, and such a piteous thing I never do remember as the girl crying out to the driver at every shudder that went through the mother's fevered frame,—'Oh! Tom, Tom, drive easy. For God's sake, drive easy. Don't go over the stones so hard, Tom.'" Information having been sent to the Swineford Union that three others, father, mother and daughter were stricken down in Charlestown, a conveyance came. Its appearance next (Sunday) night, before the house of the priest, "the chief and almost the only nurse of the plague-stricken," is thus described. It had been raining hard, and blowing gustily all day, and it was now "an awful night." But, "the cart was standing outside in the darkness, and the driver too, with his coat collar turned up and his head bent, and he soaked through and through with the rain. It was a flat common cart for carrying turf, or hay, or stable manure, and on it was shaken a lot of wet straw. This was the cart which the authorities had sent at ten o'clock at night, when it blew and rained, wherein to bring three human beings, in a raging fever, from Charlestown to Swineford, being a journey of seven miles." The Rev. Mr. Loftus orally confirmed to us the accuracy of this statement. A large heavy Crimean ambulance waggon was subsequently exhumed from some forgotten store, but it was unsuited for rural hospital service and mountain roads

mountainous places: owing probably to this cause, they have been neglected as lumber.

3rd. The position of the Medical Officers needs to be improved, in order that the services of active and talented men should continue to be acquired, especially in remote districts. A compulsory superannuation allowance should be granted, when circumstances are shown to require it. It should also be ruled that, in civil as well as in military life, exceptional services rendered in times of extra risk to life, should be duly considered and properly rewarded. The services of the Medical Officer who suffers or dies, whilst defending the population from the ravages of an epidemic, should be regarded as having the same title to recognition as those of the surgeon who is wounded or falls whilst with an army in the field. If this were done, and a proportionate encouragement given to the minor officials directly engaged, epidemics would be met more actively and thoroughly, and a greater impulse given to the eradication of infectious diseases.

4th. It seems necessary, however, that a reserve-power should be placed in the hands of the Medical Officer of requiring assistance from the police for carrying out certain urgent sanitary measures—such as the removal of the sick or the dead—in case of need. The operation of voluntary charity may sometimes act efficiently, but upon this the State has no right to depend. Yet, only for this, some of the victims of infectious disease during the past months would have been abandoned, living, and deserted, dead. To prevent such a disaster, the Medical Officer should be able to call in the aid of the State police as sanitary assistants. It is certain that the power would be judiciously used, and only employed where absolutely necessary.

General Measures.

These should be directed to the improvement of the social condition of the people. The following may here be mentioned:—

1st. Bye-roads should be made to all hamlets which at present have no proper means of communication with the high-roads. It is not conceivable that the removal of the sick could be effected from some of the villages visited without great suffering; nor is it possible for the resources of a district to be developed without proper means of communication.

2nd. In order that Poor Law Guardians should be more speedily informed of the necessities of the people, and induced to take liberal measures for their prompt relief (the surest economy), it is most desirable that clergymen should be admitted to seats at the Board. They have the most intimate and the most certain acquaintance with the needs of the poor, and to exclude them is to deprive the relief system of a great element of usefulness. Their action on the eight hundred Committees in connection with the Mansion House Relief Committee is a demonstration of their capacity, organising power, and exceptional value.

3rd. In seasons of such privations as occur in some districts, previous to the garnering of the harvest, out-door relief should be distributed to such small land-occupiers as are in need, in order to guard against the appearance of fevers, which often show themselves at these times.

4th. It is desirable that the system of Union-rating should be adopted, in order that the incidence of taxation shall not press most heavily on the districts most requiring relief, as at present.

5th. Measures should be taken to secure a more complete registration of cases of disease; at present, only a fraction of the actual number goes upon the register, and thus the basis of sanitary statistics is insecure.

6th. When an epidemic invades a given district, the power of eviction should be suspended or deferred, both because the expulsion of the suffering sick must be injurious and may be fatal, and also because the infection of a dangerous disease is certain thus to be disseminated over an enlarged area.

7th. Large tracts of the West of Ireland (especially Mayo County), bear a striking resemblance to wide districts of Ulster. The soil, in many localities, is superior, producing excellent flax. Many of the inhabitants are descendants of families who migrated thither from the North in former times. It is, however, unquestionable that the condition of the inhabitants of the Northern Province is much superior to that of the Western population. This difference is not caused by soil, climate, nor racial qualities: it arises, obviously, from a difference in the social conditions under which they live. Hence the conclusion must be, that if the customs of tenure prevalent in the North were extended to the West, the large landholders, now absentees, induced to reside on their own estates, or to spend a due proportion of their revenues in improving them; and, it may be added, if proper encouragement were given the peasants to reclaim the waste lands,*

---

* Numerous instances of the stubborn industry of the peasants came frequently before our observation throughout the West. In many places, not only had rugged and rocky declivities and wild moors been cleared and tilled, but the peasants had brought sea-wrack from the shore and carried it in creels on their backs for long distances to fertilise their poor plots of ground. In several places there were neither roads nor lanes in the immediate vicinity of the little farms. Such severe toil must affect the system, in various but often unnoticed ways. Thus, near Kilcummin, a case came before us of a peasant, noted for his industry. Some of the stones which he had collected, for fencing and building, were ready for use beside the house; but he, though dressed as though going to his work, lay in silent melancholy, on his bed. He rose, when asked, for examination; but seemed to take no interest in life. His nervous system had utterly broken down. Innumerable testimonies to the active and intelligent work of the Irish peasant where allowed to cultivate the waste land, when but slight encouragement was given, or even when the prospect of augmented rent must have disheartened, are given by Young, Wakefield, and other writers, whose evidence is quoted in the *History of Irish Land Tenures*. Mr. Tuke bears witness in the same sense. Perhaps, the most vivid picture is one given by Thackeray, in his Irish Sketch Book (ch. II.): here, the improvers of the soil had the prospect of reaping what they

the social condition of the people would steadily improve, and destitution-diseases soon be classed with things of the past.

I have the honour to remain,
My Lords and Gentlemen,
Your obedient Servant,
GEORGE SIGERSON, M.D., M.R.I.A.

should sow in security. "Stretching away from Kilcullen bridge, for a couple of miles or more, near the fine house and plantations of the L—— family, is to be seen a much prettier sight, I think, than the finest park and mansion in the world. This is a tract of excessively green land, dotted over with brilliant white cottages, each with its couple of trim acres of garden, where you see thick potato-ridges covered with blossom, great blue plots of comfortable cabbages, and such pleasant plants of the poor man's garden. Two or three years' since, the land was a marshy common, which had never since the days of the Deluge fed any bigger being than a snipe, and into which the poor people descended, draining, and cultivating, and rescuing the marsh from the water, and raising their cabins, and setting up their little inclosures of two or three acres upon the land which they had thus created. 'Many of them has passed months in gaol for that,' said my informant (a groom on the back seat of my host's phæton); for it appears that certain gentlemen in the neighbourhood looked upon the titles of those new colonists with some jealousy, and would have been glad to deprive them; but there were some better philosophers among the surrounding gentry, who advised that instead of discouraging the settlers it would be best to help them, and the consequence has been, that there are now two hundred little flourishing homesteads upon this rescued land, and as many families in comfort and plenty."

This was probably the first example of a peasant proprietary in recent times in Ireland. Its prosperous state made a contrast with the condition of the district immediately beside it, "where women were pulling weeds and nettles in the hedges" for food, "having no bread, no potatoes, no work," and where a crowd encumbered the meal-shops of Kilcullen, waiting for the weekly dole of meal contributed by the gentry.

APPENDICES.

APPENDIX I.

FIRST MEETINGS OF MANSION HOUSE COMMITTEE.

The Committee of the MANSION HOUSE RELIEF FUND held their first meeting in the Mansion House at 2.30 p.m. on Saturday, 2nd January, 1880.

The Right Hon. the LORD MAYOR in the chair.

Present:—His Grace the Most Rev. Dr. TRENCH, Rev. J. DANIEL, P.P.; V. B. DILLON, Esq., jun.; Sir GEORGE OWENS, J.P.; Sir JOHN BARRINGTON, D.L.; P. J. SMYTH, Esq., M.P.; THOMAS PIM, Esq., jun; Alderman TARPEY, C. H. MELDON, Esq, Q.C., M.P.; J. F. LOMBARD, Esq.; C. KENNEDY, Esq., and Alderman HARRIS.

The Chairman reported that he had opened an account in the names of the treasurers in the National Bank, and had lodged £553 11s. to the credit of the account as per lists submitted. Sir JOHN BARRINGTON reported that he had lodged £52 7s. 1d., as per list submitted.

After the transaction of some preliminary business the following resolutions were passed:—

Proposed by Sir ARTHUR GUINNESS, M.P.; seconded by P. J. SMYTH, Esq., M.P.; supported by the RECORDER, the Very Rev. T. J. O'REILLY, Adm., Dr. SPEEDY, and the Hon. D. PLUNKETT, M.P.:—

"That the poorer classes in many parts of Ireland must, during the coming season, suffer great distress, involving absolute destitution, if extraneous aid be not liberally and promptly supplied; and that, without interfering with the beneficent efforts for a similar purpose already instituted, a Fund be now opened for the Relief of the Distress in Ireland, to be called "The Dublin Mansion House Relief Fund."

Proposed by the Most Rev. Dr. TRENCH, seconded by Mr. P. J. SMYTH, M.P.—

"That a letter signed by the Chairman, be addressed to the Local Government Board, requesting that this Committee be supplied from time to time, and as promptly as possible, with such information as the Board can afford as to the distress in Ireland."

Proposed by Mr. PIM, seconded by Mr. KENNEDY—

"That all resolutions of this Committee be capable of being rescinded or altered after one week's notice, but not otherwise."

Proposed by his Grace the Most Rev. Dr. TRENCH, seconded by the Rev. J. DANIEL, P.P.—

"That the action of this Committee be solely through local agencies, and not through direct communication with those who seek or may need its relief."

Proposed by Mr. MELDON, M.P., seconded by Sir GEORGE OWENS—

"That the agency through which this Committee would desire to dispense its relief would be Local Committees, including, wherever practicable, the clergymen of all denominations in the district, the Chairman or Vice-Chairman of the Board of Guardians, the Chairman or Vice-Chairman of the Dispensary Committee and the Medical Officer."

Proposed by his Grace the Most Rev. Dr. TRENCH, seconded by Rev. J. DANIEL, P.P.—

"That as a condition of being recognised as an agency at whose recommendation and by whose instrumentality relief shall be imparted, the Local Committee for any district must satisfy this Committee of the existence of acute and exceptional distress in the district from which the claims to be relieved come."

Proposed by his Grace the Most Rev. Dr. TRENCH, seconded by Mr. THOMAS PIM, jun.—

"That a Local Committee, dispensing relief from this fund, must engage to keep a book in which shall be entered the names of applicants for relief, particulars as to age, occupation, number in family, extent of land held (if any), and nature and amount of relief afforded in each case; and this book shall always be open to the Committee, and also they will be expected to furnish weekly accounts of receipts from this fund and disbursements of the same."

Ordered, that the meetings for the present be held three times a week—on Tuesdays, Thursdays, and Saturdays—at the hour of three p.m.

The Committee then adjourned to Tuesday, the 6th instant, at three o'clock.

ORDINARY MEETING—COMMUNICATIONS.

The Committee met January 13th in the Mansion House.

Right Hon. the LORD MAYOR in the chair.

Members present—His Grace the Most Rev. Dr. TRENCH, T. M. HUTTON, Rev. Canon BAGOT, J. F. LOMBARD, Sir G. OWENS, Rev. J. DANIEL, V. B. DILLON, Alderman HARRIS, W. M. MURPHY, G. DELANY, D. DRIMMIE, P. M. FAY, Sir J. BARRINGTON, CHARLES KENNEDY, D. DRUMMOND.

The minutes of last meeting were read and confirmed.

The cash statement showed that the total amount of subscriptions received up to the present is £4,414.

It was resolved that such subscribers as have not yet sent in their subscriptions be requested to do so at once.

A telegram was read from Mr. R. O'GORMAN, of New York, stating that a Relief Committee had been formed in that city, and promising to give further particulars by letter.

A telegram was also received from the Mayor of New York, expressing sympathy for the great distress, and announcing that he had communicated with the Relief Committee and the Public Press of New York on the matter.

Letter received from the Mayor of Bolton enclosing £50, the first instalment from that town in aid of the Irish Relief Fund.

Letter also received from the Right Hon. the Lord Mayor of London, enclosing £500 which he had received from the Queensland National Bank—First instalment from Brisbane in aid of the Irish Relief Fund.

The Mayors of Manchester, Preston, and Chester also wrote promising co-operation.

The following letter from the Most Rev. Dr. GILLOOLY, Bishop of Sligo, was read and noted on the minutes:—

"*Sligo, January* 8, 1880.

"MY DEAR LORD MAYOR,

"Your Lordship could not inaugurate your year of office more nobly and usefully than by organising, as you have done at your meeting of last Friday, the Mansion House Central Committee for the relief of the destitution now so rapidly spreading over our afflicted country. The long roll of representative names from every class and creed, which I have read on your Committee list, is in itself a proof, not only of the necessity that exists for the action of the Committee, but of the predominating influence which Christian charity so happily exercises in our metropolis, especially in periods of public distress, over religious and political prejudices.

"As your Committee is anxious to obtain information regarding the distressed districts of the country, I feel it my duty to at once make known to you the condition of the poor people of this diocese; and I am enabled to do so with entire certainty by the detailed statements I have lately received from each of my priests respecting his own flock, statements made in every case from his own personal observations and inquiries.

"Of this diocese generally, I may say that the failure of crops, the loss and depreciation of live stock, and other causes of distress, which have been severely felt in other parts of Ireland, have pressed on us with exceptional severity. The potato crop was all but totally lost in the County Roscommon; scarcely one-tenth of it was fit for human use. The hay was lost, and the grass injured to a great extent on our low-lying, undrained lands. The sheep of Roscommon, which constitute its chief source of prosperity, perished by disease from end to end of the county, to the impoverishment, in very many cases to the utter ruin, of graziers and farmers. Business has collapsed in our towns; tenants are unable to pay their rents; landlords themselves are straitened and embarrassed; in a word, distress is universal; whilst in the cottier and small tenant class, especially along the sea-side and in worn-out bog-lands, there are thousands of families already suffering from hunger; and if relief does not speedily reach them, famine, sickness, and death will soon visit their desolate cabins. When such is the distressed condition of the classes usually prosperous and comfortable, and when the majority of our peasantry have neither money nor credit, and a large proportion of them not even the necessaries of life, it is evident beyond denial that the means of relief cannot come from the people themselves, either in the form of extra poor-rate or of private voluntary alms; and that to impose an adequate relief tax on the tenants and landlords of the destitute districts would be in reality to reduce the whole country to the same level of pauperism; whilst by the operation of this Poor Law relief, through Gregory's quarter-acre clause, the cottiers and small landholders would be doomed by thousands to eviction and death. Hence the conviction so loudly and generally proclaimed by public bodies and private individuals, without distinction of class or creed, that the means of relief should come chiefly from the Treasury. So far the Treasury remains closed against us, and there is not even a promise that it will be opened. It occurs to me, then, to suggest to your Committee that it would be clearly within the range of your duties to press the action of the Government in this matter, and to do so with all the influence that belongs to so large and representative a body. In the absence of Government relief the efforts of your Committee will barely mitigate the general destitution, and diminish the number of deaths from starvation; they will be totally inadequate to save the health of the people from hunger and cold, much more so to enable them to seed their lands and to escape another famine in 1881. On the other hand, as a supplement to State relief, your contributions will save the life and health of thousands who cannot benefit by public works, and for this very large class of destitute poor your most generous efforts would be required. You would have a perfect right, it seems to me, to press this view on the Government. * *

* * * * * *

"I cannot close this letter, long as it is, without offering an observation, suggested by certain Local Committee arrangements, lately announced in the public papers. The observation is—that the Parochial or other Local Committees, through which you will distribute your fund, although they may usefully include Poor-law Guardians, ought to be distinct from and independent of the Poor-law Union organisation; and that the selection of families for relief should not be left to landlords, agents or bailiffs, no more than to Poor-law relieving officers.

"The chief object of your Committee and of our Parochial Committees is, as I understand it, to save the destitute labourers, cottiers, and small farmers not only from death and sickness by starvation but also from the workhouse; to enable them to keep their families together until the evil days shall have passed over. Now, it is a matter of unhappy notoriety, that in Connemara and in other places that I could name, advantage is being taken of the destitution of the small landholders to evict them and get rid of them;* and a conviction prevails amongst the peasantry in every part of the destitute districts that now, as in 1847, the landlords are anxious to force them into the workhouse in order to level their cabins and free themselves from further liability for their support. Such being the case, it seems to me that the relief through which we hope to be able to keep those poor people in their homes and holdings should not be entrusted for distribution to those who are even suspected of a desire to deprive them of their homes.

"I have the honour to remain, my dear Lord Mayor,
Your very faithful servant,
" ✠ L. GILLOOLY."

A letter was also received from the Most Rev. Dr. WOODLOCK, Bishop of Ardagh, which was referred to the Sub-Committee.

Several applications for assistance to relieve distress were read, query sheets forwarded, and the letters referred to the Sub-Committee appointed to deal with applications.

The Committee were waited on by Mr. S. C. M'CORMACK, Solicitor, of Carramore, who was deputed by the clergy of his district of all denominations to request that some relief might be extended to the people in the neighbourhood of Belmullet and surrounding district. Mr. M'CORMACK stated that a small subscription had already been got up locally, but that this was barely sufficient to keep the people temporarily from starvation. He stated the people were most anxious to obtain work, and that he had known them to remain out in all weather from eight o'clock in the morning till six in the evening, working hard, for a shilling a day. Many of them were now living on turnips. The landlords of the district were non-resident, and had given no assistance.

Applications in due form for relief were entertained for the following localities, and the sums stated, respectively, were granted in each case:—

Tubbercurry, £25; Arklow, £25; Ballintubber, £20; Oughterard, £30; Caherciveen, £30.

* The return to an order of the House of Lords, issued in January, 1881, giving the number of evictions throughout Ireland which came to the knowledge of the constabulary in each quarter of the year ending December 31st, 1880, sets forth the following:—

In the quarter ending 31st March, 554 families, or 2,748 persons were evicted. Of these, 64 families, or 306 persons, were re-admitted as tenants, and 235 families, or 1,167 persons as caretakers.

In the quarter ending 30th June, 690 families, or 3,508 persons, were evicted. Of these 65 families, or 268 persons, were re-admitted as tenants, and 259 families, or 1,355 persons, as caretakers.

In the quarter ending 30th September, 671 families, or 3,447 persons, were evicted. Of these 42 families, or 197 persons, were re-admitted as tenants, and 390 families, or 2,158 persons, as caretakers.

In the quarter ending the 31st December, 198 families, or 954 persons, were evicted. Of these 46 families, or 250 persons, were re-admitted as tenants, and 63 families, or 316 persons, as caretakers.

The totals for the year were—2,110 families, or 10,657 persons, evicted. Of these 217 families, or 1,021 persons, were re-admitted as tenants, and 947 families, or 4,996 persons, as caretakers.

Taking the returns by provinces, the subjoined shows that

In Ulster there were 497 families, or 2,401 persons evicted. Of these 52 families, or 237 persons, were re-admitted as tenants, and 275 families, or 1,407 persons, as caretakers.

In Leinster there were 484 families, or 2,195 persons evicted. Of these 65 families, or 269 persons, were re-admitted as tenants, and 189 families, or 943 persons, as caretakers.

In Connaught 387 families, or 1,986 persons, were evicted. Of these, 22 families or 97 persons, were re-admitted as tenants, and 164 families, or 636 persons, as caretakers.

In Munster 742 families, or 4,075 persons, were evicted. Of these 78 families, or 418 persons, were re-admitted as tenants, and 319 families, or 1,710 persons, as caretakers. [Tenants re-admitted, forfeit their previous rights.]

APPENDIX II.

DEPUTATION TO OBTAIN SEED GRANT.

On the 29th January a deputation from the Mansion House Committee for the Relief of Distress in Ireland, waited on his Grace the DUKE OF MARLBOROUGH, and the Right Honourable JAMES LOWTHER, M.P., the Chief Secretary, at the Castle, for the purpose of urging upon the Government the necessity of supplying potato and other seed to the small farmers, in order to prevent the occurrence of a famine next year. The deputation consisted of the Right Hon. the LORD MAYOR, his Grace Archbishop TRENCH, Mr. P. J. SMYTH, M.P.; Sir JOHN BARRINGTON, Sir JAMES W. MACKEY, Sir GEORGE OWENS, Mr. JONATHAN PIM, the Rev. Canon BAGOT, Alderman PURDON, Mr. GEORGE BROWN, M.P., Mr. WILLIAM LANE JOYNT, and Mr. CHARLES KENNEDY.

The LORD MAYOR—Your Grace, at one of the earliest meetings of the Mansion House Committee for the relief of distress in Ireland, the question of the supply of seed to small farmers, more particularly seed potatoes, was brought under the attention of the Committee. They considered it as of vast importance, because they thought that probably in the distressed districts the supply of seed potatoes would be consumed as food, and that in any case the bad seed of this year would be likely, if sown, to produce a recurrence of failure of the crop next year. They referred the matter to a Sub-Committee in order to see what could be done, and the Sub-Committee reported that it scarcely came within the immediate scope of the objects of the Committee, which was appointed to collect funds for the relief of immediate destitution. In any case our funds are not sufficiently large to deal with the matter. Therefore the Committee resolved to appoint a deputation, and to ask your Grace and the CHIEF SECRETARY to confer with them on the subject; and it is with the view of pressing on your Grace as the representative of the Government, the great importance of this matter, and the necessity for immediate action, that this deputation, which is a truly representative one, has come to-day. Mr. PIM will be able to give your Grace some facts within his knowledge in connection with the famine of 1847, in the relief of which it is known that he took so active a part by the supply of seed for the subsequent harvest, the want of which was one of the causes that then produced such an amount of intense distress. Some gentlemen who are better conversant than I am with the practical details of the subject will also lay their views before you.

Mr. JONATHAN PIM—I did not anticipate that I would be called on, but I think the subject is sufficiently clear without going into details or giving any statistics. It is of paramount importance that good seed should be sown for the coming year. The LORD MAYOR has stated that the very poor farmers will be obliged to eat their potatoes, and it is very fortunate that they will. I should be almost inclined to say it would be better that the land remained unsown than that they should sow the refuse of the bad crop of last year. I may remind your Grace that there was a distribution of seed in the year 1847. The Government then took the matter in hand. I do not know to what extent the distribution took place, but it was not of potato seed alone, nor even oats, but also of turnip, cabbage, parsnip and carrot seed. The object then was to draw away the attention of the small farmers in the remote parts of Ireland from the planting of potatoes, and it was expected that great benefit would be derived from the planting of other crops. About 40,000lbs of seed were transferred by the Government to the Committee, of which I was one of the secretaries, and were distributed by us in addition to a considerable quantity—I am not sure of the exact amount, but I should say it exceeded 150,000lbs—that had been previously distributed by ourselves. The seed was distributed by agents employed almost wholly in the West of Ireland, and in very small quantities, and to a very large number of persons gratuitously.

The Lord Lieutenant—By Government officials?

Mr. Pim—I cannot say; I know that Government seed was distributed, but I cannot say how it was done. I can only speak of what was distributed by our Committee; in many cases individuals were employed as agents.

The Lord Lieutenant—Did you get a subsidy from the Government then?

Mr. Pim—We had made over to us about 40,000lbs of seed which remained over from the Government distribution. It would be easy to ascertain what was done by the Government at that time. I only wish to point out that the thing was done, and that whatever was not distributed by the Government was handed over to our Committee, and that we distributed it both in 1847 and 1848. I believe that a considerable amount of food was produced from the seed so distributed on land that would not have been sown at all but for that distribution. I think also that the beneficial result of it remains to the present day, for there is a very much larger quantity of cabbage, turnips, and other vegetables of that description grown now in the West of Ireland than there was thirty years ago. But it is clear that the object at the present time is a totally different one. It is not to alter the kinds of roots or plants which have heretofore been grown by the small farmers, but to provide them with seed which is likely to produce good crops. Your Grace must see that it is beyond the power of a Committee like ours to undertake anything of the sort.

The Lord Lieutenant—What kind of seed, in your opinion, ought to be provided? Potato seed is what the Lord Mayor has alluded to. Is it your opinion that potato and other seed should be provided, or other seed in preference to potato seed?

Mr. Pim—Our idea, I think, is that potatoes and oats are the most important crops. No doubt other crops ought to be sown, but it is of paramount importance to procure a fair potato and a good oat crop.

The Lord Mayor—Your Grace, as far as the Committee were concerned, they only took into consideration the potato and oats question.

The Lord Lieutenant—Have you gone into the matter so as to obtain any idea or estimate of the quantity of seed that would be required, either looking to the number or size of the holdings or to the number of persons to be assisted?

The Lord Mayor—They have not, because they considered that that would be a thing to ascertain accurately after a little time, and that it was desirable first to place the question of principle before you. There would then be, perhaps, sufficient time to go into the details if the deputation got any encouragement to do so.

The Lord Lieutenant—At what time ought the planting to commence?

The Rev. Canon Bagot—I might say a word with regard to the two questions which your Grace has put, having been the mover of this matter in the Mansion House Committee, and having given it a great deal of attention. At the outset I would say that I think there is a difference between the distress existing in Ireland now and the famine of 1846 and 1847. I think it will be found that the most distressed portion of the population now is a class which were not so badly off in 1846 and 1847—namely, the farmers holding from four or five to twenty or twenty-five acres. As an instance, I may mention that I visited a farmer in my own district of Kildare, who is the holder of sixteen acres, and there was not a particle of food in his house except some turnips and some Indian meal. The man had not asked for relief, and a neighbour of his told me that before he would do so he would starve. This I only give as an illustration; but, thank God, such cases are rare in my own part of the country. Your Grace asked a question as to the holdings of Ireland. I find that in the two provinces of Munster and Connaught there are 118,500 holdings of under fifteen acres.

The LORD LIEUTENANT.—What kind of rating would these have?

Rev. Canon BAGOT.—Oh, I did not go into the point of rating. I assumed that one out of every three of these holdings would require assistance in some shape or form, and I found that to give half an Irish acre of potato-seed to one-third of the total number of holdings would take £160,000. Of course this is a mere estimate, but I believe the figures are right. In order to give to all the holdings in Ireland of the same extent, potato-seed for half an English acre it would take £270,000. I jotted down these figures just to impress upon you how little any voluntary organisation could do in the way of dealing with this important matter; and I think our Committee are unanimous as to the inability of any private organisation to do so. We are quite aware of the difficulties; but the urgent and pressing question is to avert an almost worse disaster next year. I don't think there will be any potato-seed left amongst the farmers—it will have to be eaten; and that may be a very good thing, since for the last two or three years the potato crop has been getting worse and worse in Ireland. But the farmers are as much in want of oats for seed. With respect to time, it is of almost paramount importance that the potato crop should be put down, if possible, in the month of March, and certainly not later than the first week in April. Many people put potatoes down even in February, but the last fortnight in March is perhaps the very best time for sowing that crop. Of course if the Government take up this question a large amount of matters of detail will have to be settled with respect to protection and the mode of distributing the seed, so that there is really not a moment to be lost if we are to have a potato crop and an oat crop next year. I know a good deal of what landlords have been doing in the way of giving seed, but it will be a mere drop in the ocean compared with what will be required for the wants of Ireland. The question, therefore, is one of really vital importance to the country, and I hope it will receive due consideration from the Government.

The CHIEF SECRETARY—From your practical knowledge would you prefer oat seed to other seeds?

Rev. Canon BAGOT—Well, I think the simple answer to that is that the climate of Ireland is very suitable for oats. No doubt barley is largely grown in many parts of the country; but if a small farmer grows barley he sells it off his land and very often spends the money in other ways than buying food, whereas if he has grown oats he sends it to the mill, and gets it back at once in a form in which it can be used for food. Many persons in my neighbourhood are living on oatmeal.

The CHIEF SECRETARY—Having regard to the climate of Ireland, I would have expected you to suggest grass seed. I thought you were following up Mr. Pim's suggestion.

The LORD LIEUTENANT—What I gathered from Mr. Pim's remarks was, that at the time of the former famine it was the object of the Government rather to discourage the growing of potatoes, as being an uncertain crop and liable to failure, and to show that other crops might be grown to greater advantage by the small farmers and other poor people. On the other hand, the converse of that seems to be now the proposition, and potatoes and oats are now put forward—I don't give any opinion as to whether it is right or wrong—as being the crops essential for the small farmers. Potatoes seem now to have recovered their importance in the domestic agriculture of the small farmers.

The Lord Mayor—I can point out to your Grace the view taken by the Committee on this question. We did not think it would be wise to seek to interfere with the ordinary culture of the country, or to try to be wiser than the farmers themselves as to what crops suited their particular holdings. We were aware that where the potatoes have not failed the produce would be eaten. We did not wish to substitute one class of crop for another, but to secure that cultivation should proceed in its natural course uninterfered with, as far as the course of the crops is concerned, by us. We knew that oats and potatoes were the two staple crops. With reference to the question of grass seed, there is no danger that it will be eaten by hungry men.

The Lord Lieutenant—Just so.

The Lord Mayor—Potatoes may be eaten, but whatever grass seed exists will remain, and no person will eat it. Of course the grass farmers have suffered from the depression, but not to the same extent as the tenants of small holdings.

The Chief Secretary—I don't wish to be misunderstood. I asked Canon Bagot, who I know possesses a practical knowledge of the subject, whether —assuming potatoes to be disposed of, as we know they are an article of food—he preferred oats to any other crop. I asked a practical question and he gave an answer to it.

Mr. Pim—I wish to give a slight explanation. I don't think that the object thirty years ago was so much to discourage entirely the growth of potatoes as to show the people of the West of Ireland that there were other crops worthy of their attention. I do think that that object has been achieved. But it is perfectly evident that the main crops of the country have been, and continue to be, potatoes and oats; and one object now is to provide better seed for both than the people have been accustomed to sow, especially as regards potato seed. I believe there is no question that it is of great importance to change the seed, whereas the people in the West of Ireland have been in the habit of planting their own potatoes again and again. By growing a better seed in those and other districts, we should hope to secure a good crop next year, instead of a bad one.

Rev. Canon Bagot—In one respect there is an essential difference between the present time and 1847. At that time there were large numbers of labourers occupying quarter-acre holdings, and subsisting on potatoes. But now it is not merely a question as to the subsistence of a large number of labouring people, but there is a class of farmers who require assistance as regards the ordinary staple crop of the country.

The Lord Lieutenant—I suppose you will not exclude the class whose holdings are rated at under £4. These are now, as much as any other class, suffering from famine and distress, and I suppose the potato would be a very essential crop to them.

Mr. P. J. Smith was understood to say that there were large numbers of that class in Mayo.

The Lord Lieutenant—There are not so many of them as there were in the famine times; but, at the same time, they exist as a class, and they must be attended to as well as the others.

Rev. Canon Bagot—A valuation of £4 may in a great many cases represent a holding of fifteen or sixteen acres. In Munster and Connaught there are 18,800 holdings of under one acre, 59,000 of from one to five acres, and 70,500 of from five to fifteen acres.

The Lord Lieutenant—Assuming the importance of providing seed potatoes for those people, what is your opinion as to the quantity of ground that ought to be planted with potatoes in order to prevent a disaster in the way of a famine from recurring in another year?

Rev. Canon Bagot—Well, that is not a point to which I have given sufficient attention to be able to answer off book. My calculation was that half an acre of seed potatoes should be given all round; but of course many of these would be farmers holding sixteen or eighteen acres of ground, and they generally have from an acre to an acre and a half of potatoes.

The LORD LIEUTENANT—You see there is an important distinction to draw in this way. Assuming—which we have not yet granted—that it is necessary to make provision in the way of potato seed, it becomes very necessary to determine the quantity of seed to be provided. If it is to be granted, it must be by way of gift or loan, or something of that sort. I suppose you would not assume that the tenant or the small farmer should plant as much potatoes as he liked. He might, perhaps, get a quantity of seed, and might plant a considerable extent of ground, and derive a profit out of the seed so granted; whereas, I suppose your idea and contention would be, that he should have simply seed enough to prevent famine in future years. What I want to know is, on that assumption—in order to prevent famine in future years—what do you think is the quantity of ground which should be put under potatoes, the the seed being provided in some extraordinary manner?

Rev. Canon BAGOT—Taking the number of each family at six, my calculation is that half an acre of seed would be perfectly sufficient.

The CHIEF SECRETARY—Do you contemplate providing persons belonging to the classes to whom you have referred merely with the means of sustenance for themselves and families in the coming year, or do you contemplate anything in the nature of a speculation on their part?

Rev. Canon BAGOT—We ask assistance merely to enable them to supply food for themselves and their families in the coming year, and not for anything as a source of profit; however, I am only expressing my individual opinion.

The LORD LIEUTENANT was understood to ask what quantity of ground did the deputation think should be planted with oats.

Rev. Canon BAGOT—That is a very serious question, and I should rather not answer it. Of course, I could give my own opinion. If I understand your Grace, your question is—supposing that there is help to be given to the farmer in oats and potatoes, what amount of ground should be planted with potatoes and what amount with oats?

The LORD LIEUTENANT—Yes.

The Rev. Canon BAGOT—That is a question that I really think is for consideration by each district. There are some districts in which the whole of the relief should be given in potato seed. There are other districts where, no doubt, it would be found that half oats and half potatoes would be better. But with the little information that I possess, I would not like to answer the question.

The LORD LIEUTENANT—Supposing that the Government came to the conclusion of rendering extraordinary assistance, they could not be called on to render assistance to the farmers in the ordinary course of cropping their farms. Your point is simply to prevent famine in the coming year. That I understand to be the point. The distinction is a very important one to draw.

Alderman PURDON—The potato and oat crops come into consumption earlier than any others. I recollect that in 1848 the Government gave a grant for the purpose of employing thoroughly practical farmers to instruct the small farmers how to sow the seed given to them, and they were very successful. I think that was kept up for two or three years. The Agricultural Society found that the potato had been grown continuously and extensively to the exclusion of other crops, and the failure of that crop having made such ravages in 1848, that caused them to think that some remedy should be applied. But I believe there is no crop which gives more useful food to the population than the potato. It not alone feeds their families, but assists the people in rearing of the pig, which has been called the "rent-payer."

The LORD LIEUTENANT—You see it is a very important point to determine the quantity of potato seed that will be required. Canon BAGOT's contention is that half an acre would be a fairly reasonable quantity. As regards oats, it would be equally important to determine the quantity that would be necessary to prevent destitution and also to prevent famine in the coming year.

Alderman PURDON—That would depend very much on the size of the farm. The less potatoes and the less oats the more grass. The small farmer cannot afford to keep over his stock for any length of time. He must produce young stock and sell them. I am sure Canon BAGOT would rather see one acre of potatoes and two acres of oats than half an acre of each.

The CHIEF SECRETARY—I don't express any opinion as to whether the Government should give any assistance at all or not. I am merely asking questions for information, the same as his Grace has done. All parties whom I have consulted are of opinion that potatoes and oats, and, in fact, I may say almost every crop except grass, are of very doubtful investment in Ireland owing to its climate and soil.

Alderman PURDON—I would suggest a mixture of green crops, such as turnips, carrots, and parsnips.

Rev. Canon BAGOT—I am, unfortunately, in the position of having a farm on which I could not grow grass. I am afraid a great number of farmers in Ireland are in the same position.

The CHIEF SECRETARY—Of course they are.

Rev. Canon BAGOT—You must have tillage. But we are only here on the food question, and not with reference to any profit outside it.

The LORD LIEUTENANT—Does any other gentleman wish to make any remarks?

Alderman PURDON—I am sorry for having to make so many, but I rather dissent from one remark of Canon BAGOT, to the effect that this question chiefly effects small farmers, the holders of not more than five acres. In the County of Mayo the labouring classes, generally speaking, don't get employment for more than a quarter of the year, and they are supported in the winter by potatoes grown on ground which they hold in conacre from the small farmers. I think that a very undesirable state of things, but it is the fact. Although I think it has died out in Leinster, it has not died out in Connaught. But there is a large number of these men whom it would be quite as important to assist by supplying food and seed to them as the small farmers.

The LORD LIEUTENANT—I would just ask one other question, I am rather inquisitive : would there be the same difficulty, I don't mean in point of money, in providing oats for the farmers as potatoes? It would require some organisation in order to provide a considerable amount of potatoes. The potato crop has perfectly failed in many parts. In some places they have been eaten and in others they have deteriorated, so that according to the views of Canon BAGOT and the other speakers it would be desirable that the people should consume them, so as to have fresh seed to start with. That renders the case of the potato a peculiar one altogether. Is it the same with the oats? Have the oats so failed, and is there the same difficulty with respect to the crop that Government assistance and Government organisation will be necessary in order to provide for the people?

Rev. Canon BAGOT—I think we never had a finer crop in Ireland than the oats last year. I am afraid that the potato crop has been an extensive failure, and you may not be able, without enormous difficulty, to get the quantity of seed that will be required for next year's crop. In many cases I think the difficulty would be greatly lessened by relying on oats as a supplementary crop.

The CHIEF SECRETARY—It very much comes to what I thought at first—that it is your intention to encourage the growth of oats to a great extent. You not merely propose that the ordinary oat crop should continue to be sown, but you rather think it is the best crop to be grown.

Rev. Canon BAGOT—For food. It is always to be taken for granted that we come here on the food question, and it is to be remembered that the small farmers and labourers use a great deal of oatmeal. The oats can be sent to the mill and got back as oatmeal before the potatoes are ready at all.

At the close of the interview,

The LORD LIEUTENANT said—I will just say a few words, my LORD MAYOR, in answer to the deputation. Of course you will understand that in what I say now I merely speak for myself and the CHIEF SECRETARY, and that we don't at all pledge the Government to any line or course. Of course what is represented to us here it will be our duty to represent to the Government in England, and to give them every opportunity of forming a full and fair estimate of the circumstances. But as regards ourselves, I wish to say this, that it must not be supposed that this point has at all escaped our attention. I may say it is a point which for my own part—and I know I may answer for my right honourable friend the CHIEF SECRETARY also—we have been considering anxiously for some time past. But you will see, as has, indeed been stated by gentlemen here, that it is a very wide question. It may involve the expenditure of a very large sum of money, and can only be determined on a very accurate basis. Other points are involved, including the usual course of economic husbandry in the country, and it is a question which involves a request for the grant of a considerable subsidy from Government for the purpose of providing seed to a certain extent to carry out the ordinary occupations and operations of husbandry in the country. The first thing of course for you to do must be to form an accurate estimate of the sum that will be required, and of the real extent of the want that is represented. I don't think we can go a step in the direction you point out until we are able to form an accurate estimate of what are the wants in the matter. Of course the conversation that has taken place here will have pointed out how many points of difficulty there are in the matter. Canon BAGOT has very kindly given us the advantage of his great experience and knowledge of the subject as regards what he would recommend. Of course, as he stated himself, it was only his individual opinion, and on further examination it might have to be modified in various ways. Therefore I think the first point of all is to be enabled to form an accurate estimate of the real want that is before us in the country. I quite see the importance of losing no time. I believe it is a matter that we must at once consider. For my own part I am quite willing to give it my full and earnest consideration, and I may say the same for my right honourable friend, the CHIEF SECRETARY. I can see no better way of doing this than for you to appoint two or three gentlemen to confer with us on the subject. Canon BAGOT has great experience, and other gentlemen have great experience; and we shall be very happy to meet any gentlemen for the purpose of talking the matter over, with a view to arriving at a conclusion as to the actual requirements that might be necessary to be provided for. When this has been done it will then be our duty to represent the whole case to the Government, giving them all the facts, but without prejudging the question in any way, or saying what the decision of the Government in England may be. But if we get the information we want, it will be our duty to present it in the best manner we can with a view to arriving at a conclusion. But I would impress on the gentlemen present that the subject has engaged our attention, and that we are now in course of making inquiries with respect to it, and shall be in possession of a considerable amount of information in a short time; and if we can have, in addition to that information, the advantage of the experience of any gentlemen here present, with whom we shall be very willing to confer, I think it will help the matter forward, and we shall be enabled, I hope, to arrive at some kind of estimate of the actual necessities of the case. Of course, when we get that information, and have a clear view of the whole wants of the case, we shall then be enabled to make such propositions, and present the case in such a way to the Government in England that they will be able to consider it fairly, which I am sure they will do, and with a view to the best interests of the country.

The LORD MAYOR—Your Grace, on the part of the deputation, I have to thank you and Mr. LOWTHER for giving us this long and patient hearing, and for the kind and sympathetic answer which you have given to us. We shall be delighted to carry out your Grace's suggestion of appointing some gentlemen of experience to confer with you on the subject. Three or four gentlemen will do themselves the honour of waiting on your Grace whenever it suits your convenience.

The LORD LIEUTENANT—If you will let me know when the gentlemen are to come, I shall meet them.

The deputation then withdrew.

NOTE.—The following statistics, taken from "Thom's Directory," represent the extent, produce, and value of the wheat, oat, and potato crops, during the six years previous to 1880:—

Crops, and Estimated Price.	Years.	Extent of each Crop.	Average Produce Per S. Acre.	Estimated Produce.	Estimated Value.
		Stat. Acres.	cwts.	cwts.	£
Wheat, 10s. per cwt.	1874	187,978	15·4	2,885,569	1,442,784
	1875	158,995	14·6	2,318,178	1,159,088
	1876	119,700	17·0	2,023,492	1,011,146
	1877	139,297	13·6	1,901,100	950,550
	1878	154,041	15·0	2,307,685	1,153,842
	1879	157,511	11·4	1,798,931	899,465
Oats 6s. 6d. per cwt. 8s. per cwt.	1874	1,480,897	13·5	20,006,943	6,502,254
	1875	1,501,867	15·3	22,926,430	7,451,088
	1876	1,487,166	14·3	21,415,195	8,566,078
	1877	1,476,172	12·1	17,846,563	7,138,625
	1878	1,412,845	13·5	19,044,645	7,617,858
	1879	1,330,261	11·7	15,532,629	6,213,052
Potatoes, 60s. per ton.	1874	892,425	4·0	3,551,605	10,654,815
	1875	906,586	3·9	3,512,884	10,538,652
	1876	880,716	4·7	4,154,784	12,464,382
	1877	873,291	2·0	1,757,275	5,271,822
	1878	846,712	3·0	2,526,504	7,579,512
	1879	842,671	1·3	1,113,676	3,341,028

APPENDIX III.

DEPUTATION TO CHIEF SECRETARY IN REFERENCE TO DISTRESS.

On Saturday, 8th May, 1880, a deputation from the Mansion House Committee waited on the Chief Secretary, the Right Hon. W. E. FORSTER, at his offices in the Castle, for the purpose of laying before him a statement setting forth the real nature and extent of the distress in Ireland. Mr. ROBINSON of the Local Government Board, and Mr. BURKE, Under Secretary, were in attendance.

The Deputation consisted of—

The Right Hon. the LORD MAYOR, Mr. BROOKS, M.P., Mr. P. J. SMYTH, M.P., Archbishop TRENCH, the Rev. NICHOLAS DONNELLY, Administrator, Westland-row, Rev. JAMES DANIEL, P.P., Rev. Canon BAGOT, Sir JOHN BARRINGTON, Sir GEORGE OWENS, Mr. JONATHAN PIM, the Rev. Dr. KIRKPATRICK, Mr. CHARLES KENNEDY, Mr. J. F. LOMBARD, Mr. EDWARD FOX, Alderman PURDON, Alderman HARRIS, Mr. JOHN O'CONNOR, Mr. RICHARD ALLEN, Mr. MAXWELL HUTTON, Mr. V. B. DILLON, and Mr. M'CABE FAY.

The LORD MAYOR, addressing the Chief Secretary, said they appeared before him as a deputation from the Mansion House Committee, which was originated for the alleviation of distress in Ireland. They sought an interview with him at the earliest moment, being aware that he was about to return to England shortly, in order to lay before him a few facts which they consider to be of great importance. Their Committee had now been at work for some four months. They had received a very considerable sum for distribution in aid of the distress, amounting to about £150,000. They had distributed some £120,000 of that, and they had some £30,000 left in their hands. They had, more or less, depending upon them 800 Local Committees established throughout the country, and some hundreds of thousands of people were receiving relief through those Local Committees. They had distributed on an average £30,000 per month. It had been somewhat more latterly. Last month it amounted to £37,000. This month—that is the month ending last week—it amounted to £33,000. They had very strong testimony that large numbers of the people were absolutely dependent for the means of subsistence from day to day upon the relief afforded through the charitable organisation of the Mansion House, and there were many others depending on other similar organisations. They had evidence which they deemed convincing that the distress was not likely to be in any considerable degree mitigated before the end of July and the coming in of the new harvest; and the Committee did not see any reason to sanguinely hope that their resources would be maintained for that period. They thought they saw signs of the diminution of contributions to their fund. It had been decreasing rapidly of late, and the amount they now had on hands would only suffice to meet the distress for about a month. They therefore feared that for the ensuing two months there would be a cessation of the charitable relief afforded by the Mansion House Committee, and he thought the other charitable committees were in a somewhat similar condition. They believed there was no very great likelihood of the charitable contributions keeping up to an extent sufficient to deal with the distress as it had been hitherto dealt with by the charitable committees. At any rate, they believed that so far as their Committee was concerned, they would not have resources sufficient to carry on the relief up to the beginning of August, and they believed it was absolutely necessary that aid should be given up to the end of August. They thought that when the time came when they might be driven for want of funds to cease their charitable distribution, a very severe shock might occur. They feared there was no organisation at present in existence which could take up their work.

Owing to many causes—owing to the extreme, and not unnatural but laudable, reluctance of the people to accept poor-law relief, even in the shape of out-door relief—owing to various other causes which it was unnecessary to go into in detail, they feared that when their relief ceased, as they feared it must in the course of some five or six weeks, except something unexpected occurred, a large number of persons would be left in an utterly destitute condition. They thought it right to represent these facts to him (Mr. FORSTER) in order that the Government should have full notice of what they believed to be the danger likely to ensue on the cessation of their work, except full preparation was made in the meantime for some other organisation to keep the people from starvation until the coming in of the harvest. They did not think they would be justified in making to the Government any specific recommendation as to what course might be adopted, but they felt that a heavy responsibility in one sense rested upon them, because, owing to their organisation, they had brought large numbers of the destitute to look to them from week to week for the means of subsistence ; and if the day came, and he feared it must come soon, when they could give them no further supplies, they would be placed in a desperate condition during such period of transition as might be required before some other organisation was put in motion. You, Sir (added the LORD MAYOR), who were here in 1847, and took so deep an interest in the sufferings of the people then—a fact which is not forgotten by the Irish people—you are aware that there was a period at that time when the relief works ceased, and before the system of giving relief by way of food was organised, when more suffering was entailed on the people than at any other time ; and what we are anxious about is, that when our organisation, which has assumed very great proportions, comes to an end, no such shock shall take place as took place during that dreadful period in '47. We see only one way of avoiding this, by giving notice of the contingency in sufficient time to enable the Government to take the whole subject under its consideration, and to make such provision under the circumstances as may be found advisable. I could adduce many proofs to you from all quarters of the country of the character of the distress, but I do not think it is at all necessary to trouble you with them.

Archbishop TRENCH said the observations of the LORD MAYOR had so entirely anticipated the conclusions at which he had arrived, that it was almost an impertinence on his part to occupy time. At the same time it might be well that the testimony already given should be confirmed by testimony coming, as it were, from another quarter. There were two or three points which it was the purpose of that deputation to bring forward. The first was of a negative character. They did not think it desirable to suggest any scheme for meeting the present or future distress. It seemed to them that their work was, according to the nature of the case, a temporary and transient one, and that in the long run the nation, or the Government, which was the representative of the nation, should meet the terrible distress which existed through the country ; but as a deputation they had no distinct suggestion to make. Perhaps if they were to begin to make suggestions, one individual might make one, and another another, until the whole unity of the meeting would disappear. But there were two points which they especially desired to press upon the CHIEF SECRETARY. The first was that the distress was certainly—he would not say increasing, for although that might be a very defensible position, yet some might think it exaggerated —but he would say not abating. There might be some small alleviations of it here and there, but these were counterbalanced in other places by aggravation of the distress arising from the length of time it had existed, and from other causes. The settled conviction of all who were acquainted with what he should call the primary documents relating to the matter, and the letters which had passed between the different Committees, as well as of those who had the relief of the starving poor in hand, and who saw it, as it were, before their eyes—and it was a conclusion to which they were not led by any external motives, but simply by the actual facts before them—was, that the suffering of the people had not abated, but was as intense as before. If it were lightening in one place it was deepening in another. Dealing with it as a whole, it was as intense now as it had been at any time, and there were no grounds for expecting that it would be abated for two months or more. And reliance could not be placed on the coming in of voluntary subscriptions to meet the terrible gap between the present time and the coming in of the new harvest. A noble generosity of giving had shown itself in America, Australia, and elsewhere, but it would be very difficult to get that tide of contribution to flow again. It was already ebbing, and they had not made the experiment of a second appeal to the sympathies of Irish, English, and Americans all over the world. At any rate it would be extremely wrong—it would be playing with the lives of men—if they relied on voluntary contributions to meet the distress of the present and ensuing months. Under those circumstances they had thought it right to apply to the CHIEF SECRETARY, mindful of what he had done in the past to meet distress in Ireland, and confident that all that could be done would be done by the Government, of which he was the representative.

Mr. JONATHAN PIM said he really had nothing to add to what the LORD MAYOR had said. He fully agreed with the statement that the distress would for the next three months probably go on increasing in some districts, although possibly in others it might be mitigated. But, on the whole, the average would be much the same, and no reliance could be placed on the possibility of getting in any very large amount of subscriptions now. Some other means, therefore, must be taken of preparing for the future. What those means were he was not prepared to point out. He had ideas of his own, but these might be altered by information which the Government alone had power to get. He thoroughly agreed with the LORD MAYOR as to the danger there would be when the funds already collected should be run out.

Mr. BROOKS, M.P., said he entirely concurred in the opinion that the reports as to the continuing severity of the distress were thoroughly well founded. The mercantile classes of Dublin, who from their business connections had peculiar opportunities of ascertaining the state of the country, had expressed the opinion that unless some other means of relief besides voluntary contributions were provided, very great suffering and distress would arise. They felt sure that the CHIEF SECRETARY would not feel himself bound too much by economic considerations, but would take a merciful and compassionate view of the exigencies of the case.

Mr. P. J. SMYTH, M.P., said he concurred in everything that had been said as to the necessity for relief being provided. He had lately come from one of the richest counties in Ireland, where the people were certainly not wanting in independence of spirit, and where they had made the most praiseworthy local efforts to relieve the distress; but still they looked forward to a continuance of it during the next three months.

The Rev. CANON BAGOT said there was one point to which he wished specially to refer. It might be asked, how was the distress increasing? There was a large class in the country who had been more severely hit than any others by the bad harvests of the past three years and the want of credit, namely—the small farmers. They were now beginning to come into the Committees for relief. They had not been previously on the relief lists, and had had up to present their sack of oats or something to live on; but now they had nothing, and were urgently pressing for relief. Again, this class were most reluctant to ask for outdoor relief, from two causes. First, they were naturally reluctant to apply to the Unions, and, secondly, they were ratepayers themselves. The fact was, that a large number of persons who were rated to the relief of the poor were themselves actually in a state of pauperism. These facts accounted for the pressure that was so likely to be felt during the next three months.

The LORD MAYOR read a telegram he had just received from Dean M'MANUS, P.P., Clifden:—" Unless promptly relieved, many deaths from starvation are inevitable. Scenes like '47 will result." The Rev. Father RHATIGAN, who had been carrying on a separate relief organisation in the same district, telegraphed, " Great danger of deaths from starvation here. Poor creatures night and day on the streets, and no more meal to relieve them. . . . For God's sake send amount to any Committee so that the people may be saved." He was getting communications of this sort every morning from every part of the country by the score, and he was terrified at what might happen when they were able to send no more money.

Mr. PIM added that the small farmers in good years expected to raise food enough for their own consumption: but whenever the year turned out bad they had been in the habit of buying meal on credit, to be paid at the harvest. But the circumstances that had occurred for the last few years had completely destroyed their chance that way, and they could not now get food or anything else on credit.

The CHIEF SECRETARY—Well, gentlemen, I can sincerely say I am obliged to you for coming to see me to-day. I was going to say I was glad to meet you—I cannot exactly say that, for I am sorry that the first deputation I should receive in Ireland should be in reference to so very distressing a matter. But I am very glad to find that your Chief Magistrate has taken the matter up with spirit and energy in the way he has done. I do not want any argument to convince me of the existence of distress. I trust it is not what it was in '47 or '48, but I have no doubt it is now very severe. What Dean M'MANUS says of possible deaths by starvation reminds me of what I myself happened to witness in '47. In England, and perhaps to some extent in Ireland also, there has been some doubt about the extent of the distress, but I think on occasions of this sort there are always some cases regarding which there is some exaggeration, or possibly even some imposition. I am sure I feel persuaded myself, as I think everybody else must be persuaded, that exaggeration in one case does not disprove great distress in others, and that imposition even in one case does not prove that there is not dreadful misery in others. I am not at all surprised to find that you are so very much alarmed about the condition of the people during the next two or three months, because, though I know it is an advantage that we have not got the cold weather, the resources of food must be very much diminished, and I fully expect that these two months will be in some respects the worst you will have to deal with— the months of June and July, and perhaps part of August—so that I am not surprised to find that you are warning the Government of the possibility of your funds coming to an end. I hope they will not come to an end. Just a day or two before the late Parliament rose I threw the responsibility of providing for the distress in Ireland upon the late Government. I do not know whether what I said upon that occasion was reported, but, as strongly as I knew how, I said across the table of the house to Mr. LOWTHER that the Government ought to be prepared to meet any emergency that might arise supposing the charitable funds were to cease. I only allude to that simply to say that I do not wish to shirk, now that I happen to be here, words that I used when I had not the remotest expectation that I should be here. I want to state now in the strongest possible terms that I think it is the duty of the Government (and I shall endeavour that that duty shall be fulfilled) to prevent starvation. I am very glad to find, on coming here, that the permanent officials—Mr. BURKE and the administrators of the Local Government funds—are quite aware of that duty; indeed I may candidly say I have satisfied myself that they are watching anxiously and carefully almost from day to day the condition of the different distressed districts, and are assured of the dangers of the funds ceasing and of the very strong duty that devolves upon them to take care that no great calamity may happen in consequence of that cessation. I should like to tell you what I find to have been done and what is doing now, and I am rather in hopes I shall be able to give one or two facts that may give a little more feeling of security, because I think more is being done than the public generally are aware of, or are likely to be aware of. There have been large advances by way of loans promised to landlords. The amount applied for by land-

CHIEF SECRETARY'S REPLY.

owners as relief loans was £1,200,000. The amount actually issued—that is to say, the money that has actually left the Central Office for the purpose of relief employment—is already £189,720, and the sum of £26,000 is for second instalments, so that, inasmuch as no second instalment can be paid without proof that the first money has been spent in relief works, that is a pretty good proof that a good deal of it must have already got to work. I think that will increase very considerably, and increase every week.

I have got the counties from which the applications for loans have been made, and I am glad to find that in one or two of the most distressed counties the sum which has gone out is considerable. In Galway the amount actually issued is more than £25,000. In Roscommon the amount is close upon £15,000, and in Mayo it is close on £14,000. To give you an idea how much is going out, £21,000 went out last week, and that will increase. So much for loans to landlords. Then there are the relief works under presentments made with the consent of the Baronial Sessions. I found on coming here that in consequence of the change of Government the presentments were in arrear. I do not know whether anybody is to be blamed for that, but directly that I heard of it I looked into the figures as quickly as I could. I only got into a position to attend to them the day before yesterday, but I have now gone through all the presentments that are in the office, which are sixty, and the amount of the expenditure which we have authorized under these sixty presentments is £76,000. Orders for that will go out early next week. Looking through those applications, which I have done as carefully as I could with the time I had to give them, has given me some idea of the state of the country, and I find that the chief reason why they have not been authorised before is a wish not to interfere with the Spring work, and also belief that from the middle of this month up to the time of the harvest would be the time at which they would be most wanted, and I have a very real hope that they will then come in to a very considerable extent. The result of that will be—taking, for instance, such a county as Galway—there will be £40,000 probably spent under these baronial works in labour, in addition to what I have already stated has been advanced to the landlords, which is about £25,000. That will probably increase every week. It is the same in most of the other counties. I should like to state the principle upon which these presentments have been authorised. First the baronial sessions have made the presentment. Then the officials of the Board of Works have struck out those works which did not appear or which they did not believe to be works of utility. Well, I think we should all agree that we ought not to sanction useless works. I have a little experience—perhaps not a very little experience—and the experience I have had with regard to relief works in England as well as what I have heard of them in Ireland, convinces me that useless work is very little better than gratuitous relief. The next test is that the work is really wanted for employment. It is after applying these two tests that these loans have been authorised; but, while applying these tests, the Board of Works authorised more than their inspector had reported as necessary for giving employment, and they were sent back with instructions that, though the Board of Works only authorised what was approved of, yet that the remainder would be open to consideration if it should be found necessary. That is what has been actually done. I hope and really believe that it will do a good deal towards getting the people over these two or three months. All I can say is this, that if it does not, we must resort to other measures, and I know no other measures we can resort to except in the first place finding out what the boards of guardians or the ratepayers really can do for relief; and if it is quite impossible for them to meet the distress, then I think the Government must step in. I do not know that I can say more, but that I am perfectly aware of the responsibility which falls upon us, and I am very glad to find that these gentlemen, the permanent officials here—Mr. BURKE and others—are as much aware of it as I am, and are watching the condition of the country from day to day with great care and anxiety. I will simply add this, that, though I fully acknowledge the duty of the Government, I do hope and trust that the charitable funds will not cease.

P

Whatever the Government does, there will still be great room for charity, and I hope that many people will still open their hearts and purses as nobly as they have done hitherto. The Government can only relieve extreme distress. There is a great deal of misery above the degree of starvation, or of that distress which it is the duty of the Government, either local or central, to relieve; and, also, there is this class alluded to by Canon Bagot, this class of small farmers who have a very great abhorrence, and a very natural abhorrence, to receiving any Poor-law relief, and yet for whom we cannot very well break our rule, for if we did there would be an end of all rule. That class seems to be manifestly a case in which relief ought to be given by charitable means. Before you go, perhaps you will allow me to make a few suggestions—I don't know whether I have any right to make suggestions at all—I suppose I have very little—but I find that there are four funds in existence in Ireland. There is your fund, and the fund which the Duchess of Marlborough, to her very great honour, set to work, and at which she worked with such devotion. I fancy many people regret the change of Government on account of the loss of the Duchess of Marlborough. And there is the large sum that has been sent from America, and the large sum that has been sent from Canada. Would it not be possible, as there are still two or three months to be met, that there should be a complete understanding between the trustees of those funds as to that sort of energetic action that would be required to do whatever charity can do to get over this bridge, as it were? I would also venture to suggest that your Committee, with the others, should put themselves as much as possible in communication with the Boards of Guardians, and let each of them determine what class they would relieve, and if in some cases the charitable funds were to take up these small tenants, and leave the Boards of Guardians to fulfil their necessary duty of helping the labouring class, it might tend to meet the calamity rather better. I do not know that I have anything more to say. I shall be obliged to return to my Cabinet and Parliamentary duties on Monday, but I need hardly say that every suggestion I receive from your Committee on this matter of the distress will be most carefully attended to—in fact, I have no greater duty than to do so.

The Lord Mayor thanked the Chief Secretary very sincerely for the kind way in which he had received the deputation.

APPENDIX IV.

INSUFFICIENCY OF OFFICIAL RELIEF MEASURES.

MR. DILLON'S REPORT.

At a meeting of the Committee, held on the 30th April, the LORD MAYOR in the Chair, the following proceedings took place.

Mr. V. B. DILLON read the following Report:—

The Examination Committee beg to report that at their meeting of this day (28th April) they had before them and carefully considered 142 applications for relief, being a larger number than ever came before this Committee on any previous occasion at one sitting. In view, however, of the steady decrease of the Mansion House Fund, and of the increasing intensity of the destitution in many districts, especially amongst the class of small farmers, the Examination Committee were reluctantly obliged to refuse or defer no less than 63 of these applications, while in 23 instances the Local Committees to which grants were allocated were, at the same time, given to understand that such grants must be considered final. Many of those applications refused or deferred were of a most pressing character also, which this Committee would have felt it their duty promptly to relieve if the funds at their disposal permitted them to do so with due regard to other districts. In allocating the numerous grants which they did make, the Committee had special regard to those districts in which the provisions of the Poor-law Act for the distribution of out-door relief were fairly applied. On the other hand, the Committee refrained from making grants to those other districts where the Poor-law Guardians had not availed themselves of the provisions of the act except in a merely nominal sense, due regard being had, of course, by this Committee to the present amount of poor-rate levied throughout the country generally. The Examination Committee had before them for their guidance the returns of the Local Government Board showing the number of persons receiving indoor and outdoor relief in the various Unions throughout the four provinces for the weeks ending the 3rd, 10th, and 17th instant respectively, together with other sources of information, all of which were fairly referred to in examining and determining upon the merits of each application.

He (Mr. DILLON) had examined the returns furnished by the Local Government Board, and had found that out of eight unions in Donegal apparently only two had put the Act in force. In Ballyshannon Union only one person was receiving outdoor relief; in Dunfanaghy and Letterkenny Unions, none; in Stranorlar, 3; and in Milford, 24. That Committee had sent large sums to Monaghan, and yet in Monaghan Union no persons were receiving outdoor relief, and in Clones Union only two. In the Union of Scariff, county of Clare, there were 16 recipients of outdoor relief, and in Ballyvaughan Union, 48. In Bantry Union the number receiving that class of relief was 38; in Fermoy Union, 37; and in Kinsale, 7. In Dingle Union there were 2 recipients; in Listowel, 14; and in Tralee, none. In Clogheen Union, county Tipperary, there was no outdoor relief. In Gort Union there were 12 recipients of it; in Manorhamilton, 1; and in Westport, 14. Now these were amongst the most distressed Unions in the country. Gentlemen from the Manorhamilton and Westport Unions had told the Committee that the Guardians there were determined not to put the Act in force. In none of those unions was the poor-rate exceptionally high. On the other hand, in the Unions of Mayo—Swineford, Castlebar, and Claremorris—large numbers of persons were receiving outdoor relief In Clifden Union the number of persons now receiving outdoor relief was 520, as against 58 this time last year; and in Galway, Glenamaddy and Tuam Unions the numbers had increased more than a hundred per cent. since last year. He thought it was the duty of the Committee to examine into those cases and try to ascertain why it was that the law had not been put into force in the Unions to which he had referred. No doubt there might be some local circumstances to account for it. It would also be their duty to see that money went rather to those districts where the law had been actively put in force than in those where it had not.

The LORD MAYOR—Would you think well of communicating with the Local Government Board and asking them for the reasons, if any, why the act has not been put into force in the districts to which you refer?

Mr. DILLON—We might make a rule that no grants should be made to those Unions until it has been explained.

Mr. CURRAN said that principle had been already acted on.

Mr. MURPHY remarked that Boards of Guardians were very often in the hands of one or two individuals.

Mr. CURRAN thought it would be better not to refuse relief suddenly to any place.

Mr. CHARLES KENNEDY said some energetic means ought to be adopted of informing the incoming Government that the report that had been circulated that the famine had practically ceased was a living lie. On the contrary, the reports that were coming into the Committee were in a growing degree of a painful and harrowing character, and never had the pinch of famine been felt in a greater degree than it was at the present moment.

Alderman TARPEY said the Sub-Committee had reduced the grants in obedience to imperative orders from the General Committee, and yet now there seemed to be a disposition to censure them for having done so,

The LORD MAYOR—I have not heard from any gentleman a single word to that effect. The report is a very interesting and important one, and it has been discussed freely, and I have not heard the slightest suggestion of anything except that the Examination Committee have discharged their very onerous duty with the utmost ability, and in a manner for which they deserve our warmest thanks.

Dr. SIGERSON said he had had a communication from the Bishop of RAPHOE, to the effect that complaints concerning the proceedings of certain Boards of Guardians had been sent up to the Local Government Board, and that no more was heard about them afterwards. A considerable amount of time must elapse before the machinery of the Local Government Board could be brought to bear on the guardians; and, if that Committee cut off relief, people might die in the meantime.

Mr. DILLON said that the districts to which the Examination Committee had not made grants could renew their applications.

Sir GEORGE OWENS said he thought some Members of the Committee ought to wait on the Local Government Board. He was quite sure that body would insist on the law being carried out. In the South Dublin Union, outdoor relief was now given.

The LORD MAYOR—We have had communications with the Local Government Board, and they have explained to us that so long as men are on the relief list so long the guardians may consider themselves justified in not considering them destitute; and if the guardians don't relieve them under such circumstances the Local Government Board cannot compel them to do so. The preliminary to placing those persons in a position to demand relief from the guardians, and to enabling the Local Government Board to compel the guardians to give it, is that the applicants should be struck off the relief lists and therefore destitute. One dilemma is, that if we strike them off our lists they may die before the guardians can be compelled to relieve them.

Mr. CHARLES KENNEDY said he perfectly concurred with the observations of the LORD MAYOR.

The LORD MAYOR said that in one district which he visited he was told that the ratepayers were on the verge of ruin themselves. Tradesmen had got nothing from their debtors for the last two years. If too much were thrown on a Union of that sort the whole of it would be pauperised.

After some further discussion, the Report was ordered to be entered on the Minutes; a copy of it to be forwarded to the Local Government Board, with an inquiry as to why the Outdoor Relief Act had not been enforced in the districts referred to, and if the Board were prepared to compel the enforcement of it therein.*

REPORT ON RELIEF WORKS.

At a Meeting of the Committee, held on the 15th June, the LORD MAYOR in the Chair, the question of the efficacy of Official Relief Works was brought under consideration:

The Rev. Mr. M'EVILLY, P.P., of Aughagower, having appeared before the Committee to state the condition of his district and the exhaustion of his funds.

The Rev. Canon BAGOT observed: I think you spoke of public works being commenced?

Father M'EVILLY—Yes; the work has been given in sections and the contractors employ men, but up to this time I cannot say that any man except the contractors themselves had pocketed 10s.

Canon BAGOT—And the workmen have not been paid? No; unless it was done this week.

Canon BAGOT—That bears out the statement as to the works started in Clare, that the men had been working for three weeks, and many did not receive one penny.

Mr. DRIMMIE—We hear a great deal about the distribution of money for relief works. I would ask your Lordship, as a Member of the House of Commons, how much money has been distributed for relief works?

* The following table gives a comparative view of the distribution of relief in England and Wales, and in Ireland :—

ENGLAND AND WALES. POPULATION IN 1871, 22,712,266.				IRELAND. POPULATION IN 1871, 5,412,377.			
NUMBER OF PAUPERS RELIEVED.				NUMBER OF PAUPERS RELIEVED.			
On 1st of January in each Year	In-door	Out-door	Total	On 1st of January in each Year	In-door	Out-door	Total
1875	155,655	622,167	817,822	1875	49,805	30,631	80,436
1876	151,930	600,957	752,887	1876	46,214	31,078	77,292
1877	157,191	571,159	728,350	1877	45,762	32,128	77,890
1878	171,421	576,583	748,004	1878	49,305	35,500	84,805
1879	179,541	625,539	805,080	1879	51,764	39,335	91,099
1880				1880	57,455	42,735	100,190

The LORD MAYOR—Efforts have been made to elicit that information, but without avail. My belief is that very little has been distributed. Mr. FORSTER is pressing for a return even up to May, but I do not think he has been able to get it. As an inducement, I think that little or no money has been distributed in the way mentioned.

Mr. JOYNT said that those connected with the country never doubted from the beginning, that any reliance on the relief of genuine or widespread distress on what are called baronial or presentment boards would never be realised.

Father M'EVILLY then retired.

Mr. V. B. DILLON, Jun., said, that in laying on the table the Returns now before them, the object was, not that the Committee should become acquainted with facts that they already knew *ad nauseam*, but that by means of these Returns they should supply Her Majesty's Government with information as to what the Committee believed to be the actual state of the country compiled from sources the Government were not in the habit of getting information from. They knew how the Committees were constituted, that the number of persons acting on their Committees throughout the country was 15,000 or 16,000. The returns he presented were signed by the chairman or secretary of those Committees, on which were the local clergymen and respectable Protestants, Catholics, magistrates, and others well qualified to report in a non-official point of view. They had actually working now 726 committees; of these they had received returns from 630, leaving 90 from which they had received no returns. These returns were divided in this way. They had received 128 returns from Ulster, 58 from Leinster, 206 from Munster, and 198 from Connaught, making a total of 590. The actual amount expended by all the relief committees amounted to £236,000, according to these returns, of which the Mansion House Committee contributed £112,000.

THE LORD MAYOR—But there are 90 or 100 from whom no returns have come.

Mr. DILLON—Quite so. We have returns showing 384 parishes in which no relief works have been as yet authorised; that includes 128 in Munster, and 105 in Connaught. The number of parishes in which works are authorised was 206. The number of persons reported as likely to receive employment from these works was 13,187, out of a population of 358,000 reported to be in distress. Of these public works 77 had actually commenced in Munster, 38 are not yet commenced; in Connaught 41 were commenced, and 52 not yet commenced. The nature of the works was generally drainage, or cutting hills, or works of a character necessarily confined to a small area; so that the people in the remote districts will derive no benefit, the returns clearly showing that these works are valueless, except in the immediate neighbourhood where they are authorised, and there only to a very small proportion, indeed, of the people in distress. He would not take up the time of the committee by going into details, for it was not his object to have them ventilated through the Press, as that had been done; but that they should be forwarded as an authoritative document to the Government, if they chose to avail themselves of it. With that view, therefore, he moved—

"That the Secretaries send a copy of the report to the Right Honourable the Chief Secretary, calling his attention to the inadequacy of the relief-works to meet the distress, and inform him that the returns from which the information has been obtained will be placed at his disposal should he desire to avail of the information they contain."

The resolution was passed unanimously.

In accordance with this resolution, a copy of the returns was sent to the CHIEF SECRETARY.

APPENDIX V.

CLOSING ORDINARY MEETING.

The closing ordinary meeting of the Committee was held at the Mansion House on Saturday, 15th August, 1880, at three o'clock.

The Chair was taken by the Right Hon. the LORD MAYOR.
The other Members of the Committee present were —
Lord GODOLPHIN OSBORNE; Alderman TARPEY, Sir GEORGE OWENS, Sir JOHN BARRINGTON, Dr. SIGERSON, the Rev. JAMES DANIEL, P.P; and Messrs. WILLIAM L. JOYNT, J. A. FOX, V. B. DILLON, GEORGE DELANY, DAVID DRIMMIE, and EDWARD FOX.

Mr. WRIGHT read the Minutes of the last Meeting.

The weekly financial statement showed that the amount acknowledged up to that date was £179,577 5s. and that £10 had been received since the last meeting, making a total of £179,587 5s.; that the expenditure up to that date had been £176,762 8s 4d.; leaving a balance of £2,824 12s 1d.

A letter was received from Mr. A. T. MOORE, forwarding £10 from Cox & Co., of Bristol.

Letters of thanks to the Committee for their grants and assistance were received from the Rev. Canon WELDON on the part of the Glin Relief Committee; from the Rev. CHARLES O'REILLY, P.P., on the part of the Kellinkere Relief Committee; from the Rev. AUSTIN O'DWYER, P.P., on the part of the Kilkerrin Relief Committee; and from Mr. J. PRATT, of the Crossmolina Relief Committee.

Mr. DRIMMIE read and moved the adoption of the Report of Finance Committee.

Sir JOHN BARRINGTON seconded the motion. The Report contained a succinct and clear statement of their affairs, and gave a great deal of valuable information. They were much indebted to Mr. DRIMMIE for it.

The LORD MAYOR, in putting the motion, said he certainly thought they were much indebted to Mr. DRIMMIE and the Finance Committee for the clear and admirable statement of their position contained in the Report. Remembering the enormous amount of work they had had to do, and that the organisation had devolved on them to a great extent of a system which had been used by other charitable organisations afterwards, and that they had had to develop the charity of the world, in fact, by their appeals; and bearing in mind also that the greater portion of their expenditure had been enormously reproductive, he trusted it would be considered by their subscribers that they had expended their money economically and judiciously.

Mr. DRIMMIE stated that a cheque for £120 had been placed in his hands, being the amount of a deduction from usual charges for advertising in *Freeman's Journal*.

Sir JOHN BARRINGTON—I think we ought to pass a vote of thanks to the LORD MAYOR for that.

The LORD MAYOR—There is no necessity.

Dr. SIGERSON read the final Report on Destitution-Diseases in the West.

Mr. DILLON said he had great pleasure in moving that the Report be adopted and printed. It was very desirable that the entire series of Reports that had been presented by Dr. SIGERSON and Dr. KENNY, should be printed in a book form and distributed amongst the Members of the House of Commons. They threw a great deal of light on the condition of the West of Ireland. He had observed that in the discussion that took place on the previous night in the House of Commons, Mr. FORSTER recognised the value of those Reports, and stated that in many instances their recommendations had been adopted.

Sir GEORGE OWENS seconded the motion, suggesting that the Reports of Mr. Fox should be printed along with the others.

The resolution was adopted, declaring that the Reports of Drs. SIGERSON and KENNY and also those of Mr. Fox should be printed and circulated amongst the Members of Parliament, and that they should also accompany the final Report of the Committee.

Sir GEORGE OWENS said he had great pleasure in moving the following resolution:—

"That this Committee cannot conclude its labours without expressing its deep obligations to the LADY MAYORESS for the practical advantage conferred on them by placing at their disposal, for their daily work since the beginning of the year, a suite of apartments in the Mansion House."

None but the members of that Committee who had occupied so many rooms in the Mansion House could know the discomfort which the LADY MAYORESS must have suffered through her generosity in placing those rooms at their disposal. Although they were indebted to the LORD MAYOR for his munificent contributions, not only to that but to other charities of the city, they were really more indebted to the LADY MAYORESS for the use of the Mansion House.

Colonel DAVOREN seconded the proposition. He said he fully agreed with every word Sir GEORGE OWENS had uttered.

The LORD MAYOR said he felt a certain degree of awkwardness in putting this proposition. He could only say, however, that the LADY MAYORESS felt delighted in having had it in her power to place any portion of the Mansion House at the disposal of the members of the Committee. He quite recognised this fact that there was a considerable amount of inconvenience that fell, of course, upon the LADY MAYORESS and not upon him. The members would remember that when they began their work the pressure was so great that they very often did not finish business till four o'clock in the morning. If, however, in devoting any part of the Mansion House to the Committee she thus succeeded in facilitating their work of charity, the LADY MAYORESS would only feel it a pleasure. He would convey their kind resolution to her, and he was sure she would hear it with very great gratification.

The resolution was adopted.

On the motion of Mr. DRIMMIE, seconded by Mr. JOYNT, the second chair was taken by Alderman TARPEY.

Lord FRANCIS G. OSBORNE said he had been given the great privilege of moving a resolution which he was sure would recommend itself with irresistible force to them all. It was a resolution that required very little indeed to be said in its support, and in that point of view perhaps there was some excuse for its being placed in the hands of one so little fitted to make a speech. He moved—

"That the best thanks of the Mansion House Committee are due and hereby given to the Right Hon. the LORD MAYOR for the splendid and effective services rendered by him to the Committee and the people of Ireland."

They had most of them attended those Committee meetings even more regularly than circumstances had enabled him (Lord Francis) to do, and they were therefore themselves more frequently witness to the wonderful spirit of kindness, of business, and of everything in fact necessary and desirable to be brought to bear on their operations displayed by the LORD MAYOR. The success of this was all the more notable and commendable when they remembered that this Committee, over which his lordship presided, was one in which there were necessarily differing and conflicting opinions. He could not express his admiration of the kind way in which his lordship had always conducted the business, for indeed from the very commencement down to this the last day of their meeting, his every act seemed to show with increasing and deeper force the interest which he felt in the people, and consequently in the Committee which was working for the people. His lordship had that day shown in a very effective and substantial manner an example of that feeling, and to that he need not allude further. Although the LORD MAYOR refused to take any credit to himself in respect of the inconvenience necessarily occasioned by giving up the Mansion House to the use of the Committee, and although he in what they all must consider a most admirable way gave to the LADY MAYORESS, his better-half, the credit of this kind self-sacrifice, still they must all know that to his lordship this must have been a great inconvenience, and they owed to him for this a debt of gratitude. He did not wish to detain them, for he felt quite sure that no words of his could add to the willingness with which that resolution would be received. He thought he was not wrong in saying that every resolution put to this meeting had been carried unanimously, and he was sure he might with equal truth say that if the others were all unanimous, that this (although it sounded in one sense like an impossibility) would be carried with even more unanimity.

Sir JOHN BARRINGTON seconded the resolution. He said that in his capacity of Lord Mayor he (Sir John) had been early called into action with regard to this Committee, and he could bear testimony to the indefatigable and untiring zeal of the present LORD MAYOR throughout. The conciliatory manner in which he had conducted the proceedings of the Committee in every way commanded their greatest admiration. If the archives of the Committee were consulted it would be found that he (Sir John) had been very constant in his attendance. Of course he had a great deal of business to attend to in the city, but still he endeavoured to support the Committee, and was in a position to be able to speak of the assiduity and attention of the LORD MAYOR. He cordially supported the proposition.

Mr. EDWARD FOX—Sir JOHN BARRINGTON has anticipated the pleasing duty I was asked to perform in seconding this resolution, proposed with such good taste and ability by Lord FRANCIS OSBORNE. I believe that the prayers of thousands of our countrymen and countrywomen will shower down on our Chief Magistrate in grateful remembrance of the zeal, ability, and deep sympathy which was never absent from him during these critical months through which we have passed, and I believe, notwithstanding all that may be urged to the contrary, that owing to the influence of his position, his hard work and ability, thousands are now in vigour and health upon whom the grave but for him would have prematurely closed. It is a sad fact in the history of our country that these famines have proved periodical, and it is equally sad that in no one instance have they ever been met by the genius of legislature, by foresight, or by any one act of anticipation which might fairly have been expected on the part of a vigilant Administration. I sincerely hope that the necessity for similar organisations to the present will pass away; and I believe that no more certain means of realising this wish can arise than that wise counsels should at length prevail amongst those who are engaged in the agriculture of this country. It becomes absolutely a question of vital interest to every man in this land that those who live by the land should be fortified and encouraged by larger securities and by giving for that land, which is the fruitful source of sustainment, such encouragement to its development to the full extent—an encouragement which I deeply regret has not now any practical existence. I will not trench upon questions of politics. I would like to say more, but do not feel privileged to do so. I hope, however, that wise counsels will prevail, and that those who are the owners of the land will hold out such inducement to those who are endeavouring to produce food in the country as will stimulate their exertions. I have much pleasure in supporting the resolution.

Alderman TARPEY, in putting the resolution, said he heartily concurred in every word that had been said in support of the proposition. Having some practical knowledge of the working of this Committee from its infancy up to the present time, he could say with all true sincerity that the LORD MAYOR was the mainstay of the entire proceedings, anxious at all times to further its objects and increase its power for good, and that he had discharged his duties with satisfaction, not only to the Committee, but to the whole country. They could never forget his lordship's great kindness, and he was certain this resolution would be carried with acclamation.

The LORD MAYOR—Gentlemen, I need hardly say how deeply grateful I am to you for this vote of thanks, and for the particularly kind way in which the gentlemen who have spoken on it have alluded to me. Frankly, however, I feel that I scarcely deserve all the complimentary expressions made use of in my regard. I, no doubt, realised thoroughly the importance of the work in which we were engaged. It was a great national work, and we have, I think I may say without fear of contradiction, done a great national service. But, as regards the working of the Committee, I was, to a considerable extent, the mere figure-head. I was most ably seconded by gentlemen who took, I may say, the labour off my hands; and though I acted here as chairman, and endeavoured to do what I could, my multifarious duties rendered it impossible for me to give as much attention to the details of the work as I would have wished, or to have assisted as closely as I would have liked in securing that success which we all rejoice has been accomplished. I feel, therefore, that it would be culpable of me not to disclaim the full merit which your kindness would attribute to me. To you, Sir, as chairman of the Application Committee, who attended on every occasion except, I believe, one, on which the Committee met, are due the thanks of the Committee far more than to myself, for it was upon you, in conjunction with Colonel DAVOREN and two or three others, that the most serious and responsible part of the work devolved. To the Honorary Secretaries—more particularly to Mr. DILLON, who devised the organisation, which has stood the test of eight months' trial— and to Mr. CURRAN, are due especial thanks. To Mr. JOYNT, who undertook portion of the most difficult of the relief work—that of the Western Islands, where there were no Local Committees; and to Lord FRANCIS OSBORNE, who assisted in that most difficult task, and carried it out most successfully, are due the thanks of the Committee. The Most Rev. Dr. TRENCH, Mr. MAXWELL HUTTON, Canon BAGOT, Mr. C. KENNEDY, Mr. DRUMMOND, the Rev. J. DANIEL, and many other gentlemen, gave us the most devoted assistance. To Dr. SIGERSON, Dr. KENNY, and Mr. J. A. FOX our thanks are also due for their most valuable Reports; and to these gentlemen gratitude is, indeed, due, not only from the Committee, but from the country, for having, without reward, except the reward of their own consciences, given the services they did; who went and personally inspected the localities, and gave us those Reports, the value of which was recognised in the House of Commons and by the Government, who have acted on suggestions of these gentlemen. These Reports will be a lasting record of the work done by this Committee, notwithstanding the attacks which at the commencement were made on it, and which, I believe, those who made them would now be inclined to unsay, if possibly false pride did not stand in their way. These attacks we have outlived, and I think the work of this Committee will prove that Irishmen of all creeds and parties can, when a great crisis occurs, combine together for a great national object, and do it successfully.

I am very proud, indeed, as your chairman, to know that during our many meetings we never had one single division. Differences of opinion of course, arose; that must naturally be expected in a Committee composed of mixed elements. We had the representatives of the Hierarchy of different religions—we had gentlemen distinguished by strong Conservative and Tory feelings, as well as those belonging to the party with which I am identified. That, I think, is the pride of this Committee, that all parties were represented on it; and we were able to work harmoniously, without allowing our differences to mar our unity of action. I believe, indeed, that this Committee, and other charitable organisations, have saved the country from a terrible calamity. Only the other day I was looking at the returns of what the Government have done, and I can say with confidence that if we had had to depend upon the Government—and I do not use the word in a party sense, but I mean the

Executive Government—the people would have starved. It is now they are beginning to distribute money—now when the harvest is coming in. The Government were warned twelve months ago that nothing could avert this calamity. But from some cause or another—I will not say whose fault it was—their action was not sufficiently prompt to avert, or assist in averting the famine. The Relief Committees, the Duchess of MARLBOROUGH's Committee, this Committee, the Land League Committee, and the New York Herald Committee, stepped into the breach and did the work; and I have not the slightest false shame in saying that this Committee has deserved well of the country, and has done a national work of which every member should feel proud. I feel proud, for though it was a melancholy duty, it was one that must be remembered with pride by me, that I had the honour of presiding at the Mansion House during this year. It is a year which, in consequence of the famine, will be historical. I dare not trust myself to deal with the political question no more than Mr. Fox—for this being a mixed Committee, there would be a danger of a difference arising at the last moment if I were to say what is the duty of the State under such circumstances. Statesmen of all classes, however, will agree that when a terrible crisis exists it is the duty of the State to take measures for the prevention of the recurrence of such a calamity.' I need not express my opinion of what these measures should be, but it is conceded that it is the duty of the Government to take what steps lie in its power to prevent the recurrence of these periodic famines. There is only one way, in my opinion, and I hope the Government will next session face the question in a broad, comprehensive spirit. I fear I have detained you too long. I thank you deeply and sincerely for the compliment you have paid me. I feel that in presiding over the Mansion House Committee I merely discharged a duty that would have devolved upon any LORD MAYOR under the circumstances. It was a gratification, although a melancholy one, to have occupied the chair. It is a great thing to know that we have a civic house of this kind, where men of all kinds can meet together; that we had its appeal for charity recognized at the Antipodes more fully even than by our neighbours across the Channel. Men did not want to know who the individual was who occupied the chair at the Mansion House. They sent their subscriptions, conscious that whoever occupied the chair they would be well and wisely distributed. When the report of our proceedings reaches the public I do feel that it will be admitted on all hands that we did our best to deserve success, and that not one of us spared any exertion or effort to secure the proper distribution of the large sums entrusted to our care.

Mr. JOYNT proposed a vote of thanks to the Press of Dublin, the provinces, and other parts of the world for its support and advocacy of the objects of the Committee.

Mr. DRIMMIE seconded the proposition, which was carried.

APPENDIX VI.

FINAL GENERAL MEETING.

The last General Meeting of the Mansion House Relief Fund Committee was held on 7th December, in the Oak Room of the Mansion House for the purpose of receiving the Balance Sheet, considering the Draft Report of the Committee's operations, and allocating the surplus.

The Right Hon. the LORD MAYOR, M.P., presided.

Present—Messrs. M. BROOKS, M.P.; W. FINDLATER, M.P.; H. J. GILL, M.P.; Alderman CAMPBELL, J.P.; Lord FRANCIS GODOLPHIN OSBORNE; Sir JOHN BARRINGTON, D.L.; J. F. LOMBARD, J.P.; W. LANE JOYNT, D.L.; J. ADYE CURRAN, B.L.; P. M'CABE FAY, I. J. KENNEDY, T.C., J.P.; Rev. Canon FARRELL, P.P.; Professor SIGERSON, M.D.; GEORGE DELANY, Alderman PURDON, J.P.; V. B. DILLON, jun.; EDWARD FOX J.P.; Lieutenant-Colonel DAVOURS, Alderman M'DERMOTT, J.P.; Sir G. B. OWENS, J.P.; DAVID DRIMMIE, J. A. FOX, T. MAXWELL HUTTON, J.P.; T. DOWLING, AMBROSE PLUNKETT, Solicitor; DAVID DRUMMOND, J.P.; A. SHACKLETON, T.C., J.P.; Alderman TALLPEY, J.P.; Alderman HARRIS, Alderman COCHRANE, Dr. LONG, T.C.

Mr. DRIMMIE, on behalf of the Finance Committee, brought up the final Balance Sheet as follows:—

Balance Sheet of the Mansion House Relief Fund to 13th August, 1880.

Dr.	£	s.	d.	Cr.	£	s.	d.
To Amount of subscriptions received to date	180,097	5	6	By Grants made as follows:— To local committees for food, fuel, and clothing	166,899	0	0
" Fund contributed specially for grants for seed	854	5	10	" Western Islands	4,445	4	11
" Amount contributed for special distribution	535	10	9	" For Seed, as per special contributions for this purpose	932	7	1
" Interest allowed by National Bank on current account	178	7	0	" Amounts contributed for specified distribution	535	10	9
				" Special grants	732	6	4
				" Distributed by members of committee to special cases	130	0	0
				" Cost of publication of Pamphlet of Committee's Proceedings, for circulation at home and abroad	1,077	14	11
				" Expenses (including costs of appeal and of organisation and distribution of funds), salaries, &c.	1,007	4	0
				" Stationery, Printing and Scrivenery	977	13	10
				" Advertising in United Kingdom	794	19	0
				" Travelling Expenses, including cost of inspection of local committees	311	5	6
				" Telegrams	252	12	8
				" Postage	103	15	9
				" Wages (porter and messenger)	68	10	0
				" Bank charges, stamps, &c.	35	7	5
				" Incidentals, including car hire, rent of temporary offices, &c.	246	18	9
				" Balance	3,113	17	2
	£181,665	9	1		£181,665	9	1

The balance now to be disposed of by the Committee would be £3,113 17s. 2d.

On the motion of Mr. DRIMMIE, seconded by Alderman M'DERMOTT, the Report of the Finance Committee was adopted.

FINAL MEETING.

The LORD MAYOR read the following letter which he had received from His Grace the Protestant Archbishop of Dublin:—

"*The Palace, St. Stephen's-green, Dublin, Dec. 7, 1880.*

" MY DEAR LORD MAYOR,

"Nothing but business of very great importance which falls to-day exactly at the same hour as the meeting at the Mansion House, and from which I cannot absent myself, has hindered me from taking my humble share at the winding up of your work to-day. I have never gone back from my conviction not merely of the reality, but of the severity, and in many places of the intensity, of the distress which the Mansion House Committee undertook, so far as the means placed in its hands would reach, to relieve. For myself it is no small satisfaction, though I did but touch as with a little finger a burden of which others bore the full weight, to call to mind the spirit in which the whole work which is now drawing to a close was carried through. It is gratifying to remember the thought and labour which were so freely given by many, and certainly not least by yourself; the entire fairness, with no advantage sought to be snatched by any, which presided over all our arrangements—a consciousness of this preventing the slightest outbreak of jealousy in any quarter—the drawing together in friendliest intercommunion of those whom in happier times many influences keep more or less apart. I will not ask you to read this long letter, but I will ask you to say that I should have been present at the meeting to-day if other matters had not absolutely forbade me.

"I am ever, my dear Lord Mayor,
"Very faithfully yours,
"R. C. DUBLIN."

" TO THE RIGHT HON. THE LORD MAYOR.

He thought the harmonious and friendly action upon which His Grace congratulated the Committee was due to no person more than it was to His Grace himself, whose presence here, whose strong interest in the Committee, and wise and prudent advice upon many trying occasions were of the utmost possible service to the Committee. It was not merely the weight of his name that His Grace lent them, but the greatest possible assistance in the practical work of the Committee, and that assistance conduced very largely to the success on which they might fairly congratulate themselves at this winding up of their labours.

Mr. IGNATIUS KENNEDY moved, and Sir JOHN BARRINGTON seconded, that His Grace's letter be entered on the minutes.

Mr. DILLON, as one who took some little part in the business of the Committee, begged to add his testimony to the very valuable assistance given by the Most Rev. Dr. TRENCH. On very many occasions they found themselves in great difficulties out of which he alone extricated them, and he (Mr. DILLON) did not think too much could be said in praise of His Grace's very valuable aid.

Dr. SIGERSON suggested that the letter of His Grace should be inserted in the Appendix to their Report.

Sir JOHN BARRINGTON quite approved of the suggestion.

The letter was ordered to be entered on the minutes, and to be published in the Appendix of the Report.

The LORD MAYOR said he had also received the following letter from the Most Rev. Dr. M'GETTIGAN :—

"*Armagh, 6th December, 1880.*

" DEAR SIR,

"I beg to thank you for the copy of the draft Report of the Dublin Mansion House Relief Committee, which I received yesterday. I have not had time to read it all as yet. The parts I have looked over are most interesting and admirably written. It will stand as an authentic history of a most memorable year in the annals of the country, of the boundless charity of the Irish all over the world, and of the unwearied, successful labours of the Mansion House Committee in relieving distress. I regret being obliged, by engagements at home, to forego the honour and pleasure of being present at the meeting of the General Committee on to-morrow.

"Believe me, your faithful servant,
"✠ Daniel M'Gettigan."

"J. H. Wright, Esq., Assistant Secretary."

On the motion of Alderman Harris this letter also was ordered to be entered on the minutes, and the Lord Mayor was requested to acknowledge both communications.

The Mayor of Adelaide, South Australia (E. T. Smith, Esq.) forwarded £400, balance of the South Australian collections.

"The Lord Mayor of Dublin.

"*Town Hall, Adelaide, South Australia, September 4th*, 1880.

"My Dear Lord Mayor,

"By mail leaving here to-day I send you draft for £400 on the Bank of South Australia, balance of South Australia's efforts on behalf of the Irish relief movement. I can only express the hope that the efforts made in this colony (numbering a population of only about 250,000) will meet with your full approval. My telegram to your predecessor in office in the early part of last December, asking 'Whether distress in Ireland warranted special appeal here,' was, I know, the commencement of the Irish relief movement in the Australian Colonies. Immediately on receipt of replies to my telegrams, I telegraphed to the Mayors of Melbourne, Sydney, Brisbane, Hobart Town, Launcestown, and other important towns, and am delighted to know that several of the colonies have done so much better than ourselves. We feel proud to have given you a helping hand in this noble work, so well supported by all true Australians.

"Believe me, yours faithfully,
"J. Smith,
"Mayor, and Chairman of the S. A. Irish Relief Fund."

The Oriental Bank Corporation transmitted a draft for £490 from Bombay.

"To the Right Hon. the Lord Mayor of Dublin.

"*Oriental Bank Corporation, London, E.C.,*
"*20th November*, 1880.

"My Lord,

"I am advised by a telegram received to-day from our agent at Bombay of a remittance of £490 in favour of your Lordship's Fund for the relief of Distress in Ireland. I enclose, therefore, a cheque for that amount, accompanied by a form of receipt in duplicate, which kindly sign and return.

"I have the honour to remain, your Lordship's obedient servant,
"John S. Scrymgeour, *for Chief Manager*."

The Hon. P. A. Jennings, Sydney, forwarded a final instalment of £283 18s. 5d. from New South Wales.

"To the Lord Mayor of Dublin.

"*23rd September*, 1880

"My Lord,

"I have the honour to acknowledge the receipt of your letter of June 23rd, advising me of the receipt of £27,500 from Sydney on account of the Mansion House Fund, for the relief of the Distress in Ireland. Since then another remittance of £1,000 has been cabled, and I now beg to transmit a draft on the Bank of Australasia, London, for £283 18s. 5d. the balance of the fund after closing all subscription lists and defraying all charges. It cannot but prove a source

FINAL MEETING.

of great pleasure to the contributors to your Fund in Australia to be made aware, by the terms of your letter, which I have caused to be published, of the substantial nature and measure of the support rendered by them, and it is to be hoped that the good will displayed on the occasion will tend to strengthen the bonds between the mother country and Australia.

"I have the honour to be, my Lord,

"Your most obedient servant,

"(Signed), P A. JENNINGS."

Applications for grants out of the surplus in the hands of the Committee were received from the Sisters of Mercy convents at Claremorris, Gort, and Clifden. The applications were simply noted, pending the allocation of the surplus by the Committee.

The Miltown Local Relief Committee applied for payment of £28 18s., the amount of their overdrawn account for meal supplied by them in excess of the amount of the Mansion House grants. It was mentioned that various similar applications had already been received and refused, and the feeling of the Committee being against re-opening the question, the application was refused with regret.

The Publication Committee brought up the Draft Report of the operations of the Committee.

Mr. BROOKS, M.P., said he had great pleasure in moving—

"That the draft report now read be adopted, subject to the verbal revision of the Publication Committee, and be signed by the Chairman and Hon. Secretaries, and that the Publication Committee be authorised to take all necessary steps for the publication of the report with its appendices, and its circulation in such manner as they deem most desirable."

The opportunity which the Committee had kindly afforded him of perusing the report enabled him to say that it would in all probability form a prominent page in the sad literature of the history of their country. It also contained a record of the labours and liberality of those who had been engaged with the LORD MAYOR in this organisation, and it would, no doubt, be referred to by those who in future times should study the history of this period as affording the best information that could probably be afforded as to the circumstances out of which this Committee had arisen. He had much pleasure in moving the adoption of the report.

Sir JOHN BARRINGTON had great pleasure in seconding its adoption. The impression produced on his mind by the report was its wonderful comprehensiveness. It took in almost every little matter of interest that occurred during their labours, and was particular with regard to their operations in the West. He might say that from the very commencement to the end it faithfully represented the actions of this Committee. Some might say that it coloured them a little too much in one direction, and others in another direction, but in so far as he could see, it, as far as possible, kept a clear course, not favouring either one political party or the other. The gentlemen that drew it up, under the superintendence of the Publication Committee, deserved a great deal of credit for having prepared so elaborate a report of their proceedings. He found that the report alluded in the most kindly manner to the little initiative he took last year in calling together the preliminary meeting, and it would be always a pleasant thing for him to reflect that he was to a certain extent the instrument in starting a movement which was taken up by his Lordship with such assiduity and energy, supported by Mr. DILLON and others he could name, who, by their indomitable perseverance, had done so much more than he could have done, even if he had remained in office, for the success of this movement. He could not conclude without saying, that it was to the LORD MAYOR's action as Chairman a great deal of the good feeling and success of the Committee was due.

The draft report was unanimously adopted, and ordered to be published.

Sir G. OWENS said it afforded him very great pleasure to move—

"That this Committee desire to reiterate the expression of its gratitude to the various Committees and individuals who aided in the collection of the munificent sum of £181,348 2s. 8d. contributed through this organisation for the relief of distress in Ireland."

He was sure they could never sufficiently express their gratitude to the different countries for responding so nobly to their call. It was a great gratification to them all as members of this Committee, to hear the testimony borne to-day by learned prelates of both churches to the great exertions of this Committee, and it was something to know that their services as humble members of the Committee had been so thoroughly appreciated, not only by them, but throughout the length and breadth of the land. He did not think there ever was a Committee that worked more harmoniously; and though it was very difficult to pass through life without getting hard rubs occasionally, he did not think during the entire working of the Committee he ever heard a word uttered derogatory to them or to their services.

Alderman TARPEY seconded the resolution, which was carried.

Mr. FINDLATER, M.P., said the resolution he had to propose to them was one which he was sure would peculiarly enlist the sympathies of this meeting, because it was from Adelaide, in South Australia, the first suggestion came for the formation of the Mansion House Committee. He moved—

"That the Publication Committee be requested to consider the best mode of testifying the gratitude of the Irish nation to the people of Australia for the unprecedented munificence of their contributions for the relief of Irish distress, and adopt such means of conveying the thanks of the Committee to the Australian and other Committees as they think most desirable."

It really required no words from him to satisfy them that the deep gratitude of the Irish people was due to their brethren in Australia and in other countries for the manner in which they had acted towards them. He found that actually £62,875 arrived to them from Australia before they even knew who sent it. That was a fact that he thought unprecedented in the history of the world. Not only that, but the magnificent gifts received from Australia proper, Tasmania, and New Zealand amounted to the sum of £94,022 8s. 11d. Need he say one word more in support of this resolution? He must, however, refer to the able report they had just adopted, and which he had read with very great pleasure before he came here. He thought that in the whole course of his experience he never read a document more ably or more eloquently prepared. He felt sure it would be hereafter referred to as an able, eloquent, comprehensive, important, and faithful history of the famine of 1879, a philosophical and statesmanlike examination of the causes which led to it, and a moral, social, and economic treatise upon the means by which a similar calamity can be avoided in the future. He hoped there would be a resolution passed hereafter of thanks to the gentlemen who so very ably detailed the history of the labours of this Committee, as developed in this most valuable report.

Alderman PURDON, in seconding the resolution, said it would be a grave dereliction of duty on their part if they did not recognise the great exertions of their Australian friends. They must only attribute the munificence of their subscription to the great affection that existed among Irishmen abroad for their brother Irishmen at home. It was very gratifying to find that wherever their countrymen were prosperous they did not forget their brother Irishmen in the hour of need, but sent those vast sums many thousands of miles to their assistance.

The Very Rev. Canon FARRELL, P.P., supported the resolution, observing that the subject had had been so well dealt with by the admirable address of Mr. FINDLATER, that it was unnecessary for him to add another word.

Mr. BROOKS, M.P., said, before this resolution wasput he would like to say one word. He was quite sure that their fellow-countrymen in Australia were actuated by regard to the suffering and distress of the poor people at home, but he made free to think that the people of Australia, from one end of it to the other, had a knowledge of what was due by many of the Irish people in Australia to the mother of the lady who occupied a prominent position in the Mansion House, and in the affections of the people of Dublin, and though he did not like at any time on public occasions to bring the name of any lady under discussion, he could not help thinking that the daughter of Mrs. CHISHOLM, who was of all others the most eminent benefactress of Australia, and the regard, esteem, and gratitude of the people to the memory of that lady, might to a certain extent have influenced the benevolence of the people of Australia. He thought he would fail in his duty to himself, to the LADY MAYORESS, and to the memory of Mrs. CHISHOLM, if he did not mention the circumstance, that in his own heart be believed that the memory of Mrs. CHISHOLM largely influenced the charity of the people of Australia.

The LORD MAYOR, in putting the resolution, said on his wife's part he was most grateful for the kindly allusion made by Mr. BROOKS to the memory of CAROLINE CHISHOLM. Her name was still a household word, he believed, throughout the Australian colonies, and he did not himself doubt but that possibly the fact of his having the good fortune to be married to CAROLINE CHISHOLM's daughter was not forgotten by the people of Australia when this appeal was made to their benevolence.

The resolution was adopted.

Mr. LANE JOYNT moved:—

"That a grant of £150 each be made to the families of Drs. DONOVAN and ROBINSON, of Skibbereen, and GREALY, of Oranmore, who died of fever caught in the discharge of their duty as dispensary officers attending the poor during the late distress, for the relief of which this Committee was organised, and that these cases respectfully be recommended to the consideration of the Medical Benevolent Fund. The Treasurers to be authorised to make the payments to such persons on their behalf as they think desirable, without further responsibility on their part or that of the Committee."

He believed the Committee had already discussed this question, and were so well aware of the severe loss felt by the families of these gentlemen, that he need not argue the question further. The only remark he would make was that Dr. GREALY, who died in February, had only replaced his brother, who had also given his life in the same cause. They both died of typhus fever, caught in the discharge of their duty. The name of Dr. DONOVAN and his father were household words in Skibbereen. Dr. ROBINSON left a widow and six helpless children, and he believed this Committee could not better dispose of a portion of the surplus remaining in their hands than in vindicating the opinion they had always entertained of the admirable services of the noble profession to which these gentlemen belonged.

Mr. CHARLES KENNEDY seconded the resolution.

Mr. IGNATIUS KENNEDY suggested that the amount of the grants was too small.

Mr. LANE JOYNT said as the claims upon the surplus would be so many they would be quite content with a grant of £150 a piece. Mr. GLADSTONE* had recently sent £150 to the family of Dr. DONOVAN, a second grant from the Royal Bounty Fund, and a sum of £250 also to Mrs. ROBINSON, and probably there might be also a chance of an additional grant for the family of Dr. GREALY.

The LORD MAYOR said a proposal to make a grant to the families of these gentlemen was made some months ago, and at that time he was among those who, though deeply sympathising, did not feel that they would be justified in making a grant, and he felt equally strongly now that they were perfectly justified in not making these grants at the time. But he nevertheless warmly approved of giving a grant out of their surplus for this purpose. These gentlemen died distinctly in working for the poor, to relieve whom they received their funds, and he doubted that they could by any possibility select a better object to give a grant to than the families of those gentlemen who had been left unprovided for. He believed these small sums might operate as a stimulus to the dispensary medical officers through the entire country—if any stimulus were necessary—by the knowledge that if they did their duty fearlessly they would not be forgotten if they fell in its discharge.

* In response to a resolution adopted by the Mansion House Committee, and conveyed in a letter from the Lord Mayor.

At the suggestion of Sir GEORGE OWENS it was agreed that the case of the families of these gentlemen should be strongly recommended to the Medical Benevolent Fund.

The resolution was passed unanimously.

Mr. DRIMMIE proposed—

"That before closing its labours the Mansion House Committee desire earnestly to call the attention of the Government to the state of certain western districts where distress still exists, and to express its opinion that judicious measures should be taken to guard against the effects of destitution."

This Committee had received letters very recently from various parts of the West, detailing the distress which existed there, and urging the Committee to use its influence with the Government to bring some employment to the people there, in order that they might be enabled to help themselves without having recourse again to the charity of the world. It was only from a deep sense of the gravity of the situation in the West, and of the suffering and distress which still existed in many parts of it, that he was induced to propose this resolution.

Dr. SIGERSON, in seconding the resolution, said unfortunately there was ample evidence before them that distress still persisted in certain western districts, and that it would continue to persist there could not be any doubt.* He could bear personal testimony to the fact, because on some of those vast peninsulas and bleak coasts of the West he there for the first time this year saw the commencement of the potato blight. It was a melancholy thing to see the green crops touched with blackness, and even that variety of the root which had hitherto resisted the disease itself affected, and it was more melancholy still to see the peasant who had set his hopes on this year's harvest, after three years of disappointment, coming forth and wandering sadly among these blackened crops. Still more, he thought, was it painful, when they found in certain cases a man who, alone or with his family, had been stricken with fever rising out of his sick bed only to see the destruction of his crops. These were presages of distress of the most ominous kind. Succeeding events had undoubtedly occurred to confirm these unfortunate omens. They had recently occasion to observe the report of a discussion which took place at the Westport Board of Guardians, where Captain SPAIGHT, the Local Government Inspector, called the attention of the guardians to the fact that a number of people were in that district dependent on the potato crop, which had failed, and that they necessarily should be plunged into destitution without any resource to fall back upon. Hence he urged the board to use their powers of borrowing money for out-door relief. It would be in the recollection of the Committee that on several occasions they received from the relief Committee in that district information that it was difficult and almost impossible for them to increase the rates lest it should plunge the minor ratepayers into pauperism. If that were so then, *a fortiori* that must be an argument still more urgent at the present time. Finally they were aware that in many of these districts the ruin of the kelp trade, and the destruction of boats by the recent storm had added to the prevailing distress. They were aware also that it was absolutely out of the question that the charity of the world should again be appealed to, to feed the people; and if it were possible to expect it, it would be a grave misfortune that the people of this island should be taught to rely on the charity of the world, where it was alike the duty of all classes in the country and of

---

* Subsequent events have fully justified this anticipation. The following is one of several incidents which might be quoted in corroboration :—

BALLINASLOE, DECEMBER 15, 1880.—At the Ballinasloe Board of Guardians to-day, the Right Hon. the Earl of Clancarty presiding, a resolution was adopted setting out that Ballinasloe Union had been duly scheduled in pursuance of the Board of Works notice of 22nd November last, that there is want of employment in the barony of Longford, and consequent distress, and no reasonable prospect of employment being supplied either by the land proprietors, sanitary authorities, or otherwise; and that the guardians therefore resolved to ask the Local Government Board to recommend the Lord Lieutenant to convene an extraordinary meeting of the baronial sessions in the barony of Longford to present for works for the employment of the poor.—*Freeman's Journal, Dec.* 10, 1880. Other and severer cases followed.

the Government that had charge of its destiny, to take care that the possibilities of work as a resource for the people should be developed, and that the people should be enabled to look to labour, which ennobles men, instead of to pauperism, which degrades humanity.

Mr. DELANY thought that anyone who had examined the state of affairs through Ireland, and noticed the application made from many of the Boards of Guardians showing their inability to pay for seeds, would admit that before the next harvest came round there would be not only poverty, but something nearer to famine. He mentioned that in reply to queries from a large trading house in the city, magistrates, clergymen, and boards of guardians in the West of Ireland, invariably answered that God only knew what they would do for seeds next year, that before February, all their stock of potatoes would be eaten up; so that unless the Government interfered promptly things would be in a very serious position next year.

The LORD MAYOR said they would be only holding out false hopes, and doing infinitely more harm than they could hope to do good, were they to encourage the people who might be destitute this winter to look to this Committee for relief. There could be nothing clearer to his mind than that even if an appeal to public charity were to be again made—and he, for one, confessed he would have nothing to do with such an appeal—it was all very well when they were overtaken by a sudden emergency, but now there was full notice, and on the Government must rest the reponsibility. But even if such an appeal were made he did not think that it would be responded to again, and they could not expect that it should be. He did not mean to suggest that there was any danger of general destitution this winter such as existed last year, but certainly, from all the information he could gather, he was convinced that in certain isolated districts the destitution would be quite as severe as last year, and while there would be no shortness of food throughout Ireland, there would be in these districts an absence of money to buy it. He was sure the Government must have knowledge of that fact, but he certainly thought they ought formally to place it on record that they directed attention to it thus early, so that the Government might take such means as might be desirable for the relief of distress, which would be quite as severe as last year upon individuals, who would starve if they were not given some means of earning money to buy food.

Lord FRANCIS G. OSBORNE proposed the next resolution—

"That this Committee be now adjourned *sine die*. That the balance of the Fund be vested in the following nine gentlemen:—The LORD MAYOR, Sir G. B. OWENS, Alderman TARPEY, DAVID DRUMMOND, WILLIAM LANE JOYNT, CHARLES KENNEDY, Colonel DAVOREN, T. M. HUTTON, V. B. DILLON, jun., as Trustees, with full power to wind up the business of the Committee, to receive any other donations to this Fund that may come to hand, and to pay all debts due or which may accrue in connection therewith, and to devote the balance as speedily as practicable to the erection of boat-slips, and the purchase of boats and fishing gear for distressed fishermen on the Western Coast of Ireland, according to their discretion, and to incur any expenditure they think necessary for carrying out this object."

It was his firm conviction, from his experience, that though this year had been, perhaps, an exceptionally severe one, upon the Western Coast of Ireland and the Islands, there was always a state of things which was simply a disgrace to any civilised nation. He thought it was the imperative duty of this Committee to impress with all the power at their command the absolute necessity of something being done by those upon whom the responsibility for this state of things lay, so that chronic misery should be no longer permitted to exist there. It was the experience of all of them, that the miseries on the Western Coasts and Islands were particularly severe, and that being granted they could not devote the remainder of their Fund to a better purpose than relieving distress where it was greatest. Though their funds were unfortunately too scanty to enable them to make such provision for the western fishermen as the Baroness BURDETT COUTTS had made at Baltimore, they might help in some small way by supplying the fishermen with fishing gear and boat-slips, which he knew from personal experience were much needed. In conclusion, he thanked the meeting for the cordiality with which they had received him among them, and almost identified him as an Irishman. He had spent more than half of his life in Ireland, and had learned to love it the longer he lived in it, and if ever it lay in his power to assist in improving its condition, he would be as willing to do his part as when he took his place among the workers on this Committee.

Mr. MAXWELL HUTTON seconded the resolution, observing that he did not know any other way in which the money could be used so economically in the highest sense—that is, doing the greatest possible amount of good for the least amount of money.

The LORD MAYOR said he had received a letter from Mr. BRADY, one of the Inspectors of Fisheries, which showed how advantageous an allocation of their money this would be. Mr. DILLON and himself were members of the Canadian Committee, who had expended a good deal of money in the purchase of fishing gear, and perhaps the experience of the good done in this way had something to do with the suggestion that this balance should be devoted in a similar way. Mr. THOMAS F. BRADY, Commissioner of Fisheries, in his communication, thanked the LORD MAYOR, as Chairman of the Mansion House Committee, for his exertions in aiding the coast population of the West during the period of distress, and for the manner in which he called the attention of the Canadian Government to the wants of the famine-stricken people. The noble gift, he said, of the Canadian Government has done much to permanently relieve the condition of the fishery population, and most satisfactory results have arisen from the expenditure of nearly £11,000 sent across the Atlantic; still a great deal of poverty exists among the fishermen of Clare, Galway, and Donegal—an amount of poverty which can only be put aside by a supply of fishing gear, boats, and nets, and only for the Canadian Government they could not have fished at all this year. Mr. BRADY believed that if the people had the means of fishing, the occupation would become more remunerative than the tilling of land, and in hundreds of cases without which the fishery families must starve on their small holdings. Mr. BRADY now asked for a grant of £2,000 or £3,000 out of the balance of the Mansion House Fund to promote the purchase of boats and gear for those districts to which the Canadian charity did not extend. Mr. BRADY also enclosed a number of petitions for aid from poor fishermen whose boats were lost in the late gales.

Mr. E. FOX suggested that in view of the good done at Baltimore by the Baroness BURDETT COUTTS, the trustees should also be authorised to expend the money in the purchase of boats.

Mr. LANE JOYNT said the boats at Baltimore cost some £200 apiece, so that their surplus would go a short way in buying boats. With reference to Baltimore, he paid a high tribute to the benevolence of the Baroness BURDETT COUTTS, and to the exertions of the Rev. CHARLES DAVIS, P.P., to fit out a fleet there.

The LORD MAYOR said the Canadian Committee found that if they had had £100,000, instead of £20,000, they could have used it all usefully in the purchase of fishing gear.

The resolution was passed.

Mr. DRIMMIE mentioned that the final subscription to the fund was one of £280 from the Bishop of Ontario.

On the motion of Mr. DRUMMOND, the LORD MAYOR left the chair, and Mr. BROOKS, M.P., was called thereto.

Mr. DRUMMOND said he was sorry this duty had fallen upon him, inasmuch as he was quite incompetent to say what he would like to say in thanking the LORD MAYOR for all that he had done for their Committee and this country. They all owed to his lordship a very deep debt of gratitude. He had worked both in body and mind, hour after hour, day after day, and night after night, and they all knew what had been accomplished through the LORD MAYOR's presidency. He knew how much the family of his lordship must have been inconvenienced by the manner in which the Mansion House was given up to their Committee. Many a time when leaving the Mansion House late at night he thought of the inconvenience the LADY MAYORESS must have experienced, but it was all for the good of their fellow-creatures. He was sure every member of this Committee would join with him in thanking his lordship for all the care and all the trouble he had taken, and all the time he had given to the movement; and he could only hope that if ever it should please God again to send them such an ordeal as they had passed through during the last twelve months, he hoped his lordship and the LADY MAYORESS might again be the occupants of the Mansion House. He had great pleasure in moving a vote of thanks to the LORD MAYOR for all he had done in this movement.

Mr. GILL, M.P., had very great pleasure in seconding the vote of thanks to the LORD MAYOR for the manner in which he had acted while he was the head of this very influential Committee. The public ought to take into account that, in addition to the enormous amount of trouble and hard work which the LORD MAYOR took upon himself, he also assumed an enormous amount of responsibility in becoming head of this movement. In the eyes of the public he was more identified with this movement than anybody else. As it was called the Mansion House Committee the LORD MAYOR would naturally be identified with it in the most intimate manner, and the able, and dignified, and prudent manner in which he carried out all the details of the Committee's work had brought it to an end without the slightest blame having been attached to it in any respect. People of all religions and of all politics found nothing whatever to say against the manner in which the funds of this Committee were allocated, and though the LORD MAYOR had had an enormous amount of trouble and responsibility, still he would have the feeling in future times that he had done an enormous amount of good for the country in one of the most trying crisis that it ever went through. This feeling of duty well accomplished would, he was sure, always remain in his mind as one of the most pleasant, though sad (on account of its cause) remembrances a man could have. He trusted no LORD MAYOR would ever again have to undertake such a position, and that the Government by wise laws would prevent any future recurrence of the terrible calamities which required the Irish people to go before all the world as beggars.

Mr. BROOKS, M.P., in putting the resolution, said it was not necessary for him to add one word to supplement what had been said by Mr. DRUMMOND and M. GILL. He hoped, however, he might be pardoned if he bore his own humble testimony to the very remarkable assiduity and skill, and the very remarkable benevolence displayed by the LORD MAYOR in reference to the objects they had all so much at heart. They were all grateful to him. There was not a man, woman or child through the country that had not cause to feel grateful for all he had done for this organisation and in this house.

The vote of thanks was carried by acclamation.

The LORD MAYOR, in returning thanks, said this Committee had been already kind enough to pass a vote of thanks to him as chairman of the Committee, and then, in such language as he had at command—language which he certainly felt to be quite inadequate to convey his feeling in reference to the way in which they had been good enough to speak of him—he had tried to express his acknowledgment and thanks for the compliment paid him. It was very kind of them at this final meeting to repeat that vote of thanks. He thanked Mr. DRUMMOND very deeply and sincerely for the way in which he had spoken of him, and his friend Mr. GILL for his cordial references to him. He could only tell them again what he told them at their last public meeting—that he really did not deserve all the thanks and praise he had received in connection with this work. That it was a great work he would be the last to deny. That it had been a successful work he was very proud to believe; but he must repeat not with mere mock modesty, but as a simple statement of facts, that not to him but to others who were in the background, and who had not received the praise they deserved, was due really the success of this undertaking. Of course, he was, as LORD MAYOR, chairman of the Committee and the figure-head, but very often he had to be in London, and had to attend to many other avocations, and had the work been left to him as it often was left to individuals, it should have undoubtedly collapsed. But he was helped by men who knew neither fatigue nor relaxation in their efforts in the good work they had at heart. They made a fair division—they took the work, and he took the praise. With reference to the report they had just adopted, he could only see in it one defect, and that was that the acknowledgments they had made to certain individual members of the Committee were a very feeble expression indeed of the thanks which the Committee as a whole and which the Irish people owed to these gentlemen. But the Committee felt that there would be a certain difficulty in using very decided language in speaking of its own members, and they felt that the men who had really done the work with that modesty which always characterised true desert would not desire in a report to which should be appended their own names anything that might be held to pertain to mutual admiration. There was nothing of the kind here. They all worked hard; they never had a difference of opinion or a division; they did their best in a great cause, and the result was their reward With Mr. GILL he sincerely trusted that it might be the last occasion on which Ireland would have to go as a beggar to the nations. He would not attempt now to introduce what had never been introduced in their discussions, any political elements whatsoever; but he really believed it was not a political matter now to say that the land question of Ireland had reached a point at which all men, of all ways of thinking, admitted it must be dealt with in some way, and when they all recognised that the periodical famines to which this country had been subject, were due more or less to the condition of the land laws. The question must soon occupy the attention of Parliament, and he sincerely trusted that their councils might be guided by wisdom, and that they might find a true solution of a very difficult problem. He thought they would not have adequately discharged their duty if they had not warned the Government of what the condition of certain localities in the West would be during the coming winter, and he did trust that the Government, who were properly somewhat severe upon the shortcoming of previous efforts to deal with this distress, now that they had timely warning of what was approaching, would make adequate provision to meet the emergency, for there was no doubt whatever that they could not again expect any considerable aid from charitable sources. In conclusion, he asked their permission to read one passage of the report, as indicating in some manner his feelings and those of the Committee in reference to the services of certain individual members:

"Where every member of the Committee co-operated so loyally to secure the great object for which it was formed, it is hard to select names for special mention. We are restrained by this difficulty, and by the delicacy attending any reference by a Committee to its own members, from saying here much that anybody acquainted with the working of the Committee must deeply feel. But we cannot in common justice conclude this report without expressing the special obligation of the Committee especially to the Most Rev. Dr. TRENCH, for his assistance in every vicissitude of a trying time; to Alderman TARPEY, for his assiduous labour on the Examination Sub-Committee; to Mr. V. B. DILLON, jun., who planned the groundwork of the relief system; to Mr. JOHN ADYE CURRAN, who conducted the correspondence with the Local Committees; to Mr. CHARLES KENNEDY, for his constant attention to and supervision of the working of the organisation; to Lord FRANCIS G. OSBORNE, for his devoted services on the Western Coast; to Mr. W. LANE JOYNT, for his labours in connection with the supply of food and clothing to the Western Islands; to Mr. DAVID DRIMMIE, who transacted the principal part of the financial business of the Committee; to Professor SIGERSON, M.D., for his services on the Publication Sub-Committee, and on the Medical Commission in conjunction with Dr. J. E. KENNY; to the Rev. Canon BAGOT, the founder of the Seeds Fund; to Mr. J. A. FOX, for his reports concerning the condition of Mayo; to Mr. DAVID DRUMMOND, Rev. J. DANIEL, P.P., Mr. T. MAXWELL HUTTON, and Colonel DAVOREN, for their close attention to the work of the different Sub-Committees. None but their colleagues can know the labour, often extending into the night and early morning, which these and other gentlemen devoted to a work which at one time threatened to overwhelm them, and any words of thanks from their colleagues would be a trifling recompense compared with the satisfaction of knowing that their sacrifices for the alleviation of the sufferings of their fellow-countrymen have not been made in vain."

The Committee then separated.

APPENDIX VII.

APPEALS, FORMS, &c.

On the 21st of January, the following Appeal to the people of Great Britain from the Dublin Mansion House Committee for Relief of the Distress in Ireland, was transmitted to each of the several organs of public opinion at the Press :—

To the Editor,—We beg you will permit us to make this Appeal through the medium of your Newspaper.

It is now admitted that distress of an acute and exceptional character, certain to involve actual starvation if extraneous aid be not promptly and liberally forthcoming, exists over wide districts of Ireland.

This distress daily increases in area and in its intensity, so much so, that it seems impossible to avert until the next harvest an absolute famine in very many places. Every effort is being made in Ireland itself, as well by Local as by Central Relief Committees, to mitigate the calamity, but owing to the general commercial and agricultural depression, and to the wide-spread character of the distress, these efforts have proved totally inadequate to meet the crisis.

We therefore appeal with confidence to all friends of Ireland for aid in our efforts to save the people from destruction. Already munificent donations or promises of assistance have reached us from several parts of Great Britain, from the United States, from Australia, and elsewhere.

We feel that we have only to make known the sad position of the Irish people to ensure everywhere a generous response.

We would point to the constitution of our Committee, which comprises representative men of the highest character and position in the country, and of all creeds and politics, both as an assurance that this Appeal is justified, and that any funds entrusted to us shall be distributed in the manner best calculated to meet the emergency.

This Central Committee distributes its relief through Local Committees, of which the clergy of all denominations in the district, and the Poor-law Medical Officers, must be members, and requires that relief shall be given only in kind, and not in money.

We annex copy of a resolution adopted at a public meeting held here on 2nd January inst., and of a resolution adopted at the first meeting of this Committee.

We are your obedient servants,

Signed by the Lord Mayor and all the Members of the Committee.

The following Appeal was issued with a pamphlet containing an account of the proceedings of the Mansion House Committee, for ten weeks :—

Little more than two months have elapsed since the Dublin Mansion House Committee for the Relief of Distress in Ireland started into existence. At the period of its formation, there were some who were slow to believe that any pressing necessity for the organisation of such a body existed, and there were few who realised that the work before it would have proved so overwhelming in its sadness, and in its magnitude. At the commencement of the year there were, however, abundant evidences that in many districts of the West, and of the South-West and North, the shadow of a fearful calamity had settled upon the people, and that, there at least, there would be ample scope for the exercise of a benevolent charity.

With as little delay as possible the Committee applied itself to the task of sending succour to the afflicted; and as the funds for relief came in they were despatched with promptitude for distribution amongst the needy. The system adopted by the Committee for relieving the wants of those who most required assistance, is described elsewhere; and the testimony that has been offered from every quarter of the country, as to the satisfactory results that have followed upon a close adhesion to it, is the best proof of its efficiency and efficacy for all its purposes.

Three times in each week the Committee holds a Public Meeting for the discussion of its work and for the allocation of its grants, and on each of the other three days the Sub-Committees of distribution are engaged in the careful and scrupulous investigation of every application for relief. Day by day, it was found that the area of want was increasing, and that hunger and suffering and misery were creeping into households and into districts, where but a short time before their presence was but little anticipated.

The wail of woe that first came from Mayo, and Galway, and Donegal, and Clare, and Cork, and Kerry, began to come in equally harrowing tones from Sligo, and Cavan, and Roscommon, and Leitrim, and Longford, and Tyrone, and Fermanagh, and the picturesque Glens of Antrim and of Down; and it is but a short time since help was sent to the fairest spots in beautiful Wicklow, and to some of the once thriving villages of fertile Kildare. Tipperary has shared in these merciful ministrations, and Cork, and Limerick, and Dublin counties have partaken of the magnificent generosity which has so splendidly manifested itself throughout the world, in behalf our stricken and patiently-enduring people.

In truth, every day of the ten weeks that have passed since the establishment of the Committee, has intensified the distress, and to-day there is scarcely a corner of the land where famine is not impending over its inhabitants.

The prospect before them from this to August—when, as may be hoped, the fields will be ripe and rich for the harvest—is an appalling one, and but little expectation can be entertained that it will brighten till far into that month. A world's mercy and munificence have enabled the Committee up to this to save hundreds, thousands, from death by starvation; to rescue thousands of little children from premature graves, and to avert the ghastly and historic incidents of Schull and Skibbereen of three-and-thirty years ago. But as yet its work is far from done. The Committee has yet enough to keep our people alive for about six weeks more. With the expiration of that period, unless the world's mercy and munificence go on, God only knows what the result may be. The Committee makes a fresh appeal to the sympathy of the benevolent throughout the universe. The existence of a whole race depends upon the response. In her too brief and transient intervals of prosperity, Ireland was never slow in responding to appeals from afflicted nations, and out of her comparative poverty she gave with ungrudging generosity. In her present need she asks for aid, and the Dublin Mansion Committee will gladly continue to be almoners of any gifts that may be sent to it for the alleviation of Ireland's great distress.

St. Patrick's Day, 1880.

At a Meeting of the Committee, held on the 25th May, the condition of the country, the increase of disease, and the diminution of the Relief Funds were taken into consideration. The following proceedings took place:—

Dr. SIGERSON said it was his duty to bring forward the Report or Statement of the Publication Committee. They had now arrived at a somewhat critical juncture of their operations, and a few words might not be considered out of place. Various statements had been made with reference to the distress, and as to the mode of relieving it, and some doubt had even been thrown on it by persons who had kept themselves anonymous and had never authenticated their remarks by any facts. He would call their attention in the first place to one of the gravest facts in connection with this subject. They were aware that famine need not necessarily show itself at first by sudden death. The deprivation of food would manifest its influence by greatly lowering the constitution and leaving it open to attacks of disease of various kinds. Now, if that had occurred they should expect to see an increase of the death-rate. He found on looking at the Quarterly Return, which reports the death-rate of this country during the last quarter of last year, that the death-rate was "above the average for the corresponding quarter of the previous five years, the excess being 1·6 per thousand, and is the highest registered in the fourth quarter of any year since registration of deaths commenced in 1864." The Registrar proceeds—"The suffering caused by the extremely bad harvest and depression of trade is no doubt, to a considerable extent, a cause of the excessive death-rate of Ireland during the past quarter." Taking the returns for the first quarter of the present year the death-rate for the quarter was 1·3 per 1,000 under that of the first quarter of 1879 (after a rigorous winter), "although one per thousand above the average of the corresponding quarters of the past five years." The death-rate had during the first quarter decreased, as compared with that of the last quarter of last year, and what was the cause of that decrease? It was evidently due to one great cause that came into operation, and that cause was the intervention of the various associations that rose into existence to administer charity throughout the country. There had been some doubt expressed as to the accuracy of the statements that came to them, depicting the amount and intensity of the distress. But in these official documents we have the testimony of perfectly independent witnesses not biassed on the popular side, the evidence, namely, of the local Registrars. These show both the gravity of the distress and the benefit derived from the relief distributed. At Downpatrick the Registrar gave a statement showing the prevalence in one part of great sickness and considerable mortality, and towards the mountain of Slieve Croob he stated there was great privation in some cases, and extreme poverty very generally, the consequence of which was that there was "already a considerable increase of sickness and debility, and the prospects of an outbreak of fever, which usually supervenes under such circumstances." In Ballyshannon (Belleek) the Registrar said —" The deaths are much above the average this quarter, in fact exceeding any quarter since the Registration Act came into force. I ascribe much of the cause of the deaths of old people to cold and chest affections arising from the want of fuel owing to the wet summer." In Enniskillen the Registrar said—"Deaths considerably above average; chiefly old people, who suffered most from want of warm clothing and fuel. No deaths from want of food, as that was more than supplied from the Relief Funds." In the District of Milford the Registrar said—"The general health of the district was very good, considering the scarcity of food, and this was owing in a great measure to the prompt relief given in the district from the Relief Funds." In Clones the Registrar said—" Deaths have been more numerous than in any quarter I remember." Even in Carlow it was stated—" There were several slight cases of dysentery resulting from bad and insufficient diet, but no deaths occurred. A Local Committee was formed and funds obtained from the Mansion House, and I consider great relief was thus afforded to the suffering poor." From Laurencetown, Ballinasloe, it was stated—" A case of famine or relapsing fever came under my notice last week." There were several other returns of a similar kind, but those he had quoted established beyond doubt, to any sane man, that the distress had been what had been represented to them. The aid they had been enabled to give, and which had been acknowledged so gratefully, was due to the fact that they had received from various sources a sum which amounted to £161,760. How long would the balance now in hand last at their rate of distribution? During the past month, they had to diminish their grants. During the past month, the amount spent was £23,446, and they had now only £18,641 in hand—no more than would last three weeks. That being the case, it had been considered necessary that immediate steps should be taken to place the facts before the public so that all might realise the critical nature of the position in which they were placed. Hitherto a large number of people had been looking to them for relief. In a few weeks they would look in vain. The Committee could do no more than they had done, and in issuing any address to the public it should be clearly shown how urgent was the crisis. The address which he was now about to read had received the sanction of his Grace Archbishop TRENCH and his Grace Archbishop M'CABE, and the LORD MAYOR had telegraphed to him expressing his approval of it. In conclusion, Dr. SIGERSON read the following address, which was unanimously adopted by the General Committee, and ordered for publication:—

STATEMENT.

Mansion House, Dublin, May 27th, 1880.

For nearly five months we have striven with the distress which has come upon our country.

Reluctantly compelled to appeal to the generosity of the benevolent, the liberality of their response has saved the lives of thousands of our countrymen, who would have perished of famine, and the lingering diseases engendered by starvation, but for this opportune assistance.

To state the chief cause of the distress is to indicate its character, its intensity, and its duration. For three successive seasons there have been partial failures of the principal food-crop of the people, of which the greatest was that occurring last year, at a time when the general depression was most intense. The total loss from this one cause has been estimated at about thirteen millions sterling, which, falling most severely on the small cultivators, has reduced a vast multitude to utter destitution.

Thus arising, the distress must of necessity continue, as the influence of the cause continues, and even enlarge, as local resources lessen, until a new harvest shall have given a new supply of food to the people.

The agencies in operation for the relief of suffering are wholly inadequate to arrest the distress. The public works, yet to be undertaken, will be comparatively few, sparse, and of limited influence. As regards the Poor-law system, it cannot, where the need is greatest, bear even the present strain, for several Unions are already in a bankrupt condition, and very many of the humbler ratepayers have themselves become recipients of eleemosynary aid. Increase of the rates, in most of the stricken districts, means taxation of the indigent for the relief of the destitute, and thus tends to broaden the area of privation.

As it is, numbers have latterly fallen into the ranks of pauperism, after a strenuous effort for independence, and many others are even now striving desperately against the pressure of distress, rather than endure the humiliation of accepting alms.

It is a lamentable truth that the fever which follows famine has already made its appearance in several places, and when we recall the ravages caused by it, in 1847, this manifestation of the disease naturally gives rise to the most grave apprehensions.

In comparison with the immense loss suffered by the country, the sum of the funds contributed to the several charitable organizations seems but a slender pittance. Nor have we been able, with what assistance came to our hand, to do more than preserve the afflicted people from absolute starvation by scanty doles of Indian meal. But the supplies which, flowing into us during the winter season, enabled us to do thus much, have latterly decreased, and now threaten entirely to fail.

Nevertheless, an ordeal of nearly three months still remains to be undergone, during which the last provisions of many will disappear, and the full vigour of famine will fall upon suffering thousands. Our expenditure for last month, with diminished and curtailed grants, amounted to £23,446. There now remain on hand but £18,621. The demands of three brief weeks will completely exhaust our store, and if this be not soon and liberally replenished by the generosity of the humane, we can hope no longer to avert disaster.

Thus it is with us. Distress continues urgent; destitution threatens to increase; fevers make their appearance, and add the pain of disease to the pang of hunger. At the same time, to meet these enlarging evils our means are lessened, and the resources at our disposal draw rapidly to an end.

In view of a state of affairs so serious and so alarming, we deem it to be our solemn and imperative duty thus publicly to declare that, whilst ever anxious to continue our ministrations, we cannot consent even to appear to assume a responsibility which far surpasses our power efficiently to discharge. Hence, as all things combine to show that our operations must, for want of supplies, come to a close within three weeks, whilst distress shall still persist, it behoves us to give due warning that, after that period (if public generosity have not renewed our store), our assistance can no longer be expected; and that we will then formally resign into the hands of those whom the State appoints to watch over its safety, the full charge of the suffering lives which have hitherto been the subject of our care, and must still be the object of our painful solicitude.

E. D. GRAY, M.P., Lord Mayor, *Chairman*.

RESOLUTIONS

Adopted at a Public Meeting held in the Mansion House, on the 2nd January, 1880.

Proposed by Sir ARTHUR GUINNESS, M.P.; seconded by P. J. SMYTH, Esq., M.P.; supported by the RECORDER, the Very Rev. T J. O'REILLY, Adm., Dr. SPEEDY, and the Hon. D. PLUNKETT, M.P. :—

"That the poorer classes in many parts of Ireland must, during the coming season, suffer great distress, involving absolute destitution, if extraneous aid be not liberally and promptly supplied; and that, without interfering with the beneficent efforts for a similar purpose already instituted, a Fund be now opened for the Relief of the Distress in Ireland, to be called 'The Dublin Mansion House Relief Fund.'"

Proposed by C. H. MELDON, Esq., M P.; seconded by ALEXANDER PARKER, Esq., J.P. :—

"That the following Committee, with the Treasurers and Honorary Secretaries, with power to add to their number, be empowered to carry out the objects of this Meeting." (*See Committee.*)

Proposed by GEORGE BROWNE, Esq., M.P.; seconded by W. FINDLATER, Esq. :—

"That a Subscription List be now opened, and the Right Hon. E. Dwyer Gray, M.P., Lord Mayor; Sir James W. Mackey, D.L., High Sheriff; Sir John Barrington, and Mr. Jonathan Pim, be requested to act as Treasurers to the Relief Fund, and are hereby authorised to open a Banking Account in the National Bank; and they, or any of them, are empowered to draw from time to time cheques on the said Fund."

RESOLUTIONS

Adopted at the First Meeting of the Committee held at the Mansion House, Dublin, on the 3rd January, 1880.

Proposed by His Grace the Most Rev. Dr. TRENCH; Seconded by the Very Rev. J. DANIEL, P.P.:—

"That the action of this Committee be solely through local agencies, and not by direct communication with those who seek or may need its relief."

Proposed by Mr. C. H. MELDON, M.P.; seconded by Sir GEORGE OWENS:—

"That the agency through which this Committee would desire to dispense its relief would be Local Committees, including, wherever practicable, the Clergymen of all denominations in the district, the Chairman or Vice-Chairman of the Board of Guardians, the Chairman or Vice-Chairman of the Dispensary Committee, and the Medical Officer."

Proposed by His Grace the Most Rev. Dr. TRENCH; seconded by the Very Rev. J. DANIEL, P.P.:—

"That as a condition of being recognised as an agency at whose recommendation and by whose instrumentality relief shall be imparted, the Local Committee for any district must satisfy this Committee of the existence of acute and exceptional distress in the district from which the claims to be relieved come."

Proposed by His Grace the Most Rev. Dr. TRENCH; Seconded by MR. THOS. PIM, Jun.:—

"That a Local Committee dispensing relief from this Fund, must engage to keep a book in which shall be entered the names of applicants for relief, particulars as to age, occupation, number in family, extent of land held (if any), and nature and amount of relief afforded in each case; and this book shall always be open to the Committee, and also they will be expected to furnish weekly accounts of receipts from this Fund, and disbursements of the same."

APPEALS, FORMS, ETC.   221

QUERY SHEET.

The following Form was issued to be filled up by each of the Local Committees:

MANSION HOUSE,
Dublin, 1880.

GENTLEMEN,

The Committee of the Mansion House Fund has received your application, and will be obliged by your returning *this Form filled up* with answers to the following questions:—

1. By what name is your Local Committee known?
    Post Town   County
2. What is the name and extent of the district over which your Committee propose to extend their operation?
3. Are there any other Local Committees in your district? Give their names.
4. Have you made application for assistance from the "Marlborough Fund," or any other fund? If so, with what result?
5. If not, why not?
6. What is present Poor's Rate, and what has been average of last three years?
7. About what number of persons who may fairly claim assistance from the Mansion House Fund, or from some other similar fund, do you suppose to be included in your district? Is this number likely to increase?

[Write Names of your Committee, and the Names and *Addresses* of the Officers, with Religion of each Member, on this page.

N.B.—On this Committee Clergy of all Denominations should be included where practicable, and where not practicable a reason must be given.

Chairman.
Secretary.
Treasurer.]

8. What has been the condition in life of these in past time, and to what causes may their present destitution be mainly attributed?
9. What efforts have been made, and what amount of money has been subscribed, towards relieving the distress in the district? Send any documents relating to the formation of your or any other Committees in the District.
10. In what form do you propose to administer relief obtained from this fund? [*N.B.*—*You must distinctly understand that relief is to be given only in food, fuel or clothing.*]
11. Will your Committee undertake to keep a book which shall contain the names of accepted applicants for relief, particulars as to age, occupation, number in family, extent of land held (if any), amount and duration of relief afforded in each case, and to lay the same before our Committee when requested?
12. Will your Committee undertake to keep an account shewing the receipts and disbursements of any sums received from this Fund, and to furnish weekly a statement of the manner in which such grants have been expended, with the vouchers for the same?

All Local Committees are empowered to spend the money granted to them by the Mansion House Fund, as they shall deem most conducive to the ends for which this Fund exists, subject to the foregoing conditions.

To be Signed by the Chairman and Secretary

APPENDIX VIII.

CORRESPONDENCE.

In order that some idea of the condition of the country may be obtained, the following letters are here published. They represent most of the distressed Counties; but they form only a minute proportion of the immense mass of correspondence sent forward by the Committees of districts where suffering existed :—

"*Layde Rectory, Cushendall, Co. Antrim, 4th February,* 1880."

"GENTLEMEN,

"I am directed by the Committee formed in this district (extending from Garron Point to Fox Point), in the glens of Antrim, to place before you a short statement of the distress existing in this neighbourhood, and to ask for some assistance from your fund.

"Though the distress is not so widespread as in other parts of Ireland, yet so far as it goes it is quite as acute. The almost total failure of the potato crop, together with the turf already cut, and the want of employment for labourers, has impoverished the people to an extent unknown since '47, and for some time past the clergy and gentry have been besieged by people for aid, which they have relieved to the best of their ability, but it has now become too heavy for them to cope with.

"We have appointed a Committee, which includes all the magistrates resident in the district, clergy, doctors, together with a fair representation of the merchants and farmers. We have ascertained that there are upwards of fifty families, representing more than 200 persons, in immediate want of relief.

"One case reported to me yesterday, the head of a family of nine persons with not one penny, nor any food in the house. Another, a man looking for employment and going to walk thirteen miles, who had not tasted food at one o'clock in the day, leaving behind a wife and large family. Another, an old woman trying to sell brooms at one o'clock in the day, and failing to sell even one to get breakfast for herself and family. We shall make efforts to get seed potatoes, as in very many cases there are none left.

"I am, gentlemen, your obedient servant,

"WM. THOMPSON, Clk., *Hon. Sec.*

"*Crossmaglen and Creggan Relief Committee, Co. Armagh, 4th March,* 1880."

"GENTLEMEN,

"Through sheer necessity, we are obliged again to appeal to the Mansion House Relief Committee for a second donation towards relieving the distress that is becoming more widespread every day in this parish.

"Generous as has been your first donation of £25, and taking into account our local subscriptions, our funds are almost exhausted, and we have been compelled to exclude many applications.

"In our first application we gave the number of those in distress at something about 750 families, or 3,750 persons, and that number is, unfortunately, increasing On the first two days of distribution we relieved 550 families, or 2,750 people, but, as we remarked before, we were obliged to let many go unrelieved through want of funds.

"We have given relief, in the shape of Indian meal, as, owing to our want of funds, we could not afford to give anything more substantial; and to no family, no matter how numerous, have we given more than two stone of meal in the week. So, notwithstanding all our care and caution, the number of applications is daily increasing, and before many days, if some subscriptions do not reach us, I fear the consequences will be terrible.

"We will not be giving harrowing details or quoting affecting scenes to be witnessed here every day, but we simply state hard, incontrovertible facts, believing they will tell better the misery and distress prevailing here than graphic descriptions.

"Unfortunately, we have not as yet got any donations from any other fund, and we, therefore, must only appeal again to the generosity of the Mansion House Committee; and should they, in their goodness, listen to our cry for help, I need not say that the poor people of this parish will never forget them in their prayers.

"We beg to remain, gentlemen, faithfully yours.

"John M'Donnell, *Chairman.*
"James Loughran, C.C., *Secretary.*"

"*Mullagh, Kells, Co. Cavan, March 2nd,* 1880.

"Gentlemen,

"I again beg to draw your attention to application of this Committee sent you on 21st February, and to appeal to you in the strongest possible terms for your generous assistance. This parish contains a larger number of cottiers than any other in this county, together with 150 small farmers in the most distressed and destitute condition, without any visible means of supporting themselves and their families.

"Up to this there has been no employment of any account given here, and these poor people are all crying to us for relief, but for want of funds we have been unable to do anything for them this week. We beg of you, in the name of the starving poor, to send us £50 if possible.

"Obediently yours,
"Thomas P. M'Kenna, *Secretary, Mullagh P. R. Committee.*"

"P.S.—We applied to the other Funds, but got nothing. Relieved by this Committee—1,650 persons."

"*Kilnaleck, Co. Cavan, February 16th,* 1880.

"Sir,

"The Kilnaleck Relief Committee desire me to write an urgent appeal to your Committee for immediate aid. 230 heads of families got temporary relief this day, ranging from one to three stone of meal. 250 persons were obliged to go home to their helpless children without food.

"I can assure the Mansion House Committee that great destitution exists in the parish, and the cry of the poor is to give them work, for this temporary relief is not able to support them.

"Up to 500 destitute poor were in Kilnaleck this day, one-third of this number were small farmers

"Your obedient servant,
"Charles Boylan, *Hon. Secretary.*"

APPENDIX VIII.

"*Moybologue, Bailieboro', Co. Cavan, 12th February,* 1880

"GENTLEMEN,

"A meeting was this day held in the Edengora National Schoolhouse, attended by the Roman Catholic and Irish Church clergymen, and other representative gentlemen of various religious denominations.

"The following resolution, among others, was proposed, seconded and unanimously passed:—'That immediate application be made to the Mansion House Relief Fund for aid to ward off the dire destitution unfortunately existing among many in this district.'

"The materials upon which such a statement may be based are lamentably extensive. Within the limits of the parishes to which our district is confined are very many cases of whole families in such distress as borders on starvation. The inhabitants are almost all of the struggling small farmer class, depending on potatoes and turf for food and fuel. The potatoes were last year, in rare instances, not worth the digging, and the turf had to be abandoned owing to the heavy rains and consequent flooding. The scanty plots of corn sown were, in the first place, ill-productive, and next, only half saved with great difficulty.

"Owing to the excessively low market price of other farm produce, no money was realized to meet the emergency. All these causes conspiring, have reduced the small farmers here to a pitiable condition.

"What is apparent to cursory observers is not a tithe of the real distress existing, inasmuch as those very small farmers, in most cases, would suffer almost anything short of starvation before they would brook the shame of a public acknowledgment of their distress. No case of actual death by starvation has as yet, thank God, occurred, to the knowledge of the Committee; but unless immediate relief be procured from some source within a fortnight, we know not what fearful results a delay of even so short a time might bring forth. Many of the small farmers are destitute of food, of fuel, and of clothing. They are at the present moment eating, or have already eaten, their seed potatoes and seed corn, to preserve life. Many of them are perishing for want of ordinary clothes, and, what is far more serious, have no bedclothes to protect them at night from the wintry cold. It was the opinion of our meeting that at least two hundred lives are at the present moment in this perilous condition—reduced to the verge of starvation; their seed potatoes and seed corn consumed, having no fuel, their ordinary clothes, in most cases, reduced to shreds, and devoid almost of any covering at night. With this spectre of distress so excessive, brooding over so many in our district, we earnestly and respectfully request such a grant from your Committee as the statement of facts here given seems to your Committee to warrant. Pledging, on our part, that whatever sums may be entrusted to us for the relief of the distress, shall be faithfully distributed by us among those who are most necessitous, in the manner stipulated by the donors.

"I am, &c.,

"J. E. H. MURPHY, B.A., Clk., *Hon. Sec.*'

"*Dungloe, viâ Stranorlar, Co. Donegal, Jan. 14th,* 1880

"GENTLEMEN,

"As we understand that the Mansion House Fund is to be distributed amongst the poorest districts in Ireland, we deem it absolutely necessary to make immediate application to your Committee for whatever portion of the fund they may be able to allocate for this district. The parishes represented by our Committee are Templecrone and Lettermacward, Co. Donegal, large and extensive parishes, including 2,531 families, consisting of 13,372 persons, who occupy 72,230 acres, the Government valuation of which is only £4,279 10s. 0d., or 1s. 2d. per acre on an average. The distress in the above-mentioned parishes is something fearful to contemplate.

Our first instalment from the Duchess of Marlborough's Fund, amounting to £50, won't enable us to relieve for the present more than 240 out of 960 applications, giving each family ¼ cwt. of Indian meal. In fine, if relief be not forthcoming from other sources than the Duchess of Marlborough's Fund, we cannot possibly cope with the fearful destitution which prevails in this part of the country. We are, in fact, without the slightest degree of exaggeration, on the very verge of famine. Before making this application we investigated most particularly the state of the parishes referred to, and we are therefore in a position to vouch for the accuracy of the above statement. Under these circumstances we trust that your Committee will at once come to our aid.

"I am, gentlemen, yours truly,

"CHARLES M'GLYNN, P.P."

"*Letterkenny, Co. Donegal*, 16*th February*, 1880.

"SIR,

"We beg to inform your Committee that so great and so urgent have been the claims made on us for aid by the Local Committees working with us all over the county, that, in meeting them, we have all but exhausted the funds at our disposal, and we humbly beg your Committee will supplement the liberal donation already made to us by a still more liberal grant. The magnitude of the work of charity thrown upon us will be best shown by the following statistics, which for your own information we have tried to collect all over the Co. Donegal. We are glad to be able to assure you that at present we have in co-operation with us Local Committees in every distressed portion of the county, with two exceptions, Ramelton and Innishowen: and in a few days we hope to have Local Committees in these places also. Putting Innishowen down for the present as one large district to which we have already made a grant of £200, we have, in addition, twenty-eight Local or Parochial Committees. We have adopted parochial divisions, being the most practical, for many reasons, named Ballyshannon, Bundoran, Pettigo, Ballintra, Donegal, Inver, Killaghter, Killybegs, Kilcar, Glencolumbkille, Ardara, Glenties, Kiltervogue, Stranorlar, Convoy, Letterkenny, Churchill, Kilmacrennan, Rathmullen, Milford, and Carrowkeel, Carryart, Dunfanaghy, Cloghaneely, and Tory Island, Gweedore, Lower Templecrone, and Arran Island and Upper Templecrone, Lettermacward, Fintown. These Local Committees are giving relief to about 12,000 families, or 60,000 individuals, and granting each individual 6*d*. per week (surely a miserable pittance), our weekly expenditure would be about £1,500 sterling. At our last meeting we distributed about £1,100 as a weekly allowance, and the appeals are daily increasing in number, and in the urgency and extent of poverty they contain. With these facts before you, when you remember that we beg to assure you that the greatest harmony exists between the Central and Local Committees, each doing its work to the best of its power towards warding off the hand of famine from so many thousand souls now in absolute want. Further, that the Duchess of Marlborough's Committee has not up to this extended its charity to many parts of the county, and these the most distressed, namely, all the Dunfanaghy Union, including Gweedore, the Letterkenny Union, &c., and these districts are entirely dependent on us for relief, and that out of the £28,000 already distributed by your Committee only £1,200 have been sent to Donegal, though, we have no doubt, the poorest of the few counties of Ireland affected by the present distress. We feel confident your Committee will send us a generous grant from the Mansion House Fund, that thereby we may be enabled to continue to the end the noble work we have begun.

"Signed,

"✠ MICHAEL LOGUE, *Chairman, Bishop of Raphoe,*
"W. A. GALLAGHER, *Hon. Sec.*"

APPENDIX VIII.

"*Kilcoo, Co. Down, 12th February,* 1880.

"MY LORD,

"It is painful and humiliating to have to acknowledge that even in this, the premier county of Ulster, there exists distress deep-felt and widespread. Nothing but sheer necessity can force the people to acknowledge want and ask relief. They will struggle on amidst difficulties, and continue to conceal their misery until their blanched cheeks betray them and tell the observer that the gnawing pain is wearing away their vitals. Such has been the case in '46 and '47, when the gaunt spectre, Famine, stalked over the land, and decimated a famished people, and such, unhappily, is the case here now in this County of Down. At all events, such is the case in this parish of Upper Kilcoo, with a population of over 3,000, spread over thirteen townlands, situate in a mountainous district, where, owing to the inclemency of the season, the poor people did not obtain a particle of peat from the bogs—their source of fuel—and their crops were almost completely lost. Their means, which were at best but slender, have been gradually diminishing for the past few years, and are now exhausted, as is also their credit. Hence, we find that the fuel of the majority is the furze and heath which they gather from the hill-sides; and the food of many—alas! too many—an insufficient quantity of Indian meal porridge, without a single drop of milk to make it palatable. It is truly a pitiable plight in which hundreds of the poor people here now find themselves—partially without food, wholly without fuel, or means to procure it; without seed for the land, without clothing, and without credit. Knowing this, knowing that starvation is already at our doors, and claims its victims, it would be little less than criminal to allow a sense of delicacy to prevent us from proclaiming the fact, believing, as we do, that its proclamation will elicit from a generous and sympathetic public such timely aid as may possibly avert the occurrence of the harrowing scenes of the famine years.

"(Signed on behalf of the Committee),

"S. WARD, Blackcauseway, Downpatrick.
"W. P. O'CONNOR, 58, Apsley-place, Belfast.
"J. P. KINGSCOTE, J.P., Bryansford.
"CHAS. PARKHURST BAXTER, M.A., Incumbent.
"H. CONNOR, P.P.
"B. M'KENNA, C.C.
"P. FITZPATRICK, P.L.G.
"FRANCIS O'NEILL, P.L.G.
"JOHN M'ALISTER, P.L.G."

Derrylin Relief Committee, Co. Fermanagh, 28th February, 1880.

"GENTLEMEN,

"Although it was well known that distress prevailed to a great extent in this district for some months past, in consequence of the destruction of crops, meadows, and pasture land by Lake Erne floods, together with the failure of crops generally, yet it is only now, when the members of the Committee, in their several localities, have investigated the claims for relief brought before them, that they find out the dire misery which exists. The small farmers have the greatest dislike to take anything in the shape of alms; and it is only when they find the gnawing of hunger, or their children cry for food, that they come to seek relief.

"This Committee hopes your Committee will send them further help as speedily as possible. The funds at their disposal are almost exhausted, and next week will be one of suffering for many here if aid be not to hand,

"I am, gentlemen,

"Your obedient servant,

"PATRICK CLARKE, *Hon Secretary*,

"*Parochial House, Belleek, Co. Fermanagh, 12th February,* 1880.

" DEAR SIR,

" May I, through you, again be permitted to appeal to the Mansion House Committee, for another act of charity and mercy towards the many hundreds now suffering dreadfully, in my parish. In truth, the distress is now assuming here an alarming appearance. On yesterday, our day of meeting at Mulleek to afford relief, the crowd was so great, looking for anything at all we could give, that it occupied the Relief Committee up to two hours after night to get through our list of applicants, and we had to give up the task nearly in hopeless despair of knowing what to do to get the shivering creatures away. It was sad to see hundreds crowded together around the door of where the Committee met, waiting from twelve o'clock noon to eight at night, under drenching rain, for whatever little we could give. From 1s. to 2s. 6d., was our rule, and in the end had to curtail even these small sums, sooner than hear the cries of the disappointed. Really the people are on the point of dying. If something be not done very soon to give employment, alms will not at all meet the crisis much longer. On last Monday in Pettigo several poor women and strong men came to the priest's house, and some of them fainted with hunger and exhaustion. The appearance of the poor is appalling. I will also ask, with whatever the feeling consideration of the Committee will be pleased to grant our poor people here—tickets, if you have such, and sheets to make returns on—if such be required by the Committee. We have none here, and I don't know where we are to procure such. Most gratefully thanking your Committee on behalf of our Local Committee, myself, and all my poor parishioners,

" I am, dear Sir, yours very faithfully,

" J. M'KENNA, P.P., Pettigo, Belleek."

"*Scotstown, Co. Monaghan, 20th January,* 1880.

" My Lord,

" May I submit to the charitable feelings of your Lordship, and to the Committee of the Mansion House Relief Fund, the sad state of our starving people.

" I am not going to furnish you with a state of things which have their existence in my imagination. Like the poor people themselves, I would rather conceal their poverty than paint it in its horrible reality.

" The landlords here are giving no work except to the process-server; the poor have no credit, and the father and mother are in hopeless want of work, and their children in want of bread. I know of thirty-three homes—if, indeed, a tenement without a window could be called a home—in which there is neither food nor fire. I may say there are 15 of these in extreme want. Instance the following:—Yesterday evening I was called on to visit a patient. When I reached the hovel it was not dark, yet the family, seven in all, were in bed; and why? because they had eaten the scanty fare they collected during the day, they had no fire to warm them, and their remedy was to lie in a cold room, on cold beds, with cold, empty stomachs; and I fear my patient is a cold corpse now amongst them; and if I was constituted judge and jury over the cause of her death, my verdict would be 'want of food.' Such, and like pressing cases, I submit to the consideration of your Lordship.

" I have the honour to remain your faithful servant,

" THOS. CUMMINS, C.C."

APPENDIX VIII.

"*Plumbridge, Newtownstewart, Parish of Upper Bodoney,*
"*Barony of Upper Strabane,*
"*Co. Tyrone,* 13*th February,* 1880.

"GENTLEMEN,

"You may, no doubt, think it strange to have before you an appeal for relief from so prosperous a county as Tyrone. Even here not long since everyone would have thought so likewise. This parish, though situated in the heart of the mountains, without any resident gentry, large farmers, or any special industry, if not rich, had few poor. Now all is changed, especially in the eastern part of it. This consists of a mountain glen, seven or eight miles long, midway on a line between Derry and Belfast, and is used chiefly for grazing Scotch sheep and young cattle. At no time good for potatoes or even oats, the last three or four wet seasons have been the ruin of it. Nearly 400 families dwell in this glen, and fully one-half of them are now in extreme want. Their only firing is heather; they have no potatoes; their half-filled oats are sold or consumed; they are sunk in debt, from fifty to eighty per cent. of all they are worth, including their tenant-right; and the result is that they have lost their credit. Their landlords remitted them twenty per cent. in this year's payments, and, therefore, cannot be expected to do much more for them. Local contributions are not to be expected from a people on the verge of ruin. Some weeks ago, at a special meeting of the P. L. Guardians at Gortin, this state of affairs was not only acknowledged, but confirmed, by a full Board.

"The worthy Chairman, Major W. C. Hamilton, communicated with the Committee of the Duchess of Marlborough's Fund, and, from the public papers, I believe a grant was made to the Union. But how much is to be given to this locality I cannot say.

"A Local Committee has been formed, of as mixed a character as possible, consisting of the Rector of the parish, the Parish Priest and Curate, the principal representative of the Presbyterians (there being no minister just now), of the Vice-Chairman of the Board of Guardians, of the Dispensary Guardians, the Poor-rate Collector, and the P. L. Guardians of the district. In all, four Protestants, four Roman Catholics, and one Presbyterian.

"Since the formation of the Committee, and even since I began this letter, I find that in other parts of the parish also there are at least seventy or eighty families equally sunk in debt, and without credit. In the name of the Local Committee, and on behalf of these poor starving people (nearly all small farmers), may I ask you to grant us so much money as will purchase for each family at least a bag of Indian meal.

"P. MAGEE, P.P., *Hon. Secretary.*"

"*Milltown, Tuam, Co. Galway, January,* 1880.

"GENTLEMEN,

"The people of Milltown and its surrounding districts being led to believe that a system of arterial drainage, which was so much talked of taking place in this locality, would tide them over their present distress, kept secret their sufferings, and made no clamour about their destitute condition as long as there was a flickering hope.

"The inhabitants having now lost all faith in the would-be Drainage and Railway, and having almost eaten the last seed potatoes, are in utter despair about the future: how they shall exist for the next six months, and where they shall get seed potatoes and oats for setting their crops.

"I am personally aware that many families are living upon yellow meal since the last week of November.

"Many are in such straits that they have depended for the last three months on the charity of neighbours only less wretched than themselves.

"There is a class of persons amongst the Irish peasantry who disdain to mention their distress, even though famine is on the threshold; not until it comes to the hearth will they admit their sufferings.

"Of this class Milltown is not destitute, and such is another of the reasons why an appeal was not made sooner.

"Local resources there are none to cope with the distress. Credit is at an end, as the only local shopkeeper who had ever given any has, within this week, issued notices, and has told the public that he will give no more but to such as shall pay a portion of the outstanding debts.

"Poor Law relief is out of the question, for a two-fold reason : 1st,—If any further strain be put upon the Union those who would be able to struggle through the year will be pauperized. 2ndly,— Most of those in actual want would sooner die on the roadside than don a pauper's uniform.

"Within the last eight days numbers of persons have come to their respected Pastor, and detailed to him their sufferings, and earnestly implored him to apply for some of the funds that are being distributed.

"Their good Pastor, although thoroughly acquainted with their wants, still, to put it beyond all doubt, sent trustworthy men into the villages to collect accurate information of the distress prevailing in them.

"On Sunday last the leading men of the parish met at the chapel, after second Mass, for the purpose of relieving the sufferings of such as are in actual distress.

"Those engaged (some of whom were members of the Committee) in collecting accurate information as to the distress in each village, handed in their reports to the Parochial Relief Committee on Sunday evening. Two hundred families are in distress, of whom seventy are dependent for their support upon the charity of their neighbours, and, consequently, in actual want, and unless immediately assisted must necessarily die of starvation.

"The Hon. Secretary was specially requested by the members of the Committee to apply to the Mansion House Fund for relief on behalf of the Milltown Parochial Committee.

"I subscribe myself, your obedient servant,

"JAMES HEANY, C.C., *Hon. Sec.*"

"*Aran Island, Galway Bay*, 29*th January*, 1880."

"TO THE SECRETARY, MANSION HOUSE COMMITTEE

"SIR,

"Behind the fragments of the last fortress besieged by Cromwell in Ireland stands the village of Killanny with its hundred huts. It is the fishing centre of Aran, and every hut there is a fisherman's home.

"Though its inhabitants, poor fellows, point out the stone in those battlements against which Cromwell's nose was rubbed in a brief defeat, and boast of his final repulse from their walls, still worse than all, Cromwell's curse, we fear, remains.

"Nothing else could bring on the people such want and cold and nakedness as we witnessed. No later than to-day we walked through the village and saw children entirely—this is true—entirely, absolutely naked, gathering themselves around their poor old granny in the corner where the fire used to be.

"Aran grows neither turf nor timber. Fuel is supplied from Connemara, many miles distant, over one of the wildest seas around the Irish coast; and if Connemara and the whole West coast is itself in a partial fuel famine, what must inaccessible Aran be?

"We will give one instance. There are a few boats being made down on the shore, and it is really piercing to see those naked little creatures in the raw morning air, now standing on one foot and now on the other, watching the first chip that falls from the boatwright's axe.

"Would that those rich and charitable parents, whose own happy children play perhaps about them in joy whilst those lines are being noted, could see with their own eyes, in this painful condition, those shivering little ones, and the eloquence of their want would not plead in vain.

"Returning to the house where we left the old women and the naked children depending, Berkeley-like, on their imagination for heat at the quenched hearth, we find a strong man, idle and careworn, leaning against the black side-wall. After commenting mournfully on his own and his children's condition, he says, 'there are thirty men like myself in Killanny; we are too poor to get anyone to bail us for the fishery money. The people who want money most in those bad times won't get any from the Government Offices, but if we had one pound, each of us, to buy a Spillard, we'd try to put a fagot of clothes on the children, a spark on the hearth, and a bit in our mouths, with the help of God.'

"Thinking as we came away on the best mode of seeking succour for this deserving man, we said we will venture to write first to the three great Relief Funds, and we are sure they will not grudge to spend £10 each on a charity of this kind. These £30 would place the thirty wasting Killanny men in reproductive works.

"I will give them a chance of gathering, as they say, the riches that are waiting for them at the bottom of the deep.

"Signed on behalf of the Aran Relief Committee,

"JOHN A. CONCANNON, P.P.
"D. W. FAHEY, C.C."

"*Glenamaddy, Co. Galway, 28th January,* 1880.

"GENTLEMEN,

"I beg to inform you that distress to an alarming extent prevails in this district.

"The land for the most part is marshy bog—is wretchedly poor. The potatoes, the staple food of the people, could not be planted in early spring, and, in consequence, were slow in coming—never, in fact, came to maturity. Similarly the oats sown late did not ripen. A good part of this crop might be seen in the fields uncut in December, and some was never submitted to the sickle, as it was not worth the labour of cutting.

"In addition to the barren nature of the soil, the rents are very high, the land for the most part being purchased in the Incumbered Estates Court.

"Labouring under these disadvantages, it is no wonder the people are steeped in debt, many of them owing, without any fault of theirs, even two, and some of them three years' rent, and no prospect of being able to pay.

"A Committee has been formed here for their relief, but I will not attempt to describe the harrowing scenes I have had to witness since its foundation.

"Being commissioned to apply for the query sheet required to be filled before your Committee makes a grant from the funds at its disposal, I hereby request you will send it with as little delay as possible; and if you will dispense with that formula on this occasion, and be generous in granting aid to relieve as poor and afflicted a people as is to be found in any part of this ill-fated land, you will perform a real act of charity, and confer on them a favour deserving their everlasting gratitude.

"I am, gentlemen, your faithful servant,

"THOMAS WALSH, P.P."

Ballaghameehan, Garrison, Co. Leitrim, 22nd January, 1880.

"My Lord,

"This parish is partly in the Union of Ballyshannon and partly in the Union of Manorhamilton, and comprises the following divisions:—Ballaghameehan, Glenariff, and Rossinver. In these divisions, notwithstanding local exertions, there is a vast amount of destitution, bordering on starvation, consequent on the total failure of the potato crop, which is the only means of support the poor people have here.

"I do candidly believe there are not less than 100 families in the parish in deep distress. Some have a little as yet left; some have nothing.

"On visiting the sick a few days since, I entered the cabin of a poor old man, who, I believe, is bordering on eighty years old. I was grieved to see him in the miserable plight he was in—hanging over a few sods of turf, without shoe or stocking to ward off the cold from a damp floor. His hollow cheeks, penetrating looks, and emaciated visage evidently tell a sad tale. I reached another house on the same day; the inmates of this comprised four individuals—the father, an old man, unable to leave his bed unless carried; the son, the only support of the old father, and two sickly sisters, one of whom is now far advanced in dropsy, and, I believe, is dying. Having asked the son why it was that one of the girls did not look for employment, even if she were only to get her support, and his answer was, 'No one wants her.'

"I am sorry to say there are many such cases of distress as those given in this parish.

"I am, my Lord, your Lordship's obedient servant,

"John McManus, P.P."

"*Bonniconlan, Ballina, Co. Mayo, January* 19*th,* 1880.

"My Lord,

"It is with feelings of pain and regret I beg to call your attention, and the attention of the members of the Mansion House Committee, to the deplorable condition of about 200 families in the parish. They are in great distress—the most of them in absolute want. They have nothing now to live on, I might say, but Indian meal, and not enough of that same; some of them without a drop of milk, without fuel, and all without credit, having their clothes pawned and their children half naked. We were hoping day after day that the Government would come to our aid, but, unfortunately, it was hoping against hope. I trust, therefore, that you and the members of the Committee will kindly consider the sad state to which those poor creatures are reduced, and send me, for their relief, as much as you can, and as soon as you can.

"I have the honour to be, Sir, yours faithfully,

"Peter Harte, P.P., Kilgarvin."

"*Ballaghaderrin, Co. Mayo, January* 20*th,* 1880.

"Gentlemen,

"A Committee, of which our venerated Bishop, the Most Rev. Dr. MacCormack, is Chairman, has been organized for the relief of the distress which not only threatens, but actually prevails this moment, to a large extent, in this parish. The Committee had been actually working for more than a week, and every day it is besieged by crowds of strong men, and calling for something to keep away starvation. The severest inquiry is made into the destitution of each applicant, and no one has his application admitted whose destitution is not most industriously ascertained.

"After the closest investigation, there are at this moment 200 families, or about 1,000 people, receiving some relief from the very limited funds at the disposal of the Committee, and in the near future we have proof there will be 200 families, or another

1,000 people of this parish facing starvation, unless some relieving hands keep it away from them.

"May we ask you, gentlemen, in the name of the highest virtue, that your kind hand will be stretched out to us, and from one of the many hands that are wanted this moment to keep away death from the doors of our people.

"We remain, gentlemen, your faithful servants,

"Owen Stenson, Adm., *Vice-Chairman*.
"John Flannery, *Treasurer*.
"Patrick Peyton and John Cawley, *Secretaries*."

"Park, Turlough, Castlebar, Co. Mayo, 21st January, 1880.

"Gentlemen,

"As there is not a gentleman, or landlord, or any person in the parish to bring before the public the distress that prevails in this parish, nor even a poor law guardian to speak on their behalf in the board-room, I am forced to appeal to your charitable Committee on behalf of my parishioners, a great many of whom are in great distress, for there is not a poorer parish in the entire West, owing to the poor and barren nature of the soil, although the parish is very large (being 12 miles in circumference, and containing thousands of acres), there is not more than 200 acres of it that is good and arable land capable of producing meadow, the remainder consists of bog and mountain. There are about 500 families; all except three or four are small landholders, their holdings varying from three to eight acres. The greater part of the population live along the side of a cold and wet mountain; and in consequence of the wet and barren nature of the soil for the last three years, I may say the crops entirely failed, and only for the shopkeepers in Castlebar, who gave the parishioners credit last year, I am sure the greater part of them would have to leave the country. In the year 1845 there were about 1,000 families in the parish, and in 1847 the population was reduced to 500. In last May, the Archbishop, Dr. McHale, drove through a part of the parish from Castlebar, and after returning, he said that he never passed through a more wretched or poorer country, and consequently sent me £20 for the relief of the distressed. Unless the Government and the charitable public come quickly to the aid of the poor people, I fear many of them will feel the pangs of hunger, and that before long. Trusting that your charitable Committee will be so kind as to send me relief for my poor people,

"I remain, gentlemen, your obedient servant,

"Edward Griffin, P.P."

Kilmovee, Mayo, 8th March, 1880.

"Gentlemen,

"I feel, indeed, grateful to the Mansion House Committee for its noble efforts in our favour. Many of my parishioners would have perished in the past without your assistance, and, still more, will succumb in the future unless you persevere in the good work. My parish is exceptionally circumstanced. It is some twelve miles by three in area, having a population of some 7,000 to 8,000 souls. The land is ungenerous in the extreme, poor and badly cultivated, hundreds and hundreds of acres are covered with rocks or heath, while hundreds more are mere bog. I have no hesitation then in saying, did the occupiers pay no rent, the produce of their little patches would not in the best of times afford support for their families. If they have hitherto eked out a miserable existence, it is due to the money which flowed to our shores from wages earned in England and America. Imagine, then, the state to which my poor people are reduced, when I tell you that, besides losing almost the entire crop, such private aid from England and America has entirely failed us.

"I have not dwelt on the failure in the cattle trade; for, in truth, we had little to lose in that. The landlords, too, are absentees, and, like most absentees, forget the obligations of property in remembering its rights. There is no land in Mayo requires improvement more than ours. Yet, not one shilling has been expended during the winter, or is likely to be expended in the future, on public works in my entire parish. The union is sunk in debt, and hence the guardians refuse to assist the people outside the workhouse. As a result, the people, in their grim struggle with the Famine King, are deserted by those who, I suppose, should be their natural guardians—the landlord and the State. Do not wonder, then, if I assure you that, of a population of 1,400 or 1,500 families, some 1,100 or 1,200 families are reduced to the most heart-rending state, in hundreds and hundreds of cases, without food or fuel, and with the scantiest clothing. Did you enter with me one of these miserable houses, see its damp floor and fireless hearth; did you behold the poor little children huddled together, silent in their sufferings, and hear the parents' piteous tale, you would not wonder, gentlemen, that I rushed away from their midst to plead again at your door in the holy cause of charity.

"Let me add, gentlemen, that while, in the past year, you have alleviated much misery and saved many individuals from death, the future calls you to higher and holier work, for it calls you, I believe, under God, to save the West of Ireland. Enable the people to put down a good crop; give them food now so that they may give their undivided attention to their little farms; and I feel that when men come hereafter to speak of the dread season of '79 and '80 they will speak of the Mansion House Committee as the saviour of Ireland.

"I remain, gentlemen, respectfully yours,

"JOHN CANON M'DERMOT, V.F."

Attymass, Ballina, Co. Mayo, 26th January, 1880

"MY LORD,

"Among the many applications for relief that reach you, I venture to say there is hardly any district where relief is more needed than in this parish. I could say to you, even passing by train from Foxford to Ballina, look yonder east, and behold my parish, situated at the very base and beginning of the Ox Mountain. I would require no other word to convince you that distress, deep and sad, exists there. Even in better times there was pinching want in the greater part of this parish at the end of Summer; and how could it be otherwise? The land is extremely bad and awfully dear, the holdings very small, generally under five or six acres, very rarely beyond eight or nine. The parish is densely populated, a circumference with a radius of two miles enclose it, save one village of sixteen families, situated in the very centre of bogs and mountains. If you'll consider the land covered by four lakes, with bogs and small barren mountain hills within this circumference, then there remains little land to sustain 420 families, with fourteen or fifteen who live on con-acre. You'll then admit that the parishioners (Protestant and Catholic) here are in want and destitution, in testimony of which I might relate many and many a painful incident. I am a prisoner in my own house, for though I tell them again and again I have nothing to afford them, they still remain about my house hoping yet to have something with them to their empty houses and hungry families. I am pained to meet them, as I can't relieve their wants. It's the same way in every village where I have to visit. I must wait and listen to heart-rending stories, and witness sad scenes. I therefore implore yourself and charitable Committee will vote me a remittance to meet the urgent destitution of my poor parishioners, 420 families, which means about 2,000, in distress for food and clothing.

I remain, with respect, your obedient servant,

"JOHN O'GRADY, P.P., Attymass, Ballina, Co. Mayo."

"*Laherdane, Co. Mayo, January 27th*, 1880.

"GENTLEMEN,

"When, on the 19th inst., we sent you a copy of our resolutions, though even then much misery and sufferings had come under the notice of our Committee, we had no idea of the reality and the extent of the distress. We had since to learn, and, let me add, on the very best authority, the evidence of our own eyes, that many whom we thought to be in comfortable circumstances actually hold pawn-tickets for the bed clothes, so necessary in those frosty nights to shield themselves and their little ones from the bitter cold. We have the bitter scenes of '47 re-enacted, and the year of grace, 1880, calling back as a spectre from the tomb, where we had hoped it was buried for ever, the ghostly memories of the famine years. Will you believe it, gentlemen, we have seen the poor labourer wrestling with the frost to recover the potato that might have been left behind at the first digging last harvest? Gentlemen, from the fulness of our hearts we thank you for the £25 you allotted to us, and we pray God to bless you for your charity. With a population of 800 families in this (Addergoole) parish, most of them little removed from the condition of cottiers, without funds, as we are, and shut out by the negligence of Lord Lucan (who till this date had formed no Committee), from a share of the Marlborough Fund, how far can £25 relieve the distress of 4000 souls, three-fourths of whom, I declare, on the word of a priest of 49 years' standing, to be in the direst want?

"I am, gentlemen, your respectfully,

"ROBERT MACHALE, P.P."

"*Ballinlough, Castlerea, Co. Roscommon, 19th January*, 1880.

"MY LORD,

"I have been requested, as secretary of a meeting held this day in the Courthouse, Ballinlough, convened to take into consideration the present destitution in this parish (Kiltullagh), to apply to your Lordship for assistance from the Mansion House Relief Fund. On a mere preliminary list made out by the Rev. P. M'Loughlin, P.P., and A. W. Sampey, Esq., J.P., we inserted 179 families—representing about 1,000 individuals—to a few of whom we have been able to give temporary relief from a small sum (£17) allocated by the Castlerea Union Committee in connection with the Duchess of Marlborough's Fund. The population of the parish amounts to nearly 8,000, and we are within the mark in stating, that within the next few weeks fully 1,500 of these will be absolutely dependent upon the relief which the public may give them. Numbers of the unfortunate people in the parish have been compelled to pawn their clothes and bedding, so that, in addition to the starvation that stares them in the face, they are suffering keenly from want of clothing. We hope your Lordship's Committee will take our case into their immediate consideration.

"I beg to remain your Lordship's obedient servant,

"JAMES TREANOR, Rector of Kiltullagh."

"*The Kilglass Relief Committee Rooms, Enniscrone, Co. Sligo,* 19*th January*, 1880.

"MY LORD MAYOR,

"As secretaries of the Kilglass Relief Committee, we have been requested to make application through you to the Mansion House Committee, to aid us in our present endeavour to meet the awful distress now in our midst. We confess we have been too slow, if not too late, in this, our appeal, for already numbers have been starving, after having eaten not only their seed potatoes, but devoured the diseased and half-rotten roots, which are quite unfit for human use, and which, in the present instance, we fear have brought on pestilence and disease, as the natural result of such unnatural food. In one townland alone there are at present ten families suffering from fever, which, in the opinion of the medical officer of the district, is induced by cold, want of clothing, and scarcity of proper nourishment. We, in common with every well-wisher of Ireland, would prefer anything to gratuitous relief, and therefore we have earnestly appealed to the landlords of this parish to assist their tenants by means of remunerative employment in improving their own estates. We have had some favourable promises to the above effect from all; yet, with one or two honourable exceptions, these promises have never been realized; they have picked up what rents they could, and then, oblivious of their own promises, have lent a deaf ear to the pitiful entreaties of their starving tenantry.

"Many of these poor tenants who, relying on the faith of these specious promises, have paid their rents, are now the most needy applicants for the charity of strangers. We have at present some 330 families, numbering close upon 1,700 individual relief lists, and, judging from their emaciated and evidently hunger-stricken appearance, and the reports of trustworthy persons who have made house-to-house visits of their respective localities, all have been suffering the most inconceivable and dire distress. Therefore, may we most earnestly beg you will use your powerful influence in our favour, and assist us in our laborious, we might almost say, hopeless task of combatting and surmounting the difficulties of our very trying position.

"We have the honour, my Lord Mayor, to remain

"Yours very respectfully,
"J. IRVIN, P.P., Kilglass,
"R. J. FORD, Incumbent, } Secretaries."

"*Collooney Relief Committee, Co Sligo,* 19*th January,* 1880

" MY LORDS AND GENTLEMEN,

"I am directed by the Collooney, Ballysodare and Ballinacanon District Committee to apply to you for a grant to their funds. The area of the operations of this Committee is the large parish of Ballysodare, the parish of Kilvanist, and three of the largest and poorest townlands in the parish of Kilnargan—in all, about 30,000 acres. The number of our distressed is so large that at the last and only distribution of provisions we were able to make, 275 families—representing now 1,300 persons—were relieved, each family receiving orders for provisions to the value on an average of about 4s., which exhausted our funds. The rush met at the distribution was so large that it took several policemen and others to keep the passages clear. The distress is intense, and the numbers needing help at present near 2,000 souls.

"I trust you will be able to make us a large grant, and enable us to feed the starving who are crying for help.

"Your obedient servant,

"GEORGE HELEN, *Hon. Sec.*"

"*Kilshanny, Ennistymon, Co. Clare,* 22*nd January,* 1880.
"TO THE MANSION HOUSE RELIEF COMMITTEE.

" GENTLEMEN,

"Permit me to most earnestly call your attention to the sad condition of many poor homes in this parish. A state of destitution exists so fearful that in many instances cold would be the heart that would not be wrung with sharp pain at beholding it. Up to the present hour I can say we have got nothing to stop the ever-rising and spreading tide of misery; for, though this parish belongs to the Ennistymon Union, which Union has already received £125 from the Duchess of Marlborough's Fund, and though we sent to the managers of this money the names of seventy-six families, some utterly in want, the rest on the verge of absolute need, we have received to aid these hungering mouths the large sum of £2 17s. 6d.

"Besides these families, whose names are sent to the Managing Committee of the Marlborough Fund, we might add, short though the time since be, twenty more families whose condition a short fortnight ago we did not consider completely hopeless.

"You will therefore, gentlemen, readily see what a sad picture we have before us—more than ninety families all in need of a kind and helping hand, some with hunger pangs at their hearts; nay, more, poor fathers and mothers, in addition to these hunger-pangs, must behold, what to them is even more heart-rending, the child of tender years, nay, the little infant crying for food, even the poorest, and the little hungering mouth crying in vain.

"This awfully appalling state of things, which was brought home to me on yesterday more plainly and painfully than before, as I went through the parish, makes me personally appeal to you without any delay; and I have confidence that, though I had not time to form a Committee Sheet, as you suggest, you will, if possible, send us something to relieve our poor parish homes and starving labourers immediately. Let the immediate and widespread necessities of these poor people be my apology for writing to you, and I promise when I hear from you, gentlemen, that I will form a Committee such as you suggest.

"With sorrow and a bleeding heart, gentlemen, I have to confess to you that the blackness of death seems hanging over us; the awfully gaunt figure seems waiting at many a door. The strong man whose hand was brave and willing to work is growing weak at present.

"The mother, with a look of hunger in her face and eye, and a sort of unspeakable despair, more painful to see than the loudest cry, as she gazes on the little pinched and withering faces which hunger has made, wears a look of premature decay and age. May Heaven bless the kind hearts that shall feel for us in our dark hour and the hands stretched out to save.

"I have the honor, gentlemen, to remain your obedient servant,

"M. KILLEEN."

"*Corofin, County Clare, January 23rd,* 1880.

"GENTLEMEN,

"With the exception of a paragraph in the *Freeman* of last Tuesday, calling attention to the sworn evidence of the medical officer (stating that 'lately two deaths had been hastened by want of food and warmth') not a word has been heard about the distress which largely prevails in this district. I feel obliged, therefore, to ask you at the earliest opportunity to kindly place before the Mansion House Relief Committee the following statement in regard to this parish. It has a population of about 3,300, and I am under the mark when I state that 120 of these stand in want of immediate relief; in other words, they are in as bad a condition as were the two whose deaths were hastened by want of food and warmth. One family of eleven is obliged to subsist on one shilling per day, earned by the father, and such chance relief as may come from other sources. I met another lately, the mother of a large family, who told me her husband had no work for some time. She had travelled four miles (it was after two o'clock when I met her) in search of a breakfast. The children cannot come to school with empty stomachs. The heads of families have had no work until very lately, and even now the hire given is miserably small, not more than a 1s. per day. It is proposed to form a Local Committee here next week. Meantime, may I request that your Committee will, considering the necessity, at once send such a sum as may relieve pressing want. For the present I shall be happy to take charge of such sum, and to render an account of same to your Committee.

"I am, gentlemen, your obedient servant,

"JOHN McINERNEY, C.C."

LETTERS FROM DISTRESSED DISTRICTS.

Buttevant. County Cork, 20th January, 1880.

" DEAR SIR,

" In consequence of the great distress which I am daily compelled to witness among the poor and unemployed of my parish, I feel it a duty I owe to them to appeal to you for some trifling assistance. In conformity with the suggestions from your Committee, published in the *Freeman's Journal* of Tuesday, a Local Committee has been formed; the first meeting was held to-day, and, as secretary, I was directed to at once write for the " Query Sheet," which your Committee requires to be filled up by applicants for relief, will you kindly forward it immediately, as the distress is pressing and unprecedented.

" I have just been informed that a man and his wife, both about 80 years of age, who were in the habit of receiving money from their children in America, but who have not received any for the past few months, are in such terrible circumstances that they remain in bed most of the day to avoid producing an appetite, as my informant says, and that such is their horror of going to the Union that they would prefer going to die where they are breadless, penniless, and almost homeless. Similar cases I know to exist, and these certainly demand immediate relief. Anxiously awaiting your reply,

" I remain, dear sir, yours respectfully,

" MICHAEL P. NORRIS, C.C."

Castletown Bereharen, Co. Cork, 21st January, 1880.

" GENTLEMEN,

" I most respectfully beg to apply to your Committee for some substantial relief for the poor, distressed and destitute people of my parish. No doubt several such applications are being daily made to you, but I doubt much whether there are any poor people appealing for relief whose case is deserving of more consideration than that of my poor parishioners: they number 6,000, and are chiefly composed of small farmers, holding little farms capable of supporting from two to four or five cows. These poor people have the same sad and sorrowful story to tell which you have already heard from others; they have no employment, no money, no credit, and very many of them have long since consumed the last remnant of the scanty crop of bad potatoes which they grew last year. I know of several farmers who, at this moment, are starving with hunger. I know of others who were subsisting for a time at least, until they were relieved by charitable friends, on the few chance potatoes they could get out of the tillage which they dug out last year, several farmers having large families, and having nothing whatever to eat, whilst professing their shame at being obliged to do so, applied to me for relief, and were extremely obliged when I was able to give them the price of a few stone of meal out of the charity which my noble bishop, Dr. M'Carthy, placed at my disposal. I know of others who spend the greater part of the day digging up the beach in search of shell-fish, in order to help to support their families, and feel thankful if they can only procure what may suffice for a meal. To add to our misfortune, we have a great number of poor people here sick of measles, and some also sick of fever. I have every reason to know that several of these poor sick creatures are suffering the greatest privations. May I beg and implore of your charitable Committee to send us some substantial relief, and pledge myself that both the local Committee and myself will do all that depends on us to find out the most deserving objects and will dispense to them accordingly.

" I remain, gentlemen, your very obedient servant,

" THOMAS CANON CARMODY, P.P., V.F."

APPENDIX VIII.

"*Youghal, Co. Cork*, 22nd *January*, 1880.

"My Lord Mayor,

"I beg to bring under your Lordship's consideration the distress prevailing in this town and parish and the parish of Clonfrost, forming the union of parishes under my jurisdiction. The potato crop of last year was very short in quantity and defective in quality. The stock saved is nearly exhausted in many cases, and, in some instances, not even a single meal of potatoes remain. The poor farmers and labourers of this district are obliged to use Indian meal as their food, and they have neither money to buy it nor credit to get it from the dealers who sell that article of food.

"In addition to the immediate want of food, the farmers here require to be supplied with seed, both potato and corn, in order to be in a position to plant their ground. If this want is not supplied, the land must go untilled, and the consequence will be another famine next year, as I well remember the same thing occurred in 1847.

Your Lordship's most faithfully,

"T. (Canon) Murphy, P.P."

"*Drimoleague, Co. Cork*, 26th *January*, 1880.

"Dear Sir,

"The Secretary of the Committee formed in the Dispensary District of Drimoleague, Skibbereen Union, has been directed to make application to the Mansion House Committee for immediate aid for the relief of the destitute poor of this district. I have no doubt but that application has been received in good time. Permit me, in support of that application, to make a few remarks upon the state of those parishes, and the urgency of the appeal.

"The parishes of Drinagh, Drimoleague, and the greater part of Carahagh, constitute the dispensary district of Drimoleague, Skibbereen Union. It extends beyond the mountains of Owren, in the north, to within a few miles of Bantry, and this embraces near all the country to the north of Skibbereen, a tract of twenty square miles, and containing a population of near 9,000 souls.

"In all this district there is not a single resident landlord, and at the present time not one landlord giving a day's work to a labourer (except Dr. Levis, of Glenview, Skibbereen, who has taken a loan for drainage). I may say that there was a total failure of the potato crop last year, and, indeed, the year previous was very little better. The corn crops are very inferior also, and what was the main dependence of the farmers of the district—namely, the produce of the cows, became so low in price that it completed the ruin of the poor farmer. Hence the district is in a most deplorable state, and how we are to tide over these five or six months to come, the Lord alone knows.

"To tell my experiences amongst the poor would be, indeed, repeating over again what we see every day in the public papers. In short, the poor want work to earn food for their families, and, failing the work, there is dire distress upon many families, and sure to increase unless we can procure work for the unemployed. I am free to confess that but for the limited employment given to the Bantry Railway Extension, the scenes of '47 or '48 would, ere long, be enacted again in this country.

"At the meeting of the Committee on Wednesday last, there were taken down for relief 190 families, representing 1,000 souls, in want of immediate relief, and since then application has been made to me by as many poor small farmers who have not the means of procuring the seeds for their land for the season to come; and, consequently, will be as badly off next year, if any struggle out so long. I have been at the houses of this class, and I must say that it would move the heart of a Turk to see the state of them; no clothes for their beds, for the children; none for themselves—none, all gone to make something to meet the decrees and keep the bailiff from the door, and, to increase the misery, bad, very bad fires, as the turf is but half dry. I could give many cases of very severe want, where entire families are living on very insufficient food. Suffice it to say that we cannot be very much worse off unless the terrible famine-sickness comes, which, I dread, cannot be very far off in our present circumstances. Be so kind as to lay these remarks before the Committee, in hope that they may be induced to act promptly and generously in our favour.

"I am, dear sir, yours very faithfully,

"J. MURRAY, P.P."

"*Clondrohid, Co. Cork*, 28th January, 1880.

"SIR,

"This is a wild and mountainous parish of 27,000 acres. There are no resident landlords. Father Ring, R.C.C., has just been sitting with me. No one knows the distress of the people better than he does. Any relief you send us will be administered by Father Ring (Father Walsh is upwards of ninety years old), myself and Mr. Pearson.

"Father Ring told me to-day that he has visited poor, obliged to remain in bed from hunger.

"Faithfully yours,

"J. TORRENS KYLE, B.D., Rector of Clondrohid."

"*Castlemaine, Co. Kerry*, 24th January, 1880.

"MY LORD,

"May I beg your Lordship's favourable consideration for my poor people when you have any funds at your disposal for the relief of the distressed.

"In one parish, Keelgarrylander, whose valuation is only £2,000, and the rental mostly double, with a population of over 2,500, entirely agricultural, the distress is very great.

"Their dwellings are mostly wretched, they have scarcely any fuel but the heather they bring from the mountain, on whose barren slopes the most of them strive to find a livelihood by reclaiming and tilling the craggy, unproductive hillside.

"There is no employment given except by one landlord, Mr. Langford Rae, but what can one do among so many poor?

"From my own personal knowledge I can certify to your Lordship that the bedclothes of numbers of them, and whatever other clothes the pawnbroker would take in pledge, are in pawn for their support.

"The children are kept from school through want of even the scanty and ragged covering that would at other times pass muster in this backward place.

"I am sure your Lordship has appeals more than the funds at your disposal can adequately meet, but I appeal again to your Lordship's charitable heart for some help for my poverty-stricken, wretched people.

"I am, your Lordship's obedient servant.

"CORNELIUS SHEEHAN, P.P., Kiltalla and Keelgarrylander."

"*Abbeyfeale Relief Committee.*

"*Abbeyfeale, Co. Limerick*, 13th February, 1880.

"GENTLEMEN,

"The baronial works cannot commence for a good while yet, and in the meantime I apprehend very great destitution in my parish. If the Mansion House does not come to our relief with a liberal hand, the landlords of the district, as far as I know, are not inclined to borrow the money offered to them on such easy terms, though tenants are prepared to guarantee the payment of the interest on it. And we have applied to the Duchess of Marlborough's Committee, and have been told that they will give us nothing now, nor hereafter. This parish adjoins Kerry and within a short distance of the Atlantic, and exposed to its severe and withering influence, nearly as much as Kerry itself, and requiring as much external aid in the present terrible crisis. The £20 your Committee has sent us is not at all adequate to meet our orders in meal for the numbers we have given them to. But our Committee were convinced than when the Mansion House was made aware of our real sad state that they would indemnify us by sending twice or four times the amount already sent. With sincere thanks for your grant of £20, and hoping a favourable reply to this,

"I am, yours gratefully,

"M. COGHLAN, P.P., *Chairman*,
"W. WRIGHT, *Secretary*."

Clogheen, Co. Tipperary, 13th January, 1880.

"MY LORD MAYOR,

"May I submit to your Lordship and the Committee of the Mansion House Relief Fund, who have so nobly undertaken the great work of charity, that a considerable number of poverty-stricken people, living on the mountain-side called Kilcaroon, about 3½ miles from Clogheen, are this day in absolute want, a want indeed becoming hourly aggravated. I have just visited these poor people in their houses, some of their hovels without a window, and doors a little over 3 feet high. I do not in the least desire to trump up a case in their behalf, but simply state facts. They have no firing, no potatoes, in some instances the ridges have been left untouched, as the crop was not worth the trouble of rooting for it. Men, women and children met me on the way, quite in rags, asking if I brought them anything; some few creatures have struggled along, living on the produce of a few hens, which they managed to keep in the limited tenement with themselves, and invariably the donkey. The whole village seems to suffer, with perhaps two exceptions, and though ready and willing to work for a day's hire, yet no employment can they find. Your Lordship and the Committee may be disposed to take their deplorable condition into kindly consideration when the distribution of the fund takes place. In Clogheen town the distress has been much alleviated by the kindness of good-hearted Viscount Lismore, who has on several occasions driven to the door of the Presbytery and, with his own generous hands, given me parcels of warm clothing, consisting of blankets, flannels, jerseys, &c. and in addition has ordered nutritious soup from the kitchen of Shanbally Castle to be daily meted out to the poor in that locality.

"I remain your Lordship's obedient servant,

"THOMAS M'GRATH, P.P."

Telegram received from Major Percy, Resident Magistrate, Nenagh:—

"23rd February, 1880.

"Went this day with the local clergyman to visit the homes of the unemployed poor of Nenagh, and he declared he was quite unprepared, even with all his experience of distress in India, to realize the extent of the poverty and misery that met his gaze. Such was the impression made on him that he at once ordered a large quantity of bread, at his own expense, from one of the large baking establishments of that town, and is at this moment sending his views of the extent of the distress to the authorities."

"*Dungarvan, Co. Waterford, 19th February,* 1880.

"GENTLEMEN,

"When acknowledging your generous grant of £100, made to our Poor Relief Committee on the 2nd inst., we thought well to remind you that your charity would enable us to save our poor from starvation for not more than six days. You passed us a cheque on Saturday, 7th inst., for an additional sum of £50. Had we received no aid from other quarters, it would have been imperative upon us to call upon you a week ago for a renewal of your grant. Fortunately, our friends have replied to our appeals very liberally, and, accordingly, we have abstained from trespassing on your fund till now, I am confident you will not be less considerate towards us because of our unwillingness to trouble you, so long as we had any means whatever for saving our destitute thousands from starvation. I send you the return of our disbursements. Our Committee relieve daily by themselves about 250 families; by St. Vincent de Paul's Society, 25 families; by clergymen visiting houses, 90 families—365 families in all. Our disbursements (never exceeding 6s. per week in value to a family of five or less in number, and 10s. per week to a family of eight persons) have been, from 2nd Feb. (date of your grant) to 19th Feb. (this day), £313 13s. 9d.—that is, about £17 10s. per day.

"I ask you, therefore, to come to our assistance again to-morrow, for God's sake. These wretched people are entirely dependent on us. Perhaps the Board of Guardians will do something for some of them, but for the present we must keep them alive.

"I remain, gentlemen, very faithfully and thankfully yours,

"JAMES P. CLEARY, D.D., P.P., *Chairman.*"

———

"*Kildare, February* 11, 1880.

"GENTLEMEN,

"May I beg, through you, to bring before your Committee the destitute condition of a large portion of the poor people of this town, and to express a hope that your Committee will be good enough to grant us such assistance as it may deem fit to help us to tide over the present period of distress.

"Kildare is differently circumstanced from any of the other towns in the county, with very few resident gentry, a population of nearly 1,800 persons, of which nearly 100 are labourers, who work for the adjoining farmers, and about twenty-four who have passes to the camp, such as small pedlers, &c., who have been attracted hither by its proximity. Thanks to the kindness of His Grace the Duke of Leinster, a large portion of the labourers found employment during the past winter, and even now some are employed at Rathangan, Athy, and Maddenstown, but a great many, particularly those advanced in years, only got employment now and then, and their earnings were totally inadequate to the support of their families. The Camp followers live by selling small wares, vegetables, watercresses, &c. to the soldiers, or exchanging them for broken bread and waste meat, &c. When the Camp is full they are enabled to support themselves and families, but when the number of men there are much reduced, as at present, they become very poor. Both classes (the unemployed labourers and Camp followers) have suffered severely during the last winter, and their sufferings have been intensified by the severity of the weather and the want of fuel. True it is, that very many have received out-door relief, at most half-a-crown each, but what can it do to pay rent, and, it may be, support four or five in family. They will not accept relief in the Workhouse. They cling to their cabins, fearful that if once they give them up, others will take their places, or that they may be levelled and that when they are enabled (if ever) to leave the Union House, they will find themselves tramps, and looked upon as degraded.

"The inhabitants who could do so have assisted them with clothes, food, &c., but their ability to render further aid is now well-nigh exhausted. They have made

S

a collection of £40 to procure seed potatoes for those poor people who have manure and ground to put it out on:—in fine, they have done all they could, and they now appeal, through me, for your aid, and I trust I will not appeal in vain. The local clergy, P. L. Guardians, and medical men, will form a Relief Committee, and the necessary forms will be filled up as soon as received.

"I am, gentlemen, your obedient servant,
"SAM. CHAPLIN, L.K. & Q.C.P.I."

"*Urlingford, Kilkenny, February* 19*th*, 1880.

"GENTLEMEN,

"I am directed by the Urlingford Relief Committee to acknowledge the receipt of your favour, with the very generous donation. This sum will be the cause of saving many lives; indeed, until the distress was inquired into, I had no idea we had such destitution in our town. May God bless the generous donors.

"I am, gentlemen, very respectfully,
"JOHN STAPLETON, *Hon. Sec.*"

"*King's Co., January* 31*st*, 1880.

"MY LORD MAYOR,

"I am directed by the Tullamore Relief Committee to ask your Lordship to aid us in gaining funds for the relief of our poor in this locality.

"We have been exerting ourselves to the utmost to collect money, which we endeavour as far as possible to expend in useful works, suited to unskilled hands, but the demand far exceeds the supplies coming in.

"I have the honour to be, your Lordship's humble servant,
"JOHN PIERCE, J.P."

"*Edgeworthstown, Co. Longford,* 3*rd March,* 1880.

"GENTLEMEN,

"We desire to express to you our heartiest thanks for £20 grant to Edgeworthstown Local Committee.

"Our Committee has been in existence since Ash Wednesday. Our funds are again exhausted. We have relieved about 500 cases of distress. The poverty is increasing—both hunger and cold. All classes are working harmoniously on this Committee,

"We again most respectfully appeal to your most generous Committee for another grant.

"Signed, on behalf of Committee,
"W. H. LYNN, Rector, *Chairman,*
"PETER FARRELLY, Parish Priest, *Vice-Chairman,*
"PATRICK RHATIGAN, Esq., *Treasurer,*
"Messrs. JAMES FLOWER and M. KEANE, *Secs.*"

"*Inniskeen, Co. Louth,* 17*th February,* 1880.

"SIR,

"We, the undersigned residents of this locality, having met to consider the appalling distress existing in this parish, beg you will bring our case before your Committee on its next meeting.

"There are upwards of 1,300 urgent cases of destitution in this parish.

"In order to comply with the rules of your Committee, we have formed ourselves into a Local Relief Committee, to be called 'The Inniskeen Relief Committee.'

"Signed,
"PLUNKETT KENNY, *Chairman.*"

"*Drumconrath, Ardee, Co. Meath, 6th March,* 1880."

"GENTLEMEN,

"In consequence of the amount of destitution existing in this parish, the Rev. D. Monahan, P.P. for Drumconrath and Meath Hill, formed a Relief Committee in connection with your Fund, and requested me to take the position of Chairman. This I consented to do, as I considered, from my position, as by far the largest proprietor, having property exclusively in this parish, that I ought to do my utmost to further his charitable work. I wish to say that since last November I have given a large amount of labour, not only to those on my own property, but to those of others, including, I believe, some from the County Louth; but I could not be expected to find work for all, neither could I employ people residing two, three, and four miles from where I could find work for them. The parish, also, is very much divided into small properties; the whole of the landlords, except myself, being non-resident, and in very many cases, they have given abatements of rent, and I believe in many cases, also, their tenants have been unable to pay their last half-year's rent.

"The Rev. D. Monahan and myself have written to and asked subscriptions from nearly all the landlords and large tenant-farmers, as a supplement to your Fund, and have received up to the present over £80; but when we asked for this money, we distinctly stated that it was to be used as a supplement to your Fund, and not in lieu of it. We wished it to be expended on clothes, labour, seed potatoes, and the like; but we expected to get from your Committee the food.

"The Townlands of Cloughreagh, Kells Union; Drumgill, Ardee Union; Meath Hill, Kells Union; and Ardagh, Kells Union, are wretchedly poor, the inhabitants nearly all very small farmers, and the soil either a heavy, wet, cold clay, covered with rushes, where laid down to grass, or having the rock close to the surface, as in Ardagh, Ballyhill, and Carrickeleck, and in many cases having both, as in Cloughrea and Meath Hill. The land being utterly unfitted for fattening cattle, the inhabitants used to graze and rear a few calves; but in consequence of the failure of the turnip crop in Scotland last year they had to sell them for nearly half their usual price. Again, from the constant wet last summer and autumn, the cattle did not thrive, their corn stagged, their potatoes rotted in the ground, and the price of hay was also under that of late years. During the previous prosperous years, when cattle brought good prices in the autumn, I have no doubt that the small farmers found that they could pay their rent and live with a certain degree of comfort without taking much trouble with their lands, but I am afraid that last season has completely broken them down. The district, which I believe to be the poorest in Meath, and as poor as that in any part of Ireland, commences on the verge of Louth with the townland of Breslanstown, keeping the verge of the Counties Louth, Monaghan, and Cavan, from east to north and north-west, and bounded on the south by the valleys of the Dee and Blackwater; or, to be more explicit, the northern portions of the Baronies of Lower Slane, Morgallion and Lower Kells, excepting of course Cabra Castle Demesne. I wish further to state, that my own property is exclusively in the Barony of Lower Slane, and that I have no interest in the Townlands of Cloughrea, Drumgill, Meath Hill, or Ardagh. The latter is owned by a namesake, but he is no relation of my own, nor have I ever seen him in my life to my knowledge.

"I hope that you will excuse this long letter, but I feel that your Committee must be unacquainted with the circumstances of this district, or we would not have received the reply we had from you to our application for relief.

"I have the honour to be, gentlemen, your obedient servant,

"H. C. SINGLETON, J.P., D.L., Co. Meath."

"*Crettyard, Queen's County, January* 22*nd,* 1880."

"SIR,

"I beg to apply to you for some relief for some most destitute poor in this locality, and to state to you that I know at present families who have no means whatever of getting a morsel of food, or earning any wages to purchase it, especially since late severe weather set in, and are solely depending on the charity of their neighbours.

"If you kindly forward me query sheet, I shall fill up most deserving and really urgent cases, and, if required, shall get clergymen of parish, to certify as to the want of relief.

"I am, your obedient servant,
"PATRICK DELANY,
"Member of Local Committee."

"*Arklow, Co. Wicklow, 2nd February*, 1880.

"MY LORD,

"We are directed by the Relief Committee to again bring the distress in Arklow under the notice of the Mansion House Committee, and to solicit a further contribution towards our funds. We have over 500 families on our books who have been receiving relief weekly for the past month. This number represents between from 2,000 and 2,500 persons.

"Our funds will only enable us to carry on our work of charity to the end of this week, and we fear that unless we get some further help, numbers of those whom we now relieve will be in a starving condition. Our mode of distributing relief is by orders on shopkeepers for food and fuel. As we know your Lordship's Committee only requires to know that real distress exists in a locality to send aid, we earnestly trust that the assistance so urgently needed for this town will be granted.

"We remain, your Lordship's obedient servants,
"HENRY ANNESLEY,
"HUGH BYRNE, } *Hon. Secretaries.*"

"*Chapel House, Collinstown, Killucan, Co. Westmeath.*
"*February 3rd,* 1880.

"MY LORD MAYOR AND GENTLEMEN,

"On last Sunday, the 1st February, a meeting of the principal inhabitants of Fore was held in the Chapel, at which meeting they adopted resolutions, three in number, the substance of which I will give you : The first was as to the necessity of forming a Committee to collect funds to relieve the distressed poor; the second, asking Father Farrelly, P.P. and myself to appeal to the Mansion House Fund for some relief for the helpless poor here; and the third, that the Committee should consist of the Chairman, Christopher Halpin, P.L.G., the clergymen of all creeds, and the principal farmers of the place.

"I can assure you, from sad experience, that fearful distress prevails here amongst the labourers and very small farmers. The potato crop was so bad that many did not even dig them; the oats crop was very indifferent; the turnips failed altogether; and the unfortunate people have no fuel. I could give innumerable cases of fearful distress, but as I know that your time is occupied with too many communications of a similar nature, I will confine myself to one. On Saturday last, a poor starving widow came to me. Her story, which, unfortunately, is too true, was—' Father, my husband is dead for the last ten years. I have seven children. Out of half acre of oats I had only one half-hundred of meal, which is gone. Since before Christmas I have not had one potato. In the name of God, what will I do? I would rather die than give up my little place from my poor orphans.'

"I could give you many such heart-rending cases. The land in this part of the country is very poor, the holdings are small, and even those who have pretty large farms cannot afford to give employment. I implore of your Lordship and the members of the Committee to take this poor locality into consideration, and you will ever have the blessings of the poor whom you will have helped.

"I have the honour to be, my Lord and gentlemen, your humble servant,
"C. CALDWELL, C.C."

"*Taghmon, Co. Wexford, March 4th,* 1880."

"My Lord Mayor,

"We, the undersigned Relief Committee, having carefully examined the present state of small farmers and labourers in the twenty townlands comprising the electoral division of Taghmon, Co. Wexford, find that both classes are, we are pained to say, suffering very much—some reduced to acute want—having found some families in such a wretched state that they had not tasted a morsel of food for forty-eight hours! We had hoped before making this investigation, that their state was not so bad, and that we would be spared the disagreeable necessity of applying to your Committee for relief.

"We have found 59 families, or 236 persons, more or less suffering, and we are convinced that many of the farming class are in great want, but are too proud to disclose their poverty.

"The distress is nearly universal; the destitution in many families of small farmers complete, as well as the labouring class, and nothing but the most energetic exertions of the charitable will be able to save them from death by starvation.

"The total quantity of harvest produce of all kinds would, in our opinion, not suffice for the home consumption; and being compelled by landlords to sell, to pay their rents, what they should have kept for food for their families, are now reduced to deplorable suffering; without employment, without food—save what the benevolent give them—without fuel, without bed-clothing: their condition is truly wretched.

"In this locality landlords will not assist their tenants by providing seeds, &c., for the approaching sowing season; and to sow any they may have left would be madness. The fact is, the quality of the harvest, which had been so badly saved, was so inferior that it would have been folly to have used it for sowing purposes. But good or bad, the farmers could not have purchased it, as they have not the means of purchasing food for their own families during the many months to come, before the next crop will come to their aid.

"Respectfully asking your prompt succour for our suffering neighbours, which may be addressed to any of the undersigned members of the Committee,

"We are, my Lord,

"Your Lordship's obedient servants,

"M. Murphy, P.P.,
"John C. Pigott, M.D.,
"John Matthews, Clk., Incumbent of Taghmon,
"Stephen Prendergast, *Hon. Sec.*"

"*Kilmaine, Hollymount,* 14*th April,* 1880."

"Gentlemen,

"The gentlemen of your Committee will best understand the frightful state of this district by simply putting before them the following facts;—The fever patients number 103, and such is the fear entertained by the people that we have failed to get a nurse at any payment, so that in order to assist those suffering from that disease our Committee had to run into debt before they received your last instalment. Our relief list contains 441 families (2,207 individuals), whose destitution it is impossible to exaggerate and heart-rending to witness. We therefore beg your Committee to come again speedily to our assistance.

"I remain, gentlemen, yours faithfully,

"Richard Prendergast, *Secretary*."

"*Whitegate, Scariff,* 15th *April.*

"SIR,

"As I showed you on the form sent up on last Monday, our fund, at our meeting on yesterday, was only about £10 to divide amongst 1,000 poor starving creatures. Many of them had to go away, of course, without the small amount they were accustomed to get every Wednesday since the relief commenced. I do not know what they are to live on until we meet again. I can assure you that I am almost afraid to face the other side of the parish to-morrow, for the great number of starving poor that I am sure to meet will give some annoyance. To hear the different tales of distress would pierce a stone. When the poor cannot succeed in getting food enough here, they are always sure to come and make known their misery to me. In fact I am tormented every minute and hour of the day. Our Committee, one and all, were always trying to stretch our funds as far as possible. That you can see by referring to the amount given out by us every week. I appealed twice to the Land League for a grant for clothes for poor children (about 60) of this parish, who never yet entered a school door for want of clothes, and I am glad to see they have given us a grant of £20 for that purpose. We were feeding our people all through from the Mansion House funds and a few small grants from the Duchess's fund. We could not spare anything for clothes, and if you do not give us a grant at your next meeting we must turn the £20 given us for that purpose to feeding the starving. Is it not a terrible tale to tell that so many children are at home from school from want of clothes? Some of them are up to 16 years old. I am after writing everywhere I could in their behalf, and the only clothes I have been able to get for them up to this was two little boys' jackets, three pair of trousers, and five little girls' frocks, the grant from the Duchess's fund. Do now continue your generous assistance to us, for your generous grants from the commencement were the only ones given to our Committee that deserve the name of generous, save, indeed, the £20 from the Land League,

"Yours faithfully,

"HUGH MOCKLER, C.C."

Rev. W. FLEMING, Protestant Clergyman, Scotshouse, County Monaghan, wrote—" Under circumstances such as these (previously described) local aid must soon be exhausted . . . and unless some help be obtained from external sources, we fear very much that suffering will ensue—perhaps worse than that."

Rev. J. GODLEY, Protestant clergyman, Carrigallen, county Leitrim, wrote—" I am again obliged to apply to you for an immediate grant for this parish. We have about 1,500 people still on our relief list, many of whom will die of starvation unless we can obtain further relief for them."

Rev. C. WARD, Protestant clergyman, Kilcurry, county Limerick, wrote—" This Committee have been most reluctantly obliged to refuse aid in many most pressing cases, wishing to husband their resources as long as possible."

Rev. J. MOYNE, Protestant clergyman, Lurganboy, county Leitrim, wrote—" It requires at least £40 a week to afford anything like adequate relief to the half-starved and half-naked people of this poor and wide district."

Rev. A. H. HAMILTON, Protestant clergyman, Garrison, county Fermanagh, wrote—" Although there are still 500 starving families on our relief list, who are in a worse condition than they were three months ago, we could not hold any meeting of our Committee this week for want of funds."

Rev. W. M'CAUSLAND, Protestant clergyman, Castlerea, county Roscommon, wrote—" If your Committee refuse to grant relief to the starving people while funds are in their hands, upon them must rest the responsibility."

Rev. C. COONEY, Protestant clergyman, and Rev. J. MELVIN, Catholic priest, Roscommon Erris, county Mayo, wrote—" These who assert that the worst of the distress is over make a great and sad mistake relative to this part of the country.

We deliberately declare in the most solemn manner that the distress is worse here at present than it has been from the beginning . , . . Having 4,000 on our relief lists, and the supplies from all sources being insufficient to meet the demands upon us, we have been obliged to go into debt to keep our people alive,"

Rev. J. R. TARLETON, Protestant clergyman, Tyholland, county Monaghan, wrote—" Unless the Mansion House Committee give us another grant we shall have no means of saving our people from starvation during the months of June and July, when it is feared there will be great distress. Our committee earnestly entreat for further help."

Rev. W. CLARKE, Protestant clergyman, and Rev. P. WALDRON, Catholic priest, Killereran, co Galway, after speaking of the fact that no public works have been commenced, and of the great difficulty in getting the Poor-law Guardians to do their duty in the matter of out-door relief, observe—" In the meantime some of our poor people are absolutely starving."

Rev. ROBERT EVANS, Protestant clergyman, and Rev. M. HUGHES, Catholic priest, Pomeroy, county Tyrone, write—" The terrible distress which exists amongst hundreds in the Pomeroy district forces us again to appeal earnestly to you for a further grant. . . . Unless your Committee aid us we dread to contemplate the result."

———

" *Cahirciveen, May* 14*th.*

" MY LORD MAYOR,

"At a conference of the clergy of this deanery, held here last Tuesday, the present distressful state of the country, and more especially that of their own flocks, was fully and anxiously considered ; also your Lordship's generous and prompt action in laying, in union with other benevolent and influential gentlemen, the momentous subject before our Irish Chief Secretary. I have been requested by the meeting, composed of all the priests of the barony of Iveragh, to solemnly declare that your Lordship's statements, and those of your non-deputationists, are, as regards the extensive and populous districts of Iveragh, but unhappily too true, and that instant and thorough action of the Government is absolutely necessary to save the people's lives. Only yesterday one of the fathers, a parish priest, came again to me saying, in crying accents, that a farmer in his parish was becoming insane from want of food, and that it was but the beginning just seen of hundreds of like or worse cases. Iveragh, we all gratefully acknowledge, has shared liberally of the noble charities so freely sent from the ends of the earth to this poor weeping Isle of the seas ; but with troubled and anxious hearts we, who behold their saddening condition, declare before Heaven that the cries of our people are fiercer, and their efforts greater now than ever to get food. Begging, therefore, of your Lordship, and of all others who can do and feel for them, to preserve them in your humane and saving exertions.

" I am, my Lord Mayor, faithfully your Lordship's Servant,

" T. CANON BROSNAN, P.P.

———

" *Addergoole Relief Committee, Lahernane, Ballina,* 17*th May,* 1880.

" GENTLEMEN,

"At meeting of the above Committee, held here on the 15th inst., the following resolutions were proposed and unanimously adopted :—

" ' 1. Resolved—That unless we receive for the next three months constant and generous grants to relieve the alarming distress of our people, we shall have renewed in this parish, in their worst aspects, the famine scenes of '47 and '48.

" ' 2. Resolved—That our Chairman be requested to make an urgent appeal for a weekly grant to the Mansion House Committee, our only and steady friend in the hour of need.'

APPENDIX VIII.

"I have to state that a dreadful crisis is upon us, and that the sad condition of our people claims the utmost sympathy. The population consists of 800 families. In the failure of their crops they had nothing to fall back on to keep soul and body together. The parish being for the most part moor and mountain, any light description of cattle the people could rear on their small patches of land are quite unsaleable. If they searched all the fairs in the county they would not get a person to bid for them, the means of all being nigh exhausted, if not entirely gone, credit closed against them, and the clothes of a great many in the pawnshop. It is not true that the backbone of the distress is broken, nor is it true that it is on the decline. The contrary is the melancholy fact, as far as Addergoole is concerned, distress fearfully increasing: no relief from Constellation or any such source, and very little from any other source except the Mansion House. The people have no employment of any description. No works under the Extraordinary Baronial Sessions. All our applications were refused, with the exception of a few to the amount of £300, which, in the way of employment, might as well be in the moon. Unless the Government promptly discharges its responsibility, and comes to the rescue, all efforts from existing sources will prove unavailable to save the lives of the people.

"I am, gentlemen, your obedient Servant,

"PATRICK McHALE, P.P., *Chairman and Treasurer.*

"*Kilshanny, Ennistymon, County Clare, May 15th.*

"Outdoor relief will not be afforded in any case, the determination of an influential member of our Board of Guardians being not to give a single ounce of outdoor relief until the Workhouse is filled. I need hardly observe to the Mansion House Committee that most of our poor people would rather die in their poor cabins, or by the public ways, than enter the cold, inhospitable walls of that State asylum.

(Signed) "M. KILLAN, P.P."

"*Cashel, Lanesboro', 15th May, 1880.*

"Our distress has not decreased and cannot decrease in this poor district till harvest, and in point of fact, many poor families had to use during the last four weeks the Seed Potatoes obtained from the Board of Guardians. The Guardians are not willing to give out-door relief, and we cannot compel them, and so the poor must suffer. I appeal to your Committee for further assistance.

"(Signed) MICHAEL GILLYDUFF, *Chairman.*"

"*Backs, Foxford, May 17th, 1880.*

"The distress, far from diminishing, is becoming daily more widespread in this district. Many who some months ago had some little food, are now without money, without food, without credit, without earning, and consequently have no refuge but the relief list."

"*Committee Rooms, Moylough Co. Galway, May 17th, 1880.*

"Instead of distress becoming less felt now than it was three months ago, the contrary is the fact, and there are cases of fever occurring which the destitution of the poor, there is reason to fear, will predispose the people to contract and cause to spread. This parish embraces a very large area, and there are very many populous villages in it, where in the best time, especially in summer, there is very considerable suffering. This year has been the worst in my recollection; even in 1847-8 the distress in these parts was not so severe.

"A. TAIT, LL.D., *Chairman of Moylough Relief Committee.*

"*Glendarary, Achill Sound, Westport, 17th May,* 1880."

"GENTLEMEN,

"I should much regret that the Mansion House Committee should think that we were ungrateful for the large amount of assistance we have received from them—in fact, they have been our sheet anchor since the beginning of last February. My letter will show that I alluded especially to the distribution of the cargoes of the Valorous and Constellation. It is quite true that we have received from various sources over £1,200, including the Mansion House, the Duchess of Marlborough's, the Society of Friends, the Land League, the Philadelphian *New York Herald,* and other funds. The Duchess of Marlborough did not make us a separate Committee from Newport, and the share allotted to Achill from the latter is in proportion of £33 3s. 4d. to each £100 they receive from her fund. No one on behalf of any of these funds, except Mr JAMES H. TUKE, had visited us to report. The *Daily Telegraph* and the *Freeman's Journal* correspondents, however, did so, and published letters on the state of the district. In addition to the Island itself, in which there are three electoral divisions, our relief Committee has also taken charge of a fourth electoral division, Currawn, Achill, on the mainland, which is comprised in the Parish of Achill. The area of the whole is over 59,000 acres, with a population of nearly 7,000. We received some meal by the Goshawk on the 27th of last March when Lord G. OSBORNE was distributing it on this coast, on which occasion only were we able to give four stone of Indian meal to each family on our list. In ordinary weeks we give fourteen tons, at a cost of over £108, in doles never exceeding two stone to each selected family, some only receiving this once in two weeks. The week before last we could not give anything, last week only to half the number we had hitherto assisted. The question we wish to solve is, what are we to do with such an overwhelming population, of the existence of which the public do not seem to be aware? My former letter was written in the hope that we should be assisted with seed as well as provisions, as a large quantity of land was prepared which cannot now be sown, and we trust some of the American potatoes, &c., would be sent to us. We got 13 tons of potatoes from the Duchess of MARLBOROUGH, and £100 for seed. This, with a handsome donation from the Archbishop of Tuam (Dr. M'HALE) enabled us to give one cwt. of potatoes to each family, but that only. What we now anxiously look for is some assistance to send the men to England this year to earn something. Over 800 go from Achill annually, but many have not the means to pay their passage now. We have had a bale and a half of clothes by the Goshawk last March, and also some blankets and clothes from Mr. TUKE and the Dublin Friends, but there were twenty applicants for one we were able to give anything to. There are eleven National Schools in this parish, but although the inspector of the district asked last March how many suits would be required for each, none has been sent yet. Our contract price for Indian meal is £7 10s., within six miles of the Sound; and £8 beyond that. From all sources we have not been able to give two bags of meal to each family, averaging six persons, since last January.

"I am, gentlemen, yours faithfully and obliged,

WILLIAM PIKE.

Letterkenny, 18th *May,* 1880.

"GENTLEMEN,

"Though I have already forwarded a formal receipt for the very liberal grant of £3,000 which the Mansion House Committee have kindly made to us, I think it is due to your Committee that I should furnish them with a brief statement of the good which their generous efforts have hitherto effected in this county, and of the very favourable influence which they have had in our future prospects.

"During the long weary months which we have passed in a continued struggle with destitution, the position of our Committee has often been one of painful anxiety; for, though the aid we received from without, especially from America, was liberal beyond our expectations, still there were times when the ever-increasing spread of distress and the corresponding drain on our funds gave us great reason to fear that we should soon find ourselves at the end of our resources. Just at these critical times, we have always found the Mansion House Committee ready to come to our aid with a large grant, which freed us from all anxiety and enabled us to continue, with reasonable success, the work of relieving the destitute.

"But at no previous period of the distress were we in such danger of a sudden collapse as when your last generous grant reached us. All our other sources of supply had completely given out, distress spread rapidly among the small farmers and labourers, for whom there was much less employment as the spring work came to an end, and, though we had still means to last for a week or two, there were such frequent and unexpected inroads made upon them by cheques held over, charges for freight, and other expenses, that we might find ourselves, at any time, even with our very reduced scale of grants, unable to meet the calls made upon us by the Local Committees. Now, with your very liberal grant and the little that remains of our funds, we shall, I trust, be able to get on for five or six weeks longer. If we could find a soft spot in the hearts of the *New York Herald* Committee, they might enable us to tide over two or three weeks more, and then, as we would lie within sight of land, Divine Providence would inspire some one to extend a hand to rescue us.

"I make this calculation on the supposition that the distress will not increase and that the people shall be able to support life on the greatly reduced aid which we can give them. But both these contingencies are, to say the least, very doubtful. I find that, since we have been obliged to reduce our grants, the Local Committees are cutting off families from the relief lists, not because they are beyond the need of relief, but because, among the destitute, they are the least destitute. I am daily made painfully aware of this fact, because these poor people come to me from the most distant parts of the country to make known their wants and to entreat my interference on their behalf with the local Committees. Now I fear that, before August, many, if not all, of these will be reduced to a condition which will force the Committees to reverse their decision. I must now say a word of the influence which the action of your Committee has had on our future prospects; and of this I am glad to be able to speak most hopefully. During the spring our great anxiety was the want of seed. It is certain that, if left to themselves, large numbers of the people would have been without a crop or obliged to content themselves with the mere shadow of a crop. In some districts the provision made by the Unions was a hollow mockery. It was in this respect particularly that your Committee has done a work the effects of which will last. By making us large grants for food you have enabled us to devote to the purchase of seed a sum which has gone far to supply the want. What you have enabled us to spare from our own resources for this object, together with a generous subsidy from Liverpool, amounted to £9,000. I am sure there was much more than this spent on seed; for we paid freight and other expenses from the general fund, and, after the general distribution, there were extreme cases daily turning up, to which we were obliged to attend. Even about the 10th of May I intercepted, on their way to the bakehouse, three tons of Champions, which the guardians had held over, and which I purchased for half the price at which they were sold to the people. Even at that late season the poor people seized upon them most greedily for fields which they had lying waste through want of seed. The result of these efforts to provide seed is that the people have a more abundant crop, at least of potatoes, down than they have had for several years past, and the beautiful weather with which Divine Providence has favoured us gives every promise that the crop will be fruitful. In commencing this letter I had no idea of trespassing so far upon your attention, but I suppose you will bear patiently with this as one of the many troubles to which you have generously submitted for the sake of the poor. I can assure you, gentlemen, that the vote of thanks which I enclose is but a feeble expression of the gratitude we really feel towards your Committee for the splendid assistance you have given us; and our gratitude, which is merely begotten of sympathy with the sufferings of others, is very little compared with the gratitude of the poor people, which is inspired by a conviction that your noble efforts have been instrumental in saving them from want, misery, and, in many instances, even from death by starvation.

"I am, gentlemen, your faithful servant,

"✠ MICHAEL LOGUE."

"MY DEAR LORD MAYOR,

"At the request of our Relief Committee, I urge upon your benevolent Committee to come to our aid. During spring operations we forebore to importune you, as the poor struggled on to subsist; but now the present and coming months are the truly crucial months. In fact, my house for the last week is surrounded from morning to night with a clamorous and hungry crowd begging "food" or "work." Of the large sums I have received from France, America, and other parts for this diocese I have already given far more than its proportion to this parish. There is no work to be had here, though the poor people are willing to earn their bread. I appealed on their behalf to the guardians of this Union on Saturday. The reply I got was that there was no power to give outdoor relief; and as there are no works, baronial or otherwise, in this neighbourhood, the poor have no alternative but to break up home and enter the poorhouse. The poor creatures, to my certain knowledge, will elect to lie down and die of starvation rather than enter the workhouse. Though I hold strong convictions on this horrible alternative, I forbear to express further opinions from these Committee rooms. To save trouble of reference, I am requested by the Committee to furnish you with enclosed copy of the last returns sent on the 13th of March, since when this Committee have received no aid from Mansion House Committee. Again asking you to remember that 363 families, numbering 1,171 persons, appeal to you in this most trying season,

I am, with great respect and regard,

✠ PATRICK DUGGAN, *Bishop of Clonfert.*

"*Ballina, County Mayo, May 19th,* 1880.

"MY DEAR LORD MAYOR,

I received this morning the Draft Circular and your Lordship's letter of the 15th instant. The appeal cannot go forth too soon, for since the Central Committees limited their supplies to the Local Committees the latter were obliged to limit the quantities allowed to the recipients. The result has been complaints, destitution, and now consequent sickness and fever. Limited as the supplies of the Central Committees have been of late, if stopped before harvest will come to the relief of the people; famine and starvation will be the result. We heard a great deal of late about the amount of money given to landlords under the Land Improvement Act, for the employment and relief of the people. The fact of the landlords getting it and not employing the people furnishes no excuse to the Government for allowing the people to starve, and is only another development (if such were needed) of the class legislation that has brought ruin on the country. Up to this no employment has been given in this district except by one landlord, and even in that case the complaints are, that the earnings are so small as not to afford half support to the families of the employees. Other sources of employment, spoken of here during the the last four months, are held back with much craft by influential parties here until harvest will come, and will be then allowed to collapse as unnecessary. If the Government intends to save the lives of the people, let them leave them no longer to the tender mercy of either Poor-law Guardians or landlords, who have repeatedly declared that they would not burden either themselves or their properties for the relief of the people.

"I have the honour to be, my dear Lord, yours very respectfully,

"✠ HUGH CONWAY, *Bishop of Killala.*

"*Newport, May 8th,* 1880.

"MY LORD AND GENTLEMEN,

"We, the members of the Newport, Mayo, Relief Committee, respectfully beg to bring under your serious consideration the following facts in connection with the state of the poor of this district, No. 165, containing a population of 6,000 souls, is situated in the second poorest Poor-law Union in Ireland. The present rate here is 3s. 7d. in the pound, and it is only a fictitious rate; the required rate would be 7s. or 8s. in the pound, and it would be quite uncollectable. This Union is on the verge of bankruptcy, owing nearly £2,000, exclusive of loan under Seeds Act. The area is 170,383 acres; population 16,061, while the valuation is only £13,169. The general character of the land is sterile and barren, which may be inferred from the fact that it is only valued at 1s. 6½d. per acre. The district is a maritime one, and exposed to the fury of the Atlantic Ocean, the corps at best precarious and scanty, but, the successive failures for the past three seasons have reduced the population to the lowest state of poverty. There are no public works of any kind in the district, no employment for the people except the ordinary spring work, now nearly finished. Thre are only three resident landlords in the whole Union, 23 absentees. The Guardians—from being heavily in debt, their cheques have been dishonoured, contractors refusing to supply—are unable to give out-door relief to any extent, thus throwing the poor (who have an abhorrence to the workhouse), and the masses of the struggling landholders of whom there are 1,645 rated at and under £2. on the limited resources of this Committee. Add to the foregoing their indebtedness and want of credit, will complete the picture of their helplessness and poverty. This Committee is in existence since the 13th of last January (we had also a Relief Committee here to meet the distress in January, 1879), working and struggling since under difficulties of the most trying nature. All private resources are now exhausted, and this Committee now appeals to you to come to the assistance of the impoverished people of this district with liberal weekly grants from your funds, and which will be required until the 1st of August next.

"RICHARD PRENDERGAST, P.P., *Chairman.*
"SAMUEL JOHNSTON, *Clk., Incumbent.*
"GEORGE S. KEEGAN, *Clk.,* Presbyterian Minister of Newport.
"JOHN MEEHAN, C.C.
"P. GIBBONS, *Hon. Sec.*

THE DUKE OF EDINBURGH ON THE DISTRESS.

The Duke of EDINBURGH, presiding at the annual dinner of the Royal Geographical Society in London, May 31st, referring to the distress in Ireland said:— "It has been believed by many that the extent of the distress on the coast of Ireland has been greatly exaggerated, and it has even been so far believed that the relief which has been administered, perhaps might not have been necessary, and might in some cases have been misspent. I think I may confidently state, from what I have seen, and from the intimate knowledge of that relief which I have gained, that the distress in the main has not been exaggerated, and that it was excessively severe. The distress has not reached the point which it did in those celebrated years of the historical Irish famine, and that fact is due entirely to the distress having been taken in time. I cannot refrain from expressing how much of that taking in time was due to the exertions of the Duchess of MARLBOROUGH. We have also to thank the citizens of America for the great and generous help which they sent. It was my good fortune to be at Queenstown to assist in the distribution of that magnificent cargo which they so generously sent. I may say, however, that the distress is not over yet, and it will not be over for at least two months and a half, when the first crop will be taken of the potato and general harvest. Until then, in many cases actual relief, by feeding the population on portions of the West Coast and on the Islands, will have to be continually maintained. Otherwise the distress which occurred in the first instance will occur again. I hope those present will bear it in mind that the time is not completely past when the charitably inclined may do much good by still sending subscriptions to those great funds which have already done so much good. It is to be hoped that there may be other things undertaken, such as permanent works and encouragement of fisheries on the coast of Ireland. By encouragement of the fisheries I am sure there is great chance of preventing the recurrence of distress. Those fisheries, which are so much neglected, would give the population upon that coast a sure means of existence. The land is really in many parts incapable of sustaining the population, as regards its natural resources; and without the assistance of the fishing I am certain that the same thing will occur again."

"*Moygowna Relief Committee, Moygowna, Crossmolina,* June 1st, 1880.

" GENTLEMEN,

"Herewith I beg to return weekly account sheet. I am directed by the Moygowna Committee to return their most sincere thanks for your last grant of £20, received and expended the week before last. From the weekly account it will be seen that our Committee were obliged most reluctantly indeed, to take 100 families off their list—not that these families were not very much in need of relief, but lest others might actually die of sheer starvation the next week. Unfortunately this is the very first day of the really hard, severe season, June and July. The poor people have literally nothing but sheer starvation staring them in the face from this to the end of July. It is with the most intense anxiety that our Committee have seen that the Mansion House Fund, the supporter and saviour of the country, is about to bring its most useful and glorious labours to a close. Unless the Government now step in and take up, and continue in some shape or other, the work hitherto so ably and so charitably performed by the Mansion House Fund, dreadful must be the consequences. Again appealing most pressingly for a grant, faithfully yours,

"JOHN O'KELLY, P.P., *Hon. Sec.*"

"*Kilkerrin Relief Committee, Kilkerrin, Moylough, County Galway,* June 1st, 1880.

" GENTLEMEN,

"Our Committee here are not a little disappointed at having got no grant from you for either the last or the current week, though our people are indeed actually starving. It would grieve you, I am sure, if you were to see the numbers of them who flock every morning around my house asking in the name of the God of Mercy for something that will keep the life in them, and saying often that perhaps they had not a bit to eat for the four-and-twenty hours previous. This, I can assure you, is no exaggeration of their statements, but it is the literal truth, and therefore I again and again implore you not to withhold your helping hand any longer from them, for, if you do, some of them at least must surely perish, for they have now no other resource left them. Their own little means are entirely gone, and they have no credit, for no one will entrust them with anything on account of their great poverty;

and therefore, if you will not come to their assistance, and that at once, God alone can know what will be the consequence. There is no employment yet to be got; there is no outdoor relief. The Guardians would not give it, except in very rare instances to aged persons who have no land, and who are disabled by physical infirmity to provide for themselves, and even to these same they give it only with great reluctance: so you can easily see, if you or some other charitable body like you will not come immediately to their assistance, they must perish. There is nothing else left them, and therefore I implore you again not to withhold your help from them any longer, nor until some other relieving source may present itself to them; and thanking you very much for the substantial help you have already given,

"I remain, gentlemen, your very faithful servant,

"AUSTIN O'DWYER, P.P., and Chairman."

"*New Inn Relief Committee, Woodlawn, June 1st, 1880.*

(EXTRACT)

"There has not been, and cannot be for the next ten weeks, any diminution in the numbers requiring relief. In this part of the country no new provisions will be available before the middle of August. What is to become of the poor and the destitute in the meantime is a question that may well be asked, now that the Mansion House funds are all but exhausted. To this there can be but one answer, that if no other means are adopted to save the lives of the people, many will be lost in the meantime through sheer starvation. Hoping the Mansion House will enable us to postpone the evil day,

"Yours sincerely,

"(Signed) THOMAS HEAD, P.P."

"*Bangor-Erris, Mayo, June 6th, 1880.*

"GENTLEMEN,

"As there seems to be such a variety of opinion in England and in certain high quarters in Ireland as to the distress at present existing in this country—some believing it is on the wane, others that the backbone of the distress is broken, others again that it is not as bad as it is represented—will you kindly allow me to give you a brief account of how it at present exists in this parish, and how it has existed for the past three months, and to make the following remarks. There are 609 families in this parish, 150 of whom were relieved in March, 300 in April, and 580 in May. These 580 families, on an average of five to each family, will make up 2,900 individuals, all of whom are in the last stage of absolute distress, so much so that I would not be surprised at any moment to hear of death from starvation. There is no such thing to be availed of as outdoor relief in this Union, as, the relief up to this granted was supplied by the following relief funds:—The Duchess Fund, the Mansion House Fund, *New York Herald* Fund, the Land League Fund, and from the Most Rev. Dr. Conway, Ballina, the Bishop of the diocese. Any attempt on my part to depict the misery of these poor people would be out of the question. The duties of my parish have given me an opportunity for the last four or five weeks (being engaged at stations) of attesting the real destitution of the people. The scenes of wretchedness and misery that have met me on every side would make stouter hearts than mine sick. The people have neither credit, means, nor money, and what makes matters worse, the sources of relief above referred to are now nearly run out. It is quite common to see the poor people who live near the sea-board in this parish trying to drag out a miserable existence by using shell-fish and even the sea-weed.

Unless the Government step in and do something promptly, most assuredly hundreds of these poor people will die of hunger. It was most heart-rending to witness the crowd of hungry-looking people who presented themselves for relief at our Committee meeting held on Saturday last, and who had to go home empty, as we had no funds at our disposal to give relief even to one single case. Hoping your Committee will act with your usual generosity by granting us an instalment of your funds as soon as you conveniently can,

"I am, gentlemen, your grateful, obedient servant,
"JAMES DURCAN, P. P., *Treasurer.*"

"*Kilmore, Drumsna, 5th June,* 1880.

"GENTLEMEN,

"Quite a panic has been caused here by the apprehension of a probable winding up of the Mansion House Fund, which seemed inexhaustible, judging from the generosity with which you dispensed to the various Local Committees several thousand pounds a week for the last five months. On behalf of 2,200 persons on our relief lists, hundreds of whom owe their very existence mainly to the most bounteous of almoners, the Mansion House Relief Committee, I am directed to tender you our grateful acknowledgments. Since this panic set in amongst us the previous three-quarter stone of meal per head per week, amounting to £80, has been made to do service for a fortnight. A very melancholy effect of this ordeal was witnessed a few days ago by myself and another member of our Committee, when we beheld many well-to-do people of the past, tottering along at a funeral, more like skeletons than living men. These poor men cannot be persuaded that they ought to leave their houses and lands and go into the workhouse sooner than starve. Outdoor relief in Carrick-on-Shannon Union, in which four out of the five electoral divisions relieved by us are situated, is not worth naming. To my certain knowledge the guardians vie with each other as to whose division will be least taxed when the next rate is struck, while they throw on us the responsibility of relieving the poor or letting them starve, which, without the assistance of your charitable Committee, we must still do, though the storm of adversity has well nigh passed away. No Government relief has yet reached us in any shape or form. Though our resources are now exhausted, there is a prospect of a rich harvest, which affords just grounds for hope in the future; but the interval must be gloomy in the extreme without the sustaining hand which bore us up during the bitter past. With a fervent prayer that dissolution will not set in amongst the Mansion House Committee till the fulness of time has arrived.—Yours faithfully,

"P. BAMBRICK, C.C. *Hon, Sec.*"

"*Loughlynn, Roscommon, 5th June,* 1880."

"GENTLEMEN.

"I beg to acknowledge with thanks receipt of your grant, £40, for distressed in this parish. I shall not fail to communicate to the people that they are not to expect assistance from your committee to tide over the coming two months, but I am convinced that if you withdraw your generous and substantial aid from them there necessarily must be many deaths from starvation—Yours, &c.

"F. A. FLANAGAN, *Hon. Sec.*"

"*Kilkerrin Relief Committee, Kilkerrin, Moylough, County Galway,*
"*June 1st* 1880.

"GENTLEMEN,

"Our Committee here are not a little disappointed at having got no grant from you for either the last or the current week, though our people are indeed actually starving. It would grieve you I am sure were you to see the numbers of them who flock every morning around my house asking, in the name of the God of Mercy, for something that will keep the life in them, and saying often that perhaps they had not a bit to eat for the four-and-twenty hours previous. This I can assure you is no exaggeration of their statements, but it is the literal truth, and, therefore, I again and again implore you not to withhold your helping hand any longer from them, for if you do, some of them at least must surely perish, for they have now no other resource left them. Their own little means are entirely gone, and they have no credit, for no one will entrust them with anything on account of their great poverty, and therefore, if you will not come to their assistance, and that at once, God alone can know what will be the consequence. There is no employment to be got; there is no outdoor relief. The Guardians would not give it except in very rare instances to aged persons who have no land, and who are disabled by physical infirmity to provide for themselves, and even to these same they give it only with great reluctance; so you can see, if you or some other charitable body like you will not come immediately to their assistance, they must perish. There is nothing else left them; and, therefore, I implore you again not to withhold your help from them any longer, nor until some other relieving source may present itself to them: and thanking you very much for the substantial help you have already given,

"I remain, gentlemen, your very faithful servant,

"AUSTIN O'DWYER, P.P. and *Chairman*."

"*Rosmuck, Galway,* 15*th June.*

"MY LORD,

"The Rosmuck Committee in connection with the Mansion House Fund is No. 384, and on the 5th instant a letter was received from the Mansion House enclosing a grant of £40, and a letter saying this was to be the final grant. The crisis of our distress this year is at hand, and will last to middle of July. In the comparatively prosperous years of the past, from middle of June to middle of July was proverbial amongst us as one of hunger. What must it be this year? You can conceive, but I cannot describe. To say people are fasting for 24 hours, I candidly believe that poor creatures here are and have been suffering for more than 30 hours. Such a case came under my notice yesterday. The lives of the poor of Rosmuck are due to the charitable Committees of Dublin, supported by the public, but in the greatest measure to the Committee in which you so worthily move. We have struggled to keep the wolf at bay since January last, but now I fear we will have to succumb and fall easy victims. If we had £100 I am sure we would be able to foil the demon. I could not expect so much from the Mansion House at present, but as much as you could afford. Unless you help us this time, I seriously fear some will be lost, even at the eleventh hour. In your sympathy and charity represent our wretched state to the Committee at next meeting.

"I am, my Lord, yours faithfully,

"J. J. KEANE, P.P."

Letterkenny, Thursday.

At a meeting of the Raphoe Catholic Clergy held at Letterkenny to-day, the following resolutions were adopted :—

"That the present distress is most urgent, and unless Government aid be given immediately, the worst consequences must be expected; that the means hitherto adopted by the Government to meet it—viz., grants made to landlords and Boards of Guardians, have utterly failed, and that no further grants be made to them for this purpose."

"That though the amount of grants already made to landlords is very considerable, and, had it been all expended, would have gone far to meet the distress, yet in large districts where the distress is greatest no application for grants was made, whilst landlords, who have already received grants, in most instances confined the employment given to their usual staff of labourers, and but rarely employed the really destitute."

"That, believing that there has been considerable mismanagement, the portion of grants already made, yet unpaid, be withheld till due inquiry be made as to the expenditure of the money already received."

"That we have no confidence in the Poor-law system as at present administered."

"*Anacarty Relief Committee, Dundrum, Cashel, June* 18th, 1880."

"SIR,

"May I, as Chairman of the above Committee, take the liberty to ask you kindly to obtain for our exceedingly distressed poor, numbering 400, a final grant, that we may be able to keep them alive for three weeks when some work may turn up. We were obliged to refuse meal to over 100 poor last Wednesday, thereby reducing the number from 500 to 400, who will with tears press for further relief next Wednesday, but if we should fail in this application more than 260 cannot get an ounce of the Indian meal, as the few pounds—viz £5, now on hands, will not allow the Committee to give even one scanty meal of the Indian meal gruel to more than 260, the number stated above. We have a large mountain district where the potato and oat crops altogether failed last year. No work afforded by landlord or occupier of land; and since the distress has been great, yes as much as it is in Ballyvaughan or the islands around there. Dear sir, please assist me to have a final grant voted for the Committee, and you shall merit and obtain the good effect of that corporal work of mercy—the feeding of the poor starving peasantry of this miserable mountain district.

"I remain, dear sir, faithfully yours,

"JOHN FENNELLY, P.P."

"*Charlestown Relief Committee,* 18*th June,* 1880."

"GENTLEMEN,

"I am very sorry to have to say that the state of this poor parish is daily becoming more alarming. The famine fever (and a most dangerous type) is now very prevalent, and making such progress that I fear there will not be ere long a village in all the parish free of it. Of course, the destitute were the first to be visited by this awful disease, but, like death itself, it respects not persons, and very shortly makes as unwelcome visits to the well-to-do and independent. I have seen three pass by me this week to the workhouse, from the little village in which I reside. Only the week before I saw the widow borne to the grave from her orphans, and only the wall separates me from where the wife of a respected member of our Committee lies dangerously ill. Only a fortnight since, on the same day, and forth from the same house went the corpses of the grandmother and grandchild, and the son now lies dangerously ill in the workhouse. While we had only hunger to combat the work was comparatively easy, but a fear of this dreadful disease has given rise to a mutual distrust and fear of having intercourse with each other, and the danger of bringing a large number of people together, even for the purpose of distributing relief is no

T

trifling risk, and of what earthly use are a few stones of Indian meal to a family so afflicted. Such a family can get no one to employ them. Their neighbours, unfortunately, have no means to aid them, and in most cases they are bereft of all earthly means save the crop, which is at best but a hope for some future day. The crops are indeed very flourishing, and in some cases, may after four weeks bring abundance to the table of many a poor man; but there will be cases in which the 1st of August only will find them out of danger. A noble fight has been made during the past twenty-three weeks for the lives of these good, poor people, but what avails all that if they are not kept up to the end? I can compare our good priest and chairman's position to that of a home-bound mariner, who for many a day made successful headway against every storm, and over mountain billow, until he finds himself in view of the long wished for haven, and with all he loves in view and his fond hopes brightest, he suddenly finds his good ship sinking beneath him, and all his bright prospects dissipated for ever. To prevent such an end to our half-year's labour, will you take our poor people under your special care, and see, so far as in you lies, that they will not at least suffer the pangs of hunger, or be left without a drink to cool their parched and feverish lips. Begging that you will remember them at your next meeting, and allocate a grant in proportion to our wants,

"I remain, gentlemen, your obedient servant,

"MICHAEL J. DOHERTY, *Hon. Sec.*"

"*Scrabby, County Cavan, June* 24, 1880.

"GENTLEMEN,

"We are again forced to appeal to you for help to feed our people. Of the 366 families we have been trying to keep alive for the past year, by far the greater number are in as much need, some in greater need, than at any previous time during the year. We had hoped for some public relief works that would give the people employment, but although at an extraordinary presentment sessions, held for the barony, many useful works were passed for this district, and many more would have been passed but for the tone given to the meeting by the Secretary of the Grand Jury, who propounded the law for the cesspayers, yet the only works yet approved by the Local Government Board are the repairing of about a mile of an old road, repairing a piece of an old lane, and making a protection-fence that will cost £4. Then one of our landlords, who has opened relief works on a very small scale, instructs his bailiff to employ no one except those who owe him rent, and to stop the wages for the rent. As will be seen by the weekly return of expenditure, our funds are entirely exhausted. We request that you will give us some help for the next three or four weeks.

"I remain, gentlemen, yours respectfully,

"MICHAEL CORCORAN, C.C., *Secretary for the Committee.*"

"*Killala Relief Committee, Saturday, June* 26*th,* 1880.

"GENTLEMEN,

"To-day I attended a meeting of the Killala Board of Guardians for the purpose of obtaining out-door relief for some fifty of the poorest families in this parish, who are just now, and must continue for some weeks to come, in a condition of extreme distress. Owing to the shortness of funds at the disposal of the Committee we were unable to give these helpless families the usual amount of meal administered to them since the earliest period of the distress, and I very confidently hoped that my request to the Board of Guardians for relief during the crucial month of July would have been cheerfully acceded to. But I was doomed to bitter disappointment, and to-day, in impatient expectation of relief from some quarter, hungry crowds of these destitute small farmers with their families stormed the board-room and quickly packed it to suffocation. It was really lamentable, nay heart-rending, to listen to the rude but eloquent and imploring accents of those famine-stricken men and women. The pangs of hunger were not to be smothered or suppressed. And cries of agony not unmingled with muttered threats, assailed the Chairman, Colonel Knox, from all directions. I should rather not have to record my exceeding great regret that the answer of that gentleman to the famished crowd was as heartless as it was indefensible. He told them, men and women alike, and not a few of them broken and bent with age, that no 'out-door relief could be given but to such as were ready to spend eight hours each day breaking stones.' Fearing a riot, he then ordered the police to be sent for, and at this moment, as I write, the police are stationed at the entrance door to the board-room. Is it not an unseemly spectacle? And is it not intolerable that when men who represent nobody but themselves—irresponsible officers—should have thus placed in their hands almost the power of life and death over poor wretches who are starving through no fault of their own? Impossible during these present weeks that they can abandon their little homes to spend the day breaking stones. They have to mould their potatoes, to save their turf, and attend to other farm duties, which even their small holdings constantly demand at their hands. But what cares the accomplished Chairman of the Killala Board of Guardians? No out-door relief, even for a few weeks (my request only extended to that brief period), to those sixty families unless they abandon the care of those promising crops, which the charity of the world enabled them to make. In regions not very remote from Killala, eight Boards of Guardians have been abolished, and in this neighbourhood people have begun to ask themselves, is there no hope for us? Is not the hour of dissolution at hand?

'Proximus ardet Eucaligon.'

"It is my duty, gentlemen, to assure you of the abounding and lasting thanks of our poor people for the immense services rendered them by the Mansion House Committee. Had they been left to the tender mercies of the ex-officio gentlemen of the Killala board-room you may easily conjecture what would have been their fate, and for the few weeks that still intervene between them and the smiling plenty of an exuberant harvest, it is their fervent hope that the Mansion House will supply the help so unfeelingly to-day denied them by their own Guardians.

"I remain, gentlemen, your obedient servant,

"P. J. NOLAN, P.P."

"The Secretaries Mansion House Committee."

"*Aughagower, Westport, July 5, 1880.*

"We had hoped that the relief works would have tided us over July, but as they have been given to professional contractors in this locality they are a thorough sham. They are of little or no use to the poor. The contractors and their friends alone profit by them. Leaving with confidence the case of poor in your hands.

"I have the honour to be, gentlemen, yours faithfully,

"J. E. STEPHENS, C.C."

"*Bouniconlan, Ballina, July* 2, 1880.

"My Lord and Gentlemen,

"Terrible distress still rages in its intensity. The present is the supreme crisis in this locality, for fever has recently broken out in different parts of the parish, four families being now afflicted. The happy and long-expected 'Garland Sunday' seems still far away, and the golden expectations of the poor creatures have turned into gloomy anticipations, for we have in those parts for the last eight or nine days no sunshine—nothing but one continual downpour of rain. Consequently the crop which promised food to the starving about the middle of July, shows no prospect at all presently. We trust your charitable and noble Committee will still be the means of continuing their existence.

"Yours very faithfully,
(Signed) "Peter Harte, P.P., *Chairman.*"

Belmullet, 5th July, 1880.

"The promised public works have proved to be here, as in many other localities, a delusion. Up to the moment at which I write there have not been fifty men from my parish employed on those works, and this only for one week. To-day we are to have another of those meetings very properly dubbed by Act of Parliament extraordinary sessions. Had our people here been left to the tender mercies of the Government, instead of having the hand of charity, as it has been, so generously extended to them, long before this there would have been re-enacted many of those scenes of the 'bad times,' from the contemplation of which humane nature naturally recoils.

"Henry Hewson, P.P., V.F."

APPENDIX IX.

TABLE

Showing the Counties in which distress existed, the names of the Committees formed in each County, the number of persons in distress reported from each district on first application, the number returned on the 1st March, with extracts from the local appeals describing the state of the peasantry in the several districts.

PROVINCE OF ULSTER.

Counties	Districts	No. of Persons in Distress, First Local Estimate	Latest Returns of Number in Distress, March 1st.	Extracts from Appeals of Local Committees, duly authenticated.
ARMAGH	Creggan, Up.	3750	Likely to increase	All small farmers, but poverty so general that the county court judges expressed their astonishment at the vast number of civil decrees, and in many cases stayed execution.
	Derryall	250	Number increasing	In deep distress; want of meat, seed, and clothing.
	Dromante & Jonesborough	2000	Certain to increase	Small occupiers of poor land.
	Forkhill	2000	Likely to increase	Small landholders and labourers; want of employment and failure of the potato crop.
	Killeavy Up.	2455	Likely to increase	Small farmers; bad crops.
ANTRIM	Cushendall (Glens of Antrim)	200	220	People impoverished to an extent unknown since '47; clergy and gentry besieged by people for aid.
CAVAN	Arva	1225	1075	Very many have not wherewith to purchase a day's provision. They are so deeply sunk in debt, their credit gone, they are now reluctantly obliged to seek the bread of charity. Farmers, who were accustomed to employ labourers, are now themselves pressing for relief.
	Ballinagh	1000	1410	Distress in many cases amounting to absolute destitution.
	Ballintemple	583	820	General distress; failure of crops and want of employment.
	Ballyconnell	300	634	Just at present the absence of funds presses heavily on us.

Counties	Districts	No. of Persons in Distress, First Local Estimate.	Latest Returns of Number in Distress, March 1st.	Extracts from Appeals of Local Committees, duly authenticated.
CAVAN	Belturbet	1000	1039	It pains us to have nothing to alleviate their distress.
	Ballymachugh and Drumlummon	600	811	In need of the first necessaries of life.
			865	
	Bailieborough	500	850	Last week a man who held six acres died of want; if no relief, many poor struggling farmers will be driven to the workhouse.
	Billis	750	Likely to increase	Small holders of a few acres. Destitution owing to bad seasons and failure of potato crop.
	Cavan	1500	Likely to increase	Bad harvest and want of employment.
	Crosskeys	550	572	Bad harvest and want of employment.
	Castlerahan & Mt. Connaught	1000	2220	
	Castleterra		750	Small farmers; failure of crops; floods and depression in price of cattle.
	Curlough	500	990	
	Drumlane	1000	1183	Small farmers and labourers; bad harvests.
	Drumgoon	500		Want and distress increasing; if aid not soon to hand the consequences will be deplorable.
	Drung	345	490	
	Glengevlin	800		Very many are actually starving; others on the brink of starvation. For God's sake, send something at once.
	Gowna	650	1213	Failure of crops; want of work and fuel.
	Kilsherdany	800	423	Formerly in a state of comfort, now destitute from failure of crops.
	Killinkere	1500	913	Labourers; failure of potato crop; no employment.
	Killinagh	1900	1700	Small farmers and labourers; failure of potato crop; no employment.
	Kilnaleck	500	2274	Great destitution; one-third small farmers.
	Killeshandra	650	210	Poor farmers now eating their seed potatoes and last store of meal; will have nothing to maintain themselves till next crop.
	Kingscourt	1500	1400	Distress pressing fearfully on small farmers and labourers.
	Knockbride	1000	Will increase	Small farmers and labourers. A succession of bad seasons, diminished value of cattle and agricultural produce.

TABLE OF DISTRESS—ULSTER.

Counties	Districts	No. of Persons in Distress, First Local Estimate.	Latest Returns of Number in Distress, March 1st.	Extracts from Appeals of Local Committees, duly authenticated.
CAVAN	Larah	1250	221	Labourers and small farmers; causes of destitution, bad seasons and want of work.
	Lavey	750	Likely to increase	Very poor; failure of crops, especially potato, and succession of bad seasons.
	Moybolgue & Kilmainham-Wood	200	Will increase	Small farmers and labourers; failure of crops and want of employment.
	Mullagh	1480	1650	Failure of crops and want of employment.
	Shercock	550	849	Failure of crops; high rents; labourers very destitute.
	Swanlinbar	300	2000	Have had to refuse many needy applicants.
	Templeport	592	880	Distress has been borne in silence till they reached the very point of starvation.
	Virginia	300	767	Great destitution of many farmers.
FERMANAGH	Ballaghameehan	500	420	In deepest distress; potato crop totally failed; land too barren to produce oats.
	Belcoo		650	
	Blackbog	800	947	Distress is extreme.
	Boho	130	465	Farmers and labourers.
	Clenish	900		Terrible distress; in want of immediate relief.
	Derrylinn	700	1393	Total destruction of crops along Lough Erne; partial failure in all other parts. Want of fuel.
	Derrygonnelly	750	1190	In great want; no food or fuel; starvation facing them.
	Enniskillen	1000	Increasing	Our funds exhausted; all in deep distress.
	Lisnaskea		580	
	Lisbellaw		1000	
	Maguiresbridge	400	630	Private benefactions exhausted; again implore grant at earnest meeting, to relieve very great and increasing suffering from want of food; nearly 400 in a starving condition.
	Mulleek	500	634	Mostly small farmers, subsisting by turf-making; sad to see hundreds crowded at Committee door, waiting from 12 o'clock noon till 8 o'clock at night, under drenching rain; several poor women and men came to priest's house and fainted with hunger and exhaustion. The appearance of the poor is appalling.
	Newtownbutler	300	495	Small farmers and cottiers.

264　　　　　　　　　　APPENDIX IX.

Counties	Districts	No. of Persons in Distress, First Local Estimate	Latest Returns of Number in Distress, March 1st.	Extracts from Appeals of Local Committees, duly authenticated.
FERMANAGH	Roslea	713	883	Farmers and farm labourers. Successive bad harvests; failure of crops, and want of employment.
	Rossory and Cradgan		1000	
	Sallaghy	100	281	Great distress; instant relief required.
	Tempo	300	Likely to increase	No food; no fuel; no work.
DONEGAL	Ardara		2500	Distress increasing most extensively from day to day.
	Ballintra		1095	Distress daily increasing; numbers almost starving.
	Ballyshannon		3117	Committee now entirely destitute of funds.
	Bundoran		1600	Not a parish in the county more in need of aid.
	Burt		240	Distress unexpectedly breaking out.
	Churchhill, Gartan and Termon		2750	Distress and number of applicants daily increasing.
	Cloghaneely and Tory		2500	Relief entirely dependent on Central Committee.
	Convoy		1500	Earnestly appeals for assistance.
	Culdaff and Glengad		2550	425 families in great destitution.
	Clonmany		1765	150 families have no means of subsistence.
	Carndonagh		900	Individuals confined to 7lbs. of Indian meal per week.
	Dunfanaghy		1555	Distress rapidly increasing.
	Donegal		1660	200 families really in need; left unattended to from want of funds.
	Donaghmore		1750	Extensively impoverished.
	Fintown (Glenties)		1500	No employment; distress widespread and severe.
	Fahan		460	Great suffering among the small farmers.
	Gweedore		3200	The Special Correspondent of the *Daily Telegraph* has not seen "such uniform distress" in any part of the West. His time being precious, he could not wait another day to see scenes still more appalling. The distress here is becoming quite general. I fear we shall have to sink under it. It will be absolutely necessary for us to order meal to an amount of about £120. This very thing gives some idea of the magnitude of the distress in this parish. In another month it will be easy to count the families that will be free from it.

TABLE OF DISTRESS — ULSTER.

Counties	Districts	No. of Persons in Distress, First Local Estimate.	Latest Returns of Number in Distress, March 1st.	Extracts from Appeals of Local Committees, duly authenticated.
DONEGAL	Glencolumbkille		2850	Distress is becoming daily more general; some are eating the black seaweed.
	Glenties		1075	Great distress.
	Inver		2500	One of the largest and poorest parishes in the diocese.
	Innishowen		2500	
	Lettermacward		2519	The number of destitute increasing from week to week.
	Letterkenny		2500	Great distress in outlying districts.
	Killymard		950	Every day matters are becoming worse.
	Killaghtee		1290	The state of things has culminated in the most acute distress.
	Killybegs		2150	Continually telegraphing to the Central Relief Committee for aid.
	Kilcar		2500	If we fail one week in relieving, the consequences would be fearful.
	Kiltervogue		900	Distress daily increasing.
	Kilmacrenan		1230	Deep distress prevails in this parish.
	Meragh (Rosgal)		2345	Widespread distress.
	Milford		1350	The deepest distress prevails in this district.
	Moville		800	Considerable distress.
	Malin		1000	Distress exists to a very considerable degree.
	Pettigo and Belleek		3117	Many apply for relief, but cannot be relieved from want of funds.
	Rathmullen & Glenvar		1460	The people here are in the greatest distress.
	Ramelton		1160	Considerable distress.
	Stranorlar		1010	No employment; great distress.
	Tamney (Fannet)		1500	Very many people in this parish in actual starvation.
	Templecrone (Lower) & Arranmore Island		5886	The poverty of the people is such, that if immediate steps be not taken to alleviate the distress, deaths from hunger must be the immediate result. Distress attributable to almost total failure of the crops, reduction in the price of cattle and kelp, want of fuel, caused by rains, reduction in labour market of England and Scotland. Rental stated at £900; but one cow on the island; pasture reserved for sheep.
	Templecrone, Upper (Dungloe)		2000	Destitution deep and widespread.

Counties	Districts	No. of Persons in Distress, First Local Estimate	Latest Returns of Number in Distress, March 1st.	Extracts from Appeals of Local Committees, duly authenticated.
DOWN	Kilcoo	800	Must increase	Distress decidedly grave; relief urgently requested.
MONAGHAN	Anyalla	100	Will increase	External aid indispensably necessary.
	Aghabog	250	795	Small farmers, generally; suffering much from loss of crops. No credit.
	Aughamullen West	750	Likely to increase	Small farmers and labourers. Failure of crops, and rents far too high.
	Castleblayney		400	In dire distress; suffering every hardship that poverty and destitution can inflict.
	Donaghmoyne		500	
	Drum		650	Fever of a virulent type has broken out from sheer want.
	Emyvale	1000	Will increase	Distress real and widespread. People without food and fuel.
	Kilmore and Drumsnat	960	Will increase	Poverty here is most alarming.
	Killeevin	550	592	No corn, no seed potatoes, no credit; living on half the necessary amount of food. Hundreds of poor starving people looking for assistance.
	Tydavnet	150	800	Every shilling from every source exhausted. Thirty families to-day with not even a meal to help them.
	Tullycorbett		900	Small farmers and labourers; failure of potato crop.
TYRONE	Ballygawley	750	1260	Small farmers; farm labourers and their families; bad crops; failure of potatoes and fuel; little or no employment.
	Carrickmore		1158	
	Clogher		900	
	Dromore	1750	633	Distress very general; no potatoes, no seed, or such as if planted, will produce famine next year.
	Fintona	2000	1180	Condition terrible to contemplate; unless prompt and generous assistance arrives, numbers will die of hunger.
	Gortin	1200	Will increase	Great distress; no fuel; no potatoes; a miserably scanty oat crop; no credit with shopkeepers.
	Kildress	1250		Many in destitution; many small farmers in sore distress, without even the necessaries of life.

TABLE OF DISTRESS—MUNSTER.

Counties	Districts	No. of Persons in Distress, First Local Estimate.	Latest Returns of Number in Distress, March 1st.	Extracts from Appeals of Local Committees, duly authenticated.
TYRONE	Omagh	548	Likely to increase	Labourers and artisans; want of employment.
	Pomeroy	300	411	Many families in great distress; no money, no credit, scarcity of food and fuel.
	Plumbridge	1700		Nearly all small farmers, very poor, and suffering greatly for fuel and food.
	Trillick	1250	Increasing	Majority small farmers and cottiers; present distress owing to bad harvest and deficiency of employment.

PROVINCE OF MUNSTER.

Counties	Districts	No. of Persons in Distress, First Local Estimate.	Latest Returns of Number in Distress, March 1st.	Extracts from Appeals of Local Committees, duly authenticated.
CLARE	Ballyvaughan	1500	1258	
	Bodyke	300	733	The poor of this parish, willing to work and ashamed to beg, have put off the evil day as long as possible.
	Broadford		377	
	Ballina and Bohir		400	Labourers and small farmers in dire distress.
	Clondegad & Kilchreest		1000	No potatoes; no employment; no credit.
	Clonlee and Killurin	500	700	We are reluctantly compelled to make another appeal for a second grant, to enable these 173 poor families to tide over the next few weeks.
	Coolmeen	1000	1000	I can safely say that 100 people left my house yesterday, noon, ready to fall with hunger.
	Corofin	1000	2524	I believe there is great and exceptional distress this year, and in some parts of the district absolute want of the necessaries of life, and also want of fuel. I have seen two cases lately in which I consider death was accelerated by want of sufficient food and warmth.
	Clonlara		170	

APPENDIX IX.

Counties	Districts	No. of Persons in Distress, First Local Estimate.	Latest Returns of Number in Distress, March 1st.	Extracts from Appeals of Local Committees, duly authenticated.
CLARE	Carrickaholt	1250	1250	The distress among the poor people is fearful, and a great many families must starve if not immediately relieved.
	Doolin	1000	1382	The scenes I witness, the stories I hear when in discharge of my duties as pastor of the district, I refrain from telling.
	Ennistymon	2000	2790	Distress amongst the farmers is rapidly on the increase.
	Ennis	2000		A large number of artisans and tradesmen are famishing and unemployed.
	Feakle Lower	1000	660	100 families of the labouring class are unemployed, and in danger of imminent destitution, and also 150 families of small farmers in a state fast approaching to destitution.
	Feakle Upper	750	900	The whole population is suffering, and will continue to suffer for some time.
	Inagh	365	759	With one exception, the land is owned by non-resident proprietors.
	Kilbaha	350	880	148 families in a very needy condition. Many, to my own personal knowledge, are indeed in very sore distress.
	Killeedy	1200		
	Kilfenora	600	810	The small farmers are increasing in their demands for help, and it is almost impossible to conjecture when the assistance may be stopped.
	Killard	1284	1435	The people are now absolutely without food, and have no prospect of employment.
	Knock and Killimer	300	514	
	Kilmaley	1000	Likely to increase	Without money; without credit; with starvation either actually present or threatening in the near future.
	Kilrush	2000	1726	In no part of Clare is the distress so acute and so widespread as in this district of Kilrush.
	Kilshanny	450	605	More than ninety families all in need of a kind and helping hand, some with hunger pangs at their hearts. Nay more; poor fathers and mothers, in addition to their own sufferings, must behold what to them is even more heartrending—the child of tender years, nay, the little infant, crying for food—even the poorest—and the little hungry mouth crying in vain.

TABLE OF DISTRESS—MUNSTER.

Counties	Districts	No. of Persons in Distress, First Local Estimate.	Latest Returns of Number in Distress, March 1st.	Extracts from Appeals of Local Committees, duly authenticated.
CLARE	Kilmacduane	1000	Likely to increase	Appeal for immediate and timely aid to avert the inevitable and impending destitution, pauperism, and ruin, that unhappily threaten.
	Kilmihil	500	1124	The destitution is very great in our district.
	Killaloe	1250	932	Farmers and labourers; the former want seed, the latter employment.
	Kilkee	700	1700	Relief works opened some weeks since by the Board of Guardians, which gave partial employment to many families, are now suddenly closed.
	Kildysart	300	693	Over 120 families clamouring for assistance.
	Kilmurry-Ibrickane	1000	1240	Most live on sea-coast and gain a living by the sea and from small patches of potatoes; both sources have failed them.
	Labasheeda		1704	
	Loophead	500	Likely to increase	
	Liscannor	1000	1198	The distress here is very severe, and if assistance be not sent, many of my poor, patient, but sorely afflicted people must perish.
	Moneen	500		All suffering from want of food.
	Miltown-Malbay	1540	2114	I have been witness to the poor of both sexes, with spades, re-digging the potato soil, searching from morn till night for the old small potatoes left or covered by the diggers in the harvest.
	Newmarket-on-Fergus	680	806	Chiefly labourers and small farmers. Distress caused by bad harvests for three years past.
	Ogonelloe	365	Not likely	All small farmers and labourers. Destitution attributed to depression in prices of all farm produce and inability of farmers to give employment.
	Quin	680	474	300 of these in utter destitution, urging for assistance in the shape of clothing and seed potatoes.
	Ruan	500	1065	Actually starving; crops failed; no work.
	Scariff	1250	1035	Small farmers and labourers; no landlords residing in the parish; failure of crops and want of employment.

APPENDIX IX.

COUNTIES	DISTRICTS	No. of Persons in Distress, First Local Estimate.	Latest Returns of Number in Distress, March 1st.	Extracts from Appeals of Local Committees, duly authenticated.
CLARE	Six-mile-bridge	750	Certain to increase	Tradesmen and labourers; depression of trade, little or no employment, and failure of potato crop.
	Tulla (Union)	520	858	Want of employment and failure of potato crop.
CORK	Allihies Mines	2900	Increasing	Poor farmers, fishermen, and miners; general want of employment; farmers poor, and paying fully 200 per cent. over valuation; sickness prevails, owing to want.
	Aghadown	600		
	Ardfield	300		
	Barryroe	300	1150	Poor fishermen and small farmers; in a state of destitution, bordering on starvation.
	Bantry	1500	1118	Poor fishermen and labourers; in a sad state for clothing and fuel; also suffering from want of food; some going for days without even a meal.
	Bandon	1000		Principally tradesmen, who have been out of employment for some time. Local Committee working hard to relieve them.
	Buttevant	400	814	Chiefly agricultural labourers; no employment; no fuel; no credit.
	Ballynoe and Conna	1070	950	In great distress, and increasing in intensity; appealed to landlords, but with very little effect; food required for the labourers, and seed for farmers.
	Ballincollig	200		
	Ballyvourney	1500	Likely to increase	Small farmers and labourers; in terrible distress; total failure of potato crop for last three years.
	Castletown-Roche	500	650	Poor tradespeople and labourers, who are suffering from the general depression.
	Castlehaven and Myross	1600	1073	Small farmers and fishermen; three bad harvests; prices of cattle, butter, &c., very low last year; failure of potato crop.
	Caharagh	1339	1622	Small farmers and labourers; excessive rents, and failure of crops.
	Clondrohid	2000	1240	
	Cloyne	1200	1471	Farmers and labourers in distress; excessive rents; the landlords of the farmers in distress are "Absentees;" complete failure of crops.

TABLE OF DISTRESS—MUNSTER.

Counties	Districts	No. of Persons in Distress, First Local Estimate.	Latest Returns of Number in Distress, March 1st.	Extracts from Appeals of Local Committees, duly authenticated.
CORK	Carricktwohill	800		People very poor; in a most pitiable state for want of clothing, bedding, and food.
	Clonmeen	500	800	Poor farmers and labourers.
	Castletown-Berehaven	1100	2232	In a most abject state of destitution; without food, without clothes, without seed.
	Clonakilty	350	Daily increasing	Farmers and labourers, destitute through the failure of crops.
	Castlelyons	250	474	Labourers; poor householders and small farmers.
	Courceys	450	560	So pressing the distress that those who got orders for seed potatoes begged for Indian meal instead; all labourers and poor small farmers; failure of crops and want of employment.
	Clonmoyle	100	590	Labourers and small farmers; total failure of potato crop.
	Clontead and Ballynamotte	150		Labourers, who are destitute owing to poverty of farmers.
	Drimoleague	500	1313	Not a single resident landlord in the district, and only one of them giving work; failure of crops and want of employment.
	Drumtariffe	1000	1570	Distress caused by failure of crops and closing of collieries and flour mill.
	Dungourney	64	381	In extreme distress.
	Doneraile	400	820	Labourers and very few small farmers; failure of crops and want of employment.
	Dunmanway	2200		
	Eyeries	1500		
	Glengariff		414	
	Goleen	2000	Increasing	Small farmers and fishermen; failure of crops; exorbitant rents. Typhus fever has broken out, and is on the increase.
	Glounthane	1500	536	Small farmers and labourers; three bad seasons; no turf; no credit at banks or shops; very little employment.
	Innishannon		600	
	Inchigeela	535	1372	Great majority farm labourers; failure of crops and want of employment.
	Kanturk	1250		
	Kilmurry	1200		
	Kilbehenny	400		
	Killbrittain	600	336	Failure of crops and want of employment; small farmers and labourers.
	Kilmeen and Castleventry	1500	1440	Labourers, tradesmen, and small farmers. Distress owing to failure of crops and want of employment.

Counties	Districts	No. of Persons in Distress. First Local Estimate.	Latest Returns of Number in Distress, March 1st.	Extracts from Appeals of Local Committees, duly authenticated.
CORK	Kenneigh, Ballymoney, and Desertserges	500	805	Most of these people would rather succumb to starvation than complain; they have, consequently, suffered their pinching privations so long, without a murmur, that both their forbearance and bodily powers of suffering are fully exhausted.
	Kilcorney	1250	345	Some of these are farmers, who are as much in need of relief as the inmates of the Workhouse; bad harvests and want of employment.
	Kilworth	500	1000	Distress general and severe. The small farmers have no seed to sow this Spring.
	Kilcaskin	1309	1126	The people abhor relief, and would much rather work for their living. Failure of potato crop and bad Land Laws the immediate cause of distress.
	Kingwilliamstown	700	660	Labourers; cause of their present destitution is having to pay exorbitant rents for houses not fit for human beings to live in; and for gardens in which potatoes did not, of late years, grow. As to the poor farmers, high rents and unfavorable crops were the causes of their distress, and the number of this class will increase before next August.
	Kilnamartyr	400	549	Failure of potato crop and want of employment.
	Kilmichael		946	Labourers, in most cases, suffering from want of employment.
	Kilmacabea	600		
	Kinsale	750	1500	
	Killavullan	600		
	Killdorrery		1000	
	Liscarroll	500	551	Small farmers, tradesmen & labourers; failure of crops and want of employment.
	Meelin, West	300	400	Our small farmers are quite as destitute as the labourers, because they are in debt and cannot get food on credit.
	Milford	1350		
	Mitchelstown	500	1000	More than 100 families on the very verge of starvation.

TABLE OF DISTRESS—MUNSTER.

Counties	Districts	No. of Persons in Distress, First Local Estimate.	Latest Returns of Number in Distress, March 1st.	Extracts from Appeals of Local Committees, duly authenticated.
CORK	Mallow	2500	Likely to increase	Enable us to avert from hundreds, during the coming months, the awful sufferings of hunger and cold.
	Macroom	485	1163	There is a great number of families laid up in fever, which is a cause of great distress.
	Millstreet		1000	
	Ovens		560	
	Roscarberry	1500	1500	It is calculated to drive me into sickness the tales of woe coming into my kitchen.
	Skibbereen Convent	200	1325	The poor people are all coming to us, starvation depicted in their looks, and the bitterest tales of woe. We are hearing hourly enough to soften the hardest hearts.
	Skibbereen	4000	1325	Miserable, overcrowded hovels, where want of proper food—especially now—and bad air, and tattered, scanty, antiquated clothing, all tend to the production of fevers of a low type.
	Shandrum	500	1086	Without employment; without food; without credit.
	Schull	5000	Likely to increase considerably	There is no work carried on in the district; the poor have not a shilling to earn.
	Tullilease	200		
	Timoleague	720	290	The children will not go to school, being hungry and almost naked. The old and infirm are in dire distress, and would rather starve than enter the workhouse.
	Tullagh and Islands of Cape Clear and Sherkin		856	
	Youghal		1724	In addition to the immediate want of food, the poor farmers require to be supplied with seed—both potato and corn—in order to be in a position to plant their ground. If this want is not supplied, the land must go untilled, and the consequence will be another famine next year, as, I well remember, the same thing occurred in 1847.

COUNTIES	DISTRICTS	No. of Persons in Distress, First Local Estimate.	Latest Returns of Number in Distress, March 1st.	Extracts from Appeals of Local Committees, duly authenticated.
KERRY	Annascaul	1500	2120	The distress existing here at present is so intense and widespread that almost innumerable people must necessarily perish of hunger, unless we can procure them some very substantial aid.
	Ardfert	1825	2148	
	Ballyhorgan	260	560	This locality is in dire distress at this moment.
	Ballylongford	600	1617	During the past week we have relieved 1,393 souls, all in dire distress.
	Brosna	6000	2000	On yesterday I forwarded to the Registrar-General, according to order, the particulars of a case of unequivocal starvation, in which death ensued. There is no food, no fuel, no clothing.
	Beaufort	1400	1230	Many of them are in extreme want, and would almost rather die of starvation than abandon those little cabins in which they first saw the light, and felt once happy and contented.
	Bonane	500	Most likely to increase	Not one resident gentleman—not even one wealthy man—in the parish.
	Ballyduff and Causeway	1880	1923	Some of our people are long since depending on turnips and salt for their only sustenance, while others have eaten their seed potatoes, or sold them to keep away the bailiff.
	Ballymacelligot	2000	1800	From the 15th of October to the 12th of January no employment whatever was given to them, and the natural consequence was, that they were obliged to pawn and sell everything they possessed to ward off the pangs of hunger; and at this moment scarcely an article of wearing apparel or of bed-clothing is to be found in their homes.
	Ballybunion	3500	2028	Labourers and cottiers; want of work and failure of crops.
	Ballyheigue	500	1440	Farmers and labourers in great distress; want of food and clothing, also of seed.

TABLE OF DISTRESS—MUNSTER.

Counties	Districts	No. of Persons in Distress, First Local Estimate.	Latest Returns of Number in Distress, March 1st.	Extracts from Appeals of Local Committees, duly authenticated.
KERRY	Castlegregory	1600	2172	All entirely depending on charity, a good many families eating their seed potatoes, and will, of necessity, be soon appealing for relief, so that in a few weeks Four Hundred families will be without bread or work.
	Currins	800	1099	Small farmers and labourers; failure of crops; no work.
	Castlemaine	2000	1893	Present destitution to be attributed to poor and dear holdings, little employment, and failure of crops.
	Caherdaniel	1500	1090	Small farmers and labourers; failure of potato crop; low price of butter; total absence of demand for store cattle; also bad fishing season.
	Castleisland	2500	2470	Investigations into the condition of these people have revealed that hundreds are enduring terrible privations for want of bedding and clothing. The wretched rags worn during the day are the only covering they have for night, and the children are either obliged to remain away from the schools, for want of clothing, or go half-naked when they are attracted by the prospect of getting some food.
	Caherciveen	10,000	Not likely	Small farmers and labourers; succession of bad harvests; low price of cattle and butter (the staple support of the people); failure of potato crop; stoppage of all credit; want of employment, and failure of fisheries.
	Duagh		550	
	Dingle		336	The larger number are farmers, labourers, fishermen and poor widows and others, contriving to keep house.
	Dromod		1120	Distress general, owing to failure of crops; depression in price of cattle, butter, pigs, &c. No other parish in Ireland contains so much barren and waste land. The smaller farmers have consumed their seed potatoes, and are now in danger of starving, when they should be sowing their crops.

COUNTIES	DISTRICTS	No. of Persons in Distress, First Local Estimate.	Latest Returns of Number in Distress, March 1st.	Extracts from Appeals of Local Committees, duly authenticated.
KERRY	Ferriter Dingle	2000	2769	The word "distress" very inadequately describes the situation and suffering of many and many a family here. They are suffering from that most brutalizing of feelings to which humanity is subject—the gnawing of hunger. Fancy fathers and mothers going to bed supperless, that their children may have something left to stay the pangs of hunger; and, after all this self-sacrifice, these children without any food for 24 hours.
	Firies and Ballyhar	250	2000	Small farmers; their destitution is to be attributed in a great measure to too high rents and bad harvests; the labourers cannot obtain employment from farmers.
	Glenbeigh, Rosbeigh	2000	1813	The majority small farmers; failure of crops; no credit; no reduction in rents, and no employment for labourers.
	Imilaghmore	1500		Small farmers and fishermen; failure of crops, low prices of butter, and failure of fisheries.
	Kilgarvan	1000	421	No employment; no local aid; no resident landlord in the whole district; no credit to be got; the very seed has been eaten.
	Kilgobbin	300	422	General distress; not only requires present assistance, but seed to sow.
	Kenmare		3936	Small farmers, artisans, and labourers, whose destitution is owing to the failure of the potato crop and depreciation in value of cattle.
	Kilcumin	750	1098	Small farmers, labourers and servants; destitution, owing to failure of crops and want of employment.
	Kilorglynn	5000	4000	Distress general and severe; farmers and labourers; failure of crops, and almost no assistance from landlords.
	Killeentierna Kilflyn	359	1099 386	Chiefly labourers, suffering from bad harvests and want of employment; must starve if not relieved by Committee.
	Killagha and Barraduff		1060	Tradesmen and labourers; in want of food, clothing, and seed potatoes.

TABLE OF DISTRESS—MUNSTER.

COUNTIES	DISTRICTS	No. of Persons in Distress, First Local Estimate.	Latest Returns of Number in Distress, March 1st.	Extracts from Appeals of Local Committees, duly authenticated.
KERRY	Listowel	750	1006	
	Milltown	3000	1975	Distress general and severe; 300 girls attended the Nuns' School; many of them receive breakfast; no employment for labourers, and usual depression.
	Newtown-Sands		1300	These people in dire distress for want of food and clothing; out of 800 children who were attending school, one half are now unable to attend, owing to their want of clothing.
	O'Dorney and Killahan	800		
	Portmagee	590	830	Many are partly farmers and fishermen; and a great number are depending solely on fishing for support. Total failure of potatoes and small take of fish. No credit.
	Rathmore	2500	Increasing	Cottier labourers on Earl of Kenmare's estate. Total loss of potato crop, on which they staked their all.
	Sneem	2000	1626	Condition that of labourers. The barrenness of the soil in this district, all of which is either moorland, bog, or mountain. The pernicious system of rack-renting, and failure of crops.
	Spa		800	
	Tuosist	800	Likely to increase	Small farmers and labourers; their destitution is easily accounted for by the failure of the potato crop, want of employment, and the lack of fish in the harbour.
	Templenoe & Tahilla	500	Increasing	Very small farmers, holding under middlemen, whose leases have lately expired; fishermen have had a very bad season this last year; and a floating population of old women, who earned a livelihood by spinning, living with their relatives, who are now compelled to turn them out in consequence of their own necessities.
	Tralee	3000	Not likely	Chiefly the labouring classes (many artisans), out of employment; distress general and severe.

APPENDIX IX.

Counties	Districts	No. of Persons in Distress. First Local Estimate.	Latest Returns of Number in Distress, March 1st.	Extracts from Appeals of Local Committees, duly authenticated.
KERRY	Tarbet	3000	2008	Cottiers and farm-labourers; the almost total failure of potato crop and successive bad harvests; widespread distress and actual starvation exists in this locality.
	Valentia	1200	836	Distress increasing in intensity. No work, no credit, no suitable clothing for themselves or children, and are consuming their seed potatoes.
LIMERICK	Askeaton	1250	874	Small farmers and labourers; failure of crops; loss of cattle; scarcity of fuel, with want of employment.
	Abbeyfeale	3000	1300	Small farmers and labourers; failure of crops and no employment.
	Ardnacrusha	160		
	Athea	500	1427	
	Ballynecty	400		
	Bruff	800	500	Largely of labouring class, for whom there is at present no employment in this neighbourhood; failure of potatoes and badness of harvest generally.
	Cappamore	1110	1149	Wetness of last year caused turf-making, which was chief employment, to be abandoned; farmers too poor to give employment; little agriculture, district not suitable.
	Castleconnell		391	
	ChapelRussell		345	
	Caherconlish	200	407	Labourers chiefly, and a few tradespeople; distress caused by want of employment.
	Clonlara	200	170	Small farmers and labourers; the previous bad season and want of employment.
	Drumcollagher and Broadford	700	982	Labourers, with some tradesmen and a few small landholders; bad harvests and no employment.
	Effin	900		
	Feenagh and Kilmeedy	500		
	Fidamore	1000	300	Want of employment for labourers and loss of crops last harvest.
	Glin	150	1347	Agricultural labourers, artisans. The destitution may be attributed to want of employment, stagnation of business, failure of crops, and low prices.

TABLE OF DISTRESS—MUNSTER.

Counties	Districts	No. of Persons in Distress, First Local Estimate.	Latest Returns of Number in Distress, March 1st.	Extracts from Appeals of Local Committees, duly authenticated.
LIMERICK	Islandmore	50	Not likely	Labourers in want of employment.
	Kilmallock	400	400	Labourers; destitution caused by successive bad harvests and the consequent inability of the farmers to give employment.
	Kilcolman		529	
	Kileedy	300	550	Small farmers and labourers; almost total failure of all crops this year; with little or no employment.
	Knocklong & Glenbrohane	500	366	
	Knockaderry & Clowncogh		350	
	Loughill and Ballyhahill	128	830	Most of these people incapable of work; those who are able cannot procure employment.
	Mahoonagh & Fohenagh		251	
	Newcastle-West		400	
	Pallasgreen	500	Increasing	Destitution owing to loss of potato crop and the inability of farmers to give work or charity.
	Rathkeale	400	297	Labourers and poor tradesmen with large families, and a general want of employment.
	Tournafulla	950	1052	Small farmers and labourers; bad harvests for past three years; total failure of potato crop last year, and want of employment for labourers.
TIPPERARY	Annacarty	100	452	Labourers and a few small farmers, shoemakers and tailors. Depression of times, failure of crops and want of employment.
	Ardfinan	300		
	Ballinahinch & Killocully	1000	Not likely to increase	
	Ballyporeen		1497	
	Borrisoleigh and Ibeigh	1500		
	Cappawhite	200	890	A large number of labourers waited on the P.P. the day before for employment.
	Castletown-Arra	200	398	One poor woman he attended on her dying bed avowed to him that she was dying from cold caught in endeavouring to obtain a few turnips, which had been left behind by a farmer, for her starving family.

APPENDIX IX.

COUNTIES	DISTRICTS	No. of Persons in Distress, First Local Estimate.	Latest Returns of Number in Distress, March 1st.	Extracts from Appeals of Local Committees, duly authenticated.
TIPPERARY	Cloughjordan	250	480	
	Clogheen	350	550	The distress is still very great; farmers holding 20 or 30 acres of mountain land, under cover of night, came down to our chairman, applying for an order for Indian meal, to keep their children from starving.
	Dundrum	200	Likely to increase	Labourers; want of work for the past two or three months.
	Hollyford	300	400	Labourers chiefly with large families, and poor cottiers; failure of potatoes and no work.
	Holycross & Ballycahill		364	
	Killavinage	250	197	Small farmers and labourers; present distress is owing to the failure of the potato crop, the wet summer, and refusal of shopkeepers to give credit.
	Kilcommon		400	Agricultural labourers; wet seasons, failure of potato crop and want of employment.
	Lisinane	600		
	Lorrha	395	300	Small farmers and labourers; failure of crops, and want of employment.
	Loughmore & Castlerany	350		
	Nenagh	2945	Likely to increase	Labourers and tradesmen; suffering from depression of the times, failure of crops, and want of employment.
	Newbirmingham	200		
	Silvermines	1000	650	Small farmers and labourers. Their destitution is owing to rack-rents, closing of mineworks and failure of potato crop.
	Templederry	800	1000	Principally labourers and their families. The destitution is caused by failure of potato crop and want of employment, urging the necessity to supply seed to the labourers, who cannot otherwise get any.
	Templemore & Killia	1500	788	
	Templetnohy and Moyne	150	350	
	Tubrid	400	420	
	Toomavara		470	Tradesmen and labourers in need of employment. There are many aged and infirm much in need.

TABLE OF DISTRESS—MUNSTER.

Counties	Districts	No. of Persons in Distress, First Local Estimate.	Latest Returns of Number in Distress, March 1st.	Extracts from Appeals of Local Committees, duly authenticated.
TIPPERARY	Two-mile-Borris	700	500	Labourers and cottier tenants whose destitution is attributed to want of ordinary employment, failure of crops, and scarcity of turf, on which many of our cottier tenants depend.
WATERFORD	Ardmore	600	800	Some of these were tolerably independent, but are now suffering—principally from failure of potato crop and want of employment.
	Ballylaneen & Graigshoneen	40		
	Clashmore & Kinsalebeg		760	
	Cappoquin	600		
	Dungarvan	2600	1600	Great majority labourers; some tradesmen. Chief cause of distress, inability of farmers and traders to give employment.
	Kilrossanty and Fews	600	640	Principally labourers, who are now unable to obtain employment from farmers, who are themselves suffering from general depression.
	Kill, Knockmahon and Bonmahon	500	808	Farm labourers and miners. Destitution owing principally to the closing of Knockmahon Mines and general depression.
	Passage East	80		
	Portlaw	400	360	
	Rossmyre	470		
	Stradbally	350	Not likely to increase	
	Tallow	800		Mechanics and labourers. Destitution attributable to general depression and want of employment.
	Tramore	900	871	Small farmers, fishermen, mechanics and labourers; suffering from general depression.

PROVINCE OF LEINSTER.

Counties	Districts	No. of Persons in Distress, First Local Estimate.	Latest Returns of Number in Distress, March 1st.	Extracts from Appeals of Local Committees, duly authenticated.
DUBLIN	Glencullen	250	250	
KILDARE	Fontstown	60	161	Small farmers; loss of crops.
	Kilmeague	500	653	Small farmers; loss of crops.
	Kildare	100	Not likely to increase	The poor people cling to their cabins, fearful that if they give them up, others will take them, and that when they are enabled (if ever) to leave the Union, they will find themselves tramps, and be looked upon as degraded.
KILKENNY	Robertstown district		653	
	Galmoy	500	224	From the poverty of the district we have been unable to make up any money for the relief of the poor, and all our landlords are non-resident.
	Mullinavat		400	
	Urlingford	460	526	No public efforts have been made owing to the depressed state of the farmers and traders, and the scarcity of gentry living in the district.
	Johnstown	272	329	Labourers principally; failure of crops.
	Kilkenny	1500		Tradesmen and labourers; want of work.
KING'S Co.	Clonsast and Clonbollogue		300	
	Kinnetty		300	
	Shinrone		375	
	Tullamore	70	Not likely to increase	
LONGFORD	Abbeylara	700		No resident landlords.
	Bonlahy	400		
	Clonbroney	500		
	Columbkill	600	1064	
	Drumlummon and Knockduff	1250	658	
	Drumlish	1000	1750	Up to the present, landowners have not given us any money for the destitute on their estates.
	Edgeworthstown		300	
	Granard	450	1400	
	Killashee	1000	524	
	Killoe		1440	
	Lanesboro'		500	
	Newtown-Cashel	600	321	Employment expected, but has not been given, 150 families living not on their seed potatoes (for they are all consumed), but on their rotten potatoes

TABLE OF DISTRESS—LEINSTER.

COUNTIES	DISTRICTS	No. of Persons in Distress, First Local Estimate.	Latest Returns of Number in Distress, March 1st.	Extracts from Appeals of Local Committees, duly authenticated.
LOUTH	Inniskeen	1300	Certain to increase	Small farmers and labourers; extreme destitution; want of fuel; no employment.
	Faughart	500	Likely to increase	Small farmers and labourers. Destitution owing to want of employment for labourers, and total failure of potato crop, and great deficiency in all other crops.
	Carlingford	1250	Will increase	Small farmers, agricultural labourers, fishermen, failure of potato crop, and two last bad fishing seasons.
MEATH	Oldcastle	800	750	
	Kilbride and Killeagh	1300	800	Our people are in great distress.
QUEEN'S Co.	Ballickmoyler	750	Likely to increase	No public or other subscriptions have been made.
	Bor.-in-Ossory		400	
	Clonaslee	550	424	
	Durrow		400	
	Killesheir		500	
	Mountmellick		1000	
	Rathdowney & Rathsaran		1000	
	Rosenallis	480	269	Relief given by private individuals.
WESTMEATH	Athlone (St Peter's and Drum)	800	Likely to increase	The applications received this day reveal an amount of destitution greater than was anticipated.
	St. Mary's		935	
	Ballinacargy		200	
	Castlepollard	350		
	Collinstown	250	Likely to increase	I can assure you, from sad experience, that fearful distress prevails here amongst the labourers and very small farmers.
	Drumraney		400	
	Glasson		300	
	Moate	758		
	Mayne	160	140	
	Mullingar	200	1200	The labouring class and small farmers are in great distress, owing to the want of agriculture in the district.
WEXFORD	Rathowen	300	254	Deep and widespread distress prevails in the district.
	Gorey	800		Every local means has been taxed, and has been found inadequate to relieve the present distressed state of these poor people.
WICKLOW	Monomolin		70	
	Arklow	2600	2850	The continued bad weather and the dangerous state of our harbour, are keeping our poor fishermen idle.
CARLOW	Ovoca	150	600	
	Carlow	2000	Likely to increase	

APPENDIX IX.

PROVINCE OF CONNAUGHT.

Counties	Districts	No. of Persons in Distress, First Local Estimate.	Latest Returns of Number in Distress, March, 1st.	Extracts from Appeals of Local Committees, duly authenticated.
GALWAY	Abbeygormican and Killoran		677	
	Abbeyknockmoy	2000	2756	Nearly starving. Landlords principally absentees. No employment. Some have died of fever caused by starvation.
	Aughrim	750	259	Very poor; no hope save in assistance from Committee.
	Ardrahan	1000	1000	Intensity of distress likely to increase; bad harvests and want of employment.
	Ahascragh		852	
	Athenry		1480	
	Arran Islands	1600	2000	Total loss of crops and failure of fisheries, causing intense and widespread destitution.
	Annaghdown	800	1039	Potato blight cause of destitution.
	Boffin & Shark	1000	1255	Failure of fisheries and potato crop; distress intense and widespread.
	Ballymoe	500	955	Very poor tenant-farmers and labourers; failure of crops; no employment.
	Ballinasloe	1200	1197	Depending almost entirely on external aid.
	Ballinderreen	1000	876	Pressing for larger grants on account of the terrible destitution.
	Behagh	1000	935	People very poor. Failure of crops and low price of cattle, cause of distress.
	Belclare		864	
	Convent of Mercy, Gort	350	Not likely	Tradesmen and their families —no employment. Not relieved by other Committees.
	Convent of Mercy, Galway	500 children		These children are depending on the Nuns for daily food.
	Clifden (rural parish)	2000	Will be greatly increased	Principally depending on work in Scotland and fisheries; both sources unproductive last year.
	Clifden (town district)	6000	6230	With very few exceptions, the entire population is reduced to the same level of poverty, caused by bad harvests, the insecurity of tenure, and utter collapse of credit.
	Carabane		1200	
	Clarenbridge	755	849	Hope that public works will commence soon; if so, half this number will be relieved.
	Caltra		750	
	Cappard	40		
	Carna	3500	4720	Many hundreds must have died of starvation but for the aid of the Mansion House Committee.

TABLE OF DISTRESS—CONNAUGHT.

Counties	Districts	No. of Persons in Distress, First Local Estimate.	Latest Returns of Number in Distress, March 1st.	Extracts from Appeals of Local Committees, duly authenticated.
GALWAY	Cashel	1750		Hunger, distress, and disease actually exist here.
	Craughwell	300	300	Potatoes run out; no credit in bank or shop; every day reveals a new horror in the catalogue of suffering.
	Cummer	1000	1152	Will have to live for the next five months on Indian meal.
	Caherlistrane	2000	566	Distress growing intensely. Small tenants of poor and unproductive soil.
	Clonbur	3500	4200	Dependent on the produce of lands lying entirely among high mountains. Their present distress is owing to failure of crops and depression in the price of stock.
	Cloughoola & Derrybrien	1800	1000	Mountainous district; terrible distress; urging for further grant.
	Claddagh	1500	1155	Poor people in very wretched condition; failure of fisheries, and want of employment.
	Castlegar	2000	1709	In direst distress and want of food. Hundreds surrounding house of P.P., piteously asking for assistance.
	Claregalway	750	1422	Absolute destitution, unless immediately relieved; appalling consequences may be anticipated.
	Clifden Convent	320 children 20 families in which there is sickness & 30 families of respectable reduced people		These children are fed and clothed, and the sick and other families are in great distress, and entirely depending on charity.
	Clonberne	2000	1018	In deep distress; no seed for corn or potatoes.
	Crusheen and Melick		1300	
	Dunmore	6000	3093	In terrible destitution, amounting to actual starvation.
	Dysart and Taughboy	500	1450	In very great distress; half naked, with little or no bed covering; children in rags.
	Donery	1000	1080	In frightful distress, bordering on starvation.
	Errismore	300	4000	Small farmers and fishermen; failure of crop and kelp making.
	Eyrecourt and Fahy	150	200	
	Fohenagh and Killure	400		

Counties	Districts	No. of Persons in Distress, First Local Estimate.	Latest Returns of Number in Distress, March 1st.	Extracts from Appeals of Local Committees, duly authenticated.
GALWAY	Glenamaddy	3000	1700	Poor soil; total failure of crops; no employment in England nor at home.
	Glinsk	1500	1675	Small farmers, paying exorbitant rents; failure of crops, and people now only saved from starvation by assistance from Committee.
	Garbally	300	Will daily increase	Actually starving, and double the number will be in the same condition in a very short time.
	Gort	1150	Increasing	Sufferings of the people intense; small farmers, tradesmen, and labourers; failure of crops; no employment; some actually starving.
	Headford	1750	1638	Widespread distress; depending on the charity of the Committee.
	Invern		460	
	Kilkerrin	4000	1146	General and extreme destitution, bordering on starvation. Only a few landlords in the district, and their sympathy with the suffering poor is not of a very high order. The good land is in the ownership of graziers, the people living on the worst and most unfruitful parts.
	Kilmadeena & Killesteskil		750	
	Kilconnell		350	
	Kiltormer & Laurencetown		600	
	Kilthomas	35		
	Kilbeaconty	350	356	Twenty additional families, at least, will require assistance, owing to the general failure of the potato crop.
	Kilchreest	1375	1400	Struggling farmers; failure of potatoes and rot in sheep; external aid urgently required.
	Killyon and Killeroran	1500	3359	The people are living in a state of slow starvation; nearly naked; no bed clothes, or of the most squalid description.
	Killererin		1499	
	Kilmacduagh & Kiltarton	870	1432	Very many of them actually starving, and destitution daily increasing.
	Kiltullagh	100	Increasing	The small farmers are running out of their stock of provisions, and will soon be asking for relief, together with many aged and infirm now being relieved.

TABLE OF DISTRESS—CONNAUGHT. 287

Counties	Districts	No. of Persons in Distress, First Local Estimate.	Latest Returns of Number in Distress, March 1st.	Extracts from Appeals of Local Committees, duly authenticated.
GALWAY	Killalaghton and Kilreecle	400	1410	Small farmers and labourers suffering from loss of potato crop.
	Kilconla and Kilbannon	582	1770	Would prefer work to charity; assisting none but those in absolute want.
	Killimore	300	381	The worst has yet to come; no food, no employment, no credit.
	Killannin	1200	Sure to increase	Wretchedly poor; small holdings and exorbitant rents: compelled, from want of funds, to refuse relief to many who require it.
	Killeen	2500	1122	
	Kinvara	1500	2275	In absolute want of food and clothing; total failure of crops.
	Killeseobe & Menlough	1990	1209	Famine is now upon the land; great distress on a property, one of the richest in the parish, where the owner is neither giving work nor relief.
	Lacka	400		
	Letterfrack	1750	3540	
	Loughrea	1320	1197	Extreme distress; no resources; depending on Mansion House Committee.
	Leenane	560	1227	Small tenants, on bog farms, suffering from bad harvests.
	Leitrim, Kilmeen and Kilcooley	500	429	Struggling, industrious people; present destitution owing to failure of crops and want of employment.
	Lettermullen & Carraroe		1750	
	Miltown	1500	1982	Almost eaten the last seed potato. How shall they exist for the next six months? Where shall they get seed? Many of these poor people would not mention their distress till actual famine was upon them.
	Moore	1000	700	People are now commencing their Spring work, and require assistance to be kept at it; if not, crops will be neglected.
	Moycullen	500	2303	These people on the brink of starvation urgently requiring public work.
	Mountbellew Union			The Board of Guardians unanimously passed the following resolution: "We have many estates with non-resident proprietors. Some unable, and some not satisfied, to take advantage of the loans offered, and we have heard from many of the clergy, who know well the distress that exists in parts of this Union, that some who have land and cannot receive out-door relief, are in urgent need of help."

Counties	Districts	No. of Persons in Distress, First Local Estimate.	Latest Returns of Number in Distress, March 1st.	Ex... Con...
GALWAY	Moylough	750	1200	Labou... dist... men
	Mountbellew		950	Labo... fail... emp
	New Inn	350		
	Oughterard	1750	1925	In e... high... one... bad... men
	Oranmore	1250	1715	In t... fam... on,... of c... are
	Omey	598		
	Portumna	150	600	Suffe... and
	Peterswell	810	875	Peop... clin... suff... sma... fail
	Rosmuck	1980	410	Most... and... tres... and
	Rahoon	2000	640	We ... hav... dre... to s
	Roundstone	1500	1500	Stru... fail... cro
	Recess	500	1000	Terri... fro... plac... vill... and
	Spiddal (Galway)	750	1800	Tena... des... to c
	Spiddal (Tuam)	3000	4800	Urge... tan... me
	St. Patrick's Brothers (Galway)	200	207	Chil... ing... me
	St. Nicholas East, Galway		2000	
	Tuam	2000	700	Most... on... pat... No... toe
	Tynagh	400		
	Whitegate	600	800	Seed... ent... fro

TABLE OF DISTRESS—CONNAUGHT.

Counties	Districts	No. of Persons in Distress, First Local Estimate.	Latest Returns of Number in Distress, March 1st.	Extracts from Appeals of Local Committees, duly authenticated.
GALWAY	Woodford	670	823	Poor mountain land; distress severe; loss of crops.
	Williamstown	500	2610	Distress extreme, people will die of hunger unless relieved or employed.
MAYO	Achill	3000	4860	Without work, money, credit, or food; in fact starving.
	Addergoole	3000	3478	
	Ardagh	715	1077	
	Attymass	354	1073	
	Aughagower	750	4117	
	Aughamore	3000	1800	People actually starving; bad harvest, and no employment.
	Aasleagh	39	54	
	Backs	3000	1498	Three-fourths of them will be unable to ward off famine till next harvest.
	Ballintubber	2480	3168	All small farmers. Total failure of potatoes.
	Ballinrobe	2500	3000	Urgently seeking for aid from Committee, upon whose grant they are mainly depending.
	Ballindine	1200	2250	Without food, and, in many cases, without clothing; entirely depending on charity. This is not exaggeration, but fact.
	Ballyglass	360		
	Ballina	3400		
	Ballisokerry	2500	1265	Distress pressing very severely; weekly aid required.
	Ballycastle	1000	1212	
	Ballyhaunis	1000	11550	Small farmers. Total failure of crops.
	Ballycroy		782	
	Ballaghadereen	6250	3775	
	Bangor	2000	Increasing	Threatened with immediate starvation.
	Bekan	3000	2789	Fifty families in a state of starvation, the others almost as bad.
	Belmullet	240	1302	
	Bohola	2500	2685	Eating seed potatoes; pawning every available article.
	Bonnaconlan	1500	1895	
	Carracastle	4270	4562	These people, existing on one meal of Indian meal per day, provided by charity.
	Castlebar	2000	5000	
	Charlestown	5000	4136	Unless generous assistance forthcoming, the scenes of '47 will be repeated.
	Claremorris	1000	3560	Distress widespread and severe. The poor entirely depending on charity.
	Croaghpatrick	1500	1180	The poor are not only distressed for food, but for clothing also.

X

APPENDIX IX.

Counties	Districts	No. of Persons in Distress, First Local Estimate	Latest Returns of Number in Distress, March 1st.	Extracts from Appeals of Local Committees, duly authenticated.
MAYO	Crossmolina	1000	1366	Pressing for weekly grant, as the labourers and small farmers must be aided till crops are sown.
	Crossboyne & Taugheen	2000	1690	In extreme want; small cottiers and labourers in want of employment.
	Cong	1600	1850	
	Clare Island		800	
	Drum and Manulla	800	1475	
	Drummin		400	
	Foxford	3500	Increase likely	Entirely depending on Mansion House Committee; terrible destitution.
	Glenisland	1200	738	Urgently appealing for means to purchase meal.
	Islandeady	674	2008	Failure of potato crop; people in absolute destitution.
	Kilfian	1439	1005	
	Kilmaine	1000	1509	
	Kilmore Erris	4250	942	Before March will be depending on public charity.
	Knock	2000	2500	Terrible destitution; people half-starved.
	Keelogues	500	2250	Small farmers; destitution principally caused by rack rents and loss of crops.
	Killala	750	1250	
	Kilmeena and Kilmaclasson	2000	3377	Failure of crops, high rents, and want of employment.
	Kilcommon Erris	3500	1945	Distress extreme. Fever is rapidly spreading.
	Killaser	3000	3330	Failure of crops caused general and deep distress.
	Kilmovee		3720	
	Kiltymagh	2500	Increasing every day	Unless permanent relief be established, starvation will be general.
	Kilgeever	3000	2850	
	Moygounagh	1000	590	People very poor. Failure of potato crop cause of great distress.
	Mayo Abbey	800	1416	Very great poverty. People suffering from hunger.
	Mount Party	2500	1535	
	Mulrany		750	
	Newport	1500	2040	Distress will continue till after June.
	Portnahalah	500	Increasing	In absolute destitution. Threatened with death from hunger and cold.
	Rathlackan		600	
	Robeen and Kilcommon	1600	1600	
	Shrule	700	729	
	Swineford	3000	3000	Destitution owing to failure of crops and want of usual earnings in England.

Counties	Districts	No. of Persons in Distress, First Local Estimate	Latest Returns of Number in Distress, March 1st.	Extracts from Appeals of Local Committees, duly authenticated.
MAYO	Strade	2800	2800	Struggling poor people, now destitute owing to failure of potato crop.
	The Neale		975	
	Turlough	500	2843	
	Westport	8400	2910	Urgently requiring assistance; most of them in sad distress, requesting grant to supply Indian meal.
LEITRIM	Aughavass	1000	1654	Relief required to keep them from actual starvation.
	Ballinamore	571	2860	Funds exhausted; urgent requests for further assistance.
	Ballinaglera	2000		
	Cloone	1500	2202	Some families actually starving. Even should works be started, people too weak now to work.
	Carrigallen	350	1200	Privation widespread and appalling; no resident gentlemen; all small and poor farmers.
	Carrick-on-Shannon	3500	3240	Great distress. Require at least £100 per week to keep the people in Indian meal.
	Drumreilly Upper		1530	
	Drumsna	1000	Will increase considerably	Complete destruction of potato and turf crops; general distress.
	Drumreilly Lower	750	1185	These families on the verge of starvation.
	Dromahair	1000	2310	Extreme and urgent distress.
	Drumshambo	1332	1877	Widespread destitution; dire distress.
	Drumkeerin	600	12,920	Pauper farmers; provident and industrious; want food and fuel.
	Feenagh	1800	1458	Distress urgent and beyond description.
	Gortletteragh	1500	772	Lost their crops by floods; general distress.
	Kinlough	2466	2473	Number of distressed frightfully increased; suffering general, and will continue.
	Kilargue	2500		
	Kilmore and Aughrim	2500	1241	
	Kilturbride	1700	1161	Small farmers; suffering severely.
	Lurganboy		613	
	Mohill	1250	1968	These families are in a starving state.
	Manorhamilton	4000	1400	Distress so widespread that all are not receiving relief.
	Newtowngore and Lower Carrigallen	500	707	Mostly of the peasant class, and very poor.
ROSCOMMON	Ardcarne and Tumna	2490	2647	In a state of starvation.

APPENDIX IX.

Counties	Districts	No. of Persons in Distress, First Local Estimate.	Latest Returns of Number in Distress, March 1st.	Extracts from Appeals of Local Committees, duly authenticated.
ROSCOMMON	Athleague	500	511	No employment, no food, no means, no credit, being already deeply in debt; are presently in a very destitute state, and cannot possibly procure food for their families, or seed to put in the ground, without external aid.
	Ballinasloe (Roscommon)	1600	Will greatly increase	Had to refuse relief to 460 persons for want of funds.
	Ballingare & Frenchpark	1550	1177	Want of work; extreme suffering.
	Ballintubber	1500	1831	Very poor; in many cases destitute.
	Boyle	3000	2676	Destitution attributed to bad harvest and inability of shopkeepers to give credit.
	Ballymacurley		200	
	Croghan	600	540	Destitution caused by loss of crops and want of employment.
	Castlerea	1200	1920	If not supported during the next month (the time for coming tillage), they will be driven to leave in search of employment elsewhere, and thus their own land will be neglected, causing famine next winter.
	Derrane and Kilgefin	1000	1481	Labourers and small farmers. Distress caused by failure of crops and depreciation in value of cattle.
	Elphin	1800	2528	People extremely poor, and sorely pressed.
	Fuerty	400	1068	Cottiers and small farmers living on hill sides and brink of bogs: living for some time past on turnips or meal.
	Four-Mile-House	1000	Will increase	Extreme suffering; near starvation.
	Kilbegnet	1500	Certain to increase	Destitution general; many suffering from hunger.
	Kiltoom and Cam	300	1158	Severe suffering. The P.P. writes of a man dying from want.
	Kendue	1050	1218	The P.P. states that the small farmers are so poor that some of them could not afford a candle to light their Christmas dinner of Indian meal.
	Kilmore and Aughrim	2500	1241	
	Kilnamanagh and Eastersnow	1250	1843	
	Kiltullagh & Ballinlough	1000	2997	Destitution must increase; seed potatoes and oats are being consumed by the people; their clothes and bedding pawned.

TABLE OF DISTRESS—CONNAUGHT.

Counties	Districts	No. of Persons in Distress, First Local Estimate.	Latest Returns of Number in Distress, March 1st.	Extracts from Appeals of Local Committees, duly authenticated.
ROSCOMMON	Kilglass	3500		
	Lecarrow	2000	1960	Entirely depending on charity; in a desperate state.
	Loughlyn (Castlerea)	3000	2514	If not assisted, cannot escape starvation.
	Roscommon & Kelteevan	2000	1850	Threatened with starvation, unless assisted generously.
	Strokestown	1990	1329	People clamouring for relief; distress intense and spreading.
	Tybohine	1500	3084	If they do not get aid, several will starve.
	Taughmaconnell	1500	1200	The famine-stricken appearance of these poor people would make the stoutest heart feel for them.
	Tulsk	700		
	Tarmonbarry	1000	1320	
	Tissara	500	900	Distress likely to last till next August; even should baronial works be commenced, the people will not get wages sufficient to support them; they must still look for outside help.
SLIGO	Achonry	1300	1411	Oats failed; potatoes not worth digging; distress alarming.
	Ahamlish	1500	3000	
	Bunanadden	1250	6500	In extreme poverty, urgently asking for sympathy and relief.
	Ballinafad		2000	
	Ballymote	2300	2080	Pressing for relief, both in food and clothing.
	Baneda (Tubbercurry)	3000	Likely to increase	Small farmers suffering from bad harvests and general depression.
	Ballintogher	604	1458	Failure of potato crop cause of distress.
	Clogher (Ballaghaderrin)	150	Will increase	
	Collooney	2000	2075	Funds exhausted; great destitution.
	Calry and Coolera	2500	1500	The poor persons put on half allowance of food.
	Clonloo		1000	
	Castleconnor		1065	
	Curry		2000	
	Drumcliff	2000	1628	Fishermen, small farmers, labourers; loss of crops and failure of fishery.
	Dromore West	2475	1106	Present starvation only averted by the assistance of Mansion House Committee.
	Easkey		3720	
	Grange		2400	
	Gurteen	1000	2400	Funds low. People entirely depending on external assistance.

Counties	Districts	No. of Persons in Distress, First Local Estimate.	Latest Returns of Number in Distress, March 1st.	Extracts from Appeals of Local Committees, duly authenticated.
SLIGO	Geevagh	2500	1919	Cannot hold out much longer unless assisted.
	Killoran	975	1150	Funds exhausted; people quite destitute.
	Kilmactiege	4000	2700	Small struggling farmers. Crops totally destroyed.
	Keash	1250	1550	Bad seasons, bad crops, low prices, no turf, no employment.
	Kilglass	2000	1321	Entire loss of potato crop; no employment.
	Riverstown	1250	2897	Seed potatoes must be supplied or the land will lie waste.
	Screen	1500	2436	
	Templeboy		1159	
	Tubbercurry		1935	

APPENDIX X.

LIST OF LOCAL COMMITTEES,

SHOWING DATE OF FIRST AND OF FINAL GRANT, NUMBER OF GRANTS MADE, AND TOTAL AMOUNT ALLOCATED, TO EACH COMMITTEE.

PROVINCE OF ULSTER.

County	Local Committee	No. of Grants made	Date of First, and of Final Grant	Total Amount Granted
ANTRIM	Dunseverick	3	13th March to 17th June	£85
	Glens of Antrim	7	7th February to 12th June	180
	Grange and Toome	2	8th April to 1st May	45
ARMAGH	Creggan Upper	4	21st February to 29th April	£85
	Derryall	5	13th March to 24th May	75
	Dromantee and Jonesboro'	6	26th February to 20th May	220
	Forkhill	6	4th March to 13th May	165
	Killeevy Upper	5	26th February to 8th June	170
	Lisndill and Ballymacnab	1	1st April	50
	Midletown	5	18th March to 5th June	125
	Mullaglass and Tullyhappy	1	16th March	10
	Newtownhamilton	5	11th March to 21st May	80
CAVAN	Arva	10	24th February to 26th June	£210
	Ballinagh	13	5th February to 6th July	335
	Belturbet	8	12 February to 19th June	250
	Ballintemple	9	26 February to 1st July	175
	Ballyconnell	6	3rd February to 8th June	100
	Ballymachugh and Drumlummon	7	29 January to 20 May	190
	Bailieboro	8	31st January to 3rd July	160
	Billis	11	24th February to 29th July	235
	Cavan	6	14th February to 8th June	150
	Crosskeys	7	24th February to 21st May	145
	Castlerahan and Mt. Connaught	10	10th February to 22nd July	300
	Curlough	10	5th February to 24th July	285
	Castleterra	9	6th March to 22nd July	160
	Drumlane	10	29th January to 3rd June	295
	Drumgoon	10	21st February to 8th July	225
	Drung	7	4th March to 12th June	110
	Glengevlin	9	3rd February to 31st July	160
	Kilsherdany	5	21st February to 15th July	115
	Killinkere	11	10th February to 10th August	255
	Killina	13	7th February to 15th July	410
	Kilnaleck	16	25th January to 24th July	435

APPENDIX X.

County	Local Committee	No. of Grants made	Date of First, and of Final Grant	Total Amount Granted
CAVAN (Continued)	Killeshandra	6	17th February to 20th May	£145
	Kingscourt	7	10th February to 10th June	230
	Knockbride	7	24th February to 10th June	135
	Larah	9	17th February to 3rd July	225
	Lavey	4	24th February to 6th May	90
	Mullagh	10	5th February to 13th July	320
	Moybologue and Kilmainham Wood	6	21st February to 26th June	115
	Swanlinbar	11	31st February to 22nd July	290
	Scrabby	8	10th February to 13th July	270
	Shercock	7	10th February to 10th June	170
	Templeport	7	5th February to 21st May	165
	Virginia	8	24th February to 13th July	180
DERRY	Cumber	2	26th March to 13th May	£30
	Gulladuff and Rocktown	6	8th April to 17th July	60
DONEGAL	Co. Donegal Central Committee	7	23rd January to 15th June	£14000
	Ballyshannon	1	10th January	50
	Bayview	1	23rd January	20
	Clonmany	1	7th February	100
	Dungloe	1	22nd January	50
	Innishowen Union	1	27th January	100
	Killaghtee	1	25th February	25
	Killybegs	1	25th January	50
	Gweedore	1	14th August	100
DOWN	Drumgooland	2	26th March to 27th April	£35
	Kilcoo Upper	4	2nd March to 1st July	110
FERMANAGH	Ballaghameehan	6	14th February to 19th June	£120
	Blackbog	8	17th February to 10th July	185
	Belcoo	9	19th February to 29th June	255
	Boho	5	2nd March to 15th July	75
	Clonelly	9	16th March to 17th July	215
	Derrylin	12	5th February to 29th July	285
	Derrygonnelly	8	10th February to 17th June	175
	Garrison	8	11th March to 13th July	255
	Lisbellaw	5	26th February to 24th May	160
	Lisnaskea	2	2nd March to 6th April	50
	Maguire's Bridge	7	19th February to 4th May	120
	Muleek	14	3rd February to 22nd July	445
	Newtownbutler	6	20th January to 29th April	110
	Rosslea	5	24th February to 15th May	115
	Rossory and Cradgan	5	4th March to 22nd June	105
	Sallaghy	5	21st February to 27th May	85
	Tempo	10	21st February to 3rd July	235
	Whitehill	7	13th March to 1st July	.170
MONAGHAN	Annyalla	8	4th March to 26th June	£110
	Aghabog	12	10th February to 29th July	220
	Aughamullen West	7	24th February to 3rd June	110
	Castleblayney	5	27th January to 27th April	120
	Clones	7	6th March to 26th June	170
	Currin	7	6th March to 26th June	220
	Carrickmacross	3	13th March to 29th June	100

LOCAL COMMITTEES AND GRANTS—ULSTER.

County	Local Committee	No. of Grants made	Date of First, and of Final Grant	Total Amount Granted
MONAGHAN (Continued)	Drum	1	6th March	£25
	Donaghmoyne	6	2nd March to 6th July	80
	Emyvale	8	21st February to 26th June	200
	Ematris	3	8th April to 1st June	30
	Kilmore and Drumsnat	6	24th February to 17th June	75
	Killeevan	9	17th February to 13th July	180
	Mahercloone	4	6th March to 15th July	110
	Monaghan	2	6th March to 3rd April	80
	Shantonagh	3	6th March to 29th April	90
	Tydavnet	9	24th March to 24th May	205
	Tullycorbet	6	28th February to 20th May	130
	Tyholland	3	4th March to 10th June	50
TYRONE	Aughnacloy	3	4th March to 5th April	£140
	Ballygawley	4	3rd February to 22nd April	140
	Carrickmore	5	26th February to 8th June	95
	Clogher	4	2nd March to 12th June	95
	Coagh and Ardboe	1	11th March	25
	Clonoe	3	18th March to 27th April	85
	Drumquin	3	6th March to 17th April	40
	Dromore	4	19th February to 30th April	135
	Donaheady	3	20th March to 27th April	55
	English and Derrygorterry	3	8th April to 1st June	30
	Fintona	5	25th January to 10th June	140
	Fivemiletown	4	16th March to 26th June	95
	Gortin	5	23rd February to 24th May	75
	Kildress	8	24th February to 10th June	210
	Plumbridge	7	19th February to 15th July	215
	Pomeroy	12	18th February to 3rd June	255
	Rock	4	27th March to 12th June	60
	Sixmilecross	3	22nd April to 20th May	30
	Trillick	9	28th February to 22nd June	225
	Termonamongan	4	20th March to 29th July	60

PROVINCE OF LEINSTER.

County	Local Committee	No. of Grants made	Date of First, and of Final Grant	Total Amount Granted
CARLOW	Clonmore	5	16th March to 27th May	£295
	Hacketstown	1	16th March	25
	Leighlin-bridge	3	18th March to 13th May	50
DUBLIN	Cork-st. Night Refuge	1	24th January	£50
	Glencullen	1	29th January	25
	Jews' Association	1	31st January	25
	Mendicity Institution	1	26th January	50
	Presbyterian Society	1	26th January	50
	Roomkeepers' Society	1	26th January	100
	St. Vincent-de-Paul Society	1	30th January	250
	Society of Distressed Protestants	1	24th January	100
KILDARE	Fontstown	1	31st January	£14
	Kilmeague	4	14th February to 15th April	90
	Kildare	1	17th February	20
	Suncroft	1	18th March	20
KILKENNY	Ballyragget	3	11th March to 26th March	£30
	Freshford	3	9th March to 13th April	45
	Galmoy	3	17th February to 20th April	75
	Graigue	2	9th March to 1st April	70
	Innistiogue	3	13th March to 29th April	50
	Johnstown	6	31st January to 10th June	115
	Kilkenny	1	15th March	50
	Lisdowney	1	11th March	20
	Mullinavat	6	28th February to 11th May	90
	Thomastown	2	13th March to 1st April	45
	Urlingford	4	17th February to 6th April	90
KING'S CO.	Banagher	2	13th March to 13th April	£50
	Clara	2	11th March to 3rd April	30
	Clonmacnoise and Tissarn	1	20th March	25
	Clonsast and Clonbullogue	4	2nd March to 15th June	50
	Ettagh and Kilcolman	2	16th March to 22nd March	50
	Kinnetty	3	28th February to 24th May	45
	Rhode	3	11th March to 6th May	50
	Tullamore	1	3rd February	50
LONGFORD	Abbeylara	4	23rd January to 15th April	£120
	Clonbroney	3	28th February to 26th June	50
	Columbkille	10	14th February to 3rd July	345
	Clongish	6	4th March to 29th June	165
	Dromard	7	11th March to 22nd July	217
	Drumlish	13	29th January to 27th July	370
	Drumlummon and Loughduff	9	25th January to 10th June	265
	Edgeworthstown	4	24th February to 20th April	80
	Granard	6	27th January to 4th May	135
	Killashee	6	26th February to 13th May	110
	Killoe	5	6th March to 6th July	145
	Lanesboro'	5	26th February to 12th June	65
	Longford	2	15th January to 21st February	45
	Newtown-Cashel	7	24th February to 21st May	125

LOCAL COMMITTEES AND GRANTS—LEINSTER.

County	Local Committee	No. of Grants made	Date of First, and of Final Grant	Total Amount Granted
LOUTH	Darlingford	5	6th March to 12th June	£120
	Dromiskin	1	5th April	20
	Faughart	4	28th February to 18th May	85
	Inniskeen	5	24th February to 21st May	100
	Killany	5	13th March to 24th May	80
MEATH	Castletown-Kilpatrick	1	18th March	£15
	Drumconrath	4	26th February to 24th April	60
	Kilbride and Killeagh	6	21st February to 15th June	140
	Kildalkey	2	16th March to 1st April	25
	Kilberry	1	20th March	10
	Kilbeg and Carlanstown	1	20th March	10
	Moynalty and Newtown	3	4th March to 21st May	55
	Nobber	1	16th March	15
	Oldcastle	4	19th February to 1st April	85
	Rathkenny Stackallen and Grangegeeth	1	5th April	20
QUEEN'S CO.	Aghaboe	5	26th March to 12th June	£80
	Ballickmoyler	4	17th February to 30th April	130
	Borris-in-Ossory	5	6th March to 13th May	65
	Ballyfin	3	20th March to 11th May	30
	Clonaslee	7	5th February to 22nd April	115
	Durrow	3	2nd March to 24th April	45
	Killeshin	5	24th February to 29th April	105
	Mountmellick	2	28th February to 1st April	35
	Offerlane	3	11th March to 13th May	55
	Rathdowney and Rathsaran	3	4th March to 23rd March	70
	Rosenallis	4	14th February to 6th April	65
	Stradbally	4	11th March to 18th May	95
WESTMEATH	Athlone (St. Peter's)	9	20th January to 29th July	£325
	,, (St. Mary's)	1	4th March	40
	Castletown	2	24th February to 11th March	35
	Collinstown	1	5th February	25
	Clonmellon and Killalon	1	8th April	10
	Drumraney and Oughavel	3	4th March to 1st April	55
	Glasson	6	19th February to 15th May	100
	Kilbexey and Sonna	2	16th March to 22nd April	20
	Mayne	3	25th January to 18th March	60
	Moate	5	21st February to 10th April	145

PROVINCE OF CONNAUGHT.

County	Local Committee	No. of Grants made	Date of First, and of Final Grant	Total Amount Granted
GALWAY	Abbeyknockmoy	11	27th January to 15th July	£315
	Aughrim	2	3rd February to 4th March	60
	Ardrahan	10	February to 20th July	285
	Ahascragh	8	3rd February to 17th July	165
	Abbeygormican and Killoran	9	3rd February to 26th June	210
	Athenry	12	23rd January to 22nd July	345
	Arran Islands	9	29th January to 24th July	540
	Annaghadown	12	26th January to 7th August	380
	Belclare	14	18th January to 27th July	365
	Boffin & Shark Islands	6	18th January to 22nd July	250
	Ballymoe	7	24th January to 29th July	250
	Ballinasloe	13	22nd January to 12th August	470
	District of Roscommon	1	3rd February	50
	Ballymacward	6	16th March to 31st July	255
	Ballinderreen	11	3rd February to 27th July	315
	Behagh	5	7th February to 15th April	120
	Ballinakill	3	17th to 3rd July	60
	Clontuskert	2	27th March to 24th May	40
	Convent of Mercy, Gort	7	14th February to 5th August	155
	Clifden, Rural Parish	7	31st January to 22nd June	355
	Clifden Town	15	29th January to 27th July	830
	Carabane	8	21st February to 12th August	355
	Claranbridge	8	29th January to 27th July	235
	Caltra	12	29th January to 17th July	250
	Carna	17	29th January to 22nd July	1025
	Craughwell	8	7th February to 13th July	175
	Cumner	8	7th February to 1st June	250
	Caherlistrane	13	25th January to 29th July	425
	Clonbur	15	3rd February to 3rd August	705
	Cloughoola	12	31st January to 3rd August	325
	Claddagh	7	27th January to 18th May	305
	Castlegar	6	25th January to 18th May	350
	Claregalway	9	18th January to 3rd August	360
	Clifden Convent	1	15th January	25
	Crusheen and Meelick	9	10th February to 29th June	205
	Clonbern	8	10th February to 10th August	305
	Dunmore	12	5th February to 5th August	600
	Dysart and Faughboy	14	29th January to 29th July	385
	Doniry	13	29th January to 3rd August	360
	Errismore	17	29th January to 29th July	930
	Eyrecourt	6	19th February to 12th August	185
	Fohenagh and Killure	5	21st February to 27th May	110
	Glenamaddy	14	31st February to 29th July	615
	Glinsk and Kilbegnet	12	29th January to 24th July	350
	Headfort	10	31st January to 8th July	505
	Invern	7	31st January to 27th July	140
	Kilkerrin	9	5th February to 2nd August	325
	Kilbeaconty	4	5th February to 3rd June	80
	Killyon and Killeroran	13	3rd February to 12th August	495
	Kilmacduagh and Kiltartan	10	31st January to 13th July	365

LOCAL COMMITTEES AND GRANTS—CONNAUGHT. 301

County	Local Committee	No. of Grants made	Date of First, and of Final Grant	Total Amount Granted
GALWAY (Continued)	Killanin	9	27th January to 10th July	£340
	Kilescobe and Menloch	12	3rd February to 31st July	320
	Kiltullagh	3	19th February to 24th May	105
	Killaghton and Kilbreecle	7	3rd February to 5th August	135
	Kilconla and Kilbannon	10	10th February to 17th July	340
	Killerin	8	29th January to 6th July	235
	Killimore	5	24th January to 10th July	110
	Killeen, Spiddal	12	24th January to 27th July	445
	Kinvara	18	20th January to 10th August	640
	Kilchreest	6	31st January to 12th June	220
	Kilnadeena and Killesteskil	9	19th February to 5th August	190
	Kilconnell	9	19th February to 29th July	145
	Kiltomer and Lawrencetown	5	2nd March to 17th June	105
	Lackagh	7	6th March to 1st July	225
	Letterfrack	17	25th January to 5th August	1250
	Loughrea	9	22nd January to 31st July	415
	Leenane	17	15th January to 14th August	540
	Leitrim Kilmeen and Kilcooley	11	5th February to 24th July	220
	Lettermullen and Carraroe	7	26th February to 14 August	170
	Miltown	11	2nd February to to 10th July	470
	Moore	7	26th February to 9th June	200
	Moycullen	10	18th January to 6th July	460
	Moylough	13	3rd February to 15th July	380
	Mount Bellew	14	3rd February to 10th August	330
	New Inn	6	31st January to 3rd June	110
	Oughterard	17	24th January to 14th August	685
	Oranmore	9	25th January to 29th June	395
	Omey	1	17th February	25
	Portumna	7	31st January to 13th July	295
	Peterswell	9	29th January to 6th July	290
	Rosmuck	14	3rd February to 14th August	530
	Rahoon	17	3rd February to 26th June	595
	Roundstone	8	25th January to 29th July	370
	Recess	3	15th January to 23rd March	80
	Spiddal (Galway)	12	18th January to 24th July	310
	Spiddal (Tuam)	9	24th January to 15th July	265
	St. Patrick Bros. Galway	5	27th January to 1st July	145
	St. Nicholas East Galway	1	2nd March to 1st July	100
	Tuam	12	59th January to 10th August	380
	Tynagh	5	21st February to 6th May	100
	Whitegate	8	5th February to 3rd June	185
	Woodford	13	31st January to 10th August	400
	Williamstown	14	27th January to 14th August	450
LEITRIM	Aughavass	8	31st January to 24th July	£215
	Ballinamore	12	29th January to 8th July	360
	Ballinaglera	10	19th February to 7th August	410
	Barnacoola	9	20th March to 8th July	155
	Cloone	10	27th January to 13th July	285
	Carrigallen	10	3rd February to 13th July	315

APPENDIX X.

County	Local Committee	No. of Grants made	Date of First, and of Final Grant	Total Amount Granted
LEITRIM *(Continued)*	Carrick-on-Shannon	15	25th January to 22nd June	£620
	Drumrielly Upper	13	3rd February to 29th July	310
	Dramsna	6	23rd March to 27th July	190
	Drumrielly Lower	13	7th February to 13th July	300
	Dromahair	11	24th January to 5th August	295
	Drumshambo	10	23rd January to 10th July	360
	Drumkeerin	15	18th January to 7th August	680
	Fenagh	9	12th February to 22nd July	210
	Glenade	5	10th April to 1st July	85
	Gortlitteragh	11	5th February to 15th July	330
	Kinlough	13	29th January to 27th July	555
	Kilmore and Aughrim	8	31st January to 3rd August	275
	Kilturbride	16	27th January to 22nd July	465
	Lurganboy	9	29th January to 15th July	165
	Mohill	11	23rd January to 20th July	375
	Manorhamilton	14	5th February to 24th July	595
	Newtowngore and Lower Carrigallen	9	14th February to 29th July	215
MAYO	Achill	13	5th February to 3rd August	£700
	Addergoole	16	20th January to 10th August	790
	Ardagh	12	24th February to 12th August	315
	Attymass	12	5th February to 7th August	485
	Aughagower	16	23rd January to 22nd July	675
	Aughamore	11	31st January to 31st July	505
	Aasleagh	3	17th February to 6th July	45
	Backs	14	31st January to 12th August	640
	Ballintubber and Ballyglass	14	13th January to 14th August	515
	Ballinrobe	12	20th January to 13th July	645
	Ballisokerry	12	24th January to 27th July	435
	Ballyhaunis	13	27th January to 24th July	475
	Ballycastle	15	25th January to 12th August	520
	Ballycroy	14	3rd February to 29th July	420
	Ballaghaderrin	17	24th January to 14th August	960
	Bangor Erris	12	24th January to 14th August	400
	Bekan	11	3rd February to 24th July	560
	Belmullet	11	18th January to 29th July	390
	Bohola	7	27th January to 27th July	355
	Bonnaconlan	14	20th January to 5th August	585
	Ballindine	10	27th January to 22nd July	585
	Balla	4	13th April to 31st July	215
	Carracastle	23	18th January to 12th August	960
	Castlebar	12	27th January to 7th August	660
	Charlestown	20	25th January to 27th July	1070
	Claremorris	22	15th January to 14th August	665
	Croaghpatrick	15	3rd February to 22nd July	425
	Crossboyne and Tagheen	13	3rd February to 22nd July	465
	Crossmolina	19	18th January to 31st July	750
	Cong	12	24th January to 27th July	480
	Clareisland	6	26th February to 7th August	160
	Drum and Manulla	11	23rd January to 12th August	435
	Drummin	7	22nd February to 22nd July	145
	Foxford	17	25th January to 5th August	895
	Glenisland and Islandeady	11	27th January to 17th July	405
	Gowlane	8	24th April to 29th July	165

LOCAL COMMITTEES AND GRANTS—CONNAUGHT.   303

County	Local Committee	No. of Grants made	Date of First and of Final Grant	Total Amount Granted
MAYO (*Continued*)	Kilfian	7	23rd January to 29th July	£255
	Killmaine	13	10th February to 20th July	585
	Kilmore-Erris	8	25th January to 26th June	295
	Knock	5	31st January to 20th May	175
	Keelognes	15	23rd January to 3rd August	470
	Kilmeena	12	31st January to 14th August	445
	Kilmaclasser	7	1st April to 14th August	165
	Kilmovee	16	27th January to 24th July	770
	Kilcommon-Erris	12	25th January to 29th July	490
	Killala	12	15th January to 27th July	445
	Killasser	16	29th January to 12th August	800
	Kiltimagh	8	29th January to 31st July	275
	Kilgeever	10	10th February to 22nd July	450
	Moygourna	13	31st January to 12th August	350
	Mayo Abbey	11	27th January to 10th August	410
	Mulraney	12	24th February to 22nd July	240
	Newport	13	25th January to 12th August	565
	Rathlacken	14	15th January to 3rd August	410
	Robeen and Kilcommon	10	5th February to 10th July	345
	Straide	11	14th February to 14th August	350
	Swinford	19	18th January to 14th August	1080
	Shrule	9	27th January to 12th August	315
	The Neale	12	25th January to 27th August	510
	Turlough	13	23rd January to 22nd July	450
	Tourmakeedy	8	5th February to 7th August	315
	Westport	13	7th February to 22nd July	670
ROSCOMMON	Ardcarne and Tumna	8	31st January to 29th June	£310
	Athleague	5	29th January to 29th July	140
	Ballintubber	10	31st January to 24th July	385
	Boyle	13	25th January to 13th July	825
	Ballymacurly	13	20th January to 14th August	275
	Croghan	7	3rd February to 3rd July	150
	Castlerea	9	25th January to 1st July	460
	Derrane and Kilgefin	12	27th January to 17th July	515
	Elphin	9	31st January to 12th June	380
	Fuerty	6	7th February to 14th August	165
	Four-mile House	7	29th January to 29th May	155
	Frenchpark and Ballinagar	7	31st January to 26th June	175
	Kilnamanagh and Eastersnow	10	23rd January to 3rd August	330
	Kiltoom and Cam	11	25th January to 22nd July	315
	Kilglass	10	13th January to 10th July	495
	Keadue	11	15th January to 20th July	315
	Kiltullagh and Ballinlough	16	25th January to 14th August	620
	Lecarrow	9	23rd January to 19th June	345
	Loughlynn	16	15th January to 10th August	690
	Roscommon and Kiltcevan	8	27th January to 3rd June	350
	Strokestown	5	25th January to 15th July	200
	Tybohine	15	23rd January to 27th July	545
	Taughmaconnell	15	23rd January to 29th July	420
	Tulsk	10	27th January to 20th July	280
	Tissara	7	31st January to 29th July	210
	Tarmonbarry	12	31st January to 5th August	320

County	Local Committee	No. of Grants made	Date of First, and of Final Grant	Total Amount Granted
SLIGO	Achonry	10	27th January to 29th July	£295
	Ahamlish	16	15th January to 3rd August	655
	Ballintrillick	4	6th March to 19th June	115
	Bunnanadin	15	18th January to 22nd July	535
	Ballymote	12	18th January to 27th July	500
	Ballintogher	3	21st February to 24th May	70
	Ballinafad	12	29th January to 17th July	405
	Collooney	6	20th January to 20th July	305
	Calry and Coolera	10	20th January to 5th June	400
	Clonloo	8	19th February to 29th June	280
	Castleconnor	10	31st January to 17th July	305
	Curry	17	31st January to 10th August	890
	Drumcliffe	8	31st January to 8th June	270
	Dromore West	12	25th January to 14th August	500
	Easkey	19	15th January to 12th August	850
	Gurteen	12	3rd February to 27th July	445
	Geevah	13	18th January to 13th July	365
	Killoran	9	31st January to 3rd August	320
	Kilmactigue	16	29th January to 14th August	745
	Keash	8	31st January to 13th July	300
	Kilglass	13	20th January to 29th July	355
	Riverstown	12	25th January to 27th July	365
	Screen and Dromard	15	31st January to 31st July	495
	Sooey	11	11th March to 24th July	260
	Templeboy	8	15th January to 8th June	270
	Tubbercurry	16	13th January to 3rd August	770

PROVINCE OF MUNSTER.

County	Local Committee	No. of Grants made	Date of First, and of Final Grant	Total Amount Granted
CLARE	Ballyvaughan	14	18th January to 17th July	£765
	Bodyke	9	3rd February to 10th June	195
	Broadford	7	17th February to 1st July	170
	Clarecastle	2	11th March to 13th May	55
	Clondegad & Kilchreest	14	29th January to 22nd June	335
	Clonlee and Killurin	8	27th January to 24th June	215
	Coolmeen	6	27th January to 19th June	165
	Corofin	13	25th January to 13th July	295
	Carrigaholt	11	12th February to 31st July	345
	Cratloe and Kilfintinane	1	13th May	25
	Doolin	5	27th January to 6th May	135
	Doora and Kilraghter	6	16th March to 29th June	130
	Ennistymon	9	27th January to 26th June	365
	Ennis	4	24th February to 19th June	170
	Feakle (Lower)	7	29th January to 17th June	220
	Feakle (Upper)	9	7th February to 29th May	170
	Inagh	12	5th February to 10th June	325
	Kilkeedy Boston and Kells	9	19th February to 1st July	210
	Kilbaha	11	3rd February to 27th July	225
	Kilfinora	7	3rd February to 3rd July	220
	Knock and Killimer	6	31st February to 18th May	125
	Killard	8	31st January to 15th July	310
	Kilmaley	6	21st February to 3rd June	185
	Kilmurray Ibricane	13	5th February to 13th July	440
	Kilrush	12	14th February to 8th July	455
	Kilshaney	7	25th February to 29th July	140
	Kilmacduane	11	5th February to 24th June	295
	Kilmihil	11	7th February to 17th July	295
	Killaloe	8	20th January to 3rd June	185
	Kilkee	11	23rd January to 13th June	415
	Kildysart	9	18th January to 12th June	215
	Labasheeda	9	27th January to 15th July	225
	Liscarrow	11	20th January to 8th July	260
	Miltown Malbay	12	18th January to 29th June	465
	Newmarket-on-Fergus	8	29th January to 20th May	165
	O'Gonelloe	1	17th February	30
	Quin	5	10th February to 21st May	80
	Ruan	10	24th January to 22nd July	215
	Scariff	10	24th January to 6th July	345
	Six-mile-bridge	7	14th February to 27th May	155
	Tulla	5	3rd February to 15th June	170
CORK	Abina	1	20th March	£25
	Allihies	7	2nd March to 13th July	265
	Aghadown	7	19th February to 29th June	190
	Ardfield and Rathbarry	2	21st February to 11th May	35
	Ballinahassig	1	11th March	15
	Barryroe	12	18th January to 19th June	275
	Bantry	8	27th January to 8th June	295
	Bandon	3	1st April to 29th May	60
	Buttevant	1	29th January	30

Y

APPENDIX X.

County	Local Committee	No. of Grants made	Date of First, and of Final Grant	Total Amount Granted
CORK *(Continued)*	Ballynoe and Conna	4	5th February to 4th May	£110
	Ballyvourney	7	26th February to 19th June	150
	Ballincollig	1	19th February	20
	Charleville	2	9th March to 26th March	60
	Carrigaline and Crosshaven	6	21st February to 17th June	90
	Castletown-Roche	8	18th March to 24th June	160
	Castlehaven and Myros	7	5th February to 12th June	185
	Caharagh	4	31st January to 1st July	140
	Clonrohid	1	31st January	50
	Cloyne	11	3rd February to 3rd July	285
	Clonmeen	7	10th February to 20th July	120
	Castletown Bere	6	25th January to 6th May	270
	Clonakilty	4	24th January to 27th April	145
	Castle Lyons	2	19th February to 13th March	50
	Courceys	5	5th February to 29th April	100
	Clonmoyle	3	28th February to 1st April	40
	Clontead and Ballynomotte	2	19th February to 13th May	30
	Colmanswell	2	9th March to 23rd March	20
	Drimoleague	7	27th January to 24th June	195
	Drumtarriff	7	5th February to 21st May	205
	Dongourney	4	25th January to 24th April	120
	Doneraile	3	10th February to 3rd July	60
	Dunmanway	4	14th February to 20th July	110
	Fyeries	7	19th February to 22nd June	230
	Freemount	1	5th April	10
	Glengarriffe	10	22nd January to 24th July	365
	Goleen	8	7th February to 13th July	270
	Glountane	5	10th February to 29th April	110
	Inchigeela	6	5th February to 24th June	200
	Innishannon	2	2nd March to 8th June	30
	Inniscarra	1	1st June	15
	Kilbehenny	4	21st February to 24th June	65
	Kilbrittain	4	5th February to 18th May	85
	Kilbrin	1	16th March	20
	Killeagh	3	6th March to 1st June	55
	Kilmeen and Castleventry	7	5th February to 8th July	180
	Kilmeen No. 2	2	18th February to 16th March	50
	Kennoigh Ballymoney and Desertserges	6	7th February to 24th June	155
	Kilcorney	7	7th February to 10th June	70
	Kanturk	3	20th January to 2nd March	85
	Kilworth	4	18th January to 27th May	105
	Kildorrery	4	4th March to 13th May	75
	Kilcaskin	11	24th January to 26th June	365
	Killavullen	6	26th February to 3rd June	90
	Kingwilliamstown	9	5th February to 27th May	195
	Kilmurry	3	26th February to 11th May	70
	Kilnamartyr	4	7th February to 8th June	85
	Kilmicheal	5	10th February to 22nd June	125
	Kilmacabea	8	24th January to 1st July	235
	Kinsale	3	19th February to 15th May	75
	Liscarroll	2	19th February to 4th March	45
	Lisgoold	3	18th March to 10th June	60
	Midleton	2	24th April to 11th May	40

LOCAL COMMITTEES AND GRANTS — MUNSTER.

County	Local Committee	No. of Grants made	Date of First, and of Final Grant	Total Amount Granted
CORK (Continued)	Milford	8	3rd February to 6th July	£135
	Meelin	9	27th January to 26th June	175
	Mitchelstown	4	27th January to 1st April	110
	Mallow	5	27th January to 10th April	225
	Minteravaragh	5	25th January to 1st May	160
	Macroom	3	23rd January to 4th May	125
	Millstreet	6	18th January to 20th May	145
	Mourne Abbey	2	11th March to 29th May	70
	Ovens	1	24th February	25
	Queenstown	1	20th March	25
	Roscarberry	9	20th January to 18th May	295
	Shanbally	1	11th March	10
	Skibbereen	13	15th January to 8th June	625
	Shandrum	7	24th January to 8th June	180
	Schull	10	24th January to 29th July	550
	Timoleague	9	29th January to 3rd July	220
	Tullalease	1	10th February	25
	Tracton	2	11th March to 8th May	70
	Tullagh & Islands of Cape Clear & Sherkin	5	12th February to 3rd June	160
	Youghal	6	31st January to 11th May	225
KERRY	Ardfert	7	31st January to 13th July	£250
	Anniscaul	12	29th January to 22nd July	335
	Ballyhorgan	1	20th January	25
	Ballylongford	9	24th January to 10th June	220
	Brosna	5	24th January to 15th May	140
	Beaufort	9	26th January to 24th June	215
	Bonane	4	20th January to 20th May	90
	Ballyduff and Causeway	7	29th January to 13th July	275
	Ballymacelligott	7	25th January to 5th June	150
	Ballybunion	11	29th January to 22nd June	410
	Ballyheigue	9	5th February to 17th July	195
	Castlegregory	13	31st January to 1st July	420
	Cunens	4	7th February to 24th June	125
	Castlemaine	9	27th January to 1st July	290
	Caherdaniel	7	23rd January to 1st May	185
	Castleisland	7	20th January to 10th June	270
	Caherciveen	11	13th January to 8th July	425
	Duagh	3	12th February to 29th May	75
	Dingle	9	24th February to 10th July	350
	Dromod	6	31st January to 1st June	190
	Ferriter	10	23rd January to 24th June	500
	Ferries and Ballyhar	10	7th February to 1st July	325
	Glenbeigh	9	10th February to 17th July	355
	Imelaghmore	7	2nd March to 3rd July	160
	Kilgarvan	6	5th February to 6th July	210
	Kilgobbin	4	3rd February to 20th April	105
	Kenmare	7	29th January to 5th June	245
	Kilcommon	8	27th January to 3rd June	190
	Killorglynn	4	29th January to 13th May	175
	Killarney	4	9th March to 20th July	90
	Kilflyn	6	17th February to 3rd June	100
	Killaha and Barraduff	5	4th March to 13th July	130
	Listowel	2	5th February to 2nd March	45
	Miltown	11	14th February to 29th June	285
	Newtownsands	5	19th February to 5th June	130

APPENDIX X.

County	Local Committee	No. of Grants made	Date of First, and of Final Grant	Total Amount Granted
KERRY *(Continued)*	O'Dorney and Killahan	4	24th February to 17th June	£100
	Portmagee	9	18th January to 15th June	200
	Rathmore	7	12th February to 21st May	220
	Sneem	7	31st January to 13th May	200
	Spa	6	19th February to 3rd July	135
	Tuosist	8	29th January to 27th May	190
	Templenoe	2	31st January to 26th February	75
	Tralee	5	28th February to 8th June	155
	Tarbert	9	14th February to 22nd June	255
	Valentia	5	3rd February to 12th June	195
LIMERICK	Ardagh	3	27th March to 27th April	£70
	Askeaton	5	7th February to 4th May	140
	Athlacca	2	26th March to 13th May	25
	Athea	2	26th February to 1st April	45
	Abbeyfeale	4	7th February to 8th May	80
	Ardnacrusha	1	24th February	10
	Ardpatrick	2	11th March to 1st April	20
	Banogue	1	20th March	10
	Ballinavan and Bulgaden	1	16th March	25
	Ballingarry	1	13th March	40
	Ballylanders	3	9th March to 22nd April	80
	Ballyneety	1	24th February	20
	Ballygran and Castletown-Conyers	1	27th March	20
	Bruff	4	23rd January to 10th April	85
	Cappamore	5	25th January to 7th April	230
	Chapel Russel	2	12th February to 6th March	75
	Caherconlish	6	5th February to 6th May	85
	Clonlara	4	21st February to 7th June	85
	Castelconnell	2	19th February to 15th June	35
	Crecora	2	9th March to 10th April	40
	Dromkeen and Boherroe	1	24th March	10
	Dromcollogher	3	29th January to 10th April	110
	Effin	3	19th February to 1st May	80
	Fenagh and Kilmeedy	6	26th February to 3rd June	100
	Fedamore	7	31st January to 3rd June	210
	Glenroe	3	6th March to 22nd June	30
	Glin	5	14th February to 8th May	105
	Hospital and Herbertsown	2	13th March to 29th April	40
	Islandmore	2	25th January to 23rd March	100
	Kilfinane	1	8th May	25
	Kilmurry Mondleen and Derrygalvin	5	11th March to 17th June	60
	Knockaderry and Cloncough	4	2nd March to 18th May	90
	Kilmallock	3	27th January to 4th March	105
	Kileedy	4	7th February to 3rd June	70
	Kilcolman	3	21st February to 13th April	95
	Knocklong and Glenbrohane	2	26th February to 26th March	30
	Knockahinuy	2	11th March to 3rd April	30
	Kilteely	2	11th March to 7th April	50

County	Local Committee	No. of Grants made	Date of First, and of Final Grant	Total Amount Granted
LIMERICK (*Continued*)	Loughill and Ballyhahill	5	27th January to 8th June	£105
	Mahoonagh and Fohenagh	5	19th February to 29th April	80
	Murroe	3	6th March to 4th May	50
	Newcastle West	2	21st February to 13th March	50
	Pallasgreen	4	24th January to 22nd April	90
	Rathkeale	5	27th January to 27th May	160
	Rockhill and Bruree	1	29th April	15
	Tournafulla	4	19th February to 29th April	110
	Templeglantine	3	20th March to 3rd June	55
TIPPERARY	Annacarty	7	3rd February to 22nd June	£110
	Ardfinane	1	21st February	20
	Ballinahinch and Killosully	7	25th January to 1st May	150
	Ballingarry	3	18th March to 13th May	70
	Ballyporeen	9	5th February to 3rd July	330
	Boherlahan	6	18th March to 26th June	95
	Borrisoleigh and Ibeigh	4	2nd March to 20th April	75
	Burgess and Youghal-arra	3	9th March to 20th May	85
	Ballina and Bohir	4	4th March to 6th May	85
	Cappawhite	5	7th February to 1st June	105
	Castletown-arra	8	24th January to 20th May	175
	Cashel	2	3rd April to 13th April	50
	Cloughjordan	4	24th January to 23rd March	95
	Clogheen	4	15th January to 4th March	100
	Drangan	8	11th March to 22nd July	125
	Drom and Inch	3	13th March to 1st April	30
	Emly	2	13th April to 11th May	20
	Hollyford	8	27th January to 10th June	130
	Holycross and Ballycahill	4	19th February to 15th April	70
	Killinavinage	7	10th February to 24th May	150
	Kilcommon	7	29th January to 24th May	165
	Killenaule and Moyglass	5	10th April to 10th June	85
	Kilcooley	3	4th March to 15th April	50
	Lorrah	2	27th January to 11th March	75
	Loughmore and Castleraney	2	24th February to 27th March	30
	Monsea and Killadangan	2	20th March to 22nd April	30
	Mullinahone	1	4th May	25
	Nenagh	3	25th January to 23rd March	225
	Newport	4	25th January to 1st April	174
	New Inn and Knockgriffin	1	13th April	10
	Seskinane and Lickoran	4	2nd March to 22nd April	70
	Silvermines	4	26th February to 3rd June	75
	Templederry	8	18th January to 21st May	190
	Toomavara	6	27th January to 27th May	150
	Two-mile-Borris	6	14th February to 1st May	135

County	Local Committee	No. of Grants made	Date of First, and of Final Grant	Total Amount Granted
TIPPERARY (*Continued*)	Templetuohy and Moyne	4	17th February to 17th April	£85
	Tubrid	6	21st February to 1st May	125
	Templemore and Killea	5	21st February to 24th April	140
WATERFORD.	Aglish	3	6th March to 6th May	£50
	Ardmore	6	12th February to 15th June	145
	Ballylaleen and Graigshooneen	5	2nd March to 22nd June	65
	Ballyduff (Lismore)	2	6th March to 15th April	80
	Ballyduff (Kilmeaden)	1	12th March	25
	Clonea	2	6th March to 7th April	50
	Clashmore and Kinsalebeg	2	17th February to 13th May	75
	Cappoquin	3	24th February to 29th April	125
	Colligan Kilgobnit and Kilbryan	1	24th April	25
	Dungarvan	5	3rd February to 15th April	325
	Kilrosantry and Fews	3	29th January to 11th May	95
	Kill Knockmahon and Bonmahon	3	27th January to 9th March	130
	Knockanore and Kilwatermoy	5	18th March to 20th July	155
	Lismore	1	6th March	25
	Passage East	1	28th February	10
	Old Parish and Ringville	2	6th March to 24th April	45
	Portlaw	2	24th February to 11th March	40
	Rossmyre	4	2nd March to 26th June	70
	Stradbally Kilmacthomas	5	29th January to 12th June	90
	Tallow	4	12th February to 10th June	115
	Tramore	3	14th February to 20th March	85

TOTAL AMOUNT GRANTED BY MANSION HOUSE COMMITTEE TO EACH COUNTY.

	£	s.	d.
ANTRIM	310	0	0
ARMAGH	980	0	0
CARLOW	170	0	0
CAVAN	7,035	0	0
CLARE	9,905	0	0
CORK	11,060	0	0
DERRY	90	0	0
DONEGAL	14,395	0	0
DOWN	145	0	0
DUBLIN	650	0	0
FERMANAGH	3,160	0	0
GALWAY	30,195	0	0
KERRY	9,415	0	0
KILDARE	144	0	0
KILKENNY	680	0	0
KING'S COUNTY	350	0	0
LEITRIM	7,765	0	0
LIMERICK	3,275	0	0
LONGFORD	2,195	0	0
LOUTH	405	0	0
MAYO	31,105	0	0
MEATH	435	0	0
MONAGHAN	2,345	0	0
QUEEN'S COUNTY	890	0	0
ROSCOMMON	9,440	0	0
SLIGO	11,065	0	0
TIPPERARY	3,910	0	0
TYRONE	2,205	0	0
WATERFORD	1,830	0	0
WESTMEATH	1,090	0	0
WEXFORD	95	0	0
WICKLOW	165	0	0
	166,899	0	0
SPECIAL GRANTS FOR WESTERN ISLES, FOOD, CLOTHES, &c.	6,085	18	9
	£172,984	18	9

TABLE SHOWING THE NUMBER OF COMMITTEES IN EACH COUNTY IN IRELAND.

Province	County	No. of Committees to whom Grants were made	No. Amalgamated or to whom no Grants were made
ULSTER	Antrim	3	—
	Armagh	9	—
	Cavan	33	2
	Donegal	46	16
	Down	2	—
	Fermanagh	18	1
	Monaghan	19	3
	Tyrone	20	2
	Derry	2	—
CONNAUGHT	Galway	93	19
	Leitrim	23	2
	Mayo	63	15
	Roscommon	26	13
	Sligo	26	5
MUNSTER	Clare	41	8
	Cork	85	13
	Kerry	45	5
	Limerick	47	2
	Tipperary	38	3
	Waterford	21	1
LEINSTER	Carlow	3	4
	Kildare	4	2
	Kilkenny	11	3
	King's County	8	2
	Longford	14	2
	Louth	5	1
	Meath	10	1
	Queen's County	12	3
	Westmeath	12	3
	Wexford	4	2
	Wicklow	2	3
	Dublin	—	9
		745	145

SUMMARY OF FOREGOING TABLE.

Province	No. of Committees to whom Grants were made	No. of Committees Amalgamated or to whom no Grants were made
Ulster	152	24
Connaught	231	54
Munster	277	32
Leinster	85	35
	745	145

TABLES SHOWING THE CONSTITUTION OF LOCAL COMMITTEES.

PROVINCE OF ULSTER.

County	Catholic Clergymen	Clergymen of other Denominations	Medical Officers	Poor Law Guardians	Other Lay Members
Antrim	4	7	2	—	19
Armagh	13	20	7	14	76
Cavan	69	62	28	64	367
*Donegal	85	88	46	66	322
Down	4	3	—	5	31
Fermanagh	28	30	11	25	175
Monaghan	39	36	15	21	132
Tyrone	36	45	14	24	174
Derry	4	4	2	4	13
	282	295	125	223	1,309

* The Donegal Central Committee had forty-six Sub-Committees, composed of members as above, and six hundred and thirty-eight grants were made by the Central Committee to these Sub-Committees.

PROVINCE OF CONNAUGHT.

County	Catholic Clergymen	Clergymen of other Denominations	Medical Officers	Poor Law Guardians	Other Lay Members
Galway	161	69	56	94	647
Leitrim	54	30	18	64	143
Mayo	95	43	26	44	568
Roscommon	63	24	21	41	252
Sligo	47	29	20	47	243
	420	195	141	290	1,853

PROVINCE OF MUNSTER.

County	Catholic Clergymen	Clergymen of other Denominations	Medical Officers	Poor Law Guardians	Other Lay Members
Clare	83	32	35	67	356
Cork	171	94	52	106	690
Kerry	82	21	29	72	296
Limerick	90	38	23	49	364
Tipperary	68	33	25	43	364
Waterford	39	20	19	24	172
	533	238	183	361	2,242

PROVINCE OF LEINSTER.

County	Catholic Clergymen	Clergymen of other Denominations	Medical Officers	Poor Law Guardians	Other Lay Members
Carlow	6	6	1	1	40
Kildare	11	6	4	5	37
King's County	18	9	7	9	82
Kilkenny	23	11	6	10	95
Longford	26	16	3	13	107
Louth	11	7	4	12	38
Meath	12	9	6	14	116
Queen's County	26	22	13	18	102
Westmeath	22	13	9	12	109
Wexford	8	5	3	4	18
Wicklow	3	2	2	3	19
Dublin	3	1	1	2	4
	169	107	59	103	767

SUMMARY OF FOREGOING FOUR TABLES.

Province	Catholic Clergymen	Clergymen of other Denominations	Medical Officers	Poor Law Guardians	Other Lay Members
Ulster	282	295	125	223	1,309
Connaught	420	195	141	290	1,853
Munster	533	238	183	361	2,242
Leinster	169	107	59	103	767
	1,404	835	508	977	6,171

APPENDIX XI.

LETTERS OF IRISH BISHOPS.

At a Meeting of the Committee, held on Saturday, January 31st, the Lord Mayor mentioned that he had received a telegram from New York, stating that its "character, motives, and mode of distribution of money had been publicly questioned there, and that it would be desirable to send out a sanction of the Committee's proceedings by the Catholic Archbishops, which could be published in America." In reply to the above, the following letter was issued to the Bishops:—

"MANSION HOUSE FUND FOR THE RELIEF OF DISTRESS IN IRELAND.

"*Dublin, 30th January*, 1880.

"MY LORD,

"I am informed that it has been publicly asserted in America that this Committee is influenced in the distribution of its funds by other motives than the desire to relieve distress, and that it is desirable we should have the express approval of the Catholic Hierarchy of our proceedings. In Ireland such statements would not be made, for everyone would know them to be without foundation, but when made elsewhere it becomes necessary that they should be formally corrected. Your Lordship is aware that every Catholic, as well as every Protestant Bishop in Ireland, is a member of this Committee. Our proceedings are public, and we have already had on our books nearly 500 Local Committees to which we have granted relief. Of these, I need hardly say, the Catholic Priests are in all instances members, and in nearly every instance the Protestant Clergymen are associated with them. Our rules require that, when practicable, the clergy of all denominations shall be represented, but we do not delay sending relief in any case that appears urgent. We have already distributed over £12,000 without any complaint in Ireland as to our *bona fides* or impartiality. I enclose your Lordship a printed list of the members of our Committee, our Rules and our Query Sheet. As the statements that are being made would be calculated to stop the flow of subscriptions to our fund, and discredit our exertions if these statements obtained credence, I have now, in the cause of honesty and of justice, and in that of the famine-stricken people of this country, in whose service the Committee is working, to ask you to state, by return of post, whether, in your Lordship's opinion, this Committee is worthy or not of public confidence.

"I have the honour to be, your Lordship's obedient servant,

"E. DWYER GRAY, Lord Mayor, *Chairman*."

To this letter the following replies were received:—

The Most Rev. DANIEL M'GETTIGAN, Primate of All Ireland, wrote:—

"*Armagh, 2nd February*, 1880.

"MY DEAR LORD MAYOR,

"The Mansion House Committee for the Relief of the Distress in Ireland is engaged in the noblest work under the sun. The amount of good already done by it is marvellous. Everyone must have confidence in the integrity, honour, impartiality, and benevolent motive of its members. It is cruel to throw discredit on it. To bring that Committee under suspicion is a crime akin to poisoning the wells that supply a besieged city with pure water. It is idle for me to add, that I have a firm trust in the fairness of your excellent Committee.

"Believe me to remain, my dear Lord Mayor, your faithful servant,

"✠ DANIEL M'GETTIGAN."

The Most Rev. Dr. MACCABE, who attended the next meeting, said :—

"I thought it better to come here myself and personally enter my solemn protest against the charge brought against this Committee. I myself have not come in contact with it in so far as being an applicant for money, but I have had an opportunity of meeting a great many bishops in Maynooth, and I may tell you that I have heard from themselves the statements you have now heard from their letters, and their feeling, as mine, is one of complete satisfaction and unbounded confidence in the operations of the Committee. As some of the letters reminded us, it would be perhaps a miracle to find all the gentlemen around this table agreeing upon any subject except that of charity. I am sure we would not all agree on religious doctrines, on politics, and on a great many social subjects; but what brings us all here is the one great cause, the cause of Godlike charity. Though it may seem strange, I think that, assuming these telegrams are correct, perhaps it is very fortunate the charge has been made, for it has given an occasion for a great and generous outburst of approval of the proceedings of the Committee. Had you gone on unchallenged there never would have been such a unanimous expression of opinion. There is no evil so purely evil from which great good may not come, and I think you may rather congratulate yourself on this charge having been made. Had the charge been confined to Ireland, the Lord Mayor might have indeed afforded to despise it, but under the circumstances of its having been made in foreign parts, it was right they should now protest against it. For myself, I have the most unbounded faith in this Committee, and I am glad to know with confidence that we all rejoice at being able to work harmoniously."

His Grace the ARCHBISHOP OF TUAM wrote :—

"*St. Jarlath's, Tuam, January 31st,* 1880."

"MY DEAR LORD MAYOR,

"Very willingly I bear testimony to the efficiency with which the Mansion House Committee has hitherto laboured in mitigating the distress of our sorely afflicted people, and in averting for the present, in certain localities, the horrors of the famine of thirty years ago.

"I remain, my dear Lord Mayor, your faithful servant,

"✠ JOHN, Archbishop of Tuam."

The Most Rev. Dr. CROKE, Archbishop of Cashel, wrote :—

"*The Palace, Thurles, February 2nd,* 1880."

"MY DEAR LORD MAYOR,

"I am in receipt of your circular, and beg to say in reply that I have no reason to think that the moneys placed at the disposal of the Mansion House Committee have not been judiciously applied. It is true, indeed, that I have no special fancy for certain members of the Committee, whose sympathies with our people I would be strongly disposed to question. But your name and other names are ample guarantee to me that no substantial wrong can be done our people in the distribution of the Mansion House Fund.

"I have the honour to be, my dear Lord Mayor,

"Your faithful servant,

"✠ T. W. CROKE, Abp

The following letter was also received from His Grace the Protestant ARCHBISHOP of DUBLIN :—

"*The Palace, Stephen's Green, Dublin, Jan.* 30*th*, 1880.

"Having had some practical share from the beginning in the work of the Committee of the Mansion House Relief Fund, and in the distribution of the money of which it has been made the almoner, I feel called to bear witness to the spirit of entire fairness which has presided over all its arrangements, and to the absence of all considerations save only the necessities of the applicants, which has governed its distribution of the funds entrusted to it.

"RICHARD C. DUBLIN."

"*St. Jarlath's College, Tuam, January* 30*th*, 1880.

"MY DEAR LORD MAYOR,

"Your letter literally astounds me. How it is any man, or men, could concoct such a calumny as that referred to in your letter passes my comprehension. Why, it is as notorious as any public fact can be, that the praiseworthy exertions and labours of your Committee are all undergone in the interests of the poor struggling tenants and starving poor of Ireland, without distinction of creed, and have already saved the lives of thousands of our afflicted poor. Your Committee, composed of gentlemen of every creed, who merge every other consideration in the interests of charity, dispense the charities confided to you with the greatest fairness, and, as far as I know, have secured public confidence in your judgment and impartiality.

"With sincerest esteem, believe me, very sincerely yours,

"✠ JOHN M'EVILLY."

The Most Rev. Dr. DUGGAN, Bishop of Clonfert, wrote :—

"*Loughrea, January* 30*th*, 1880

"MY DEAR LORD MAYOR,

"I am deeply pained to learn from your inquiry that imputations have been cast upon the integrity, or impartiality, or the motives actuating your Committee in their desire to afford relief to the distressed poor in this crisis. My means of information are extensive. The Committees to whom you are entrusting your funds in this district are composed of men of all political and religious shades. The utmost care is taken in distribution. The only test is destitution. I am astonished to hear of the imputations to which you refer. Already by your contributions to this quarter much misery has been alleviated, and as the season moves into spring, deaths without number will be the consequence unless some aid comes through a charitable public. It is quite true that our rulers should institute a system of public works. Our people want work, and not alms. In the absence of this aid from Government any one who would, by imputing unworthy motives to your Committee, check the hand of charity, will incur a dreadful responsibility before God and the country. No one here questions the honour, the motives, or the judicious action of your Committee. On the contrary, all approve and are deeply grateful.

"I am, my dear Lord Mayor, sincerely yours,

"✠ PATRICK DUGGAN."

The Most Rev. Dr. CONWAY, Bishop of Killala, wrote :—

"*Ballina, Co. Mayo, February* 1*st*, 1880.

"MY LORD,

"I am favoured by the receipt of your lordship's communication of the 30th ult., stating that 'it has been publicly asserted in America that the Mansion House

Relief Committee is influenced in the distribution of its funds by other motives than the desire to relieve distress.' In replying, I beg to state that I believe that assertion to be a most unfounded calumny. In the famine years of 1846, 1847, and 1848, and since then, I had a good deal to do with relief committees. I corresponded with most of them, formed during that time for the relief of distress, and I candidly say that I never experienced a more benevolent disposition and a greater desire to ascertain the extent and urgent nature of the distress to be relieved than I found among the gentlemen who form the present Mansion House Committee. Any other cement than that of pure charity and sympathy for afflicted humanity could not unite into one harmonious body the conflicting religious and political elements of which your Committee is composed. It has to deal with local committees composed of the same conflicting elements, and it would be impossible that any other motive (if such existed) than the desire to relieve the poor could escape notice. The local committee here, of which I am chairman, is composed of clergymen of all denominations, of landlords, poor-law guardians, medical officers, merchants, and gentlemen of different creeds and politics. They all bear most willing evidence to the prompt, courteous, and kind attention paid to their applications by your Committee, and never have I heard any other motive assigned for this courteous conduct than that of pure benevolence. In fact, the Mansion House Committee is more popular than the Executive Committee of the Duchess of Marlborough's Fund; for, while the latter don't allow their fund to be applied for the relief of those who in ordinary circumstances could be relieved by the poor-rates, the Mansion House Committee makes no distinction, but leaves the application of their funds to the judgment of the local committees, a thing that has kept thousands out of the workhouse.

" I have the honour to be, my Lord, your most obedient servant,

"✠ HUGH CONWAY."

The following letter was received from the BISHOP of RAPHOE:—

Letterkenny, January 31st, 1880.

" MY DEAR LORD MAYOR,

" I am surprised and pained to learn that the motives of the Mansion House Committee have been questioned in America. Such charges as that to which you allude should not be lightly made. To cast, without clear grounds, even a breath of suspicion on the Committee, and thereby impair its efficiency, is a crime against the famine-stricken people of Ireland. The crime is still greater when such suspicions tend to shake the confidence of the generous-hearted American people, to whom we already owe so much, and from whom we expect still more effectual aid in battling with the terrible distress under which our poor country suffers. Surely the authors of such charges would be more cautious did they remember that in making them they snatch the scanty dole of charity from the mouths of weak women and helpless children; yes, and from the mouths of famishing stalwart men, to whom the hunger-pang is a trifle compared with the unspeakable torture of beholding their wives and children pining away through want before their eyes.

" I am happy to express my belief that these charges are groundless, and to testify that I have never heard the motive of your Committee questioned by those who have had the best opportunities of observing its action. I have myself carefully examined its constitution; I have read its rules; I have day by day taken an interest in its proceedings, like to that with which Lazarus watched the crumbs as they dropped from the rich man's table; yet, neither in its constitution, nor rules, nor daily action, could I detect anything which was not honestly directed, according to the best judgment of its members, to the effectual relief of distress—anything which was not calculated to win the confidence of those most deeply interested in the welfare of the poor sufferers.

" It would be deplorable, indeed, should jealousies or misunderstandings creep in to paralyse the action of the various bodies who so nobly devote themselves to the relief of distress. The field is large; there is more than enough work for all; there is crying need that the efforts of all should be directed to the one great end of saving the people's lives. Hence, humanity, patriotism, charity, and every other motive which can influence an upright mind, demand that each of us should sacrifice his private likings for the common good.

"I am, my dear Lord Mayor, your faithful servant,

"✠ MICHAEL LOGUE, Bishop of Raphoe."

The following was received from the BISHOP OF ELPHIN :—

"*Sligo, January 31st*, 1880.

"MY DEAR LORD MAYOR,

"This evening's post has brought me your esteemed favour of yesterday, and I am glad you have given me the opportunity of expressing my opinion of the Mansion House Committee, over which you preside. In Ireland it need not be observed that its members are men of respectable position, high character, and considerable influence. They hold strong and widely-diverging opinions in religion and politics; yet they have never, that I know or have heard, manifested the slightest religious or political bias in their discussions, or the Lord Mayor of Dublin's decisions as a Committee. Their bond of union, and the sole object for which they are associated, appears unmistakably to be the relief and prevention of distress amongst our poor people; and considering the fearful, bewildering crisis with which your Committee has to deal, and the countless claims it has to weigh and decide, on information often unavoidably incomplete, it has, in my humble opinion, dispensed the funds entrusted to it with as much prudence and efficiency as could be expected from any Central Committee, no matter how constituted. I have had many opportunities for forming the opinion I here express—and to express it, under the circumstances that call for it, is to me a duty of justice as well as of gratitude. It would be a public calamity if your Committee were allowed to be robbed of the confidence it has hitherto so justly enjoyed.

"I have the honour to remain, my dear Lord Mayor,

"Your faithful servant,

"✠ L. GILLOOLY, Bishop of Elphin."

The Most Rev. Dr. WALSHE, Bishop of Kildare and Leighlin, wrote :—

"*Braganza, Carlow, February* 1, 1880.

"MY LORD,

"I have the honour to acknowledge the receipt of your lordship's respected communication of the 30th ult. I was painfully surprised at hearing the statement which was reported to you. It is certainly without foundation. I am confident that your excellent Committee possesses, as it eminently deserves, the confidence of the public, and is justly entitled to our warm gratitude for its generous and laborious exertions to relieve the great distress now so general, and pressing so very sorely in many places upon our afflicted people.

"I have the honour to be, my Lord,

"Your Lordship's faithful servant,

"✠ JAMES WALSHE."

The Most Rev. Wm. FITZGERALD, Bishop of Ross, wrote :—

"*St. Patrick's College, Maynooth, January* 31st, 1880.

"MY DEAR LORD MAYOR,

"I am in receipt of your Lordship's letter which duly reached me here, and in which you ask me to state whether, in my opinion, the Committee of the Mansion

House Fund is worthy or not of public confidence. Whilst, for the sake of the suffering and hunger-stricken poor, I regret exceedingly that there should be any need of testifying to the *bona fides* of your Committee, I lose no time in stating that, as far as I know, the members of your Committee are justly considered to be working with impartiality and success for the alleviation of the prevailing distress. Whatever moneys you have sent to the Diocese of Ross, and, from all that I have heard and read, whatever moneys you have sent elsewhere, are being disbursed for one particular purpose, and that the intended and meritorious one of relieving the distressed poor. Anything said or done to diminish the confidence which the public, up to this, has felt in the energy and honesty of your Committee, tells heavily against the famine-stricken people whom all should strive to serve, and who, as long as the Government refuses to hear their cry for help, have no other resource left than that which is found in the union and co-operation of their patriotic fellow-countrymen, and in the compassionate sympathy of the charitably-disposed all over the world.

"I have the honour to remain, my dear Lord Mayor,

"Your Lordships's obedient and faithful servant,

" WM. FITZGERALD.

The BISHOP of KILMORE wrote :—

" *Cullies House, Cavan, February 1st*, 1880.

" MY DEAR LORD MAYOR,

"I beg to say that I have the utmost confidence in the Mansion House Committee, and consider that its members deserve the gratitude of the country for the noble and generous efforts they are making to relieve its distress.

"I am, my dear Lord Mayor, faithfully yours.

" ✠ N. CONATY, Kilmore.

The following was received from the Most Rev. Dr. M'CARTHY, Bishop of Kerry :—

" *The Palace, Killarney, February 1st*, 1880.

" MY DEAR LORD MAYOR,

"I have no hesitation in expressing my opinion that your Committee is worthy of public confidence.

"I remain your Lordship's most faithful servant,

" ✠ D. M'CARTHY "

The Most Rev. Dr. BUTLER, Bishop of Limerick, wrote :—

" *The Palace, Limerick, February 1st*, 1880.

" MY DEAR LORD MAYOR,

"In reply to your letter I hasten to say that I never entertained the slightest doubt, nor did I ever hear a doubt expressed, of the honour and impartiality of the 'Mansion House Committee' in carrying out the great work of charity to which they have so nobly devoted themselves. The country from end to end has the most absolute confidence in their honesty and ability.

"Believe me to be, yours most faithfully,

" ✠ GEO. BUTLER."

The Bishop of Achonry wrote :—

"*The Abbey, Ballaghaderin*, 1st February, 1880.

"My dear Lord Mayor,

"In my opinion, the Dublin Mansion House Relief Committee is worthy of confidence; and I am sorry to learn that any statement should be made, at home or abroad, that would be calculated to arrest the course of charity, or discredit the unsparing labour of your Committee.

"In the distribution of a relief fund to remote districts it is very difficult to hold the balance so evenly as not to seem to incline one way or the other. I would suggest as standard—the relative distress and population of districts—information on both heads being derived from trustworthy sources.

"I remain, my dear Lord Mayor, your faithful servant,

"✠ F. J. MacCormack, Bishop of Achonry."

The Most Rev. Dr. Leahy, Bishop of Dromore, wrote :—

"*Violet Hill*, February 2nd, 1880.

"My dear Lord,

"In answer to your Lordship's question, I have great pleasure in stating that I consider the Mansion House Relief Committee entitled to the fullest confidence of the clergy and people.

"I am, my dear Lord, your Lordship's obedient servant,

"✠ John P. Leahy."

The Most Rev. Dr. MacCarthy, Bishop of Cloyne, wrote :—

"*Queenstown*, January 31st, 1880.

"My dear Lord Mayor,

"In reply to the circular of the Mansion House Relief Committee, received only this evening, I lose not a moment in saying most emphatically that it is deserving not only of the confidence but of the gratitude of every one (no matter what his creed or politics) who has a heart to feel for the unparalleled sufferings which hundreds of thousands of our poor fellow-countrymen are enduring at this moment from the process of slow starvation in Ireland. Formed on the broadest basis of Christian charity, in which, thank God, members of every denomination can unite, the sole object it proposes to itself, I am firmly convinced, is the relief of distress wherever it is to be found: and its action up to this, as far as I have been able to observe it, has been in perfect keeping with this sublime object. I regret exceedingly that any doubts should have arisen, either at home or abroad, on this point—doubts, whose only effect can be to check the flow of Christian charity to those who are sorely in need of it; but as far as my single testimony can go, I again assert emphatically that such doubts are unfounded.

"I am, my dear Lord Mayor, yours faithfully,

"✠ John MacCarthy."

The following telegram was received from the Most Rev. Dr. Kelly, Bishop of Derry :—

"Most Rev. F. Kelly, Derry; the Right Hon. the Lord Mayor, Dublin.

"Lord Mayor may add Bishop's name to list of prelates who have confidence in the Mansion House Committee."

The BISHOP of FERNS wrote :—

"*Enniscorthy, February 2nd*, 1880.

"MY LORD,

"I am most happy to state my belief that the Dublin Mansion House Committee deserves the fullest public confidence in its distribution of the funds entrusted to its care, as well as the lasting gratitude of the suffering people of Ireland.

"I have the honour to be, my Lord, yours faithfully,

"✠ M. WARREN, Bishop of Ferns."

The BISHOP of WATERFORD wrote :—

"*Waterford, 2nd February*, 1880.

"MY LORD MAYOR,

"I regret exceedingly to learn that it has been publicly stated in America that the Mansion House Committee for the relief of distress in Ireland is influenced in the distribution of the funds at its disposal by other motives than the desire to relieve distress. Such a statement is utterly groundless and most unwarrantable, and must be painful to the feelings of the gentlemen comprising the Committee, who give so much of their valuable time in receiving and examining the numerous applications for relief. There is no hesitation in stating that the Committee is deserving in the highest degree of public confidence, and I trust that the reckless assertions referred to shall not have the effect of damaging the good work in which the members of the Committee are benevolently engaged.

"I am, my dear Lord Mayor, yours very sincerely,

"✠ JOHN POWER, Bishop of Waterford."

The following was received from the VICAR-GENERAL of KILLALOE :—

"*Killaloe, 2nd February*, 1880.

"MY LORD MAYOR,

"As the Bishop, Dr. Flannery, is in Paris, no communication can be received from him in reply to either your letters or your telegrams within the time specified.

"I am, my Lord Mayor, your obedient servant,

"F. J. REDMOND, P.P., V G."

The BISHOP of ARDAGH wrote :—

"*Bishop's House, Newtownforbes, Co. Longford,*

"*31st January*, 1880.

"MY LORD MAYOR,

"In reply to your Lordship's favour of yesterday, I beg to assure you and your worthy co-operators in the holy work of relief of distress in Ireland, that I deem your Committee worthy of the fullest confidence. Your efforts on behalf of our destitute poor deserve the heartfelt gratitude of every friend of Ireland and humanity.

"I have the honour to remain, my dear Lord Mayor,

"Very faithfully yours,

"✠ BARTH. WOODLOCK, Bishop of Ardagh."

The BISHOP of CORK wrote and telegraphed:—

"*Cork, February 2nd, 1880.*

"MY LORD MAYOR,

"I received a circular regarding the Mansion House Fund Committee, signed by your Lordship, and as no other name appears in the document, I trouble your Lordship with my reply. I place the most implicit confidence in the benevolence, the impartiality, and the prudence of the Mansion House Committee.

"I have the honour to be, your Lordship's faithful servant,

"✠ WILLIAM DELANY."

(TELEGRAM.)

"*Feb. 3rd, 1880.*

"Right Rev. Dr. DELANY, Blackrock; the Right Hon. the LORD MAYOR, Dublin.

"I place the most implicit confidence in the benevolence, the impartiality, and prudence of the Mansion House Committee."

The BISHOP of CLOGHER wrote:—

"*Monaghan, 2nd Feb., 1880.*

"MY LORD MAYOR,

"I very willingly testify that the Dublin Mansion House Committee, established for the relief of Irish distress, has my unbounded confidence. No one here entertains the smallest misgiving as to the *bona fides* and impartiality of your Committee, and vast good has been already done by it throughout the famine-stricken districts of the country, without manifesting the slightest political or religious bias. As to certain statements, alleged to have been made in America, calculated to injure the character of your organisation, I would hope and be half inclined to believe there may be some mistake or misunderstanding.

"I am, my Lord Mayor, your faithful servant,

"✠ JAMES DONNELLY, Bishop of Clogher."

The BISHOP of OSSORY wrote:—

"*Kilkenny, 2nd Feb., 1880.*

"MY DEAR LORD MAYOR,

"In reply to the query which has come to hand, whether I consider the Mansion House Committee for the relief of distress in Ireland deserving or not of public confidence, I hasten to reply that your Committee has already effected an immense amount of good, and, in my opinion, merits in the fullest manner the public confidence. It is only to be expected that when great good is being effected, and when all our leading men, whatever their political opinions may be, are found united in promoting the work of charity, some persons should be found anxious to sow dissensions and to introduce elements of discord into your deliberations. I trust that your Committee will pay no attention to such persons, but will continue to promote with the same energy as in the past this great work of public beneficence and true Christian charity in which you have so meritoriously taken a leading part.

"Believe me to remain your faithful servant,

"✠ PATRICK FRANCIS, Bishop of Ossory."

The following letter was read from Most Rev. Dr. NULTY, Bishop of Meath :—

"MY DEAR LORD MAYOR,

"In the circumstances in which I happened to be placed I could not reply to your circular of yesterday in time for last evening's post. In the chorus of approval which that circular has evoked to-day I heartily concur. That the Mansion House Relief Committee enjoys the confidence, and is entitled to the gratitude of the country, seems a truism to which everyone seems willing to bear testimony, and to which I most cheerfully and sincerely subscribe.

"I remain, my dear Lord Mayor, ever respectfully yours,

"✠ THOMAS NULTY."

The following letter was received from the Most Rev. Dr. DORRIAN :—

Chichester Park, Feb. 4, 1880.

"MY DEAR LORD MAYOR,

"On my return from County Down this evening, I beg to acknowledge the receipt to-day of your Lordship's letter in reference to the Relief Committee. Up to the present we received no aid in this diocese from the Mansion House Committee, though in the parish of Kilcoo, County Down, the clergy had to provide for 150 of the labouring adults who had not their dinner on Christmas Day. Your Committee knew nothing of this, and is not to blame. These poor fellows, having no work at home, went to England, but their employment ceased there from the slackness in the iron works, and they had to come home penniless. This will show your Committee how far you are from knowing the extent of the distress over the whole country. However, I am glad to say I heard no complaints of partiality in the distribution of the funds; nor do I for a moment believe any member could be influenced by any other motive than to relieve real want. Still, the question is, was the right thing done? Could not your Committee have started by using its influence to force the Government to give employment and save us from a gigantic system of soup kitchens, which perpetuate misery and do very little to allay hunger. Work brings wages, and wages wants no alms. If your Committee had turned to this way of relieving distress they were too influential to have failed, and no little jealousies would disedify the public. Wages in the beginning; alms, alas, now! I have had no experience of your Committee, but would agree with the Bishop of Elphin that diocesan, not county, committees are more workable for the distribution of relief. Here we made a collection in our churches as soon as we saw alms to be inevitable, and we sent them, like the Christians in the famine under Claudius Cæsar, by the hands of Barnabas and Saul, to help the Christians in Judea—to the bishops.

"I have the honour to remain, my dear Lord Mayor,

"With great esteem, faithfully yours,

"✠ P. DORRIAN."

APPENDIX XII.

REPORT OF THE DONEGAL COUNTY COMMITTEE.

The Donegal Central Committee held its first meeting on January 4th, 1880. It owed its origin to the alarming reports of destitution which daily came in from every part of the county, and to a belief that funds would be more successfully collected and more equally distributed, and that thus the distress could be more effectually met by a central body, in the chief town, than if each locality were left to appeal on its own behalf, with the probable result of receiving not as much in proportion to its needs as to the earnestness of its demands.

At first discouraged by the magnitude of the work before them, and fearing to wound local susceptibilities, the members resolved to confine their action to the northern half of the county, leaving the leading residents of the southern half to organise a similar Central Committee in the town of Donegal. Several causes, however, soon led to the abandonment of this plan. In the first place, so far from encountering any local jealousy, except on the part of a small knot of gentlemen in one district, the Committee received assurance of ready and zealous co-operation from every part of the county. Secondly, the funds then at the disposal of the Committee being almost exclusively made up of contributions sent to the Bishop from America and elsewhere, it was found practically impossible to distribute them in due proportion between two central bodies. Thirdly, the Mansion House Committee, having decided to distribute through our Central Committee the portion of its funds which should be granted to Donegal, very properly required that we should take charge of the whole county.

Accordingly, at a meeting held on January 19th, it was resolved that the Committee should act as a Central Committee for the whole county.

At first the Barony of Innishowen created a difficulty. As it belongs to the Diocese of Derry, an accurate knowledge of the condition of the people, for which the Committee had to rely very much on the experience of its clerical members, could not be easily obtained in the case of Innishowen. Then there was a serious doubt whether the Bishop of Raphoe could distribute outside its limits the large funds sent to him expressly for his own diocese. This difficulty, however, was overcome by the Bishop's leaving entirely to the wisdom of the Committee the decision of the question of justice, and by the Committee trusting to the well-known honesty of the clergy and leading residents of Innishowen for the necessary local knowledge.

Henceforth the Committee extended its action to every part of the county, and soon had in connexion with it forty-six Parochial Committees. Both the Central and Parochial Committees were constituted according to the strictest requirements of impartiality, following, in this respect, to the letter, the rules laid down by the Mansion House Committee. The Central Committee included among its members the Catholic Bishop of the Diocese, the Protestant Bishop of Derry and Raphoe, the clergy of all denominations, medical men, the county members, deputy lieutenants, magistrates, public officials, poor-law guardians, the leading merchants of the town, together with the chairmen of all the Parochial Committees.

From January till the end of July, the Committee had from 60,000 to 70,000 individuals on its relief lists. In providing for the necessities of this multitude of sufferers, over £34,000, with the exception of a small balance remaining in bank, have been expended. Nor does this large sum represent all that has been done for the relief of distress through the agency of the Committee. Considerable quantities of food, seed, and clothing, of which the Committee could not easily take account in making out a balance sheet, have been forwarded to the Committee for distribution. In addition to these, large sums were occasionally sent to the Chairman with directions from the donors to apply them to particular districts. As these sums were not left at the disposal of the Committee to be voted by them in the ordinary way, they naturally were excluded from the balance sheet of the Committee, but will be accounted for in a separate balance sheet to be prepared by the Chairman.

The greatest care has been taken by the Committee that the large sums committed to them for the relief of distress should be administered with the strictest economy. They cannot give a better proof of their success in this respect than the fact that their working expenses, up to the time when their accounts were submitted for audit, was only £48. To this sum £8 has since been added for printing, and a small fee, not yet determined, must be paid to the auditor.

Of the working of the Committee it may not become a member to speak in complimentary terms; still I may be permitted to state that it has been characterized throughout by harmony, cordiality, zeal for the welfare of the sufferers and remarkable unanimity on every question which has come before it.

Whilst the Committee believe that they have laboured conscientiously for the alleviation of distress, they feel that the success of their efforts is mainly due to the generous charity of the American people and the aid which they received from the Mansion House Committee, the New York Herald Committee, and the Liverpool Committee. To the Mansion House Committee they are under a special obligation not only for a chief part of their funds, but also for advice and direction, and for the generous and active sympathy which its members have shown throughout for the suffering people of Donegal.

I enclose copies of the abstract of accounts.

✠ MICHAEL LOGUE, Bishop of Raphoe, Chairman.

Letterkenny, 28th October, 1880.

Balance Sheet of the Donegal Central Relief Fund.

Dr.

1880			£	s.	d.	£	s.	d.
January...Private Subscriptions			103	15	3			
February	,,	,,	97	18	11			
March	,,	,,	548	17	11			
April	,,	,,	6	1	0			
May	,,	,,	6	9	0			
June	,,	,,	5	0	0			
						768	2	1
Londonderry Contribution		...	824	11	0			
Kilmacrock	,,	...	94	12	6			
New York Herald		...	2,000	0	0			
Liverpool Irish Distress Fund Contribution		...	1,500	0	0			
The Land League		...	44	14	4			
The Mansion House Relief Committee		...	14,000	0	0			
Subscriptions per the Right Rev. Dr. Logue		...	14,285	0	0			
						33,288	17	10
						£34,056	**19**	**11**

Cr.

T.	C.	Q.	Committees.		Seed		Provisions		
25	12	0*	Mevagh	...	£150	...	£1,001	0	0
			Gweedore	...	400	...	1,200	0	0
			Lower Templecrone	...	550	...	1,490	0	0
			Dungloe	...	250	...	810	0	0
			Lettermacaward	...	300	...	715	0	0
25	12	0*	Churchill	...	300	...	1,145	0	0
			Kilcar	...	300	...	945	0	0
			Glencolumbkill	...	300	...	995	0	0
9	16	0*	Kilmacrenan	...	70	...	415	0	0
			Ennishowen	...	250	...	200	0	0
			Killybegs	...	250	...	775	0	0
			Kilbarron	...	200	...	665	0	0
			Bundoran	...	130	...	520	0	0
6	8	0*	Convoy	...	100	...	670	0	0
3	4	0*	Stranorlar	...	50	...	320	0	0
15	16	0*	Milford	...	100	...	205	0	0
			Ardara	...	300	...	780	0	0
			Killaghtee	...	150	...	408	0	0
			Dunfanaghy	...	120	...	616	0	0
6	4	0*	Kilcuvogue	...	80	...	501	0	0
			Glenties	...	180	...	545	0	0
			Fintown	...	200	...	550	0	0
			Inver	...	330	...	1,025	0	0
			Dunerana	...	60	...	440	0	0
			Pettigo	...	90	...	370	0	0
6	8	0*	Rathmullan	...	70	...	331	15	0
			Ballintra	...	130	...	370	0	0
			Clonmany	...	100	...	687	0	0
			Clonchanedy	...	350	...	920	0	0
			Donegal	...	250	...	515	0	0
			Killymard	...	130	...	380	0	0
			Fahan	...	25	...	153	0	0
6	8	0*	Fannett	...	50	...	475	0	0
			Moville	...	60	...	335	0	0
			Ramelton	...	90	...	270	0	0
			Culdaff	...	150	...	650	0	0
			Carndonagh	...	90	...	218	0	0
			Malin	...	90	...	340	0	0
6	8	0*	Donaghmore	...	50	...	325	0	0
			All Saints	...	55	...	103	0	0
			Taughboyne	...	55	...	165	0	0
			Burt	...	20	...	77	0	0
23	2	2*	Conwall	...	200	...	815	0	0
			Raymochy	...	30	...	57	0	0
			Desertegney	...	40	...	175	0	0
			Muff	...	50	...	35	0	0
134	18	2*			£7,245		£25,079	15	0
							7,245	0	0

SPECIAL GRANTS.

	£	s.	d.
Right Rev. Dr. Logue, Clothing (15th and 29th March) Supplemented ...	£25	8	0
John M'Devitt (Emigration) ...	4	0	0
Seed paid for and sent to the various Committees, as in margin, 134 tons 18 cwts. 2 qrs.	1,306	14	1
Freight on Seed and Meal, and Expenses of Distributing same	111	11	7
Stamps, Stationery, Printing, &c., &c. ...	48	10	5
Balance in Bank ...	236	0	10
	£1,732	4	11
	£34,056	**19**	**11**

* Seed bought and given to these Committees.

I hereby Certify that I have examined the foregoing Abstract, and find that it contains an accurate Statement of the Receipts and Expenditure of the Donegal Central Relief Fund, from its formation to its close.

Adopted and approved by the Committee.

HUGH STEVENSON, *Auditor*.
✠ MICHAEL LOGUE, *Chairman*.

LETTERKENNY 28*th October*, 1880.

APPENDIX XIII.

AUSTRALIAN CORRESPONDENCE.

"*Town Hall, Geelong, January 20th,* 1880.

"Dear Sir,

"We have the pleasure to remit the accompanying Draft for £650 to the 'Irish Relief Fund.' This sum, cheerfully contributed by the inhabitants of Geelong and its vicinity, represents various classes, creeds and countries. It is hardly necessary to express the desire that it may be distributed on the same broad and benevolent basis.

"We have the honor to be, dear Sir, yours faithfully,

"J. H. Connor, Mayor, *Chairman.*

"Signed on behalf of the Committee.

"Denis O'Brien, Town Councillor, *Hon. Treasurer.*

"Borough Geelong West.

"The Right Honorable The Lord Mayor of Dublin."

"My Lord, "*Town Hall, Melbourne, 22nd January,* 1880.

"I have much pleasure in officially notifying to your Lordship what you have already been made acquainted with by telegram, that a subscription has been commenced in Victoria, to raise funds for the relief of the distress now unhappily prevailing in Ireland.

"A requisition numerously and influentially signed, was presented to me as Mayor of Melbourne, to convene a public meeting in the Town Hall, which was held on the 9th instant. I beg leave to enclose an account of the proceedings, as recorded in the daily papers of the 10th instant.

"On the 15th instant, in conjunction with the Chairman of the Executive Committee, Sir John O'Shanassy, K.C.M.G., M.P., I had the satisfaction of telegraphing to your Lordship through the Union Bank of Australia, London, an intimation that the sum of five thousand pounds was placed to your credit at call in that institution as a first remittance. Subscriptions from all classes continue to pour in to the Central Committee, Melbourne, from all parts of Victoria, and great liberality and generosity are manifested, so that further sums will be transmitted to you by the same channel of communication, and in a similar manner, with as little delay as possible.

"It will afford me satisfaction to be enabled to furnish to the subscribers, such reports as your Lordship may favour me with of the proceedings of the Central Committee over which you preside, and which will doubtless gratify the feeling expressed at the public meeting here, that the distribution should be impartially made throughout Ireland.

"I have the honor to be, my Lord, your Lordship's most obedient servant,

"George Meares, Mayor of Melbourne, *Treasurer.*

"The Right Honorable the Lord Mayor of Dublin."

"*International Exhibition*, 1879, *Offices, Macquarie-street,*
"Sydney, 29th January, 1880.

"My Lord,

"I have the honor to state for your information, that the inauguration of the movement for the collection of funds to alleviate the distress in Ireland, the City of Sydney and the Colony of New South Wales have sent in large donations, and the sums received have been remitted to you by wire as follows:—

Through Bank of Australasia	£1,000
London Chartered Bank	1,000
Bank of New South Wales	1,500
Commercial Bank	2,000
Union Bank of Australia	1,000
Joint Stock Bank	1,000
English and Scottish Bank	1,000
"Eight thousand five hundred pounds.	£8,500

"This amount has been sent free of exchange by the above Banks, and has been contributed by all classes and creeds of the community.

"Further sums will be remitted as received, and it is estimated that three or four thousand pounds are yet to come in.

"It is hoped that the response made by the Australian Colonies to the appeal for help from Ireland will materially mitigate the existing distress, and be accepted as a testimony of the good will felt in Australia towards the Irish people.

"I have the honor to be, my Lord, your most obedient servant,
"P. A. Jennings, *Hon. Treasurer Irish Relief Fund.*
"The Right Honorable the Lord Mayor of Dublin."

"*Court House, Charters Towers, Queensland, 30th March,* 1880.

"Sir,

"As Honorary Secretary to the Irish Distress Relief Fund I now have the pleasure to hand you first of Exchange pro £108 2s. 9d.; second of Exchange by following mail.

"The amount now remitted is the balance in our hands of the contributions (amounting in all to £708 2s. 9d.) given by the people of Charters Towers for the relief of our distressed fellow-countrymen in Ireland.

"Trusting that the national response made throughout these colonies, and from all parts of the British Empire, may be found ample to meet all claims, and relieve the existing distress.

"I have the honor to be, your Lordship's obedient servant,
"Edmund Morey, Police Magistrate, *Hon. Secretary to Fund.*
"The Right Honorable The Lord Mayor of Dublin."

"*Sandhurst, County of Bendigo, Victoria, Australia, April* 1st, 1880.

"My Lord,

"We have now the honor to remit per this mail a further sum of £725, as the second contribution of the people of Sandhurst and District towards the relief of the distressed poor in Ireland. We need not express to you the regret which we feel at the continued distress which still exists there, and we trust that the previous remittance of £700, together with that now made, may be the means, in some degree, of tending towards its alleviation.

"We have the honor to be, your Lordship's most obedient servants,
"John Woodward, *Mayor,*
"Andrew Thunder, *Treasurer.*
"John Nelson, *Hon. Secretary.*
"The Right Honorable The Lord Mayor of Dublin."

"*Sydney International Exhibition*, 1879, *Office of the Commission*,

"153, *Macquarie-street, Sydney*, 24*th April*, 1880.

"My dear Lord Mayor,

"The enclosed lists show the amount forwarded by me up to the present date, and also indicate the agencies through which these cable remittances have been made.

"It is proposed to hold a full meeting of the Committee on Monday, the 26th instant, to wind up the affairs of the Fund, and I hope to be able to transmit you about £2,000 more a little after that date, which will make £27,000 altogether from Sydney, being the contribution of New South Wales.

"I am glad to see our prosperous offshoots, Victoria and Queensland, have also contributed largely to your fund.

"Believe me, my dear Lord Mayor, yours most faithfully,

"P. A. Jennings.

"The Right Honorable The Lord Mayor of Dublin."

"*Carlton House, Perth, Western Australia*, May 1*st*, 1880.

"My Lord,

"I had the honor of addressing you on the 22nd of March, informing you that I had instructed the Manager of the Branch of the Union Bank here to remit by telegram to your credit, with their head office in London, the sum of £500, and also on the 5th of April I had again the pleasure of informing your Lordship that a further remittance of £400 was forwarded to the same Bank to your credit, and I have now, my Lord, the great pleasure of remitting to your credit at the same Union Bank of London, the sum of £275, as our final remittance to the Mansion House Fund, for the relief of our famine-stricken fellow-subjects in Ireland, and I trust to hear that by this time all cause for anxiety has been removed by the liberality of all parts of Her Majesty's dominions, and the kindness of our American kinsmen. It has, my Lord, been a great source of gratification to myself and the Committee, that our appeal to our fellow-colonists of all *creeds* and *denominations* for giving a helping hand (however small) to this *national* and praiseworthy work has been so generally responded to, and trust, that with God's blessing this mutual good feeling will have the effect of more closely cementing the bonds of union between all parts of the British dominions. I see that numbers of people are emigrating to America. I hope some day to see the tide of emigration turned to this part of the Empire, as I fully believe there are few places where an honest, sober and able-bodied working man *can do better*. We are still suffering from the want of farm-labourers and domestic servants, and I should be glad to see some of my suffering fellow-countrymen come and try their fortunes with us.

"We may, my Lord, have perhaps a small sum to transmit after this, which will be forwarded in the same way, and I hope in due time to hear that all these remittances have duly come to hand.

"I have the honor to remain, my Lord, with all respect,

"Your Lordship's obedient servant,

"Samuel Evans Burgess,

"*Chairman of Committee for the Irish Relief Famine Fund.*

"The Right Honorable The Lord Mayor of Dublin."

"*Corporation of Hobart Town, Town Hall, Hobart Town, June 8th,* 1880.

"MY LORD,

"I have the honor to enclose to your Lordship a Draft on the Bank of New South Wales, London, for the sum of £259 6s. 3d., being the balance of the sum collected here in aid of the above fund, which, with the sum of £2,000 before transmitted, makes the total amount subscribed £2,259 6s. 3d.

"Permit me to say I have not received any acknowledgment of the two sums of £1,000 respectively referred to in my letters of the 3rd March and 26th April, which certainly would have been satisfactory, the omission being a matter of surprise.

"I have the honor to be, my Lord, your Lordship's obedient servant,

"J. M. BURGESS, Mayor of the City of Hobart Town.

"The Right Honorable The Lord Mayor of Dublin."

Summary for Tasmania.

Hobart Town	...	...	£2,259	6	3
Launceston	...	...	1,437	0	10
		Total,	£3,696	7	1

IRISH DISTRESS RELIEF FUND.

COMMITTEE ROOMS, TOWN HALL, SYDNEY.

List of Remittances forwarded from Sydney, New South Wales, to Lord Mayor of Dublin.

January,	13th, Bank of Australasia	£1,000
	14th, London Chartered Bank	1,000
	17th, Bank of New South Wales	1,500
	22nd, Commercial Bank	2,000
	30th, Union Bank	1,000
	30th, Australian Joint Stock	1,000
	30th, English and Scottish	1,000
	31st, Oriental Bank	1,000
February,	5th, Mercantile Bank	1,000
	6th, Bank of New Zealand	1,000
	6th, City Bank	1,000
	12th, Bank of New South Wales	2,500
	19th, Bank of Australasia	1,500
	20th, Union Bank	1,500
March,	1st, Commercial Bank	1,500
	2nd, Oriental Bank	1,000
	8th, Australian Joint Stock	1,000
	8th, English and Scottish	1,000
	19th, London Chartered Bank	1,500
	19th, Mercantile Bank	1,000
		£25,000

"N.B.—A sum of nearly £2,000 is available for remittance after the 26th inst

"P. A. J."

REPORT OF IRISH RELIEF FUND, SOUTH AUSTRALIA.

Owing to a series of unavoidable delays I have been compelled to postpone, until I had everything complete, my Report of the Irish Relief Fund movement in this colony. It is now a little over nine months since South Australia took the lead of all the Australian Colonies in organizing practical initiatory steps towards helping Ireland in her then melancholy state of distress.

On Friday, December 19, 1879, a public meeting was held in White's Rooms, Adelaide, presided over by His Worship the Mayor (E. T. SMITH, Esq., M.P.), at which resolutions were adopted, expressing sympathy with the Irish people, and a large and influential Committee was formed to give effect to those resolutions. His Worship the Mayor was chosen Chairman ; Sir GEORGE KINGSTON, Treasurer; and M. T. MONTGOMERY, Hon. Secretary. This Committee shortly after appointed a Sub-Committee, consisting of the MAYOR (Chairman). Hon. H. SCOTT, M.L.C., Messrs. J. C. BRAY, M.P., W. K. SIMMS, M.P., HUGH FRASER, M.P., W. C. BUIK, C. C. KINGSTON, D. M'NAMARA, F. WHOLOHAN, P. HEALEY, J. J. LAFFIN and M. H. DAVIS. to whom was entrusted the real work of carrying on the movement. At first the information to hand bearing on the distress being of a somewhat meagre character, it was decided to postpone prompt action until a reply was received from the Lord Mayor of Dublin (then about to retire from office) to a cablegram sent him by the Mayor of Adelaide, enquiring if the distress in Ireland warranted public appeal here. After an unaccountable delay of ten days, an answer was received in the affirmative, which was followed in a few days by a telegram from the then Lord Mayor elect, the Right Hon. E. DWYER GRAY, M.P., stating—" Distress severe ; assistance urgent." This itself was sufficient evidence to work upon ; but all doubt was, however, dispelled by the announcement the following morning in the telegraphic columns of the *Register* and *Advertiser* that the Duchess of Marlborough, wife of the Lord Lieutenant of Ireland, had started a fund for the relief of the distress in Ireland, and that Her Most Gracious Majesty the Queen had contributed the handsome donation of £500 towards it. The Sub-Committee lost no time, but commenced their very onerous task with a zeal and earnesness which they continued to exercise until the fund was closed. The same plan was decided on which made the Indian Famine Fund such a success, the details of which were supplied to me by Mr. A. ABRAHAMS, whose courtesy I am here desirous of gratefully acknowledging. Acting under the directions of the Sub-Committee, I sent a circular to every Mayor and Chairman of District Council in the colony, requesting them to call a public meeting in their particular districts, with the view of forming local committees to co-operate with the Central Committee in enlisting the sympathy of the public, and raising subscriptions for so noble a purpose. To these meetings it was decided to send delegates from the Central Committee, but a difficulty was experienced in finding a sufficient number who could spare the time, and consequently on my shoulders was thrown almost exclusively the very arduous but pleasing task of advocating the cause of my suffering countrymen upon the public platform. The telegrams which appeared from time to time in the daily papers, together with extracts from home journals on the arrival of each mail, presented a state of poverty and suffering in Ireland, little less in its terrible effects than the melancholy period of 1847 and 1848. The tales of woe were such as to arouse the universal sympathy of the Australian people, in proof of which I would call attention to a remark made by the Lord Mayor of Dublin at a recent public gathering, viz., that of the £180,000 collected altogether by the Dublin Mansion House Committee, fully £90,000 had been contributed by the Australian Colonies.

I now approach the practical portion of the work, and in doing so intend to give a detailed account of the lists sent out, and also a comparison, showing the gross amounts collected in the principal neighbouring colonies and the average donation per head, taking as the basis of my calculation the latest census returns. In lists and books there were distributed altogether 2,427, as follows:—Municipalities, 18; District Councils, 102; newspapers, 25; establishments, 140; institutes, 90; postmasters, 437; managers of stations, 190; banks, 101; hotels, 618; lighthouses, 16; schools, 319; police stations, 89; various committees, 282. Total, 2,427. Of this number there were returned with cash 682; blank, 737; not returned, 1,008.

The total receipts were £8,456 4s. 6d. In the above sum I have not included the amount collected at Kapunda, which reached the handsome figure of £420, and was forwarded direct, making a total realized in this colony of £8,876 4s. 6d.

On June 30, 1879, the population of Victoria was 887,435, and her contributions to the fund amounted to close on £33,000, being an average per head of 8¾d. On the same date the census returns show that New South Wales had a population of 712,019 persons, and her gross contributions came to a little over £31,000, or an average of 10¾d. per head. On December 31, 1878, the population of South Australia was roughly estimated at 252,000, making an average donation per head of 8½d.; and Queensland, with her 210,510 persons, gave over £11,000, or an average of 13¼d. Taking into consideration the relative wealth of each of the above colonies, the result is, that Queensland was the largest contributor, South Australia stands second, New South Wales third, and Victoria fourth.

Of the warm sympathy with which the people of this and the adjoining colonies took up this movement from the start, it is impossible to speak in too high terms of praise. I feel it difficult to refer in sufficiently complimentary terms to the kind feeling displayed by the Press, whose editorial columns were freely used for the purpose of enlisting popular sympathy. The entertainments got up for the benefit of the fund were with one exception financial failures; but I think it only just to make special mention of the kindness shown by Mr. JAS. ALLISON, who gave the use of his Theatre for a night's performance, and Mr. ARTHUR GARNER, who gave the services of his company. Amongst others deserving of special notice I must not forget Messrs. R. CLELAND & SONS, of Port Adelaide, who stored, free of charge, for several months, some two hundred and odd bags of wheat; also Mr. J. C. BRAY, M.P., and Mr. W. K. SIMMS, M.P., who made a vigorous personal canvas of the city in connection with the Mayor, to whom I shall have occasion to refer later on. The Hon. the CHIEF SECRETARY, in giving £25 worth of postage stamps, and the Hon. the Commissioner of Public Works, in allowing all contributions of wheat to be transmitted free on the Government railways, exhibited kindly feeling, which should not be forgotten by the Irish people. The fund had another warm supporter in Mr. J. W. B. CROFT, of the Telegraphic Department, who was instrumental in collecting £141 16s. 6d. from the operators on the Port Darwin line, £50 of which was obtained by a young lady (Miss LITTLE). But the heart and soul of the movement was our present popular Mayor of Adelaide (Mr. E. T. SMITH, M.P.) The eagerness with which he worked from the very commencement of the fund, stamps him as the most genuine and ardent friend the suffering poor of Ireland have had in the Australian Colonies. When I mention that by his own individual labours he collected over £600, I think this statement falls far short of the compliment he is entitled to. In him the Irish people have had a good kind friend, who laboured hard to rescue them from their miserable position. The amount actually remitted from the colony was £8,029 17s. 5d. There is yet a small balance to the credit of the fund in the bank, which will be forwarded in a few days.

I have endeavoured to make this Report as complete as possible, and when it is read, as it will be, by millions of my countrymen, I have no doubt that there will run through every Irish heart a feeling of gratitude and thankfulness towards those who held out a helping hand to save them from the fearful scurge of famine.

M. T. MONTGOMERY,
Hon. Secretary, Irish Relief Fund.

Adelaide, October 11, 1880.

REPORT OF IRISH RELIEF FUND, SOUTH AUSTRALIA.

Amounts Received.

From—	£	s.	d.	From—	£	s.	d.
Adelaide	2,109	13	0	Robe	43	9	6
Mount Gambier	512	7	10	Laura	42	17	6
Norwood	274	18	5	Oulnina Station	40	0	0
Burra	268	5	4	Yongala	39	19	6
Port Augusta	243	8	0	Rapid Bay	38	17	7
Jamestown	237	5	7	Melrose	37	6	2
Port Adelaide	215	7	2	Condowie	36	8	4
Gawler	204	15	0	Moonta	36	2	8
Sevenhills and Clare	201	15	9	Yarcowie	32	10	0
Saddleworth	189	18	11	Strathalbyn	31	18	6
Narracoorte	174	16	2	Alma	31	16	8
Georgetown	154	14	3	Port Pirie	31	4	3
Millicent	151	10	0	Narridy	30	5	0
Operators on Port Darwin Line, per J. W. B. Croft, Esq.,	141	16	6	Blanchetown	29	0	0
				Keyneton	26	15	6
				Virginia	26	1	6
Beautiful Valley	136	18	0	Callington	24	16	4
Yarcowie	112	15	0	Yorketown	23	15	9
West Torrens	99	9	4	Balaklava	23	8	4
Caltowie	97	14	3	Spalding	22	1	0
Port Lincoln	93	11	8	Canowie Station	21	8	0
Koolunga	92	7	0	Yatina	21	5	0
Kadina	88	12	3	Kenton Valley	20	16	10
Nairne	86	11	6	Angaston	19	18	0
Morphett Vale	80	6	4	Mount Bruce Station	18	10	0
Redhill	80	4	3	Terowie	17	16	0
Lancelot	79	1	10	Hoyleton	17	18	6
North Adelaide	74	3	6	Two Wells	17	14	0
Milang	69	18	10	Salisbury	17	9	6
Crystal Brook	69	10	0	Bramfield Station	17	2	0
Gladstone	67	15	0	Light	17	1	6
Mintaro	66	9	0	Waterloo	15	15	6
Glenelg	63	15	11	Farrell's Flat	15	7	6
Riverton	63	12	6	Undalya	15	2	9
Willunga	61	9	6	Yattala	13	16	0
Beltana	59	11	0	Yardea	13	15	0
Teatree Gully	56	3	3	Canowie Station	13	12	6
Pekina	54	19	0	Booyoolie	13	3	0
Warnertown	54	17	4	Limestone Ridge	13	0	0
Border Town	52	2	0	Pinda	12	15	6
Maitland	52	2	0	Warooka	12	12	0
Quorn	52	1	3	Hamilton	12	11	0
Mannum	51	6	3	Keilli	12	11	0
Marion	47	10	0	McEwin	12	2	6

From—	£	s.	d.	From—	£	s.	d.
Stirling, East	11	10	6	Para Wirra	4	5	0
Curnamona	10	15	0	Middleton	3	17	6
Tanunda	10	12	0	Nalpa Station	3	14	0
Hallett	10	0	0	Warcowie Station	3	4	6
Palmer	9	8	6	Mudla Wirra	2	10	0
Freeling	9	4	8	Minlaton	2	5	4
Mount Torrens	9	3	6	Unley	2	4	6
Ediowie	7	17	6	Gepp's Cross	2	2	0
Truro	7	13	0	Kangarilla	1	15	0
Mingibbe	7	10	6	Armagh	1	14	0
Apoinga	7	5	0	Eudunda	1	12	0
Modbury	6	18	6	Portallock Station	1	11	4
Gumeracha	6	17	6	Willowie	1	11	0
Kanyaka	6	14	0	Finniss Point	1	10	0
Myrtle Spring Station	6	13	0	Matt Station	1	10	0
Portee Station	6	5	6	Venus Bay	1	5	8
Brimbago Station	6	3	6	Cradock	1	2	6
Joyce Station	6	0	6	Upper Sturt	1	1	0
Hermitage	6	0	0	Wiston	0	14	2
Streaky Bay	5	18	6	Navan	0	10	0
Minbury Station	5	15	0	Salem	0	2	0
Blyth Plains	5	12	0				
Second Valley	5	6	2	Total	£8,456	4	6

LETTER OF THANKS.

The following Letter of Thanks was addressed by the LORD MAYOR of DUBLIN to the Chairmen of the various Committees and others in Australasia whose generous labours had been so magnificently made known to Ireland, whilst yet their names were withheld :—

MANSION HOUSE FUND FOR THE RELIEF OF DISTRESS IN IRELAND.

Dublin, March 6th, 1880.

" DEAR SIR,

"In sending you a list of subscriptions to this fund, I find it is impossible adequately to express my sense of gratitude to the people of Australia for their unbounded munificence towards this country. When I reflect that from the Australian Continent and the isles, the subscriptions up to this reach the sum of £54,070, it is little to say that the memory of such generosity will never be effaced from the mind of the Irish Nation. The generosity becomes still more remarkable when it is remembered that all the information that has reached your country was contained in a few meagre telegrams, and that without pausing for detailed information, regardless of every consideration save that Ireland was in distress, the hearts of your people were opened, and the tide of generosity which set in, in a few hours after the first communication was sent from this Committee, has continued to flow uninterruptedly to the relief of a stricken land. So rapidly have the contributions come, so little did any consideration of self weigh with your generous people, that I have not received sufficient information to enable me to thank the Committees by the names of their chairmen or secretaries. I postponed from time to time making this acknowledgment, in hope that some information of that nature would reach me, but as yet it has not arrived. One of our Melbourne communications bore the respected name of JOHN O'SHANASSY, and I have asked him to be the medium of making this communication to the other cities and places from which contributions have so bounteously come. According to the entries in the books of this committee the contributions from Australasia stand as follows :—

Melbourne,	£19,000	} For Victoria.
Ballarat,	1,000	
Sydney,	18,000	For New South Wales.
Charters Towers,	600	} For Queensland.
Brisbane,	7,500	
Adelaide,	4,500	For South Australia.
Launceston,	500	For Tasmania.
Wellington,	200	
Dunedin,	1,200	
Invercargill,	300	} New Zealand.
Christchurch,	600	
Oamaru,	200	
Hokitika,	470	

making a grand total of £54,070, and this, as I have said, in response to a few meagre telegrams.

"Our hearts are filled with admiration for such a people. I would ask as a favor that lists of your Committees and of the subscriptions to your funds be sent us here, that they may be preserved with the records of this Committee, as a bright example of generosity to succeeding generations. Our entire fund now amounts to

£100,647, of this we have distributed through local Committees, up to this date, the sum of £50,432. These local Committees are now spread over 29 out of the 32 Counties of Ireland, so you will see that the area of our operations is not limited to any part of the country. Wherever distress of an exceptional nature exists, we have endeavoured to relieve it. Of course the distress is greatest in the counties along the Western and North Western coasts, but in some of our midland counties and in wide portions of the North and South, the pressure of famine is keenly felt. A list of the grants made out in counties accompanies this letter. The local Committees, of which over 600 are now working, comprise (with very rare exceptions) the clergymen of the Catholic and Protestant churches, the dispensary doctors, and guardians of the poor. We can refer with pride to the testimony recorded in our favor on a recent occasion by the Catholic Hierarchy of Ireland, and by His Grace the Protestant Archbishop of Dublin, to whose constant co-operation we are much indebted. This testimony, coupled with that borne by clergymen and laymen from all parts of the country, to the worth of our organisation, enables me to assure you that your contributions have not failed to answer the noble purpose for which you, I am confident, wish them applied, namely, the relief of distress, without distinction of creed or party. This has been and will continue to be the aim and object of this Committee.

"The total of the persons who are dependent for weekly supplies on this Committee, according to the returns of the local Committees, numbers considerably over 300,000. But this Committee fears the worst has not yet come. During the period that has elapsed since the formation of our Committee the inclemency of the weather, and the absence of all employment in the fields and in the farmyard, necessarily intensified the people's suffering, and they demanded our constant and most generous attention. We have spared neither labour nor money in relieving the afflicted. Thank God, we have succeeded in saving hundreds, thousands of lives.

"The funds now in hands will enable us to continue our work during the months of March and April.

"But we are painfully convinced that the most trying period of this year of bitter trial for our people will be that comprised in the Summer quarter (May, June, and July,) when field-work will not be required, and the harvest is ripening. Such has been the history of former famines. Many persons in Australia will remember the expression so familiar in the mouths of our peasantry, "the year of the Dear Summer." We have, however, great confidence that the generous friends of humanity throughout the world symphathising with our poor people, will enable us to continue our operations to the end.

"In my own name and in that of the Mansion House Committee, and in the name of a country not unmindful of its benefactors, I thank you and all the people of Australasia,

"And have the honor to be yours faithfully,

"E. DWYER GRAY, Lord Mayor of Dublin.

"Since writing, I have received the following additional subscriptions, not included in the list before given:—

Melbourne,	£3,000	Geelong,	£650
Sydney,	2,500	Christchurch,	400
Hobart Town,	1,000	Waimate,	315
Wellington,	500	Kapunda and Light Relief Fund, Victoria,	300

"The last Melbourne subscription included the munificent donation of the Victorian Railway employés of £1,100.

"This makes the total subscriptions from Melbourne £22,000, and from Sydney £20,500, and the entire sum received up to date from Australasia £62,735.

"8th March, 1880."

NEW ZEALAND CORRESPONDENCE.

"MY LORD,   "*Greymonth, New Zealand, 23rd February,* 1880.

"We have the honour on behalf of the 'Greymonth Irish Distress Relief Fund Committee' to remit the accompanying Bank Draft for four hundred pounds sterling (£400), being the second instalment of the sum contributed by the residents of the Borough of Greymonth, and the surrounding district of Grey Valley, towards the alleviation of the distress unhappily existing in Ireland.

"The first instalment of £200 was remitted by Bank Draft also by the January mail, through the National Bank of New Zealand in Auckland; advice of which was forwarded by telegram.

"We may add that the amount raised here has been ungrudgingly and cheerfully given by persons of various classes, creeds, and countries, and feel confident that we need scarcely express the desire, that the relief which it can seasonably afford may be distributed consistently with the same broad and philanthropic spirit as that by which the contributors were actuated.

"When the list shall have been closed, the final instalment will be duly transmitted, and meantime, requesting the acceptance of the total amount remitted (£600) as a proof of the sympathy and benevolence of the colonists of this portion of the British Empire.

"We have the honour to be, my Lord, your obedient servants,

"RICHARD MANCORROW, Mayor, *Hon. Treasurer.*
"C. C. M'CARTHY, *Hon. Secretary.*

"The Right Honorable the Lord Mayor of Dublin."

         "*Kemard Goldfield, Westland, New Zealand, February 23rd,* 1880.

"MY LORD,

"We have the honor to forward Draft for one hundred and ninety pounds (£190), as a second instalment, making a total of £330 towards the relief of the sufferers in Ireland.

"We would specially mention that of the above sum £59 19s. has been subscribed in Goldsborough (Old Waimea), £37 8s. 6d. in Stafford, and £15 5s. in Christchurch Road. The balance has been subscribed in this town and surrounding districts.

"Our population being comparatively small, and chiefly composed of the working class, this amount is a sufficient testimony of the deep sympathy we, in this land of comparative prosperity, have for the famine-stricken people of Ireland.

"That the present calamity is mainly due to the abominable land system, and to the recurrence of bad seasons, is evident to the world; and we trust that the constitutional agitation which is now being carried throughout the length and breadth of the land, will culminate in establishing improved Land Laws. This would secure Ireland from these periodical scourges, and enable the tiller of the soil to live in prosperity and contentment.

"In conclusion we have much pleasure in stating that the appeal made in these localities to alleviate the distress in Ireland, has been most cheerfully responded to by all creeds and classes of our community.

"We have the honor to be, my Lord, your obedient servants,

"JOHN S. PRAUN, Mayor.
"JOHN O'HAGAN.
"PETER DUNGAN.
"PATRICK MORAN
"PATRICK DUGGAN, *Hon. Sec.*

"The Right Honorable The Lord Mayor of Dublin."

NEW ZEALAND CORRESPONDENCE.

"*Mayor's Office, Auckland, New Zealand, 2nd March*, 1880.

"MY LORD MAYOR,

"I have the honour to intimate that in accordance with the request contained in your telegram relative to the distress in Ireland, I took steps, through a public meeting, to raise funds in aid of the unfortunate sufferers. I have much pleasure in stating that a good response has been given to the appeal made, and I have now the honour to forward to your Lordship a Draft for eleven hundred and fifty pounds, of which you will have received telegraphic advice in order to its prompt disbursement.

"There are some further sums yet to come in, and I shall endeavour to have the Fund closed and the balance forwarded to your Lordship by next mail.

"In the hope that the efforts so laudibly put forth by your Relief Committee will be productive of much good in mitigating the severity of this calamity.

"I have the honour to be on behalf of the Committee,

"Your Lordship's obedient servant,

"THOMAS PEACOCK, Mayor.

"*Charleston, West Coast, New Zealand, March 2nd*, 1880.

"MY LORD,

"You will be pleased to accept, in response to your Lordship's most noble and timely appeal, the enclosed Draft on the Bank of New Zealand for one hundred and five pounds seventeen shillings (£105 17s.) sterling, which, on behalf of the Irish Relief Committee, we have the honour of transmitting, as an addition to the General Relief Fund, now so universally and liberally subscribed to. The amount, we need hardly say, is the generous and almost spontaneous offerings of the people of the Charleston and Brighton districts (whose names we enclose), without distinction of race, creed, or nationality; and though small in comparison with larger and perhaps more favoured localities, in this portion of the British Dominions, we hope it may in some measure tend to alleviate the dire distress which apparently at present unhappily prevails in Ireland.

"Sympathising with the Irish people in the trying ordeal through which they are passing, and trusting to your Lordship's wisdom and discretion for an equitable distribution, where most needed, of the enclosed remittance,

"We have the honour to remain, &c.,

"RICHARD DELANY, *Hon. Sec.*
"HENRY W. LUTTON, County Chairman. } *Hon. Treasurers.*
"PHILIP MCCARTHY,

"The Right Honorable The Lord Mayor of Dublin."

"*City Council Chambers, Nelson, New Zealand, 5th March*, 1880.

"MY LORD,

"To-day I had the great pleasure of forwarding the sum of £300 by cable to your Lordship, for the relief of my starving countrymen at our antipodes. Having learned of the awful distress I wrote a letter in one of our local papers, and immediately afterwards the Mayor called a public meeting, which was attended by clergymen of all denominations, who expressed their sympathy with the poor sufferers, and organised a Committee to collect funds to assist the distressed. I have the honor to be the Honorary Secretary to the Relief Committee, and I need not state I felt proud in being able to forward such a good cause, and used every means in my power to make the collection a success. Dreading the awful consequence of a famine, I thought it desirable to forward the amount immediately to alleviate the poor people. I expect to be able to forward an additional £70 or £80 by next mail

The people of Nelson have acted nobly in the great work of charity, and the amount collected speaks very creditably for a little colonial town of about 20,000 inhabitants the majority of whom are working men. God bless them! Thank God, we don't know what poverty is out here, and if ever we can assist you let us know. To give you an idea of the attachment of Irishmen to the 'Old Country,' and their readiness to assist you in any way possible, five gold-diggers left their claim, and walked about 40 miles into town to me with their mite (£5) to help to buy food for the poor souls.

"Poor Ireland! What must proud England's feeling be? Standing listlessly by at the door of our famine-stricken country, while all Christendom cries *shame!* Even out here, I see that England's treatment of Ireland is looked into by people who were staunch upholders of her Government, and they now think differently from what they did.

"Some discussion arose as to who the money would be forwarded to, and when I informed the meeting I had the pleasure of knowing you, and that you were son of the illustrious Sir John Gray, they were perfectly satisfied. If you have time an acknowledgment of this letter would be gratefully received.

"I have the honour to be, your obedient servant,
"ARTHUR M'MURROUGH KAVANAGH.

"*Council Chambers, Otago, New Zealand, Cromwell,* 10*th March,* 1880.
"MY DEAR LORD MAYOR,

"I have the honour to enclose Draft in your favour for £140 towards the 'Irish Relief Fund.' I regret being unable to make the amount £10 more without further delay in forwarding the money.

"The sympathisers of the Colonies have been very general in the matter, and when you recollect that this locality contains only a small proportion of Irishmen, you will find additional pleasure in discovering the kindly sympathy of the English and Scotch colonists.

"The acquaintance which I had the honour to enjoy of your uncle, Judge Gray, whose name has been revered by all whose privilege it was to come in contact with him, renders the present correspondence with you the more happy, and doubtless the connexion between you and our late district judge has not been without its effects in inducing liberality of donations from those who still cherish their memory.

"Hoping that our mite may be acceptable, and may, even to some small extent, relieve the distress now prevailing in the land that I, at least, am proud to call 'land of my birth,'

"I have the honour to be, my dear Lord Mayor, your most obedient servant,
"CHARLES COLCLOUGH, Mayor of Cromwell.
"Edmund Dwyer Gray, Esq., M.P., Lord Mayor of Dublin."

"*Bank of New Zealand, Hokitika,* 10*th March,* 1880.
"MCLEAN W. JACK, ESQ., Chairman, Irish Famine Relief Fund.
"DEAR SIR

"In answer to your inquiry as to the terms of the telegram sent to London on account of the first payment by your Committee, I have to say that the following is a copy of the cablegram—'Pay Lord Mayor Dublin from Mayor Hokitika four hundred seventy pounds.'

"Yours faithfully, JOHN P. HARRIS, Manager."

"Received from J. GRIMMOND, Esq., Mayor of Ross, the sum of forty-four pounds (£44), 'for Irish Relief Fund.' Said payment being included in telegraphic remittance of £470, referred to on opposite side.

"H. D. RAE, *Hon Secretary.*

NEW ZEALAND CORRESPONDENCE.

"*Borough Council Chambers, Ross, New Zealand, 20th March*, 1880.

"RIGHT WORSHIPFUL SIR,

"Please find enclosed Bank Draft for forty-four pounds, thirteen shillings, sterling (£44 13s.), collected in this borough on behalf of your Irish Famine Relief Fund. A sum of forty pounds I forwarded to you through the Mayor of Hokitika some time ago by cablegram, being a portion of four hundred and seventy pounds, sterling (£470), remitted from Hokitika, as per acknowledgment from his Secretary herewith enclosed.

"This is only a small borough of about four hundred inhabitants, but it has given them the greatest pleasure to be enabled to contribute their mite to the relief of a suffering people, and I sincerely hope that before long the period of depression may pass away for ever from Ireland.

"I have the honor to be, Worshipful Sir, your obedient servant,

"JOSEPH GRIMMOND, Mayor, *Hon. Treasurer.*
"JOHN B. LOPAS, *Hon. Secretary.*"

"*Town Clerk's Office, Westport, 24th March*, 1880.

"SIR,

"I have the honor to forward you the enclosed (first solo of exchange) for the sum of one hundred and fifty pounds sterling, being first instalment of public subscriptions from the town of Westport and County of Buller, in aid of the 'Irish Famine Relief Fund.'

"Trusting that the amount may be opportune and serviceable, and that the Irish distress may soon be alleviated.

"I have the honor to be your most obedient servant,

"JOHN MUNRO, Mayor, *Borough of Westport, Hon. Treasurer.*"

"*Council Chambers, Thames, New Zealand, April 7th*, 1880.

"MY LORD,

"I have the pleasure to enclose Draft for one hundred pounds (£100) in aid of the distress in Ireland, said amount being the second contribution of the people of Thames for that purpose.

"I trust that with the advancing summer and relief afforded, the hardships of the poor may be greatly if not entirely removed.

"I have the honour to be, my Lord, your obedient servant,

"LOUIS EHRENFRIEOL, Mayor.

"The Right Honorable The Lord Mayor of Dublin."

Municipal Offices, Invercargill, New Zealand, April 15th, 1880.

"MY DEAR LORD MAYOR,

"I have the honor to transmit to you a Bank Draft for £80 5s. 2d. I have already forwarded to you through the Union Bank of Australia, by cablegram, the sum of £500 : namely, on the 5th February, £300, and on the 9th March, £200. The Draft now enclosed will make the subscription from the district of Southland, of which Invercargill is chief town, £580 5s. 2d.

"This amount is sufficiently large to warrant my expressing the opinion, that with the commercial depression which has affected the Colony, as indeed it has the whole Empire, and with the ordinary calls upon colonists, who have to support wholly, or in part, all the social and religious institutions in their midst, which in many parts of the United Kingdom are maintained from endowments, the residents of this southern district of New Zealand have subscribed very liberally, whilst the expressions of sympathy with the distress that has unhappily existed, but which, I hope, may pass away as your summer approaches, have been universal. The cause of the distress has not been asked or spoken of; it was simply, did it exist? and that being affirmed, the donors forthwith gave according to their means.

"I enclose you a newspaper, the *Southland Times*, which contains the subscription list.

"I should like to add, in conclusion, that although I have the privilege of forwarding the sum collected, yet that the honor attached to a successful appeal to our colonists, must be shared with me by the two gentlemen who filled the honorary positions of treasurer and secretary, namely, Mr. DAVID ROCHE, and Mr. W. B. SCANDRETT, the Town Clerk of Invercargill.

"I have the honor to be, my dear Lord Mayor,

"Your Lordship's obedient servant,

"G. GOODWILLIE, Mayor."

"The Right Honorable The Lord Mayor of Dublin."

"*Ruthin, West Coast of New Zealand, 17th April,* 1880.

"EDMUND DWYER GRAY, Esq., Lord Mayor of Dublin.

"SIR,

"Herewith please find two Bank Drafts, one for £193 9s., the other for £8, making a total of £201 9s., which you will kindly place to the credit of the 'Irish Relief Fund.' The amount was contributed by the inhabitants of this remote corner of the world, who are principally engaged in mining, and who have earned for themselves a character for generosity whenever an appeal has been made to them for the relief of suffering humanity. Hoping that the sufferings of the poor people in our native country will have lost most of their intensity by the time this letter will reach you,

"I have the honour to remain, your obedient servant,

"PATRICK BRENNAN.

"P.S. Please acknowledge receipt in the *Freeman's Journal.*"

"*Bank of New Zealand, Waimate, 23rd April,* 1880.

"MY LORD,

"On the 28th February last, I wrote you advising having forwarded to our Christchurch branch the sum of £315 sterling, to be cabled direct to you as a first instalment from this place on account 'The Irish Famine Fund.' I now beg to enclose first exchange of Draft on our London office, in your favour for £5 13s. 1d., being balance of subscription to date for same purpose.

"I am, my Lord, yours most respectfully,

"ROBERT M'OWEN, *Hon. Treasurer, Irish Famine Relief Fund.*

"The Right Honorable The Lord Mayor of Dublin."

"*Oamaru, New Zealand, April 23rd,* 1880.

"MY LORD,

"At a public meeting of the inhabitants of this town, held on January 21st, 1880 (and presided over by the Mayor), for the purpose of expressing their sympathy with the people of Ireland in their great distress, it was unanimously resolved that a Committee be formed to obtain subscriptions. On the 13th February the Committee had the pleasure of sending you (per cable) through the National Bank of New Zealand, the sum £200 as their first instalment.

"I have now the pleasure of enclosing herewith a Draft on the Bank of England for the sum of £100, being the balance of the amount collected in this part of New Zealand towards the alleviation of the distress in Ireland.

"I have the honour, my Lord, to be your most obedient servant,

"W. J. SMITH, *Treasurer, Irish Famine Relief Fund, Oamaru.*

"The Right Honorable The Lord Mayor of Dublin."

"*Christchurch, New Zealand, April 24th,* 1880.

"MY LORD,

"In response to your circular asking for subscriptions to the 'Irish Famine Relief Fund,' I had the honour to forward by cablegram on February 3rd last, through the Bank of New Zealand, the sum of six hundred pounds, and again on March 5th, an additional sum of four hundred pounds. I now enclose a Bank Draft for the sum of four hundred and fifty pounds, eighteen shillings and three pence, being the balance left in my hands after paying the expenses of advertising and collection, These sums have been subscribed by the citizens of Christchurch and surrounding country, during a period of great commercial depression, otherwise I have reason to think the amount would have been much larger; however, I hope this donation will be acceptable, and I shall rejoice to hear that the worst is over so far as the distress in Ireland is concerned.

"I have the honour to be your Lordship's most obedient servant,

"C. J. JETZ, Mayor.

"The Right Honorable The Lord Mayor of Dublin."

"*Wellington, New Zealand, May 3rd,* 1880.

"MY LORD,

"I have the honour to inform you that a public subscription in aid of the Irish distress, was opened in this city, and, considering the commercial depression which has for some time prevailed here, I think it may be said that the invitation to subscribe was very fairly responded to. The total amount subscribed was £761 12s., of which £402 4s. 11d. was the balance of a subscription list previously opened by Messrs. BLUNDELL, Brothers, our proprietors of the *Evening Post* here, see copy, they having previously sent £300 direct to your Lordship. I had the pleasure to forward £500 on the 3rd of March, and £165 on the 11th March, both by cable. the Bank of New Zealand making no charge for remission. £14 8s. 11d. was paid for the two telegrams, and £13 8s. 1d. for canvassing, advertising and other necessary expenses. The balance amounts to £67 15s. for which I have now the pleasure to send a Draft payable at sight, it not being thought necessary to send such a small amount by cable. The Committee direct me to express their hope that the effort they have made will have contributed in some slight degree to mitigate the great distress unfortunately prevailing in Ireland.

"I have the honour to be, my Lord, your Lordship's most obedient servant,

"J. E. PAGE, *Hon. Secretary.*"

"*Dunedin, New Zealand*, 13*th August*, 1880.

"MY DEAR LORD,

"I have much pleasure in enclosing herewith a draft for £44 17s. 11d., being the balance (less charges) of the sum of £1,892 14s. 5d., collected by the Dunedin Committee, in aid of the 'Irish Relief Fund.' I should have liked to have forwarded the balance earlier, as the object of the Fund was one where despatch was of all importance, but it is only within the last few days, that the last county subscription, amounting to £30 16s. 2d., came to hand, and I seize now the first opportunity of remitting it. I also have to acknowledge the kind recognition of our efforts as conveyed in the letter of the Secretary of your Committee of the 10th May last, and in reply I am sure I only express the feelings of all who have contributed towards the Fund, when I say that we are amply repaid for our efforts in the consciousness that we have in some small degree helped towards the alleviation of the great misery brought about by the Famine.

"I am, my dear Lord, faithfully yours,

"HENRY J. WALLER, Mayor

"The Right Honorable The Lord Mayor of Dublin."

APPENDIX XIV.

LIST OF SUBSCRIPTIONS.

Name		Address		£	s.	d.
"A. B."	..	per T. M. Hutton, Esq.	..	2	0	0
"A. B. C."	..	per Rev. Canon Bagot	..	1	0	0
Abbitt, Samuel	..	Redruth, Cornwall	..	5	0	0
Abdon, De Goity Gerain	..	Calle del Prado, 3 Vittoria	..	10	0	0
Abraham, H.	..	per P. Walsh, Dublin	..	1	1	0
Abraham, John	..	Dublin	..	2	0	0
Abraham, Mrs. Jane	..	Dublin	..	2	0	0
Addington & Co., S.	..	London	..	5	0	0
Adelaide	..	Australia, South	..	7,400	0	0
Aden (Collection)	..	Arabia	..	82	0	0
A Dublin Man	..	Derry	..	3	0	0
A Friend	..	Scotland	..	0	5	0
Do.	..	per Jonathan Pim	..	1	0	0
Do.	..	Newcastle-on-Tyne	..	10	0	0
Do.	..	per Mitchell & Son, Dublin	..	5	0	0
Do.	..	per William Rollo, Arbroath	..	5	0	0
Do.	..	Chapelizod	..	0	5	0
Do.	..	Canada	..	1	0	0
Do.	..	Arbroath, N.B.	..	20	0	0
Do.	..	per Royal Bank	..	0	5	0
Do.	..	per Ash & Lacy, Birmingham	..	5	5	0
Do.	..	Kilmarnock	..	3	0	0
A Friend	..	Pittsburg, U.S.A.	..	1	0	0
A Fellow-countryman	..	2, Anson-road, London, N.	..	1	10	0
A Few Workmen	..	Pinkerton, Ontario	..	2	0	0
"A. G."	..	per National Bank (Rathmines Branch)	..	1	0	0
"A. G. A."	..	Norwood	..	3	0	0
A Harrow Man	..	per Sir John Barrington	..	10	0	0
Alexander, G. J.	..	Dublin	..	10	10	0
Allen, C.	..	10, Norton, Tenby	..	25	0	0
Alliance Gas Company	..	Grafton-street, Dublin	..	50	0	0
Allistan (Collection)	..	Toronto, Canada	..	29	13	0
Allsopp & Sons	..	Burton-on-Trent	..	105	0	0
A Lady	..	per W. L. Copplestone	..	0	10	0
A Lady	..	per W. L. Joynt	..	0	5	0
A Little North Carolina Girl	..	per A. Sprunt	..	0	15	5
A Lighthouse-keeper	..	—		1	0	0
A Poor Widow	..	per Sir John Barrington	..	0	2	0
A Married Constable	..	R. I. C.	..	0	2	6
Ambleside Church	..	per Rev. W. Aston, Ambleside	..	20	11	0
Amer, E.	..	Ranelagh, Dublin	..	1	0	6
Amiers, J. F.	..	22, Eden-quay, Dublin	..	5	0	0
Amis, Societe des, France	..	per Samuel Brun, Pontefract, Yorkshire	..	2	6	1
Andrews, Robert	..	—		5	0	0
An English Workman		—		0	2	6
An English Academician	..	per Rev. Dr. Tisdall, Dublin	..	25	0	0
An Irishman	..	London	..	0	5	0
		Carried forward	.. £	7,804	19	6

346   APPENDIX XIV.

			£	s	d
	Brought forward		7,864	19	6
Anonymous	per Rev. M. A. Fricker		3	0	0
Do.	per Rev. N. Donnelly		1	0	0
Do.	per National Bank		3	0	0
Do.	Camden Town, London		5	0	0
Do.	per William Fleming, Dublin		1	1	0
Do.	per H. J. Gill		1	0	0
Do.	—		0	10	0
Do.	—		10	0	0
Do.			1	0	0
Do.	Dublin		1	0	0
Do.	per Most Rev. Dr. Trench		2	0	0
Do.	per Most Rev. Dr. Trench		3	1	9
Do.	per Sir John Barrington		1	0	0
Do.	per Rev. J. Daniel, P.P.		1	0	0
Do.	per Charles Kennedy		0	10	0
Do.	per Captain M'Innery, R.I.A.		2	0	0
Do.	per Duffy, Mangan & Butler		50	0	0
Do.	Ardee		10	0	0
Do.	per Royal Bank		10	0	0
Do.	Blandford		0	1	0
Do.	Bristol		0	5	0
Do.	Carlisle		0	1	0
Do.	Dublin		10	0	0
Do.	per Mrs. Day, London		0	12	6
Do.			50	0	0
Do.	Germany		2	0	0
Do.	do.		1	0	0
Do.	Glasgow		5	0	0
Do.	do.		0	2	11
Do.	Hardcastle, per Alderman Tarpey		1	0	0
Do.	per Rev. J. F. Knox, South Kensington, London		10	0	0
Do.	per Rev. J. F. Knox, South Kensington, London		1	2	6
Do.	Sheffield, per Jonathan Pim		23	0	0
Do.	"Toast"		1	10	0
Do.	per W. Thorp		1	0	0
Do.	Shilling Collection in *one* Establishment		2	5	0
Do.	—		0	2	0
Apothecary's Hall	per Sir George B. Owens		10	10	0
A Widow			0	1	0
"A R."	per Archd. Robinson, 11, Dawson-st., Dublin		1	1	0
Armstrong, Surgeon-General	—		2	2	0
Arnott & Co. (Limited)	Dublin		50	0	0
Do. (Collections)	do.		297	16	0
Arnott, D. T.	Woodlands Cork		10	0	0
Arnott, Sir John	do. do.		100	0	0
A Surgeon			0	2	0
A Scotchman			1	0	0
Ash & Lacy	Birmingham		5	5	0
Ashdown & Parry	per Pigott & Co., Dublin		2	2	0
Ashburton	Canterbury, New Zealand		71	3	6
Asken, Paul	Dublin		5	5	0
Ashton R.	per National Bank, King's Cross, London		0	10	6
Ashville, North Carolina	per Brown, Shipley & Co., Liverpool		23	13	8
Askwith, F. W.	per Vincent P. Healy, London		0	10	0
Auckland	New Zealand		1,081	13	10
Austin, G. J.	per Messrs. Coutts & Co.		5	0	0
Avery, Mrs.	Tatton		0	2	6
A Widow's Mite			0	1	0
A Working Man	—		0	2	0
A Young Collegian	—		0	1	0
	Carried forward	£	10,348	7	2

LIST OF SUBSCRIPTIONS. 347

		£ s. d.
	Brought forward	10,314 7 2
"B."	—	20 0 0
Baddeley, Messrs.	Chapel-street, Whitecross street, London	1 0 0
Babra (Collection)	Demerara, per J. C. R. Hill	57 18 10
Bagot, John	28, William-street, Dublin	10 10 0
Baggulleys, Mestall & Spence	per P. Walsh, Dublin	5 0 0
Baker, William	per National Bank, King's Cross, London	1 0 0
Baillie, E.	—	0 10 0
Baillie, H. A. G.	per Bank of South Australia	1 0 0
Ballarat	Australia	1,000 0 0
Baltimore	—	825 0 0
Baltimore, Easton	(*see* Easton, Baltimore)	
Banbridge Catholic Church	Banbridge	31 1 0
Barber & Co., J. J. (Employés Collection)	Cutlers, Sheffield	11 11 0
Barcham, John	Statham, Norfolk	0 10 0
Barcroft, F.	Redford, Moy	2 0 0
Barcroft, J. W.	do.	3 0 0
Barker, Rev. Alleyne	7, Hale-crescent, Farnham, Surrey	2 0 0
Barker, Boam & Co., William	per National Bank, King's Cross, London	1 0 0
Barnemoor Church (Collection)	per Rev. M. Norman	6 1 0
Barnewell, Mrs. H. C.	London	1 0 0
Barnsley	—	60 0 0
Barrett, A.	Vale Grove, Chelsea	0 10 0
Barrington, Richard	per Sir John Barrington, Dublin	14 7 3
Barrington, J. & Sons	Dublin	20 0 0
Barrow Bros., Samuel	per J. J. Kennedy	10 0 0
Barrons, Sir Henry T. P.	Park-view, Waterford	5 0 0
Barry, Norton & Co.	Dublin	20 0 0
Barton	—	21 0 0
Bartlett & Sons	Redditch	5 0 0
Bass & Co.	—	105 0 0
Bate, Capt.	Greenhall, Carmarthen	2 2 0
Bateman & Sons, Robert	per P. Walsh, Dublin	2 2 0
Bates, F.	per Wilts & Dorset Banking Co., Malmesbury	0 10 0
Batt, William	Milnthorpe	0 10 6
Battin & Gaynor, J. & J.	London	10 0 0
Batty, Espine	per Sir John Barrington, Dublin	5 0 0
Bax, Frederick	London	3 3 0
Bean, F. S.	93, Goodramgate, York	0 13 0
Beard, M. R.	Lily's-place, Doncaster-road, Barnsley	2 1 0
Beare & Son	per Pigott & Co., 112, Grafton-st., Dublin	2 2 0
Bedford Roman Catholic Church	Bedford	15 0 0
Bedlington	Northumberland	5 3 0
Belin, Mons. P.	Dublin	2 2 0
Bell, Sarah & Elizabeth	Lougham, Hants	5 0 0
Bender, Rev. P.	73, Lower Mount-street, Dublin	1 0 0
Bennett, Mrs.	London, per J. Pim, Esq.	10 0 0
Benson, Robert	Preston	5 0 0
Bentley, Mark C.	per Sir John Barrington	1 0 0
Bentley, J.	161, Capel-street, Dublin	5 0 0
Bentley & Burn	per Dublin (South) City Market Co.	2 2 0
Benyon, Mrs. Crowther	Dale-house, Camden-hill, Up. Norwood, S.E.	5 5 0
Bergin, Margaret A.	New York	20 12 0
Berkeley, William King	10, Southampton-buildings, London	5 5 0
"Bertico"	Demerara	75 0 0
Beveridge, J. J.	per Charles Kennedy, Dublin	5 5 0
Beresford, The Right Hon. and Most Rev. Marcus	—	10 0 0
Bibby & Baron	Burnley	1 0 0
Biggs, Thomas	Messrs. Ward & Co., London	1 0 0
Biggs, Mrs. L.	per Jonathan Pim, Esq.	1 1 0
Billington, Ed.	per National Bank	10 0 0
Bilston	per Staffordshire Joint Stock Bank	89 3 7
Bingley (Collection)	Yorkshire	81 8 5
	Carried forward £	12,914 15 6

348 APPENDIX XIV.

		£ s. d.
	Brought forward £	12,914 15 6
Binyon, Mrs.	Worcester	5 0 0
Binyon, Miss	do.	5 0 0
Birchall, Mrs. K. & O.	Briscot Rectory	2 0 0
Birch, Rev. John	Kilkenny	3 0 0
Bird, Rev. Charles	Chollerton, Wallsend-on-Tyne	5 0 0
Birmingham	per Richard Chamberlain, Esq., Mayor	477 15 9
Bispham	Poulton le-Fylde (Entertainment)	4 0 0
Black, D.	per National Bank	5 0 0
Blackburn	per Adam Dugdale, Mayor	507 2 2
Blackie & Son	Glasgow and Dublin	10 0 0
Blackwood & Co.	per M. & S. Eaton	2 2 0
Blake, John A.	Algiers	5 0 0
Blizard, Conway	per National Bank	0 10 0
Blyth Church Offertory	Worksop	2 0 0
Board of Trade (Collection)	Chicago	210 5 2
Bolger, Richard, T C.	Dublin	25 0 0
Bolton	per Mayor	500 0 0
Booley, E. J. D.	per Mrs. Leetch, Dublin	1 1 0
Bombay	India	3,000 0 0
Bomford, D. W.	Fenagh-house, Bagnalstown, Dublin	10 0 0
Bonasse, Lebel et Fils	Paris	1 0 0
Bond, Mrs. Harriett	Winchester	1 0 0
Bond, Right Rev. Bishop	Montreal	0 17 1
Booth, Alderman J.	Castlemere, Rochdale	2 2 0
Boulenger, Mons. A.	Rouen	4 4 0
Bowley, Chr.	per Jonathan Pim	1 0 0
Boucher, Rev. H.	Thornhill-house, Stalybridge, Blandford	10 10 0
Boyd, J.	Argostob, Borham-road, South Croydon, Surrey	2 2 0
Bosanquet, Mr. & Mrs. F. B.	Buckfastleigh, Devon	75 0 0
Boyd, Samuel	per Sir J. Barrington	10 10 0
Boylan, Patrick	46, William-street, Dublin	5 0 0
Boys, St. Vincent's Home	London	20 0 0
Bracken, W.	—	10 0 0
Bradford "Star Inn" Concert	Bradford	10 0 0
Bradley & Sons, W. G.	Dublin (per J. A. Curran)	2 2 0
Brady, Dr. James	Dublin	5 0 0
Brady, Miss E.	Birmingham	1 0 0
Brady, Thomas F.	11, Percy-place, Dublin	2 2 0
Brady, Mrs. Bedford	Birmingham	1 0 0
Bramley, W. T.	Killiney, Co. Dublin	10 0 0
Brand, R. J.	per National Bank Branch, Oxford-street, London	0 2 6
Breen, Thomas	Hibernian Bank, College-green, Dublin	3 3 0
Brenner, F.	per National Bank Branch, Bayswater, London	0 10 0
Brenon, E. St. John	25, Crosthwaite-park, Kingstown	5 0 0
Brewen, Robert	Cirencester	5 0 0
Brewis, Brothers	per National Bank Branch, King's Cross, London	1 0 0
Briddlecombe, Miss	Bridgewater	0 5 0
Briggs, M. J.	Bridport Harbour, Bridport	0 15 0
Briggs, Mrs.	do. do.	0 5 0
Brisbane (Collection)	Australia	11,361 0 0
British Co-operative Society	Wellington-street, Barnsley	20 0 0
Broad, M. A. J.	Paris	5 0 0
Brock, Thomas	—	5 5 0
Broke, Lady	—	5 0 0
Brooks, Thomas & Co.	Dublin	50 0 0
Brooke, The Misses	Summerhill-house, Clones, Monaghan	25 0 0
Broomhead, Rev.	per Sir John Barrington	4 1 1
Brown, M.P., George	Kilternagh, Co. Mayo	5 0 0
Brown & Thomas	Dublin	10 10 0
Brown, Westland & Moore	Cauldon-place, Staffordshire Potteries	5 0 0
Brown, Miss A. M.	34, Palmerston-road, Dublin	0 10 0
	Carried forward £	30,071 7 3

LIST OF SUBSCRIPTIONS. 349

			£ s. d.
	Brought forward	£	30,071 7 3
Browne, W. J.	Gloucester-terrace, London		10 0 0
Brownfield & Sons, W.	per Mrs. Leetch		2 2 0
Bruce, Rev. T. Cyril	Leicester		0 17 0
Bruce & Gibson	6, Bachelor's-walk, Dublin		38 1 6
Buchanan, Mrs. H. Cross	Happyland-park, Bishop Auckland, Durham		1 1 0
Buckland, Stephen	per London Tramways Company		2 0 0
Buenos Ayres	River Plate, South America		3,802 0 8
Bulfin, Joseph	2, Trinity College, Dublin		1 0 0
Bullock, Rev. George M.	The Rectory, Clareloot, St. Peter's, Slough		2 10 0
Bunton & Co., J.	Kidderminster		20 0 0
Burke, D.	Innsbruck, Germany		2 7 0
Burke, Martin	per John A. Curran		1 1 0
Burlington	Iowa		100 0 0
Burnett, Charles F.	London		5 0 0
Burnett, Thomas	per National Bank Branch, King's Cross, London		1 0 0
Burnley	—		56 7 0
Bury (Collection)	Lancashire		73 10 0
Butler, C. S.	Hotel de Russia, Rome		10 10 3
"Buzy"			0 4 6
Byrne, E. O.	Corville, Roscrea		5 0 0
Byrne, P.	91, Lower Camden-street, Dublin		5 0 0
Byrne, P. J.	Dublin		5 5 0
Byrne, W. H.	52, Dame-street, Dublin		3 3 0
Byrne & Sons, J. J.	6, Henry-street, Dublin		3 3 0
Cadby & Co., Charles	London, per Pigott & Co.		2 2 0
Caithness, G. T.	—		1 0 0
Calcutta	per Oriental Bank Corporation, London		4,000 0 0
Calderwood, G. Henry	Sion Hill, Drumcondra		3 0 0
Callander, Miss	per Wilts and Dorset Banking Company, Malmsbury		1 0 0
Caledon Presbyterian Church	per Rev. A. J. Wilson		2 12 6
Calumel	Haughton County, Michigan		206 10 0
Calvin Church (Collection)			10 0 0
Campbell, E.	Portland-place, London		2 2 0
Campbell, J. & G.	Dublin		10 0 0
Campbell, Mrs. & Miss	per National Bank, Dublin		3 0 0
Campbell & Son, S.	Glasgow		1 0 0
Candahar Force	Calcutta		239 11 1
Cannon, Rev. F. G.	Hoo-road, Kidderminster		1 0 0
Cantrell & Cochrane	Dublin		50 0 0
Capel, Frank C.	—		20 0 0
Caplin, J.	London		0 10 0
Cardiff	South Wales (per Mayor)		583 4 6
Carlos & Son	Madrid		1 0 0
Carolan, L.	per Rev. J. Daniel		1 0 0
Carville, William	Rathgar		25 0 0
Casey & Clay	Dublin		10 10 0
Catholic Registration	Stalybridge (see "S")		
Catteral, R.	Agricultural Seedsman, Kirkham		1 0 0
Cayley & Cayley	London		5 0 0
"C. B."	per D. Allingham, 100, Capel-street, Dublin		2 0 0
"C. E."	Exeter (per Jonathan Pim, Dublin)		5 0 0
"C. H."	Tottenham (per Jonathan Pim, Dublin)		1 0 0
Chadwick, William	(See Oldham)		
Chamberlain, M. & C.	36, Arran-quay, Dublin		21 0 0
Chanther, William	Newport (per Jonathan Pim)		0 10 0
Chantier, Rev. J. M.	Ilfracombe		26 6 4
"Charity"	—		1 0 0
Chapman, William	Bushfield-avenue, Dublin		5 0 0
Charleston (Collection)	West Coast, New Zealand		105 17 0
Charter's Towers	Queensland, Australia		708 2 9
Charlton Church (Collection)	Malmsbury		2 7 0
	Carried forward	£	40,281 0 4

			£ s. d.
	Brought forward		40,281 6 4
Chatham (Collection)	Montreal		310 13 8
Cherry & Smalldridge	Dublin		77 4 0
Cherry, Miss	Teignmouth		2 2 0
Chester (Collection)	—		178 10 5
Child, A, Sacred Heart Convent	Quimper, France		2 0 0
Chrisholm, William	Kimberley, South Africa		20 0 0
Chivot, E.	Abbeyville, Rotterdam		1 0 0
Christchurch (Collection)	New Zealand		1,250 18 3
Christchurch	West Virginia, U.S.		4 0 0
"C. H. S."	—		1 0 0
Churcher, Mrs. M.	Broadwater-road, Worthing, Sussex		1 0 0
Churchill, J. & A.	Publishers, London		2 0 0
Cincinnati	Chamber of Commerce		8 5 0
Cincinnati Collection	—		103 0 0
Cirencester (Collection)	per Jonathan Pim		16 2 0
City Market Co., (South)	Employés		2 3 0
Civil & Military Gazette	Lahore, India		14 6 3
Clarke & Son	per M. & S. Eaton		2 2 3
Clenvestra, Alfred	Preston		3 0 0
Cleveland (Collection)	Ohio		64 13 2
Clitheroe	Proceeds of Concert		15 12 0
"C. M."	per F. O'Brien, Castleknock		2 0 0
"C. M."	—		1 0 0
"C. M."	Clonmel		1 0 0
"C. M."	—		2 0 0
Coates, Brothers	London		1 0 0
Cocks & Co., R.	per Pigott & Co., Dublin		5 5 0
Coffee Palace Company	Proceeds of Entertainment		6 6 0
Coffey, H. J.	Ferney, Stillorgan		10 0 0
Coghlan, H. T.	—		52 10 0
Cohen & Co., A.	per National Bank, London		0 10 6
Coleman, J.	35, Golden-square, London		5 5 0
Coleridge, Minnie	Royal Marine Barracks, Plymouth		3 3 0
Colgan, V.G., Right Rev. J.	Mysore, India		40 0 0
Collard & Collard	per Pigott & Co.		21 0 0
Collins, Mrs.	3, St. Catherine's-ter., Clonliffe-road, Dublin		1 0 0
Collum, Hugh R.	Leigh Vicarage, Tonbridge, Kent		5 3 10
Coll, Patrick	4, Palace-street, Dublin		2 0 0
Colusa (Collection)	California		67 0 0
Colthurst, D.	Cork Club, Cork		5 0 0
Colville, J. C.	Dublin		10 0 0
Comerford, Thomas N.	10, Devonshire-road, Holloway, London		1 0 0
"Commercial Traveller"	—		5 0 0
Commins, William	Custom House, Londonderry		20 0 0
Commissariat Department	Shorncliffe Camp		1 16 0
Common Pleas Jury	—		3 3 0
Do.	—		1 1 0
Congregational Church	York-street, Dublin		10 10 0
Connor, Hon. Sir. H.	Chief Justice of Natal		5 0 0
Conway, J. F.	per National Bank, Dublin		0 10 0
Connaught Rangers	proceeds of Concert given by Bandsmen		15 0 0
Conyers & Son, Joseph	7 Water-lane, Leeds		25 0 0
Cooke & Son, J.	per M. & S. Eaton		1 1 0
Cooke, G. H.	37, King's-road, Brighton		10 0 0
Cooke, Leonard	Harwich		1 1 0
Cooke, M.	Portarlington		1 0 0
Coonoor, Madras	per Stanes & Co.		116 3 0
Co-operative Society (Limited)	(Wholesale) Manchester		200 0 0
Cooper, W. J.	per National Bank, Dublin		3 0 0
Coopersburg Lodge	Saucina Encampment		4 0 0
Cupplestone, Mrs.	15, Denmark-terrace, Brighton		5 0 0
Corbett, Miss A. B.	per Sir John Barrington		1 0 0
Corcoran, James	—		20 0 0
Corry & Soper	91, Shad Thames, Dockhead, London		5 0 0
	Carried forward	£	43,057 15 8

LIST OF SUBSCRIPTIONS.

			£ s. d.
	Brought forward	..	43,057 15 8
Cosslett, Mrs.	St. Leonard's	..	10 0 0
Cotton, S. V.	per National Bank, Dublin	..	5 0 0
Courteney, Captain D. C. ..	Royal Engineers, Dublin	..	50 0 0
Cousin, A.	Paris	..	1 0 0
Cousins, Rev. J. F. (Family and Friends)	North Hykeham, Lincoln	..	1 16 0
Coven Church	Wolverhampton	..	3 3 0
Coventry, Joseph F. ..	Birkenhead	..	1 0 0
Coventry (Collection) ..	per the Mayor ..	..	57 2 0
Coventry	Proceeds of Concert on St. Patrick's Day	..	88 5 8
Coventry Elastic Weaving Co. (Limited)	Coventry	..	5 5 0
Cowper, His Excellency Earl	Lord Lieutenant of Ireland	..	500 0 0
Cox, Henry	Chard, Somerset ..	..	10 10 0
Cox, Miss E. S.	Fursden, Plympton, South Devon	..	0 10 6
Cox & Co., J.	Bristol	..	10 0 0
Craig, Samuel	Liscolman, Dervock, Co. Antrim	..	4 0 0
Cranfield & Sons	Dublin	..	3 3 0
Creak, A. S.	The Wick, Brighton ..	..	2 0 0
Crewe (Collection)	per Richard Whittle, Esq., Mayor	..	43 13 2
Crine & Wyld	per F. Smith & Son, Dublin	..	0 10 6
Crompton Co-operative Provident Society	—	..	5 0 0
Crook, M.	Dublin	..	20 0 0
Cromwell (Collection) ..	Otago, New Zealand ..	..	140 0 0
Crosby, Lockwood & Co. ..	London	..	3 3 0
Cross & Donaldson	per G. J. Alexander, Dublin	..	5 5 0
Crotty, Rev. John	Powerstown	..	1 0 0
Crotty, R. D.	15, Sherrard-street, Dublin	..	1 0 0
Crowe, Wilson & Co. ..	Lower Bridge-street, Dublin	..	10 0 0
Crowley, Elizabeth	Croydon	..	5 0 0
Crowley, E. S. & E. ..	do.	..	1 0 0
"C. S."	per National Bank ..	..	1 0 0
Cullen, H.	Oakhill Park, Old Swan, Liverpool	..	50 0 0
Curran, John A.	Dublin	..	5 5 0
Curwen, H. F.	Estate Office, Workington	..	10 0 0
D'Abbadie, Antoine ..	per National Bank ..	..	15 0 0
Dalhousie, Earl of	—	..	10 0 0
Dallas, Miss	31, Castle-street, Farnham, Kent	..	2 0 0
Daniel, Arthur	Abersychan, Mon. S. Wales	..	0 10 0
Daniel, J.	Paris (per H. J. Gill) ..	..	0 10 0
Daniel, Rev. J.	—	..	3 3 0
Daniel & Sons	44, Grafton-street, Dublin	..	5 0 0
Daniel, T.	Paris (per M. & S. Eaton)	..	0 10 0
D'Arcy, Charles T. ..	Sandymount-green, Dublin	..	1 0 0
D'Arcy, M. P.	Dublin	..	50 0 0
Darley, J. H.	per National Bank ..	..	5 0 0
Darfield Main Collieries ..	Barnsley	..	15 0 0
Darlington, John ..	4 Highfield-terrace, Rathgar, Dublin	..	2 0 0
Do. (Collection) ..			3 0 0
Darlington (Collection) ..	per F. Swinburne, Esq., Mayor	..	103 8 0
David & Co.	per G. J. Alexander, Dublin	..	2 2 0
Davoren, Colonel	Dublin	..	5 0 0
Davoren, Richard ..	13, Dame-street, Dublin	..	5 5 0
Daw, Joshua	Exeter	..	2 2 0
Dawson, Charles, T.C. ..	27, Lower Stephen-street	..	10 0 0
Day & Martin	97, High Holborn, London	..	57 10 0
"D" Company 2nd Infantry	Camp Chelan, Washington Territory	..	25 14 3
Dean, William	Cape Town	..	1 0 0
Dearham, Colliery (Collection)	per Matthew Walton, Esq.	..	1 10 0
De Brett's Peerage, Proprietors of	London	..	1 1 0
Deed & Co., J. S. ..	London	..	1 1 0
De Ferrand, Mons. ..	Pauillac, Gironde, France	..	1 11 8
	Carried forward	..	44,502 5 5

352   APPENDIX XIV.

			£ s d
	Brought forward	£	44,502 5 5
De Groot, M.	48, Lower Gardner-street, Dublin		2 2 0
Delany, George	Dublin		10 0 0
De La Rue & Co.	per M. & S. Eaton, Dublin		5 0 0
Demerara County			77 12 6
Demambay, Miss	per Wilts & and Dorset Bank		1 0 0
De Moleyns, E. H.			5 0 0
Denham, W.	per F. Smith & Son, Dublin		1 1 0
Dennehy, T.	7, Northumberland-road, Dublin		2 2 0
Derham, Brothers	Bristol		5 5 0
Devine, F.			5 0 0
Dicks, H.	London (per H. J. Gill)		1 1 0
Dickie, W. D. (Collection)	per A. Plunket, Esq.		33 1 0
Digby, W. A.	47, Wellington-road, Clyde-road, Dublin		5 0 0
Dillon, V. B. Junior	7, Rutland-square, Dublin		10 0 0
Dingnan, M.	104, Albion-road, Stoke Newington, London		1 0 0
Dingnan, Michael	London		2 0 0
Disabled Volunteer Soldiers	Milwaukie		82 1 0
Distlimmau, A.	—		1 1 0
Dixon, Miss	per A Wilson, Halifax		2 0 0
D. M.	Charing Cross Hotel, London		100 0 0
Dobbin, George	Cyprus		1 0 0
Dobell & Co.	per G. J. Alexander, Dublin		2 2 0
Donagher, Owen	Tullamore		2 0 0
Dollard, Joseph	Dublin		5 0 0
Do. Employees of	Dublin		10 0 0
Donegan, P. (Collected by)	Dame-street. Dublin		70 0 0
Dooner, Mrs.	Barton, Rathfarnham		1 0 0
Donegal County	Collections in Parish Churches		184 8 5
Doorman, M.	Croydon		0 3 0
Dormeuil, Freres	10, New Burlington-street, London		5 5 0
Dove & Willes	—		20 0 0
Doyle, John	Dublin		5 0 0
Drake & Son, John	Bristol		10 0 0
Drimmie, David	Dublin		10 10 0
Drummond & Co.	58, Dawson-street, Dublin		25 0 0
Du Bedat & Son, W. G.	2 & 3, Foster-place, Dublin		5 5 0
Dublin Man, A.	Derry (*see* "A")		
Dublin Whiskey Distillery Co.	Dublin		50 0 0
Dudgeon, Brothers	103, Great Brunswick-street, Dublin		5 5 0
Duncan, W. W.	London		10 0 0
Dunedin (Collection)	New Zealand		1849 17 11
Dungerfield, W.	per F. Smith & Son		1 0 0
Dunhill Parish (Collection)	Waterford		7 1 0
Dunn, Rev. R.	Hunt-town, Bampton, Devon		24 10 0
Dunne, Jos. J.	Northumberland-road		3 0 0
Durham (Collection)	—		113 8 2
Durmicliff & Smith	Nottingham		2 2 0
Eason, Charles	30, Kenilworth-square, Rathgar		5 0 0
East, James	per G. J. Alexander, Dublin		2 2 0
Easton (Collection)	Baltimore		73 13 1
Eaton, M. & S.	95, Grafton-street, Dublin		5 0 0
Eccles Sunday Schools			5 10 0
Echelay, Mrs.	Netherwood, Godalming		2 0 0
Edge, James	per Jonathan Pim, Esq.		1 0 0
Edgson, G. W.	per National Bank, Bayswater		0 3 6
Edinburgh (Collection)	—		404 4 10
Edmundson & Co.	Capel-street, Dublin		10 0 0
Edwards, Rev. A.	per Most Rev. Dr. Trench		2 10 0
Edwards, Mr. & Mrs. T. P.	3, Elm View, Shaw Hill, Halifax		1 1 0
Edwards, Miss	per Sir John Barrington		2 0 0
E. G.	per Rev. Canon Bagot		1 0 0
Egan, Rev. J.	Dublin		1 0 0
Eighty-fifth Regiment	Collection		42 2 4
	Carried forward	£	47,834 16 8

LIST OF SUBSCRIPTIONS.

			£	s.	d.
	Brought forward		47,834	10	8
Elrington, C. A.	Cuddesden College, Oxford		0	10	0
Elliott, Cooke & Co.	Thomas-street, Dublin		20	0	0
Elliott, Samuel	Liskeard, Cornwall		1	0	0
Elmes, Robert H.	per National Bank, Dublin		1	0	0
Ely, Marquis of	Hotel de la Grande Bretagne, France		20	0	0
Ely, Marchioness of	Do. Do.		10	0	0
Emmens, William	London		10	0	0
Ennis, E. A.	Dublin		5	5	0
Erard	per Pigott & Co., 112, Grafton-st., Dublin		5	0	0
Etchemin & New Liverpool	Quebec		61	19	7
Evans, Henry	Dublin		5	0	0
Evans, John	40, Dawson-street, Dublin		1	0	0
Evans & Co., Richard	London		2	2	0
Exeter (Collection)	—		9	8	7
Exeter Cathedral Church Collection	—		42	15	0
Evans, Miss F.	Sandymount		2	0	0
Fahie, J. A.	23, Leinster-square, Rathmines, Dublin		2	2	0
Falconer, John	53, Upper Sackville-street, Dublin		5	5	0
Falk & Son, Henry	Newcastle-on-Tyne		0	10	6
Family Herald, Proprietors of	London		5	5	0
Fanagan, William	—		5	0	0
Fardan, Mrs.	per Jonathan Pim, Esq.		1	0	0
Faris, J. C. & Friends	Medaryville, Indiana		1	0	0
Farquharson, R.	Dublin		5	5	0
Fay, P. M.	Dublin		50	0	0
Fellowes, Charles	6, Tettenhall-road, Wolverhampton		5	0	0
Fenerhead, Jun. & Co., D. M.	Oporto		10	0	0
Fennell, S. J.	Dublin		5	0	0
Ferguson, M.D., Robert	per Bank of Ireland		2	0	0
Ferre & Co.	10, Glasshouse-street, London		5	5	0
Fetchburg (Collection)	Massachusetts		172	12	7
F. G.	Charing Cross, London		1	0	0
Fibbin, J.	per National Bank, Bayswater		0	1	0
Fiji (Collection)	—		315	0	0
Findlater & Co., Alexander	Upper Sackville-street, Dublin		50	0	0
Findlater, William	Stephen's-green Club, Dublin		20	0	0
Findon, Miss Elizabeth	London		1	0	0
Fitzgerald, Charles	per John A. Curran		2	2	0
Fitzgerald, D. & T.	20, St. Andrew-street, Dublin		25	0	0
Fleming, The Misses	Windermere		2	0	0
Fleming, William	Stephen's-green, Dublin		5	0	0
Flint (Collection)	North Wales		120	2	9
Flood, Robert L.	East-street, Dorking		50	0	0
Flynn, John	Blackrock		1	0	0
Fogarty, Owen	Dublin		2	0	0
Foley, J.	per M. J. Briggs		0	5	0
Ford Parish (Collection)	Northumberland		17	17	0
Ford, J. A.	Rathmines		1	0	0
Fordham, H. G.	—		1	1	0
Foresters, Ancient Order of	Dublin		51	0	0
Fortress, Monroe (Collection)	Virginia		38	9	6
Forster, Captain	Swords		10	0	0
Forster, Right Hon. W. E.	Chief Secretary for Ireland		50	0	0
Fottrell, Junior, George	8, North Great Georges-street, Dublin		5	0	0
Four Workmen	Gateshead		0	4	0
Fox, E.	Dublin		5	5	0
Fox, Joseph H.	Wellington, Somerset		5	0	0
Fox & Co., Samuel	per F. Smith & Son, Dublin		2	2	0
Frank	per National Bank, Bayswater		0	2	6
Frankland, Mrs.	Kendal		5	0	0
Franklin, William A.	per V. B. Dillon, Junior		2	0	0
Fraser, G. R.	Newcastle West, Limerick		5	0	0
	Carried forward	£	49,100	13	8

2 B

354   APPENDIX XIV.

		£ s. d.
	Brought forward	49,106 13 8
Frazer, G. R.	7, Homefield-road, Wimbledon	5 0 0
Fredericton (Collection)	Toronto, Canada	250 0 0
Freeman, William G.	London	10 0 0
French Relief Committee	Paris	3,996 3 1
Friendly Sons of St. Patrick	New York	500 0 0
Friends, Society of	Ackworth School	2 7 6
Do.	Bath	6 19 0
Do.	Bishop Auckland	13 17 0
Do.	Dover	2 15 10
Friends (per W. Scott & Co.)	England & Scotland	20 10 0
Do. Do.	Do.	5 5 0
Do. (per Todd, Burns & Co.)	Do.	60 0 0
Do. Do.	Do.	50 0 0
Friends, Society of	Kettering	7 15 0
Do.	Swarthmore	8 8 0
Do.	Stourbridge	10 0 0
Do.	Thaxted	52 6 2
Do.	Warwickshire	0 5 8
Do.	Zealand Conyers	16 11 0
Friends, Two	per National Bank, Oxford-street, London	1 1 0
Do.	Tytherton, England	2 5 6
Frisco (Collection)	Southern Utah, North America	66 11 2
Fry, Charles M.	New York	10 0 0
Fry, Rev. G. A.	Dodsworth, Beasley	8 5 5
Fry & Sons, William	13, Lower Mount-street, Dublin	25 0 0
Furnival & Co.	London	2 2 0
F. W.	per National Bank, Bayswater	0 2 6
G. A. D.	Roden-street, London	0 2 0
Gaelic Church	Inverness	5 0 0
Galbraith, Rev. Jos. A.	Dublin	5 0 0
Gardiner, George	per National Bank, Dublin	3 0 0
Garland, George V.	Wimberne	5 5 0
Gateshead (Collection)	—	245 5 0
Geelong (Collection)	—	971 19 11
Geelong & Western District	St. Patrick's National Benefit Society	50 0 0
General Advertiser, Proprietors of	Fleet-street, Dublin	10 0 0
Georgetown (Collection)	Demerara	275 14 2
Gent, L. C.	London	1 1 0
Gernon, William	53, Lansdowne road, Dublin	2 0 0
Gerty, Miss	24, Rathgar-road, Dublin	1 0 0
Gerty & Rorke	134, Lower Bagot-street, Dublin	2 2 0
Gesu Church	Philadelphia	45 0 0
Gibbons, Miss E. M.	46, Lower Dominick-street, Dublin	2 0 0
Gibbons, W. B.	per National Bank, Dublin	30 0 0
Gibbons, Mrs.	Bootle, Liverpool	35 0 0
Gibbons, Miss	Do.	35 0 0
Gibbs & Co.	per G. J. Alexander, Dublin	10 10 0
Gibson, E., Rt. Hon.	per National Bank, Dublin	2 0 0
Gibson, George S.	—	50 0 0
Gibson & Co., W.	per F. Smith & Son, Dublin	1 1 0
Giles, William Henry	21, Fair-street, Drogheda	0 7 6
Gill, H. J.	Dublin	20 0 0
Do. (Collection)	—	6 1 0
Gilley, Junior & Co., F. W.	New York	10 0 0
Gilligan, P.	78, Middle Abbey-street, Dublin	10 0 0
Glasgow (Collection)	per William Collins, Esq., Lord Provost	1,279 2 11
Gleeson, P. M.	Dublin	5 0 0
Glennon, J.	per National Bank, Dublin	10 10 0
Glovemaker, A	—	1 0 0
Godley, R.	Moordown, Bournemouth, Hants	0 10 0
Gonin, The Most Rev. L.	Port of Spain	20 0 0
Goodman, J. F.	Dublin	2 2 0
	Carried forward	£ 57,302 13 0

LIST OF SUBSCRIPTIONS. 355

		£ s. d.
Brought forward		57,392 13 0
Good Templars (Independent Order of)	Hatcham	0 10 0
Goore, Rev. Edward	Darlington	1 0 0
Gossett, Rev. J. F.	The Priory, Westward, Ho! Bideford, Devon	5 0 0
Gowland, Thomas	Dublin	5 5 0
Grattan, Lady Laura	Ham House, Petersham, Surrey	5 0 0
Graves, Rev. R. P.	1, Winton-road, Leeson-park, Dublin	1 0 0
Gray, Rt. Hon. Edmund Dwyer	Dublin	270 0 0
Gray, Mrs.	Dublin	10 10 0
Gray, Rev. H. R.	Holt Vicarage, Wrexham	1 1 0
Gravesend (Collection)	per F. B. Nettingham, Mayor	20 0 0
Green, Charles	Savannah, Georgia	10 0 0
Green, J.	London (per H. J. Gill)	3 3 0
Greenock (Collection)	per Provost Campbell	550 15 0
Greer, Rev. G. S.	The Glebe, Kilcullen	1 0 0
Greer, Rev. S. M'Curdy	3, Gardner's-place, Dublin	10 0 0
Gregory, Sophia	Tatton	0 10 0
Gregory, W. & F.	Tatton	1 0 0
Greymouth (Collection)	New Zealand	686 0 0
Grice, Grice & Booth	Birmingham	1 0 0
Griffith & Farran	Publishers, London	2 2 0
Groom, Miss Georgina	Charleywood, Herts	1 1 3
Groves, Rev. C. W.	Tewkesbury	2 2 0
Guildford (Collection)	—	9 14 6
Guinness, Sir Arthur	Dublin	200 0 0
Guinness, Edward C.	5, Grosvenor-place, London, S.W.	200 0 0
Guinness, Olivia	Dublin	10 0 0
Guitoriann, S.	per F. Smith & Son	1 1 0
Gundry, Joseph	Tatton	1 0 0
Gunn, M. J.	Gaiety Theatre, Dublin	25 0 0
Haig, C. E.	6, Queen's-parade, Windsor	2 0 0
Haigh, Marcus H.	Aberia, Wales	20 0 0
Haigh, Carton	Grimsby Hall, Grimsby	2 0 0
Haigh, Hedley	Do.	2 0 0
Haigh, Ernest	Do.	2 0 0
Haigh, Arnold	Do.	2 0 0
Haigh, Claude	Do.	2 0 0
Halder & Halder (Limited)	Wantage	1 1 0
Halifax	Nova Scotia	815 4 3
Halifax (Collection)	per Matthew Smith, Esq., Mayor	200 0 0
Halifax	per A. Wilson, Halifax	1 0 0
Hall, Edwin	St. John's Wood, London	0 5 0
Hall, Rev. John	per Sir Barrington	5 0 0
Hall & Son, John	London (per G. J. Alexander)	10 10 0
Hallinan, J.	per National Bank	5 5 0
Hamerton, Charles	Maidstone	0 10 0
Hamilton, Alexander J.	Dublin	5 0 0
Hamilton, J. J. D.	Upper Mount, Shanklin, Isle of Wight	0 9 1
Hanagan, J.	Dublin	2 0 0
Handcock, D.	Handsworth, Birmingham	1 0 0
Hannon, Mons.	9, Rue Neuve Chaussée, Boulogne	0 8 0
Hares, 30	—	3 2 6
Hare, Miss	9, Argylle-road, London	3 0 0
Harold & Co., Charles	Birmingham	1 1 0
Harris, Alderman	Dublin	20 0 0
Harris, Rev. H.	Winterbourne, Bassett, Swinbourne	1 1 0
Harrison, Mrs. E.	London	1 1 0
Harrison, Rev. A. H.	Maidstone	1 0 0
Harrison & Crossfield	per Jonathan Pim	100 0 0
Hartnell, J. Esq.	—	5 0 0
Harvey, Edmund	Waterford	2 0 0
Harvey, F. L.	per Bank of Ireland	1 0 0
Carried forward		£60,045 6 1

APPENDIX XIV.

		£ s. d.
	Brought forward £	00,645 6 1
Harvey, Thomas	Leeds	10 0 0
Harvey, Mrs.	Grange, Waterford	1 0 0
Harvey, Mrs. A.	8, Brunswick-Villas, Windsor	1 0 0
H. A. S.	—	1 0 0
Haskell, C. B.		2 2 0
Haslam, Roger	Manchester	1 0 0
Hastings County (Collection)	Ontario	102 14 2
Hatch, Miss	per Oxford-street Branch, National Bank	0 5 0
Haughton, B.	Eversleigh, Cork	5 0 0
Haughton, Samuel	Torquay, South Devon	10 0 0
Haughton, The Misses	Dublin	10 0 0
Haughton-le-Spring (Collection)	—	24 4 3
Hawarden Church	—	7 7 7
Haworth & Co., Richard	Manchester	20 0 0
Hayes & Co., William		1 1 0
Hayhurst, H. H. F.	Wrockwardine, Shropshire	5 5 0
Hayman	Bristol	0 5 0
Hayward, M.P.	Cheltenham	10 0 0
H. B. N.	Norwich	2 2 0
H. C...	—	0 2 6
Healy, V. P.	1, Thornsett road, Anerley, S.E.	1 0 0
Heberden, Rev. J.	Hinton Rectory, Alveston, Hants	1 0 0
Hemphill, J. H., Q.C.	23, Merrion-square, South, Dublin	10 0 0
Henderson, J.	Publisher, London	5 0 0
Hengler, Charles C.	Argylle-street, Regent-street, London	21 0 0
Do.	Proceeds of benefit night at Circus	117 12 0
Hennell, Frank S.	107, London road, King's Lynn	1 1 0
Hennessey & Co.	Cognac	25 0 0
Hepburn & Sons	Leather Market, Southwark, London	5 0 0
Herite, Mons.	French Consul, Dublin	20 0 0
Herschell, Farrar	40, Grosvernor Gardens, London, S.W.	10 0 0
H. G.	—	1 0 0
Hibernian Bank	Dublin	50 0 0
Hicks, Alexander	per National Bank	0 10 0
High Sheriff, The	Dublin	10 10 0
Highflatts Meeting (Collection)	Yorkshire	18 0 0
Hildesheimer & Faulkner	London	0 10 0
Hill & Sons	Blue Bell Factory, Inchicore	5 5 0
Hills, F. C.	Redleat, Penshurst, Kent	20 0 0
Hilton, T.	Wellingborough	0 10 0
Hilton (Collection)	Cansenburgh, New Zealand	10 19 11
Hines, Thomas	1, Brisbane-street, Douglas, Isle of Man	2 0 0
Hiogo (Collection)	Japan	108 0 0
Hislin, Christopher	Dublin	5 0 0
Hitchcock, Williams & Co.	London	5 5 0
H. M. M.	—	0 10 0
Hobarttown (Collection)	New South Wales	2,259 6 3
Hobhouse, Ven. Archdeacon	Liskeard	2 0 0
Hobson, Rev. G, F.		4 17 4
Hoddeston (Collection)	Herts	5 0 0
Hodgkinson & Co., W. S.	Wells, Somerset	2 2 0
Hodgson, James	per National Bank, Bayswater	0 2 6
Hodgsons, Surgeon-Major	Barracks, Devonport	1 1 0
Hogg & Co. William	Cope-street, Dublin	50 0 0
Hokitika	New Zealand	470 0 0
Holmes, John	Castlewood House, Rathmines	5 0 0
Hong Kong (Collection)	China	2,000 0 0
Hooper, George N.	Elmleigh, Beckenham, Kent	5 0 0
Hopkinson	per Pigott & Co., Dublin	2 2 0
Horchitz & Co.	per G. J. Alexander, Dublin	5 0 0
Horniman, John	Croydon	10 0 0
"Hornsen"	Hedon, Hull, England	0 10 0
Horsnail, H.	Bulford Hill, near Braintree, Essex	1 0 0
Houston, Arthur	per John A. Curran	5 5 0
Houstain & M'Nairn	15, Ingram-street, Glasgow	10 0 0
	Carried forward £	66,152 13 7

LIST OF SUBSCRIPTIONS. 357

			£ s. d.
	Brought forward		66,152 13 7
Howell, G. R.	11, Tavistock-st., Bedford-square, London		1 1 0
Howitt & Co.	Glasgow		5 0 0
Howth, Earl of	Howth Estate Office, 68, Lower Gardiner-st., Dublin		5 0 0
Huddersfield (Collection)	—		212 6 0
Hudson, T. H. B.	Publisher, London		1 1 0
Huges, Mr.	per Rev. J. Daniel, P.P.		1 0 0
Hughes, Frederick	33, Edith-road, Peckham, London		1 1 0
Hughes, M.	17, Eustace-street, Dublin		1 0 0
Hull (Collection)	—		1,135 10 2
Hull, Rev. J. & Mrs.	—		2 0 0
Hunter, L.	Dublin		3 0 0
Huntingdon (Collection)	—		33 13 0
Hurst, Messrs.	Ballinahinch, Co. Down		10 0 0
Hurst & Son	per G. J. Alexander, Dublin		10 10 0
Hussey, W. H.	Dublin		1 0 0
Hutchings, Miss	Ealing, W., London		5 0 0
Hutchinson, Hon. Mrs. C. H.			10 0 0
Hutchinson, George	per Windsor Thorp, Esq.		1 0 0
Hutton, H. S.	per National Bank		2 0 0
Hutton, R. J.	13, Sloane-terrace, London, S.W.		5 0 0
Hutton & Sons, J.	Dublin		20 0 0
Hyam, B.	per National Bank		10 0 0
Hyderabad	India		2,786 0 10
Illustrated Sporting and Dramatic News	London		21 0 0
Independence Collection	Missouri		108 7 8
Inglelow, W. F.	—		10 10 0
Ingram, J. K.	2, Wellington-road, Dublin		5 0 0
Inland Revenue Officers (Collection)	Dundee		12 0 0
Do. do.	Halifax		17 5 0
Do. do.	Kilkenny		14 10 0
Do. do.	Kirkcaldy, N. B.		1 5 0
Do. do.	Waterford		15 5 0
Do. do.	York		8 14 0
Invercargill	New Zealand		580 5 2
Irish Farmers' Gazette	Dublin		10 10 0
Isacke, Captain	—		2 0 0
Isbister & Co.	London		5 5 0
Ivers, Rev. Canon B.	St. Peter's, Broad-street, Birmingham		1 1 0
Jackson, Miss	per Miss Tisdall		3 0 0
Jackson & Co., J.	—		2 0 0
Jackson & Co., J.	Lynn		1 1 0
Jacob & Co.	Riga (per G. J. Alexander)		20 0 0
Jacob & Co., W. & R.	Peter's-row, Dublin		25 0 0
Do. (Employés)	Do.		6 8 6
Jarrow (Collection)	—		238 19 1
J. C.	Horwood House, Guildford, Surrey		5 0 0
Jersey City, U.S.	U. S.		351 12 0
J. F. S.	—		1 0 0
J. J.	Exeter		35 0 0
J. L. B.	per National Bank		3 0 0
J. L.	—		1 0 0
J. M.	—		1 0 0
J. M.	York		0 6 6
J. M. C.	—		1 0 0
Johnson, James	15, Southwark-st., Cambridge-sq., London		2 0 0
Johnston, J. B.	8, Clyde-road, Dublin		10 0 0
Johnson, Maziere	London & Lancashire Fire Insurance Co.		2 0 0
	Dublin		5 0 0
	Carried forward	£	71,042 14 4

358 APPENDIX XIV.

			£ s. d.
	Brought forward		71,042 14 4
Johnson, Mrs. (Collection)	Baden-Baden		
Johnson, W. L.	26, Lower Leeson-street, Dublin		10 0 0
Johnson, W. & A. K.	Publishers, London		3 3 0
Jones, Mrs. Annie	Portslade-by-Sea, Sussex		0 3 0
Jones, H. M. T.	—		0 10 0
Jones, P.	15, Westmoreland-street, Dublin		2 0 0
Jones & Sons, George	Stoke		1 1 0
Jones, Ward & Co.	per National Bank, King's Cross, London		2 2 0
Joynt, William Lane	Dublin		10 0 0
J. P.	Dublin		1 0 0
Jury, "Healy v. Rountree"			1 1 0
Jury, Nisi Prius Court	—		1 1 0
Jury, "Plunket v. White"			12 12 0
J. S. S.	per Oxford-street Branch, National Bank		0 5 0
J T.	England		10 0 0
Kane, John	Leeson-park House, Dublin		10 0 0
Kane, R. D.	Claremount, Howth		5 0 0
Kane & Son, J. F.	London		2 0 0
Kapunda & Light	South Australia		432 0 0
Kavanagh, J. W.	Rathgar		1 1 0
Kavanagh, Michael	10, Stephen's-green, Dublin		5 0 0
Kearney, Simon	Fair street, Drogheda		2 0 0
Keeling, Beville & Co.	London		2 2 0
Kehoe, T. B.	Kilcumney, Kildare		2 2 0
Keighley (Collection)	—		141 3 10
Kekewich, Lieutenant-Colonel	per Sir John Barrington		5 0 0
Kelly & Co.	per Pigott & Co., Dublin		1 1 0
Kelly, B. D.	10, Upper Rutland-street, Dublin		5 0 0
Kelly, Madame	Sacred Heart Convent, Quimper, France		4 0 0
Kelly, James	1, Bath-avenue, Dublin		20 0 0
Kelly, Rev. John	St. John's, Pelling-on-Tyne		30 0 0
Kelly, P. S.	Peoria, Illinois, U.S.		0 0 0
Kelly, Thomas A.	Monkstown		5 0 0
Kennaway, W. B.	3, St. James's-place, Exeter		15 0 0
Kennedy, Charles	Dublin		50 0 0
Kennedy, George O'B.	86, Lower Leeson-street, Dublin		3 3 0
Kennedy, Mrs. M.	1, Prince Arthur-terrace, Rathmines		0 10 0
Kennedy & Son	Dublin		10 0 0
Kennedy, Thomas	Trim		10 0 0
Kenny, Dr. E.	Dublin		1 0 0
Kenny, Mrs.	Dublin		1 0 0
Kenny, Patrick	4, North Earl-street, Dublin		5 0 0
Kent (Collection)	Ontario		100 0 0
Kenyon & Son, James	Bury, Lancashire		10 0 0
Keogh, Madame	Rue de Rivoli, Paris		6 0 0
Keswick (Collection)	—		18 19 10
Do.	Amateur Performance		5 0 0
Kidderminster (Collection)	—		157 8 7
Kiernan, Dr.			1 0 0
Kiely, J.	per M. J. Briggs		0 2 0
Kildare & Leighlin	per Most Rev. Dr. Walsh		80 0 0
Kiely, W. T.	Toronto, Canada		20 0 0
Kilmore, Most Rev. the Bishop of			2 0 0
King, James	94, Bishopgate-st., Wavertree, Liverpool		1 0 0
King, L. M. & E. E.	Wateringbury, Kent		1 0 0
Killala (Collection)	per Most Rev. Dr. Conway		22 14 9
Killaloe, Bishop of	—		10 0 0
Kimberley	South Africa		1106 0 0
Kintore, Earl of	Keith Hall, Inverin, Aberdeen		5 0 0
King's Cross Branch, National Bank	London		2 10 0
Kingston (Collection)	Ontario		95 0 0
Kingston, Mrs. George	Exmouth, Devon		2 2 0
	Carried forward	£	74,510 12 4

LIST OF SUBSCRIPTIONS. 359

		£ s. d.
	Brought forward .. £	74,519 12 4
Knight, Craig & Co.	per M. & S. Eaton, Dublin ..	2 2 0
Knight, Thomas	London	1 1 0
Kobnstamm, Leopold ..	Furth, Bavaria	1 1 0
Kumara	Westland, New Zealand	334 0 0
Kumser Valley	Proceeds of Concert	35 9 9
Kyle, Ven. Archdeacon ..	37, Upper Fitzwilliam-street, Dublin ..	2 0 0
Labour Loan Society ..	London	3 13 0
La Grange, H.	Dublin	1 1 0
Lahore (Collection) ..	India	38 8 10
Laird & Co., Alexander A. ..	Glasgow	20 0 0
Lahore, Rt. Hon. the Bishop of ..	Dalhousie, Punjaub	100 0 0
Lalor, J. J.	Drummartin Castle, Dundrum ..	1 1 0
Lambe, J. D.	Lakerren, Bessbrook, near Newry ..	1 10 6
Landy, Thomas P. ..	Collection, Telegraph Clerks, G. P. Office ..	10 0 0
Lane, Rev. R. T.	156, Albany, London, N.W. ..	1 0 0
Langan, F. H.	Dublin	5 0 0
Lange	Pigott & Co. Dublin	2 2 0
Langston, Miss	—	1 0 0
Larkin, Michael	51, Dame-street, Dublin ..	20 0 0
La Touche, J. J. Digges ..	1, Upper Ely-place, Dublin ..	5 0 0
Launceston (Collection) ..	Tasmania	1360 0 0
Law, H., Q.C.	9, Fitzwilliam-square, Dublin ..	10 0 0
Lawe's Chemical Manure Company ..	Dublin	10 10 0
Lawlor, Joseph, M.D. ..	Richmond Lunatic Asylum, Dublin ..	3 0 0
Leaf, Sons & Co.	Old Change, London	1 1 0
Lecomtre, Mons.	Poitiers, France	6 0 0
Lee, W. H.	per Mayor of Wakefield	5 0 0
Leech, A.	per M. J. Briggs, Bridport Harbour ..	0 2 0
Leetch, Thomas	Dublin	10 0 0
Leeson, Henry	per Sir John Barrington	10 0 0
Leith Town Council ..	—	20 0 0
Lennon, William	Dublin	5 0 0
Lethielleux P.	Paris	0 8 0
Lever, John O.	Adelaide Buildings, London Bridge, E.C. ..	25 0 0
Lewis, H. K.	London	1 1 0
Lewis, Richard	per National Bank, Dublin	1 1 0
Lewis, W. L.	per National Bank, Charing Cross, London ..	0 10 0
L. H.	—	0 6 9
Lichwitz, L.	per National Bank, Bayswater, London ..	0 5 0
Liefmanne & Sohune, R. ..	Hamburg	2 0 0
Lincoln, Henry	6, Emorville-terrace, South Circular-road, Dublin	2 0 0
Lincoln, Mrs.	6, Emorville-terrace, South Circular-road, Dublin	1 0 0
Littleboy, Richard	Newport, Bucks	5 0 0
Littledale, R. F.	—	2 0 0
Liverpool & Birkenhead Wholesale Potato Salesmen's Association ..	—	25 0 0
Liverpool Victoria Legal Friendly Society	—	0 2 1
L. K.	—	1 0 2
Llanrwst (Collection) ..	North Wales	16 0 0
Llewellyn & Son, G. ..	Haverfordwest	1 1 0
Lloyd, Altuee & Smith ..	London	1 0 0
Lloyd, Miss Emly	Ripley, York	1 0 0
Locomotive Works (Collection) ..	Broadstone Railway, Dublin ..	6 6 3
Lodge, Felix (Collection) ..	India	26 10 0
Lombard, J. F.	South Hill, Upper Rathmines ..	10 10 0
Lombard, Mrs.	do. do. ..	5 0 0
London (Collection) ..	Ontario	343 12 6
Lord Mayor and Lady Mayoress ..	Dublin (*see* "G")	
Lossiemouth, N.B. (Collection) ..	Proceeds of Concert	1 10 0
	Carried forward .. £	77,040 5 2

APPENDIX XIV.

			£ s. d.
	Brought forward	£	77,040 5 2
Low, Alfred	per National Bank, Dublin		1 1 0
Lowry, John	do. do.		2 0 0
Lowry, Major-General R. W.	25, Warrington-crescent, London, W.		2 2 0
Luce, Charles	per Wilts & Dorset Banking Company		1 0 0
Luce, W. H.	do. do.		2 0 0
Luxmore, P. B.	Timaru, New Zealand		5 0 0
Lyle, Major	per National Bank, Dublin		4 0 0
Lyle, Robert	do. do.		2 0 0
Lynch, George	43, Lower Sackville-street, Dublin		1 0 0
Lynch, J.	per M. J. Briggs, Bridport Harbour		0 2 0
Lynch, Nicholas	20, Wicklow-street, Dublin		10 10 0
Lynch, Stanislaus	Luton		5 0 0
Lyons & Son	per National Bank, Dublin		4 4 0
Lynchbury (Collection)	Virginia		207 12 8
Macauley, G. C.	Rugby		5 5 0
Mackay, H. W. Boyd	16, Queen-street, Exeter		1 1 0
Macken, H. M. & P.	5, Burgh-quay, Dublin		20 0 0
Macken & Sons, James	Poolbeg-street, Dublin		20 0 0
Mackie, Charles	Little Cote, Harpford		1 0 0
Mackie M.P., Robert B.	per Mayor of Wakefield		5 0 0
Macpherson, C.	St. John's, Newfoundland		1 0 0
Madden, M.D., R.R.	Booterstown		1 0 0
Madden, P. (Collection)	Bradford		13 0 0
Madison, County (Collection)	Indiana		37 0 3
Madras (Collection)	India. (*see Appendix*)		6898 8 0
Maffett, Rev. R. S.	Grenville Cottage, Madeira road, Ventnor		1 0 0
Magee, James	per Alderman Tarpey		10 0 0
Magrath, Surgeon, Major E.	India		5 0 0
Mahon, Mrs.	Tours, France		27 8 8
Mahalm, & Co., William	Dublin		10 0 0
Mahon, Mrs. A.	Chateau de St. Wolstan		28 19 5
Maharajah of Vizianagram	India		1000 0 0
Maher, Mrs.	Enniscorthy		10 0 0
Mainez	per National Bank, Bayswater		1 0 0
Mallett, Mr. & Mrs. Charles	7, Queensboro'-terrace, London, W.		3 3 0
Malone, Lawrence	36 & 37, Lower Ormond-quay, Dublin		10 0 0
Malton, (Collection)	York		46 2 3
Main et fils	Tours		2 0 0
Manchester, (Collection)	—		1470 7 8
Manitoba, (Collection)	North West Territory, Canada		308 4 4
Mapother, Dr.	Dublin		5 0 0
Marks, Benjamin	per National Bank, King's Cross, London		1 0 0
Marshall, Robert	Glasgow		10 0 0
Marston Low & Co.	Publishers, London		5 5 0
Marlborough, Duchess' Committee	towards Grant to Western Islands		129 15 10
Martin, Florence	66, South George's-square, London		20 0 0
Martin & Co., R.	28 to 33, Sir John Rogerson's-quay, Dublin		50 0 0
Martin, T.	Manchester		0 5 0
Martin, T. & C.	North Wall, Dublin		50 0 0
Martin, W. J., M.D.	60, Harcourt-street, Dublin		2 2 0
Maryport (Collection)	—		22 5 0
Massey, W. N.	13, Old Broad-street, London		20 0 0
Masters & Co., J.	London		0 5 0
Mathews, Rev. P. T.	Gateshead-on-Tyne		63 1 0
Matson, J. F.	10, North Great George's-street, Dublin		1 0 0
Matthews, Jehu	32, Lower Ormond-quay, Dublin		5 5 0
Matthewson, Alexander	per Robertson & Arnott, Dundee		2 0 0
Matthewson, John	do. do.		0 5 0
Matthewson, Allen	do. do.		0 5 0
Maudesley, John	Stoke		0 5 0
Maunders & Co.	James-street, Dublin		50 0 0
Maunsell, G. W., D.L.	Dublin		5 0 0
Mev ard Brothers	London		1 0 0
	Carried forward	£	87,667 15 3

LIST OF SUBSCRIPTIONS. 361

			£ s. d.
	Brought forward		87,067 15 3
Mayo, County	Collections in Parish Churches		57 7 6
Mayo, George	Adelaide, Australia		100 0 0
M. B. N.	Norwich		0 5 0
M. C.	per Bank of Ireland		5 0 0
Mead, J.	per M. & S. Eaton		1 1 0
Meara, Rev. H. G. J.	Newbury, Berks		5 0 0
M. E. C.	—		5 0 0
Mees & Moens	Rotterdam		2 2 0
Melbourne (Collection)	Australia		27500 0 0
Meldon, Charles and Mrs.	Dublin		10 0 0
Member, R.I.C.	per Rev. J. Daniel		0 6 9
Menuell, Henry T.	Croydon		2 2 0
Metropolitan Loan Company	Dublin		20 0 0
Meyyett, A.	Croydon		0 2 6
M. F.	Hilltown		1 0 0
M. F.			0 1 0
M. G.	per Rev. F. Antrobus, South Kensington		20 0 0
M. H.	per Rev. J. Daniel		1 0 0
M. H.			1 0 0
Miggeron & Co.	London		2 2 0
Miller & Co., A.	Thomas-street, Dublin		50 0 0
Milwaukee (Collection)	Indianapolis		45 0 0
Minneapolis do.	United States		63 6 4
Mintons, Messrs.	Stoke-upon-Trent		10 0 0
Mitchell & Son, S.	10, Grafton-street, Dublin		10 0 0
Mitchell & Son, John	Newhall-street, Birmingham		5 0 0
Mitchell, Miss	Grove-cottage, Spring-road, Southampton		2 2 6
Mitchell, James	Dublin		0 5 0
Mitchell, William	per M. & S. Eaton		5 0 0
M. K. W.	—		1 0 0
M. L.	—		1 0 0
M, L.	—		0 10 0
M. N.	50, Richmond-terrace, South Lambeth		3 0 0
Modiligo Parish (Collection)	per Most Rev. Dr. Power		9 0 0
Mogg & Co., Joseph	Adelaide Works, Redditch		5 0 0
Mollineux & Webb	Manchester		0 10 6
Molloy, J.	55, Harcourt-street, Dublin		100 0 0
Molloy & Co., P. J.	Dame-street, Dublin		10 10 0
Monas Herald	Isle of Man		1 0 0
Monson, Robinson & Co.	94, Talbot-street, Dublin		5 5 0
do. Employés	do. do.		3 13 6
Mooney, F.	—		2 2 0
Mooney, William	per John A. Curran		10 0 0
Moore, A. T.	23 and 24, High-street, Dublin		50 0 0
Moore, Dr.	Southport		1 0 0
Moore, M.	Dervock, Co. Antrim		5 0 0
Moran, William	St. Edmondsbury, Lucan, Dublin		5 5 0
Moravian Church	Bishop-street, per Royal Bank		8 17 0
Moreau, Monsieur Frederick	—		2 0 0
Morgan, Priscilla	per Jonathan Pim		1 0 0
Morgan & Co., C.	London		10 0 0
Morland, Hannah	Croydon		5 0 0
Morrison & Co.	per National Bank, King's Cross, London		0 10 0
Muller & Co.	per G. J. Alexander		5 0 0
Mulligan, John	Dublin		5 0 0
Mullock, T. H.	per National Bank, Dublin		5 0 0
Munster Banking Company	Dublin		50 0 0
Murland, Lucy	Croydon		3 0 0
Murphy Brothers	Rathangan		5 0 0
Murphy, James, Q.C.	—		5 5 0
Murphy, John	—		2 2 0
Murphy, Robert F.	10, Upper Mount-street, Dublin		1 0 0
Murphy, Very Rev. Canon	Dublin		3 3 0
Murphy, Mrs. Mary	10, Upper Mount-street, Dublin		1 0 0
Murphy, W. M.	30, Dame-street, Dublin		20 0 0
	Carried forward		£115,936 11 10

362   APPENDIX XIV.

		£ s. d.
	Brought forward	115,936 11 10
Murphy & Sons, J.	Dublin	10 0 0
Murray, Mrs. E. F.	do.	5 0 0
Murray, E. F.	do.	5 0 0
Murray, Children and Servants	do.	2 0 0
Murtagh, Surgeon Major	Camp, Colchester	1 0 0
Musvier, Madame S.	Paris	4 0 0
M. W.	Charing Cross	0 10 0
M'Cabe, Most Rev. Dr.	Archbishop of Dublin	10 0 0
M'Cabe, Charles	New York	1 0 0
M'Cann, J.	per National Bank, Dublin	25 0 0
M'Cann, Thomas L.	—	10 0 0
M'Clean, H.	16, Leeson-park, Dublin	5 0 0
M'Cleverty, Rev. R.	Edgemond, Newport, Salop	10 0 0
M'Comas & Son, Samuel	15, Lower Sackville-street. Dublin	3 3 0
M'Dermott, John	64, Mountjoy-square, West, Dublin	50 0 0
M'Devitt, E. O.	per J. A. Curran	1 0 0
M'Donald, Lieutenant Col. John		11 5 0
M'Donnell, John R.I.C.	Scots House, Clones	0 10 0
M'Eachen, Mrs.	Cork	0 10 0
M'Evoy, T.C., John	Dublin	3 0 0
M'Farlane, Strang & Co.	Glasgow	13 5 0
M'Gauran, E.	Dublin	3 0 0
M'Gloin, Esq., Henry	—	1 0 0
M'Gee, P.	per Rev. J. Daniel	0 10 0
M'Govern, Thomas	College-green, Dublin	2 0 0
M'Hale, Most Rev. Dr.	(*see* Tuam, Archbishop of)	
M'Hale, P. W.	per M. J. Briggs, Bridport Harbour	0 5 0
M'Kenzie & Sons, T. (Limited)	(Collection Dublin)	64 12 0
M'Kenzie, William	—	5 0 0
M'Kerlie, James	Edinburgh	10 0 0
M'Knight and friends of "Northern Whig"	Belfast	11 5 0
M'Laren, D. M.P.		5 0 0
M'Master, Hodgson & Co.	Capel-street, Dublin	25 0 0
M'Mullen	per M. J. Briggs, Bridport Harbour	0 2 0
M'Namara & Son, M.	5, Eden-quay, Dublin	10 0 0
M'Niven & Cameron	per M. & S. Eaton	2 2 0
M'Rahan, C. P.	Ceylon	5 1 3
M'Sheehy, John	per J. A. Curran	5 0 0
Naish, John		5 5 0
Nalty, S.	Dublin	2 0 0
Nanson, Rev. R. N.	Aldham, Colchester	0 10 0
Nash, R.	Anglesea-street, Dublin	5 5 0
Nash, Surgeon-Major	per National Bank, Dublin	2 0 0
National Bank Branch	Bayswater, London	1 13 6
do. do.	Belgravia, London	1 17 0
National Bank	Dublin	100 0 0
do. (Collection)	London	15 7 6
National Discount Company	26, St. Andrew-street, Dublin	25 0 0
Nawab Abdul Gunny	Decca, Bengal	125 0 0
Nawab Khajah Ahumgolah	do.	125 0 0
Neil, Christiana	per Jonathan Pim	0 5 0
Neale, Richard	Mountrath	4 0 0
Nelson (Collection)	New Zealand	327 8 2
Nelson & Sons, T.	Edinburgh	5 0 0
"Nemo"	per V. B. Dillon, Junr.	2 2 0
Neville, Rev. Canon	Stow Rectory, Lincoln	1 0 0
Newark (Collection)	New Jersey	569 10 7
New Bandon	Co. Gloster, Bathurst, N.B., Canada	5 11 5
Newbold, David	per National Bank, King's Cross, London	0 10 0
Newcastle-on-Tyne (Collection)	—	549 5 5
Newfoundland do.	—	1800 0 0
Newmarket do.	Ontario	26 0 8
Nutt, D.	Publisher, London	2 2 0
	Carried forward £	119,959 14 4

LIST OF SUBSCRIPTIONS. 363

			£ s. d.
	Brought forward	£	119,959 14 4
Newtown Parish (Collection)	Waterford		5 0 0
Newport do.	Monmouthshire		75 0 0
New York do.	—		3,810 0 0
Niall, M.D., Eugene	London		1 0 0
Nicholson, John	—		1 0 0
Nicoll & Co.	Arbroath		1 1 0
Nixon, John	Dublin		5 0 0
Nobles & Hoare	Cornwall-road, Stamford-street, London		25 0 0
Non-subscribing Church			2 19 6
Northwood, E. J.	106, Offord-road, London, N.		0 5 0
Norris, J.	per National Bank		30 0 0
Norris, William G.	per Jonathan Pim		1 0 0
Northampton (Collection)	—		150 0 0
Norwood, Upper do.	—		34 1 9
N. O. S.	per National Bank, Bayswater		0 2 6
Novello, Ewer & Co.	Publishers, London		5 5 0
Nugent, Michael	Dublin		10 0 0
Ninety-sixth Regiment	Aldershot		0 16 0
Oamah (Collection)	Wellington, New Zealand		300 0 0
Oastler, Palmer & Co,	London		5 5 0
Oldham (Collection)	per William Chadwick (Mayor)		225 18 9
Olive Brothers	Bury, Lancashire		2 2 0
Olive & Partington	Glossop		2 2 0
Oliver, G. B.	Glasgow		1 0 0
Oliver, William	Birmingham		1 1 0
Olwin, Amsden & Co,	London		2 2 0
One who regrets he cannot give more	—		0 10 0
One who feels for the distress	—		1 0 0
Ontario (Collection)	—		130 15 11
Ormsby, H, L,	Dublin		3 3 0
Orr, R. J,	Belfast		2 2 0
Osborne, Ashby G.	2, St, Martin's-place, Dover		5 0 0
Ottawa (Collection)	—		500 0 0
Otter, Rev. John	52, York-road, Brighton		40 0 0
Owen, S. R,	per Hardy Brothers, William-street, Dublin		2 2 0
Owens, Sir George B.	Dublin		5 0 0
Oxford (Collection), University and Citizens	£100 transferred to Seed Fund		136 17 5
O'Brien, Lieut.-Col., and Officers of the Metropolitan Police Force	—		28 11 0
O'Brien, M	per National Bank, Dublin		0 0 0
O'Brien, Patrick	Hotel de la Minerva, Rome		50 0 0
O'Brien, William	Dublin		2 0 0
O'Callaghan, A. P.	T.C.D., Dublin		1 0 0
O'Carroll, The Most Rev. W. D,	Port of Spain		10 0 0
O'Connor, John	Dublin		60 0 0
O'Connor & Co., Michael, and Friends	Indianapolis		46 0 0
O'Donnell, Thomas	Dublin		3 3 0
O'Gilligan, G. R,	3, Castle-avenue, Clontarf		2 0 0
O'Hagan, Lord	Dublin		200 0 0
O'Halloran, George W.	85, Kensington Gardens-square, London		0 10 0
O'Hanlon, Rev. J,	Dublin		1 0 0
O'Keeffe, Edward	3, Mill-street, Dublin		5 0 0
O'Keeffe & Co.	Toronto		20 0 0
O'Neill, George	7, Henry-street, Dublin		5 0 0
O'Rorke, J,	Lindon House, Ballyragget		1 0 0
O'Shaughnessy, Andrew	per National Bank, Dublin		1 0 0
O'Shaughnessy, Mark	10, Gardiner's-place, Dublin		3 3 0
O'Sullivan, J.	Shamrock-villa, Stamford		2 1 6
Page, Draper & Co.	Liverpool & London		10 0 0
Paisley (Collection)	—		300 0 0
	Carried forward	£	126,202 14 ~

APPENDIX XIV.

			£ s. d.
	Brought forward	£	120,292 14 8
Palestine East, (Collection)	Ohio		11 10 0
Palgrave, Murphy & Co.	17, Eden-quay, Dublin		100 0 0
Pallas, C. Lord Chief Baron	—		20 0 0
Palmer, Mrs.	Taunton		5 0 0
Palmer, Martha	Tatton		1 0 0
Parnell, J. T. A.	Exploit River, Newfoundland		3 0 0
Paris, St. Patrick's Society	Ontario West, Canada		20 0 0
Parsons, The Misses	Elmgrove, Dublin		6 0 0
Parsons & Co.	per National Bank, King's Cross, London		1 1 0
Patterson, Malcolm	Dewsbury		3 3 0
Patriotic Assurance Co.	9, College-green, Dublin		50 0 0
Patterson, B. T.	11, Kildare-street, Dublin		10 0 0
Pau, Proceeds of Concert	France		85 3 0
Pavy, Lister & Henderson	London		1 0 0
Payne, Philip & George	Shipston		0 15 0
Pears, Henry	Weston Cottage, Malvern		1 1 0
Pease, Arthur	Darlington		25 0 0
Pease, M.P., Joseph W.	Darlington		25 0 0
Peckover, Algernon	Wisbech		20 0 0
Peckover, Mrs.	Wisbech		5 0 0
Peel, William	Cintra, Ryde		1 0 0
Perola (Collection)	South Australia		4 10 0
Penon, R.	per G. J. Alexander, Dublin		2 0 0
Perinet Fils	Rheims		5 5 0
Perrin, Richard	Dublin		20 0 0
Perry	per National Bank, Dublin		10 0 0
Perry, J.	Holborn Viaduct, London		21 0 0
Perry, George	—		2 2 0
Perry, George	per Aldermon Cochran		2 0 0
Perkins, R.	per Oxford-street Branch, National Bank		1 1 0
Perth (Collection)	Ontario		200 0 0
Perth (Collection)	Western Australia		1214 17 5
Peters, J. C.	Austwick, Clapham, Lancaster		1 0 0
Pettifer, E. H.	189, Culford-road, London N.		2 0 0
Petvin, Joseph A.	Tatton		5 0 0
Phayre, General Sir A.	National Bank, Dublin		10 0 0
Phillips George, Junr.	Liverpool		2 2 0
Phillips & Co., J. & N.	35, Church-street, Manchester		105 0 0
Phipps, Rev. William	68, Upper Gardiner-street, Dublin		5 0 0
Phœnix Brewery Co, Employés	Dublin		10 1 6
Picard & Co.	London		5 5 0
Pierson, D.	per Sharples & Co.		1 0 0
Pietermaritzburg	Natal		71 0 0
Pigott & Co.	112, Grafton-street, Dublin		10 10 0
Pim Brothers & Co., Limited	South Great George's-street, Dublin		50 0 0
Pim, Henry	—		10 0 0
Pinching, C. J.	5, The Terrace, Gravesend, Kent		5 0 0*
Pincot, Proceeds of Concert	Ontario		42 2 5
Pirie & Sons, A.	Aberdeen		5 0 0
Plantenga, J. H.	per G. J. Alexander, Dublin		2 0 0
Planter's Stores and Agency Co.	Ditrugash, Upper Assam		20 5 0
Plunket, Ambrose	Dublin		5 5 0
Plunkett, Hon. D.	1, Merrion-square South, Dublin		20 0 0
Plunkett, G. N.	14, Palmerston road, Rathmines		5 0 0
Polman, M.	Haarlem		1 1 0
Pontypridd Constabulary	South Wales		1 3 9
Poor Brewery Boy	—		0 2 6
Pope, Rev. Canon	St. Andrew's Church, Dublin		5 0 0
Portarlington, Right Hon. Earl	Portarlington		10 0 0
Poussielgne, Messrs.	London		0 8 0
Powell & Sons, J.M.	London		1 1 0
Powell, William	48, Wood-street, London		0 5 0
Powell, William (Collection)			3 0 0
Pratten, Rev. B. P.	Hazlemere, Surrey		0 10 0
Prendergast, J. P.	127, Strand-road, Sandymount		2 2 0
	Carried forward	£	128,587 7 3

LIST OF SUBSCRIPTIONS.

			£	s.	d.
	Brought forward		128,587	7	3
Preston (Collection)	Working Men's Relief Committee		56	0	0
Preston, E. W.	per National Bank, Dublin		3	0	0
Presbyterian Church	Ballina		1	2	0
Preston & Co., R. W.	Liverpool		2	0	0
Price & Sons, J. & C.	per National Bank, Liverpool		1	1	0
Prideaux, The Misses	Joy Bridge, Devon		2	0	0
Provincial Bank	Dublin		100	0	0
Provincial Legislature of Ontario	Canada		4,000	17	4
Provost, Trinity College	Dublin		10	0	0
Puller, Miss	Harley-street, London		0	10	0
Pumphrey, Edwin (Collected)	Sunderland		57	12	6
Pumphrey, Mrs.	Great Malvern		0	10	0
Pumphrey, Mrs.	Worcester		2	0	0
Purser & Co.	per G. J. Alexander		10	10	0
Quaile, J. R.	—		5	0	0
Quebec (Collection)	—		1,350	0	0
Quill, Thomas	Hammersmith, London		0	5	0
"R."	5, Leinster-road, Dublin		2	0	0
Rainsford, John	Dublin		1	0	0
Rait, Mrs.	Sydenham		0	5	0
Ram, Richard F.	Kilndown, Essex		10	0	0
Ramsay Brothers	per Robertson & Arnott, Dundee		1	0	0
Rangoon (Collection)	British Burmah		70	17	1
Rankin, Charles	Dublin		1	0	0
Ransome, Sims & Head	London		10	10	0
Rath, Mrs. M.	Blackwater, Gorey		1	0	0
Rath, Miss	do. do.		1	0	0
Rathbone & Sons (Sunday Schools)	Millpoint, Canada		32	1	0
Ray, W.	per Canon Bagot		2	0	0
Raymond, Oliver	Middleton Rectory, Sudbury, Suffolk		5	0	0
"R. B."	Edinburgh		1	1	0
R. D. T.	per Oxford-street National Bank Branch		0	5	0
Read, M.P., Clare Sewell	—		5	0	0
Reading (Collection)	—		280	16	0
Recorder, The, and Mrs. Falconer	—		20	0	0
Reefton (Collection)	West Coast, New Zealand		220	18	6
Regan, C. J.	per Vincent P. Healy		1	0	0
Registry of Deeds Office (Collection)	—		10	0	0
Renault & Co,	Cognac		10	0	0
Reynolds & Co., Charles	London		1	1	0
Reynolds & Son, James	London		5	0	0
Richards & Co.	per G. P. Walsh, Dublin		1	1	0
Richardson & Son	Derby		0	10	0
"Ringwood"	per Royal Bank		0	10	0
Risci, C. R.	per Wilts & Dorset Banking Company		1	0	0
River Church	Dover		5	0	6
Rix, George R.	Somerleyton, Lowestoft		0	2	6
Roberts & Son	—		2	0	0
Robertson & Arnott (Collection)	Dundee		3	9	0
Robinson, J.	—		1	0	0
Robinson, R.	per National Bank		0	10	0
Rock & Remington (Collection)	—		1	15	0
Roe, Henry, Junr.	per Bank of Ireland		100	0	0
Rogers, R. J.	Charing Cross, London		0	10	0
Romney, M. A.	per National Bank, King's Cross		0	10	0
Rooney, J.	Rathgar		5	0	0
Ross (Collection)	New Zealand		44	13	0
Ross, David, LL.B.	—		2	2	0
Rossiter, J. H.	Oatlands, Lewes		5	0	0
Roth, Joseph	per Mrs. Leetch, Dublin		2	2	0
Rothe, H.	London		1	1	0
	Carried forward	£	135,145	5	11

APPENDIX XIV.

		£ s. d.
	Brought forward .. £	135,145 5 11
Routledge & Sons, G.	London	5 5 0
Rowhane & Co.	per P. Walsh, Dublin	1 1 0
Rowley, J. W.	per National Bank, Bayswater ..	0 10 0
Rowney & Co., George ..	per M. & S. Eaton	5 0 0
Roxburgh, Lieutenant-Colonel ..	1, Clarendon-street, Kensington ..	1 1 0
Royal Bank of Ireland ..	per David Dromm	116 0 0
Royal Yacht Club	Jersey	3 6 6
Royal Artillery, H Battery ..	3rd Brigade	11 8 9
R. T. R.	London	5 0 0
Rule, Peter	Cornhill-on-Tweed	0 5 0
Russell, J. W.	per John A. Curran	1 0 0
Russell, P.	per Vincent P. Healy, London ..	0 10 0
Russell, T. W.	Temperance Hotel, Stephen's-green, Dublin	2 0 0
Russell & Co., William ..	—	10 0 0
Rutter, T. A.	More, Wilts	1 0 0
Ryder, Canon, D.D. ..	per National Bank, Dublin ..	2 0 0
"S"	Enniscorthy	1 0 0
Sabel & Co.	per M. & S. Eaton ..	1 1 0
Sacramento (Collection) ..	—	550 0 0
Salter & Sons, H.	41, Lower Sackville-street, Dublin ..	2 2 0
Salter H., Junr.	—	1 1 0
Samuel, B.	40, Fitzroy-square, London ..	5 0 0
Samuelson, B., M.P. ..	Lupton, Brixham, Devon ..	25 0 0
Sanderson, Thomas Kemp ..	per Mayor of Wakefield ..	5 0 0
Sandhurst (Collection) ..	Australia	1,500 1 7
Sankey, William	Coalbrookdale	1 0 0
Santley, Charles	per Rev. J. Daniel	5 0 0
Sardis Independent Church ..	Pontypridd	3 0 0
Saul, Edward	Peckham, Rye	3 0 0
Saunders, F. G.	per John A. Curran	1 1 0
Saunders, Gilbert	Albany-road, Monkstown ..	2 2 0
Saunders, James	Wolverhampton	1 1 0
Savannah (Collection) ..	Georgia	511 5 0
Seaton, H. S.	Kingsbridge, Devon	0 5 0
Selton, Colley & Co. ..	Newcastle-on-Tyne	50 0 0
Servants, Two	—	0 5 0
Scallan, Eugene, V.P. ..	1, Brunswick-place, Dublin ..	0 10 0
Scallan, J. L. & W. ..	17, Bachelor's-walk, Dublin ..	10 0 0
Scanlan, P.	Rosemary-street, Bristol ..	0 10 0
Scarborough, (Collection) ..	Yorkshire	125 0 0
Scarth, Mrs.	Guisborough	1 0 0
Schofield, Miss	Southport	0 2 6
Schofield, Thomas	Mayor of Rochdale	3 3 0
Shomberg, Ontario	Proceeds of Dramatic Entertainment ..	7 10 2
Solanders, Brothers & Co. ..	per A. Shackleton	10 10 0
Scott, Bell & Co.	Wellington-quay, Dublin ..	5 0 0
Scott, Bell & Co., Employés ..	do. do. ..	5 0 0
Scott & Strickland	Island-bridge Mills, Dublin ..	2 2 0
Scott & Co., William ..	—	7 7 0
Scott, Miss	Ealing	50 0 0
Scrimgiven & Sons, John ..	per Robertson and Arnott, Dundee ..	1 1 0
Scully, Vincent	—	25 0 0
Shalders, Robert, and Mr. Shalders	Vice-Consul, Parniba, Brazil ..	10 0 0
Shabbington Church ..	Thame, Oxfordshire	1 12 6
Shackell & Edwards ..	London	2 2 0
Shackleton & Son, George ..	35, James's-street, Dublin ..	5 0 0
Shangway, H.	per M. J. Briggs, Bridport Harbour ..	0 2 0
Shanklin Church	Isle of Wight	2 0 0
Shanks, James	50, Townsend-street, Dublin ..	2 0 0
Shannon, Mrs. William ..	5, Sydenham Villas, Bray ..	2 0 0
Sharpe, H. & F.	Wisbeach	5 5 0
Shaw, G. F., F.T.C.D. ..	—	3 3 0
Sharples & Co.	Hertford	1 13 6
	Carried forward .. £	138,283 11 11

LIST OF SUBSCRIPTIONS.

			£	s.	d.
Brought forward			138,263	11	11
Shaw, J. J.	114, Lower Baggot street, Dublin		1	0	0
Shaw, William	Dublin		20	0	0
Sheepshed, Proceeds of Concert	—		53	0	0
Sheffield, (Collection)	—		1,186	2	6
Shiel, R.	22, Elgin-road, Dublin		10	0	0
Sheldon, Dr. Charles	2, Buckingham Vale, Clifton, Bristol		5	0	0
Sheldon, Thomas	per G. I. Alexander, Dublin		3	3	0
Sherbrooke, (Collection)	Quebec, Canada		141	15	7
Sherlock, R. A.	Dublin		2	2	0
Shipley, (Collection)	—		29	0	0
Sholl, James	Tatton		0	10	0
Sholl, Nathaniel	Tatton		0	2	6
Shute, W.	per National Bank		0	10	0
Sills, Edward	do. do.		1	0	0
Simpkin, Marshall & Co.	London		10	0	0
Sims, W. D.	per Jonathan Pim		5	0	0
Sims, W. G.	13, Old Broad-street, London		2	2	0
Six Sergeants	Royal Artillery, Barrackpore		0	15	0
Simcoe, (Collection)	Norfolk, Ontario		41	1	11
Sixth Regiment, (Collection)	Cawnpore		1	19	6
Sixth Regiment, (Collection)	—		8	8	4
Skipton-on-Craven, (Collection)	—		54	13	7
Slaney & Son	Wellington, Shropshire		1	1	0
Smallman, J. T.	Dublin		10	0	0
Small Sums	per Jonathan Pim		0	3	0
S. M. G.	per Sir George B. Owens		5	0	0
Smith, Baron	per H. Horsnail		0	5	0
Smith, Brabazon	per J. A. Curran		1	0	0
Smith, Brothers	31, Blackstock-street, Liverpool		50	0	0
Smith, Frank	Toronto, Canada		20	0	0
Smith & Lester	per P. Walsh, Dublin		10	10	0
Smith & Sons, W. H.	Employés, Dublin House		0	10	6
Smith & Sons, W. H.	Clerks, Railway Book Stands		5	1	0
Smith, T.	Tramore		3	0	0
Smith, William	Oxford-street, London		1	0	0
Smyth & Son, F.	Collection, 75, Grafton-street, Dublin		5	0	0
Smyth, R. G.	Dublin		1	0	0
Solomons, M. E.	19, Nassau-street, Dublin		2	0	0
Solomons, Mrs.	do. do.		1	0	6
Soper, John	per Oxford-street Branch, National Bank		0	10	0
Southall, R.	Surbiton		5	0	0
Southampton, Bruce & Co.	Ontario		17	18	4
Sparks, Alfred	Great Malvern		1	10	0
Sparks, William	do.		3	0	0
Speedy, Dr.	Dublin		2	0	0
Spradbergs, Mr. Children	Dublin		0	5	0
Sprickley, White & Lewis	London		5	5	0
Springfield (Collection)	Pittsfield, Massachusetts		465	6	5
Squire, D. & S. A.	Berkhamstead, Hants		10	0	0
Squire, Edward L.	per Jonathan Pim		0	10	0
Squire, William	Berkhamstead, Hants		5	0	0
S. S. and Family	Tatton		0	10	0
Stacy, Barton	Stockbridge, Hants		0	5	0
Stagg, W. H.	Wetheravon, Annesbury, Wilts		2	2	0
Staleybridge Catholic Registration	Staleybridge		84	0	0
Staples & Co.	10, Argylle-place, London		2	2	0
Stapley & Smith	148, London Wall, London, E.C.		5	0	0
S. T. B	York		5	0	0
Stein, Robert	7, Clarinda Park, Kingstown		15	0	0
Stenbenville, (Collection)	Ohio		134	16	8
Stephens, C.	The Willows, Bourke End, Maidenhead		1	1	0
Stephens & Haynes	Publishers, London		1	1	0
Stephenson, Clarke & Co.	London		25	0	0
Stevenson, John S.	43, Upper Leeson-street, Dublin		5	5	0
Stewart & Co., James	Dale-street, Liverpool		10	0	0
Carried forward		£	139,890	15	9

APPENDIX XIV.

		£ s. d.
Brought forward		139,890 15 9
Stillwell & Sons	London	1 1 0
Stirling, James	19, Fitzwilliam-place, Dublin	5 0 0
Stockton, (Pollection)	California	341 0 0
Stockville, (Collection)	—	2 19 5
Stockwith Church	Gainsborough, Lincolnshire	2 6 2
Stoke Edith Church	Hereford	3 16 0
Storey, G.	Crowle	1 1 0
Stourbridge, (Collection)	Worcester	47 5 0
Stuart, Mrs. M.	—	0 3 6
St. Saviour's Church	Waterford	8 5 0
Stubbs & Co.	1, College-green, Dublin	5 0 0
St. James' Church	Glossop	11 8 6
St. Andrew's Pic Nic Club	New Brunswick	21 6 0
St. Etolwold School Chapel	per Rev. S. E. Gladstone	0 14 5
St. Helen's (Collection)	Lancashire	533 2 3
St. Ishmael's Church	Milford Haven	0 10 6
St. John's Parish (Collection)	Telling-on-Tyne	20 0 0
St. Saviour's Church	Poplar	3 17 9
St. Joseph's Church	Greenhill, Swansea	40 0 0
St. Matthew's Church	Willesden	6 4 8
St. Margaret's Orphanage	East Grimstead	1 0 0
St. Saviour's Schools	Poplar	5 4 0
St. Marie's Catholic Sick and Burial Society	Oldham	20 0 0
St. Mary's (Collection)	Exeter	0 10 0
St. Patrick's Society	Brooklyn, New York	200 0 0
St. Patrick's (Collection)	Auckland, New Zealand	100 0 0
St. Paul's do.	Princeton, New Jersey	20 0 0
St. Thomas's do.	Ontario	37 0 6
Subscriber to Freeman's Journal	29, Upper Gloucester-street, Dublin	5 0 0
Sub-Constable, R.I.C.	—	1 0 0
Sudbury (Collection)	Suffolk	5 0 0
Suffield, Rev. R.	29, London-road, Reading	1 2 0
Suffolk, Earl of	per Wilts and Dorset Banking Company	1 0 0
Suffolk, Countess of	do do. do.	1 0 0
Sullivan, Barry	London	50 0 0
Sullivan, Brothers	per William Layne Joynt, Esq., D.L.	5 0 0
Sullivan, J. C., and Friends	Blackheath, London	3 10 0
Sullivan, Patrick	per National Bank, King's Cross	10 0 0
Sullivan, Robert	New York	50 0 0
Sunderland (Collection)	—	324 13 5
Sundry Subscriptions	per National Bank, King's Cross, London	7 6 1
Supple, James	per Sir John Barrington	5 0 0
Sutton & Co.	London	5 5 0
Sweeny, M.	Kingstown	10 0 0
Sweeting, Miss E.	Grange-over-Sands, Lancashire	0 10 0
Sydney (Collection)	Australia	28,000 0 0
"Sympathy"	—	1 0 0
Do.	—	2 10 0
"Tablet," The	72, Wellington-street, Strand, London	257 16 10
Taggart, Boyson & Slee	London	20 0 0
Tallon, J.	Kingstown	2 0 0
Tarpey, Alderman H.	Dublin	10 0 0
Tatham & Son, William	17, Old Broad-street, London	5 5 0
Taunton (Collection)	Massachussetts	100 0 0
Taylor, A. & E.	Tottenham	0 10 6
Taylor, C.	London	1 0 0
Taylor & Son	Edinburgh	5 0 0
T. B. H.	Brondesbury Road, London	3 0 0
T. C. D.	Dublin	1 0 0
Thames (Collection)	New Zealand	250 0 0
Thomason, William, M.P.	London	50 0 0
	Carried forward	£ 170,974 0 3

LIST OF SUBSCRIPTIONS.

			£ s. d.
	Brought forward		170,974 0 3
Thompson, Miss C.	per Wilts and Dorset Banking Company		0 2 0
Thomas, John, C.B.	Acting British Consul, Greytown, Nicaragua		5 0 0
Thompson, John	Chester		50 0 0
Thompson, Richard	York		3 3 0
Thompson & Collins	Bridgewater		1 1 0
Thompson & Co., J. G.	—		2 0 0
Thompson & Co., Thomas	Birmingham		1 0 0
Thonaiski, Count Alexandre	per the Marchioness of Ely		1 0 0
Thornley & Knight	Birmingham		10 0 0
Thorp, John Hall	Dublin		5 0 0
Thorp, Windsor	Dublin		1 0 0
Threlfall, Lazarus	Colne, Lancashire		2 2 0
Tischler & Co.	Bordeaux		10 0 0
Tisdall, Miss	Sunnyside, Clontarf		3 0 0
"T. O."	—		1 0 0
Tobias, M.	per John A. Curran		1 0 0
Todd, Burns & Co.	Mary-street, Dublin		50 0 0
Do. Employés	—		18 13 0
Todd, James	Louisville, Kentucky, U. S.		5 0 0
Torkington, J.	Dublin		1 0 0
Torquay (Collection)			12 10 0
Tosar, Nephews	London and Cadiz		2 2 0
Trainer, Thomas, and Few Friends	Milner's Bridge, Huddersfield		1 6 0
Trench, Archbishop	Dublin		135 0 0
Trenton (Collection)	North Jersey		225 11 8
Trotter & Son, Y.	Chirnside		2 0 0
Truell, W. H. A.	Blandford, Dorset		1 1 0
Tuam, His Grace the Archbishop of	Portion of the American Contributions		3,000 0 0
Tuke, J. H.	Hitchin		50 0 0
Turgis, Mons. Z.	Paris		1 0 0
Turner, Ellen	York-place, Brighton		2 2 0
Turner, Luke	Richmond House, Dane's Hill, Leicester		10 0 0
T. W.	per National Bank, Bayswater		0 2 6
Tynemouth (Collection)	—		41 17 0
Tyrrell & Co., James	—		20 0 0
Tyrrell, Ward	per National Bank		1 0 0
Ulster Banking Company	Dublin		50 0 0
Urlin, Denny	per Sir John Barrington		2 2 0
Uitenhage, Collection	South Africa		140 0 0
Vallyo (Collection)	California		15 0 0
Veale, A. H.	St. Austell		1 0 0
Veale, James	do.		1 0 0
Verdon & Co., R.	Dublin		3 3 0
Verry, William	36, Dagmar Road, London		1 1 0
Vesey, The Misses	Tunbridge Wells		1 0 0
Vesey, W. M.	Bagnalstown		2 0 0
Vickers, George	London		1 1 0
Vickers & Sons, T.	Manchester		5 0 0
Vilmorin, Andrieux & Co.	Paris		4 4 0
Waimate (Collection)	New Zealand		320 13 1
Walker, Miss Lydia B.	Elm Hall, Wanstead, London		1 1 0
Walker, J. J.	University Hall, London, W.C.		2 2 0
Wall, Rev. F. H.	per National Bank, Dublin		1 0 0
Wall, F. S.	per National Bank, Bayswater		2 2 0
Walla-Walla (Collection)	Wyoming, United States		102 9 3
Wallaceborough do.	Kent, Ontario		28 11 4
Wallingford Church	per Rev. F. Chalker		3 4 0
Wallsend-on-Tyne	Collection		45 10 0
Walpole Brothers	per Bank of Ireland		10 0 0
	Carried forward	£	175,393 17 1

APPENDIX XIV.

			£ s. d.
	Brought forward	£	175,393 17 .
Walsh, P.	Dublin		20 0 0
Walsh, P. (Collection)	do.		13 7 0
Walters & Son	per F. Smith & Son, Dublin		2 2 0
Walton, Miss	Southport		1 0 0
Warburton Church	Warrington		2 5 10
Ward & Co., A.	Leek		1 1 0
Ward, Lock & Co.	London		2 2 0
Wardle, C. S.	Dublin		1 1 0
Wardrope, John	per Robertson & Arnott, Dundee		0 8 0
Waring Church	Reading		8 8 9
Warne & Co., Frederick	London		5 0 0
Washington (Collection)	United States		500 0 0
Waterloo Station	Collection in Box		1 3 6
Watkins & Co., J.	Ardee-street, Dublin		50 0 0
Waterford and Lismore	Collections in Diocese		730 7 3
Watson, Robert	per Robertson & Arnott, Dundee		2 2 0
Watson, S.	4, Burgh-quay, Dublin		5 5 0
Watson, Mrs.			1 0 0
Weaver, W.	19, Albert-square, Clapham Road, London		5 5 0
Webb & Co., J. H.	Dublin		5 0 0
Wedgewood & Co.	Tunstall		2 2 0
Weekes, Chas.	London		2 2 0
Weir, James	per Thomas Leetch		10 0 0
Welch, H.	Camelford		0 3 0
Weldon, C. & J.	London		2 2 0
Wellington, (Collection)	New Zealand		1,532 15 0
Wells & Holohan	Dublin		5 0 0
Wells, Wm. F.	Stoke, Newington		2 2 0
Wesleyan Chapel	—		0 10 0
West Cumberland Iron and Steel Co. Employés	Workington		21 7 0
West Hartlepool	Collection		276 11 9
West, E. & L.	Tatton		0 5 0
West, Henry, J. P.	19, North Great George's-street, Dublin		21 0 0
West, Henry W.	10, King's Bench Walk, Temple, London		10 0 0
West, Very Rev. Dean	Dublin		3 0 0
Western Australia (see "A")			
Westport (Collection)	New Zealand		150 0 0
Weston, Philip	per Jonathan Pim		0 10 0
West Lexham Church	Swaffan, Norfolk		0 10 0
Wethered, George	Maidenhead		5 0 0
W. F. H.			2 0 0
W. H.			1 0 0
Whalley, Thomas	per G. J. Alexander, Dublin		2 2 0
Wharton & Sons, Henry	per National Bank, Dublin		1 0 0
Wheeler, Fredk.	Rochester		5 0 0
Wheeler, S.	per M. J. Briggs, Bridport Harbour		0 2 0
White, H. K.			2 0 0
White, Morris & Co.	New York		10 0 0
Whitehaven (Collection)	—		100 0 0
Whittard, Cuxp & Co.	Market-street, Bermondsey, S. E.		2 2 0
Whittle, J. Lowry	3. Harcourt Buildings, Temple, London		3 3 0
White, R. N. Capt. W. H.	New-street, London		5 0 0
Wiggin, & Co., Henry	Birmingham		3 3 0
Widnes Choral Society	Proceeds of Concert		10 0 0
Wilkinson, Jonas J.	Staleybridge		5 0 0
Wigan, Collection	per Mayor		150 0 0
Willand Parish	Collumpton, Devon		0 2 9
Williams, J. R.	Liverpool		1 0 0
Williams & Sons, D.	12, Birchin-lane, Manchester		10 0 0
Wills, W. S.	Charing-cross, London		1 1 0
Wilmot, M. B.	Tatton		0 2 0
Do., R. & A.	Tatton		0 5 0
Wilmington (Collection)	North Carolina		203 15 0
Wilmslow, do.	per Jonathan Pim		7 17 0
	Carried forward	£	179,325 11 2

LIST OF SUBSCRIPTIONS.

		£ s. d.
	Brought forward	179,325 11 2
Wilson, A.	Halifax	2 0 0
Wilson, Charles	Glendoran House, Cheltenham	100 0 0
Wilson, Effingham	London	0 10 6
Wilson, Mrs.	Southport	5 0 0
Winnipeg (Collection)	Manitoba, Canada	206 8 5
Winstanley, James	Roebuck	10 0 0
Wise, Ada C.	Croydon	0 5 0
Wise, Charles	do.	5 0 0
Wise, E. L. & J. P.	do.	0 2 0
Wittman & Co., J. F.	per Mrs. Leetch, Dublin	5 0 0
Wittman & Roth	do. do.	3 0 0
Wolff, Theodore	Paris	1 1 0
Wood, F. J.	53, Bow-street, Dublin	5 5 0
Wood, Miss	per Oxford-street Branch National Bank	0 2 0
Wood & Co.	per M. & S. Eaton	0 10 0
Woodfield & Hanbury	Mark-lane, London	25 0 0
Woodhouse, Rev. E.	The Elms, Taunton	5 0 0
Woodlock, Wm.	—	2 0 0
Woods, Webb & Phœnix	Dublin	10 0 0
Woolfenden & Co., J.	Denton, near Manchester	1 1 0
Do., & Sons	Bolton	5 5 0
Worcester Porcelain Co. Employés	Worcester	28 2 9
Worthington, A.	Kilmainham, Dublin	5 5 0
Wright, Agnes	Villa Foraldo, Mentone, France	0 10 0
Wright, Mrs.	Quinta de Castella, Villa Nova de Gaia, Portugal	10 0 0
Wright, Mr.	Southport	0 5 0
Wright, R. S.	Temple, London	1 1 0
W. S.	per National Bank, Bayswater	0 1 0
W. T.	do. Oxford-street	1 1 0
W. T.	do. do.	0 5 0
Wymer, Edward R.	per National Bank, King's Cross	1 1 0
"W. Z. H."	—	1 0 0
"X. Y. Z."	—	0 10 0
Young Men's Bible Class	St. John's, Paddington	0 11 0
Younger & Co., Wm.	Edinburgh	10 10 0
York street Unitarian Church	Belfast	5 18 0
Zion Baptist Chapel	Mirfield	12 0 0
Add Subscriptions since received—		£ 179,796 2 4
Garrison, Mauritius		29 0 5
Madras		33 15 1
Bombay		490 0 0
Sydney		283 18 5
Total Subscriptions received, per Balance Sheet		£ 180,632 16 3

Note.—All Subscriptions received since 2nd December, 1880, will be acknowledged by the Trustees.

BROWNE AND NOLAN, PRINTERS, DUBLIN.

www.ingramcontent.com/pod-product-compliance
Lightning Source LLC
Chambersburg PA
CBHW030406230426
43664CB00007BB/774